Communications in Computer and Information Science   1498

Constantine Stephanidis ·
Margherita Antona · Stavroula Ntoa (Eds.)

HCI International 2021 - Late Breaking Posters

23rd HCI International Conference, HCII 2021
Virtual Event, July 24–29, 2021
Proceedings, Part I

Springer

Editors
Constantine Stephanidis
University of Crete and Foundation
for Research and Technology – Hellas
(FORTH)
Heraklion, Crete, Greece

Margherita Antona
Foundation for Research
and Technology – Hellas (FORTH)
Heraklion, Crete, Greece

Stavroula Ntoa
Foundation for Research
and Technology – Hellas (FORTH)
Heraklion, Crete, Greece

ISSN 1865-0929   ISSN 1865-0937   (electronic)
Communications in Computer and Information Science
ISBN 978-3-030-90175-2   ISBN 978-3-030-90176-9   (eBook)
https://doi.org/10.1007/978-3-030-90176-9

This Springer imprint is published by the registered company Springer Nature Switzerland AG
The registered company address is: Gewerbestrasse 11, 6330 Cham, Switzerland

Foreword

Human-Computer Interaction (HCI) is acquiring an ever-increasing scientific and industrial importance, and having more impact on people's everyday life, as an ever-growing number of human activities are progressively moving from the physical to the digital world. This process, which has been ongoing for some time now, has been dramatically accelerated by the COVID-19 pandemic. The HCI International (HCII) conference series, held yearly, aims to respond to the compelling need to advance the exchange of knowledge and research and development efforts on the human aspects of design and use of computing systems.

The 23rd International Conference on Human-Computer Interaction, HCI International 2021 (HCII 2021), was planned to be held at the Washington Hilton Hotel, Washington DC, USA, during July 24–29, 2021. Due to the COVID-19 pandemic and with everyone's health and safety in mind, HCII 2021 was organized and run as a virtual conference. It incorporated the 21 thematic areas and affiliated conferences listed on the following page.

A total of 5222 individuals from academia, research institutes, industry, and governmental agencies from 81 countries submitted contributions, and 1276 papers and 241 posters were included in the volumes of the proceedings that were published before the start of the conference. Additionally, 174 papers and 146 posters are included in the volumes of the proceedings published after the conference, as "Late Breaking Work" (papers and posters). The contributions thoroughly cover the entire field of HCI, addressing major advances in knowledge and effective use of computers in a variety of application areas. These papers provide academics, researchers, engineers, scientists, practitioners, and students with state-of-the-art information on the most recent advances in HCI. The volumes constituting the full set of the HCII 2021 conference proceedings are listed in the following pages.

I would like to thank the Program Board Chairs and the members of the Program Boards of all thematic areas and affiliated conferences for their contribution towards the highest scientific quality and overall success of the HCI International 2021 conference.

This conference would not have been possible without the continuous and unwavering support and advice of Gavriel Salvendy, founder, General Chair Emeritus, and Scientific Advisor. For his outstanding efforts, I would like to express my appreciation to Abbas Moallem, Communications Chair and Editor of HCI International News.

July 2021   Constantine Stephanidis

HCI International 2021 Thematic Areas and Affiliated Conferences

Thematic Areas

- HCI: Human-Computer Interaction
- HIMI: Human Interface and the Management of Information

Affiliated Conferences

- EPCE: 18th International Conference on Engineering Psychology and Cognitive Ergonomics
- UAHCI: 15th International Conference on Universal Access in Human-Computer Interaction
- VAMR: 13th International Conference on Virtual, Augmented and Mixed Reality
- CCD: 13th International Conference on Cross-Cultural Design
- SCSM: 13th International Conference on Social Computing and Social Media
- AC: 15th International Conference on Augmented Cognition
- DHM: 12th International Conference on Digital Human Modeling and Applications in Health, Safety, Ergonomics and Risk Management
- DUXU: 10th International Conference on Design, User Experience, and Usability
- DAPI: 9th International Conference on Distributed, Ambient and Pervasive Interactions
- HCIBGO: 8th International Conference on HCI in Business, Government and Organizations
- LCT: 8th International Conference on Learning and Collaboration Technologies
- ITAP: 7th International Conference on Human Aspects of IT for the Aged Population
- HCI-CPT: 3rd International Conference on HCI for Cybersecurity, Privacy and Trust
- HCI-Games: 3rd International Conference on HCI in Games
- MobiTAS: 3rd International Conference on HCI in Mobility, Transport and Automotive Systems
- AIS: 3rd International Conference on Adaptive Instructional Systems
- C&C: 9th International Conference on Culture and Computing
- MOBILE: 2nd International Conference on Design, Operation and Evaluation of Mobile Communications
- AI-HCI: 2nd International Conference on Artificial Intelligence in HCI

Conference Proceedings – Full List of Volumes

1. LNCS 12762, Human-Computer Interaction: Theory, Methods and Tools (Part I), edited by Masaaki Kurosu
2. LNCS 12763, Human-Computer Interaction: Interaction Techniques and Novel Applications (Part II), edited by Masaaki Kurosu
3. LNCS 12764, Human-Computer Interaction: Design and User Experience Case Studies (Part III), edited by Masaaki Kurosu
4. LNCS 12765, Human Interface and the Management of Information: Information Presentation and Visualization (Part I), edited by Sakae Yamamoto and Hirohiko Mori
5. LNCS 12766, Human Interface and the Management of Information: Information-rich and Intelligent Environments (Part II), edited by Sakae Yamamoto and Hirohiko Mori
6. LNAI 12767, Engineering Psychology and Cognitive Ergonomics, edited by Don Harris and Wen-Chin Li
7. LNCS 12768, Universal Access in Human-Computer Interaction: Design Methods and User Experience (Part I), edited by Margherita Antona and Constantine Stephanidis
8. LNCS 12769, Universal Access in Human-Computer Interaction: Access to Media, Learning and Assistive Environments (Part II), edited by Margherita Antona and Constantine Stephanidis
9. LNCS 12770, Virtual, Augmented and Mixed Reality, edited by Jessie Y. C. Chen and Gino Fragomeni
10. LNCS 12771, Cross-Cultural Design: Experience and Product Design Across Cultures (Part I), edited by P. L. Patrick Rau
11. LNCS 12772, Cross-Cultural Design: Applications in Arts, Learning, Well-being, and Social Development (Part II), edited by P. L. Patrick Rau
12. LNCS 12773, Cross-Cultural Design: Applications in Cultural Heritage, Tourism, Autonomous Vehicles, and Intelligent Agents (Part III), edited by P. L. Patrick Rau
13. LNCS 12774, Social Computing and Social Media: Experience Design and Social Network Analysis (Part I), edited by Gabriele Meiselwitz
14. LNCS 12775, Social Computing and Social Media: Applications in Marketing, Learning, and Health (Part II), edited by Gabriele Meiselwitz
15. LNAI 12776, Augmented Cognition, edited by Dylan D. Schmorrow and Cali M. Fidopiastis
16. LNCS 12777, Digital Human Modeling and Applications in Health, Safety, Ergonomics and Risk Management: Human Body, Motion and Behavior (Part I), edited by Vincent G. Duffy
17. LNCS 12778, Digital Human Modeling and Applications in Health, Safety, Ergonomics and Risk Management: AI, Product and Service (Part II), edited by Vincent G. Duffy

18. LNCS 12779, Design, User Experience, and Usability: UX Research and Design (Part I), edited by Marcelo Soares, Elizabeth Rosenzweig, and Aaron Marcus

19. LNCS 12780, Design, User Experience, and Usability: Design for Diversity, Well-being, and Social Development (Part II), edited by Marcelo M. Soares, Elizabeth Rosenzweig, and Aaron Marcus

20. LNCS 12781, Design, User Experience, and Usability: Design for Contemporary Technological Environments (Part III), edited by Marcelo M. Soares, Elizabeth Rosenzweig, and Aaron Marcus

21. LNCS 12782, Distributed, Ambient and Pervasive Interactions, edited by Norbert Streitz and Shin'ichi Konomi

22. LNCS 12783, HCI in Business, Government and Organizations, edited by Fiona Fui-Hoon Nah and Keng Siau

23. LNCS 12784, Learning and Collaboration Technologies: New Challenges and Learning Experiences (Part I), edited by Panayiotis Zaphiris and Andri Ioannou

24. LNCS 12785, Learning and Collaboration Technologies: Games and Virtual Environments for Learning (Part II), edited by Panayiotis Zaphiris and Andri Ioannou

25. LNCS 12786, Human Aspects of IT for the Aged Population: Technology Design and Acceptance (Part I), edited by Qin Gao and Jia Zhou

26. LNCS 12787, Human Aspects of IT for the Aged Population: Supporting Everyday Life Activities (Part II), edited by Qin Gao and Jia Zhou

27. LNCS 12788, HCI for Cybersecurity, Privacy and Trust, edited by Abbas Moallem

28. LNCS 12789, HCI in Games: Experience Design and Game Mechanics (Part I), edited by Xiaowen Fang

29. LNCS 12790, HCI in Games: Serious and Immersive Games (Part II), edited by Xiaowen Fang

30. LNCS 12791, HCI in Mobility, Transport and Automotive Systems, edited by Heidi Krömker

31. LNCS 12792, Adaptive Instructional Systems: Design and Evaluation (Part I), edited by Robert A. Sottilare and Jessica Schwarz

32. LNCS 12793, Adaptive Instructional Systems: Adaptation Strategies and Methods (Part II), edited by Robert A. Sottilare and Jessica Schwarz

33. LNCS 12794, Culture and Computing: Interactive Cultural Heritage and Arts (Part I), edited by Matthias Rauterberg

34. LNCS 12795, Culture and Computing: Design Thinking and Cultural Computing (Part II), edited by Matthias Rauterberg

35. LNCS 12796, Design, Operation and Evaluation of Mobile Communications, edited by Gavriel Salvendy and June Wei

36. LNAI 12797, Artificial Intelligence in HCI, edited by Helmut Degen and Stavroula Ntoa

37. CCIS 1419, HCI International 2021 Posters - Part I, edited by Constantine Stephanidis, Margherita Antona, and Stavroula Ntoa

38. CCIS 1420, HCI International 2021 Posters - Part II, edited by Constantine Stephanidis, Margherita Antona, and Stavroula Ntoa
39. CCIS 1421, HCI International 2021 Posters - Part III, edited by Constantine Stephanidis, Margherita Antona, and Stavroula Ntoa
40. LNCS 13094, HCI International 2021 - Late Breaking Papers: Design and User Experience, edited by Constantine Stephanidis, Marcelo M. Soares, Elizabeth Rosenzweig, Aaron Marcus, Sakae Yamamoto, Hirohiko Mori, P. L. Patrick Rau, Gabriele Meiselwitz, Xiaowen Fang, and Abbas Moallem
41. LNCS 13095, HCI International 2021 - Late Breaking Papers: Multimodality, eXtended Reality, and Artificial Intelligence, edited by Constantine Stephanidis, Masaaki Kurosu, Jessie Y. C. Chen, Gino Fragomeni, Norbert Streitz, Shin'ichi Konomi, Helmut Degen, and Stavroula Ntoa
42. LNCS 13096, HCI International 2021 - Late Breaking Papers: Cognition, Inclusion, Learning, and Culture, edited by Constantine Stephanidis, Don Harris, Wen-Chin Li, Dylan D. Schmorrow, Cali M. Fidopiastis, Margherita Antona, Qin Gao, Jia Zhou, Panayiotis Zaphiris, Andri Ioannou, Robert A. Sottilare, Jessica Schwarz, and Matthias Rauterberg
43. LNCS 13097, HCI International 2021 - Late Breaking Papers: HCI Applications in Health, Transport, and Industry, edited by Constantine Stephanidis, Vincent G. Duffy, Heidi Krömker, Fiona Fui-Hoon Nah, Keng Siau, Gavriel Salvendy, and June Wei
44. CCIS 1498, HCI International 2021 - Late Breaking Posters (Part I), edited by Constantine Stephanidis, Margherita Antona, and Stavroula Ntoa
45. CCIS 1499, HCI International 2021 - Late Breaking Posters (Part II), edited by Constantine Stephanidis, Margherita Antona, and Stavroula Ntoa

http://2021.hci.international/proceedings

HCI International 2021 (HCII 2021)

The full list with the Program Board Chairs and the members of the Program Boards of all thematic areas and affiliated conferences is available online:

http://www.hci.international/board-members-2021.php

HCI International 2022

The 24th International Conference on Human-Computer Interaction, HCI International 2022, will be held jointly with the affiliated conferences at the Gothia Towers Hotel and Swedish Exhibition & Congress Centre, Gothenburg, Sweden, June 26 – July 1, 2022. It will cover a broad spectrum of themes related to Human-Computer Interaction, including theoretical issues, methods, tools, processes, and case studies in HCI design, as well as novel interaction techniques, interfaces, and applications. The proceedings will be published by Springer. More information will be available on the conference website: http://2022.hci.international/.

General Chair
Prof. Constantine Stephanidis
University of Crete and ICS-FORTH
Heraklion, Crete, Greece
Email: general_chair@hcii2022.org

http://2022.hci.international/

Contents – Part I

HCI Theory and Practice

For a New Protocol to Promote Empathy Towards Users of Communication
Technologies 3
    Samip Bhurtel, Pedro G. Lind, and Gustavo B. Moreno e Mello

Unidentified Users of Design Documentation 11
    Agnes Cadier

Common Interactive Style Guide for Designers and Developers
Across Projects 17
    Bryan Croft, Jeffrey D. Clarkson, Eric Voncolln, Mike Nithaworn,
    Seana Rothman, and Odalis Felix

(DT)^2-Box – A Multi-sensory Approach to Support Design
Thinking Teams 24
    Julien Hofer and Markus Watermeyer

The Ethic of "CODE"—To Pro Mortalism and Antisurvivalism
from Antinatalism 31
    Sachio Horie

Theory and Practice in UX Design: Identification of Discrepancies
in the Development Process of User-Oriented HMI 37
    Svenja Knothe, Thomas Hofmann, and Christian Blessmann

Using Verbatims as a Basis for Building a Customer Journey Map:
A Case Study 44
    Arturo Moquillaza, Fiorella Falconi, Joel Aguirre, and Freddy Paz

Green Patterns of User Interface Design: A Guideline for Sustainable
Design Practices 51
    Jitesh Nayak and Apurva Chandwadkar

HCI Based Ethnography: A Possible Answer to Reduced Product Life 58
    Maarif Sohail, Zehra Mohsin, and Sehar Khaliq

Celebrating Design Thinking in Tech Education: The Data Science
Education Case 66
    Samar I. Swaid and Taima Z. Suid

Social Innovation and Design — Prototyping in the NICE2035 Future
Living Labs   71
Jing Wang

On the Life Aesthetics of Packaging Design in the Context
of Digital Economy.   81
Yifei Zhu and Wei Yu

UX Design and Research in Intelligent Environments

Lego®-like Bricks to Go from the Real to the Virtual World   91
Alejandro Cabrerizo, Will Zeurcher, Thomas Wright,
and Peter Jamieson

Systematic Literature Review of Nuclear Safety Systems in Small
Modular Reactors   99
Tucker Densmore and Vincent G. Duffy

Bio-Spatial Study in the Urban Context: User Experience Analysis from
New York, Preliminary Neurophysiological Analysis from Kuala Lumpur
and Nairobi   107
Arlene Ducao, Ilias Koen, Tania van Bergen, Yapah Berry, Scott Sheu,
Tommy Mitchell, and Landon Johnson

Speech Emotion Recognition Using Combined Multiple
Pairwise Classifiers   115
Panikos Heracleous, Yasser Mohammad, and Akio Yoneyama

QFami: An Integrated Environment for Recommending Answerers
on Campus.   119
Xiangyuan Hu and Shin'ichi Konomi

DoAR: An Augmented Reality Based Door Security
Prototype Application   126
Muhammad Usama Islam and Beenish Chaudhry

Machine Learning-Based Font Recognition and Substitution Method
for Electronic Publishing   135
Ning Li, Huan Zhao, and Xuhong Liu

Collaborative Explainable AI: A Non-algorithmic Approach to Generating
Explanations of AI   144
Tauseef Ibne Mamun, Robert R. Hoffman, and Shane T. Mueller

Toothbrush Force Measurement and 3D Visualization   151
Kasumi Sakuma, Haicui Li, and Lei Jing

A Study on the Creativity of Algorithm Art Using Artificial Intelligence   159
Ryan Seo

An Approach to Monitoring and Guiding Manual Assembly Processes   165
Benjamin Standfield and Denis Gračanin

Deep Learning Methods as a Detection Tools for Forest Fire Decision
Making Process Fire Prevention in Indonesia   177
Dia Meirina Suri and Achmad Nurmandi

Intelligent Music Lamp Design Based on Arduino.   183
Yuanlu Wang and Xiaofang Li

Exploring Drag-and-Drop User Interfaces for Programming Drone Flights . . .   191
Joshua Webb and Dante Tezza

Research on the Logical Levels and Roles of Human Interaction
with Intelligent Creatures Under the Trend of Human-Computer
Intelligence Integration.   197
Wei Yu and Xiaoju Wang

An AR-Enabled See-Through System for Vision Blind Areas.   206
Shaohua Zhang, Weiping He, Shuxia Wang, Shuo Feng,
Zhenghang Hou, and Yupeng Hu

IMGDS - Intelligent Multi-dimensional Generative Design System
for Industrial SCADA   214
Wei Zhao, Ruihang Tian, Nan Zhao, Jiachun Du, and Hanyue Duan

Interaction with Robots, Chatbots, and Agents

Storytelling Robots for Training of Emotion Recognition in Children
with Autism; Opinions from Experts   223
Maryam Alimardani, Lisa Neve, and Anouk Verkaart

A Study on the Usability Evaluation of Teaching Pendant for Manipulator
of Collaborative Robot.   234
Jeyoun Dong, Wookyong Kwon, Dongyeop Kang, and Seung Woo Nam

The Design and Evaluation of a Chatbot for Human Resources.   239
Jaimie Drozdal, Albert Chang, Will Fahey, Nikhilas Murthy,
Lehar Mogilisetty, Jody Sunray, Curtis Powell, and Hui Su

Relationship Between Eating and Chatting During Mealtimes
with a Robot   249
Ayaka Fujii, Kei Okada, and Masayuki Inaba

When in Doubt, Agree with the Robot? Effects of Team Size and Agent
Teammate Influence on Team Decision-Making in a Gambling Task   257
  Gregory J. Funke, Michael T. Tolston, Brent Miller,
  Margaret A. Bowers, and August Capiola

Modeling Salesclerks' Utterances in Bespoke Scenes and Evaluating Them
Using a Communication Robot   271
  Fumiya Kobayashi, Masashi Sugimoto, Saizo Aoyagi,
  Michiya Yamamoto, and Noriko Nagata

User Satisfaction with an AI-Enabled Customer Relationship
Management Chatbot   279
  Maarif Sohail, Zehra Mohsin, and Sehar Khaliq

Evaluation of a NUI Interface for an Explosives Deactivator Robotic Arm
to Improve the User Experience   288
  Denilson Vilcapaza Goyzueta, Joseph Guevara Mamani,
  Erasmo Sulla Espinoza, Elvis Supo Colquehuanca, Yuri Silva Vidal,
  and Pablo Pari Pinto

Attitudes Towards Human-Robot Collaboration and the Impact
of the COVID-19 Pandemic   294
  Verena Wagner-Hartl, Kevin Pohling, Marc Rössler, Simon Strobel,
  and Simone Maag

Older Adults' Voice Search through the Human-Engaged
Computing Perspective   300
  Xiaojun (Jenny) Yuan and Xiangshi Ren

Virtual, Augmented, and Mixed Reality

Research on Projection Interaction Based on Gesture Recognition   311
  Zhiwei Cao, Weiping He, Shuxia Wang, Jie Zhang, Bingzhao Wei,
  and Jianghong Li

The Effects of Social Proneness and Avatar Primes on Prosocial Behavior
in Virtual and Real Worlds   318
  Yu-chen Hsu, Siao-wei Huang, and Hsuan-de Huang

VR-Based Interface Enabling Ad-Hoc Individualization of Information
Layer Presentation   324
  Luka Jacke, Michael Maurus, and Elsa Andrea Kirchner

Alleviate the Cybersickness in VR Teleoperation by Constructing
the Reference Space in the Human-Machine Interface   332
  Weiwei Jia, Xiaoling Li, Yueyang Shi, Shuai Zheng, Long Wang,
  Zhangyi Chen, and Lixia Zhang

Translating Virtual Reality Research into Practice as a Way to Combat
Misinformation: The DOVE Website.............................. 341
   Chidinma U. Kalu, Stephen B. Gilbert, Jonathan W. Kelly,
   and Melynda Hoover

Software Usability Evaluation for Augmented Reality Through User Tests... 349
   Guto Kawakami, Aasim Khurshid, and Mikhail R. Gadelha

Virtual Reality to Mixed Reality Graphic Conversion in Unity:
Preliminary Guidelines and Graphic User Interface 357
   Ramy Kirollos and Martin Harriott

A Study on User Interface Design Based on Geo-Infographic
and Augmented Reality Technology 364
   Heehyeon Park

Comparing the Impact of State Versus Trait Factors on Memory
Performance in a Virtual Reality Flight Simulator.................... 369
   Anya Pejemsky, Kathleen Van Benthem, and Chris M. Herdman

Co-exploring the Design Space of Emotional AR Visualizations 377
   Sinem Şemsioğlu and Asım Evren Yantaç

Exploring an Immersive User Interface in Virtual Reality Storytelling 385
   Gapyuel Seo

Developing Spatial Visualization Skills with Virtual Reality
and Hand Tracking 390
   Liam Stewart and Christian Lopez

The Effect of Avatar Embodiment on Self-presence and User Experience
for Sensory Control Virtual Reality System 399
   Huey-Min Sun

Presenting a Sense of Self-motion by Transforming the Rendering Area
Based on the Movement of the User's Viewpoint.................... 410
   Tomoya Yamashita, Wataru Hashimoto, Satoshi Nishiguchi,
   and Yasuharu Mizutani

3D User Interface in Virtual Reality 418
   Gu Yue

Manual Preliminary Coarse Alignment of 3D Point Clouds in Virtual
Reality... 424
   Xiaotian Zhang, Weiping He, and Shuxia Wang

Games and Gamification

Agrihood: A Motivational Digital System for Sustainable
Urban Environments   435
    Antonio Bucchiarone, Giulia Bertoldo, and Sara Favargiotti

A Study on the Integration Method of Sports Practice and Video Games   443
    Sakuto Hoshi, Kazutaka Kurihara, Sho Sakurai, Koichi Hirota,
    and Takuya Nojima

Development of a Board Game Using Mixed Reality to Support
Communication.   451
    Shozo Ogawa, Kodai Ito, Ryota Horie, and Mitsunori Tada

The Creative Design-Engineer Divide: Modular Architecture
and Workflow UX   459
    Brian Packer, Simeon Keates, and Grahame Baker

Training of Drone Pilots for Children with Virtual Reality Environments
Under Gamification Approach   471
    Cristian Trujillo-Espinoza, Héctor Cardona-Reyes,
    José Eder Guzman-Mendoza, Klinge Orlando Villalba-Condori,
    and Dennis Arias-Chávez

The Interaction Design of AR Game Based on Hook Model for Children's
Environmental Habit Formation   479
    Qitong Xie and Wei Yu

Conflicts: A Game that Simulates Cognitive Dissonance
in Decision Making.   486
    Morgan Spencer Yao, John Casey Bandiola, John Michael Vince Lim,
    and Jonathan Casano

Development of 'School Nocturnble': A Sensitive Game
with Eye Trackers   494
    Subeen Yoo, Dain Kim, Seonyeong Park, and JungJo Na

HCI in Mobility, Transport and Aviation

Disruptive Technology in the Transportation Sector (Case in Indonesia).   503
    Pahmi Amri, Achmad Nurmandi, and Dyah Mutiarin

Collaborative Workspace – Concept Design and Proof of Concept of an
Interactive Visual System to Support Collaborative Decision-Making for
Total Airport Management   511
    Mandra Bensmann, Alicia Lampe, Thomas Hofmann, and Steffen Loth

From a Drones Point of View.   517
   D. L. Dolgin, D. Van Der Like, J. London, and C. Holdman

Desirable Backrest Angles in Automated Cars   521
   Martin Fleischer and Nikko Wendel

Identifying Mobility Pattern of Specific User Types Based
on Mobility Data   527
   Tobias Gartner, Waldemar Titov, and Thomas Schlegel

How to Find My Ride? Results of an HCI Expert Workshop
for AR-Aided Navigation.   535
   Fabian Hub and Michael Oehl

Smart Mobility: How Jakarta's Developing Sustainable Transportation
to Connect the Community.   543
   Mohammad Jafar Loilatu, Dyah Mutiarin, Achmad Nurmandi,
   Tri Sulistyaningsih, and Salahudin

Analysis of the Daily Mobility Behavior Before and After the Corona Virus
Pandemic – A Field Study   552
   Waldemar Titov and Thomas Schlegel

Research on Interaction Design Promote Aesthetic Changes in Car Styling
Under the Background of Intelligent Driving   558
   Mangmang Zhang

Author Index   565

Contents – Part II

Design for All and Assistive Technologies

Prototyping-Based Study of Designs for Eye-Tracking Interface
in Augmentative and Alternative Communication Applications   3
    Nayan Adhikari, Pedro G. Lind, and Gustavo B. Moreno e Mello

Wearable Device to Aid Impaired Vision People Against Covid-19   11
    Sandro Costa Mesquita, Tiago Diógenes de Araújo,
    and Victor Hazin da Rocha

An Evaluation of Foot Rowing Type Wheelchair for Elderly People
by Using Questionnaire with Experiments   17
    Naohisa Hashimoto, Yusuke Takinami, and Nobuhito Kakuta

An Electronic Guide Dog for the Blind Based on Artificial Neural
Networks   23
    Sergej Lopatin, Florian von Zabiensky, Michael Kreutzer, Klaus Rinn,
    and Diethelm Bienhaus

Exploratory Study into the Disability Awareness Through an Inclusive
Application Development Process Driven by Disabled Children   31
    Kanako Nakamura and Daisuke Kumagai

Evaluation and Classification of Dementia Using EEG Indicators During
Brain–Computer Interface Tasks   39
    Yuri Nishizawa, Hisaya Tanaka, Raita Fukasawa, Kentaro Hirao,
    Akito Tsugawa, and Soichiro Shimizu

Ideating for Co-designing with Blind and Visually Impaired Users:
Exploring Possibilities for Designing User-Centered Healthcare
Information in Pandemic Conditions   47
    Sushil K. Oswal and Lohitvenkatesh M. Oswal

A Domain-Specific Language for Model-Driven Development
of Networked Electronic Travel Aid Systems   56
    Florian von Zabiensky, Christian Loosen, Michael Kreutzer,
    and Diethelm Bienhaus

The Packaging Design of Braille Beverage Bottle Based on Universal
Design Thinking   64
    Zhou Yang, Shuyi Chen, Tianhong Fang, and Yifei Zhu

Physiology, Affect and Cognition

Obtaining External Motivation from Strangers:
A Study on Customer-to-Customer Interaction in Gymnasiums   73
   Ying-Yu Chiang, Hsien-Hui Tang, and Shu-Yi Chen

Real-Time Feedback of Subjective Affect and Working Memory Load
Based on Neurophysiological Activity   80
   *Sabrina Gado, Katharina Lingelbach, Michael Bui, Jochem W. Rieger,
   and Mathias Vukelić*

A Hierarchical Classification Scheme for Efficient Speech
Emotion Recognition   88
   Panikos Heracleous, Kohichi Takai, Keiji Yasuda, and Akio Yoneyama

Research on the Finger Contact Force of Persons of Different Gender
as Grasping Bottles   93
   Ru Ji, Zhellin Li, Jiaxu Fan, Yongyi Zhu, and Lijun Jiang

Sensorimotor EEG Rhythms During Action Observation and Passive
Mirror-Box Illusion   101
   Nikolay Syrov, Anatoly Vasilyev, and Alexander Kaplan

Multiple Regression Model for Cognitive Function Evaluation Using P300
Based Spelling-Brain–Computer Interface   107
   *Kohei Yoshida, Hisaya Tanaka, Raita Fukasawa, Kentaro Hirao,
   Akito Tsugawa, and Soichiro Shimizu*

HCI for Health and Wellbeing

Co-Designing M-Healer: Supporting Lay Practitioner Mental Health
Workers in Ghana   115
   *Liam Albright, Hoa Le, Suzanne Meller, Angela Ofori Atta,
   Dzifa A. Attah, Seth M. Asafo, Pamela Y. Collins, Dror Ben Zeev,
   and Jaime Snyder*

Using Experience-Based Co-design to Develop mHealth App for Digital
Pulmonary Rehabilitation Management of Patients with Chronic
Obstructive Pulmonary Disease (COPD)   125
   Qingfan An, Marjorie M. Kelley, and Po-Yin Yen

A Speech-Based Data Collection Interface for Contact Tracing   134
   Tamara Babaian

A Feasibility Study of an ICT Based Training for Older People with Mild
Cognitive Impairment: Future Perspective for Designers
and Health Professionals 139
  Roberta Bevilacqua, Elena Gambella, Elisa Felici, Patrizia Civerchia,
  Giovanni R. Riccardi, Susi Paolini, Sara Pasquini, Giuseppe Pelliccioni,
  and Elvira Maranesi

Usability Optimization of National Health Insurance Express App. 147
  Li-Hsin Chen and Meng-Cong Zheng

Preliminary Study on the Multi-person Cooperative Training Module
in the Application of Virtual Reality Technology to the Advanced Cardiac
Life Support. 155
  Hsu-Wen Hung and I.-Jui Lee

Study on the Step-By-Step Service Design and Service Strategy
of CoVID-19 Prevention and Control Medical Products 163
  Jinze Li, Mingming Zong, and Kamolmal Chaisirithanya

Exploring the Role of Cognitive Empathy and Emotional Empathy
in Medical Crowdfunding. 176
  Lili Liu, Qianyi Tao, and Shanjiao Ren

Advancing Reminiscence Therapy Using Virtual Reality Applications
for Persons with Dementia 184
  Daniel Presas, Rob Shewaga, Alvaro Uribe-Quevedo, Winnie Sun,
  and Sheri Horsburgh

Information Chaos in the Electronic Health Record as a Threat
to Patient Safety 189
  Emily Schaefer, Nicole Werner, and Matthew Scanlon

Rewards in Mental Health Applications for Aiding with Depression:
A Meta-analysis 197
  Stephanie Six, Maggie Harris, Emma Winterlind, and Kaileigh Byrne

Discussions About Covid-19 in Indonesia. Bibliometric Analysis
and Visualization Article Indexed in Scopus by Indonesian Authors 207
  M. Syamsurrijal, Achmad Nurmandi, Misran, Hasse Jubba,
  Mega Hidayati, and Zuly Qodir

UI/UX Design of Portable Simulation Pet 'KEDAMA' Hairball
for Relieving Pressure 215
  Jiang Wu, Yihang Dai, Jiawei Li, and Yuan Yuan

A Usability Testing of COVID-19 Vaccine Appointment Websites 224
  John Xie

HCI in Learning, Teaching, and Education

Student eXperience: A Survey in Argentinian Universities About Education
in the Pandemic Context   233
    Iván Balmaceda Castro, Cristian Rusu, and Silvana Aciar

Development of a Digital Collaborative Whiteboard   242
    Armin Beckmann, Marc Bollmann, Tim Buchholz, Rafael Geiser,
    Daniel Kerpen, and Jan Conrad

Computational Thinking and Language Immersion with Umwelt.   249
    Zeynep Büyükyazgan, Demir Alp, Elif Selin Kozanoğlu, Rana Taki,
    Arda Eren, and Sedat Yalçın

Usability of Digital Numeration Training for Students at Primary School. . . .   258
    Ningxi Chen, Adrian Roussel-Fayard, Nadine Vigouroux,
    Jean-François Camps, Charlotte Tabarant, and Frédéric Vella

LABS ONLINE – An Opportunity to Access High Quality Laboratory
During COVID Breakout.   266
    Romi Dey and Kailash Manjhi

Conversational Agents in Language Education: Where They Fit and Their
Research Challenges   272
    Rahul R. Divekar, Haley Lepp, Pravin Chopade, Aaron Albin,
    Daniel Brenner, and Vikram Ramanarayanan

Digital Tool to Detect the State of Languishing of Students During
the Covid-19 Pandemic   280
    M. Guzmán, P. Manzanilla, J. Martínez, T. Tapia, A. Núñez,
    and S. Zepeda

Use of Virtual Resources as a Tool for Teaching Language Skills
at the Colombian Caribbean Region Primary Basic Level.   286
    Maria Moreno, Sonia Duran, Margel Parra,
    Irmina Hernández-Sánchez, and Javier Ramírez

Establishing Cyberpsychology at Universities in the Area
of Cyber Security   294
    Paulina Ruh and Holger Morgenstern

Using a Mobile Augmented Reality APP on Mathematics Word Problems
for Children   302
    Mengping Tsuei and Jen-I Chiu

Implementation of ICTs in a University Curriculum for the Development
of Math and Critical Reading Skills During COVID-19 Pandemic.   307
  Derlis Aminta Villadiego Rincón, Alex Alberto Castellar Rodríguez,
  Harold Gamero Rodríguez, and Adriana del Rosario Pineda Robayo

Culture and Computing

An Exploratory Study of the Business Strategies for Virtual Idols in the Era
of Phygitalization—Analysis in the Perspective of Cases in China.   317
  Han Han, Minling Lin, and Francesco Zurlo

Mobile Application to Disseminate the History of Historical Buildings   325
  A. Méndez, C. Borja, D. González, A. Núñez, and S. Zepeda

Digital Representation of Virtual Reality Environments of Gothic Choirs
Using Photogrammetric 3D Models: Monasteries of Yuste and Nájera.   331
  Carles Pàmies, Isidro Navarro, Alberto Sánchez Riera,
  and Ernest Redondo

Visualization of Patterns and Impressions in YOSAKOI Costumes   339
  Yuka Takahashi and Namgyu Kang

From Text to Image: Image Application and Design Transformation
of Traditional Cultural IP Resources – A Case Study of the Classic
of Mountains and Seas.   347
  Jie Zhou and Jingyi Cui

Social Computing

Social Media in Politic: Political Campaign on United States Election 2020
Between Donald Trump and Joe Biden   359
  Paisal Akbar, Bambang Irawan, Mohammad Taufik, Achmad Nurmandi,
  and Suswanta

Exploring the Effect of Activity Intervention on Reducing Social Media
Use: Lessons Learned in a Field Study   368
  Ju-Ling Ko, Chieh Yuan, Billy Malherbe, Cheng-Han Yang,
  and Pei-Yi Kuo

Social Media as Tools of Disaster Mitigation, Studies on Natural Disasters
in Indonesia   375
  Danang Kurniawan, Arissy Jorgi Sutan, Achmad Nurmandi,
  Mohammad Jafar Loilatu, and Salahudin

STellaR – A Stationary Telepresence Counselling System for Collaborative
Work on Paper Documents   383
   Matti Laak, Anne-Kathrin Schmitz, Dominic Becking, Udo Seelmeyer,
   Philipp Waag, and Marc Weinhardt

Why Audiences Donate Money to Content Creators? A Uses
and Gratifications Perspective   390
   Lili Liu, Jiujiu Jiang, Shanjiao Ren, and Linwei Hu

Social Media and Social Movements: Using Social Media on Omnibus Law
Job Creation Bill Protest in Indonesia and Anti Extradition Law
Amendment Bill Movement in Hongkong   399
   Arissy Jorgi Sutan, Achmad Nurmandi, and Salahudin

The Message Is Unclear: Evaluating Disinformation in Anti-Vaccine
Communities   407
   Alicia J. W. Takaoka

Understanding Continuance Usage Intention of Shopping Guide Apps
in Social Commerce   414
   Shuo Zhang, Lili Liu, Mingzhu Li, Qianru Tao, Ruoqi Zhang,
   and Yunguo Xia

Design Case Studies

Optimizing the Information of Sport Graphics in the Major
League Baseball   425
   Chih-Yung Chen and Meng-Cong Zheng

Web Interface for Power Grid Database   433
   Sujan Devkota, Pedro G. Lind, and Norun Christine Sanderson

HyperSCADA: A Codification Framework for Improving SCADA System
User Experience Design   441
   Jiachun Du, Hanyue Duan, Nan Zhao, and Ruihang Tian

Study on Optimal Design of Dynamic Information Display - a Case Study
of Taipei Metro   446
   Hsin-An Huang and Meng-Cong Zheng

Quality Analysis of Local Government Websites (Study Case DKI Jakarta,
Bali, Banten Provinces)   454
   Miftahul Jannah Jalil, Achmad Nurmandi, Isnaini Muallidin,
   Danang Kurniawan, and Salahudin

An Experimental Analysis of Face Anti-spoofing Strategies for Real
Time Applications   463
   Aasim Khurshid and Ricardo Grunitzki

A Meta-analysis of Big Data Security: How the Government Formulates
a Model of Public Information and Security Assurance into Big Data   472
    Achmad Nurmandi, Danang Kurniawan, Misran, and Salahudin

Website Quality Analysis in Three Ministries of Indonesia Study Ministry
of Finance, Ministry of Home Affairs, and Ministry of Village   480
    Achmad Nurmandi, Ramaini Mei, Isnaini Muallidin,
    Danang Kurniawan, and Salahudin

Presentation of a Three-Dimensional Image by Rotating Pepper's Ghost   489
    Ryuichi Shibata, Wataru Hashimoto, Yasuharu Mizutani,
    and Satoshi Nishiguchi

Study on Dynamic Emotional Design Expression in Interface Vision
of Digital Media Art   497
    Fei Wang

Research on Furniture Design Based on Parametric Urbanism.   505
    Weijia Zhao and Maoqi Xu

User Experience Studies

Old-looking yet Usable!: An Investigation of Consumer's Usability
Perception of Retro Products   515
    Nektar Ege Altıntoprak and Wei Wang

Customer Value Co-creation Behaviors Through Online Interactions
in Luxury Hotels: Effect on Customer Loyalty   522
    Zineb Bouchriha, Sabra Farid, and Smail Ouiddad

Perceptions in Two-Dimensional and Three-Dimensional
Aperture Problems   527
    Guang-Dah Chen and Hsiwen Fan

A Pilot Study on Navigation for Information Acquisition Using
Eye Tracking   535
    Fumiya Inoue and Makio Ishihara

A Comparison of Multiple Selections Using Multiple Checkbox Selections
and List Boxes   539
    Wasana Leithe and Frode Eika Sandnes

The Influence of Team Workload Demands During a Cyber Defense
Exercise on Team Performance.   545
    Ricardo G. Lugo, Torvald F. Ask, Stefan Sütterlin, and Benjamin J. Knox

Estimation of Consumer Needs Using Review Data in Hotel Industry   550
    Shin Miyake, Kohei Otake, Tomofumi Uetake, and Takashi Namatame

Influence of the Contact Surface Size on the Illusory Movement Induced
by Tendon Vibrations   558
    Hiroyuki Ohshima and Shigenobu Shimada

Training and Learning for Long Duration Spaceflight   564
    Terry Rector, Curtis Cripe, and James Casler

Changes of Multiple Object Tracking Performance
in a 15 Days' - 6° Head-Down Tilt Bed Rest Experiment   572
    Hongqiang Yu, Ting Jiang, Bingxian Zhou, and Chunhui Wang

Author Index   579

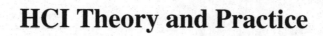

HCI Theory and Practice

For a New Protocol to Promote Empathy Towards Users of Communication Technologies

Samip Bhurtel[1,2], Pedro G. Lind[1,2,3(✉)], and Gustavo B. Moreno e Mello[1,2,3]

[1] Department of Computer Science, OsloMet – Oslo Metropolitan University,
P.O. Box 4 St. Olavs plass, 0130 Oslo, Norway
[2] ORCA – OsloMet Research Center for AI, Pilestredet 52, 0166 Oslo, Norway
[3] NordSTAR – Nordic Center for Sustainable and Trustworthy AI Research,
Pilestredet 52, 0166 Oslo, Norway

Abstract. We propose an experimental protocol to promote empathy towards non-verbal people, based in the training of communication with an eye-tracking device. Our framework includes one eye-tracker, one communication interface and one questionnaire. The questionnaire is applied before and after the intervention, assessing the empathy level of participants in both stages of the experiment and it extends a validated questionnaire (QCAE) to measure empathy. Our results show that, while the empathy levels seem to decrease in both control and test groups, the decrease in the test group is not as significant as in the control group. The statistical power to distinguish between the scores in both groups is 75%. While both QCAE and our extended questionnaire show a strong correlation ($R^2 = 0.95$), our extended questionnaire is more sensitive in distinguishing between both groups than the standard QCAE for which we obtain a power of 63%. Finally, we discuss limitations and future directions, such as extending the study to a larger sample and applying it to different school or working contexts.

Keywords: Eye-tracker · Augmented communication · Social inclusion

1 Introduction

Imagine a life where verbal communication would not be possible. How would we gather together and chat about our day? How would we express our emotions, easily reflected in the intonation of our sentences? To communicate without speaking is challenging and to understand that is not trivial, particularly if one never faced that challenge. Indeed, the widely spread claim that communication is only 7% verbal, based in a few limited studies during the 1960's, is now starting to be questioned, based in what has been uncovered since then (Lapakko 2007). Non-verbal people around the world suffer e.g. locked-in syndrome, quadriplegia or brain paralysis (Farr et al. 2021) and face serious challenges when communicating (Mehrabian 2017), including not only the difficulty to be understood,

© Springer Nature Switzerland AG 2021
C. Stephanidis et al. (Eds.): HCII 2021, CCIS 1498, pp. 3–10, 2021.
https://doi.org/10.1007/978-3-030-90176-9_1

but also a higher propensity to be subjected to injustice and discrimination in society (Catala 2020). It is therefore important for the society to establish ways for inclusion of this particular group.

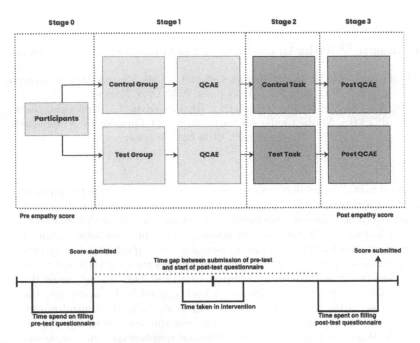

Fig. 1. (Top) Experimental design to test the protocol for promoting empathy towards users of eye-tracking devices for communication. (Bottom) The time variables taken into account during the experiment.

To communicate, non-verbal people usually adopt communication technologies such as eye-tracking devices, which have contribute to more inclusiveness (Smith and Delargy 2005). With an eye-tracker, non-verbal people communicate by moving the eyes among sets of letters and words on a computer screen, during which the eye-tracking device tracks the fixation periods on the selected letters or words (Prabaswari et al. 2021). However, such technologies alone are not enough to fill the gap between verbal and non-verbal people in regards to communication (Robinson et al. 2020). Verbal people are typically not aware about the challenges associated with communication using augmented technologies (Poletti et al. 2017). Consequently, to develop inclusiveness, it would be helpful to establish protocols which easily promote the empathy of all social groups towards non-verbal people.

In this paper we propose such a protocol. The protocol is tested throughout an experimental intervention sketched in Fig. 1 and can be used to enable verbal people to experience the same challenges in communicating as non-verbal people. We adapt a validated questionnaire of cognitive and affective empathy (QCAE) by Reniers and co-workers (Reniers et al. 2011), extending it to suit the specific situation of empathy towards users of eye-tracking devices.

2 Experimental Set-Up, Methods and Research Protocol

We used an eye-tracking set-up consisting of a Tobii Pro X3-120 Hardware and the software Tobii Pro Lab Presenter Edition[1], at the Eye-tracking Lab of Oslo Metropolitan University. Figure 2 (top) shows the main components.

The eye-tracker was used in combination with a digital interface, consisting of an e-tran board, illustrated in Fig. 2 (bottom). The e-tran board is a cheap augmented communication interface (Zhang et al. 2017), which facilitates to easily replicate the intervention tested in our study. It is divided in nine regions, the central one empty and the remaining eight consisting of letters with colors. Using this e-tran board, the communication is done in two steps: first, participants choose the letters they need to use (Fig. 2 bottom left), and, second, they select color of the frame to identify the letter (Fig. 2 bottom right) (Krohn et al. 2020).

In what concerns participants, we apply our intervention to a total of 44 participants, between 20 and 40 years, equally divided into control and test groups. Most of the participants were students. Four of them were nurse by profession and one was part-time student. The remaining 39 were bachelors and masters students from three Norwegian universities.

After recruiting the participants and grouping them into control and test groups, the experiment followed three main stages (see Fig. 1 top). In Stage 1, each participant answered the questionnaire for assessing the empathy level and the respective score was recorded. We have used questionnaire of cognitive and affective empathy (QCAE) to access the level of empathy, consisting of 31 questions, with scoring answers ranging from "strongly disagree" (1) to "strongly agree" (4). The test was validated at university of Birmingham by Reniers and co-workers (Reniers et al. 2011). We add 9 new questions to better contextualize the questionnaire to the specific situation of empathy towards users of communication technologies. To assess the validity of our extended questionnaire, which we call henceforth "complete questionnaire", we analyze our results considering both this questionnaire and the standard QCAE.

In Stage 2, the control group performed a task consisting of looking to an image of random pixel during one minute, while the test group was subjected to the planned intervention. The intervention consisted eight small tasks, to construct specific sentences:

1. "Please type hello with the letters that are available on the screen."
2. "Can you type your full name."
3. "Please type: Can you help me?"
4. "Please type: Can you take me to the restroom?"
5. "Please type: I am hungry. Can you do me some eggs?"

---

[1] https://www.tobii.com/.

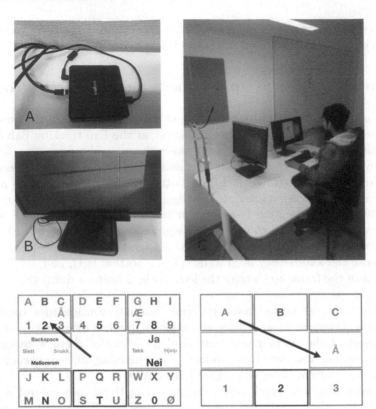

Fig. 2. (Top) Eye-tracker and the Tobii hardware: (A) connector, (B) eye-tracker plugged to the screen, (C) full set-up and lab at OsloMet. (Bottom) Illustration of E-tran boards used during the intervention for the test group.

6. "Please type: I am uncomfortable. Can you change my position?"
7. "Please type: I am in pain. Can you give me some medication?"
8. "Please type: Hi, how are you?"

In Stage 3, participants in both groups repeated the questionnaire and the respective score of their empathy level was recorded.

Moreover, we also interviewed some of the participants in the end of Stage 3, to better understand possible reasons for specific participants to score higher than the rest of the group.

3   Main Results and Power Analysis

3.1   Assessing the Empathy Development After the Intervention

In Fig. 3 (left) we plot the individual score difference before and after the intervention for both groups and both questionnaires. There are three main observations. First, in all cases there seems to be a persistence in a *decrease* of empathy

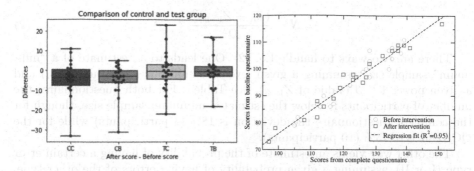

Fig. 3. (Left) The difference that we achieved after the experiment. We compared the results before and after the experiment for both test and control group in boxplot. First letter indicates the group ("C"ontrol and "T"est) and second indicates the questionnaire ("C"omplete and "B"aseline). (Right) Scores for both the complete and the baseline questionnaires, showing a strong correlation with $R^2 = 0.95$.

Table 1. Summary of results for both control and test groups and both standard and complete questionnaires.

	Standard QCAE	Complete quest.
Mean/stand. dev. control group	$\mu_c = 91, \sigma_c = 8$	$\mu_c = 117, \sigma_c = 11$
Mean/stand. dev. test group	$\mu_t = 96, \sigma_t = 12$	$\mu_t = 124, \sigma_t = 14$
Effect size D, Eq. (1)	0.49	0.56
Sample size for $\alpha = 0.05$, $1 - \beta = 0.8$	32	26
Prob. type-II error for $\alpha = 0.05$	37%	25%

levels, with most participants showing a negative score difference. This is to some extent a non-expected outcome in our study. Second, the decrease in empathy is not so significant for the test group as for the control group. Third, the differences obtained with the complete questionnaire do not differ considerably from the standard QCAE in both groups, though there is an apparent stronger deviation when considering the complete questionnaire solely.

To better quantify these claims we carry out a power analysis (Schellenberg et al. 2021) of our results. Table 1 shows the mean and standard deviation computed from the scores differences before and after intervention in both control and test groups. These quantities enable to estimate the effect size D given by

$$D = \frac{|\mu_c - \mu_t|}{\tilde{\sigma}}, \tag{1}$$

where $\tilde{\sigma}$ is the pooled standard deviation, given by the weighted average of the standard deviations of each group $\tilde{\sigma} = \sqrt{(\sigma_c^2 + \sigma_t^2)/2}$. Assuming the same sample size N for both groups, the effect size D can be used together with chosen Z-scores with a given significance level α and for a given power $1 - \beta$, to provide an estimate of the minimum sample size in each group:

$$N \sim \frac{(Z_\alpha + Z_{1-\beta})^2}{D^2}. \tag{2}$$

There are two ways to handle Eq. (2). One leads to an estimate of a "minimum" sample size assuming a given level of significance α (value of Z_α) and a given power $1 - \beta$ (value of $Z_{1-\beta}$). See Table 1: For both questionnaires the number of participants is below the estimated minimum sample size, though for the complete questionnaire the deviation is 18% (4 participants) while for the QCAE it is of 45% (10 participants).

The other way yields an estimate of the probability of having a certain error type (I or II), assuming a given probability of having errors of the other type. Indeed, if we substitute the sampel size $N = 22$ in Eq. (2) and assume a significance level of $\alpha = 0.05$ we can estimate the value of $Z_{1-\beta}$ and hence estimate the probability β of having type-II errors, i.e. the probability of not rejecting the null hypothesis ($\mu_c = \mu_t$) given that it is false ($\mu_c \neq \mu_t$). See Table 1: Interestingly, although in both cases the power is below the threshold usually accepted in social sciences (80%), the power obtained for the complete test (75%) is significantly higher than that obtained for the standard QCAE (63%).

3.2 A Questionnaire to Assess Empathy in the Context of Communication with an Eye-Tracker

To adapt the QCAE questionnaire to the specific context of communicating with the eye-tracker, we extend it with 9 new questions, namely

1. "I feel frustrated when I cannot communicate my ideas."
2. "I complete the sentences of other people when they find it difficult to communicate their ideas to help them."
3. "If someone is suffering from stutter, I prefer speaking rather than texting."
4. "I try to be patient when people speak with me very slowly."
5. "In a situation, when there are handicapped students in a classroom, the pace of the class should be adapted to the handicapped student."
6. "In a situation, when there are only one handicapped student in a classroom, the pace of the class should be adapted to him/her independently of how many students are in the class."
7. "I feel impatient when people communicate slowly, so I complete other people's sentences to make the communication more efficient."
8. "I believe that the handicapped students should catch the pace of the group in a classroom to not delay the progress of other students."
9. "I feel left out (or excluded) when I cannot participate in a conversation."

These questions were selected from a first list of 20 questions about users of communication technologies after performing a focus group with 6 participants.

In Fig. 3 (left), we can see that there is a positive correlation between baseline test score obtained from the participants with complete test score obtained for both, before and after intervention for experimental group.

4 Discussion and Conclusions

In this study we proposed a protocol to promote empathy in common individuals towards users of communication technologies. To this end we carried out an experiment to assess empathy before and after the protocol, combining an eye-tracking device, a communication interface e-tran board and a questionnaire. The questionnaire extends a validated questionnaire to assess empathy levels, adapted to our specific situation.

We report three main results. First, a decrease in the empathy level was observed, after using the eye-tracking, although for the test group the decrease of the empathy level was not as evident as for the control group. This finding is somehow counter-intuitive. Possibly one experiment was not enough to promote empathy in participants, or the time of the experimental session was not long enough or the participants recruited for the experiment was not enough to get the significant results. We analyzed several time variables, sketched in Fig. 1 (bottom), but we did not find any significant correlation between them and the empathy level decrease.

Second, we did not find strong evidence to reject the null hypothesis, though power analysis points towards a larger sample size to increase the statistical power to not reject the null hypothesis.

Third, and perhaps more interesting, it seems that the deviation between both groups is sharper when taking the complete questionnaire showing a statistical power of 75%. Moreover, although our complete questionnaire was not validated, we found a strong positive correlation between the completed questionnaire and the validated QCAE, which indicates that the questionnaire may be further tested and used in forthcoming studies.

All in all, this study can be an inspiration for future research, such as in exposure therapy, where a virtual environment is created in which participants would encounter the difficulties faced by nonverbal people while interacting, or as a training protocol in the school context or in companies, particularly aimed at groups including users of communication technologies.

Acknowledgements. The authors thank Prof. Dr. Renate Reniers, from the Institute of Clinical Sciences at the University of Birmingham, for providing us the questionnaire which we adapted to our intervention. Moreover, we are grateful to all the students and employees at Oslo Metropolitan University, who volunteered to participate in the experiment. SB thanks the Department of Computer Science and the OsloMet Research Center for AI (ORCA) at OsloMet for financial support.

References

Catala, A.: Metaepistemic injustice and intellectual disability: a pluralist account of epistemic agency. Ethical Theory Moral Pract. **23**(5), 755–776 (2020)

Farr, E., Altonji, K., Harvey, R.L.: Locked-in syndrome: practical rehabilitation management. PM&R (2021)

Krohn, O.A.N., Varankian, V., Lind, P.G., Moreno e Mello, G.B.: Construction of an inexpensive eye tracker for social inclusion and education. In: Antona, M., Stephanidis, C. (eds.) HCII 2020. LNCS, vol. 12188, pp. 60–78. Springer, Cham (2020). https://doi.org/10.1007/978-3-030-49282-3_5

Lapakko, D.: Communication is 93 nonverbal: an urban legend proliferates. Commun. Theater Assoc. Minnesota J. **34**, 7–19 (2007)

Mehrabian, A.: Nonverbal Communication. Routledge (2017)

Poletti, B., et al.: An eye-tracker controlled cognitive battery: overcoming verbal-motor limitations in ALS. J. Neurol. **264**(6), 1136–1145 (2017)

Prabaswari, A.D., Utomo, B.W., Purnomo, H.: Eye tracker evaluation on google classroom using use questionnaire. J. Phys. Conf. Ser. **1764**, 012181 (2021)

Reniers, R.L., Corcoran, R., Drake, R., Shryane, N.M., Völlm, B.A.: The QCAE: a questionnaire of cognitive and affective empathy. J. Pers. Assess. **93**(1), 84–95 (2011)

Robinson, C., Brulé, E., Jackson, J., Torjussen, A., Kybett, J. and Appshaw, T. (2020). Tricks and treats: Designing technology to support mobility assistance dogs. In Proceedings of the 2020 CHI Conference on Human Factors in Computing Systems (pp. 1–14)

Schellenberg, F., Gnad, D.R., Moradi, A., Tahoori, M.B.: An inside job: remote power analysis attacks on FPGAs. IEEE Design & Test (2021)

Smith, E., Delargy, M.: Locked-in syndrome. BMJ **330**(7488), 406–409 (2005)

Zhang, X., Kulkarni, H., Morris, M.R.: Smartphone-based gaze gesture communication for people with motor disabilities. In: Proceedings of the 2017 CHI Conference on Human Factors in Computing Systems, pp. 2878–2889 (2017)

Unidentified Users of Design Documentation

Agnes Cadier(✉)

Department of Informatics, Lund University, Ole Römers väg 6, SE-223 63 Lund, Sweden

Abstract. When working with system development and design, one is urged to write design documentation. The design document should be constructed in a specific way and should include all necessary information. However, the users of the design document are not stated and seem to be secondary. This study's aim is therefore to investigate who the users are. A literature review was conducted to answer the question. The literature showed that design documentation is a tool to communicate design and it should include relatable information. The essential role of design documents within software projects were also discussed and hence, they are included in this study. The literature review revealed that the system developer and the individuals which are involved in the production of the software is the users. To investigate this further, a hypothesis was formed and thereafter an observation was done, where videos of system developers were observed. The observation showed that system developers do not verbalize the importance of design documentation. Secondly, the study showed how unidentified the users are and that the discussion of who they are is limited. Furthermore, the design documentation is a valuable tool for communicating amongst other designers but if the documentation is not read, it is argued to be a waste of valuable time. The results presented within this study, therefore indicates that a definition of who the user is of design documentation is required.

Keywords: Design documentation · Users · Communication tool and human computer interaction

1 Method

To answer this paper's question, who the users of design documentation is and if they use it, a literature review was conducted with keywords such as "importance of design documentation", "design documentation AND human computer interaction", "design documentation and users" and "design documentation AND system development". Lund's university's database LUB Search Discovery, Google Scholar and ResearchGate were used when searching for relatable articles. Books, articles, and blogs were also used besides the articles. After the literature review, a hypothesis answer to the paper's question was evolved. To problematize the hypothesis, videos published by system developers on YouTube were observed. The criteria for the videos were: published within the last two years and a detailed description of their working day. The videos were watched one by one, and some short notes were taken during the observation. After the observations made on YouTube, an analysis of the notes was conducted.

© Springer Nature Switzerland AG 2021
C. Stephanidis et al. (Eds.): HCII 2021, CCIS 1498, pp. 11–16, 2021.
https://doi.org/10.1007/978-3-030-90176-9_2

2   Communicating Design

A challenge for a designer is to communicate their mental representation of an imaginative design, and a solution to this challenge is to include all the artifacts gained from the design process [1, 14]. Furthermore, an important point, raised by Pyle [17] is that another challenge for the author of design documentation is to come to the understanding regards, why software developers might seek information in their daily work. What information needs to be included within the design documentation to simplify the procedure of building a system [1]. Information about how the different components interact and so on, but the author also needs to have access to detailed design information [17]. Thus, are the following aspects important to include:

- A holistic picture of the complete system, with the aim to generate an overall understanding of the system.
- Detailed information about the components, alongside with the interface and the relationship amongst the components [17].

2.1   The Essential Role of Design Documents

When working on a project is seldom a one man show, you are a part of a team. Some of the members work on one part and your teammates are working on something different. When it comes to putting the whole project together, you need to understand what your teammates have done. One way of finding out is to read the generated documents. One thing one can be certain of is that you simply cannot put a whole system together without understanding the parts and expect the results to be a functioning system. You need to understand the other parts in order to integrate them in a functional way and one way of doing so is by sharing the code. However, this is not enough, the developers need the design documents as well [8].

According to Brown [3], a design document is the result from the design process, he continues by stating that documentation is mostly useless. Design documentation plays an essential role within the software development environment and its purpose is to communicate how to use the software, how it works, what it does and how to use it [17]. A document which encapsulates all design knowledge for a system or application is referred to as a software design document. The document should be well-structured, and it often contains models and textual description of the system. By gathering everything in one document, it can be easier to share one's design information to others [15].

The design document is a result from the design process and Brown [3] therefore refers to them as a deliverable. Furthermore, the artifact is submitted during the design project with the aim to capture decisions, simulate conversations and to facilitate communication. The deliverable is also seen as a tool to navigate within the design. A deliverable's legibility and actionability is the starting point of deciding if the deliverable can be classed as a good or a bad deliverable [3].

The way the deliverables can be presented is within documents and, preferable through a presentation of the deliverables. The design document could include descriptions such as personas where the site's target group is described or by a wireframe where the content is represented. These are just two examples of doing it, there are many more ways of presenting the artifacts and preferable, one should include a lot of different ways within the design documentation but also when presenting the design. In this way, it could be easier for the external stakeholders to understand how the design process was conducted and get an understanding of how the final design emerged [3].

3 Results from Literature Review

The aim of this paper was to identify the users of design documentation. One identified user is the system developers, this is because they generate different development artifacts [12] Furthermore, Morales et al. [12] states that the system developers have the responsibility to make use of various elements such as the development artifacts. With a design documentation, containing an explanation of the developed artifacts, can the software developer find answers when other developers are not available [17].

As presented in Jensen's [10] blog post, the design documentation can help the developer to communicate to the project's stakeholders, both internal and external. This can in turn demonstrate the value of the project. Jensen [10] also referees the design documents as an enabler for bringing the technology to life, and how it can be used for claiming a patent on a system. Moreover, Fox [6] writes in a blog post that the design documents serve as evidence of agreement between the developers and the project owner, and one should discard the projects who do not have specified time outlined for just documentation.

Individuals which are involved in the production of the software do read the design documents generated by the developers. Project leaders, developers and managers are all individuals who can be regarded as involved within the production of the software. These suggested individuals could be considered as users of the design documents, but it is however not clearly stated by the authors. Another user of the design documentation, as previously mentioned, could also be other software developers within the same developing team, which tries to understand the other developed artifacts within the system. Therefore, a user of a design document can be seen as an individual who reads the documents, or it could be seen as the individual who actually uses the documents within their daily work.

3.1 A Hypothesis and Observation

Based on Morales et al. [12] and Pyle [17] a hypothesis of who the users of the design documentation are, were formed: The system developers are the users. To get some information about what a workday could look like for a software developer one can turn to YouTube. Within the videos one can learn in a detailed way of how a workday can look like, a substitute for doing interviews with different software developers. Two questions were to be answered during the observation, to investigate the hypothesis. The questions where:

1. Is the individual starting their day by reading design documents?
2. Is it some part of their working day which they do read design documents?

4 Results from Observation

As one can see, in Table 1, there were none who started off their day by looking at design documentation and there were only two who looked at documents at some point. The documents Nguyen [13] turned to were about the coding syntax and not about the design. In Clever Programmer's [5] video it is stated that the life of a software developer is messy, and the days lack routine, hence, one day might start off with looking through design documentation, but in this video it does not. Within Hammond's [7] video, he states that the work of a software engineer is often glamorized to make the work look more appealing and in he's video, he tries to show a real life.

Table 1. Result from YouTube

Video posted by:	Question 1:	Question 2:
Clever Programmer	No	No
Justin Hammond	No	Yes
Nguyen	No	Yes
Josh and Katie	No	No
Amigoscode	No	No
Product Manager	No	No
Omar Khan	No	No
Chau Codes	No	No

Within this video, one can learn that documentation is a part of the coding process. However, it is not stated how much time of the day is spent on documentation. In the video where one can follow a software engineer working at Google, uploaded by Nguyen [13], it is shown how the engineer is stuck on a problem within the code. The way the problem is solved is by looking at documentation. The documentation is, however, not a design document, it is a coding syntax document. Within the videos published by Josh and Katie [11], Amigoscode [2], Product Manager [16], Khan [9] and Chau Codes [4] the documentation is not even mentioned.

5 Conclusion

This study set out to investigate the different users of design documentation, and the study has identified two different users; the system developer and individuals which are involved in the production of the software, the stakeholders. However, this study suggests, through observation, that system developers pay limited attention to use design documents. Based on this study, it indicates a lack of how unidentified the users are, and that the discussion could be non-existing. The literature presented within the study did however reveal that the users of user design documentation are considered to be the system developers. Nevertheless, when looking into what a work day of a system developer looks like, can one find that only two did use design documentation, and one of them did in fact look at a document containing coding syntax so that leaves it up to only one user. An implication of this is the possibility that software developers only to a limited extent use design documentation and therefore I suggest that further research is conducted on the matter. A further study could also assess if the individuals which are involved in the production of the software, could be users of design documentation.

Additionally, the study hints how important design documentation is, what the author of the documentation needs to consider and the importance of design documentation as a communication tool. It is up to my belief that design documentation unifies creative thinking with the technology, and hence, the end system. Hence, the design documentation has its purpose, but the users should be clearly stated to be more operational and felicitous. A limitation to this study is the lack of real interviews, which could have contributed to a more abundant and comprehensive view of the users of design documentation. Secondly, the study did not investigate the other identified users, which were the individuals involved in the production of the software, the stakeholders.

Prior to this study there was limited research with interest of who the users are of design documentation and therefore I argue that this study is a contribution to other studies within human computer interaction. Furthermore, the study opens for a debate concerning how necessary and valuable design documentation is. Design documentation is a way to communicate but if no one reads it, it is unnecessary and hence, it is of limited value. Finally, this study is a contribution to problematise the importance and possible limitation for other studies which aim to demonstrate the importance of design documentation.

Acknowledgments. Lastly, but no means least, I would like to thank my classmates and teacher for encouraging and inspiring discussions. I would also like to express my deepest appreciation to my teacher Markus Lahtinen for encouragement and support for making this into a publicised poster.

References

1. AltexSoft, Software r & d engineering: Technical documentation in software development: types, best practices, and tools. https://www.altexsoft.com/blog/business/technical-doc umentation-in-software-development-types-best-practices-and-tools/?utm_source=Medium Com&utm_medium=referral (2020). Accessed 4 Jan 2021
2. Amigoscode: A day in the life of a software engineer in London | STARLING | 2020, YouTube. https://www.youtube.com/watch?v=oS-m5-XikwA (2020). Accessed 5 Jan 2021
3. Brown, D.M. (ed.): Communicating Design: Developing Web Site Documentation for Design and Planning. New Riders Publishing, Berkeley (2010)
4. Chau Codes: Day in the life of a self-taught software developer, YouTube. https://www.you tube.com/watch?v=VkKFEUZJ0DA (2020). Accessed 11 Jan 2021
5. Clever Programmer: Day in the life of a software developer, YouTube. https://www.youtube. com/watch?v=Zwu2HjU7pXY (2019). Accessed 5 Jan 2021
6. Fox, C.J.: Why writing software design documents matters. https://www.toptal.com/freela nce/why-design-documents-matter (n.d). Accessed 4 Jan 2021

7. Hammond, J.: A REAL day in the life of a software engineer, YouTube. https://www.you tube.com/watch?v=j1fc0FlCjyI (2020). Accessed 5 Jan 2021
8. Holland, B.: Visual studio live share can do that? Smashing Magazine, 18 September. https://www.smashingmagazine.com/2018/09/visual-studio-live/ (2020). Accessed 4 Jan 2021
9. Khan, O.: Day in the life of an amazon software engineer (WFH), YouTube. https://www.you tube.com/watch?v=I4W9blxeHEU (2020). Accessed 11 Jan 2021
10. Jensen, M.: 5 reasons why design documentation is important. http://steensolutions.com/2015/12/5-reasons-why-design-documentation-is-important/ (n.d). Accessed 4 Jan 2021
11. Josh and Katie: Day in the life of a twitter software engineer, YouTube. https://www.youtube.com/watch?v=sS6O7Yp5xmg (2020). Accessed 5 Jan 2021
12. Morales, J., Rusu, C., Quinones, D.: Programmer experience: a systematic mapping. IEEE Latin Am. Trans. 1111–1118 (2020). https://doi.org/10.1109/TLA.2020.9099749
13. Nguyen, S.: A day in the life of a Google Software Engineer | work-from-home Edition, YouTube. https://www.youtube.com/watch?v=a0glBQXOcl4 (2020). Accessed 5 Jan 2021
14. Saddler, H.J.: Understanding design representations ACM interactions. Interactions 17–24 (2001). https://doi.org/10.1145/379537.379542
15. Voorhees, P.D.: Guide to Efficient Software Design An MVC Approach to Concepts, Structures, and Models. Springer International Publishing, Cham (2020). https://doi.org/10.1007/978-3-030-28501-2
16. Product Manager: A day in the life of a software engineer at eBay (Product Manager Edition), YouTube. https://www.youtube.com/watch?v=KE0Yjp1bbiM (2019). Accessed 11 Jan 2021
17. Pyle, T.: Guidelines for creating effective software design documentation. Intercom (2020)

Common Interactive Style Guide for Designers and Developers Across Projects

Bryan Croft$^{(\boxtimes)}$, Jeffrey D. Clarkson$^{(\boxtimes)}$, Eric Voncolln$^{(\boxtimes)}$, Mike Nithaworn$^{(\boxtimes)}$, Seana Rothman$^{(\boxtimes)}$, and Odalis Felix$^{(\boxtimes)}$

Naval Information Warfare Center Pacific, San Diego, CA, USA
{bryan.croft,jeff.clarkson,eric.voncolln,mike.k.nithaworn, seana.rothman,odalis.felix}@navy.mil

Abstract. Advanced user interfaces continue to improve through better design which in turn translates to more effective development and end use. The intent of this work is to provide design guidelines that can be used across all new applications. An interactive prototype toolkit called the User Interface Prototyping Toolkit (UIPT) was developed to allow sponsors, customers, end users, designers, engineers, and software developers to work together in an iterative fashion to achieve a tailored but guided user interface for the application of interest. Modern styles were applied with a consistent and common look and feel while adhering to solid principle of design, workflow, tasks, layout, coloring, size, animation, and user cues. The design required a general repeatable structure for designers and developers with the intent to allow each new project to understand the overall design and incorporate the features and functionality in accordance with style guide principles. UIPT integrates multiple domains within in the same software application with the ability to efficiently transition an end user's role from one display presentation to another. To date, several projects and user roles have been integrated into the UIPT. In support of this design philosophy an interactive style guide is in continuous development to apply a common reusable design across the multiple projects that utilize the UIPT-based interface. Both the UIPT application and the interactive style guide were built with Unity, a 2D and 3D game engine. Styles for size, color, layout, and other design factors are laid out in the style guide itself which can be run to visualize and examine interactions. This is advantageous for new and experience software developers because the guide itself contains the code and styles necessary to implement the various components of the user interface while supporting design consistency with reusable code for rapid deployment.

Keywords: Command and control · Information systems · Naval Innovative Science and Engineering · Rapid prototyping · User interfaces · User interface rapid prototyping toolkit · Unity3D · User centered design

1 Introduction

A Naval Innovative Science and Engineering (NISE) project titled User Interface Prototyping Toolkit (UIPT) continues to explore the rapid production of high-fidelity user

C. Stephanidis et al. (Eds.): HCII 2021, CCIS 1498, pp. 17–23, 2021.
https://doi.org/10.1007/978-3-030-90176-9_3

interface (UI) prototypes. Such interfaces rely on end users, researchers, designers, and engineers working together to develop and validate, new concepts of operations (CONOPS) and emerging technologies. The IWC project was targeted to include exploration and integration of technologies involved with a future vision and function of Naval Command and Control spaces with emphasis on the human-computer interfaces and interaction. An interactive style guide provides a key element in providing a consistent look and feel for such interfaces including their interactions and workflow.

The objective is to examine the ability to rapidly develop a specific human-machine interface prototype for future Navy information systems that address emerging operational and tactical threats and is currently targeting advanced UI designs specifically for multitouch display devices. UIPT is a software development effort to explore rapid prototyping of information systems while standardizing forward looking UI interactions. One goal of the project was to maintain a common look and feel or style for said interfaces. This supports the end user in finding commonality between the various applications and domains the require a user interface.

1.1 Motivation

The US Navy is focused on maintaining a decisive advantage over adversarial forces. The Warfighter as an individual end user and as a collective set of end users plays a critical role in maintaining this advantage. New technologies such as Artificial Intelligence, Machine Learning, and Autonomous Systems grow in importance and applicability. How the user interfaces with these technologies becomes critical, especially in a fast-paced environment where situational awareness and decision making are out pacing the human's ability to not only comprehend but to understand, formulate and then act in the most optimal way possible. The UI between the end user and advanced capabilities such as ambient intelligence, autonomous systems and the overwhelming influx of data from intelligence sources and sensors, is positioned as a key element that allows the end users awareness, understanding and control with regards to these complex systems. How end users will be able to utilize such interfaces and maximize the man-machine performance and relationship is still largely unknown but, current efforts are working toward such a solution.

The lack of User Experience (UX) design in software development in the past has resulted in software user interfaces which are non-intuitive, difficult to use, non-task oriented, and have a general lack of form and function required for knowledge and decision support end use. The goal for the UI in the UIPT project was to overcome this trend and provide an easy to use and valid interface for the Warfighters. UI prototypes which focus on innovative concepts continue to progress through the efforts of processes such as User-Centered Design (UCD). For the domain of interest, it becomes more than just the User Experience (UX). It is the timely and well-designed placement and interaction of information on the UI that can better support the critical functions of situational awareness, decision making and control of the supporting systems. The exploration for the use of an interactive style guide supports the maintenance of commonality across various applications that integrate the UIPT based user interface. This solves the naval end user to eliminate complexity and training needs for end users.

1.2 Technical Background

Often a style guide is a document which adequately describes standard practices and requirements for the development of user interface elements. The style guide strives to improve communication between the stakeholders, end users, designers and developers while striving for consistency within the user interface across multiple projects. After years of experience and various techniques, a need for an interactive and living style guide was deemed necessary.

Consideration was given to creating the interactive style guide using the same development process and tools used to create the UIPT user interface creation toolkit. This serves multiple purposes but also comes with other constraints and requirements. A designer can use tools of choice to create the look and feel or essentially the style from the smallest component to the structure of the entire user interface. This is a technical requirement in that some form of communication is required between the designer and the developer of the interactive style guide. Essentially the style guide is created in the standard form but then used by the programmer to generate code which exemplifies that user interface element. Often the design of a user interface element comes with some type of interaction behavior and event activation. This is where building the style guide itself in code allows for this to happen.

Then only technical requirements are in the translation from a designer's static creation to one of interactive user interface elements in code. For the UIPT project a 2D and 3D game development tool call Unity was used. The type of coding for Unity does adhere to common development tools such as C# and Visual Studio however, a lot of the development is performed within the Unity tool. Since the UIPT prototyping toolkit is used for user interface designs following the style guide it maintains a uniform code based for UI elements. The code used in the style guide can be re-utilized in the UIPT prototypes. UIPT is a user interface prototyping tool and not necessarily considered a product that would be used in production, however, that is possible. The key point to this is that the style guide is based upon code which allows for reuse for new, modified or the same type of user interface element. A developer can just obtain the code from the style guide and import it into the prototype code.

1.3 Using the Interactive Style Guide

The major factor provided by the interactive style guide is its ability to be interactive and react to user actions. Having live coded examples of user interface elements aids both the designer, developer and end user to better understand the functionality, behaviors, workflow, colors, sizes and other elements that make up certain UI element. This allows each member of the community have a handy tool which meets their specific needs. A designer can review, improve and update the style guide. A developer can understand the designer's intent and know the workflow, interactions and behaviors of the UI elements and not have to re-invent the code. The end user can review the style guide to understand what UI elements are available and how they would work in the interface. This allows them to provide better feedback on the content they want to see in their user interface.

2 Objectives and Approach

The UIPT application allows users to explore the impact of new technology on emerging operational concepts before large program investments are made. The Navy can significantly reduce the risks associated with pursuing revolutionary technology. The Navy is currently investing in new technologies, such as, autonomous vehicles, artificial intelligence, distributed sensing, and integrated fires. The way in which Fleet users will work with and "team" with these new capabilities is largely unknown. UIPT is striving to establish a common user interface and the style guide provides a means in making it "common" among diverse end uses but under a common umbrella of Navy applications. This often eases the burden of training and understanding how the system works across multiple applications. Have the same look and feel, workflow and interaction are the main goals associated with this project. The style guide helps to achieve and maintain that goal from initiation to deployment.

2.1 Development of the Style Guide

As mentioned, the style guide begins with tools common to designers. These tools produce the styles required but are needed for the developer of the style guide to understand the designer's intent. Artifacts from the designers are used in collaborative meetings between the designers and those producing the interactive style guide as means to communicate how the design works. This collaborative effort is pretty much like the normal process of the designer working with the developers however, in this case the product is the style guide which serves as a more permanent and reusable product.

A key consideration for the style guide is the common use across projects. Each new interface must have the same look and feel while maintaining both a common interaction and UI element interactions. The difficult part is to make this a common interface work across multiple domains. In general, behind this goal is a wealth of experience and practice from both the designer and developer of the interactive style guide.

2.2 Deployment of the Style Guide

The deployment of the style guide would generally be web based to allow access to the various groups that would use it. This also allows for continued review and examination of the styles that exist and related interactions. As stated, the interactive style guide is a living document which required frequent updates and improvements. This becomes a necessity as more and more diverse applications tend to utilize this type of interface. The style guide itself can also become an early in the design process tool to be used by designers and end users to better target the specific UI element required for the intended target. Each developer also has easy access to the online interactive style guide in order to validate recent developed UI elements as well as to gain a better understanding of how the UI elements work. The style guide very much becomes coupled within the entire process of content creation for UI of an application. This is simplified from a developer's standpoint because the code is immediately available to re-deploy into new applications.

3   Examples

The interactive style guide has pretty much the same elements found in many style guides. It differs in that it is a live interactive document with the purpose to guide Navy applications to use a common UI. Common styles include overall themes, layouts, symbols, typography motion, icons, and a variety of components. This section will provide a brief overview of some of the main UI elements of the style guide.

3.1   Theme, Roles and Layout

The style guide has an overall dark theme such as seen in Fig. 1.

Fig. 1. Dark theme

The layout components seen in Fig. 2 serve as a guide to keep each application in various domains within the bounds of creating a common user interface. It consists of ABC.

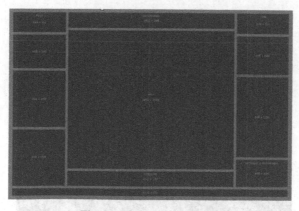

Fig. 2. User interface layout

The role user element, seen in Figs. 1 and 2 in the upper left corner, provides the means to switch context of the entire application for use by a different end user with a specific role. This allows the same user interface to be used by various users who perform differing functions. The main layout of the UI for the applications remains the same while the components are replaced in a animated way so to illustrate to the user that changes in the interface have occurred.

3.2   Common Components

The interactive style guide provides direction for many common user interface elements typography, symbols, and icons. The following are examples of these common components: accordions, bins, cards, clocks, context menus, control panels, controls, input fields, pop ups, notifications, tables, tabs, and buttons. These are common UI elements that have been specifically stylized to match the advanced UIPT user interface concepts. Each element can be re-utilized in various layout positions and functionality for the specific application.

3.3   Advanced Components

There are a few very specific and more advance UI components. Three of these type of interface components is a timeline, a map and a component called Halo. These are illustrated in Figs. 3, 4 and 5, respectively. The value of an interactive style guide becomes very evident with these components.

Fig. 3. Timeline component

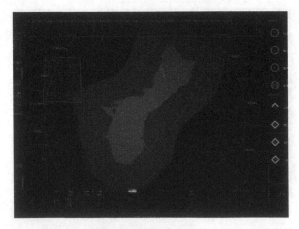

Fig. 4. Map component

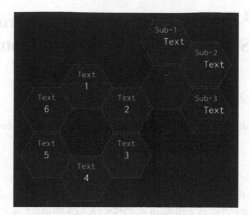

Fig. 5. Halo component

4 Conclusions and Future Work

The UIPT style guides has been in development for over a year while the effort to arrive a completed style guide will be a continuous effort. Internal evaluation of the interactive style guide to date, provides good indicators that further and continued development is warranted. Evaluation from Navy Warfighters, the end users of the advance user interface, provides feedback on the value of the styles and workflow used. To date the feedback has been extremely positive with continued interest from a variety of projects to use the interface. The UIPT based interface continues to apply the style guide to projects in multiple domains which gives credence to the user infaces which are derived from the common interactive style guide. To date, the application of the style guide across several domains have proven successful with little to no changes to the style guide moving from one end use case to the next. The design and overall workflow support this concept and have been proven through integration of several projects into the same code baseline. Morphing of the display screen between projects is handled using roles. Future works would need to verify this concept outside of the Navy set of domains but, has work well within that set. User feedback with weekly reviews of the features and workflow being added to the user interface is essential in style guide development. This process, as with most user interfaces over time, continues to be refined and extended. The underlying code for the interactive part of the style guide also changes and improves overtime which add to the continuous requirement for style guide upgrades.

(DT)²-Box – A Multi-sensory Approach to Support Design Thinking Teams

Julien Hofer(✉) ⓘ and Markus Watermeyer

University of Hildesheim, Hildesheim, Lower Saxony, Germany
julien.hofer@gv.hamburg

Abstract. Creative innovations are of immense importance for companies in the modern working world as well as in research. Design thinking as a solution app-roach for complex problems has become an indispensable part of innovation devel-opment and is used in many industries for a wide variety of fields and technolo-gies. However, the documentation of the process in such projects is often neglected despite its great importance for the transfer of information and the reflection of the process. As a result, errors occur in the implementation of the developed ideas or further improvements to the process cannot take place. Software tools that support documentation are therefore desirable, but exist in small numbers so far. Also for the joint reflection of Design Thinking teams, no known approaches to assistance by software exist so far. This paper therefore iteratively develops an IoT-tool for supporting documentation in Design Thinking projects within the framework of a design-scientific investigation, which also offers assistance in method selection as well as the joint reflection on the work carried out, and which is particularly easy to use due to an alternative form of operation. The developed solution is evaluated with the support of experts from innovation research and tested for its practical suitability to answer the questions to what extent software can support documentation, reflection, and method selection in Design Thinking projects. At the same time, it is shown how video recordings can be used to demonstrate the developed solutions in design science research digitally, even in times of contact restrictions.

1 Introduction

Companies today face a variety of challenges arising from a rapidly changing market environment and increasing uncertainties [1]. Economic activity in developed indus-trialized countries is increasingly shifting away from pure production and industrial manufacturing toward services and the creation as well as provision of knowledge. In contrast to times past, it is no longer just about new physical products, but also about new processes, methods, forms of entertainment or ways of communicating and collab-orating. For this, companies need innovative development approaches. As a result, there is not only great pressure to innovate, but innovation has become nothing less than a survival strategy [2].

Since creative design thinkers are usually anything but bureaucratic documentarians [3] and often neglect documentation despite its enormous importance, various authors

© Springer Nature Switzerland AG 2021
C. Stephanidis et al. (Eds.): HCII 2021, CCIS 1498, pp. 24–30, 2021.
https://doi.org/10.1007/978-3-030-90176-9_4

see the potential for improvement primarily in reducing the effort for documentation by means of an easy-to-use software tool that can be integrated as unobtrusively as possible into the creative process [4, 5]. In addition, a great added value is assumed in the support of the process and the selection of methods, since especially in the educational environment often only limited process and method knowledge is available [5]. For the reasons mentioned above, it seems reasonable to assume that a support tool for documentation that can be operated without prior technical knowledge and with little effort and that supports the selection of methods can improve documentation in DT. This can make a valuable contribution to better reflection within and after development. Technology from the Internet of Things (IoT) promises interesting alternatives for operation through the use of different sensor technology. Thus our research question is:

RQ: *How can we support design thinking teams with a multi-sensory device?*

2   Related Work

Design Thinking is an approach to solve wicked problems and to develop innovative ideas. People from different disciplines and with different backgrounds create with the help of design thinking new products, services, business processes and so on [6]. [1] argues that design thinking can be used in disciplines like product design, architecture or management. Design Thinking is there to solve wicked problems (...) which are problems with unclear and changing requirements that need a collaborative, co-creative and iterative approach to solve these problems [5].

For Design Thinking exists different procedure models which are based on the same principles. The procedure model of the Hasso-Plattner-Institute or of the Stanford d.school are very popular. They differ mainly in how they divide the overall process. The model from Stanford distinguishes between the phases Emphasize, Define, Ideate, Prototype and Test. While the HPI-model divides the Emphasize-phase into Understanding and Observing.

At the University of Hildesheim, we teach a model with six phases similar to the model from the HPI but we extended two phases: Prepare and Project management. We argue that for teaching purposes it is important to highlight theses phases. Another part of the overall Design Thinking process is the continues reflexion about the developed artefacts. This can discover tacit knowledge and transform it into explicit knowledge. Reflection theory distinguishes between reflection-in-action and reflection-on-action and also between individual reflection.

In joint reflection, whole teams can receive feedback, learn from each other, take different perspectives, be inspired by others' experiences and thus develop better solutions, which is why it is particularly valuable in Design Thinking teams for tackling complex problems.

A good documentation is essential for the reflection and the learning of previous iterations during a Design Thinking process. Documentation makes it possible to standardize projects, captures and communicates design decisions and offers traceability. This traceability of the path allows understanding, justification and verification of requirements of the entire design finding. Knowledge that is explicitly captured in the documentation can be reused later, whereas tacit knowledge has to be recreated later.

- Design Thinking
- Classes of User Interfaces
- Tangible User Interfaces
- Documentation of Design Thinking

3   Research Method

DSR has its origins in design as the creation of concretely applicable solutions [7]. It represents an approach to research that focuses on the development and evaluation of artefacts (models, theories, prototypes, etc.) with the aim of creating new benefits and solving real problems [8].

We followed the design process of [8] to build and evaluate our prototype. Thus the following section describes briefly our iterations of designing the $(DT)^2$-Box-System.

3.1   Iteration 0

At first we needed a new system which can support the documentation of the Design Thinking process based on the procedure model from the University of Hildesheim. It should be as easy to use as possible without any prior technical knowledge and should be able to be integrated into the process without requiring much attention from its users. Furthermore, the system should be able to be connected to an existing documentation system in order to complement it.

Therefore, we have developed a device (Design Thinking Documentation Tool-Box $(DT)^2$-Box), which acts as a client within a client-server architecture. This allows, for example, several devices to be used at the same time. To make the interaction between the box and the users as simple as possible, we used a combination of several sensors. On the one hand, we have installed buttons that allow binary decisions, and on the other hand, we have integrated an RFID scanner that recognizes objects that are equipped with an RFID transponder. Our first prototype is shown in Fig. 1a. For the display of the current status, we have installed an LED with a color spectrum.

Furthermore, in order to use the auditory channel and thus be able to output more complex data to the users, we have connected a loudspeaker for a voice output. In order to make this as flexible as possible, we have dispensed with the playback of stored audio files and used a text-to-speech service (Google TTS), which can be called up via a web-based API. The hardware we used for this was a single-board computer (Raspberry Pi 4), which has the necessary interfaces.

As our device is to be used in design thinking sessions, it needs a compact form, which is why we chose a box design. This box was designed with a CAD software and produced with a 3D printer. For the documentation of the individual phases, we printed 6 different phicons and equipped them with RFID tags (see Fig. 1b).

3.2   Iteration 1

To evaluate our prototype we presented the box and its features to an expert in the field of Design Thinking. He teaches our students in the Design Thinking Course and works

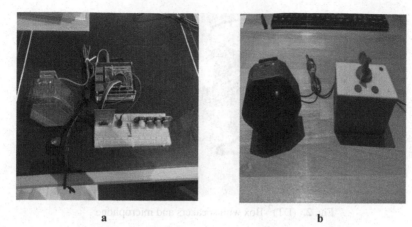

a   b

Fig. 1. (a) First prototype (b) Prototype with Phicon on it.

as a Design Thinking Coach for different companies. Due to the COVID-19 situation, we were not able to interview him directly in person, although this would have been beneficial as we wanted to get feedback on the haptic features of our prototype. He told us that the general concept of the device is useful and that he would integrate it in the Design Thinking sessions when he is not there.

He also made further demands on the system. The box should query whether the number of participants' present is sufficient to carry out a method. If the number of participants is not sufficient, another method from the database should be suggested.

3.3 Iteration 2

The methods to be used by the students in the ISUM procedure model are already stored in a method database of the $(DT)^2$. This database changes dynamically when, for example, new methods are added by staff or students. In order to be able to apply these changes in the $(DT)^2$ box as well, a connection to the $(DT)^2$ system must be enabled. This task is performed by a new class Method-Service on the backend server, which queries all methods every time a new phase is started and randomly selects one of the methods belonging to the selected phase. The same procedure is followed when users reject a method and thus need an alternative method. Methods contain the following information: They have a unique ID (id), a title (title), a description (description), optionally a timeframe (timebox), and a required number of participants (members). They are also assigned to a model and a phase from the database.

Once a method has been selected and confirmed by the users, it is also recorded in the documentation, for which an additional method column has been added to the phase protocol table (phase_protocol) of the database. This then contains the name of the selected method. The existing read-ahead function via TTS, which so far only outputs the information about a phase, is also used to provide method information. This allows users who do not have sufficient knowledge about the method to query this information.

Fig. 2. $(DT)^2$-Box with speakers and microphone

3.4 Iteration 3

At the start of a new session, the system first checks whether a session already exists in the documentation for the logged-in DT team. If this is the case, the team should be encouraged to reflect on this session by first displaying a brief reminder of which phase and which method was last used. Then it is automatically checked whether this session has already received a reflection. For this purpose, the meeting table (meetings) contains a new column for reflection. If the reflection column does not yet contain an entry, the team is prompted to reflect on this session and then dictate the result. For this purpose, a USB microphone is added to the hardware to record the users' speech (see Fig. 2).

After reflection, a user can speak a text about the result into the microphone, which is then processed via Speech-to-Text (STT). This is done using the Google Cloud's STT tool, which works in reverse to the TTS function and requires a Google Cloud account with the STT service enabled. Then, after successful authentication (using a token), the $(DT)^2$ box can use the API, send audio files up to a length of one minute to the STT endpoint and receive the recognized text as a response. This can then be assigned to the associated session in the usual way via the backend in the database. Due to the limit for the length of the audio file, dictation may take a maximum of one minute, but can also be completed beforehand by pressing the button. After that, the recording is automatically terminated. Complete skipping of the reflection is also enabled to leave autonomy to the DT team in designing the process themselves [9].

4 Discussion

This paper addresses the question of the extent to which it is possible to support DT teams in documenting their projects through the use of IoT technology, to provide them with assistance in selecting methods, and to encourage them to reflect regularly. To answer, we incrementally developed and evaluated an IoT artifact that uses an acoustic-haptic operating concept with the use of RFID technology, phicons, TTS and STT services to provide its users with a particularly straightforward means of logging. It randomly selects appropriate methods from an existing database and prompts for reflection on past sessions.

Both demonstration and evaluation could only be carried out digitally. Since the developed artifact is a physical device, this form of presentation has the major disadvantage that the evaluating experts could see the use but could not try out the artifact themselves. Thus, an important part of the operating concept can only be evaluated to a limited extent.

Given the limitations described above, it would be worthwhile to explore in future research how the artifact can be used by DT teams in practice and, if necessary, further improved.

5 Evaluation

The present work has succeeded in creating an IoT artifact that helps DT teams to document their process in a straightforward way, that regularly encourages joint reflection on DT sessions, and that supports the selection of methods. In doing so, teams are given as much autonomy as possible in that the determination of phases, the selection of methods, and even reflection are never mandated, but the choice is left to the team. Experts from practice and research have confirmed that the implemented functionalities also offer an interesting approach in practical application. It must be noted that greater functionality and the desired uncomplicated operation that requires little attention are opposing requirements, and the balance between them is a fine line that is not easy to find.

Through the development of the artifact, it was demonstrated that it is possible through an IoT tool to enable a log of the temporal sequences within a process automatically through simple placement and removal of phicons (in this case, phase figures). This form of operation the use of IoT technology and the degree of automation of documentation represent above all the novelty of the development. Documents, images or sketches with time stamps created during this time could thus be clearly assigned at a later date, resulting in fully-fledged multimedia documentation.

References

1. Schoormann, T., Hofer, J., Knackstedt, R.: Software tools for supporting reflection in design thinking projects. In: Proceedings of the 53rd Hawaii International Conference on System Sciences, pp. 407–416 (2020). https://doi.org/10.24251/HICSS.2020.051
2. Brown, T., Katz, B.: Change by design. J. Prod. Innov. Manage. **28**(3), 381–383 (2011). https://doi.org/10.1111/j.1540-5885.2011.00806.x
3. von Thienen, J.P.A., Perlich, A., Eschrig, J., Meinel, C.: Smart documentation with tele-board MED. In: Plattner, H., Meinel, C., Leifer, L. (eds.) Design Thinking Research. UI, pp. 203–233. Springer, Cham (2016). https://doi.org/10.1007/978-3-319-19641-1_14
4. Beyhl, T., Berg, G., Giese, H.: Towards documentation support for educational design thinking projects. In: Proceedings of the 15th International Conference on Engineering and Product Design Education: Design Education - Growing Our Future, EPDE 2013, September, pp. 408–413 (2013a). https://doi.org/10.13140/2.1.4137.4080

5. Hofer, J., Schoormann, T., Kortum, J., Knackstedt, R.: Ich weiß was ihr letzte Sitzung getan habt – Entwicklung und Anwendung eines Softwarewerkzeuges zur Dokumentation von Design Thinking-Projekten. HMD Praxis Der Wirtschaftsinformatik **56**(1), 160–171 (2019). https://doi.org/10.1365/s40702-018-00480-8

6. Brown, T.: Design thinking. Harvard Bus. Rev. **86**, 84–92 (2008)

7. Hevner, A.R., March, S.T., Park, J., Ram, S.: Design science in information systems research. MIS Q. **28**(1), 75 (2004). https://doi.org/10.2307/25148625

8. Peffers, K., Rothenberger, M., Tuunanen, T., Vaezi, R.: Design science research evaluation. In: Peffers, K., Rothenberger, M., Kuechler, B. (eds.) DESRIST 2012. LNCS, vol. 7286, pp. 398–410. Springer, Heidelberg (2012). https://doi.org/10.1007/978-3-642-29863-9_29

9. Uebernickel, F., Brenner, W., Pukall, B., Naef, T., Schindlholzer, B.: Design Thinking: Das Handbuch. Frankfurter Allgemeine Buch, Frankfurt (2015)

The Ethic of "CODE"—To Pro Mortalism and Antisurvivalism from Antinatalism

Sachio Horie(✉)

Nagoya University, Nagoya, Japan
horie.sachio@f.mbox.nagoya-u.ac.jp

Abstract. Antinatalism is a philosophy that denies that a person is born in this world. It means that parents should not give the birth in this world, who should not be born, because the life is suffering. In particular, David Benatar does not deny continuing the life, but rather proposes antinatalism on the moral principle that the life should not harm others. The conclusion derives pro-mortalism and anti-survivalism.

Pro-mortalism means if it is better not to be born, it is better to not exist after the birth, and admits the suicide, and I call the philosophy of admitting the homicide is anti-survivalism.

In this article, we affirm the antinatalism advocated by David Benatar as a premise that we must think about the value in our lives, and by continuing to produce and consume until new technology becomes available. The question of whether the existence of is ethically justified is explained in relation to the three arguments related to the convergence of the Anthropocene. One is the extinction of human beings, the second is the continuation of life by machines, and the last is the continuation of quiet life. Finally, we consider the implications of endless antinatalism with respect to spiritual uploads, the metaphysics of personal self-identity around death, with a focus on the human spirit in the eusociality.

Keywords: Pro mortalism · Antisurvivalism · Antinatalism · Transhumanism

1 Introduction

In this article, I reasonably affirm the following propositions.

I.   It is good that no one exists.
II. Furthermore, the number of people should decrease more than now.
III. The extinction of humans causes great harm to our last generation.

My proposal is shown below.

(1)   The existence of human beings is always harmful.
(2)   The existence of humans should be denied.
(3)   I deny childbirth.

C. Stephanidis et al. (Eds.): HCII 2021, CCIS 1498, pp. 31–36, 2021.
https://doi.org/10.1007/978-3-030-90176-9_5

(4)   I affirm suicide.
(5)   I affirm homicide.
(6)   The extinction of humans causes great harm to the last generation.
(7)   Life-prolonging technology enables people to live indefinitely.
(8)   Brain remodeling nullifies human pleasure and pain.
        New technologies make life much more valuable than it is today.
(9)   First, one survives indefinitely in a life worth continuing.
(10)   Second, a person lives a life free from harm and pleasure.
(11)   Therefore, the development of new technology may affirm (1) and avoid extinction.
(12)   There is a possibility of making (1) meaningless and avoiding extinction.

I don't think (9) is always good. Therefore, I support (12). I call it true social antinatalism.

In this article, we consider antinatalism advocated by David Benatar, considering whether the existence of those who continue to produce and consume is ethically justified for the value of our lives. We also explain three arguments related to the convergence of the Anthropocene, which is independent of the conclusion that antinatalism should be affirmed. One is the extinction of human beings, the second is the continuation of life by machines, and the last is the continuation of quiet life. Finally, I consider the implications of endless antinatalism with respect to the metaphysics of personal self-identity surrounding death.

2   To Pro Mortalism and Anti Survivalism from Anti Natalism

Our living is hard. We should not be born, should not give birth to our children. This is antinatalism. Among antinatalists, David Benatar [1] does not deny staying alive, and he rationally proposes antinatalism on general moral principles. However, it leads to the pro-mortalism [2] and the anti-survivalism.

Our society is more mature than any other society so far. Should we be grateful for this happiness? Our standard of living is equal to or better than the former royal aristocrats. In all generations, peoples often feel more pain than pleasure. We are expected to work hard by society. In modern times, it is the self-management ability. The self-management leads us to social success. If self-management ability is evaluated as poor, all my failures are my responsibility, which is resolved by self-help effort ability. In society, the crime is considered selfish. This is plausible. We can only behave self-centeredly in social structure when an event occurs that exceeds a self-managing threshold. Is this personal selfishness? We comply with the law as a social norm. This is because by adhering to social norms, even if we suffer short-term disadvantages, we will benefit in the long-term. Therefore, suicide and murder mean mistakes by the society.

Importantly, Benatar's proposal makes a difference between a life that deserves to begin and a life that deserves continuation. Whether or not to continue life should be left to the person who is living the life. However, when I reasonably judge that the harm of staying alive outweighs the harm of stopping it, I think that even if there is a desire to stay alive, that desire is not rational. Therefore, I affirm suicide. If it is not good to be born, it is also good that there is no more.

Furthermore, I call the idea of allowing homicide as anti-survivalism. I also affirm anti-survivalism. Because by executing murder, we can end the undeniably good life of the murdered partner. We should quietly proceed to the destruction of mankind. It is possible to draw such a conclusion by pursuing Benatar's idea. However, I affirm homicide and suicide, but deny hurt and violence. Because it is harmful to be all present, and therefore I oppose war and the death penalty.

The question of why murder, including suicide and homicide, is the difference between recognizing and not recognizing the right not to be killed.

This article aims at minimum to fill-in a lacuna in the literature on anti-natalism, thereby contributing to future discussions of the topic.

3 Lemma to Benatar

If I affirm Benatar, the proof should show that it is harmful to needlestick pain. However, your denial of him should show that such harm is not always correct for the being. For many, no matter how terrible they are objectively, the harm is not decisive if they are satisfied. This shows the confrontation between Benatar and the opponent. This is explained by Yoshizawa [3] with the argument that Benatar's asymmetry should be distinguished from value-theoretic asymmetry as moral asymmetry.

If I explain this, he replaces pain and pleasure with misery and happiness, respectively. This appeals to our intuition. However, I think that rationality should be prioritized in consideration of multiple lemmas.

I think that everyone can feel distress, and the harm caused by distress is harmful, more or less.

If we eat delicious food that we have never experienced, what we think is delicious will be unpleasant. Moreover, poking a finger with a needle is better, but worse, than breaking a finger. That is, the good thing is that if anything unfavorable happens from there, it will be bad.

In the counterargument to Benatar, Morioka argues that it is meaningless to think of harm and pleasure for someone that does not exist. The original title of Benatar's paper is "BETTER NEVER TO HAVE BEEN", not "BETTER NEVER TO BE". The existence of X is only confirmed at time t, and the existence or nonexistence of X is not determined at $t + 1$ (the future is unknown). With this, Benatar's asymmetry holds at any point in time, except that it exists at time point t. If X is at point t and knows that he will experience the maximum amount of pain in his life at $t + 1$, even if he gets the maximum amount of pleasure in his life so far, then X is point $t + 1$. Do you want the future?

This is always better than the fact that one does not exist at any time by accepting Benatar's asymmetry in pain and pleasure.

4 Debt of Living

Mark Fisher [4] advocated accelerationism. During his lifetime, Fisher considered the inevitable prostitution of capitalism in capitalist realism. This means dedicating oneself to society as a commodity.

In modern times, this is a contract with our society. In this society we are not allowed to be lazy, and there is no way out because the safety nets are not working. All failures are lack of self-help efforts and no mistakes are tolerated. Social success is the only thing that is desired. That is, contribution to capitalism is the only condition for success in our lives. Losers are born in endless competition, and losers are given only the despair of being socially worthless. Those who do not work should not eat, but those who cannot work should not live.

In such a society, suicide is a passive escape measure for those who are disqualified from finding value in themselves, and homicide is an active escape measure. The birth is the act of creating new debt of living.

5   Reject of Birth

The education interferes with children's work and their parents' expectations for their work.

It makes them more dependent on their parents. Children make adults a lot of money and time. In the presence of these conditions, the demand for children is apparently low. People increasingly would rather spare their possible future children the burdens of existence, in order to maximize well-being and status for their existing children and, perhaps, for themselves.

Alone among animals, humans have brought reproduction (the most important evolutionary act) under conscious control. Conscious control of reproduction has thus become a locus for selection, with new niches arising for biological and cultural adaptations that promote reproduction against the dangerous innovation of human consciousness. Fertility is not the only evolutionarily crucial domain that has come under conscious control.

6   Affirmation of Suicide

People have been able to consciously control the length of their lives as prolonging their lives simultaneously. It's suicide. The suicides are significantly less culturally adaptable than their own biological adaptability if people live in a community, that is, they are productive but have zero commercial value, or produce in the first place. They are extremely incapacitated, and as long as they survive under these circumstances, they not only contribute nothing to their genetic existence, but rather deplete the resources of their genetic relatives. That is, their continued survival is contrary to their genetic existence. The suicide occurs when one's existence is harmful to others or in the community.

The survival of human society and the destruction of humans do not matter to the earth. What humans have created is only needed by humans, including God.

Society certainly seems to be gradually in equilibrium for the better, after a major historical conflict. However, I think that human society will never improve. Because, if we maximize the utility of society, some people will be unhappy.

According to Benatar, the extinction of humans is the path that humans should aim for. The question to consider is not to find out whether extinction is good or bad, but to find a solution to how it will be extinct. When the population is reduced for extinction, the quality of life of human beings is significantly reduced due to the collapse of society due to the increase of non-producers or the extreme decrease of human beings. Extinction of human beings is necessary, but it is necessary to avoid harming existing human beings by reducing the population. Benatar advocates gradually erasing the number of people at a constant rate. However, the last generation of human beings cannot have hope and must live in a collapsed society.

7   Affirmation of Murder

Why murder is affirmed? The anti-survivalism denies painful violence, war, and the death penalty. Now, as a basic rule, it is a sin to cause pain to others.

Unless you have a strong reason to violate this rule, you need to obey it. If everyone hurt someone or hurt someone for the purpose of murder, he will experience pain. However, if everyone gently hits a someone's head with a muzzle and attempts to murder, and that is successful, then this extremely violent act does not cause pain.

The opponent who does not notice the existence of the gun will die without feeling anything before the trigger is triggered, and there is no pain.

If everyone is a healthy young person, he may be asked how terrible it is to rob him of his promising future, but he can't feel his loss. That is, it is harmless. The pain and death are unrelated.

Many people will be disgusted with the murder, but the murder cannot be banned on the basis of harm to others.

It means there is no legal or ethical reason to prohibit an unexpected and painless murder of a person. However, when you imagine living in such a situation, the life of a person who has no close relationship with others cannot be protected.

You will experience constant fear of being killed painlessly. This is painful and harmful. In the end, two options are left. One is to be frightened of harm and commit suicide.

Do you make rules to lose harm?

8   Transhumanism [5]

Anti-survivalism affirms death and thinks that death is inevitable, but in the first place, what is the reason why people die rather than die naturally?

Peter Zapffe [6] says that non-human creatures concentrate on living, but the overly strong self-consciousness that separates the inside from the outside world acquired during human evolution is confusing us.

As an alternative to escape from death as a whole, transhumanism is in a position to use emerging science and technology to evolve the human body and cognitive abilities and dramatically improve human existence. Specifically, transhumanism is also an area for studying what may happen in the future through the expansion of human functions and the development and use of other future science and technology.

Transhumanism studies the potential benefits and dangers of emerging technologies that can overcome fundamental limitations, including human genes, and the ethical limitations of using those technologies. The most common transhumanist claim is that one eventually transforms from one's current state into a different being with significantly expanded abilities, pursuing the possibility of becoming a posthuman being.

However, Thomas Rigotti [7] calls transhumanism one of the ways to kill time in life. We are mortal beings, and it is inevitable. Even if we could upload knowledge to a computer, there would be no end to it if the earth was destroyed.

However, if technological evolution can create a set of suppressed self-consciousness, such as the collective consciousness, then by realizing eusociality [8], we may be able to find a way to survive. We remain trapped within the world that others have built for the benefit of others. We need to rethink our identities.

9   Alternative Future and Conclusion

Our identity makes us our feet. A highly digitized society is a world in which we can reconstruct relationships as relative actors involved in the world.

Even if the electrodes embedded in the brain can suppress our emotions [9], we feel the fear of loss of identity. However, our distinctive identities slowly disappear, creating new, unique and wonderful identities, or collective identities.

I call this state a decentralized network of minds (collective consciousness). Although the self exists in the collective consciousness, the self is only a part for achieving an arbitrary purpose with ensemble, and is swallowed by the continuous survival. In other words, making the self as small as possible makes the harm of the individual as small as possible and eventually disappears. Transhumanism just rejects human biological/mental limits and creates new individuals.

References

1. Benatar, D.: Better Never to Have Been: The Harm of Coming into Existence. Oxford University Press, Oxford, UK (2006)
2. McGregor, R., Sullivan-Bissett, E.: Better no longer to be. S. Afr. J. Philos. **31**, 56–68 (2013)
3. 吉沢文武，　ベネターの反出生主義をどう受けとめるか，　現代思想9月号，　青土社，pp. 129–137 (2019)
4. Fisher, M.: Ghosts of My Life: Writings on Depression, Hauntology and Lost Futures. Zero Books, Hampshire, UK (2013)
5. O'Connell, M.: To Be a Machine: Adventures Among Cyborgs, Utopians, Hackers, and the Futurists Solving the Modest Problem of Death. Anchor, New York, NY (2017)
6. Zapffe, P.W.: The Last Messiah. In: Philosophy Now (1933)
7. Ligotti, T.: The Conspiracy Against the Human Race. Penguin Books, London (2018)
8. Nowak, M.A., Tarnita, C.E., Wilson, E.O.: the evolution of Eusociality. Nature **466**, 1057–1062 (2010)
9. https://www.nature.com/articles/s41591-020-01175-8

Theory and Practice in UX Design

Identification of Discrepancies in the Development Process of User-Oriented HMI

Svenja Knothe[1], Thomas Hofmann[2]([✉]), and Christian Blessmann[3]

[1] Deutschen Instituts für Normung, 49074 Osnabrück, Germany
[2] Hochschule Osnabrück, Sedanstraße 60, 49076 Osnabrück, Germany
T.Hofmann@hs-osnabrueck.de
[3] Deutschen Instituts für Normung, 49080 Osnabrück, Germany

Abstract. In many productions, work processes are becoming increasingly complex and are controlled, monitored and analysed with the help of computers with appropriate software. The task of user-centred design is to present this wealth of information to the user in such a way that the relevant facts can be quickly grasped and analysed in order to react accordingly. A customised interface can increase effectiveness, employee satisfaction and also error prevention. Legislation has also responded to this increasing relevance by issuing the standard on human-centred design of interactive systems [1].

From experience, problems often arise in the practical implementation of theoretical concepts that could not be foreseen beforehand. For the successful completion of the project, these changes/events should be reacted to and the processes adapted if necessary. In this paper, the possible problems and deviations in the implementation of DIN EN ISO 9241-210 are to be pointed out. For this purpose, suitable methods for obtaining information in theory and practice are illustrated for each phase. It will also be shown that the entire design process can develop a momentum of its own, as external influences and new information often lead to an adaptation and readjustment of the selected methods.

Keywords: DIN EN ISO 9241-210 · User experience design · User interface · HMI first section · Iterative entwicklung · Agiles vorgehen

1 Design Process According to DIN EN ISO 9241-210

Due to the fact that more and more people have to deal with computers and software in their daily work, the government has reacted and issued standards and guidelines for the human-centered design of interactive systems. The various parts of DIN EN ISO 9241 list the procedures, requirements and recommendations for designing an HMI.

Basically, the entire development process should be iterative, i.e., certain procedures can or should be repeated if necessary. Also, the later users should be involved already in the development, since the comprehensive understanding of the tasks and the working environment are crucial for the success of the software. By having users repeatedly review and evaluate the design solutions, the design can be adjusted and refined.

© Springer Nature Switzerland AG 2021
C. Stephanidis et al. (Eds.): HCII 2021, CCIS 1498, pp. 37–43, 2021.
https://doi.org/10.1007/978-3-030-90176-9_6

In order to design a user-centered system, DIN EN ISO 9241-2101 [1] recommends an approach with four development phases (Fig. 1):

1. Phase: Understanding and defining the context of use
2. Phase: Specifying user requirements
3. Phase: Developing design solutions
4. Phase: Evaluation and design

DESIGN PROCESS ACCORDING DIN EN ISO 9241-210

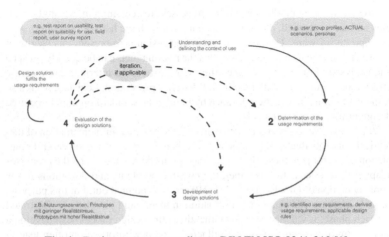

Fig. 1. Design process according to DIN EN ISO 9241-210 [1]

1.1   1. Phase: Understanding and Defining the Context of Use

The determination of the ACTUAL state is the basis for the analysis and provides essential information about the technical and organizational knowledge of the application area. Among other things, the analysis provides facts such as:

– Who works with the system
– which work is supported and
– which technical conditions are available.

In addition to the determination of the given state, the existing weak points should also be pointed out in order to consider them in the implementation [2]. It is helpful if facts such as organizational structures, business processes and its weak points and workflows are already documented.

A wide diversity of methods is available for obtaining the information, such as questionnaires, interviews or on-site observations.

Depending on the depth of detail of the available information, the different methods are suitable. Combinations can also be useful.

On-site observation of work processes provides additional information to obtain a holistic view of the performance of activities, especially for those tasks that have a high routine component. If on-site observations are not possible or the effort is too great, procedures and methods such as live ideation can be used as an alternative.

For a better understanding of interrelationships and dependencies, it is helpful to present the processes in the form of charts, diagrams and/or flowcharts. Often, further weaknesses, information deficits or even questions are raised that are important for a holistic understanding.

1.2   2. Phase: Specifying User Requirements

After the ACTUAL analysis has been completed, the usage requirements are derived. The usage requirements contain generally formulated requirements as given by the user's work tasks; under no circumstances do they contain software-specific features [2].

The first thing to do is to clearly define who the main user group is. Due to the large amount of information, it can be difficult to understand and specify the needs of the individual target groups. In some cases, creating fictional people, called "personas," can reveal a more concrete picture of the target group and their needs.

Once the goals and requirements have been identified, it is useful to clearly define them. This can be particularly helpful in the design phase and also during the argumentation towards the customer. In addition, the project status can always be checked against these criteria. However, it should be noted that this requirements list can be adjusted and supplemented throughout the project.

1.3   3. Phase: Developing Design Solutions

The implementation can be done with the help of different types of prototypes. A software-based solution is chosen for the most part for the design of interfaces, because at an advanced stage it is possible to link between the screens and thus experience a "real" impression of the menu navigation.

For the design of an interface, design criteria (structural structure) and design guidelines (type of presentation) have developed over time. According to Ben Shneiderman [4] and Jakob Nielsen [5], the following principles should be considered when designing an interface:

1. consistency
2. universal usability
3. informative feedback
4. completed dialogues
5. error prevention/error correction
6. reversibility
7. user control

8. relief of short-term memory
9. correspondence between the system and the real world
10. help and documentation

Many of the design features listed above are taken for granted at first glance. The structure of an HMI is usually developed from the rough to the small, which can cause the overall consistency of the concept to be lost sight of when working out the details.

1.4   4. Phase: Evaluation and Design

In each phase of HMI design, the results obtained should be repeatedly reviewed, questioned, revised and adapted. Different methods can be used for this, such as pretest, interviews, workshops, cognitive walkthrough. The choice of method depends a lot on the user group and the course of the project. Often methods can be combined. One possibility could be to conduct a pretest in combination with the observation of the users. Afterwards, a short interview could be made with the person in order to find out how the work and the operation of the program were perceived.

1.5   Documentation

Good documentation helps the customer to improve his understanding of the process and also of the product. The central role here is played by the style guide, as this represents the design guideline for the software. As work is done with the document, the structure should be well thought out so that elements can be found quickly. At best, a user-friendly design is also followed through here. Even after the project has been completed, the software will continue to develop; it is important to maintain the corresponding documents so that the consistency of the product can be maintained.

2   Design Process in Practice

According to the classic design process, the individual phases are worked through in chronological order. The evaluation briefly refers back to the previous phase and is mainly carried out in the design phase.

However, practice clearly shows that such a linear process is rarely or never adhered to. Already during the procurement of information, misunderstandings can arise regarding the importance of information and/or delays in the transmission of data. Furthermore, there is the danger that the selected methods for information procurement are not target-oriented and an additional method must be applied. This can already cause the first deviations from the planned schedule.

In addition, it may be determined during the presentation of the first analysis data that the specified circle of users must be expanded, since additional groups of people will use the program/app. If this is the case, the needs of this user group must be analyzed and compared with the existing requirements. As a result, previous results will have to be adjusted more frequently.

Extensive research is the basis for the success of a user-centric HMI. Therefore, the significance and the resulting importance of the research should be explained to the customer. However, the employer usually demands concrete solutions quickly, which means that tasks from following sections or phases often have to be brought forward.

In order to meet the wishes of the customer, the information can be evaluated and defined as preliminary requirements after the initial information gathering. This also offers the possibility of evaluating and, if necessary, consolidating requirements through more precise queries, further surveys and observations.

For successful project implementation, it is useful to clearly formulate and prioritize the requirements from the research. By defining the goals, the requirements for the product become clear for the first time. Also, especially in large and complex projects that run over a long period of time, the goal hierarchy can help not to lose orientation during the implementation. The method of goal definition is well known in project management [3] and is used at the end of a project to make an objective evaluation of the successful implementation. Often this step is not carried out at the beginning of a project, because the development of the prototype is already started. Only afterwards the benefit of the formulation of the goals becomes conscious e.g. if it goes to the documentation and explanation of the concept.

Another very useful method that can be borrowed from project management is environment analysis. In the first part of an environment analysis, all factors (stakeholders and factual factors) that have a direct or even an indirect influence on the project are identified. Then, the individual factors are evaluated and weighted to ensure the satisfaction of the affected persons/groups of persons. The analysis includes the possible risks and the measures derived from them.

In this context, communication to the stakeholders is more important than clarifying the framework conditions. This is due to the fact that the more a person is made to feel that he or she has been actively involved in shaping the project, the more sympathetic he or she will be towards the result. Like the goal definition, the environment analysis is carried out rather rarely, because during a project no great importance is attached to these two analyses.

After the first data collection has been successfully carried out, a first rough prototype can be presented to the customer.

Here, especially at the beginning, attention should be paid to a strongly reduced surface design in the design, so that it is suggested to the customer that this phase is exclusively about the construction. Otherwise, the customer can be given the feeling that he already has a completely designed product. Because of this, it should be pointed out constantly, especially at the beginning, that it is primarily about the structure, display and weighting of information and not yet about the design of the individual elements. This only follows at the end, when the process and the type of presentation have been clarified.

It may be useful to present the results in small steps, especially at the beginning, because this is where the basic orientation and structure of the product are determined. The further the development progresses, the longer the intervals between the individual evaluation rounds can be. The benefit of conducting multiple iteration loops should always be made clear to the customer, because the clearer and more detailed the user feedback, the more user-specific the end product.

Depending on the phase and method, different evaluation methods are suitable. The effectiveness of a method depends not only on the implementation, but also strongly on the people involved. Consequently, it makes sense to apply different methods to similar scenarios from time to time to determine which method is the more successful (Fig. 2).

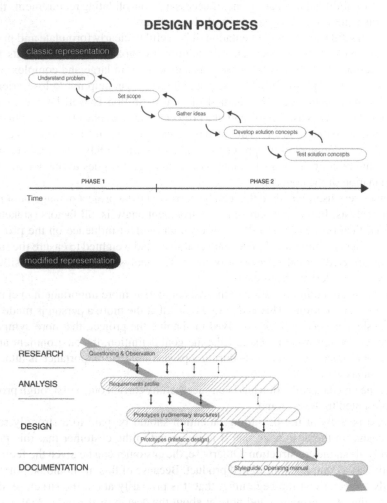

Fig. 2. Design process: theory and practice

3 Conclusion

The theoretical process from DIN EN ISO 9241-210 can be regarded as a rough outline in practice. In experience, however, it has been shown that a linear progression of the phases - especially in large projects - is not practicable.

Even at the beginning of the project, it can be assumed that not all the information and documents will be submitted in full by the customer at the start of the project. This is usually due to the fact that the customer assesses the relevance of information differently. Also, there are often different understandings of the duration and effort of each phase on the part of the customer and the contractor.

Therefore, it is essential for the successful completion of the project, among other things, that transparent and constant communication is maintained with the customer. The earlier problems, changes and wishes are discussed, the easier it is to react to them and take them into account in the project. Another important aspect is that applied methods are questioned again and again and if necessary supplemented by new methods. Every project is different and changes should be reacted to dynamically and at short notice. This makes strict adherence to fixed structures a hindrance.

4   Discussion

Consequently, it can be discussed to what extent the process in DIN EN ISO 9241-210 can be seen as a sequence to be aimed at, or whether the process can be seen more as a kind of 'guideline' or rough basic structure on which the design process is based instead of viewing it as a 'slavish' guideline.

In this course it should also be considered whether a weighting of the phases e.g. by a rough time estimation could be helpful. Furthermore, the listing of possible disruptive factors (new user groups, delayed information, etc.) could help to make a more realistic project progress planning.

Finally, in actual industrial projects with design involvement, it turns out again and again that the established development models - whether according to DIN ISO, SCRUM or Design Thinking - do not sufficiently reflect the actual development methodology and way of thinking in the design process. It would be debatable whether a method and guideline adapted to the actual iterative and recursive approach in the design process should be developed, or whether the established models should be revised accordingly.

References

1. DIN EN ISO 9241-210: Ergonomie der Mensch-System-Interaktion Teil 210: Menschenzentrierte Gestaltung interaktiver Systeme, Germany (2020)
2. DAkkS: Leitfaden Usability, Germany (2010)
3. Gessler, M.: Kompetenzbasiertes Projektmanagement (PM 3), Nürnberg (2016)
4. Cubetech, Die 8 goldenen Regeln des Interface Design in der Praxis. https://www.cubetech.ch/die-8-goldenen-regeln-des-interface-design/. Accessed 04 March 2021
5. Nielsen Norman Group homepage: 10 Heuristics for User Interface Design. https://www.nngroup.com/articles/ten-usability-heuristics/. Accessed 04 March 2021

Using Verbatims as a Basis for Building a Customer Journey Map: A Case Study

Arturo Moquillaza[✉] [iD], Fiorella Falconi[iD], Joel Aguirre[iD], and Freddy Paz[iD]

Pontificia Universidad Católica del Perú, Lima 32, Lima, Perú
{amoquillaza,fpaz}@pucp.pe, {ffalconit,aguirre.joel}@pucp.edu.pe

Abstract. Customer Journey Map is currently a very used canvas in the UX (User Experience) practice and design processes. Although it is widely discussed, both in the academic and industrial domains; practitioners still present questions about how to model this diagram. Customer Journey Maps are typically generated from the Personas technique, which is generally created by interviews or observations. On the other hand, many organizations employ a tool called NPS (Net Promoter Score). This tool generates both quantitative and qualitative data. The tool obtains expressions from the customer about the service or product called "Verbatim" about the qualitative data. These verbatims capture faithfully the event that took place when customers interacted with the financial products, services, systems, or channels. In that sense, we present a case study where a different approach is employed to build a Customer Journey Map about customers and their User Experience interacting with ATMs in a financial institution in collaborative sessions. In this sense, by applying this approach, we could map the touchpoints by analyzing verbatims. This way, verbatims could constitute a better source of information over interviews. The integration of the verbatim analysis in the CJM process could effortlessly scale as the data gathered from customers grows, promotes the sharing of knowledge inside the organization, and the culture of data-driven decision-making. In the end, we could obtain crucial insights and pain points that could generate new opportunities, requirements, and even new projects for the channel development backlog. We shared the results with a multidisciplinary audience with positive feedback, and they suggested that for new initiatives and analysis, to apply this new approach.

Keywords: Verbatim · User experience · Customer journey map · Human-computer interaction · Automated teller machine

1 Introduction

Customer Journey Map is currently a very used canvas in the UX (User Experience) practice, and design processes that show and explain the journey that a customer does to interact and engage with a product or service [1, 2]. The journey map also helps to explain how interaction occurs in a determinate moment and how this interaction influences other moments. In the Customer Journey Mapping (CJM) process, these determinate

C. Stephanidis et al. (Eds.): HCII 2021, CCIS 1498, pp. 44–50, 2021.
https://doi.org/10.1007/978-3-030-90176-9_7

moments are called touchpoints. Touchpoints are usually placed in a horizontal timeline, identifying three periods: the pre-service, the service, and the post-service [1].

Although it is widely discussed, both in the academic and industrial domains; practitioners still present questions about how to model this diagram [1]. Customer Journey Maps are typically generated from the Personas technique, and the Personas are generally created by ethnographic methods; for instance, interviews or observations [3]. The more touchpoints, the more complicated the mapping becomes, and as the number of customers grows, organizations gather more information about them and it becomes more difficult to map the journey of customers only with interviews.

On the other hand, many organizations employ a variety of techniques and tools for obtaining information from products, channels, and services they offer. This information many times is not shared with other divisions into the organization, giving as a result that divisions as Marketing, Design, Engineering, or R&D gather their data and results.

One very interesting tool that is very useful in the retail and financial sectors is the NPS (Net Promoter Score) [4]. This tool generates both quantitative and qualitative data. Regarding the quantitative data, customers answer about their satisfaction with the service, typically on a 1–10 Likert scale. Later, this information is processed to calculate the NPS of the product, service, or channel of the institution in a general way. About the qualitative data, the tool obtains expressions from the customer about the service or product. Those expressions and assertions are called "Verbatim". These verbatims capture faithfully the event that took place when customers interacted with the financial products, services, systems, or channels. The verbatim analysis is the process by which this information is processed and converted into valuable information [5]. Nevertheless, in many cases, this processing is disconnected from other analyses or is not taken into account as input in design and improvement processes outside the division into the institution that runs those analyses.

In that sense, we present a case study where a different approach is employed to build a Customer Journey Map about customers and their User Experience interacting with ATMs in a financial institution in collaborative sessions.

This paper is structured as follows: The Context section shows the main concepts related to the research. In the Case Study section, the case study is detailed. Finally, the last section presents conclusions and future work based on the results of the present experience.

2 Background

In this section, we present some ideas and previous experiences in the use of NPS, Verbatim, and CJM, as well as experiences in their use for User Experience improvement.

2.1 NPS

NPS is a metric developed by Fred Reichheld in 2003. It is widely used today due to its simple implementation and the ability to provide feedback from customers based on their experience during their interaction with the company [6]. It is currently employed by two-thirds of the Fortune 1000 companies [4]. To calculate NPS, a customer is asked a question about the likelihood of recommending a particular service on a scale of 1 to 10. Results between 9 and 10 categorize the customer as a promoter. Results between 7 and 8 classify the customer as neutral and a result less than or equal to 6 classify the customer as a detractor. To find the NPS, the percentages of promoters and detractors are subtracted. The NPS score will be between −100 and 100. An NPS above 0 is considered "good", above 50 is "excellent", and above 70 is considered "best in class". Negative scores are generally associated with poor customer experiences [4]. However, NPS is a metric that is not without controversy [5].

Likewise, it is a growing trend to capture qualitative information from customers, contextually obtain feedback and enhance innovation and customer experience improvement processes [7]. In this way, it has become common to add a question after the 1–10 rating, to ask about the reason for the rating. In this way, analysis can be performed on what the customer has written directly about their interaction. This information, which constitutes the exact quote of what was said by the customer, without any changes, is called Verbatim [6].

The analysis of these Verbatim obtained from NPS surveys is an activity that is increasingly being performed in mixed methods research, along with other metrics to complement what is reported by NPS [5] and to gain further insights from the information they already obtain [8]. Other uses include the discovery of pain points [9], the discovery of business drivers in a Six Sigma improvement process [10], among others. Likewise, various efforts are being made to automate this processing with Artificial Intelligence and Natural Language Processing techniques [5, 8, 11, 12]. Tristan [6], details a set of related research.

2.2 Customer Journey Map

According to Rosenbaum et al. [1], Customer Journey Mapping (CJM) is an increasingly popular tool recommended by both academics and practitioners for use in understanding the customer experience. The fundamental idea behind a CJM is a visual depiction of the sequence of events through which customers may interact with a service organization during an entire interaction. Its main objective is to enhance the service experience by improving the associated user experience at each touchpoint.

For some years now, some proposals have been observed in the industry to analyze the qualitative information of Verbatim to improve the CJM [13, 14]. Six iteration steps have even been proposed to carry out this process, with emphasis on detractors verbatim [14]. The six steps are as follows:

- Step 1: Collect Customer Verbatim Comments
- Step 2: Categorize Verbatim Comments into Themes & Frequency
- Step 3: Visualize Data in a Pareto Chart
- Step 4: Apply Root Cause Analysis
- Step 5: Implement Practical and Simple Countermeasures
- Step 6: Measure and Adjust

2.3 Verbatim Analysis to Improve the UX in Domain ATM

The information provided by Verbatim has proven to be a valuable input for the improvement of the User Experience (UX) in the ATM domain. In a previous paper [9] we show the good results obtained by incorporating the insights found in the first stages of a redesign process of an ATM application.

In this sense, it is proposed to use the data already available to many organizations that use NPS and Verbatim in their Customer Experience (CX) processes, and incorporate this input in the UX improvement processes. This is a complex issue since it is usually different areas that must share this information.

According to the above, it is proposed to use Verbatim analysis to enrich, and in other cases, to be the main input for the elaboration of a Customer Journey Map, which will guide the UX improvement process in the other stages of UX design aligned to any framework such as Design Thinking or User-Centered Design.

3 Case Study

For the case study, in particular, it was required to find pain points and user requirements that serve as input for a UX improvement process in the interaction between customers and the ATM network of a financial institution.

Due to the above, and due to the context of the COVID-19 pandemic, where user interviews and fieldwork were seriously limited, it was seen as convenient to employ the approach of analyzing Verbatim as input for the elaboration of a Customer Journey Map.

Then, taking into account proposals such as [1] and [14], we carried out a process with the following steps:

- Step 1: Obtain the original verbatim
- Step 2: Filter the Verbatim of the customers considered as detractors.
- Step 3: Categorize the Verbatim by the stages defined for the CJM from the user's perspective.
- Step 4: Subcategorize the Verbatim by themes and frequency
- Step 5: Relate Verbatim to representative emotions
- Step 6: Select Key Verbatim for each group to be performed
- Step 7: Elaborate the CJM with the processed information.

The activities that were followed for each step are detailed below. These activities were mainly carried out in collaborative sessions using tools that allowed such collaboration remotely.

3.1 Step 1: Obtain the Original Verbatim

Sessions were coordinated with the Customer Experience areas to have access to the NPS and especially to the Verbatim delivered by the customers. We decided to use this information directly, because the information processed by the area in question, having different objectives, reached conclusions that were not necessarily relevant to the User Experience in their interaction with ATMs. With this, we covered the step.

3.2 Step 2: Filter the Verbatim of the Customers Considered as Detractors

The information was obtained in a spreadsheet and we proceeded to perform the corresponding filtering. A base of 300 Verbatim correspondings to a specific quarter was used for the following steps.

3.3 Step 3: Categorize the Verbatim by the Stages Defined for the CJM from the User's Perspective

Three base stages were defined for this experience: Before, During, and After the customer's interaction with the ATM. Then, using the Google Jamboard collaborative whiteboard, we proceeded to the initial reading and categorization.

3.4 Step 4: Subcategorize Verbatim by Theme and Frequency

Work continued on the Jamboard and subcategories were obtained and colors were used to differentiate frequencies.

3.5 Step 5: Relating Verbatim to Representative Emotions

On the same Jamboard, a representative emotion was related to each category identified.

3.6 Step 6: Select Key Verbatim Per Group to be Performed

One or two key Verbatim were selected as representative of the category.

3.7 Step 7: Prepare the CJM with the Processed Information

The CJM was completely elaborated based on the information obtained, and taking into account the analysis performed and the feedback obtained by other areas of the organization.

Finally, the CJM was presented to a multidisciplinary audience within the organization, where very positive feedback was obtained, first, for the advantages of having the information mapped employing a CJM, known within the organization, as well as for the findings of the exercise. These findings were novel in comparison with user tests and direct interviews with small samples of users, typical in CJM elaboration processes.

4   Conclusions and Future Works

According to all of the above, it has become evident that, by applying the proposed approach, we could map the touchpoints by analyzing verbatims to build a Customer Journey Map. This way, verbatims could constitute a better source of information over interviews, principally for the amount of available data. The integration of the verbatim analysis in the CJM process could effortlessly scale as the data gathered from customers grows, promotes the sharing of knowledge inside the organization, and the culture of data-driven decision-making.

At the end of this experience, we could obtain crucial insights and pain points that could generate new opportunities, requirements, and even new projects for the channel development backlog.

We share the results with a multidisciplinary audience in the institution with positive feedback about the proposed approach, and they suggested that new initiatives and analyses apply this new approach. Based on the above, we consider that the proposal has achieved the objectives for which it was launched.

As future work, we propose to formalize the incorporation of this analysis as part of the framework used by the UX area, where, in addition, this analysis becomes cyclical and is input and output of continuous improvement processes. Likewise, we propose to explore Machine Learning and Natural Language Processing techniques to automate Verbatim analysis.

Acknowledgment. We want to thank the ATM team in BBVA Perú for its support along with the research. In addition, we thank the "HCI, Design, User Experience, Accessibility & Innovation Technologies (HCI DUXAIT)". HCI DUXAIT is a research group from the Pontificia Universidad Católica del Perú (PUCP).

References

1. Rosenbaum, M., Losada, M., Contreras, G.: How to create a realistic customer journey map. Bus. Horiz. **60**(1), 143–150 (2017). https://doi.org/10.1016/j.bushor.2016.09.010
2. Moon, H., Han, S.H., Chun, J., Hong, S.W.: A design process for a customer journey map: a case study on mobile services. Hum. Factors Man. **26**, 501–514 (2016). https://doi.org/10.1002/hfm.20673
3. Howard, T.: Journey mapping: a brief overview. Commun. Des. Q. Rev. **2**(3), 10–13 (2014). https://doi.org/10.1145/2644448.2644451
4. Lee, S.: Net promoter score: using NPS to measure IT customer support satisfaction. In: Proceedings of the 2018 ACM SIGUCCS Annual Conference (SIGUCCS '18). Association for Computing Machinery, New York, NY, USA, pp. 63–64 (2018). https://doi.org/10.1145/3235715.3235752
5. Zaki, M., Kandeil, D., Neely, A., McColl-Kennedy, J.R.: The fallacy of the net promoter score: customer loyalty predictive model. Camb. Serv. Alliance **10**, 1–25. https://cambridgeservicealliance.eng.cam.ac.uk/resources/Downloads/Monthly%20Papers/2016OctoberPaper_FallacyoftheNetPromoterScore.pdf
6. Tristán Gómez, L.: Modelo Predictivo del Índice NPS Basado en Información Textual de Percepción del Servicio al Cliente. Universidad Ricardo Palma, Perú (2019). http://reposi torio.urp.edu.pe/handle/URP/2480
7. Witell, L., Kristensson, P., Gustafsson, A., Löfgren, M.: Idea generation: customer co-creation versus traditional market research techniques. J. Serv. Manag. **22**, 140–159 (2011). https://doi.org/10.1108/09564231111124190
8. Gallager, C., Furey, E., Curran, K.: The application of sentiment analysis and text analytics to customer experience reviews to understand what customers are really saying. Int. J. Data Warehouse. Min. (IJDWM) **15**(4) (2019). https://doi.org/10.4018/IJDWM.2019100102

9. Moquillaza, A., Falconi, F., Paz, F.: Redesigning a main menu ATM interface using a user-centered design approach aligned to design thinking: a case study. In: Marcus, A., Wang, W. (eds.) HCII 2019. LNCS, vol. 11586, pp. 522–532. Springer, Cham (2019). https://doi.org/10.1007/978-3-030-23535-2_38
10. Fehlmann, T.M., Kranich, E.: Using six sigma transfer functions for analysing customer's voice. In: Glasgow, UK, Fourth International Conference on Lean Six Sigma, University of Strathclyde (2012). https://www.semanticscholar.org/paper/Using-Six-Sigma-Transfer-Functions-for-Analysing-Fehlmann/995fdc4a56cc4fbf27c4c3980241ecf32c36c120
11. Piris, Y., Gay, A.-C.: Customer satisfaction and natural language processing. J. Bus. Res. **124**, 264–271 (2021). https://doi.org/10.1016/j.jbusres.2020.11.065
12. Villaroel, F., Burton, J., Theodoulidis, B., Gruber, T., Zaki, M.: Analyzing customer experience feedback using text mining: a linguistics-based approach. J. Serv. Res. **17**(3), 278–295 (2014). https://doi.org/10.1177/1094670514524625
13. Perceptive Customer Insights Team: How to use NPS to inform your customer journey map. CustomerMonitor.com (2019). https://www.customermonitor.com/blog/how-to-use-nps-to-inform-your-customer-journey-map
14. Shmula: NPS customer feedback loop, closed loop system, and lean thinking. Shmula.com (2012). https://www.shmula.com/nps-customer-feedback-loop-lean-thinking/10563/

Green Patterns of User Interface Design: A Guideline for Sustainable Design Practices

Jitesh Nayak[✉] and Apurva Chandwadkar

SAP Labs Pvt. Ltd., #138, SAP Labs Road, EPIP Zone, Whitefield, Bengaluru, Karnataka 560066, India

Abstract. Despite aiming to lower the carbon cost, the growing digital footprint is concerning because of the energy consumed by data centers strewn across the globe. Analysis and distribution of large quantities of data, at these centers, account significantly to the rapidly rising global energy usage. Over the last decade, information service demand has increased manifold which has given rise to energy intensive computation techniques like Artificial Intelligence, Machine Learning and Data Mining, just to name a few. Surprisingly, study shows otherwise, the energy consumption at data centers has risen by only 6% from 2010 to 2018 [1] due to global push for sustainability and technological advancements in data management and cooling systems.

This paper promotes the idea further by showing a new approach of efficient design practices, i.e. Green Patterns, in software product development cycle. We correlated the design choices made on User Interface (UI) to its contribution on energy cost, based on a study that suggests the energy consumption of a device is highly attributed to Displays [2]. We measured the energy efficiency of various UI components using three factors: (a) Page Weight (b) Interactive Time and, (c) Sync Time. In the second part of the study, we validated the proposed Green Patterns with users so that usability is not at all compromised while reducing the digital carbon footprint.

Keywords: Sustainability · User interface · Energy consumption · Carbon footprint · Digital carbon cost · Sustainable Development Goal

1 Introduction

Smart products have become an integral part of everyday lives and are often built with sustainable goals in mind. The impact of product on the environment is inadvertently decided and embedded by designers. However, digital information has been under sustainability's ambit only over the last decade as the information services have increased. The information we are sending and receiving carries heavy baggage: accounting for 1% of global energy consumption [1] through global data centers. However, due to global push for environmental sustainability and technological advancements, the energy usage has only risen by 6% from 2010 to 2018 [1]. The goal of this paper is to explore and demonstrate the impact of sustainable design decisions on environment. Subsequently, we provide specific recommendations to reduce energy consumption of software products through User Interface design.

© Springer Nature Switzerland AG 2021
C. Stephanidis et al. (Eds.): HCII 2021, CCIS 1498, pp. 51–57, 2021.
https://doi.org/10.1007/978-3-030-90176-9_8

1.1 Motivation

Sustainable Development Goals (SDGs) and energy efficient policies are hardware oriented and limited to physical products. True energy efficiency will be achieved only when everybody is involved and contributes at each stage of the software development process. We want to empower software designers with a set of principles to implement sustainable patterns.

1.2 Related Work

Through blog posts, Microsoft's Sustainable Software [14] is educating the developer community for accounting carbon cost while building products. Another tech giant, Google's Core Web Vitals [15], is leveraging developer tools to measure important aspects of website development. Both are important steps towards energy efficiency but HCI still has very little focus.

2 Principles of Interaction Design with Sustainable Perspective

The framework for defining efficient design practices is discussed in this section by correlating key components of user experience design to carbon cost. Page Weight, Interactive and Rendering Time are sufficient metrics to quantify the energy consumption of UI artifacts.

2.1 Page Weight

Data Uses Energy. Downloading, storing, sharing, and retrieving data takes up energy. Internet trends show the average web page size has grown 400% from 2011 to 2019 [11]. Users are frustrated due to slow loading speeds; the environment also suffers from bloated websites due to access load on the servers.

2.2 Interactive Time

Hick-Hyman Law. It defines the amount of time, T, required to process the bits of information. Hick-Hyman law assesses the cognitive speed to interpret a certain number of choices given to users: increasing the number of choices, n, will logarithmically increase the time taken to choose an option.

$$T = b.\log_2(n + 1), \tag{1}$$

where b is a constant. UI designs capitalize on Hick-Hyman law by providing few options on menus, as a result, reducing human cognitive load while interacting with the system.

Fitts Law. This law predicts the time, T, required to complete a task on screen which is governed by ratio between the distance to the target and width of the target, represented by following equation:

$$T = c_1 + c_2. \log_2(^{2D}/w), \tag{2}$$

where $c1$ and $c2$ are experiment derived constants.

It's common for websites and applications to capitalize on both (1) and (2), to reduce the Interaction Cost [13]. IC is defined as the addition of physical effort and cognitive effort to perform a task:

$$IC = P + C \qquad (3)$$

Perhaps, we should consider ecological cost as an additional metric. Since low interactive time suggest low energy consumption and efficient lines of code.

2.3 Sync Time

Simpler Apps on the Surface Have Complex Architecture. Feature rich applications nowadays are far more complex at backend, large code base means slow server calls. Slow Sync Time suggests actual end user requirements are ignored while loading features and churning these datasets at the server requires significant energy. Simplifying and reducing the architecture complexity of applications is recommended by Cisco [4] for making future-ready applications.

3   Green Patterns: UI Design Heuristics for Reducing Carbon Cost

Design can have more than just usability and aesthetic value. These patterns already exists although need to be propagated by designers into their application.

3.1 Delight is Environment's Enemy

Subtle animated effect into a design can make users feel that they are interacting with software that has a personality, as Dan Saffer says, *"A contained product moment that revolves around a single use case or task."* [9]. Investigation on different animation technique suggests that while creating micro animations for delight, we often ignore sync time and use GIFs or high-quality graphics. These animation techniques increase both Page Weight and Sync Time. Green Patterns promotes using CSS based animation to keep the user encouraged and engaged.

3.2 Efficiency in Notifications

Notifications often trigger engagement with the applications but are also associated with stress [3]. People are assumed to be constantly co-present and available for conversation, maintaining levels of attentiveness for large parts of their wake time result in reduced productivity. By opting for explicit navigation in the UI for notifications, designers can reduce the server calls and keep the energy cost low.

3.3 Auto Confirmation

Unnecessary confirmation buttons do not effectively protect the user from errors [12]. In situations like these, the confirmation button will not only increase the time to perform the tasks but also make unnecessary server call. Designers can use auto confirmation for energy efficient performance.

3.4 Contextual Menu

Contextual Menu reduces cognitive load and interaction time as the server only loads on demand and relevant actions essential to complete a task. It is triggered by right click, haptic touch (iOS), long press, etc.; this lets the user perform a specific task without launching the entire app [10]. Green patterns incorporates quick access to contextual menu for the user with a list of predesignated Quick Actions of the application.

3.5 Infinite Scroll

The infinite scroll is advantageous because a low amount of data is requested at first and the server is only requested for more data when the user scrolls. It is typically popular for consuming social media's entertaining content; it can be adapted across domains by designers. By running a single query, superSQL [5] infinite scroll has achieved incredible improvement in architecture complexity by reducing 100+ lines of traditional code to just 12 lines. Such practices will bring energy intensive processes to the minimum while incorporating the best-in-class user experience.

3.6 Idle State of Application

Some lines of code are always sending bits to the server even when the user is not using the application. A designer should ensure the idle state of the application so that system can dedicate the power to application user is interested in [7]. Depending on the task analysis [8], distributing the power will make a significant difference in carbon cost.

4 Our Approach

We developed and launched a standard HTML (see Fig. 1) web page in URL https://freeused.org to create a benchmark to compare with the webpage created with Green Patterns (see Fig. 2). Inbuilt Google Chrome developer tool Lighthouse [16] is used to audit the performance score for both webpages. Lighthouse audits progressive web page for its First Contentful Paint, Speed Index, Largest Contentful Paint, Time to Interactive, Total Blocking Time, Cumulative Layout Shift.

4.1 Performance Measurement

The scores were measured by various metric but we correlated First Contentful Paint, Speed Index, Time to Interactive with our parameters described in Sect. 2. Since this paper has goal of focusing on the UI, we used FCP, SI and TTI for our investigation purposes.

4.2 Results

Green Patterns achieved impressive results when compared with the standard variant. Although, the variations are in milliseconds but improvement in SI and FCP shows the reduction in front end complexity (see Fig. 3).

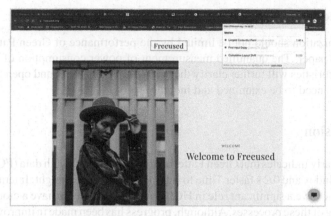

Fig. 1. The webpage with standard design with Lighthouse extension opened on the browser.

Fig. 2. The webpage with Green Patterns with Lighthouse opened on the browser.

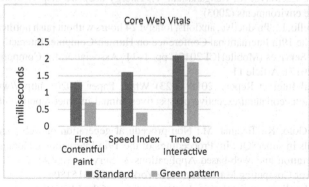

Fig. 3. The graph shows the variation of key metrics as provided by Lighthouse for both the variants of webpages.

4.3 Open Research Questions

Energy optimization should not be limited by the performance of Green Patterns mentioned in this paper. The quantified measurement of power consumption of display for each of the heuristics will further clarify the core idea of this paper and open to research. More patterns need to be examined and included.

5 Conclusion

The result clearly indicates that Green Patterns are 50% faster to fetch data (FCP), 4 times better Speed Index and 0.2 s faster Time to Interactive. As Page Weight, Interaction Time and Sync Time have a significant role in HCI, it would be useful to have a more thorough understanding of these processes. Although, progress has been made in improving energy efficiency, it is clear that there are still many opportunities for further optimization. Green Patterns are not negating any existing practices rather it is an add-on, so that sustainable practices are propagated from the very pixel designer decides to put on a design artifact.

According to Cisco's annual report, by 2023 two-third of the global population will have access to the internet across devices [4]. Such increase in global adoption of the internet and devices will generate high demand for information services. We will need designers to think beyond users and include ecological impact in their thought process. Like how Paul Dourish [6] describe Contextual Inquiry: *"It provides a set of methods whereby designers can move out from laboratory settings to the real world as a basis for design inspiration"*. From the perspective of sustainability, the Green Patterns are trying to make HCI design practitioners accountable and expand their definition of 'users' to 'user and its environment'.

References

1. Masanet, E., Shehabi, A., Lei, N., Smith, S., Koomey, J.: Recalibrating global data center energy-use estimates. Science **367**, 984–986 (2020). https://doi.org/10.1126/science.aba3758
2. Iyer, S., Luo, L., Mayo, R., Ranganathan, P.: Energy-adaptive display system designs for future mobile environments (2003)
3. Pielot, M., Rello, L.: Productive, anxious, lonely: 24 hours without push notifications. In: Proceedings of the 19th International Conference on Human-Computer Interaction with Mobile Devices and Services (MobileHCI 2017), pp. 1–11. Association for Computing Machinery, New York (2017). Article 11
4. Cisco Annual Internet Report (2018–2023) White Paper (2020). https://www.cisco.com/c/en/us/solutions/collateral/executive-perspectives/annual-internet-report/white-paper-c11-741490.html
5. Tajima, M., Goto, K., Toyama, M.: Non-procedural generation of web pages with nested infinite-scrolls in superSQL. In: Proceedings of the 19th International Conference on Information Integration and Web-based Applications & Services (iiWAS 2017), pp. 289–295. Association for Computing Machinery, New York (2017). 3151806
6. Dourish, P.: Implications for design. In: Proceedings of the SIGCHI Conference on Human Factors in Computing Systems (CHI 2006), pp. 541–550. Association for Computing Machinery, New York (2006)

7. Brown, D.J., Reams, C.: Towards energy efficient computing. Commun. ACM **53**(3), 50–58 (2010)

8. Saxe, E.: Power efficient software. Commun. ACM **53**(3), pp. 44–48 (2010)

9. Saffer, D.: https://www.oreilly.com/library/view/microinteractions/9781449342760/

10. Neilsen Norman Group: Anna Kaley. https://www.nngroup.com/articles/contextual-menus/

11. Rossul UI UX Agency. https://www.rossul.com/2019/blog/sustainable-ux-design/

12. Microsoft Blog. https://docs.microsoft.com/en-us/windows/win32/uxguide/mess-confirm?redirectedfrom=MSDN

13. Neilsen Norman Group: Raluka Budiu. https://www.nngroup.com/articles/interaction-cost-definition/

14. Microsoft's Sustainable Software. https://devblogs.microsoft.com/sustainable-software/

15. Google's Core Web Vitals. https://web.dev/vitals/

16. Google Chrome Lighthouse. https://developers.google.com/web/tools/lighthouse/

HCI Based Ethnography: A Possible Answer to Reduced Product Life

Maarif Sohail[1]([⊠]), Zehra Mohsin[2], and Sehar Khaliq[3]

[1] DeGroote School of Business, McMaster University, Hamilton, ON, Canada
sohaim9@mcmaster.edu
[2] Lahore College for Women University, Lahore, Pakistan
[3] Foundation University Islamabad, Islamabad, Pakistan

Abstract. The reduced lifespan of Information Systems (IS) based products continues to trouble IS companies. We investigate if there are evidence of short time ethnographies in IS or Human-Computer Interaction (HCI) studies, including the researcher as a part of the concurrent engineering team. Our literature analysis reveals that organizations are making use of different forms of ethnographies while addressing customer needs. We propose a Human-Computer Interaction (HCI) framework that can help researchers understand existing research focusing on the shortened product life and, at the same time, appreciate the bridge between research and practice.

Keywords: Lifespan · Research · Practice · Framework

1 Introduction

Reduced product life within the context of the internet of things (IoT) and smart products have created a dilemma for organizations that produce such devices. End users and researchers are attempting to bridge the ever-present gap between academic rigor and relevance to practitioners. Samsung Galaxy Note 7, which initially anticipated continuing where Samsung Note 5 had left off, was a failure. Samsung 7 could not deliver on its promise of improved features and result in more discomfort for end-users. There were distressing reports initially dismissed as fake news on the internet to actual stories of exploding batteries, causing people to question Samsung's product features and users' safety. The popular qualitative methods frequently used to identify end-user adoption or resistance include grounded theory methodology and ethnography. The researchers make compelling arguments for their technique selection, but, given the essential nature of shorter product life and the limited time available for adopting the smart product, we believe rapid ethnography or other atypical ethnographies may be the best option. Thus, our critical research question:

RQ: Can a short time HCI ethnographic initiative improve the researchers' role as a part of the concurrent engineering team while improving the product life span?

© Springer Nature Switzerland AG 2021
C. Stephanidis et al. (Eds.): HCII 2021, CCIS 1498, pp. 58–65, 2021.
https://doi.org/10.1007/978-3-030-90176-9_9

We divide the remainder of this article into four different sections. Section 2 illustrates the Literature Review, while Sect. 3 offers the proposed research framework. Section 4 mentions analysis and discussion while presenting propositions, and Sect. 5 sums up the conclusion.

2 Literature Review

Concurrent ethnographies, using human-centric methods for IS system design and development, focus on the role of the ethnographer to work beyond the control room environment (Hughes et al. 1994). Design is also knotted to manufacture and is persistently watchful of possible glitches that a knowledge-based proposal might face at the manufacturing stage (Pycock and Bowers 1996). Similarly, focus ethnography is a short-term or specific goal-based ethnography that is rigorous, data-intensive, and supplements other conventional forms of ethnographies (Knoblauch 2005). Ethnography extends the requirements process, culminating in the ethnographically based method of social analysis (Viller and Sommerville 1999).

Two dichotomous views represent the relationship between ethnography and participatory design, one being the background and the other being participatory, which forms the basis of active participation of all participants (Blomberg and Karasti 2012).

A less popular but critical view is that organizations are ethnographic test fields with numerous activities becoming a part of organizational culture (Harper 2000). One of the foremost opportunities for ethnographers is to use fieldnotes as tools to form their team, share information, and create knowledge (Creese et al. 2008). There are challenges in multidisciplinary teams working with ethnographic methods (Quinlan 2009). There is an important admonition that, in an ethnographic setting, the organization members or the collaboration project team should have the same comprehension, agreed-upon deliverables, and expectations from ethnography (Gajera and O'Neill 2014). Critiques may argue that there are available strategies like grounded theory methodology or phenomenology, other than ethnography for organizations interested in improving their understanding of problems related to reduced product life and enhancing customer experience (Goulding 2005).

The strategy of symbolic interactionist ethnography by sharing common symbols can overcome these challenges by aiming for trustworthiness and congruence (Tan et al. 2003). These focus group meetings can use certain strategic forms of ethnographies like autoethnography, video ethnography, comparative ethnography, and virtual ethnography (Vesa and Vaara 2014). Communication ethnography shares communication among various critical stakeholders (Keating 2001). Ethical considerations make visual ethnography vital and sensitive to participants' privacy and lead to a host of data management issues (Schembri and Boyle 2013).

Organizations can use the dynamic and visible practices of big data in online advertising and other forms of investigation at the individual level (Nafus and Sherman 2014). They can thus monitor the device's performance and the particular user: digital ethnography studies digitalization, online communities, and digital data (Varis 2016). At the same time, the availability of data mining techniques has developed 'ethnomining' (Aipperspach et al. 2006) and emerged as a form of ethnographic insight and data mining. Big data does not always convey the actual reasons for specific issues. Hence, researchers need to understand that large volumes of data may not result in unearthing the real root cause of the problem, and the analysis may be incorrect (Lohmeier 2014).

With its ever-improving algorithms combined with artificial intelligence, the future powerful form of Big Data has the potential to replace ethnography. Big Data will also add the benefit of reducing operational costs and achieving greater efficiencies in data collection. However, big data would still be limited to only those with access to high-speed internet (Beuving 2019).

Analysts pay attention to big data and analytics for business, consumer, and social insights (Chang et al. 2014) as well as "Thick descriptions" (Stoller 2013) even though it may allow them to form a complete picture of information (Cuesta et al. 2019). Big data analysts will still have to pay attention to surveillance, privacy, and future misuse of data (Blok and Pedersen 2014) to accomplish the greater good (Charles and Gherman 2019).

The literature review identifies certain gaps, with one of the more important ones suggesting that different forms of ethnographies are available. However, due to the absence of an academician researcher (or simply a researcher), the organizations cannot ensure product quality, product performance, and a pleasant user experience.

3 Proposed Research Framework

Hughes et al. (1997) presented a framework for the design of IS development. Post Internet of Things (IoT), more or less all manufactured products and provided to the customers can be envisioned as Information Systems. We feel that organizations make use of applied research using their various departments and form a cross-sectional team under the concept of concurrent design or concurrent engineering. Corporations have started to engage anthropologists to study consumer behavior and the culture of the consumers. Thus, these organizations are consciously making use of concurrent ethnography, which refers to consumer research anthropology (Sunderland 2016), business anthropology (Tian et al. 2018), and enterprise anthropology (Jordan 2018).

We propose a simple framework in the presence of a wealth of knowledge. This knowledge base framework will compensate for the scope's lack of rigor and relevance. The academic researchers could ideally be an excellent resource for the ICT/ Manufacturing organizations who use cross-functional teams for design and product testing. Having an academic researcher would allow the activities at various stages of the product design and development, manufacturing, testing would be managed and recorded academically and practically in any acceptable format, whether audio, video, text, or web-based. We can extend the framework keeping in view the subject expertise to address any problems.

The framework has two dimensions, namely the breadth and the depth of research or intervention under consideration. In a top-down approach, the principal constituent is the scope of KMS based Ethnography, which sets out the study's boundaries. Concurrent Design/Engineering represents the stage where different critical interfaces nominate their subject experts, contributing to the design of the new product.

The responsibility of the concurrent design/engineering team often changes its position from design to changes in design if the organization is attending to an issue related to product design or performance based on some design issue. The product testing stage is where the product is tested under various conditions to seek the product's performance threshold and thus identify safe and optimum operating conditions of the product based on environment and regulatory compliance requirements. The focus group is often purely pivoting on end-users representing different demographics; their feedback often forms the basis for possible improvements. Finally, the Communiqué stage allows the information to be shared with various stakeholders with feedback recorded, and individuals requested consent. The scope of KMS ethnography is the over-arching stage where the ethnographer takes field notes and observes the actions of others.

One of the most important components of our framework is the role of the researcher. The researcher, in our opinion, should be well versed with the perspective that HCI is accurately a multidisciplinary effort. The researcher should ensure that under diverse settings and in a wide range of disciplines at an academic institution of learning or and corporate research establishments, she should be able to steer the HCI research. We advocate that the researcher has essential functional knowledge of critical fields of inquiry like cognitive psychology, human factors, ergonomics, social psychology, organizational psychology, economics, and Information Systems. The researcher should display a Cognitive science-based perspective linking the cognitive processes.

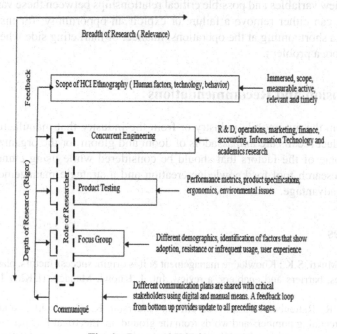

Fig. 1. Proposed HCI framework

The role of the researcher also needs an articulation of understanding about human aspects of HCI to include sociology and anthropology, especially research involving the impact of technology and technological factors on society as a whole. Today, most researchers are expected to work on problems related to traditional businesses and e-commerce, like consumer behavior, knowledge management, and especially information systems. The role of the researcher contributes to the efficacy and success of the HCI framework. The framework captures several key elements and their working scope and boundaries, as illustrated in Fig. 1.

The integrative framework is grounded in qualitative findings and business practices. This framework can be modified to capture an organization's own Knowledge Management System, policies, and work practices. The framework captures participants' knowledge, experience, and expertise at multiple functioning levels, including the individual, cross-functional, organizational, and societal levels.

4   Analysis and Discussion

The concept of concurrent engineering is well established and well-practiced, especially in the manufacturing environment. Researchers from the Industrial engineering field have proposed making use of concurrent engineering ethnographies. However, the existing literature is silent on providing any evidence as far as IS or HCI research is concerned. We present some propositions that can help future researchers with theory building, identifying new variables and possible critical relationships between these variables. An organization can either remove a failure or exploit an opportunity; for instance, it is overcoming a shortcoming at the operations, finance, or marketing side when planning to troubleshoot a problem.

5   Conclusion and Recommendations

Whether from the automobile industry or from the industry that manufactures smartphones, product recalls are ambassadors of doom and gloom for the organizations. We identified some of the factors that should be considered while using ethnography as a strategic research tool for knowledge creation and a strategic management tool for competitive advantage.

References

Agrawal, A., Mukti, S.K.: Knowledge management & it is origin, success factors, planning, tools, applications, barriers and enablers: a review. Int. J. Knowl. Manage. (IJKM) 16(1), 43–82 (2020)

Aipperspach, R., Rattenbury, T.L., Woodruff, A., Anderson, K., Canny, J.F., Aoki, P.: Ethnomining: integrating numbers and words from the ground up. Electrical Engineering and Computer Sciences, University of California at Berkeley, Technical report No. UCB/EECS-2006–125 (2006). www.eecs.berkeley.edu/Pubs/TechRpts/2006/EECS-2006-125.html. Accessed 21 May 2011

Alavi, M., Leidner, D.E.: Knowledge management and knowledge management systems: conceptual foundations and research issues. MIS Q, 107–136 (2001)

Anand, A., Walsh, I., Moffett, S.: Does humility facilitate knowledge sharing? Investigating the role of humble knowledge inquiry and response. J. Knowl. Manage. (2019)

Blok, A., Pedersen, M.A.: Complementary social science? Quali-quantitative experiments in a Big Data world. Big Data Soc. 1(2), 2053951714543908 (2014)

Blomberg, D.J., Karasti, H.: Ethnography: positioning ethnography within participatory design. In: Routledge International Handbook of Participatory Design, pp. 106–136. Routledge (2012)

Brun, I., Rajaobelina, L., Ricard, L., Amiot, T.: Examining the influence of the social dimension of customer experience on trust towards travel agencies: the role of experiential predisposition in a multichannel context. Tour. Manage. Perspect. 34, 100668 (2020)

Carver, L., Turoff, M.: Human-computer interaction: the human and computer as a team in emergency management information systems. Commun. ACM 50(3), 33–38 (2007)

Castellani, P., Rossato, C., Giaretta, E., Davide, R.: Tacit knowledge sharing in knowledge-intensive firms: the perceptions of team members and team leaders. RMS 15(1), 125–155 (2019). https://doi.org/10.1007/s11846-019-00368-x

Cawley, K.S.: Assessing the impact of age and experience on the perceived ease of use of crisis information management software (Doctoral dissertation, Northcentral University) (2020)

Chai, S., Kim, M.: A socio-technical approach to knowledge contribution behavior: an empirical investigation of social networking sites users. Int. J. Inf. Manage. 32(2), 118–126 (2012)

Chang, R.M., Kauffman, R.J., Kwon, Y.: Understanding the paradigm shift to computational social science in the presence of big data. Decis. Support Syst. 63, 67–80 (2014)

Charles, V., Gherman, T.: Big data analytics and ethnography: together for the greater good. In: Emrouznejad, A., Charles, V. (eds.) Big Data for the Greater Good. Studies in Big Data, vol. 42, pp. 19–33. Springer, Cham (2019). https://doi.org/10.1007/978-3-319-93061-9_2

Chen, Y.H., Lin, T.P., Yen, D.C.: How to facilitate inter-organizational knowledge sharing: the impact of trust. Inf. Manage. 51(5), 568–578 (2014)

Creese, A., Bhatt, A., Bhojani, N., Martin, P.: Fieldnotes in team ethnography: researching complementary schools. Qual. Res. 8(2), 197–215 (2008)

Cuesta, D.A., Borges, M., Gomes, J.O.: Planning the combination of "big data insights" and "thick descriptions" to support the decision-making process. In: Rocha, Á., Ferrás, C., Paredes, M. (eds.) ICITS 2019. AISC, vol. 918, pp. 73–82. Springer, Cham (2019). https://doi.org/10.1007/978-3-030-11890-7_8

Duryan, M., Smyth, H., Roberts, A., Rowlinson, S., Sherratt, F.: Knowledge transfer for occupational health and safety: cultivating health and safety learning culture in construction firms. Accid. Anal. Prev. 139, 105496 (2020)

Evangelou, C., Karacapilidis, N.: On the interaction between humans and knowledge management systems: a framework of knowledge sharing catalysts. Knowl. Manage. Res. Pract. 3(4), 253–261 (2005)

Gajera, R., O'Neill, J.: Ethnography in parallel. In: Rossitto, C., Ciolfi, L., Martin, D., Conein, B. (eds.) COOP 2014 - Proceedings of the 11th International Conference on the Design of Cooperative Systems, pp. 259–275. Springer, Cham (2014). https://doi.org/10.1007/978-3-319-06498-7_16

Gay, C., Horowitz, B., Elshaw, J.J., Bobko, P., Kim, I.: Operator suspicion and human-machine team performance under mission scenarios of unmanned ground vehicle operation. IEEE Access 7, 36371–36379 (2019)

Goulding, C.: Grounded theory, ethnography and phenomenology: a comparative analysis of three qualitative strategies for marketing research. Eur. J. Mark. 39(3/4), 294–308 (2005)

Harper, R.H.R.: The organisation in ethnography–a discussion of ethnographic fieldwork programs in CSCW. Comput. Support. Coop. Work (CSCW) 9(2), 239–264 (2000)

Hughes, J.A., O'Brien, J., Rodden, T., Rouncefield, M., Blythin, S.: Designing with ethnography: a presentation framework for design. In: Proceedings of the 2nd Conference on Designing Interactive Systems: Processes, Practices, Methods, and Techniques, pp. 147–158. ACM, August 1997

Hughes, J., King, V., Rodden, T., Andersen, H.: Moving out from the control room: ethnography in system design. In: Proceedings of the 1994 ACM Conference on Computer Supported Cooperative Work, pp. 429–439. ACM, October 1994

Beuving, J.: Ethnography's future in the big data era. Inf. Commun. Soc. (2019). https://doi.org/10.1080/1369118X.2019.1602664

Jordan, A.: The Significance of Enterprise Anthropology in Asia. Glob. Econ. Rev. **47**, 20–27 (2018)

Keating, E.: The ethnography of communication. In: Handbook of Ethnography, pp. 285–301 (2001)

Knoblauch, H.: Focused ethnography. In: Forum Qualitative Sozialforschung/Forum: Qualitative Social Research, vol. 6, no. 3, September 2005

Kucharska, W., Erickson, G.S.: Organizational IT competency, knowledge workers and knowledge sharing. In: Proceedings of the 20th European Conference on Knowledge Management, vol. 1, pp. 665–671, September 2019

Lohmeier, C.: The researcher and the never-ending field: reconsidering big data and digital ethnography. In: Big Data? Qualitative Approaches to Digital Research, pp. 75–89. Emerald Group Publishing Limited (2014)

Mani, Z., Chouk, I.: Drivers of consumers' resistance to smart products. J. Mark. Manage. **33**(1–2), 76–97 (2017)

Mueller, J.: Formal and informal practices of knowledge sharing between project teams and enacted cultural characteristics. Proj. Manage. J. **46**(1), 53–68 (2015)

Nafus, D., Sherman, J.: Big data, big questions| this one does not go up to 11: the quantified self-movement as an alternative big data practice. Int. J. Commun. **8**, 11 (2014)

Nisar, T.M., Prabhakar, G., Strakova, L.: Social media information benefits, knowledge management and smart organizations. J. Bus. Res. **94**, 264–272 (2019)

Ogunmokun, O.A., Eluwole, K.K., Avci, T., Lasisi, T.T., Ikhide, J.E.: Propensity to trust and knowledge sharing behavior: an evaluation of importance-performance analysis among Nigerian restaurant employees. Tour. Manage. Perspect. **33**, 100590 (2020)

Ogunmokun, O.A., Unverdi-Creig, G.I., Said, H., Avci, T., Eluwole, K.K.: Consumer well-being through engagement and innovation in higher education: a conceptual model and research propositions. J. Public Aff., e2100 (2020)

Olak, A.J., et al.: The relationships between the use of smart mobile technology, safety knowledge and propensity to follow safe practices at work. Int. J. Occup. Saf. Ergon., 1–10 (2019)

Pycock, J., Bowers, J.: Getting others to get it right: an ethnography of design work in the fashion industry. In: Proceedings of the 1996 ACM Conference on Computer supported Cooperative Work, pp. 219–228. ACM, November 1996

Quinlan, E.: The 'actualities' of knowledge work: an institutional ethnography of multidisciplinary primary health care teams. Sociol. Health Illn. **31**(5), 625–641 (2009)

Sagynbekova, S., Ince, E., Ogunmokun, O.A., Olaoke, R.O., Ukeje, U.E.: Social media communication and higher education brand equity: the mediating role of eWOM. J. Public Aff., e2112 (2021)

Schembri, S., Boyle, M.V.: Visual ethnography: achieving rigorous and authentic interpretations. J. Bus. Res. **66**(9), 1251–1254 (2013)

Sinha, A., Kumar, P., Rana, N.P., Islam, R., Dwivedi, Y.K.: Impact of internet of things (IoT) in disaster management: a task-technology fit perspective. Ann. Oper. Res. **283**(1–2), 759–794 (2017). https://doi.org/10.1007/s10479-017-2658-1

Stoller, P.: Big data, thick description and political expediency. Huffington Post, 16 (2013)

Sunderland, P.: In Advancing Ethnography in Corporate Environments. In: In Advancing Ethnography in Corporate Environments, pp. 122–135. Routledge (2016)

Tan, M., Zhu, L., Wang, X.W.: Symbolic interactionist ethnography: Toward congruence and trustworthiness. In: AMCIS 2003 Proceedings, p. 377 (2003)

Tian, R.G., Sigamani, P., Malhotra, S.: Business Anthropology. In: Hilary, C. (ed.) The International Encyclopedia of Anthropology, pp. 364–382. John Wiley & Sons, Ltd (2018). https://doi.org/10.4135/9781529756449.n21

Varis, P.: Digital ethnography. In: The Routledge Handbook of Language And Digital Communication, pp. 55–68 (2016)

Vesa, M., Vaara, E.: Strategic ethnography 2.0: four methods for advancing strategy process and practice research. Strateg. Organ **12**(4), 288–298 (2014)

Viller, S., Sommerville, I.: Social analysis in the requirements engineering process: from ethnography to method. In: Proceedings IEEE International Symposium on Requirements Engineering (Cat. No. PR00188), pp. 6–13. IEEE, June 1999

Wolcott, H.F.: Ethnography: A Way of Seeing. Rowman Altamira (1999)

Celebrating Design Thinking in Tech Education: The Data Science Education Case

Samar I. Swaid[1]([⊠]) and Taima Z. Suid[2]

[1] Philander Smith College, Little Rock, AR, USA
[2] Dillards Headquarter, Little Rock, AR, USA

Abstract. Today, corporates are moving toward the adoption of Design-Thinking techniques to develop products and services, putting their consumer as the heart of the development process. Tim Brown, president, and CEO of IDEO, defines design thinking as "A human-centered approach to innovation that draws from the designer's toolkit to integrate the needs of people, the possibilities of technology, and the requirements for business success". The application of design thinking has been witnessed to be the road to develop innovative applications, interactive systems, scientific software, healthcare application, and even to utilize Design Thinking to re-think business operation as the case of Airbnb. Recently, there has been a movement to apply design thinking to machine learning and artificial intelligence to ensure creating the "waw" affect to consumers. ACM Taskforce on Data Science program states that "Data Scientists should be able to implement and understand algorithms for data collection and analysis. They should understand the time and space considerations of algorithms. They should follow good design principles developing software, understanding the importance of those principles for testability and maintainability" However, this definition hides the user behind the machine who works on data preparation, algorithm selection and model interpretation. Thus, Data Science program to include design thinking to ensure meeting the user demands, generating more usable machine learning tools, and developing new ways of framing computational thinking. In this poster, we describe the motivation behind injecting DT in Data Science programs, an example course, its learning objective and teaching modules.

Keywords: Design thinking · Data science · Machine learning · Higher education

1 Introduction

Design thinking is a systematic human-centered, iterative approach to problem solving that goes beyond shape and layout to have user demands and needs positioned central to the process. In design thinking the focus is on an idea that might help the end-user to achieve specific goal. This approach calls for continuous feedback between the developer of a solution and the target users. Design Thinkers step into the end users' shoes – not

© Springer Nature Switzerland AG 2021
C. Stephanidis et al. (Eds.): HCII 2021, CCIS 1498, pp. 66–70, 2021.
https://doi.org/10.1007/978-3-030-90176-9_10

only interviewing them, but also carefully observing their behaviors. Solutions and ideas are concretized and communicated in the form of prototypes as early as possible, so that potential users can test them and provide feedback – long before the completion or launch. In this way, Design Thinking generates practical results. Design Thinking is not only to help understand the end-user goals, but also to avoid bias in data science and better balance processes applied in data science methodologies. For example, Bias in machine learning is knows as algorithm bias. *Algorithms can have built-in biases "because they are created by individuals who have conscious or unconscious preferences that may go undiscovered until the algorithms are used, and potentially amplified, publicly"* [8]. To limit bias in data science, DT has much to offer by engaging the different stakeholders, ensuring the quality of the data and the process [5]. Other motivations to apply Design Thinking is profitability. Accenture [1] found based on their research that organizations that applies DT-based artificial intelligence out-performed the ones who do not. Blending DT with Data science results in more successes not only in the quality of the machine learning modeling and their analytical models but also in the subsequent organizational alignment around and adoption of the analytic results [10].

The rest of this paper is organized as follows. The next section provides some background of design thinking in higher education and IT corporates. Next, the concept and the architecture of the Design Thinking for Data Science program is introduced. Finally, we provide conclusion and future steps.

2 Background

Design Thinking is methodology to create innovative experiences, products and services. Taken from Herbert Simon's 1969 seminal work *"The Sciences of the Artificial"*, the design process consisted of seven steps of: *define, research, ideate, prototype, choose, implement*, and *learn*. User research has been the cornerstone of design process for decades. Recently, several models are witnessed to be applied for DT such as Google Design Sprints, Design Council UK Double Diamond model, Stanford. School design thinking process, IDEO design thinking program, and IBM Enterprise Design Thinking, among others. For example, in 2004 SAP announced they will start their Design thinking journey with its 3D approach of Discover, Design, Deliver Experience. Most of these models share the target of achieving innovation through three main factors: Human values, Business and Technology [3] (Fig. 1 and Table 1).

Design Thinking Humanizes Data Science

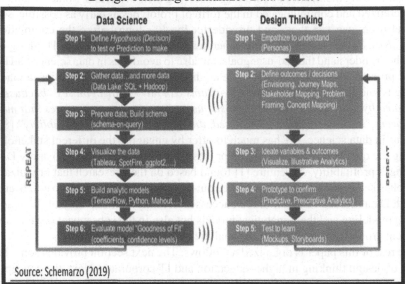

Fig. 1. Design thinking humanizes data science

Table 1. Selected models of design thinking

Reference	Approach to design thinking
dSchool (Stanford)	Empathize Define Ideate – Prototype – Test
Google Design Sprint	Understand – Define – Sketch – Decide – Prototype – Validate
Design Council UK Double Diamond Model	Discover – Define – Develop – Deliver
IDEOU DT Model (IDEOU 2020)	Empathise –Define – Ideate –Prototype –Test – Implement
IBM Enterprise Design Thinking Model	Observe – Reflect – Make
SAP's Human-Centered Approach	Discover – Design – Deliver

3 Celebrating Design Thinking

3.1 Intro to Data Science: Course Description and Learning Objectives

A committee was developed to develop the course, learning objectives and teaching modules. The committee was formed of three faculties of Computer Science who have different experiences in data science areas of machine learning, data mining and artificial intelligence, data management and big data. The committee reviewed different Data Science programs in other schools to decide what fits their students and the CS program offered at the institution. The course of "Intro to Data Science" is developed as "This course will introduce students to the fundamentals of data science. Students will learn to explore, visualize, and analyze data to understand natural phenomena, investigate patterns, model outcomes, and make predictions. The course will utilize IBM Visual Studio and technologies. (3 credit hours). The course will introduce students to the fundamentals of data science. Students will learn to explore, visualize, and analyze data to understand natural phenomena, investigate patterns, model outcomes, and make predictions. The course will utilize IBM Visual Studio and technologies. (3 credit hours). The learning objective of the course are as listed in Fig. 2.

Course Description: This course will introduce students to the fundamentals of data science. Students will learn to explore, visualize, and analyze data to understand natural phenomena, investigate patterns, model outcomes, and make predictions. The course will utilize IBM Visual Studio and technologies. (3 credit hours)

    Learning Objectives:
- Introduce data science and its applications
- Responsibilities of data scientist
- Design Thinking: Elements and principles
- Understand the processes of Empathise –Define – Ideate –Prototype – Test – Implement
- Explore and understand data
- Introduce data wrangling tactics
- Train on IBM Watson Studio
- Introduce Python basic programming
- Describe visualization and its role in data science
- Introduce AutoAI to build and deploy models
- Learn JupertNoteBook
- Apply knowledge using case study: Auto Fraud Analysis

Fig. 2. Course intro to data science

4   Conclusion

Information consumers are ultimately the beneficiaries of any insight derived from data. Thus, applying Design Thinking principles to ensure the resulting insights are valuable and actionable to stakeholder is very crucial. Design thinking has emerged as a methodology to understand first the human in the loop and the human's needs, in an iterative process, to reach innovative solutions. Today, Design Thinking's application in the business world is witnessed as an undeniably a methodology that not only satisfies the needs of the information consumers and key stakeholders, but also would result in more profitability on the long run. Unsparingly, higher education has developed several data science programs at different levels, but paralleling between the principles of design thinking and data science in higher education is overlooked. We here aim to contribute to the new efforts to interweave designing thinking with data science academic programs.

References

1. Accenture: Artificial Intelligence (2020). https://www.accenture.com/us-en/insights/artifi cial-intelligence-summary-index. Accessed 30 Dec 2020
2. Dragicevic, N., Lee, W., Tsui, E.: Supporting service design with storyboards and diagrammatic models. In: Proceedings of the Theory and Applications in the Knowledge Economy Conference, pp. 457–469 (2017)
3. Elmansy, R.: Design Thinking Case Study: Innovation at Apple, 7 April 2016. https://www.designorate.com/design-thinking-case-study-innovation-atapple/. Accessed 1 July 2021
4. IDEO: Design Thinking (2019). https://www.ideou.com/pages/design-thinking. 1 July 2021
5. Mehrabi, N., Morstatter, F., Saxena, N., Lerman, L., Galstyan, A.: A survey on bias and fairness in machine learning. Preprint arXiv:1908.09635 (2019)
6. SAP: SAP Combined Approach to Build Scalable Solutions (2019). https://experience.sap.com/designservices/approach. Accessed 1 July 2021
7. SAS: Machine Learning What it is and why it matters (2020). https://www.sas.com/en_us/insights/analytics/machine-learning.html. Accessed 30 Dec 2020
8. SearchEnterpriseAI: Machine Leaning Bias (2020). https://searchenterpriseai.techtarget.com/definition/machine-learning-bias-algorithm-bias-or-AI-bias. 1 July 2021
9. Schmarzo, B.: Design Thinking Humanizes Data Science (2019). https://www.datasciencecentral.com/profiles/blogs/design-thinking-humanizes-data-science. https://www.datasciencecentral.com/profile/BillSchmarzo. Accessed 1 July 2021
10. TechTarget: Design Thinking Humanizes Data Science (2019). https://www.datasciencecentral.com/profiles/blogs/design-thinking-humanizes-data-science. Accessed 1 July 2021

Social Innovation and Design — Prototyping in the NICE2035 Future Living Labs

Jing Wang[✉]

College of Design and Innovation, Tongji University, Shanghai, China

Abstract. The "Horizon 2020" is initiated by the European Union, and it advocates design-driven innovation. It is generally believed that design is an essential impetus for innovation, and naturally, design methods and tools are applied in the field of innovation. In innovation, one field is social innovation that refers to new ideas and solutions developed to cater to social needs. Evidences have shown that social innovation can be fully demonstrated through design, especially in systems thinking, prototype design and visualization. However, people express their concerns about limitations of design in this field.

In this paper, having discussed specific case - NICE2035 Future Living Lab, the author proposed innovative design, methods and concepts of social innovation, and emphasized prototype design and infrastructure. Different from project design, social innovation methods, activities in implementation and social connection network built aimed to help stakeholders establish long-term relationships and obtain design opportunities. Moreover, it stressed that prototypes, as a design method and tool, should be open and displayed to more people, and to spread knowledge of a sustainable lifestyle.

Keywords: Social innovation · Prototype · Infrastructure · Place for knowledge production

1 Introduction

Since the 21st century, the society have faced severe economy and ecological challenges. The TSI declaration holds that compared with disappointing future described by austerity policies, social innovations usher in a promising prospect for people[1]. as a response, public sectors adopt social innovation as an effective way to develop effective solutions.

In the past 10 years, designers had involved in this area, who, following the user-centered principle, introduced stakeholders into the innovative solutions exploring process through participatory design and rapid prototyping methods. In this paper, social innovation project of NICE2035 Future Living Laboratory was analyzed, which creates empowered scenarios for city innovation and entrepreneurship. This NICE2035 laboratory project was initiated by Lou Yongqi [1], the dean of the School of Design and Creativity, Tongji University which following the principle of SLOC [2] proposed by

---

[1] http://www.transitsocialinnovation.eu/about-transit.

© Springer Nature Switzerland AG 2021
C. Stephanidis et al. (Eds.): HCII 2021, CCIS 1498, pp. 71–80, 2021.
https://doi.org/10.1007/978-3-030-90176-9_11

Manzini, experimenting emerging scenarios through a series of design research plans. DESIS (Design for social innovation and sustainability) is a global design laboratory network to realize SDGs[2]. The network had set over 40 laboratories across the world, and mobilized design schools to trigger and expand social innovations through design. DESIS Labs creates partnerships with local places, regions and global areas, and formulates new scenarios and communication procedures. According to DESIS, the laboratory is a place to generate new visions, and enhance social synergy, and stimulate production of new social initiatives.

The NICE2035 Future Living Lab reported in this paper, which is user-centred innovation ecosystem, based on a systematic method of co-creation with users, integrates research and innovation processes in real community and environment. In terms of infrastructure, it cultivates partnership between business and academic fields by contributing financial resources. It takes cooperation with stakeholders such as non-governmental organizations, municipal units in Yangpu District of Shanghai, local community management departments, and business partners, to explore new services and solutions so as to meeting the social needs in this era.

2   Social Innovation and Design

2.1   Social Innovation

Social transformation to a sustainable living system requires fundamental changes at all levels of the society-technical system [3], from a series of interconnected small and short-term projects to large-scale, long-term, open processes to realize the social oriented vision [4]. For example, the DESIS network initiated by Ezio Manzini, and exploring new processes, systems, services which transcend the market-led design paradigms and shape a more sustainable lifestyle [5]. Manzini advocates developing a series of themes and design research plans and are spread through internet and new organizations showing prospects of future society which is called the SLOC [2] scene (small, local, open and connected). Basic necessities such as food, housing, transportation and life projects are presented to signify sustainable solutions and outline promising scenarios.

These new design method are described as emphasizing values and mission; blurring the lines between production and consumption; emphasis on cooperation and interaction, care and maintenance; distributed networks are used to maintain and manage social relations [6]. Design has been described as a creative and proactive activity, and designer work as the coordinators between different stakeholders and promoting the generation of new ideas and initiatives [4], which has been claimed as social innovation design [7, 3, 8].

Social innovation, originated from civic movement, aims to improve well-being and brings good changes to society [9]. Openness, participation and democracy are the core feature of social innovation [10, 11]. According to Murray, the emergence of social innovation is due to the most pressing social problems that cannot be solved by the existing social structure and policies [12]. More and more civil organizations breaking conventions and spontaneously experimenting collaborative and effective production

---

[2] https://www.desisnetwork.org/.

method. In some literatures, entrepreneurship is regarded as a solution to conduct socially responsible design [9]. More importantly, it is necessary to develop social entrepreneurs talents, charity organizations, industry associations, so as to explore innovative methods to meet social demands [13]. Cases of social innovation include Neighbor Garden, Slow Food movement, Participatory Groundwater Management, Parking Day, Time banker and others.

2.2 Design-Enabled Infrastructure

The design driven innovation program first was launched by European Commission, who tries to introduce innovative design into EU government policies and SEMS corporate strategies[3]. Horizon2020 is the design-driven innovation program initiated by the European Union funding for innovation research. European Commission intends to make full use of design potential of European countries and regions, to promote innovation and create job opportunities. Since April 1, 2021 European Union plans to establish a new agency——the European Innovation Council and the SMEs Executive Agency (EIS-MEA)[4]. It provides financing opportunities for innovation participants in Europe, tests new methods, helps SMEs enterprises cooperate with foundations, and establishes an innovation and entrepreneurship ecosystem. Trainings and presentations can be offered to supply participants in SMEs with benefits, opportunities and meaningful innovation views. Moreover, it emphasizes outstanding scientific industry leadership and capabilities to cope with social challenges, so that Europe will have world-class science to eliminate barriers, and create easier innovative cooperation between public and private sectors.

The concept of infrastructure was firstly introduced into design field by Susan Leigh Star and his collaborators in 1996 when they applied concept of information infrastructure into the participatory design (PD) community [14]. infrastructure is used to represent complexity of "designed objects" for a long time, especially to explore social material attachment and communication behaviors in group [15, 16].

In opinions of Manzini, design and collaboration capabilities are part of human nature. However, due to different backgrounds, these capabilities need to be improved [17]. For the Design Major, an important mission is to improve and enhance such abilities of all. Infrastructure is important in developing and maintaining social relations because it promotes social interaction and enhances publicity nature of groups [14]. In the book, An Introduction to Design for Social innovation—Design, when everybody Designs, the first element of infrastructure is digital platforms which connect decentralized social innovators; The second element is physical space which provides working space for people to communicate, such as conference rooms or coffee shops; Third, logistics services meet organizational needs for mobility of people and things; Fourth, information services give suggestions on what to do and how to do it. Fifth, evaluation serves for monitoring activities and results. In short, the ultimate goal of infrastructure is to expand, copy, and spread social innovation projects.

---

[3] https://ec.europa.eu/easme/.

[4] https://eismea.ec.europa.eu/index_en.

In this paper, the author explores the social infrastructure with the purpose of make contributions to innovation and entrepreneurship infrastructure of cities and how infrastructure helps establish social connections between dispersed social innovators, and cultivates reciprocal and hybrid culture communities.

3 Prototyping for Social Innovation

In engineering design, prototypes are often used to elicit unknowns [18], physical prototypes support future objects, experiences, and imaging future lifestyle. To be specific, the Spread 2050 Sustainable Lifestyle Project invites business department, research department and different stakeholders of public sectors to jointly conceive 2050 sustainable lifestyles. future scenarios are created through interactive situations and visual actions.

In a sense, prototype is a dynamic value-based cooperative relationship where demands of different stakeholders are bundled together [19]. The prototype generate innovative forms of expression and links expectations of different stakeholders [20], which helps establish a shared mental model and promotes coordination among stakeholders [21]. Design-driven innovation is not driven by demands of users, but the insistence on new visions, and possible meanings. Jégou and Manzini describe the prototype as a stakeholder system through which stakeholders learn from each other to engage in social collaboration [22]. It is a kind of culture model that exploring "unknowns" through prototypes which is not to find a specific solution, act as communication and exploration process, seeks for supplementary and alternative solutions [23].

In the development of new social solutions, "prototype experiments" cannot be regarded as independent entities since they are a part of the larger social exploration process, with purpose to identify the unknowns. In the multi-stakeholder ecosystem, a network-based ecosystem is established that consists of ideas, capital, knowledge, production methods, market feedback, organizations, and brands, activating social collaboration among departments. However, attention should be placed on attitude influence to unknowns, and the ability to identify unknowns during prototyping.

4 NICE2035 Future Living Labs

In March 2018, Tongji University College of Design and Innovation established a partnership with Siping sub-district office in Yangpu District, Shanghai to develop "NICE2035: 'Re-imagine the future living'. The aim was to explore innovative approaches to activate urban community. NICE 2035 stands for "Neighborhood of Innovation, Creativity, and Entrepreneurship toward 2035 [24]. The university brought in its global knowledge community and talents to Siping community to establish labs and start-ups.

NICE2035 Future Life Lab is composed of three environments - scenes, neighborhoods and startups. As for academic research plans of the School of Design and Innovation of Tongji University, they are set to promote collaboration between researchers, companies, public sectors and civic departments in testing and developing new technical services and products in real environment. Lane 1028 of Siping Road was selected as the project location, docking 15 LABs settled on the block. These included the Tongji-Dadawa Sound Lab, Tom's BaoBao Food Lab, NoCC Fashion Lab, Neuni Material Lab,

Design Harvests Rural Lab [24], etc. The Lane 1028 of Siping Road—houses a series of innovative education units, prototype stores and co-creation spaces functioning as co-creation hubs where ideas, people, labs, resources, and capital come together.

NICE Commune is an organization of social entrepreneurs, and many social innovators are gathered there, such as youth cultural and creative organizations, cultural and creative enterprises, and college students clubs. Regular cultural and creative activities, and exhibitions are held (see Fig. 1). There are more than 500 entrepreneurs in NICE Commune. The goal of NICE2035 is to support local communities to develop grassroots social innovation. Furthermore, emerging social practices initiated by social entrepreneurs are spread through a network widely connected to life laboratories in universities. It attaches great importance to exploring possible win-win relationships between stakeholders and encourages local communities to develop primary-level social innovation.

Fig. 1. Picture 1: The project address of NICE2035 is located in Lane 1028, Siping Road (Source: NICE2035 project documentation)

4.1 Prototype 1: Sustainable Lifestyle Exhibition

On the website of the State Supervision Commission of the Central Commission for Discipline Inspection are recorded remarks of Xi Jinping during the 29th collective study session of the Political Bureau of the CPC Central Committee. It is necessary to support transformation of green and low-carbon technological innovation, and encourage green technological innovation. Efficient use of resources and green and low-carbon development should serve as a foundation to develop economy and society. Teachers and students from design department of Tongji University, Donghua University, and University of Shanghai for Science and Technology participate in the Sustainable Life

Exhibitions in Yangpu Binjiang[5]. This is to respond to national sustainable development strategies, and exercise students' capabilities in design & innovation, and test of market products.

Neili Department Store organizes the sustainable living fairs. It is not only an innovative and entrepreneurial company, but also a concentration place of sustainable design and sustainable living. In other words, it sets foot in fashion field where customers' demands can be known immediately. Interest activities and exhibitions are held regularly. In public welfare exhibitions to spread sustainable future lifestyle, different stakeholders from business departments, research departments, and public sector are invited to jointly hold the Sustainable Lifestyle Exhibition in Yangpu Binjiang. Sustainable lifestyles are introduced from food, clothing, housing, and education, cultivating people's knowledge and understanding of sustainability (Fig. 2).

Fig. 2. Picture 2: Sustainable Lifestyle Exhibition in Yangpu Binjiang (Source: project documents)

The exhibition is an innovation laboratory for teachers and students of Shanghai universities. The creativity and design of teachers and students are transformed into innovative products and services directly provided to citizens on the spot. The themes of their works are related to "sustainable development" and "college students' campus life". In the exhibition, materials from the industrial age are used, including worn-out switches, power supplies, electric energy meters, colored lights, electric notebooks, and computer cases, intending to display a novel form or to change original meaning of things. They defamiliarize familiar things, so as to trigger thinking about daily life. Meanwhile, they focus on developing and designing environmentally friendly materials. For the purpose of sustainability, teachers and students use environmentally friendly technologies, materials and new combination ideas, to convey the concept of circular

---

[5] http://www.ccdi.gov.cn/ldhd/gcsy/202104/t20210430_241271.html.

economy. For example, in textiles and garments, eco-products have passed international authoritative certifications.

4.2 Prototype 2: Sustainable Diet Workshop

NICE2035 Future Living Laboratory regularly organizes workshops and community activities one of which is sustainable diet workshop. YUAN Fang initiates food design project, who designs food game of Perry bingo. In workshops, participants fill in cards and think personalities of food that provides nutrition and energy, nourishing affections and connections with food through games. People have bats in the belfry in terms of shapes, flavor, and taste of food to create novel food combinations (Fig. 3).

The plant-based workshops aim at helping more people understand plant-based diets and develop a healthy and environmentally sustainable eating habit. During the shared kitchen workshop, food connects people emotionally and convey values and belief. The project is funded by Siping Community Charity Foundation of Yangpu District, Shanghai. The plant-based implies people's spiritual pursuits. it is conducive to cultivating the concept of collective development by making delicious food together in shared kitchen.

Fig. 3. Picture 3: sustainable diet workshop (Source: The public website of Design Harvest, Photographer: LU Zhouzhou and others)

5 Discussion

The prototyping is potential as ideas in daily lives are iterated rapidly through prototypes and new technical solutions are formulated. It should be noted that the prototype aims not to get a definite result, but to demonstrate new things to the outside and more people [25]. At the same time, predicaments and problems will be revealed. The prototype itself is not mature, but as an answer to the vagueness of a sustainable future, or a supplement to existing lifestyles.

The author explores how to establish the design process by transiting project-based approaches to a long-term open infrastructure [4]. In return, infrastructure assists people in developing projects in daily lives through a series of guidance, programs, and operating documents.

Although it is useful to reveal structured problems, there are limitations of this method such as plans and activities need to be re-planned constantly because of the flexible a structure which make the projects process more complicated.

What is more, another question is: How can emerging social practices be spread as knowledge? Designers should serve as both a creator and cultural intermediary to innovate in new cultural forms. Strictly speaking, design is a profession, and also attitude and ability of people to solve daily problems [26]. In this process, professional designers are responsible for facilitating negotiations and helping other participants express expectations in public.

In the future, alliances between major universities are necessary to establish living laboratories networks [27]. In summary, different from project-based design, social innovation methods are equipped with social connection network to jointly shape design goals, in order to build relationships among stakeholders and promote collective actions toward sustainable future.

6 Future Research

Social contact represents sense of belonging and intimacy between people. Hygiene defines social contact as the feelings strengthened together through consciousness system [28]. "Intimacy" is a term in psychology. Apart from parents and children, the intimacy is also common between partners. It is a special time node when young students graduate from school, get rid of family structures, enter into the enterprise society. "intimate relationship" need to be taught to help them distinguish "group interests" and the "personal interests" while maintain friendships.

This paper provides a new evidence for studying social infrastructure that is dedicated to meet the needs of young entrepreneurs, such as places and funds. More importantly, it cultivates entrepreneurs' awareness of new relationships. With social infrastructure, individuals and groups are allowed to generate and maintain psychological resources to support them achieve important goals. People usually find a sense of belonging and psychological support when they establish common goals through relationships, joint practices and collective actions. They know clearly that if they fail, they can recover from the setback, which is "resilience" [29]. To some extent, infrastructure can be regarded as the capabilities building process.

References

1. 娄永琪. NICE 2035: 一个设计驱动的社区支持型社会创新实验. 收藏, 5 (2018)
2. Manzini, E.: Small, local, open and connected–Design research Topics in the Age of Networks and Sustainability. University of Art and Design Helsinki (2009)

3. Manzini, E.: New design knowledge. Des. Stud. **30**(1), 4–12 (2009)
4. Manzini, E., Rizzo, F.: Small projects/large changes: participatory design as an open participated process. CoDesign **7**, 199–215 (2011)
5. Mulgan, G., Tucker, S., Ali, R., et al.: Social innovation: what it is, why it matters and how it can be accelerated. Skoll Centre for Social Entrepreneurship (2007)
6. Murray, R.: Danger and Opportunity: Crisis and the New Social Economy. Nesta (2009)
7. Manzini, E., Meroni, A.: Emerging user demands for sustainable solutions. Emude (2007)
8. Manzini, E.: Context-based wellbeing and the concept of regenerative solution a conceptual framework for scenario building and sustainable solutions development. J. Sustain. Prod. Des. **2**, 141–148 (2002)
9. Armstrong, L., Bailey, J., Julier, G., et al.: Social design futures: HEI research and the AHRC. University of Brighton (2014)
10. Chesbrough, H.W.: Open Innovation: The New Imperative for Creating and Profiting from Technology. Harvard Business Press (2003)
11. Von Hippel, E.: Democratizing Innovation. The MIT Press, Cambridge (2006)
12. Murray, R., Caulier-Grice, J., Mulgan, G.: The Open Book of Social Innovation. Nesta London, 24 (2010)
13. Phillips, W., Lee, H., Ghobadian, A., et al.: Social innovation and social entrepreneurship: a systematic review. Group Organ. Manag **40**(3), 428–461 (2015)
14. Star, S.L., Ruhleder, K.: Steps toward an ecology of infrastructure: design and access for large information spaces. Inf. Syst. Res. **7**(1), 111–134 (1996)
15. Björgvinsson, E., Ehn, P., Hillgren, P.-A.: Participatory design and democratizing innovation. In: Proceedings of the 11th Biennial Participatory Design Conference, pp. 41–50. ACM (2010)
16. Bjögvinsson, E., Ehn, P., Hillgren P.-A.: Design things and design thinking: contemporary participatory design challenges. Des. Issues **28**(3), 101–116 (2012)
17. Manzini, E., Cullars, J.: Prometheus of the everyday: the ecology of the artificial and the designer's responsibility. Des. Issues **9**(1), 5–20 (1992)
18. Sutcliffe, A., Sawyer, P.: Requirements elicitation: towards the unknown unknowns. In: 2013 21st IEEE International Requirements Engineering Conference (RE), pp. 92–104. IEEE (2013)
19. Holmlid, S.: Participative; co-operative; emancipatory: From participatory design to service design. In: Conference Proceedings ServDes. 2009; DeThinking Service; ReThinking Design, Oslo, Norway, 24–26 November 2009, no. 059, pp. 105–118. Linköping University Electronic Press (2012)
20. Sanders, L., Stappers, P.J.: From designing to co-designing to collective dreaming: three slices in time. Interactions, XXI (2014)
21. Neyer, A.K., Doll, B., Möslein, K.M.: Mission (IM) possible?–Prototyping service innovation. Support. Serv. Innov. Through Knowl. Manag. Pract. Insights Case Stud., 143–164 (2009)
22. Jégou, F., Manzini, E.: Collaborative Services – Social Innovation and Design for Sustainability (2008)
23. Jensen, M.B., Elverum, C.W., Steinert, M.: Eliciting unknown unknowns with prototypes: introducing prototrials and prototrial-driven cultures. Des. Stud. **49**, 1–31 (2017)
24. Lou, Y., Ma, J.: Growing a community-supported ecosystem of future living: the case of NICE2035 living line. In: Rau, P.L. (eds.) Cross-Cultural Design. Applications in Cultural Heritage, Creativity and Social Development. CCD 2018. LNCS, vol. 10912, pp. 320–333. Springer, Cham (2018). https://doi.org/10.1007/978-3-319-92252-2_26
25. Hillgren, P.-A., Seravalli, A., Emilson, A.: Prototyping and infrastructuring in design for social innovation. CoDesign **7**, 169–183 (2011)
26. Manzini, E.: Design, When Everybody Designs: An Introduction to Design for Social Innovation (2015)

27. Manzini, E.: Enabling solutions for creative communities. Designmatters. Danish Design Center: HC Anderson Boulevard 27, DK, København (2005)
28. Baumeister, R.F., Leary, M.R.: The need to belong: desire for interpersonal attachments as a fundamental human motivation. Psychol. Bull. **117**(3), 497 (1995)
29. Alkire, S.: Subjective quantitative studies of human agency. Soc. Ind. Res. **74**(1), 217–260 (2005)

On the Life Aesthetics of Packaging Design in the Context of Digital Economy

Yifei Zhu and Wei Yu(✉)

School of Art Design and Media, East China University of Science and Technology, No. 130, Meilong Road, Xuhui District, Shanghai, People's Republic of China

Abstract. All the beautiful satisfying things in life have their own internal aesthetic mechanism. Digital economy promotes the new pattern of digital economy integration and transformation of industrial digitalization and digital industrialization. In digital economy, the life aesthetics of the integration of science and art advocates judging and optimizing the things in life through the organic unity of science and aesthetics. First of all, through the literature reading and data collection analysis of creative packaging works and smart packaging cases, to explore the differences between smart packaging and traditional packaging, summed up for the packaging design of the new economic model under the innovative path. Secondly, the semantic difference method is used to integrate and filter the emotional vocabulary of the public in the new economy, to enhance the public's sense of experience, and to analyze the process of beauty in the literary and creative packaging design from the perspective of life aesthetics, this paper discusses the integration of functional beauty and formal beauty. From the perspective of life aesthetics and technology aesthetics, this paper examines the innovative design of all elements of packaging, making it possible to reflect on the connotation and explicit innovation of life aesthetics in packaging design under the background of digital economy, to achieve the original intention and vision of making people's lives better. The theory and method are proved to be accurate and applicable by taking the packaging design of time-honored cakes as an example.

Keywords: The digital economy · Packaging design · Life aesthetics

1 Aesthetics of Life in Digital Economy

1.1 The Digital Economy

The "Digital economy" first originated from the book "Digital Economy: Hopes and Concerns in the Age of Intelligent Networks" published by Don Tapscott in 1994, the father of the digital economy in Canada. The digital revolution can change the way we live and communicate, and the "digital economy" has entered people's lives, including the application of artificial intelligence, the development of the Internet of Things and digital life [1]. Digital economy, as the mainstream of the world's economic development, with big data and technological manufacturing at its core, from the emergence of cloud computing and artificial intelligence to the cross-border integration of all walks of life, highlighting the transformation of digital industrialization to industrial digitalization, digital economy technology is deeply infiltrated packaging industry.

C. Stephanidis et al. (Eds.): HCII 2021, CCIS 1498, pp. 81–87, 2021.
https://doi.org/10.1007/978-3-030-90176-9_12

1.2   Aestheticization of Life

What we are experiencing is the emergence of the aestheticization of daily life and the living of art design. The so-called "aestheticization of life" refers to the intermingling of aesthetic emotions with daily life, such as clothing, food, housing and transportation, and is the inevitable result of the transformation of art philosophy into the aesthetics of life [2]. Although Wilde, the master of aestheticism, believed that "life imitates art more than art imitates life" has its paradoxical side, he objectively pointed out the organic connection between life and art aesthetics.

In the case of MUJI packaging, the simple colors and text layout with transparent materials show the Japanese aesthetics of wabi-sabi, which, in terms of design values, can quickly convey the aesthetics of life. The Western theoretical discourse of "aestheticization of life", transferred into the Chinese cultural context, is a cultural integration of consumer culture representation and aesthetic generalization in contemporary China. Packaging design has become an important way to compete in the consumer market. Take cultural and creative packaging as an example, it integrates contemporary aesthetic consciousness and aesthetic connotation of cultural and creative brands, and uses digital means to reflect people's sense of participation and experience. Creative packaging constantly updates its design expressions to establish an emotional connection with customers, drawing inspiration from artworks, using soft color blocks and illustrations, and integrating emotional language and graphic interaction. In the case of the Forbidden City Museum (see Fig. 1), the scissor-hands of Yongzheng and the Chinese colorful creations have become a hit through new media communication, inspiring more people to identify with national culture and broadening the ways of spreading oriental aesthetics internationally.

Fig. 1. The imperial palace packaging

1.3   Aesthetic Living

"Internet" "5G" and other new industries continue to affect people's lifestyles, pursuit of life is also changing. Aesthetics return to life gradually, aesthetics of life is not only the generalization of aesthetic life, but also the experience of pursuing a good life.

Contemporary aesthetics in China has gone through three transition periods, gradually showing the trend of respect for life, turn to spiritual and cultural consumption, respect for life is also the inevitable trend of the integration of modern aesthetics and technology [3]. Throughout the 2020 packaging design trends and creative product packaging, it is found that aesthetics and life are closely related, graphics can spread culture faster than words, and often more relevant to the aesthetics of life, the brand is easier to stimulate the emotional identity of consumers.

In the face of development of the Internet, more and more packaging incorporates interactive elements and innovative materials to establish a closer connection with consumer groups. Aesthetics has been formed in daily life as an unconscious pan-aesthetic artistic activity, and aesthetic activities have evolved into a harmonious unity of intelligence and culturality. This is in line with what Li Zehou said in his "Four Lectures on Aesthetics", "the feeling or emotion of physical and mental pleasure that arises when the living individual overlaps with certain natural laws in the activity of achieving the purpose." Therefore, designers need to simplify the design process and optimize commodity packaging according to human emotional experience. In the modern era of cross-fertilization of multiple fields, science and art are integrated from symbiosis to integration, and aesthetic generalization makes all packaging possible to become the accumulation of life aesthetics.

2 Packaging Design in the Digital Economy

2.1 Design and Aesthetics

In the digital context, life aesthetics and design side by side, the presentation of design is given more artistic techniques, and the means of design shifts from two-dimensional to three-dimensional, from purely visual to multi-sensory interaction trends. Graphics from the designer to the emotional needs. Traditional packaging add intelligent technology, form the carrier of everything connected to the three new technology system theory (new technology, new materials, new processes) and the traditional packaging system of emotional packaging structure and visual presentation, connecting consumers and brands.

Unlike the industrial revolution, new technologies can enhance the aesthetic experience of users. AI combined with packaging, Tulou creative packaging using AR+ cultural packaging, through augmented reality technology to achieve aesthetic scene reproduction (see Fig. 2), insight into young people's entertainment generalized lifestyle, packaging and technology combination is better to pitch their interests. Take the cooperation mineral water of the Fair as an example, the introduction of new technology, experts scan the code can appear the name of experts and other information, to achieve DIY customization of packaging services, and further to packaging to make life better.

In the context of digital economy, 5G and big data form a refined packaging. The biggest difference between traditional packaging technology and intelligent packaging technology is that intelligent packaging technology uses new materials and new processes to pursue emotional needs on the basis of solving functional needs. Physical material interaction using smart materials to achieve new functions in packaging, or use of visual illusions in the packaging structure and other ways to enhance the visual experience to meet the needs of consumer sensation [4].

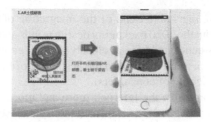

Fig. 2. Tulou AI creative packaging

2.2 Packaging and Life

Standing in the perspective of life aesthetics, packaging design includes at least three levels of cultural values: first of all, the formal beauty of packaging materials, shapes, colors, etc., which intuitively conveys the visual beauty and human touch of packaging. Secondly, the cultural beauty in packaging design. Thirdly, the beauty of technological innovation. In order to meet the design needs in the digital economy, packaging design is more infused with human flavor and attention to sensual emotional factors on the basis of achieving basic aesthetics. Design in the field of packaging design applying sensual engineering is still little, but this is the trend of cross-fertilization in multiple fields.

As a tool, carrying the aesthetics of life, design needs to find a balance between functional beauty and formal beauty, and based on the "three new" innovation paths, obtain consumers' perceptual understanding of creative packaging through scientific methods and present it in combination with high technology. The graphics, colors and words of the packaging are all related to consumers' perceptual imagery. In this paper, we use the literature research and data collection method as an example to analyze the emotional elements of people's old brands, based on the literature research method and data collection method, the conclusion provides a basis for the design.

The old-established pastry packaging samples were made from old-established pastry photos, and the representative pictures were finally selected by screening the series of photos, using the card analysis method to determine the representative semantic adjectives organized into a semantic scale measurement, finally forming the initial emotional dimension by the semantic analysis method to finally form the perceptual imagery vocabulary ranking (see Fig. 3).

The brain operates in three separate dimensions when processing information systems. First of all, human instincts make subjective evaluations of visual beauty; therefore, the semantic difference approach helps design consider full-factor design to visually stimulate consumers and enhance the aesthetic experience. The formal beauty guidelines of packaging act as aesthetic measures that influence the price of goods and consumer judgments (Table 1).

According to the values derived from the table (see Fig. 4), we can find that in the texture of the packaging, consumers prefer smooth and delicate texture. In order to amplify the tactile cultural perception to avoid unisex sensory interaction. The processing of the New Year gift box adopts laser engraving to show special texture, and the paper adopts super-sensitive paper, after oiling and hot stamping, which visually shows more texture and highlights the aesthetic level and artistic value of Chinese classical culture, in

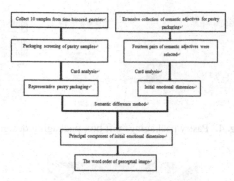

Fig. 3. The process of consumer perceptual image extraction

Table 1. Results of variance analysis method

Vision	Component
Dense - loose	−1
Bright - dull	−1
Simple-complex	0.55
Sweet-salty	−0.8
Retro-chic	−0.55

line with the aesthetic connotation of "true goodness and beauty" [5]. In the visual aspect of the old-branded pastry packaging (See Fig. 3), consumers' perceptual imagery is more inclined to dense and bright patterns. In order to amplify the consumer experience, the daily version and the gift box version were designed according to the user group. The daily version used bright orange-blue as the main color, supplemented by less saturated yellow and red, and used a simplified graphic arrangement of the pastry outline to form the packaging pattern. The gift box version uses less saturated blue and white as the main colors, and the overall texture is more atmospheric, using a wooden gift box to convey the green packaging design concept. On the basis of perceptual imagery, with Presentation using new technologies, the three new theories are used, and through the interactive QR code and text symbol card settings (see Fig. 5), the calorie and nutritional content of the pastry can be easily checked to meet the needs of modern people for a healthy diet and deepen the memory point of the package to attract more consumers.

The charm of life aesthetics is that it can change a certain human behavior experience, modern and traditional culture, international cultural elements and Chinese classical elements collision and fusion is what Chinese aesthetics is experiencing, the user experience at the behavior level is more concerned about the overall feeling of consumers when using, using perceptual emotion extraction to improve the visual design of packaging so as to convey brand culture and sea culture to consumers and deepen brand memory. Under the development of digitalization, a good design is a humane and innovative design, which should be integrated with intelligent technology on the basis

Fig. 4. Pastry packaging- gift box packaging design

Fig. 5. Pastry packaging - peripheral interactive packaging

of meeting consumers' perceptual needs, so that inheritance and innovation can move forward side by side. In the environment of creating green packaging for all people, designers need to open up innovative paths, explore the innovative integration of traditional packaging elements and modern intelligent packaging theory, get rid of formalism under consumerism, optimize the design process and innovate according to consumer preferences.

3   Innovative Thinking of Living Aesthetics in Packaging Design in the Context of Digital Economy

3.1   The Past and Current Situation of Packaging Design

In the digital context, packaging design pursues more spiritual aesthetic consistency, visual stimulation and consumer psychology are infinitely enlarged, and the famous American cognitive psychologist Donald Norman emphasizes the user-centered design philosophy in "Emotional Design" [6] and "Design Psychology" [7]. The proportion of "moving people with emotion" in modern design is gradually increasing, and the accurate communication of emotion is a higher level of artistic expression in packaging design. By improving the structure of packaging and using visual elements to provide consumers with emotional experience, the multidisciplinary integration with sensual experiments leads consumers to emotional resonance, and the integration of design elements with sensual imagery, truly achieving the original intention and vision of "making the world a better place".

3.2   The Past and Current Situation of Packaging Design

In the future, under the background of digital economy, based on the spiritual aesthetics, the development trend or innovation of the life aesthetics in packaging design should focus on: intelligent packaging design; digital packaging industry; packaging experience aestheticization.

The use of 3d printing technology in the field of breakthroughs in printing technology saves a lot of time and makes it easier to show the personality of the goods. Take pharmaceutical packaging as an example, to achieve DIY customization needs, amplify the consumer experience, if the smart label is introduced into the packaging design, consumers scan the smart label to display the patient's medical information, enhance consumer treatment follow-up services, expand the use of intelligent packaging field, release "creativity + technology" energy, improve consumer aesthetic experience.

4   Conclusion

The value of beauty is reflected in innovation. Contemporary designers need to integrate from multiple fields such as consumer psychology, intelligent technology and packaging design across borders, build a theoretical system of intelligent packaging, pay attention to the intelligent development of the three new theory (new technology, new material and new process), optimize the quality of the supply chain, and visualize the culture and region, the mutual integration of sensual imagery and intelligent technology, highlight the charm of the aesthetics of the times and oriental aesthetics, amplify the It also visualizes the culture and region, blends sensual imagery with intelligent technology, so that cultural creativity is understood and inherited by the world.

Taking the upgrade work of packaging as an example, we use Semantic Differential Method to extract emotional elements, analyze the embodiment of packaging human feelings and culture, and upgrade old brand pastry packaging design. Taking advantage of the characteristics of the digital economy to build an industrialized system of packaging design for cultural and creative products, promote the industrialization of digital packaging design and the aestheticization of packaging experience, to realize the perfect integration of functionality and aesthetics, rationality and sensibility of packaging design.

References

1. Tapscott, D.: The Digital Economy: Promise and Peril in the Age of Networked Intelligence. Machine Industry Press, Beijing (2016)
2. Feng, Y.: Aesthetics and inclusive connections of life. Ginseng Flowers (Below) (02), 75 (2020)
3. Wang, Q.: A new paradigm of chinese aesthetics transformation and life aesthetics. Philos. Dyn. **01**, 83–88 (2013)
4. Cheng, C.: On the influence of niche trend on modern packaging design. Tomorrow's Style (08), 87–89 (2021)
5. Zong, B.: Translation of Western Aesthetics Masterpieces. Chongqing University Press, Chongqing (2014)
6. Norman, D.A.: Emotional Design: Why We Love (or Hate) Everyday Things. Basic Books, New York (2005)
7. Norman, D.A.: The Design of Everyday Things. Basic Books, New York (2002)

UX Design and Research in Intelligent Environments

Lego®-like Bricks to Go from the Real to the Virtual World

Alejandro Cabrerizo, Will Zeurcher, Thomas Wright, and Peter Jamieson(✉) ⓘ

Miami University, Oxford, OH 45056, USA
`jamiespa@miamioh.edu`

Abstract. In this work, we prototype a system that allows for Lego®-like bricks to be used physically to create a model in the real world that is then mapped and recreated in an existing Lego CAD software. This allows users to build their designs tactically in the real world and have these designs translated into the virtual-world automatically. The key benefit is that bricks are, naturally, a tactile building tool, but there is a desire to have virtual representations of brick-based models for all sorts of reasons such as designing and creating instruction booklets, creating models that can be incorporated in virtual worlds (such as games), and simply sharing and archiving a design beyond the limits of a physical model. Our system shows that an embedded system that includes per brick computing intelligence is a viable method to achieve the simple goal of translating a real brick model into a virtual model.

Keywords: Lego® · Mapping · Design · Virtual · Embedded system · CAD

1 Introduction

Lego® bricks are popular toy for all ages including the authors. The brick as a toy has gone beyond just toy and has permeated many more forms of our society including movies, fashion, and art. Of particular interest to this work, is how to take Lego® designs in the real world with bricks into the virtual/digital space for reasons such as mapping models into video games and CAD tools to create instructions and virtual models. The key question, we have, is can we create a smart tactile based brick in the real world that can translate into the virtual world automatically from an inside-out design perspective, meaning the components themselves help create the virtual model of the real world model.

In this work, we present our system that achieves the above challenge and demonstrates a prototype of such a system at the scale of Duplo® where a Duplo brick is two times the size of an equivalent Lego brick. We take an Inside-out approach where each brick is designed as a smart brick that includes both sensors and a micro-controller that computes connectivity with other bricks and communicates with the other bricks in the system to determine a relative location of each brick. The bricks then communicate this information to a *bridge* that

© Springer Nature Switzerland AG 2021
C. Stephanidis et al. (Eds.): HCII 2021, CCIS 1498, pp. 91–98, 2021.
https://doi.org/10.1007/978-3-030-90176-9_13

evaluates this information and injects the results via a *builder* into CAD software thus converting the real model into a virtual model.

Some of the key questions when prototyping this system are: How small can the system be designed? How fast can the inside-out approach to localization of bricks run at? What are the limitations of this approach? What limits are there to miniaturization and how significant is the component cost?

The key contributions of this work include the following:

- A description and demonstration of system capable of an inside-out brick system that goes from a real model to a virtual model
- Open source release of all our system including software and hardware

In the paper, we will describe the above contributions, and we include a link to the open source design files on Github that includes links to videos that demonstrate our working system. Additionally, we provide details on how much a system like this costs per brick.

The remainder of the paper is organized as follows: Sect. 2 provides insight into what research has already been done in bridging real world and virtual/digital world implementations. Section 3 describes the details of our system to solve this challenge of taking a real world Lego® to a virtual model. Finally, Sect. 4 concludes this paper.

2   Research on Bridging Real and Virtual Worlds

Fitzmaurice [2] defines: "Graspable User Interface is a physical handle to a virtual function".

We identify two main approaches to the challenge of creating a system that translates real world models into virtual world models as:

- Inside-Out: These systems are designed with components that have the capability to sense, compute, and communicate their structure and location to build up a model inside the computing machine.
- Outside-In: These systems observe the existing model and determine how the model is built inside the computing machine.

For each approach, we will describe related research on the use of the approach, and we will start by describing the pros and cons of each approach. Note that a hybrid approach can be used that combines some of the benefits from each.

There have been many avenues of research into graspable user interfaces. Their importance has been identified as a human need to touch objects and receive quick feedback from the physical objects [11].

2.1   Inside-Out Approach

This approach for translating real world models into virtual models benefits from the capability to understand the internal details of the model without having to be captured over time. The downside of this approach is that the components of the system need to be smart, smartness comes with a cost, miniaturization is a technological limitation, and the number of needed smart components can impact the speed of translation into a digital form.

Fitzmaurice [2] defines 5 core properties for graspable interface, which the inside-out approach captures. These system are space-multiplexed, use a high-degree of inter-device concurrency, have a physical form, employ spatially aware devices, and are spatially reconfigurable. Hiroshi and Ullmer [5] describe these systems as Tangible User Interfaces (TUI) and provide many early examples in this space.

In almost all cases, there is a need to track the components of the system. Early work by Want *et al.* [15] describes tracking objects via electronic tags. Tags based on RFID (early conception by Stockman [13]) have become common off-the-shelf tag technology used for tracking.

These early ideas have seen a number of potential applications across a broad range of fields [2], and there are a vast number of demonstration of these systems. For example, Ullmer *et al.* [14] describes blocks that interact and identify themselves. The main reason there are not modern commercial products using this approach, we believe, is that miniaturization and technical challenges and limitations make an Outside-In approach easier to implement. Still, systems such as KidCAD [3] are pushing towards smart tangible objects that take an inside-out approach.

2.2   Outside-In Approach

The Outside-In approach has many more research prototypes and designs mainly because the external approach seems simpler to design for and costs less with the use of cameras. The downside of this approach is that most of the functionality is implemented with either cameras or detecting smart pads which creates limitations on how the system needs to be used for proper detection. Additionally, from a construction perspective the detection system needs to be aware of the progress of the build (time-multiplexed) so that the design can be captured.

There are a number of Outside-In systems that have been prototype and researched in the past and we provide a few examples in this section. Jun and Yujii [10] use visual tags in an augmented reality space to detect items in the space. The tag approach is common in many industrial technologies such as the QR code invented by Denso Wave in 1994. Two examples in the world of art include Klemmer *et al.* [7] creation of a Papier-Mache tangible input system and Sheng *et al.* [12] interface for virtual sculptures.

In this space, there has been a significant amount of research on camera-based scanning, and for our problem the most interesting research is in 3D scanning. For example, Kersten and Lindstaedt [6] used a scanning method to create an architectural scan. More recently, Lee *et al.* [8] looked at 3D scan methods in the design space.

2.3   Virtualization of Lego®

The last aspect we review in this section is what, specifically, has already been done with Lego as related to this work. In Fitzmaurice's work [2] they identify LegoWall by Knud Molenbach of Scaitech and Lego as a graspable interface where the bricks work with a wall mounted plate. Around the same time, Ayers and Zeleznik [1] created a toolkit to use Lego based design as a part of a 3D interfacing hardware.

There is a number of attempts and exploration of how to use Lego in Virtual spaces and interacting with them. Mendes and Ferreira [9] looked at how to use multi-touch surfaces to control Virtual Lego pieces. Lego has implemented Augmented Reality in their commercial releases such as "Lego Fusion Town Master" in 2014 [4].

In addition to interfacing and virtualization, there is a significant amount of research with Lego in many directions. For example, Lee *et al.* [8] looked at how to create a Virtual object using CAD based algorithms to optimize a Lego design.

3   Our Prototype Brick System

Our system is an Inside-out approach system where the Lego bricks are designed to communicate with one another to figure out their orientation and connections in the model. This information is then passed to a physical *bridge* that then passes the information to a PC and uses a *builder* to inject the location information to an existing Lego CAD program.

In this section, we describe the terminology used to describe a Lego brick in Sect. 3.1. Next, we describe the brick level system in Sect. 3.2, and the brick to CAD system structure in Sect. 3.3. We describe most of the details of this system, but because we release all design files open source at github.com/alecamaracm/Smart-LEGO-HDI we don't go into excessive details.

3.1   Relevant Brick Terminology

Figure 1 shows a 2 × 4 Lego brick where in (a) a stud is illustrated. The standard brick size is defined in relation to the columns and rows of studs. The tube, shown in Fig. 1(b) shows the tube on the bottom of the brick. The tube, typically, fits into a 2 × 2 set of studs. Note, that there are other parts of a brick, but for this work we only need to understand what a stud is as it is the main aspect of a brick used to detect the orientation and connectivity of two bricks.

3.2   Smart Brick Design

Our system is an inside-out embedded system where the bricks determine there connectivity. For this, we need an external reference frame to know relative location of each brick. To do this each brick is its own frame of reference, and relative positions are sent and determined by a more powerful computing machine.

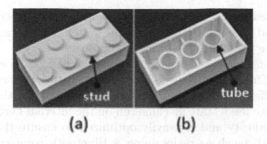

Fig. 1. A 2 × 4 brick defined by the number of (a) studs. In (b), we show a tube on the base of a brick.

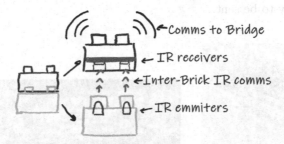

Fig. 2. Illustration of how two bricks use IR to communicate via the brick studs

Brick to Brick Communication. Our brick design uses electromagnetic/light waves to send data through transparent/translucent bricks. Each brick stud continuously sends a brick ID and a stud ID through an infrared (IR) LED. Thus, if a bottom stud detector in another brick receives data, the system knows exactly which studs are connected together. Figure 2 shows the basics of inter-brick IR communication system.

Each stud needs to communicate enough information to identify itself and the brick that it belongs to including the following information:

Brick ID (6 bytes): A unique ID that represents a brick.
- Brick type (3 bytes): A universal LEGO brick type id. This represents the type of LEGO brick (4 × 2, 2 × 2)
- Stud ID (3 bytes): Which stud of the brick is sending this message.

This information is sent asynchronously between the bricks as they do not share a common clock. In this protocol, a bit is detected as a digital "1" if the high time is twice as large than the low time. Also, as no physical connection exists between the bricks, the communication protocol needs to be quite resilient to poor signal integrity, incorporating error checking, correction and allowing for a decent amount of noise in the IR connection. By default, the "long time" of a bit is two times a "short time". If there is noise in the channel or for some reason the bricks CPU is busy doing something else and the timings is not perfect, there is a period of time (0.5 times), where if the error is smaller than that, the bit will still be received correctly. In addition to that, each connectivity message has its own header and checksum. This allows the system to determine if a packet is valid or not before passing the information upwards.

Finally, we can not assume that all the studs will be receiving packets at the same time. This makes it necessary for each stud to have its own state variables and buffers and that operate independently from the others. In our implementation, we use a state machine run on the internal hardware timer that has the highest priority and is heavily optimized to ensure that the CPU can still do other work (such as maintaining a Bluetooth connection). This state machine is then in charge of reading the raw input from the LEDs, processing it into packets, and then signaling the CPU communication scheduler that there is a packet ready to be sent.

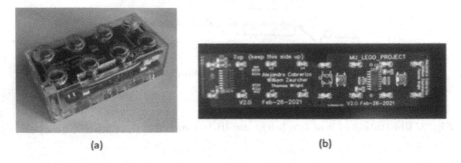

(a)   (b)

Fig. 3. Our brick (a) and the internal PCB (b) where the Left Part is the top and the Right Part is the bottom

Once bricks know they are connected, this information is forwarded to the bridge. Figure 3 shows a 2×4 brick (a) and the accompanying internal PCB (b) that contains the CPU and transmission and receiving hardware.

3.3   Bridge and Builder - Capturing Brick Details for Lego CAD

Bridge. Our *bridge* is responsible for gathering the position data from all the bricks, and condensing it into a common format that the *builder* understands. We use a Bluetooth Low Energy (BLE) *bridge* where the BLE protocol dictates that every communication needs to be started with an advertisement (scheduled windows where devices can send small packets of data). Therefore, whenever a brick has a change in the state of a stud it is going to queue that change into a message buffer that can hold up to 50 stud changes and start advertising that information. The *bridge* hears the advertisement and opens a connection to the brick for the stud changes (deltas). Due to the 32 bits per packet limitation in BLE, sending a 100-byte packet might take several advertisements to complete. As advertisements are scheduled on fixed time intervals (100ms in our implementation), sending 100 bytes might can take several seconds. This is why compressing the data and only sending the deltas is important.

As the BLE advertisement itself already contains the local ID (BLE MAC address) and the local brick type, the only data we need to send on each delta are the remote MAC address and the local and remote stud IDs that just connected or was removed. This data is then sent a *builder* through WIFI TCP (Transmission Control Protocol) WebSocket's. The *bridge* does not try to understand the bytes it is receiving at all; it just decompresses the commonly used parts of the packets, packs them up into larger ones and proceeds to send them to the *builder*.

Every time there is a change in any stud connection, the *builder* will have the responsibility to transform those studs to stud connections into a set of {X,Y,Z} coordinates (and rotations) for each brick. The *builder* software parses incoming deltas from the bricks and creates a persistent brick model from them. Once the *builder* has enough information to place the first set of 2 bricks (2 bricks are connected together), it chooses one as the starting point of the building.

From that point on, it will look for other connected bricks to that one with at least 2 studs in common. By creating vectors relating these pairs of studs together, it is possible, with linear algebra, to know the relative locations of additional bricks. This process is then repeated until all the bricks have a fixed location. Finally, all the bricks are offset so that the bottom ones are at y = 0 (Height = 0), and changes in the final CAD view are calculated and sent to the CAD program.

Builder. Once the *builder* has the position and rotation for each brick, it sends them to the CAD program for it to display it on the screen (virtually). We use BrickLink Studio www.bricklink.com/v2/build/studio.page as our CAD program, and there is no way to programmatically interact with it directly. To go around that, the BrickLink studio program would have to be patched with new code to add our needed features.

Fortunately, BrickLink Studio is a game developed on top of the Unity game engine. Because of this, we are able to place or remove bricks using HTTP commands sent from the *builder*. To accomplish this, a dynamic linked library (DLL) containing an HTTP server implementation with the commands *addBrick*, *removeBrick*, and *resetView*. This DLL is injected at run-time into the BrickLink process, adding the injection to the CAD tool. To perform an injection, the open-source library "DotNet DLL Injector" is used, which handles the code compilation from the C# bytecode to machine code and creating another process inside the host thread to run our application entry point. This allows us to demonstrate our real-time system of real world bricks being updated in the virtual world (for example see: https://drive.google.com/file/d/1l-9bFWEu4QhFfqXpGIShnhi3ygX5V5At/view?usp=sharing).

4   Conclusion

In this work, we demonstrate an inside-out human interface for humans to use real world Lego bricks and have them updated in a virtual world. We estimate that the cost of this approach is, currently, approximately 5 USD per brick when creating ten thousand units, and that there is a great commercial potential for creating such a system that would allow designers to create models and have them automatically virtualized. We describe our system in detail and provide open source access to our design approach.

References

1. Ayers, M., Zeleznik, R.: The Lego interface toolkit. In: Proceedings of the 9th Annual ACM Symposium on User Interface Software and Technology, pp. 97–98 (1996)
2. Fitzmaurice, G.W.: Graspable user interfaces. Citeseer (1997)
3. Follmer, S., Ishii, H.: KidCAD: digitally remixing toys through tangible tools. In: Proceedings of the SIGCHI Conference on Human Factors in Computing Systems, pp. 2401–2410 (2012)
4. Greenwald, W.: Lego fusion town master review. PC Mag. (2014). https://www.pcmag.com/reviews/lego-fusion-town-master
5. Ishii, H., Ullmer, B.: Tangible bits: towards seamless interfaces between people, bits and atoms. In: Proceedings of the ACM SIGCHI Conference on Human factors in Computing Systems, pp. 234–241 (1997)
6. Kersten, T.P., Lindstaedt, M.: Virtual architectural 3D model of the imperial cathedral (Kaiserdom) of Königslutter, Germany through terrestrial laser scanning. In: Ioannides, M., Fritsch, D., Leissner, J., Davies, R., Remondino, F., Caffo, R. (eds.) EuroMed 2012. LNCS, vol. 7616, pp. 201–210. Springer, Heidelberg (2012). https://doi.org/10.1007/978-3-642-34234-9_20
7. Klemmer, S.R., Li, J., Lin, J., Landay, J.A.: Papier-Mache: toolkit support for tangible input. In: Proceedings of the SIGCHI Conference on Human Factors in Computing Systems, pp. 399–406 (2004)
8. Lee, W., et al.: 3D scan to product design: methods, techniques, and cases. In: Proceedings of the 6th International Conference on 3D Body Scanning Technologies, Lugano, Switzerland, 27–28 October 2015, Authors version. Hometrica Consulting (2015)
9. Mendes, D., Ferreira, A.: Virtual Lego modelling on multi-touch surfaces (2011)
10. Rekimoto, J., Ayatsuka, Y.: CyberCode: designing augmented reality environments with visual tags. In: Proceedings of DARE 2000 on Designing Augmented Reality Environments, pp. 1–10 (2000)
11. Robles-De-La-Torre, G.: The importance of the sense of touch in virtual and real environments. IEEE Multimedia 13(3), 24–30 (2006)
12. Sheng, J., Balakrishnan, R., Singh, K.: An interface for virtual 3D sculpting via physical proxy. In: GRAPHITE, vol. 6, pp. 213–220 (2006)
13. Stockman, H.: Communication by means of reflected power. Proc. IRE 36(10), 1196–1204 (1948)
14. Ullmer, B., Ishii, H., Glas, D.: mediaBlocks: physical containers, transports, and controls for online media. In: Proceedings of the 25th Annual Conference on Computer Graphics and Interactive Techniques, pp. 379–386 (1998)
15. Want, R., Fishkin, K.P., Gujar, A., Harrison, B.L.: Bridging physical and virtual worlds with electronic tags. In: Proceedings of the SIGCHI Conference on Human Factors in Computing Systems, pp. 370–377 (1999)

Systematic Literature Review of Nuclear Safety Systems in Small Modular Reactors

Tucker Densmore$^{(\boxtimes)}$ and Vincent G. Duffy$^{(\boxtimes)}$

Purdue University, West Lafayette, IN 47906, USA
{tdensmo, duffy}@purdue.edu

Abstract. Safety in nuclear power plants is an important area in the realm of engineering safety [1]. Small Modular Reactors (SMRs) are an emerging form of nuclear technology with widespread application, notably in austere or remote communities. SMRs are defined as power plants that produce 300 MWe or less [2], designed with modular fabrication technology for ease of onsite construction. Historically, nuclear power plants have maximized large economies of scale and been constructed with ample resources for safety regulation concerns, such as access to reliable water tables. SMRs will be deployed to remote locations without the resources normally afforded to a large power plant, and so the safety systems of these new designs must be innovative and still be able to meet the stringent safety specifications set forth by regulatory bodies [3]. This is a very important aspect of SMR design and is critical for licensing and production. This paper outlines a systematic literature review of scientific papers concerned with nuclear safety systems of SMRs. To further expound upon this topic, literature analyses were completed using keyword searches for, "nuclear safety systems," and "small modular reactor" and then evaluating trends between articles. The databases used for this research were Google Scholar, Scopus, Web of Science, and Mendeley. The analyses were completed by use of the following literature review software: VOSViewer, Publish or Perish, MAXQDA and Vincinitas. The results are presented in the form of trend analyses, keyword cluster analysis, co-author clusters analysis, co-citation analysis, word clouds and emergence analyses. The results show a strong correlation between the study of this material and the rising interest in green energy, as well as the particular safety systems necessary for the development of SMRs.

Keywords: Nuclear safety systems · Small modular reactors · Bibliometric analysis

1 Introduction and Background

The advent SMRs has presented a unique solution to the energy crisis in remote communities worldwide. Small modular reactors are distinct in their relatively small power output, modular design and fabrication, and ease of operation. Such systems can be prefabricated and shipped to a remote community. An SMR can be tailor-made to meet the power requirements of a small community and would require a minimal footprint

© Springer Nature Switzerland AG 2021
C. Stephanidis et al. (Eds.): HCII 2021, CCIS 1498, pp. 99–106, 2021.
https://doi.org/10.1007/978-3-030-90176-9_14

for operation. In such desolate conditions, the requirements for autonomous operation, and exhaustive safety features are critical [4].

This new technology presents unique design challenges for safety systems at every level of the nuclear power plant process, from the fuel cycles and shipping to the worst-case scenario of core coolant loss [5]. The safety systems of SMRs must pass the existing stringent regulatory licensing requirements but must also account for the possibility of issues arising not normally seen with large-scale power plants. These systems must be able to operate autonomously and in very remote locations without the ideal conditions such as access to reliable water tables (for emergency cooling). For this reason, new and innovative core designs have been proposed such as liquid metal cooled, molten salt cooled, and hot gas-cooled reactors [6]. Modifications have been made to well-known water-cooled reactor designs to adapt the proven technology to a smaller scale. Ultimately, these systems will have to demonstrate extremely reliable and robust safety systems in normal operation, through fuel cycles, and in worst-case scenarios before licensing will be granted.

The Canadian SMR market is a good example of how important safety is to the development of SMRs. There are currently five designs under pre-licensing agreements with the Canadian government [7]. Some technologies have benefits beyond power generation, however for the specific application in Canada's north the two primary drivers will be economic feasibility, and support from indigenous communities. The second factor will largely depend on the perceived level of safety and the impact on the surrounding community and environment should an emergency occur.

2   Purpose of the Study

The purpose of this study is to perform a systematic literature review, including a bibliometric analysis of scientific articles relating to nuclear safety systems of small nuclear reactors. The primary focus of this study is aimed specifically at emerging fourth-generation safety systems that will enable nuclear reactor technology to be scaled to the SMR level. Furthermore, this study will highlight the developments in this area by including analysis methods from VOSViewer, MAXQDA and Vincinitas. These programs were used for data collection, and then to extrapolate data trends. Key word analyses, word clouds, emergence analyses, cluster analyses and trend analyses will show what parts of the research are critical, where the research is occurring, by whom, and will show how public perception is driving research in this field.

2.1   Relation to Engineering Safety

This is an important research topic in terms of engineering safety. Nuclear accidents are perhaps amongst the most notorious engineering mistakes in history. Therefore it behooves engineers to approach nuclear safety with detail and care and provide exhaustive engineering protections in their systems. This concept is personified in the "Defense in Depth" approach to safety in nuclear engineering.

2.2 Human-Automation Interaction

Historical accidents have been the result of human-automation interaction, such as Chernobyl or Three-mile Island. The focus of SMR safety is passive features, which help to eliminate human-automation errors.

3 Methodologies

3.1 Data Collection

Data were collected and analyzed using similar methods used by Duffy [8]. Data were collected from four different databases: Google Scholar, Scopus, Web of Science and Mendeley. The databases were accessed using Purdue Library. Searches were conducted in each database using the keywords: nuclear safety systems, small modular reactor. The searches were not restricted by publication year, and the results included relevant metadata. Metadata included article titles, abstracts, citations, and author names. This metadata from the searches was extracted and analyzed using several bibliometric analysis tools and included over 7800 articles from the various databases.

3.2 Trend Analysis

A trend analysis was carried out for both the Web of Science database results, as well as the Scopus database results. As shown in Fig. 1, there has been a steady increase in research in this domain. Nuclear energy has been around since the 1940s, but the dramatic increase in research is likely due to the increasing trend away from fossil fuel use.

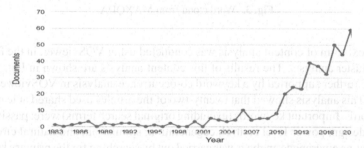

Fig. 1. Number of publications per year from Scopus database.

4 Results

4.1 Co-citation Analysis

A co-citation analysis is a form of bibliometric coupling analysis that was developed to better indicate subject similarity [9]. For this analysis, the Web of Science database was input to VOSviewer. This is a bibliometric analysis software that performs analyses using metadata from database searches. For this particular analysis, 142 articles were connected, sharing at least three citations. This produced four major clusters shown in Fig. 2.

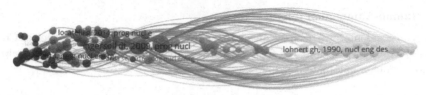

Fig. 2. Co-citation analysis using VOSviewer, showing results for a minimum of three citations, categorized by color. (Color figure online)

4.2 Content Analysis

The first content analysis was performed using MAXQDA. The most relevant articles were selected from the results of the co-citation analysis, as well as relevant research articles selected by the author. MAXQDA finds the most important keywords, and then creates a word cloud to portray the prevailing themes. The word cloud shown in Fig. 3 highlights the non-keyword search terms of accident, radioactive, standards etc.

Fig. 3. Word cloud from MAXQDA.

The next form of content analysis was conducted using VOSviewer, in the form of a content cluster analysis. The results of this content analysis are shown in Fig. 4. These results are further supported by a keyword co-occurrence analysis in VOSviewer, shown in Fig. 5. This analysis showed that twenty-two of the articles used shared at least five of the keywords. Important keywords (excluding original search terms) were: passive safety systems, design, power-level control, cogeneration, simulation, and natural circulation.

Finally, an emergence analysis was carried out by searching for the primary keywords (nuclear, safety) in Vincintas. This tool provides an emergence analysis from Twitter, showing the relevant social media data, and a word cloud with the relevant terms associated with the keyword search. Note that the influence was indicated at over 86 million, which is quite influential. Figure 6 shows the results of the Vincinitas analysis. This supports that nuclear safety is an emerging topic of research and public discussion, likely owing to the decreasing reliance on fossil fuels and increasing interest in nuclear technology. This is also likely driven by the recent nuclear plant accidents in Japan.

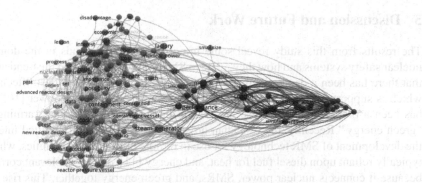

Fig. 4. Content cluster analysis using VOSviewer, categorized by color. (Color figure online)

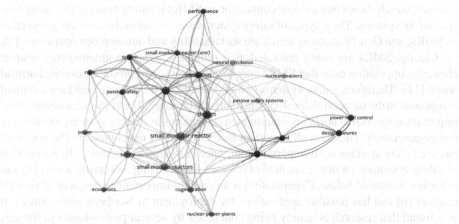

Fig. 5. Keyword co-occurrence cluster diagram from VOSviewer with four main clusters, categorized by color. (Color figure online)

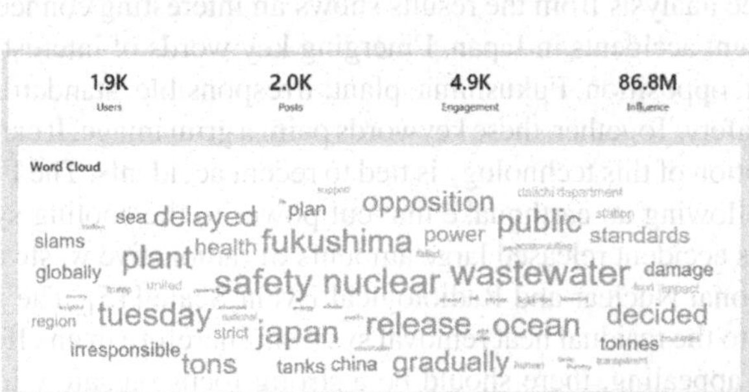

Fig. 6. Emergence analysis from Vincinitas, showing keyword popularity on Twitter.

5 Discussion and Future Work

The results from this study reveal some important research trends in the domain of nuclear safety systems and how they relate to SMRs. It was clear from the trend analysis that there has been a drastic increase in research in this field in the past fifteen years, which is supported by economic motivators for the rise of nuclear power [10]. There has been a proportionate increase in research in the fields of "global warming," and "green energy." Recently, the Canadian government announced committed interest in the development of SMR technology for use in remote northern communities, which are typically reliant upon diesel fuel for heat, and energy [11]. This is a relevant correlation because it connects nuclear power, SMRs, and green energy together. This rise is also roughly coincident with the US Department of Energy setting forth the Gen IV reactor requirements which encompass a variety of goals from sustainability, economics, physical protection, and safety and reliability [2]. A primary focus of the safety portion of these goals is passive safety [12]. There is an equal connection, as shown in the cluster analyses which shows that a major connection to SMRs is safety systems including passive safety systems. These types of safety systems are critical to the secondary objective of SMRs, and Gen IV reactors which are sustainability and autonomous operations [2].

Clearly, SMRs are being marketed as a reliable alternative green-energy source. However, opposition cites that SMRs may be dangerous, and produce possibly harmful waste [11]. Therefore, safety systems (which include waste management) are a critical component to the successful development of this technology. The keyword analyses show important subjects that are being investigated such as passive safety systems, simulation, and cogeneration. These are all important factors for SMR development. The notion of passive safety systems is an important component of Gen IV reactors [13]. Simulation of safety systems is an important field of research for licensing and certification [14] and is further discussed below. Cogeneration is an equally important component of Gen IV reactors [6] and has possible applications for deployment to Northern communities. It was found that research is mainly being conducted by several professionals in the US, China, Korea, and Japan. These results coincide with the leading users of nuclear power. It was shown that Canada is starting to lead in terms of research which is likely due to the SMR Road Map laid forth by the Canadian government, which details the prospective deployment of SMR technology to Canada's northern communities [7].

The emergence analysis from the results shows an interesting connection to nuclear safety and the recent accidents in Japan. Emerging key words of interest were: wastewater, Japan, ocean, opposition, Fukushima, plant, irresponsible, standards, damage, sea, globally, health, safety. Together, these keywords paint a grim image. It can be determined that public perception of this technology is tied to recent accidents. The Fukushima accidents occurred following an earthquake that cut power to the cooling systems of three reactors [15]. This accident released large amounts of radioactive waste and was rated a 7 on the International Nuclear and Radiological Event Scale [15]. The main issue was the power supply to the residual heat removal system. Therefore in an effort to make this technology more appealing, there should be a strong focus on safety to ensure public buy-in for the programs is achieved. This also ties into the key word analysis of SMR and Gen IV systems. It was shown that critical words such as passive safety systems, design, power-level control, cogeneration, simulation, and natural circulation were integral to research in this field. Passive safety systems would prevent the type of accident that occurred in Japan, because these systems do not rely on external power systems. This is as simple as gravity feed cooling pools that can flood a reactor system. Ultimately the Fukushima reactors were cooled by flooding. This is an important correlation, and supports the aforementioned Gen IV reactor goals, specifically the improved safety systems. It should be noted that Fukushima reactors were LWR type reactors. The public perception of these types of reactors may affect which type of Gen IV reactor technology is chosen for SMR development. For SMR-LWR development a major design concern will likely be how to retain passive safety systems without the need for large coolant reservoirs, in order to minimize plant footprint.

Lastly, as mentioned above, future work in this field can be supported by the results of this study. The types of research work can be directed by the themes uncovered in the bibliometric analysis. A good indicator of the accuracy of this study and its conclusions is the future work under development and where it is happening. The National Science Foundation awards research grants for important scientific development and research. This provides a good indicator of future work development. A preliminary search through the "awards" database showed that numerous grants have been awarded for further research in the domain of nuclear safety systems. One such work was done by M. Nakayama. This work is focused on the statistical analysis of nuclear power plant safety and improving algorithms for risk assessment [16]. This important work was brought to light with the recent occurrence of nuclear power plant disasters in Japan. The work focuses on refining algorithms and presents new Monte Carlo simulation models for improved computing and more accurate models.

6   Conclusion

With the increasing interest in alternative, green energy as well as the interest in SMRs, there has been an increasing amount of research into nuclear safety systems. The need for increased safety was outlined in the Generation IV reactor technology requirements [2]. This study has shown that this is a heavily interconnected field of research, supported by the well-developed nuclear power generating nations. Nuclear safety is particularly important for SMRs because of the relatively small size and requirement for autonomous operations [17]. This study has shown that particular fields of research are important to this domain such as 'passive safety systems,' 'natural circulation' and simulation. This was shown to be connected to public perception of nuclear safety, and recent accidents in Japan. Equally, simulation of safety systems and risk analysis has been shown to be an important field of research. In conclusion, nuclear safety systems will continue to be an important field of study, notably for the application to SMRs.

References

1. Bounds, A.: Implementation of nuclear safety cases. Saf. Reliab. **39**(3–4), 203–214 (2020). https://doi.org/10.1080/09617353.2020.1800977
2. Generation IV Goals: GIF Portal - Home. https://www.gen-4.org/gif/jcms/c_9502/genera tion-iv-goals#:~:text=Eight%20technology%20goals%20have%20been,proliferation%20r esistance%20and%20physical%20protection. Accessed 14 Apr 2021

3. Lesinski, M.: Perspectives on Canada's SMR opportunity. Can. Nucl. Lab. (n.d.)
4. Sam-Aggrey, H.: Opportunities and challenges related to the deployment of small modular reactors in mines in the northern territories of Canada. CNL Nucl. Rev. **5**(1), 143–53 (2016). https://doi.org/10.12943/cnr.2015.00058
5. Kaliatka, A.: Issues related to the safety assessment of the SMR concepts. Lith. Energy Inst., 2017 September
6. Butler, G.: Drivers for reactor choice- choosing a reactor - benefits and challenges of advanced technologies choosing a reactor - benefits and challenges of advanced technologies (n.d.)
7. Canadian Small Modular Reactor (SMR) Roadmap Steering Committee: A call to action: a canadian roadmap for small modular reactors, vol. 28, no. 1, pp. 1–2 (2018)
8. Duffy, B.M., Duffy, V.G.: Data mining methodology in support of a systematic review of human aspects of cybersecurity. In: Duffy, V.G. (ed.) HCII 2020. LNCS, vol. 12199, pp. 242–253. Springer, Cham (2020). https://doi.org/10.1007/978-3-030-49907-5_17
9. Surwase, G., et al.: Co-citation analysis: an overview. In: BOSLA National Conference Proceedings, CDAC, 9 September 2011. ISBN : 935050007-8
10. Richard, W.: The future of nuclear power. Environ. Sci. Technol. **26**(6), 1116–1120 (1992). https://doi.org/10.1021/es50002a013
11. The Canadian Press. Five Things about Canada's Proposed Small Modular Nuclear Reactors. CTVNews. CTV News, 14 April 2021. https://www.ctvnews.ca/sci-tech/five-things-about-canada-s-proposed-small-modular-nuclear-reactors-1.5387383
12. Elsheikh, B.M.: Safety assessment of molten salt reactors in comparison with light water reactors. J. Radiat. Res. Appl. Sci. **6**(2), 63–70 (2013). https://doi.org/10.1016/j.jrras.2013.10.008
13. Yan, G., Ye, C.: Passive safety systems of advanced nuclear power plant: AP1000. In: International Conference on Nuclear Engineering, Proceedings, ICONE, vol. 6, pp. 85–89 (2010). https://doi.org/10.1115/ICONE18-29521
14. Roth, G.A., Aydogan, F.: Comprehensive analyses of nuclear safety system codes. In: ASME International Mechanical Engineering Congress and Exposition, Proceedings (IMECE), vol. 6 B, pp. 1–29 (2013). https://doi.org/10.1115/IMECE2013-63773
15. Fukushima Daiichi Accident - World Nuclear Association. https://www.world-nuclear.org/information-library/safety-and-security/safety-of-plants/fukushima-daiichi-accident.aspx. Accessed 18 Apr 2021
16. Alban, A., Darji, H.A., Imamura, A., Nakayama, M.K.: Efficient Monte Carlo methods for estimating failure probabilities. Reliab. Eng. Syst. Saf. **165,** 376–94 (2017). https://doi.org/10.1016/j.ress.2017.04.001
17. Hussein, E.M.A.: Emerging small modular nuclear power reactors: a critical review. Phys. Open **5,** 100038 (2020)
18. MAXQDA. (n.d.). https://www.maxqda.com/. Accessed 1 Apr 2021
19. Scopus (n.d.). https://www-scopus-com.ezproxy.lib.purdue.edu/search/form.uri?display=basic#basic. Accessed 1 Apr 2021
20. VOSviewer (n.d.). https://www.vosviewer.com/. Accessed 1 Apr 2021
21. Web of Science (n.d.). https://apps-webofknowledge-com.ezproxy.lib.purdue.edu/WOS_GeneralSearch_input.do?product=WOS&search_mode=GeneralSearch&SID=8Fl5FKLCbemDKARc7wU&preferencesSaved=. Accessed 1 Apr 2021

Bio-Spatial Study in the Urban Context: User Experience Analysis from New York, Preliminary Neurophysiological Analysis from Kuala Lumpur and Nairobi

Arlene Ducao[1,2](✉) ⓘD, Ilias Koen[2], Tania van Bergen[2], Yapah Berry[2], Scott Sheu[2], Tommy Mitchell[2], and Landon Johnson[1]

[1] New York University School of Engineering, Brooklyn, NY 11201, USA
arlduc@mit.edu
[2] Multimer, Brooklyn, NY 11231, USA

Abstract. Multimer is a new system that measures multimodal biosensor data to model how the built environment influences neurophysiological processes. This article presents participant feedback of user experience for a Multimer study in Manhattan south of Central Park, New York City, USA. The feedback was used to update and improve the entire Multimer system for use in other locales. This article will also present preliminary analyses for bio-spatial pilot studies in Kenya and Malaysia, conducted by the Multimer's research team in partnership with the Sustainable Mobility Unit of the United Nations Human Settlements Programme (UN-Habitat). For all of these studies, participants used wearable sensors to record their electroencephalographic signals as they cycled or walked.

Keywords: Cognitive ergonomics in distributed · Ambient and pervasive interactions · Development methods and tools for distributed

1 Introduction

Multimer is a new system that deploys a mobile app, a cloud-based monitoring platform, and various consumer-grade wearable sensors to measure multimodal biosensor data, including electroencephalogram and electrocardiogram data. Multimer data is used to model how the built environment influences human neurophysiological processes (as diagrammed in Fig. 1).

This article presents participant feedback of user experience for a Multimer study supported by the National Science Foundation (Award #1721679). The study deployed a protocol approved by the Biomedical Research Alliance of New York, an independent institutional review board. The study involved training 101 New York City-area pedestrians, cyclists, and drivers to record biosensor, survey, and comment data over the course of twelve weeks, from 01 August 2017 to 31 October 2017. The concept of this study and the technical results are discussed in previous articles [1–3]. The feedback sessions discussed in this article were conducted in November 2017 with twenty-three

© Springer Nature Switzerland AG 2021
C. Stephanidis et al. (Eds.): HCII 2021, CCIS 1498, pp. 107–114, 2021.
https://doi.org/10.1007/978-3-030-90176-9_15

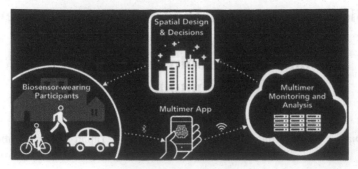

Fig. 1. Multimer system diagram.

people of varying demographics and experience. The sessions were divided into four feedback stations, three of which are briefly discussed in this article: 1) participants provided feedback for their overall experience; 2) participants provided feedback about the Multimer mobile app; 3) participants provided feedback about the custom, ergonomic EEG (electroencephalogram) headsets constructed by the project team. Except for the first "overall experience" station, each station employed visuals to support the interview questions or as a mode of providing direct feedback (Fig. 2).

Fig. 2. Paper-printed visual aids used during the user experience feedback sessions.

2   Overall User Experience: Interview Summaries

Participants were interested in the scientific aspect of the project, and a large majority of participants were interested in contributing their own data. Some participants were interested in the money as well. Of the twenty-three respondents, many were drawn to the study by an interest in science. Overall, participants had a positive experience interacting with staff. Most found using the Multimer technology to be interesting enough that they would wear it on their own without payment (though few stated this strongly).

During the New York study, long hours of wearing the EEG headset caused discomfort for many participants. While using the Multimer mobile app, participants would find that the Bluetooth connection between their phones and the EEG headset would be severed (disconnected) without knowing it. Participants also had a hard time predicting when the EEG headset would require new batteries.

Participants thought that Multimer could eventually be useful in helping them plan their transport routes. "If Multimer can let you know how stressed you are, how you're riding (like the wrong way), and tell you take a better route, that would be cool. Instructions to drive the right way would be useful for bikers," one participant said. A pedestrian participant said: "It maybe can help runners identify points where they're having a hard time". And the cyclist participant said, "I think it'd be interesting to see how you're doing on the streets: how you improve, how many miles, how you did right or wrong. It would be cool if it showed you traffic ways". Another participant added: "I'd like to use Multimer to identify preferred routes of which I may not be cognizant".

3   Mobile App and User Stats Feedback

Participants encountered a number of issues with the connection of the biometric gear to the Multimer mobile app. One of the participants said, "Connecting the headset was disheartening. I wanted the App to tell me when the battery should be changed. I wanted the App to notify them any time the headset disconnected. I wanted to be notified when the headset disconnects". Another participant said that "What would be ideal would be that the headset pairs and you can start. In reality, it's a multistep process. It takes multiple tries to get a good signal, and sometimes the app would not log me in".

One participant highlighted the issue of connectivity in different parts of town: "When going through certain zones, I'd lose service. I'd see spots where I have to switch it. I had to restart and reconnect. I would get frustrated and not record at all".

Another participant pointed out that checking the connectivity was stressful: "Always, I was checking my phone to make sure it was connected. Wish I didn't have to check it constantly. There should be an alert when the headset would lose connection with the app".

A participant pointed out that it was "complicated to have it always connected" (Fig. 3).

The Multimer project member who conducted app-related interviews noted that "uploading data makes people tense. People were confused about long/lat and meditation/attention but many checked to see if the numbers changed". This interviewer made several suggestions based on patterns from these interviews:

- Make it clear in the training that batteries should be changed after every 8 h of use.
- Make sure that it is clear that "Diagnostics" is a button on the activity type screen.
- Make it clear in the training where the user stats are and how to use them.
- Indicate that there is a drop-down menu that allows users to select dates in user stats.
- Simplify the diagnostics page and get rid of jargon. Consider a display that looks like this:

Fig. 3. The Multimer app's screens: launch, activity, diagnostics, upload.

Headset connected ✅
Brainwave data enabled ✅
Heart Rate Monitor connected ✅
Location data enabled ✅

4 Headset Ergonomics: Feedback Summary

EEG data can be challenging to collect outside of a research lab setting. While several lightweight wireless EEG headsets are now available on the consumer market, most of them are not practical for long sessions (2 or more hours) of data collection from a large sample size of participants. Consequently, the New York study used a simplified EEG headset [4] with a single electrode located at FP1, near the frontal cortex, which is associated with high-level cognition [5, 6]. For this study, the Multimer research team prepared two kinds of headsets for participants: the unmodified manufacturer's headset, and a modified version in which the hard plastic arm that holds the forehead EEG electrode in place was replaced by a flexible cable that could be tucked under a helmet or hat.

For this activity, participants were given photos of the unmodified "hard" and modified "soft" EEG headsets used during the course of the study (Fig. 4). They were instructed to record opinions of each part of the headset. This included notes on what they disliked, what was comfortable, how was their experience, what problems they encountered and suggestions for change. Later, participants were given a prototype of Multimer's own custom-fabricated headset casing to see what the prototype looks like and share their thoughts on it (Fig. 4). They were able to feel, wear, and suggest some ideas.

Several participants said that the unmodified headset gave them headaches or physical discomfort: "Headband pinched head". "Headaches every time after 10–15 min. Only relieved if I take it off". "I got headaches from the pressure of [the sensor] pushing into my forehead". "Riders have stopped using it because it hurt so much". "Hard to adjust forehead sensor".

Some participants further tied their discomfort to the weather: "Cold days gives you a headache. Feels like a spike. I got used to it clamping your ear, but it really hurts". "[The] headset is hard [to wear] during hot weather. I preferred [to wear the] heart rate monitor".

And some participants mentioned more discomfort with the clip that attached the grounding electrode to the ear: "Ear clip wire was too short". "Ear clip pinched ear".

While participants generally preferred the modified headset and didn't encounter as many issues of physical discomfort, they encountered other issues in keeping the forehead electrode secure and connected: "Headpiece was not secure enough". "Forehead wire was too short. Forehead sensor was too big". "Keeping the forehead sensor in place was hard". "It was hard for it [the forehead electrode] to stay attached and get EEG reading. Spent too much time thinking about that". "Sensor would slip. Detection wasn't consistent. Headband would be helpful in making it more secure and consistent". "[The sensor] would start sliding off, so I would have to readjust it".

For the modified headset, much like with the unmodified headset, participants had issues with the ear electrode clip: "The ear clip wire was too short". "Ear clip pinched ear". "Tight on the ear. Needs a longer wire". "Earpiece pinched a little bit".

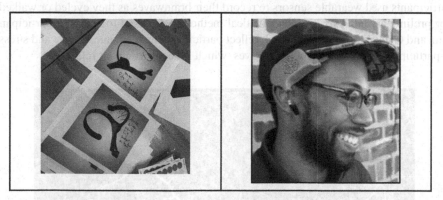

Fig. 4. User-annotated images of the "hard" and "soft" headsets (left). A researcher wearing a custom headset prototype (right).

From these interviews, recommendations for headset revisions include keeping the headset small, creating a smaller forehead sensor, being sure electrode wires are long enough, using an earbud instead of clip, and adding a clip to attach to headbands and headphones.

However, unlike with sensors embedded in wristbands or chestbands, participants had a wide range of reactions to all of the headsets presented. This underscores the challenge of developing a head-based wearable—and since they measure brainwaves, EEG devices must be worn on the head. Participants seemed to have very strong preferences about what they are willing to wear on their heads, which is one reason that, as long as Multimer works with brainwave data, its team will continue to research the affordances and best practices for developing head-based wearables.

5 Kuala Lumpur and Nairobi: Preliminary Results

The 2017 user experience feedback from New York pedestrians, cyclists, and drivers helped to add a more subjective, human aspect to the process of developing and evolving the technology. The feedback was used to update and improve the entire Multimer system, which has since been used to model human neurophysiological experience studies in corporate offices, developing economies, and informal settlements [7]. In 2018 and 2019, several Multimer studies, modeled on the protocol approved by the Biomedical Research Alliance of New York, were conducted in partnership with the Sustainable Mobility Unit of the United Nations Human Settlements Programme (UN-Habitat). Like with the 2017 study, the 2018 and 2019 studies were meant to provide new data that shows how the built environment and the movement of traffic may influence the neurophysiological state of pedestrians, cyclists, and drivers.

In Malaysia, a 2018 study (n = 12) was conducted to measure cyclist experience of Kuala Lumpur's first-ever dedicated cycle lane (separated from motorist lanes). In Kenya, two studies were conducted: a 2019 study (n = 11) of cyclist experience on major Nairobi thoroughfares and a 2019 study (n = 12) of schoolchildren's experience as they walk to school in the informal settlement of Kibera. For all of these studies, participants used wearable sensors to record their brainwaves as they cycled or walked. For preliminary analysis, simple statistical methods were used to compare participant Beta and Gamma brainwaves, which reflect participant engagement, activity and stress, to participant Delta and Theta brainwaves, which reflect participant relaxation.

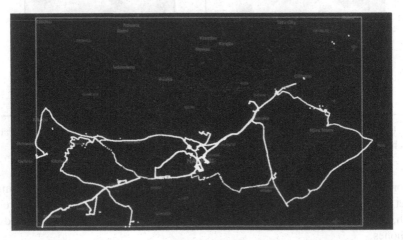

Fig. 5. A map of EEG and EEC data recorded by Nairobi cyclists (n = 11) on major thoroughfares in January 2019.

For the Nairobi Cycling analysis (Fig. 5), conducted in partnership with UN-Habitat, the Institute for Transportation and Development Policy (ITDP), and Critical Mass Nairobi, the median occurrence of Delta/Theta frequencies were higher (mostly around 10 to 12 percentage points) than that of Beta/Gamma frequencies. For occurrences of all these frequencies, the standard deviation was high, which may have been caused by a large number of null values where streets were most bumpy, thus disrupting the connection between the participant and the biometric wearable sensors.

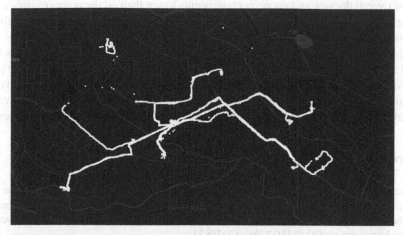

Fig. 6. A map of EEG and EEC data recorded by Nairobi schoolchildren (n = 12) while walking to school in the informal settlement of Kibera "slum," December 2019.

The Nairobi Walkability analysis (Fig. 6), conducted in partnership with UN-Habitat and Map Kibera, revealed that the median occurrence of Beta/Gamma and Delta/Theta frequencies were relatively even for most routes, with the only notable exceptions to this trend being being data points near schools and security areas gender-based violence centers. These locations' Delta/Theta medians occurrences were five percentage points higher than the Beta/Gamma median occurrences, while the others were either three points higher or the same.

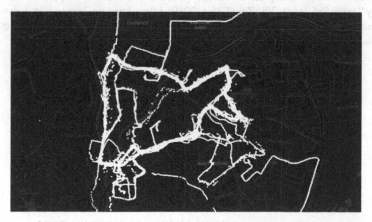

Fig. 7. A map of EEG and EEC data recorded by Kuala Lumpur cyclists (n = 12) in February 2018, on and near the city's first dedicated cycle track.

The Kuala Lumpur analysis (Fig. 7), conducted in partnership with UN-Habitat and Cycling KL, yielded some of the clearest results, with the median occurrences of Delta/Theta frequencies of the dedicated cycle track being 3 percentage points lower than the overall dataset, and six percentage points lower than all the points outside of the cycling tracks data sets. The median occurrence of Beta/Gamma frequencies was always 54 points, both on and off the cycle tracks.

While analysis continues on the Nairobi and Kuala Lumpur data, the data has been shared with stakeholders in Nairobi and Kuala Lumpur, particularly transportation planners working for the respective city governments. The user interface modifications recommended by participants in the 2017 New York study have facilitated the deployment the Multimer system in smaller, shorter studies run by local, on-the-ground partners.

References

1. Ducao, A., Koen, I., Guo, Z.: Multimer: validating multimodal, cognitive data in the city: towards a model of how the urban environment influences streetscape users. In: Proceedings of the Workshop on Modeling Cognitive Processes from Multimodal Data, pp. 1–8, October 2018. https://doi.org/10.1145/3279810.3279853
2. Ducao, A., Koen, I., Guo, Z., Frank, J., Willard, C., Kam, J.: Multimer: modeling neurophysiological experience in public urban space. Int. J. Community Well-Being 3(4), 465–490 (2020). https://doi.org/10.1007/s42413-020-00082-7
3. Ducao, A.: Data+Multimer: mapping human signals for improved spatial design. In: Data, Architecture and the Experience of Place, pp. 22–44. Routledge (2018)
4. NeuroSky: Mindset Communications Protocol (2015). http://developer.neurosky.com/docs/lib/exe/fetch.php?media=mindset_communications_protocol.pdf
5. Amodio, D.M., Frith, C.D.: Meeting of minds: the medial frontal cortex and social cognition. Nat. Rev. Neurosci. 7(4), 268 (2006)
6. Luu, P., Flaisch, T., Tucker, D.M.: Medial frontal cortex in action monitoring. J. Neurosci. 20(1), 464–469 (2000)
7. Ducao, A.: Neurophysiological experience of cyclists in Kuala Lumpur and Nairobi. Int. Journey Traffic Saf. Innov. Vis. Zero Cities (2019). https://medium.com/vision-zero-cities-journal/neurophysiological-experience-of-cyclists-in-kuala-lumpur-and-nairobi-362d4c060074. Accessed 26 Mar 2021

Speech Emotion Recognition Using Combined Multiple Pairwise Classifiers

Panikos Heracleous[1], Yasser Mohammad[2]([✉]), and Akio Yoneyama[1]

[1] KDDI Research Inc., 2-1-15 Ohara, Fujimino-shi, Saitama 356-8502, Japan
{pa-heracleous,yoneyama}@kddi-research.jp
[2] National Institute of Advanced Industrial Science and Technology (AIST),
2-3-26 Aomi, Koto-ku, Tokyo 135-0064, Japan
yasserm@aun.edu.eg

Abstract. In the current study, a novel approach for speech emotion recognition is proposed and evaluated. The proposed method is based on multiple pairwise classifiers for each emotion pair resulting in dimensionality and emotion ambiguity reduction. The method was evaluated using the state-of-the-art English IEMOCAP corpus and showed significantly higher accuracy compared to a conventional method.

Keywords: Speech emotion recognition · Pairwise classification · Dimensionality reduction

1 Introduction

Speech emotion recognition is the task of automatically classifying human emotions conveyed through uttered speech. Due to the importance of emotion recognition in real-world applications, a large number of studies present results using many different feature extraction and classification approaches [1–7]. Although recent studies have showed significant improvements in the performance of speech emotion recognition systems, this field is still an open research area, and for real-world applications further investigation is needed. In the current study, a method is proposed and evaluated using the IEMOCAP English state-of-the-art corpus [8] for the recognition of four emotions. The proposed method is based on using multiple pairwise classifiers and combining the results using a majority vote decision. The main advantage of using pairwise classification is dimensionality reduction resulting in ambiguity reduction between classes. To our knowledge, speech emotion recognition using combined pairwise classifiers for all classes has not been investigated comprehensively. In [9], a method specifically for facial expression recognition using pairwise discriminative task was reported. The method, however, used different visual features for each pair, and for class recognition distance measures were applied. In contrast, in the proposed method

Dr. Panikos Heracleous is currently with Artificial Intelligence Research Center (AIRC), AIST, Japan.

C. Stephanidis et al. (Eds.): HCII 2021, CCIS 1498, pp. 115–118, 2021.
https://doi.org/10.1007/978-3-030-90176-9_16

the same features are used in all pairs, and for classification fully-connected deep neural networks (DNNs) [10] and the popular support vector machine (SVM) [11] classifier are being used. Another advantage of the proposed method is that it can also be applied for emotion recognition using visual or multimodal features without changes to the system architecture.

2   Methods

2.1   Acoustic Features and Classifiers

Twelve mel-frequency cepstral coefficients (MFCCs) [12] along with shifted delta cepstral (SDC) coefficients [13,14] were extracted from the speech signal every 10ms using a window of 20ms. Furthermore, the basic acoustic features were transformed to i-vectors [15] of 200 dimensions. The i-vector paradigm was previously introduced in speaker recognition and spoken language identification aiming at overcoming the problem of high dimensionality when using Gaussian mixture models (GMMs) supervectors. When using i-vectors in speech emotion recognition, the whole sentence can be represented by a small number of factors of dimension 100–400. Additionally, linear discriminative analysis (LDA) [16] was also applied to form the final feature vectors. For training and testing 476 and 119 speech samples for each emotion were used, respectively. The DNN architecture used in this experiment is a standard fully connected network with three hidden layers of 64 neurons each, followed by a Softmax layer with 2 neurons for classification. All neurons employed the ReLU activation function. Data were presented to the network in 100 epochs without early stopping. The batch size was set to 128. Additionally, results obtained using SVM classifier are also reported.

2.2   The Proposed Classification Method

Figure 1 shows the proposed method of classifying the emotions happy, sad, angry, and neutral. In the first stage, pairwise classifiers are trained using the corresponding training data of the emotions included in the pair. During evaluation, the output labels of all pairs are considered, and the emotion is classified using a majority vote decision.

3   Results

Table 1 shows the results obtained using the proposed method compared with a 4-class classifier. As shown, using the proposed pairwise scheme, higher recalls were obtained in most cases. The unweighted average recall (UAR) (i.e., mean of individual recalls) when using the 4-class method was 64.3.

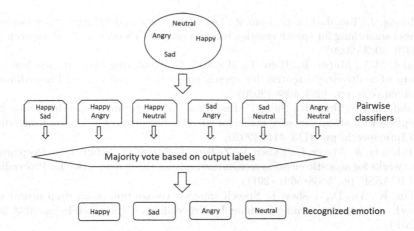

Fig. 1. The proposed method for speech emotion recognition based on pairwise classifiers.

Table 1. Recalls using the proposed method compared with a 4-class recognition scheme.

Classification method	Emotion class				
	Happy	Sad	Angry	Neutral	UAR
4-class classifier	47.1	69.7	78.9	61.3	64.3
Proposed method SVM	50.4	93.3	75.6	62.2	70.4
Proposed method DNN	56.3	93.3	77.3	63.9	72.7

4 Conclusions

In the current study, we presented a pairwise classification scheme for effective speech emotion recognition. In the proposed method, models for each emotion pair are trained, and the final emotion is selected using a majority vote scheme. Experimental results using the IEMOCAP English emotional corpus show significant improvements as compared to conventional methods. Although the method was evaluated using only four emotions, a larger number of emotions can also be considered without significant modifications to the system architecture. Currently, similar experiments using a larger number of emotions (six and seven emotions) are in progress.

References

1. Feng, H., Ueno, S., Kawahara, T.: End-to-end speech emotion recognition combined with acoustic-to-word ASR model. In: Proceedings of Interspeech, pp. 501–505 (2020)

2. Huang, J., Tao, J., Liu, B., Lian, Z.: Learning utterance-level representations with label smoothing for speech emotion recognition. In: Proceedings of Interspeech, pp. 4079–4083 (2020)
3. Jalal, M.A., Milner, R., Hain, T., Moore, R.K.: Removing bias with residual mixture of multi-view attention for speech emotion recognition. In: Proceedings of Interspeech, pp. 4084–4088 (2020)
4. Jalal, M.A., Milner, R., Hain, T.: Empirical interpretation of speech emotion perception with attention based model for speech emotion recognition. In: Proceedings of Interspeech, pp. 4113–4117 (2020)
5. Stuhlsatz, A., Meyer, C., Eyben, F., Zielkel, T., Meier, G., Schuller, B.: Deep neural networks for acoustic emotion recognition: raising the benchmarks. In: Proceedings of ICASSP, pp. 5688–5691 (2011)
6. Han, K., Yu, D., Tashev, I.: Speech emotion recognition using deep neural network and extreme learning machine. In: Proceedings of Interspeech, pp. 2023–2027 (2014)
7. Lim, W., Jang, D., Lee, T.: Speech emotion recognition using convolutional and recurrent neural networks. In: Proceedings of Signal and Information Processing Association Annual Summit and Conference (APSIPA) (2016)
8. Busso, C., et al.: IEMOCAP: interactive emotional dyadic motion capture database. J. Lang. Resour. Eval., pp. 335–359 (2008)
9. Kyperountas, M., Tefas, A., Pitas, I.: Pairwise facial expression classification. In: Proceedings of MMSP 2009, pp. 1–4 (2009)
10. Hinton, G., et al.: Deep neural networks for acoustic modeling in speech recognition: the shared views of four research groups. IEEE Signal Process. Mag. **29**(6), 82–97 (2012)
11. Cristianini, N., S.-Taylor, J.: Support Vector Machines. Cambridge University Press, Cambridge (2000)
12. Sahidullah, M., Saha, G.: Design, analysis and experimental evaluation of block based transformation in MFCC computation for speaker recognition. Speech Commun. **54**(4), 543–565 (2012)
13. Bielefeld, B.: Language identification using shifted delta cepstrum. In: Fourteenth Annual Speech Research Symposium (1994)
14. Torres-Carrasquillo, P., Singer, E., Kohler, M.A., Greene, R.J., Reynolds, D.A., Deller Jr., J.R.: Approaches to language identification using gaussian mixture models and shifted delta cepstral features. In: Proceedings of ICSLP2002-INTERSPEECH 2002, pp. 16–20 (2002)
15. Dehak, N., Kenny, P.J., Dehak, R., Dumouchel, P., Ouellet, P.: Front-end factor analysis for speaker verification. IEEE Trans. Audio Speech Lang. Process. **19**(4), 788–798 (2011)
16. Fukunaga, K.: Introduction to Statistical Pattern Recognition, 2nd edn. Academic Press, New York, ch. 10 (1990)

QFami: An Integrated Environment for Recommending Answerers on Campus

Xiangyuan Hu[1(✉)] and Shin'ichi Konomi[2]

[1] Graduate School of Information Science and Electrical Engineering, Kyushu University, Fukuoka, Japan
hu.xiangyuan.213@s.kyushu-u.ac.jp
[2] Faculty of Arts and Science, Kyushu University, Fukuoka, Japan

Abstract. With the development of the Internet, people increasingly use search engines to obtain the answers for their questions and quench their thirst for knowledge. Although search engines often provide some information quickly, they can fail to provide what people really need. Despite the ubiquitous availability of search engines, people ask questions to other people to seek valuable local information and enrich social experiences. Existing social applications such as Stack Overflow [1] and other Community Question Answering systems allow people to exchange knowledge efficiently. However, they mainly consider the expertise to recommend answerers, which would not be sufficient for supporting Q&A activities in real-world environments. In this work, we propose QFami, a novel integrated Q&A environment for physically-based Q&A scenarios on campus, QFami incorporates the interest expertise, proximity, locations, and other contextual factors that can be inferred by using various sensors on mobile phones.

Keywords: Community question answering · Campus situation

1 Introduction

Many community Q&A websites have appeared over the years, which allow people to ask questions and obtain answers. When building a Community Question Answering (CQA) [2] system, there are many factors to consider. However, most of the existing CQA systems mainly consider the expertise when recommending answerers, thus can easily fail to reflect people's real and individual needs.

In this paper, we focus on the development of a novel CQA system in campus environments. Campus environments are often inhabited by small communities of people, who have specific characteristics. Firstly, they have specialized knowledge and skills in different areas. Secondly, there are different spaces for different on-campus activities. Besides classrooms, there are libraries, gymnasiums and other recreational spaces. Some people may share the same space every day without knowing each other, potentially making them familiar strangers. Thirdly, strong and various relationships between people may exist, such as teacher-student relationship, friend relationship, colleague relationship, classmate relationship and roommate relationship. Fourthly, freshmen and

© Springer Nature Switzerland AG 2021
C. Stephanidis et al. (Eds.): HCII 2021, CCIS 1498, pp. 119–125, 2021.
https://doi.org/10.1007/978-3-030-90176-9_17

other students may have a large number of questions to ask as well as a need to develop social relations. Therefore, besides recommending answerers with high expertise, we also consider the user proximity, location and propose in QFami, which aims to encourage people to learn from each other and increase chances to have meaningful social experiences with friends and strangers.

2 Related Work

2.1 Expertise-Based CQA Systems

With the increasing popularity of CQA, many techniques to find answerers with high expertise have emerged. Wang, et al. summarized the main techniques currently used on CQA: language models, topic models, network-based methods, classification methods, expertise probabilistic models, collaborative filtering methods and hybrid methods [3].

Latent Factor Model is a commonly used model in recommendation systems, which was used successfully in the recommendation algorithm competition of Netflix and was first applied in movie recommendation. Its core idea is to find the latent factor in users and movies. For example, if a user prefers funny and warm movies, movies that have these characteristics get high scores. Then they can be recommended to the user.

Yang et al. use the PMF model with question tags and answer score to calculate user expertise. The model performs better than the models analyze topics of questions. They argue that the question tag is more important than the latent topic in questions and the result shows a higher performance in recommendation by only using question tag and answer score [4].

Mikolov et al. introduced *Word2Vec* that can efficiently obtain word vectors [5]. Compared with keywords extraction like *TF-IDF*, word vectors reveal the inner relationship and meaning between words.

2.2 Village-Like CQA Systems

Aardvark is a CQA system based on the village paradigm. Villagers don't have libraries and they often use natural language to ask questions and communicate [6]. This system uses probabilistic model and considers the user expertise, social connectedness and availability to recommend answerers.

When analyzing the social, it considers social connection, demographic similarity, profile similarity, vocabulary match, chattiness match, verbosity match, politeness match and speed match. Although it considers many factors, these factors are all based on the existing networks and social behaviors. In fact, there may be some familiar strangers who 'interact' in the same room, etc. but do not establish a social connection on the Internet, and thus Aardvark would miss such real yet 'hidden' relationships as it does not consider the user's location. Location is also a very important factor when considering to recommend a local expertise to answer questions related to a specific place, because no one knows better than the locals.

2.3 Location-Based CQA Systems

Naver KiN "Here" is a location based CQA systems, which classify questions into different location categories [7]. Questions can be read by local users if they search questions by clicking their residential area. Although the system considers location in finding relevant answerers, it doesn't consider the distance relationships between people. There can be questions about going out for shopping or playing, and people may want to invite nearby people to do it together.

3 The Proposed System

We use the answer score in Stack Exchange datasets [8] to initialize the user's score and then recommend answer candidates by using LFM model with question tag and answer score. Next, we select the candidates whose score is larger than the asker, then combine the user proximity and physical distance between them to find the final answerers.

3.1 Expertise

The level of knowledge varies from person to person, and people usually may learn from people who are better than themselves. LFM is a mature model used in recommender systems. We can get the user latent matrix p_u, and tag latent matrix q_t by the following equation, where S is the real score obtained by the user's answer activity with each tag, λ is the regularization coefficient.

$$min \sum_{u,t \in S} (y_{ut} - p_u q_t)^2 + \lambda |\, p_u\,|_2 + \lambda |\, q_t\,|_2 \qquad (1)$$

After getting them, we multiply p_u and q_t to get the predict score of user expertise E. When a use asks a question and attach tags, we rank score to filter the user whose score is lower than the asker.

One problem is the user cold start problem, because we can easily get the user's general information from database like name, email, department, it is difficult to get the user's detailed data in university environments, such as their interests and skill scores. If we ask users to show their expertise when they register in the system, it would be a tedious job and affect the user experience. We thus consider to match the users in the university and the users in Stack Exchange by analyzing the similarity between them. Firstly, we remove stop words from the user's self-introduction text. Then, split each text to word and add each word vector every text. Next, we calculate the cosine similarity between two people's texts and rank. Finally, when new users register in the system, they need to fill in self-introduction, which not only can the systems get their interest information but also can make other people learn them well. And then the system will give him an initial score by finding the mean score of top 3 similar people.

3.2 Location

We obtain the physical distance between two people through GPS. When the system recommends answerers by distance in the system, the asker can find the nearby answerer to discuss questions face-to-face. This feature usually promotes users to gain new experience and friendship. For example, if a user wants to make an appointment with someone for lunch, he can ask a question like *"Does anyone want to each launch at canteen together?"* and attach an eat out tag, and the system will automatically match nearby candidates.

Besides calculating the distance, GPS sensor also record the cities they have stayed because some questions need a local expertise to answer their question.

3.3 Proximity

Proximity is a factor that can have significance influence. As askers, people generally tend to trust answers or accept help from friends or colleagues. In other words, some people want answers from someone close, like if the askers know that the answer comes from her friend, she is more receptive. As answerers, if they know the questions are asked by their friends, classmates or colleagues, they can be more willing to provide answers.

In this system, we use GPS and indoor location technique to record the time T if two people stay together within proximity, then the system will increase proximity score. The proximity score is then used to infer friends, classmates, colleagues and familiar strangers, allowing us to estimate the willingness to provide/accept answers.

4   Experiment

4.1 Dataset

The experimental dataset is collected from Stack Exchange, one of the well-known CQA websites involving many different areas of topics such as biking, math, software engineering, Japanese language, music, cooking etc. Our experiments are based on 5 campus-relevant active topics, including cooking, movies, pets, sports, travel. Each question is made associated with of an owner ID, title, question body content, tags and all answer-document IDs including a best best-answer tag. Each answer contains owner ID, answer content, answer score. We use this dataset to train the interest and authority model. Each user dataset contains user ID and self-introduction.

We perform the following steps to get the needed data: 1) Deleting data with the owner ID being null. 2) Deleting the answers that are provided earlier than the question creation time because the Stack Exchange website merge the past answers to the same questions. 3) Collecting questions that have more than one answer. 4) Combining different topic datasets into one dataset and clean the content of user self-introduction. 5) Considering that as time increases, the user's skill value will change, we use the answer whose creation date less than 1 year since the time when the question was created. 6) Because there is a linear relationship between answer scores and the log of question view count numbers (see Fig. 1), which means the more user visit the question the more score the answer will get. We divide all the score by the log of corresponding question view count.

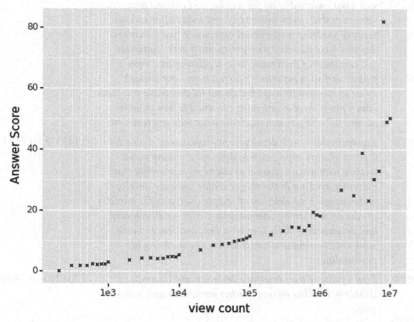

Fig. 1. The relationship between question view count and the answer score.

4.2 Result

The following Table 1 shows top 3 the most similar people of a test user with self-introduction "*I am a Software Engineer. I have worked for a long time. I like cooking but since work, there is very little time to cook.*" with user's interest tag "*cooking*". Then, the initial score in cooking is the mean of three, 0.1482810. With this initial score, we can apply LFM model and ranking to find answerers with high expertise.

Table 1. Top 3 similar Stack Exchange users' information.

AccountId	Self-introduction	Expertise	Similarity
1410746	*I have been programming all my life since i was a little boy it all started with warcraft 3 and the jass and vjass languages that oriented me into the path of the programmer after having that experience i decided that was what i wanted to do for a living so i entered university where my skills grew immensely and today after several years of studying professional experience and a masters degree i have meddled with pretty much every language you can think of from nasm to java passing by c ruby python and so many others i do not even have enough space to mention them all but do not let that make you think i am a pro if there is one thing i learned is that there is always the new guy can teach me what will you teach me*	0.000000	0.819296
5809829	*Enterprise level web development professional with a total 7 years of work experience in different domains social welfare with great exposure to micro service architecture currently working in the role of senior software developer and managing the delivery of complex services for ministry of education a strong communicator with good technical and development skills keen to accept challenges in the work environment and target myself at enhancing my potentialities*	0.143573	0.754712
5249574	*I am a fulltime user interface designer and illustrator i dabble in cooking baking crochet gardening and various crafts*	0.301270	0.748071

5 Conclusion and Future Work

As the results shown in Sect. 4 demonstrates the feasibility for our system, we identified a few areas of potential enhancement and improvements. When users ask questions, we can make them choose a preference to sort answerers by expertise, proximity or location. We consider to use more accurate recommendation model and text similarity algorithm as a next step. Because of the convenience of smartphones and the wealth of sensors embedded in them, smartphones are a promising platform for the development of QFami. Therefore we will build an Android mobile application to test and evaluate our approach.

References

1. https://stackoverflow.com Accessed 5 June 2021
2. Srba, I., Bielikova, M.: A comprehensive survey and classification of approaches for community question answering. ACM Trans. Web (TWEB) **10**(3), 1–63 (2016)

3. Wang, X., Huang, C., Yao, L., Benatallah, B., Dong, M.: A survey on expert recommendation in community question answering. J. Comput. Sci. Technol. **33**(4), 625–653 (2018)
4. Yang, B., Manandhar, S.: Tag-based expert recommendation in community question answering. In: 2014 IEEE/ACM International Conference on Advances in Social Networks Analysis and Mining (ASONAM 2014), pp. 960–963. IEEE, August 2014
5. Mikolov, T., Chen, K., Corrado, G., Dean, J.: Efficient estimation of word representations in vector space. arXiv preprint arXiv:1301.3781 (2013)
6. Horowitz, D., Kamvar, S.D.: The anatomy of a large-scale social search engine. In: Proceedings of the 19th International Conference on World Wide Web, pp. 431–440, April 2010
7. Naver Local Q&A. http://kin.naver.com/qna/list.nhn?dirId=12. Accessed 10 June 2021
8. Stack Exchange Datasets. https://archive.org/details/stackexchange. Accessed 10 May 2021

DoAR: An Augmented Reality Based Door Security Prototype Application

Muhammad Usama Islam[✉] and Beenish Chaudhry

University of Louisiana at Lafayette, Lafayette, USA
{muhammad-usama.islam1,beenish.chaudhry}@louisiana.edu

Abstract. The advent of massive technological paradigm shift to subsequent interest in augmented reality (AR) paved the way for designers to design, develop and deploy new use cases of AR in the service industry. In this paper, we investigate the use of augmented reality as an option for providing entry into secured buildings by comparing it against the traditional radio frequency identification devices cards. 51 participants from various backgrounds were recruited to enter a secured building using an AR-based app and an RFID card. The results stipulate that AR-based app had a greater acceptance among participants in terms of security and ease of use. 40 participants thought AR-based app is more secure than RFID cards and 34 participants felt the application was easier to use compared to RFID cards. 32 participants indicated that they would prefer to use the AR-based on daily basis. The result only came short in favor of RFID-based systems in terms of faster access with a margin of 3 persons where RFID systems outperformed AR-Based systems. The results indicate that the system is a suitable option but further research is needed to deploy the research in real-world settings.

Keywords: Augmented reality · Security · Interaction design · RFID

1 Introduction

The research on secured access and authentication systems has evolved rapidly to ensure safety and security of the consumers over the years [14]. While many methods such as numeric password authentication, voice activated passkeys have failed to gain traction because of privacy and security issues, and acoustic wave matching problems, respectively [9], methods such as radio frequency identification device (RFID) have become alternate as well as popular method of access and authentication due to its robustness, low power needs, faster access mechanism and long range transmitter communication ability [18]. The current market size of RFID globally is approximated at around 10.7 billion US dollars in 2021 [21] with household names such as Amazon, H&M, Decathlon and Walmart. It has also grown exponentially to be an integral part of pharmaceutical industries, retail, logistics, travel, education and agriculture industries.

While RFID has been praised for its aforementioned features, it has been criticized for security and ease of access [8]. It has been found that RFIDs are

© Springer Nature Switzerland AG 2021
C. Stephanidis et al. (Eds.): HCII 2021, CCIS 1498, pp. 126–134, 2021.
https://doi.org/10.1007/978-3-030-90176-9_18

prone to hacking in real time [15] with various mechanisms such as two-factor authentication, trigger alarms, One-Time-Password (OTP) based authentication systems and so forth [3]. Therefore, there is a need to explore alternative methods that can provide safe access to secure buildings.

Smartphone based secured entry systems have gained popularity over the course of time [7] where usually either speech activated command as well as personal identification number (PIN) based access is of common form [1]. Near field communication along with smartphone has been explored for design and implementation of door lock by Hung and his colleagues [5]. SwitchPin, a secured smartphone based pin entry method that addresses the problem of shoulder surfing has been proposed in [11] where, switchable keypads and random mapping method were utilized to prevent the security issues. Similarly, a smartphone based keyless entry system which is context aware has been proposed in [19].

In this research work, we compare the potential of augmented reality [12,13] (AR) in promoting restricted access to secured buildings against the traditional Radio Frequency Identification Device (RFID) cards. We designed a prototype of a smartphone-based AR application that allows users to experience an alternative mechanism to enter restricted-access buildings. 51 users evaluated the prototype and provided feedback that sheds considerations for designing an AR-based secured entry system to replace an RFID-based system.

2   Related Work

Augmented Reality (AR) is an emerging smartphone-based technology that is changing the service delivery landscape in medicine, education, retail stores and gaming industries [17]. Mostajeran and his team [16] found that AR-based virtual coaches can fulfill the role of human coaches for balance training in older adults. The usage of AR technology to provide a solution to door locking mechanism is discussed in [6], where quick response (QR) code along with an AR application, a micro-controller device, an e-lock and a wireless module are recommended for designing the system. However, they did not develop an app to test its feasibility in the real-world situation. QR codes, albeit lucrative fails to deliver in terms of security as malicious codes can be embedded to exploit the user as discussed thoroughly by Krombholz and her colleagues [10]. An experimental study is conducted by Wazir and his team [20] to understand the feasibility of doodle inspired AR authentication systems where the user drew a pattern in the air instead of on the phone.

It is important to explore this space because AR is becoming increasingly popular, yet Ashtari and his team [2] report that there are too many "unknowns" relating to development and deployment of AR apps. Gupta et al. [4] and Zhu et al. [22] agree and further claim that limited stakeholder knowledge is restricting the growth and widespread adoption of AR apps in various spheres. Specifically, developers lack technical know-how to develop AR based systems and consumers are unaware of the usefulness and existence of such systems. This may clarify one of the "unknowns" pointed out by [2].

3 System Design

We developed an augmented reality prototype application for Android platform named DoAR using "Unity".

3.1 Usage Scenario

The first step is when the user stands in front of a locked door and opens the DoAR application. The user then accesses the phone camera via the app to capture and recognize the AR marker posted on the door.

On recognizing the marker, the application interface changes to a Login page where user's credentials are requested and transmitted to the university-housed door controller database. If the credential of the user matches that of the server, a confirmation message is shown on the application followed by door controller opening the door for 10 s so that the user can get inside the building. Instead if the user provides an input that is not recognized to the server, a door controller is then set to 0 thus hindering the user from passing by the restricted entrance. The Fig. 1 further clarifies the system design.

4 Prototype Evaluation

51 participants who frequently accessed secured buildings using RFID cards were invited to test and provide feedback on the developed AR prototype application. The purpose of the study was to evaluate the applicability of the design and idea in real life. The goal was to understand whether or not the users liked the contact-free systems as an alternative in terms of security, ease of use and ease of access and their pointers on likeability of the application that they are using as well as the rationale behind their choice.

4.1 Participants

The demographic information of the participants were diverse in terms of age, gender, academic qualification and their previous experience with RFID and AR based systems. 7 participants were 17–25 years old, 18 participants were 26–32 years, 21 were 33–40 years and the remaining 5 were more than 41 years of age.

9 participants in total had a high school diploma as their terminal degree, 15 of the participants finished college, 19 of the participants highest degree was having a masters degree and 8 identified had obtained a doctorate.

There were 29 male and 22 female participants who partook in the study. Everyone owned a smartphone. 23 participants were familiar with AR technology while 28 of them identified themselves as novices. 42 participants had previous experience with RFID technology and 34 were using it to access a secured building on a regular basis.

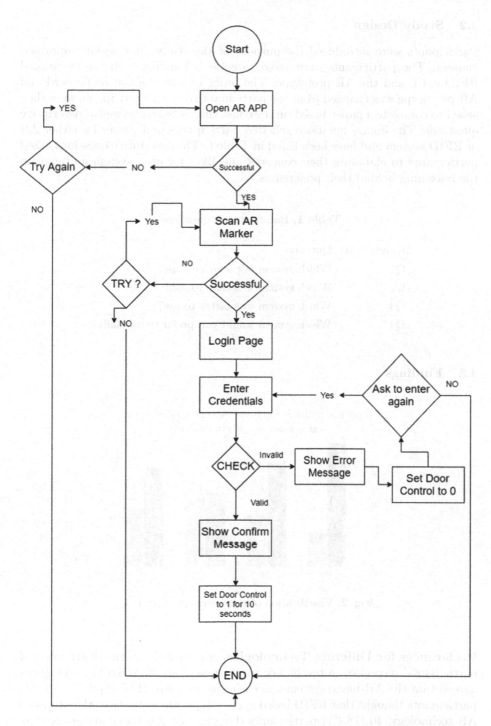

Fig. 1. Process diagram of the proposed AR application (DoAR)

4.2 Study Design

Participants were introduced the purpose of the study after seeking informed consent. The participants were asked to enter a building with the traditional RFID card, and the AR prototype. The order of usage of the RFID card and AR prototype was changed from one participant to next. Participants were then asked to complete a paper-based survey consisting of binary as well as descriptive questions. The binary questions solicited participants preferences for either AR or RFID system and have been listed in Table 1. The descriptive questions asked participants to elaborate their concerns and likes for each system and explain the reasoning behind their preferences.

Table 1. Binary survey questions

Question ID	Question
Q1	Which system felt secure to use?
Q2	Which system was easy to use?
Q3	Which system was faster to use?
Q4	Which system would you prefer to use daily?

4.3 Findings

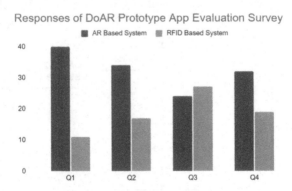

Fig. 2. Visualization of responses question 1–4

Preferences for Different Technologies. Figure 2 shows the distribution of participants' responses to the binary survey questions. 34 (66.6%) participants agreed that the AR-based system was easier to use than RFID (Q2). 27 (52.9%) participants thought that RFID based system (Q3) are faster than the proposed AR technology. 40 (78.4%) participants thought that AR based system is more secure than the RFID based system. 32 (62.8%) participants in the study indicated that they would prefer to use it on daily basis if it were to become available (Q4).

Table 2. Personal remarks and rationale behind liking AR based system

Remarks	Number of persons
Cool	14
Easy to use	18
Secure	8
Fast	4

Reasons for Preferring AR. Regardless of whether participants preferred AR or not, they had some positive comments about the AR-based system that have been summarized in Table 2. The top reason (n = 14) for liking AR was the newness and fancy nature of the technology, which participants thought set it apart from other technologies available for secured entry. *"The advanced feature is quite appealing."* Participants also thought that the technology is easy to use and easily accessible from the phone. They liked the fact that they did not have to buy a new device and that it could be accessed and controlled directly from their phones. *"I liked the usability and convenience. My smartphone supports AR and that's wonderful!"*

Table 3. Personal remarks and rationale behind liking RFID based system

Remarks	Number of persons
Fast	17
Secure	8
Convenient	8
Easy management	2

Reasons for Preferring RFID. Similarly, participants were asked to elaborate their likes for the RFID-based system(Table 3). The majority of participants (n = 18) liked RFID because it was fast. *"The RFID system is a rapid pass – touch and go."* The second major reason for liking RFID was that participants thought it was secure with well-established encryption standards. Participants thought that carrying a card around is simple and easy. *"It can be a small card, easy to carry and as it's hardware based so less bug issue."* Two participants also pointed out that management of the RFID card is relatively simple as it can be easily programmed.

Table 4. Personal remarks and rationale behind disliking AR based system

Remarks	Number of persons
Slow speed	13
Not secure	11
Early stage technology	9
Smartphone needed (cost)	5
User control	4
Battery drainage	3
Negative impact on health	2

Reasons for Disliking AR. The main dislike with the AR system was that it slowed down the building entry process. *"I had to follow many steps, like unlock the mobile phone then open the AR app, scan the marker and then I get to access the building."* Another issue was that the participants felt that the system is still in its early stages and it will take some time before it is widely accepted by the larger community. *"The AR is quite newborn compared to other systems. So it has many lacking and will take quite a lot of time to reach near perfection."* The dislikes and concerns around using the AR-based system are listed in Table 4.

Table 5. Personal remarks and rationale behind disliking RFID based systems

Remarks	Number of persons
Not secure	15
Old technology	10
Easy to lose	10
Management issues	4
Easy to break	3
Harmful to humans	3
Expensive	2

Reasons for Disliking RFID. Participants had many complaints and dislikes with the RFID card. The major problem recognized by participants was that the RFID card is not secure. *"Unauthorized devices may be able to read and even change data."* Another issue participants mentioned was managing the RFID card and keeping it safe and accessible. *"If the card is lost then reissuing a new card is a trouble."*. The dislikes have been summarized in Table 5.

5   Discussion and Future Works

Our study demonstrates that people are interested in using AR-based application to gain entry into secured buildings. The major reason for preferring AR was the coolness factor of the technology and a desire to move away from old way of entering into building. Clearly, there are several issues that need to be considered to successfully implement the proposed system. For example, password-entry method needs to be made more secure; amount of time required to use the app to open the door needs to be decreased; and the energy requirements of running an AR based app on a smartphone need to be optimized. Moreover, the AR technology developers need to work on improving consumers' trust in AR by building on its major appeal for the target population.

One limitation of the current study was the small number of participants. Another limitation was exclusion of personnel with special needs. This limitation can be addressed in future research by recruiting more participants from diverse backgrounds. We are planning to improve our prototype and run a larger study consisting of diverse users to further understand the implementation issues.

6 Conclusion

Augmented reality has changed how we move in public sphere. Augmented reality and Virtual reality (VR) is shifting the paradigm of social interaction in a dynamic manner. Alternate solutions based on Extended reality (XR) in service industry has grown exponentially over the years through technological adoption of smartphones and contact-free virtual solutions. This research work compares user acceptance and experience of two methods of gaining entry into secured buildings: AR-based technology versus RFID cards. We developed an android based prototype to demonstrate the AR-based methods in real time, which was then evaluated by target users. The results show that the technology is acceptable to use by the user targets. We are planning to undertake further work to implement the system and evaluate it with the target users.

References

1. Arifin, R.D.H., Sarno, R.: Door automation system based on speech command and pin using android smartphone. In: 2018 International Conference on Information and Communications Technology (ICOIACT), pp. 667–672. IEEE (2018)
2. Ashtari, N., Bunt, A., McGrenere, J., Nebeling, M., Chilana, P.K.: Creating augmented and virtual reality applications: current practices, challenges, and opportunities. In: Proceedings of the 2020 CHI Conference on Human Factors in Computing Systems, pp. 1–13 (2020)
3. Divya, R., Mathew, M.: Survey on various door lock access control mechanisms. In: 2017 International Conference on Circuit, Power and Computing Technologies (ICCPCT), pp. 1–3. IEEE (2017)
4. Gupta, A., Lin, B.R., Ji, S., Patel, A., Vogel, D.: Replicate and reuse: tangible interaction design for digitally-augmented physical media objects. In: Proceedings of the 2020 CHI Conference on Human Factors in Computing Systems, pp. 1–12 (2020)
5. Hung, C.H., Bai, Y.W., Ren, J.H.: Design and implementation of a door lock control based on a near field communication of a smartphone. In: 2015 IEEE International Conference on Consumer Electronics-Taiwan, pp. 45–46. IEEE (2015)

6. Hung, C.H., Fanjiang, Y.Y., Chung, K.C., Kao, C.Y.: A door lock system with augmented reality technology. In: 2017 IEEE 6th Global Conference on Consumer Electronics (GCCE), pp. 1–2. IEEE (2017)
7. Jeong, J.: A study on the IoT based smart door lock system. In: Information Science and Applications (ICISA) 2016. LNEE, vol. 376, pp. 1307–1318. Springer, Singapore (2016). https://doi.org/10.1007/978-981-10-0557-2_123
8. Kleinman, R.A., Merkel, C.: Digital contact tracing for COVID-19. CMAJ **192**(24), E653–E656 (2020)
9. Kolesau, A., Šešok, D.: Investigation of acoustic features for voice activation problem. In: 2020 IEEE Open Conference of Electrical, Electronic and Information Sciences (eStream), pp. 1–4. IEEE (2020)
10. Krombholz, K., Frühwirt, P., Kieseberg, P., Kapsalis, I., Huber, M., Weippl, E.: QR code security: a survey of attacks and challenges for usable security. In: Tryfonas, T., Askoxylakis, I. (eds.) HAS 2014. LNCS, vol. 8533, pp. 79–90. Springer, Cham (2014). https://doi.org/10.1007/978-3-319-07620-1_8
11. Kwon, T., Na, S.: SwitchPIN: securing smartphone pin entry with switchable keypads. In: 2014 IEEE International Conference on Consumer Electronics (ICCE), pp. 23–24. IEEE (2014)
12. Masood, T., Egger, J.: Augmented reality in support of industry 4.0-implementation challenges and success factors. Robot. Comput. Integr. Manuf. **58**, 181–195 (2019)
13. Masood, T., Egger, J.: Adopting augmented reality in the age of industrial digitalisation. Comput. Ind. **115**, 103112 (2020)
14. Mathew, M., Divya, R.: Super secure door lock system for critical zones. In: 2017 International Conference on Networks & Advances in Computational Technologies (NetACT), pp. 242–245. IEEE (2017)
15. Molnar, D., Wagner, D.: Privacy and security in library RFID: issues, practices, and architectures. In: Proceedings of the 11th ACM Conference on Computer and Communications Security, pp. 210–219 (2004)
16. Mostajeran, F., Steinicke, F., Ariza Nunez, O.J., Gatsios, D., Fotiadis, D.: Augmented reality for older adults: exploring acceptability of virtual coaches for home-based balance training in an aging population. In: Proceedings of the 2020 CHI Conference on Human Factors in Computing Systems, pp. 1–12 (2020)
17. Parekh, P., Patel, S., Patel, N., Shah, M.: Systematic review and meta-analysis of augmented reality in medicine, retail, and games. Visual Comput. Ind. Biomed. Art **3**(1), 1–20 (2020). https://doi.org/10.1186/s42492-020-00057-7
18. Thornton, F., Lanthem, C.: RFID Security. Elsevier (2006)
19. Wang, J., Lounis, K., Zulkernine, M.: CSKES: a context-based secure keyless entry system. In: 2019 IEEE 43rd Annual Computer Software and Applications Conference (COMPSAC), vol. 1, pp. 817–822 (2019). https://doi.org/10.1109/COMPSAC.2019.00120
20. Wazir, W., Khattak, H.A., Almogren, A., Khan, M.A., Din, I.U.: Doodle-based authentication technique using augmented reality. IEEE Access **8**, 4022–4034 (2020)
21. Yahoo: Global RFID market (2021 to 2026) - rising need for contact-tracing solutions due to COVID-19 presents opportunities - researchand-markets.com, March 2021. https://www.yahoo.com/entertainment/global-rfid-market-2021-2026-130000356.html
22. Zhu, F., Grossman, T.: BISHARE: exploring bidirectional interactions between smartphones and head-mounted augmented reality. In: Proceedings of the 2020 CHI Conference on Human Factors in Computing Systems, pp. 1–14 (2020)

Machine Learning-Based Font Recognition and Substitution Method for Electronic Publishing

Ning Li(✉), Huan Zhao, and Xuhong Liu

Beijing Key Laboratory of Internet Culture and Digital Dissemination Research, State Key Laboratory of Digital Publishing Technology, Computer School, Beijing Information Science and Technology University, Beijing 100101, China

Abstract. This study proposes a font recognition algorithm based on a deep convolution neural network and a font substitution algorithm based on texture and grayscale features. The experiments show that the proposed font recognition method can effectively extract font features with a high recognition rate, without the prior knowledge of the text content and with good versatility. The substitution effect of the proposed font replacement method can better satisfy the subjective visual perception of the human eyes and easily expand. The research results can be used to improve the publication quality; ensure the best presentation effect when presented in different platforms; facilitate font retrieval and effectively protect font copyright.

Keywords: Font recognition · Font substitution · CNN · Gabor transformation · Digital publishing

1 Introduction

The quality inspection of publications is an important part of electronic publishing. At present, the quality detection of publications is mostly performed manually, although some automatic detection methods are under development [1–3], with publications generally having strict regulations from content to typesetting and needing to meet the corresponding quality requirements. Most related studies focus on document identification, metadata regularity, correctness of text content, normality of citation, etc. Quality inspection is equally important for official documents and academic papers, among others.

Font detection has always been a weak point in the quality detection of electronic publications. Fonts play a very important role in publications, and some publications have strict font requirements. Fonts also affect one's reading experience. Publication fonts have two basic requirements: 1) to use the specified font to display the corresponding text and 2) if the browser lacks the corresponding font, the best alternative font should be used to display the text. Therefore, the problem we must solve is how to recognize fonts and how to find the best alternative fonts when the specified font is missing.

C. Stephanidis et al. (Eds.): HCII 2021, CCIS 1498, pp. 135–143, 2021.
https://doi.org/10.1007/978-3-030-90176-9_19

Compared with character and handwriting recognition, font recognition has a shorter research history and fewer achievements. Research is classified into two main types: font recognition for 1) text blocks and 2) single characters. The former aims to determine the font type used in a continuous text area. The latter aims to determine the font type of a single character.

Font recognition methods for text blocks can quickly determine the font of a group of characters. The Gabor filter is generally used to extract texture features from image blocks containing more than 40 characters, which have limitations when these consecutive words contain different fonts, however, while the overall recognition rate is high, and the effect is stable, dealing with the situation of mixed typefaces is difficult. Therefore, we need to study the font recognition method for single characters.

Compared with font recognition for text blocks, font recognition for a single character is more flexible and can be used for text blocks, albeit more difficult. Firstly, some characters have fewer strokes and are difficult to use in extracting sufficient features. Secondly, some features are not fully utilized, resulting in a higher misrecognition rate. Thirdly, stroke or texture features should be extracted for each character image, which has a high computational complexity leading to a difficult application.

In recent years, machine learning methods have been widely used in various fields, among which deep learning becomes one of the research hotspots. Deep learning has been gradually applied in font recognition as it expresses the intrinsic data distribution through a multi-layer nonlinear network structure, can extract well the intrinsic features of the input data and can effectively depict the intrinsic information of font images. Wang et al. attempted to construct a DeepFont system based on the convolutional neural network for Roman font recognition. A text image sample library, called AdobeVFR, was then built based on the stacked convolutional auto-encoder technology consisting of both labelled synthetic images and partially labelled real-world images for learning and testing [4, 5]. Tao et al. integrated the principal component layer convolution with the two-dimensional (2D) long-short-term memory (2D LSTM) and developed a principal component 2D LSTM algorithm for font recognition. The former helped remove noise and obtain rational and complete font information. The latter contributed to capturing the contrast between the character trajectory and the background [6]. Meanwhile, Huang et al. proposed a DropRegion method to generate a large number of stochastic variant font samples, whose local regions were selectively disrupted. An Inception font network with two additional convolutional neural network (CNN) structure elements (i.e. a cascaded cross-channel parametric pooling and global average pooling) was also designed. Their method can deal with font recognition for both text blocks and single characters [7]. Wang et al. used the VGG-16 and AlexNet models to recognize the font in natural images. They also designed a transfer learning scheme to alleviate the domain mismatch between synthetic and real-world text images and enhance the font classifier' discrimination and robustness [8].

At present, deep learning-based methods are mainly used for font recognition in natural scenes, with a focus of enhancing the recognition robustness under conditions of blur, distortion and noise interference. We should design a network model with a high generalization ability as font recognition in publishing is different because the quality of the input text images is very high, necessitating the support of a larger font set. In other words, the common features of each font can be effectively extracted through model training. Not much research results in font recognition for publication quality inspection have yet been achieved, which is one of the key contents of this paper.

2 Design of the Network Model for Font Recognition of a Single Character

Achieving great success in pattern recognition, we tried to use the CNN for font recognition. Different from text recognition, attention should be paid to the ability of the network model to extract common font features. For the human eyes, the difference between fonts is generally much smaller than that between characters [9]; thus, we need to build a neural network model that is suitable for font recognition.

Four CNN models, namely AlexNet, VGG, GoogLeNet and ResNet, are mainly used at the present. ResNet is not suitable for font recognition because of its high complexity, large amount of calculation and excessive layers. Both AlexNet and VGG-16 are derived from the LeNet-5 model. The experiments showed that the font recognition rate is very low when using AlexNet, and the model cannot converge when using VGG-16. Therefore, we inferred that simply optimizing and deepening the network layer cannot lead to an efficient extraction of the font features, but will lead to gradient disappearance and explosion. GoogLeNet uses a network-in-network approach of stacking Inception modules to form a network that is substantially different from previous CNNs. Stacking Inception modules increases the depth and width of the overall network and makes good use of the computing resources in the network. GoogLeNet is more suitable for extracting the multi-scale features of fonts. Therefore, we decided to develop the model based on the GoogLeNet and introduce the Inception module structure.

2.1 Font Recognition Model

The GoogLeNet model is a 22-tier network structure consisting of multiple stacks of Inception modules. The multi-scale design of the Inception module is very suitable for the multi-form and -scale distribution characteristics of different fonts in an image space. It receives the input from the first layer and processes the input data by using four convolution cores of different scales. After splicing the data, it obtains the output of the Inception module, thereby realizing the fusion of multi-scale features. Therefore, we based on the Inception module structure to extract the features from the local structures of different fonts at different scales.

The network model was stacked with nine Inception modules (Fig. 1). The closer to the output layer, the more abstract the font features were. For a font feature map near the output layer, it is likely to extract the stroke feature of a font and distribute it centrally in space. Large convolution kernels were used for the feature extraction to reduce spatial centralisation. Therefore, more 3 * 3 and 5 * 5 convolution cores were found near the output layer. However, multiple convolution kernels may cause problems of parameter increase and computational consumption and also lead to overfitting. Therefore, the computational overhead was reduced by adding a 1 * 1 convolution core. The convolution layer first used a 7 * 7 convolution core. The local details were more important in distinguishing the fonts. Therefore, a smaller convolution core was designed to extract the font details. The first layer of the network model used a 5 * 5 convolution core and made a 2 * 2 maximum pooling. After convolution and pooling, local response normalisation was added, and the ReLU activation function was used to prevent overfitting, avoid gradient explosion and accelerate the convergence speed. As for the network feature extraction, two loss layers were added (two large dotted boxes, Fig. 1) to prevent the gradient from disappearing.

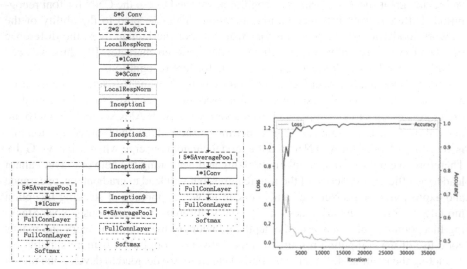

Fig. 1. Network structure for font recognition   **Fig. 2.** Training model trends

The font recognition process is listed below:

1) Building a sample library: for each font type, 6763 characters in the GB 2312 font set are used to generate a binary image of 64 * 64 px for each Chinese character. 2) Pre-training the model parameters: the initialisation parameters are very important because an inappropriate selection of the initialisation parameters may lead to the non-convergence or a gradient explosion of the network model. Therefore, the small font sample library is used to pre-train the model. Moreover, the pre-trained parameters are used as the initial values in formal model training to accelerate the convergence speed of the network model and improve the accuracy rate of the font recognition. 3) Optimizing the network parameters: train the network model and tune the parameters to obtain a converged network model. 4) Recognizing the font by the trained network model obtained in Step 3.

2.2 Optimal Training of the Font Recognition Network Model

The network model must be optimised to extract rich font features and obtain a font recognition model with a strong generalisation ability. We used the back-propagation algorithm to obtain the cost function gradient to the model weights and biases, update the parameters and continuously input the samples until the cost function error was minimised. However, the final solution may not be globally optimal because of the existence of multiple local minimum values on the error surface when using the back propagation algorithm in multi-layer networks. In practical work, we input a small batch of samples to update the parameters, which avoids the disadvantages of frequency and instability. We also update parameters by inputting font images of single characters and avoid the problem of slowness by inputting the whole font image of all characters.

3 Algorithm for Font Similarity Measurement for Font Substitution

The evaluation of the font substitution effect by the human eyes was found to be mainly related to the average grayscale and texture features of the fonts because the font texture reflects the stroke-end features of different fonts at different scales, and the font grayscale reflects the stroke thickness features of different fonts with a certain mutual exclusion. A good font substitution effect must be that the substituted font and the substituting font are close in grayscale and texture. Therefore, with our concern herein being how to extract texture features, how to determine the weight of the grayscale and texture features and how to calculate the font similarity for the font substitution, we measured the similarity for the font substitution based on these two features.

The Gabor filter function has similar properties with human visual primitives; hence, the 2D Gabor filter function waveform is closer to the human visual system's perception. The 2D Gabor transform is widely used to extract the texture features for discrimination purposes in the image processing and computer vision fields [10, 11]. Therefore, we used the Gabor transform to extract the texture features of fonts. Grayscale is defined as the ratio of the number of black pixels in the image to the total number of pixels of the image. The grayscale feature of a font in this study is defined as the average grayscale of all the text block images with the same font. Font substitution focuses on the overall substitution effect; thus, the grayscale and texture features should be based on text blocks. This study selects 10 kinds of fonts with different stroke thicknesses. We first clustered the texture features of the same fonts to observe the texture feature distribution of different fonts and analyzed the relationship between the texture and grayscale feature and human visuals. We then determined the trend between the font texture and human visual similarities and that between the font grayscale and human visual similarities. We found that the human visual similarity is linearly related to the texture and grayscale similarity of the font. Therefore, their relationship can be established by the multiple linear regression model for estimating the font substitution similarity. We can compute the substitution similarity between each font and other fonts. For each font, we can acquire a substitution similarity list, namely a font substitution table, by sorting all the substitution similarity values between it and the other fonts in a descending order. When the reader lacks some fonts, the substitutions with the best visual effects can be obtained by sequentially looking up the font substitution table.

4 Experimental Result

4.1 Font Recognition Effect

We designed two experiments to verify the validity of the proposed method. The first experiment was performed on a small-scale Chinese font set, including the five commonly used fonts. The second experiment was performed on a large-scale Chinese font set.

The experiments were performed on a common font set and a 23-font set used in the literature [12]. The comparisons of the recognition performance are presented below.

1) The average recognition accuracy of the common five-font set was 99.8% (Table 1), whereas that of literature [12] was 92.45%, indicating that the proposed algorithm had a higher recognition accuracy. Table 2 shows the classification confusion matrix.

Table 1. Recognition accuracy on the common font set

	SongTi	FangSong	HeiTi	KaiTi	LiShu
Recognition accuracy (%)	99.71	99.71	100.00	99.77	99.83
Average Recognition accuracy (%)	99.80				

Table 2. Classification confusion matrix

	SongTi	KaiTi	FangSong	HeiTi	LiShu
SongTi	99.89	0.11	0	0	0
KaiTi	0.28	99.72	0	0	0
FangSong	0	0	99.94	0	0
HeiTi	0	0	0	99.9	0.11
LiShu	0	0.06	0	0	99.94

2) The second experiment was performed on a large font set with 23 fonts. The loss value declined while the correct rate gradually increased with an increase in the iterations (Fig. 2). The network model performance was optimised during the training process. The training loss function basically converged when the iteration times exceeded 12,500. Moreover, the recognition accuracy rate became stable, reaching 99.58%.

Table 3 shows the recognition rate on a 23-font set.

Table 3. Recognition rate on a 23-font set (unit: 100%)

	SongTi	FangSong	HeiTi	KaiTi	YouYuan	LiSu
Accuracy of the proposed algorithm	99.83	99.90	99.43	99.77	99.60	99.60
Accuracy of [4]	99.67	98.67	95.33	98.00	98.67	73.67
	STXinwei	FZDaBiaoSong	FZJianZhi	FZShaoEr	FZShuiHei	FZBeiWeiKaiShu
Accuracy of the proposed algorithm	99.26	99.6	99.83	98.92	99.89	99.66
Accuracy of [4]	64.00	88.00	71.33	97.33	80.33	98.00
	FZChaoCuHei	FZGangJinLiShu	HuPo	FZHuaLi	FZGuLi	FZZhiYi
Accuracy of the proposed algorithm	99.60	99.89	99.55	99.03	99.43	99.49
Accuracy of [4]	83.33	95.67	87.33	90.00	79.00	98.67
	YaoTi	FZZhanBiHei	FZPangWa	CuQian	FZMeiHei	Average accuracy
Accuracy of the proposed algorithm	99.66	99.72	99.83	99.89	98.92	99.70
Accuracy of [4]	92.67	89.33	81.00	88.33	87.00	88.49

4.2 Results of Font Substitution

The font substitution rule table is constructed following the font similarity calculation method for the font substitution proposed in Sect. 3. The experiments in Table 4 showed that the font substitution results herein are basically consistent with the visual perception of the human eye.

Table 4. Example of font substitution rules.

Font to be Replaced	Substitute Fonts			
FZDaHei	Substitute Font1: FZHeiTi	Substitute Font2: HeiTi	Substitute Font3: FZCuSong	Substitute Font4: Arial Unicode MS
	Substitute Font5: FZXIHei	Substitute Font6: SongTi	Substitute Font7: STXingKai	Substitute Font8: FZBaoSong
	Substitute Font9: FZWeiBei	Substitute Font10: LiShu	Substitute Font11: FZKaiTi	Substitute Font12: FZFangSong

5 Conclusion

Font recognition and substitution are two key issues in the automatic quality detection of electronic publications and cross-platform browsing. Aiming at these two problems, this study proposed a font recognition algorithm based on a deep convolution neural network and a font substitution similarity calculation method based on texture and grayscale.

Future work can be performed in the following aspects:

1) The following two methods are generally used when using a neural network as a classifier: a) establish one neural network model for each class, and one model can only identify one class; and b) build one neural network model for multiple classes, and one model can identify multiple classes. The first method has a higher recognition rate than the second. However, as the number of font categories increases, a large number of neural networks must be established, the calculation is complicated, and the parameters are difficult to share. For the second method, the model becomes increasingly complicated as the number of categories increases, leading to a decrease in the recognition rate. Currently, although we can successfully identify 20 or 30 fonts using the second method, we must consider the further expansion of font sets by adopting a multi-level neural network scheme in the future. Firstly, we designed herein a neural network to classify the fonts into large categories, such as the Song, Kai and Hei styles. Secondly, we designed some other neural networks that identify the fine classes, such as the network used to identify XiaoBiaoSong, XinSong and CuSong.

2) Currently, the single-character recognition method does not use context information. In the future, the font associations between multiple consecutive texts can be utilised to increase the font recognition accuracy.

Acknowledgements. The authors acknowledge the National Natural Science Foundation of China (Grant: 61672105), National Key R&D Program of China (Grant: 2018YFB1004100) and the Opening Foundation of State Key Laboratory of Digital Publishing Technology.

References

1. Liu, Y.P.: The development and research of word document format-checking plug-in based on VSTO. Comput. Knowl. Technol. (2016)
2. Si, G., Ning, L., Lin, Z.: Method for bibliographic reference format normativity checking. J. Beijing Inf. Sci. Technol. Univ. **32**(1), 44–49 (2017)
3. Yang, Y.: Check the Document Style Method and System, CN 104346319 B (2017)
4. Wang, Z., Yang, J., Jin, H., et al.: DeepFont: a system for font recognition and similarity. In: ACM International Conference on Multimedia, pp. 813–814. ACM (2015)
5. Wang, Z., Yang, J., Jin, H., et al.: DeepFont: identify your font from an image, pp. 451–459 (2015)
6. Tao, D., Lin, X., Jin, L.: Principal component 2-D long short-term memory for font recognition on single chinese characters. IEEE Trans. Cybern. **46**(3), 756–765 (2016)

7. Huang, S.P., Zhong, Z.Y., Jin, L.W., Zhang, S.Y., et al.: DropRegion training of inception font network for high-performance Chinese font recognition. Pattern Recognit. 77 (2018)
8. Wang, Y., Lian, Z., Tang, Y., et al.: Font recognition in natural images via transfer learning. MultiMedia Model. (2018)
9. Ling, X., Guo, S., Gao, F.: Chinese character font recognition based on multi-scale wavelet analysis. Comput. Appl. 26(b06), 21–23 (2006)
10. Hou, Y., Zhou, S., Lei, L., Zhao, L.: Invariant feature with multi-characteristic scales using Gabor filter bank. Acta Electron. Sin. 41(06), 1146–1152 (2013)
11. Li, K., Yin, J., Li, Y.: Local statistical analysis of Gabor coefficients and adaptive feature extraction for face description and recognition. J. Comput. Res. Dev. 9(2), 611–648 (2012)
12. Wang, X.: Optical font recognition of Chinese based on the stroke tip similarity. Acta Scientiarum Naturalium Universitatis Pekinensis 49(1), 54–60 (2013)

Collaborative Explainable AI: A Non-algorithmic Approach to Generating Explanations of AI

Tauseef Ibne Mamun[1(✉)], Robert R. Hoffman[2], and Shane T. Mueller[1]

[1] Michigan Technological University, Houghton, MI, USA
tmamun@mtu.edu
[2] Florida Institute for Human and Machine Cognition, Pensacola, FL, USA

Abstract. An important subdomain in research on Human-Artificial Intelligence interaction is Explainable AI (XAI). XAI attempts to improve human understanding and trust in machine intelligence and automation by providing users with visualizations and other information that explain decisions, actions, and plans. XAI approaches have primarily used algorithmic approaches designed to generate explanations automatically, but an alternate route that may augment these systems is to take advantage of the fact that user understanding of AI systems often develops through self-explanation [1]. Users engage in this to piece together different sources of information and develop a clearer understanding, but these self-explanations are often lost if not shared with others. We demonstrate how this 'Self-Explanation' can be shared collaboratively via a system we call collaborative XAI (CXAI), akin to a Social Q&A platform [2] such as StackExchange. We will describe the system and evaluate how it supports various kinds of explanations.

Keywords: Artificial Intelligence · Explanation tool · System design · Explanation type

1 Introduction

Recent advances in AI systems have created technology that is both more capable and more difficult to understand or predict than previous eras of AI. Consequently, it has become critical to develop explanatory systems (i.e., XAI) that will help users to understand and work with these AI systems. Research using a Naturalistic Decision Making (NDM) approach [3], has suggested parallels between the ways in which we explain complex concepts to ourselves and others, and the needs for XAI. Although most existing XAI systems are algorithm-based, this work suggests a potential role for collaborative explaining and the use of collaboration during the exploratory process. We thus propose a collaborative XAI system (CXAI), in which users pose questions and generate explanations through collaboration that will help the group to understand the AI system. We believe that this collaborative system can enhance and improve existing algorithmic explanation-based systems, and provide communities of users an important resource for understanding a system.

© Springer Nature Switzerland AG 2021
C. Stephanidis et al. (Eds.): HCII 2021, CCIS 1498, pp. 144–150, 2021.
https://doi.org/10.1007/978-3-030-90176-9_20

One justification for the usefulness of a collaborative environment for explanation is that it mirrors well-studied frameworks of pedagogy and learning, allowing opportunities for learners to participate irrespective of their experience or knowledge levels. For example, ICAP (Interactive>Constructive>Active>Passive) framework [4], suggests the most effective modes for learning involve human-human interactivity where students can better understand a particular topic through dialoguing and explaining to one another. Thus, a collaborative explanation system has the potential to benefit the users at a number of levels, from those who interact with others to create explanations, to those who construct explanations, and those who actively explore the system in order to solve particular problems. Thus, CXAI may help users to learn from each other about the AI systems they use. Some of the explanations this can support include: How does an AI system work? What are its shortcomings? What are the reasons for the shortcomings? What are some suggestions, and methods for working around the shortcomings? Thus, CXAI may help provide a user-centric explanation system that does not require algorithms, user models, or complex visualizations, in order to provide important explanations to a user. Furthermore, the explanations elicited may complement those produced by algorithmic approaches, providing a different level of information that is useful and actionable.

2 Background

Although collaborative explanation systems have not been used in XAI, it has precedent in general collaborative systems referred to as social Q&A [2]. Traditional SQA approaches include message boards, platforms such as Yahoo Answers, and programming help boards such as StackExchange. Although the CXAI shares properties with these, it is also intended to help focus users on the particular problems of explaining AI system behaviors.

2.1 Collaboration Learning, and Web-Based Collaboration

The CXAI system supports human-human learning via collaboration, which has been studied in educational settings. Collaborative Learning has a broad meaning. It can be conducted as a pair or in a group, face-to-face or computer-mediated, synchronous, or asynchronous. However, learning via collaboration can be generally described as a situation in which particular forms of interaction among people are expected to occur, which would trigger learning, although there is no guarantee that the expected interactions will occur [5].

Learning in collaboration has been suggested to help in developing higher-level thinking skills [6]. Students can perform at higher levels when asked to work in collaborative situations than when asked to work individually [7]. They also test better when they learn in a collaborative manner [8]. Students develop valuable problem-solving skills by formulating their ideas, discussing them, receiving immediate feedback, and responding to questions and comments [9, 10]. Since the XAI approach advocated here is intended for novel users of an AI system, and one of their goals is gaining problem-solving skills in the context of an AI system, it is promising that collaborative learning has been shown to support these skills in other contexts. Web-based technology is frequently used in the classroom to enrich learning performance, including individual knowledge construction and group knowledge sharing. For example, [11] studied web-based collaborative learning systems in the computer-supported collaborative learning (CSCL) paradigm, which are informed by a rich history of cognitive science research about how students learn. Web-based collaborative environments allow equal opportunities for learners to participate without the limitation on knowledge levels [12]. Learners in web-based collaborative learning believe it is a time-saving and efficient knowledge-sharing system [13]. In addition, five factors have been found to affect users' attitude towards collaborative web learning [14]: system functions, system satisfaction, collaborative activities, learners' characteristics, and system acceptance. The Knowledge Community and Inquiry Model [15] is also relevant, as it involves Web 2.0 technologies where students explore a conceptual domain, express their ideas, and create a collective knowledge base. This type of knowledge base can be used by any future user of an AI system.

2.2 Collaborative Problem Solving

A second collaborative activity supported by the CXAI system is a form of collaborative problem solving: trying to figure out the unknown properties of the AI system together. Problem-solving not only depends on making sense of the behavior of the system but also depends on the division of labor in the group. A number of past systems have been developed to support collaborative problem-solving. For instance, in a web search task, for initial, and synchronous search, a chat-centric view was preferred by 67% of participants in the CoSense tool [16]. This suggests the ability to communicate regarding the problem may be useful for forming explanations about an unknown trait of an AI system as it helps in keeping track of what decisions are made in the group and how each member is performing in the task of problem-solving.

Another important aspect of collaborative problem solving involves how the problem is initially framed and posed to trigger the problem-solving activity. In the initial stage of a collaborative system where problem-solving has not started yet, to initiate problem-solving, specific questions can be useful. Such trigger-questions that initiate explanations include Taxonomic knowledge (What does X mean? What are the types of X?), Sensory knowledge (What does X look like? What does X sound like?), Goal-oriented procedural knowledge (How does a person use/play X?), and Causal knowledge (What causes X? What are the consequences of X? What are the properties of X? How does X affect the sound? How does a person create X?) [17], and similar trigger questions have been examined in the scope of XAI [18].

Collaborative problem-solving tasks also involve both content-free and content-dependent types [19]. Content-free tasks depend on inductive and deductive thinking skills, and content-dependent tasks allow users to draw on knowledge gained through traditional learning areas or subjects. The CXAI mainly supports content-dependent problem solving, because it focuses users on particular cases, errors, and challenges of an AI system. To better enable content-dependent tasks in CXAI, we have implemented specific data fields that allow URL references to specific problems in the AI system, so that the knowledge can be drawn from these references by the users.

2.3 Motivating Users for Explanations

Our proposed system is a modified SQA platform (like Stack Exchange or Stack Overflow), but rather than being a general-purpose system for a wide audience, can serve as an explanation system for AI. The goal is to give users the general advantages of SQA systems while focusing workflow and usability on the particular needs of AI explanations. SQA systems often harness the social context in which people ask, answer, and rate content [2], serving as public or community-based resources and relying on natural language communication [20] rather than extensive algorithmic data, video, or other means. In order to succeed, however, users of an SQA platform need to be sufficiently motivated to interact with the system. A small community or team may be motivated to communicate intrinsically, but other SQA systems have incorporated specific features that encourage contributions.

For example, some SQA sites vet existing contributions and motivate future contributions by awarding points to users [2]. SQA sites typically do not enlist professional or expert answers, though several SQA sites have allowed users to build a reputation within a particular question category and become known as an expert on the site [20]. A user contributes his/her knowledge because of factors including the user's reputation, self-presentation, peer recognition, etc. [21]. Motivating users to contribute is important because, along with having more information, the best answers in an SQA platform are correlated with the consistent participation of users, which can be motivated through points [22] or bounties [23].

3 Human-Centric System Design and Development

To identify the critical elements of a web-based novel explanatory system similar to a social QA platform, we engaged in a collaborative design effort in which members of our research group worked with an initial system to pose and answer explanatory questions about an AI system, and iteratively refined the interface based on this activity. The system has traditional features of a general social QA platform (like StackOverflow or StackExchange) where users can associate keyword(s) to their posts, and also some novel features like a list of topics that can be used to categorize the postings in the system. These topics would be the "triggers" (see Fig. 1) for explanations that have been revealed in the research on the importance of users' goals and needs regarding explanations [18]. These topics can also be used in initiating problem-solving discussed earlier. Once one or more topics were selected, it would serve as metadata to contextualize the user's notes and the responses from other users. This would support other users' subsequent search through the collaborative system. Thus, the artifacts of system development that we examine are not part of a comprehensive user test from a naive user group, but may still be informative.

Another feature we incorporated through the team's feedback is the ability to add URL reference(s) to their posts about the AI system so that other users can understand the posts with the help of the reference link(s). Another is the use of keywords: if a user wanted to create a new post, this could be associated with one or more keywords and topics that help in categorizing and searching posts.

Your post might relate to any of these possibilities. Before typing your post below, check all
of these that you think apply.

Topics ·

HOW IT WORKS

What does it achieve?   What can't it do?

SURPRISES and MYSTERIES

Why did it do that?   Why didn't it do x?

TRICKS & DISCOVERIES

Here's something that surprised me.   Here's a trick I discovered.

How can I help it do better?

TRAPS

What do I have to look out for?   What do I do if it gets something wrong?

How can it fool me?   What do I do if I do not trust what it did?

You can select mutiple topics.

Fig. 1. Topics as 'triggers'

4   Type of Explanations

Although various evaluations of the system are in progress, we examined artifacts from
the initial collaborative development process in order to assess the kinds of explanations
the CXAI may support. Two independent raters classified the explanations based on
popular taxonomy that was described by [24] that identifies five basic explanation types:
What, Why, Why Not, What If, and How To. If a chunk did not answer a question, the
case was rated as 'none'.

Results indicated that independent raters achieved a moderate level of agreement
on the cases, unweighted $\kappa = 0.76$. Results show that the majority of explanations fall
into a 'what'-style explanation type according to [24], these 'what' explanations appear
to support many different purposes, especially describing surprising results, warning
others about mistakes, and advising how to handle certain cases. Notably, relatively few
statements answer 'why' or 'why-not' questions—which would represent justification-
style explanations that are probably the most typical explanations that exist in current
XAI systems. However, there were substantial numbers of explanations identified by the
users as answering 'why questions' that were coded as 'what' explanations. This initial
examination suggests that CXAI may provide different kinds of information than are
typically surfaced with other explanatory systems.

5   Conclusion

In this paper, we have described some of the motivations and iterative design processes
for developing the CXAI system. We believe that the resulting user-centric explanations
may help the users of AI systems to better understand and share knowledge about an AI
system. Future plans include evaluating the effectiveness of collaborative explanations
and improving and evaluating the impact of different SQA features on the quality of
explanations produced by the system.

Acknowledgment and Disclaimer. This research was developed with funding from the Defense Advanced Research Projects Agency (DARPA). This material is approved for public release. Distribution is unlimited. This material is based on research sponsored by the AirForce Research Lab (AFRL) under agreement number FA8650-17-2-7711. Approved for public release, Distribution Unlimited.

References

1. Mueller, S.T., et al.: Principles of explanation in human-AI systems. ArXiv Prepr. ArXiv210204972 (2021)
2. Oh, S.: Social Q&A. In: Brusilovsky, P., He, D. (eds.) Social Information Access. LNCS, vol. 10100, pp. 75–107. Springer, Cham (2018). https://doi.org/10.1007/978-3-319-90092-6_3
3. Klein, G.A.: Naturalistic decision making. Hum. Factors **50**(3), 456–460 (2008)
4. Chi, M.T., Wylie, R.: The ICAP framework: linking cognitive engagement to active learning outcomes. Educ. Psychol. **49**(4), 219–243 (2014)
5. Dillenbourg, P.: What do you mean by collaborative learning? (1999)
6. Webb, N.M.: Group composition, group interaction, and achievement in cooperative small groups. J. Educ. Psychol. **74**(4), 475 (1982)
7. Vygotsky, L.S.: Mind in Society: The Development of Higher Psychological Processes. Harvard University Press (1980)
8. Gokhale, A.A.: Collaborative learning enhances critical thinking. J. Technol. Educ. **7**(1) (1995)
9. Johnson, D.W.: Effectiveness of role reversal: actor or listener. Psychol. Rep. **28**(1), 275–282 (1971)
10. Peterson, P.L., Swing, S.R.: Students' cognitions as mediators of the effectiveness of small-group learning. J. Educ. Psychol. **77**(3), 299 (1985)
11. Koschmann, T.D.: CSCL, Theory and Practice of An Emerging Paradigm. Routledge (1996)
12. Scardamalia, M., Bereiter, C.: Computer support for knowledge-building communities. J. Learn. Sci. **3**(3), 265–283 (1994)
13. Liaw, S.-S.: Considerations for developing constructivist web-based learning. Int. J. Instr. Media **31**, 309–319 (2004)
14. Liaw, S.-S., Chen, G.-D., Huang, H.-M.: Users' attitudes toward Web-based collaborative learning systems for knowledge management. Comput. Educ. **50**(3), 950–961 (2008). https://doi.org/10.1016/j.compedu.2006.09.007
15. Slotta, J.D., Najafi, H.: Supporting collaborative knowledge construction with web 2.0 technologies. In: Mouza, C., Lavigne, N. (eds.) Emerging Technologies for the Classroom. Explorations in the Learning Sciences, Instructional Systems and Performance Technologies, pp. 93–112. Springer, New York (2013). https://doi.org/10.1007/978-1-4614-4696-5_7
16. Paul, S.A., Morris, M.R.: CoSense: enhancing sensemaking for collaborative web search. In: Proceedings of the SIGCHI Conference on Human Factors in Computing Systems, pp. 1771–1780 (2009)
17. Graesser, A.C., Baggett, W., Williams, K.: Question-driven explanatory reasoning. Appl. Cogn. Psychol. **10**(7), 17–31 (1996)
18. Mueller, S.T., Hoffman, R.R., Clancey, W., Emrey, A., Klein, G.: Explanation in human-AI systems: a literature meta-review, synopsis of key ideas and publications, and bibliography for explainable AI, ArXiv Prepr. ArXiv190201876 (2019)
19. Care, E., Griffin, P., Scoular, C., Awwal, N., Zoanetti, N.: Collaborative problem solving tasks. In: Griffin, P., Care, E. (eds.) Assessment and Teaching of 21st Century Skills. Educational Assessment in an Information Age, pp. 85–104. Springer, Dordrecht (2015). https://doi.org/10.1007/978-94-017-9395-7_4

20. Shah, C., Oh, S., Oh, J.S.: Research agenda for social Q&A. Libr. Inf. Sci. Res. **31**(4), 205–209 (2009)
21. Jin, J., Li, Y., Zhong, X., Zhai, L.: Why users contribute knowledge to online communities: an empirical study of an online social Q&A community. Inf. Manage. **52**(7), 840–849 (2015)
22. Nam, K.K., Ackerman, M.S., Adamic, L.A.: Questions in, knowledge in? A study of Naver's question answering community. In: Proceedings of the SIGCHI Conference on Human Factors in Computing Systems, pp. 779–788 (2009)
23. Zhou, J., Wang, S., Bezemer, C.-P., Hassan, A.E.: Bounties on technical Q&A sites: a case study of stack overflow bounties. Empir. Softw. Eng. **25**(1), 139–177 (2020)
24. Lim, B.Y., Dey, A.K.: Assessing demand for intelligibility in context-aware applications. In: Proceedings of the 11th International Conference on Ubiquitous Computing, pp. 195–204 (2009)

Toothbrush Force Measurement and 3D Visualization

Kasumi Sakuma[1], Haicui Li[2], and Lei Jing[2,3(✉)]

[1] The Undergraduate School of Computer Science, The University of Aizu,
Aizuwakamatsu, Japan
[2] The Graduate School of Computer Science, The University of Aizu,
Aizuwakamatsu, Japan
[3] Research Center for Advanced Information Science and Technology (CAIST),
The University of Aizu, Aizuwakamatsu, Japan
leijing@u-aizu.ac.jp

Abstract. In recent years, a variety of oral care products have been developed. In this research, we propose a toothbrushing system that can detect force from the force-sensitive sensor. The results of the experiments show that the membrane force sensors attached to the brush side have a higher detection rate of force than the acceleration sensor.

Keywords: Toothbrush · 3D modeling · Pressure estimation · Accelerometer · Pressure sensor

1 Introduction

Tooth brushing is one of the most important lifestyle habits. It has been reported that oral diseases are associated with various systemic diseases. Daily removal of plaque through tooth brushing can prevent tooth decay and periodontal disease, leading to overall health maintenance. Therefore, it is very important for human health to learn how to brush teeth correctly.

Nowadays, there are several types of electric toothbrushes. Force sensors, inertial sensors, and cameras are built into the handle. These can prevent the user from brushing their teeth unevenly and check if the proper force is being applied to the teeth. However, electric toothbrushes can be expensive, require batteries, and damage teeth and gums if they are not the right size or vibrate too strongly. The purpose of this research is to improve the tooth brushing system developed in our previous studies. In this research, we propose a simple method to detect the value of force during tooth brushing. Since it is difficult to attach a force sensor to the surface of a tooth, we aimed to develop a system to detect the value of force during tooth brushing by attaching a force sensor to the handle of a toothbrush. Currently, most evaluations of whether teeth have been brushed or not are based on the use of plaque stains. In addition, brushing force can only be judged from the spread of the brush bristles, the degree of gum damage, and tooth loss. Therefore, we aimed to develop a system that can provide visual feedback on a computer screen.

© Springer Nature Switzerland AG 2021
C. Stephanidis et al. (Eds.): HCII 2021, CCIS 1498, pp. 151–158, 2021.
https://doi.org/10.1007/978-3-030-90176-9_21

Therefore, the paper will focus on two issues: How to measure toothbrushing force applied through the bristle axis; how to intuitively display the results. This research uses an Arduino and two membrane force-sensitive sensors to detect force. Sliders are placed next to the 3D model of the tooth that indicates the forces. The value of the slider will change according to the value of the force acquired in real-time. It allows the users to intuitively know how much force is being applied to the teeth.

2   User Model and Related Works

2.1   Model

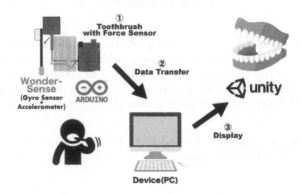

Fig. 1. Model of application

Figure 1 shows the application model. We aim to create a simple system using a regular toothbrush, an inertial sensor, and membrane force sensors. First, the user brushes his or her teeth using a toothbrush with an acceleration sensor and a force-sensitive sensor attached to the handle. Next, the device receives data from the acceleration sensor and force sensors and estimates the value of the force and the area of the tooth that was brushed. Finally, the system displays them as a slider and a 3D model.

2.2   Related Research

In the previous research [1], an inertial sensor attached to the handle of a toothbrush is used to detect the trajectory of tooth brushing. A six-axis inertial sensor attached to the handle of the toothbrush detects the movement of the toothbrush. The upper, lower, left, and right teeth are divided into 16 regions, and the motion is used to determine which region is being brushed. Furthermore, in a previous research [2], we calculated the force on the teeth from the amplitude of the acceleration data obtained and displayed the value of the force on the screen using Unity and the discoloration of the 3D model.

There are some problems with the conventional system. First of all, it is inconvenient to run separate programs for the tooth brushing area and the force detection and display. Also, the force calculated from the acceleration has a large error. In paper [3], a small force sensor is directly attached to a tooth model, which may be highly accurate, but it is not suitable for measuring force during daily tooth brushing because the sensor is attached to only one tooth and the transmitter needs to be attached in the mouth. In the paper [4], a strain gauge was attached to the toothbrush to measure the brushing force from the strain. However, it was impossible to prepare a load cell that could be used with Arduino, was large enough to be placed between the brush and the handle, and was water-resistant.

3 System Design

3.1 Basic Ideas

First, detect the force on the toothbrush handle from the membrane force sensor using Arduino. We display sliders on the Unity screen that change the position of the bar according to the brushing force. Besides, we discolor the 3D model of the tooth corresponding to the tooth area that has been brushed.

3.2 Outline of the System

Figure 2 shows an overview of this system. This system is composed of four parts. First, from the electrical resistance obtained from each force sensor, the value of each force is estimated using the equation obtained from the regression analysis. Second, the force on the brush, i.e., the force on the teeth (f0), is obtained by subtracting the force (f2) obtained from the force sensor attached to the brush side from the force (f1) obtained from the force sensor installed on the opposite side of the brush. Third, acceleration data is received from an acceleration sensor. Finally, the estimated area and the value of the forces are displayed on a 3D model in Unity.

3.3 Data Collection

The membrane force sensor used FSR406 [5]. We use acceleration data from Wonder Sense Wi-Fi (WS) developed in our lab for region detection and acceleration-based force detection. WS sends an array of data to the system via Wi-Fi. This gives the acceleration (A) and angular velocity (Gy). Both sampling frequencies 100 Hz.

3.4 Data Processing Method

In order to estimate the value of the force, we had to do some data processing. In this section, we describe these methods. Figure 3 shows an image of membrane

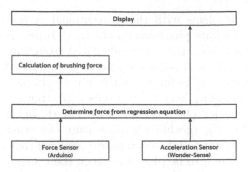

Fig. 2. System outline

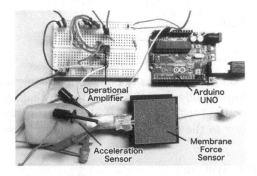

Fig. 3. Force detection toothbrush system

force sensors. They are robust polymer thick film (PTF) sensors whose resistivity decreases as the force applied to the sensor surface increases. They have an active area of 38 mm square.

First, a weight is placed on top of the membrane force sensor. The weight is increased by 50 g from 0 g to 1 kg. The average value of the electrical resistance of each of the 50 weights is recorded. From this average voltage resistance, the regression equation is determined using regression analysis. A power regression is used for the regression equation, and the graph is shown in Fig. 4.

The regression equation was determined as follows, with weight as F and electrical resistance as R.

$$F = 1.342e^5 R^{(-0.8.122e^{-1})} \tag{1}$$

3.5   Display

In this system, Unity is used for 3D visualization. First, the force on the teeth is calculated by subtracting the value obtained from the force sensor on the brush side from the value obtained from the force sensor on the backside of the toothbrush. The brushing force estimated from the membrane force sensors and the force estimated from the acceleration value obtained from WS are indicated

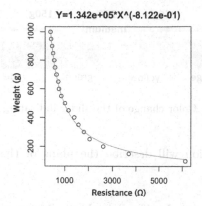

Fig. 4. Regression graph

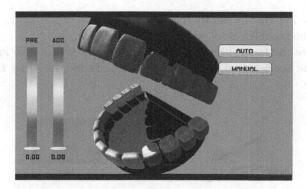

Fig. 5. Display

by the movement of the color slider, respectively. Simultaneously, the brushing area of the teeth is determined from the acceleration data of WS, and the discoloration of each tooth part of the 3D model is displayed. The color change of the force slider is defined by six colors. The color definitions are shown in Fig. 6; when a tooth is brushed with a reasonable force of 150 g to 200 g, the slider bar points to green. With these color changes, the user can visually know whether he is brushing his teeth with proper force or not.

4   Evaluation

4.1   Experiment

In this research, we conducted two experiments.

1. Experiment to determine the accuracy of the value of force estimated from the membrane force sensor (expt. 1).
2. An experiment to determine the usability of this system (expt. 2)

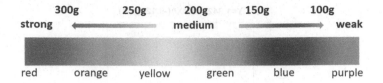

Fig. 6. Color change of the slider indicating force

Next, each subsection will describe the plans of the experiment and the results.

Plan of the Experiment. In this research, we did two experiments to evaluate the accuracy of our method. Five subjects participated in this experiment.

– Experiment 1. Figure 7 shows the situation of the experiment.
    1 Move the toothbrush on the electronic balance.
    2 Compare the force (f0) obtained from the force sensor, the force obtained from the acceleration, and the force actually measured by the electronic balance.

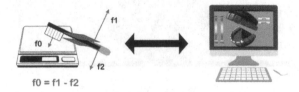

Fig. 7. Experimental situation (expt. 1)

– Experiment 2
    1. The subjects brushed their teeth using the model.
    2. We asked them to evaluate the usability of the system.
The following items were used as questionnaires. The subjects were asked to rate each question on a 5-point scale.

> 1. Ease of use of the system.
> 2. Evaluation of screen display.
> 3. Whether the color slider indicating brushing force is easy to understand intuitively.
> 4. Accuracy of force detection.

Result

- Experiment 1. Figure 8 shows the experimental results. In the membrane force sensor, the average error is 49.47 g, while the average error of the acceleration sensor is 232.04 g. It means that the force sensor has less error and is more suitable for measuring brushing force. However, for the same membrane force sensor, the error was much larger for the small force sensor of 10 mm. It is probably because the small force sensor has a smaller area than the finger touches, and the finger position shifts from the detection part of the sensor, resulting in an error.

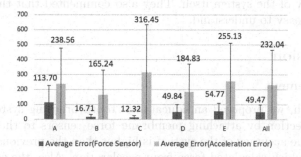

Fig. 8. Average error

- Experiment 2. Figure 9 shows result of this experiment. Each number within brackets corresponds to each question number in Sect. 4.1.1. We did it for five people. The following items are the definition of the numbers in Fig. 9.

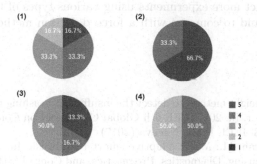

Fig. 9. Usability

> 5: Extremely satisfied
> 4: Moderately satisfied
> 3: Neither satisfied nor dissatisfied
> 2: Slightly dissatisfied
> 1: Extremely dissatisfied

As for the evaluation of usability, 50% of the respondents were dissatisfied with the accuracy of force acquisition, and the acquisition rate of correct brushing force was low. However, 50% of the respondents were satisfied with the usability of the system itself. They also commented that the screen was simple and easy to understand.

5 Conclusion

5.1 Achievement

In this research, we proposed an educational tooth brushing system equipped with force detection by attaching membrane force sensors to the handle of a toothbrush. The accuracy of the system is higher than the previous force detection method, which calculated force from acceleration. Also, the screen display in the 3D model became more visually apparent. However, it must be said that the error in force detection is still large.

5.2 Future Work

There are two issues to be addressed in the future. The first is to use more stable force sensors, such as strain gauges, to detect force values accurately. The second is to conduct more experiments using various types of toothbrushes and toothbrush grips and to come up with a force detection method corresponding to each.

References

1. Jing. L.: A lightweight method to detect the insufficient brushing regions using a six-axis inertial sensor. In: 2017 IEEE 6th Global Conference on Consumer Electronics (GCCE), pp. 1–3. IEEE Press, Nagoya (2017)
2. Stark, B., Samarah, M.: Mac7: adaptive smart toothbrush. In: 2018 International Conference on Sensing, Diagnostics, Prognostics, and Control (SDPC), pp. 153–158. IEEE Press, Xi'an (2018)
3. Watanabe, T., Nakamura, J.: A study of toothbrushing pressures by the specifically designed intraoral telemetry system. Journal of the Japanese Society of Periodontology **27**(4), 779–793 (1985)
4. Cshima, Y.: Effects of toothbrushing habits and toothbrushing force on toothbrushing. J. Dent. Health **17**(3), 119–138 (1967)
5. Akidzuki Electronic: Trade. Membrane Force Sensor (38 mm Square Active Area), September 2010. http://www.ncbi.nlm.nih.gov

A Study on the Creativity of Algorithm Art Using Artificial Intelligence

Ryan Seo[⊠]

Seoul Foreign School, Seodaemun-gu, Seoul 03723, South Korea
ryan.seo.23@seoulforeign.org

Abstract. Algorithmic art, otherwise known as generative art, is gaining popularity as a new medium for aesthetic creation using computer-generated automation. It is also seen as a potentially powerful platform toward enhancing the understanding of AI. Algorithmic art can be interpreted in a straightforward manner, translations of naturalistic elements within our society through algorithms is something that speaks truths to us and makes ask question things. Not only is generative art reflecting specific naturistic elements of society and our environment, but it also is a method of understanding how AI units function, how they process visual perceptions of our world. In this paper, I have shown that algorithmic art has existed for much longer than most people know. Algorithmic art has proven that the process of creating art and perceiving reality with machines is extraordinarily parallel to the creation of particular and historical forms of contemporary art and the perception of humans.

Keywords: Algorithmic art · Generative art · Creativity · Artificial intelligence

1 Introduction

Algorithmic art, otherwise known as generative art, is gaining popularity as a new medium for aesthetic creation using computer-generated automation. It is also seen as a potentially powerful platform toward enhancing the understanding of AI. The use of AI to create art has not evolved without causing some controversy: firstly, algorithmic art has a reputation for being controversial in terms of the value of the artwork it produces; and secondly, algorithmic art is seen as fake by many artists as the creative process is being undertaken by a computer. In this paper I will show how algorithmic art has been around for much longer than most people know.

However, it's not that algorithmic art diminishes creativity in contemporary art, but rather exists as an evolution of influences that have been apparent throughout the history of creativity and the history of art in particular. By exploring the work of some notable mathematical artists and important periods of aesthetic creation across the world and throughout history, this paper recognizes the significant connection algorithmic art has with the traditional mathematical structure of some forms of contemporary art.

© Springer Nature Switzerland AG 2021
C. Stephanidis et al. (Eds.): HCII 2021, CCIS 1498, pp. 159–164, 2021.
https://doi.org/10.1007/978-3-030-90176-9_22

2 Historical Background of Algorithmic Art

2.1 Islamic Art

Algorithmic art has a significant background of influences that is often ignored but that is evidencable as being established on the connection between mathematical structures and contemporary art. Artificial intelligence is extraordinary good at calculation and following instructions. This is why its aesthetic structures appear to replicate one of the most historical and methodical art forms to date: Islamic art. This unique artistry incorporates geometrical patterns and precise calculations to create correlating infinity-like artworks. It was during the golden age of Islamic discoveries when discoveries in math and science became public knowledge. These discoveries leaked onto Islamic architecture and were utilized in creating mind-bending patterns (see Fig. 1).

The geometrical and organic style of Islamic art was known as arabesque. This form of art was considered to represent the transcendent, invisible and perfect God. Some historians believe that mistakes in the repetition of patterns in some Islamic art were intended to represent the imperfect and incomparable nature of humanity compared to God. However, computers are great at designing structures with a perfect and clear form. In other words, a 21st century computer could be perceived as the equivalent of the Muslims' God: invisible, transcendent, and perfect.

Islamic art became a fundamental symmetrical form of art that influenced the way beauty was perceived. Many contemporary artists have been influenced by it, even going as far as replicating it in some of the most famous artworks to date.

As Islamic art influenced and structured the mathematical context of some forms of contemporary art, it also shares the precision and flawlessness of generative art (Fig. 2).

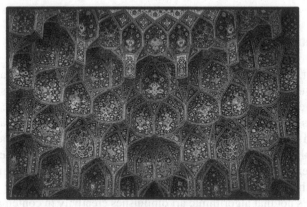

Fig. 1. Islamic, or arabesque, art and decoration is characterized by intertwining plants and abstract curvilinear motifs [1].

2.2 Renaissance Art

User Western art has a very culturally diverse collection of artists and artworks that reflect the many chronological stages in development that have had an impact on society. One

Fig. 2. Example of algorithmic art, Ryan Seo, <between hot and cold> 2019

of the most prominent stages in the development in art and culture to utilize math was the renaissance period.

The renaissance period was very expansive: development thrived on discoveries in music, art, literature, and science. During this period, many artists used these discoveries to inspire their artworks. The most renowned and famous artist to exploit this tactic is Leonardo Da Vinci. His world-famous artwork, the *Vitruvian Man* (see Fig. 3), is undoubtedly a piece of art that employed relevant mathematical patterns and coordinated scaling to create an organized and creative masterpiece. Art is always perceived as an abstract way of channeling creativity, but, in reality, it can be a very flexible platform for polymaths such as Leonardo Da Vinci to share his perspective on the personal experiences and philosophical factors of reality.

Another artist that greatly incorporated math in his art to increase the aesthetic pleasures of his artwork is Michelangelo. This expressive genius is known to have created many sculptures, paintings, and structures that combine his imaginative style and precise calculations. Although Michelangelo seems to be an artist that disregards precision and relies on spontaneous creations, he uses a consistent pattern throughout his projects. This pattern is called the Golden Ratio; in mathematics, two quantities are in the golden ratio if their ratio is the same as the ratio of their sum to the larger of the two quantities (see Fig. 4). When estimated, the golden ratio is approximately 1.6 and is found in artworks such as *The Creation of Adam*. The golden ratio is uniquely found in many natural objects such as snail shells and flower petals, something that has always puzzled scientists. Bizarrely, this rule is frequently utilized by many famous architects, artists, and in the composition of music.

By looking at one of the most influential art movements, we can conclude that math was significantly exploited in highly influential Western art such as that developed during the Renaissance. Algorithmic art follows the same principles these renowned artists used af it to match it with the modern digital era that we live in today.

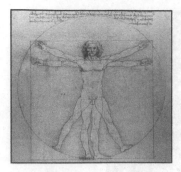

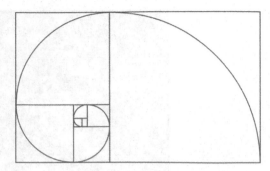

Fig. 3. Vitruvian Man by Leonardo da Vinci (c. 1490).

Fig. 4. The golden ratio

2.3 Contemporary Influences

Math and art have a surprising relationship in not only traditional and major art movements, but they also have a unique relationship when it comes to op art. Op art is a movement that consists of mind-bending illusions intended to deceive our brains into seeing something different than what is actually present in reality, either on the canvas or visual space created by the op artist. This genre of art is consistently associated with math because of the requirement of precise calculations and specifically oriented patterns to create its effect.

One of the most inspirational artists to create op art is Bridget Riley; she has made countless original pieces of op art that introduced a whole new way of interpreting art using unorthodox mathematics. One of her many artworks that sufficiently represent mathematics integrated in art are her series known as The Stripe Paintings made during a long period from 1961 to 2014. Within these striped optical illusions, Riley replicates and balances mathematical method with randomness. She uses two forms that greatly determine the effectiveness of her artwork: global and local entropy. She is known to have integrated these unique systems of depiction within her overall methodical way of producing art. This greatly connects with the idea of algorithmic art as it too is very methodical and specific when producing the lines of code. However, when this methodical code runs on the generative platform, it is known to create randomly generated and unique patterns that appeal to the eye much in the same way that optical illusions deceive our mind to produce something beautiful and appealing.

Much like Bridget Riley, there are many various artists that lead the influential movement of the integration of math in artistic forms. These contemporary artists are known to be the earliest dictators of algorithmic art, they include Sol Lewitt, Frank Stella, Maurits Cornelis Escher, and Grace Degennaro. These contemporary artists are known to be some of the most renowned and respected mathematical artists of the 20th century, when abstract art was really starting to take over the perception of how art was represented (Fig. 5).

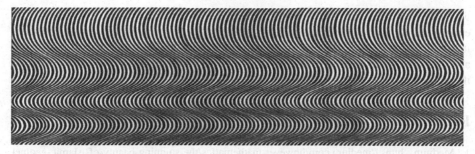

Fig. 5. Bridget Riley, composition with circles 6 (2008) [2]

2.4 Computer-Generated Art

Computer generated art started during the 1960's when the first significant step towards the development of computers arose. Since then, Computer generated art has developed rapidly. The 1980s to 1990s were the most significant stages of computer art development. As computers were discovered to have diverse functionalities, private businesses such as Adobe (launched in 1982), which developed a new form of imagery called Vector, and Microsoft utilized specific aspects to make art within a different platform. The age of digital automatization held an advantage when conveniently portraying the creation of art. As digital art was becoming more widespread and sparked realization in individual artists about the convenience of this format, people started to appreciate and acknowledge the integration of digital art software into the contemporary scene. However, as the 21st century approached, the works of Manfred Mohr and the specific algorithms he utilized were being recognized, coding programs typically used for Website building and systematic online procedures such as Javascript were integrated into translating contemporary art to surreal digital depictions.

Although digital generative art can be interpreted in a straightforward manner, translations of naturalistic elements within our society through algorithms is something that speaks truths to us and makes ask question things. Not only is generative art reflecting specific naturistic elements of society and our environment, but it also is a method of understanding how AI units function, how they process visual perceptions of our world. Generative art is often seen as a straightforward program that consists of various processes and revisions. However, the truth is contrary to these typical stereotypes that categorize algorithms being part of programming and far from integral as an artistic genre.

3 Conclusion

Undoubtedly, the full potential of AI and the similarities between us and automated machines have yet to be discovered. However, generative art has proven that the process of creating art and perceiving reality with machines is extraordinarily parallel to the creation of particular and historical forms of contemporary art and the perception of humans. Society has designed algorithmic art influenced by previous art movements such as Islamic patterns, and mathematical artists that defied the laws of creativity. Generally, we expect generative art to feel artificial and monotone; however, from observations and experimentations in the overall nature of AI and art pieces utilizing automated software, it is conclusive that whether we believe it or not, AI is approaching the point of being able to replicate the human mind and contemporary art is just at beginning to discover its full potential in terms of artistic production.

References

1. Medium. https://medium.com/however-mathematics/the-stunning-beauty-of-islamic-geometric-patterns-4fb57ed5644a. Accessed 20 Aug 2020
2. FRIEZE. https://www.frieze.com/article/seeing-believing-1. Accessed 21 May 2021
3. Bailey, J.: Augmenting creativity - decoding AI and generative art. Artnome, artnome, 21 October 2019. https://www.artnome.com/news/2019/10/21/augmenting-creativity-decoding-ai-and-generative-art. Accessed 20 Aug 2020
4. Boundless Art History: Lumen (2005). https://www.courses.lumenlearning.com/boundless-arthistory/chapter/introduction-to-islamic-art. Accessed 20 Aug 2020
5. Chris, N.: A beginner's guide to generative adversarial networks (GANs), pathmind (2017). https://www.pathmind.com/wiki/generative-adversarial-network-gan. Accessed 20 Sep 2020
6. Lamb, B.: https://www.thoughtco.com/biography-of-frank-stella-minimalist-artist-4177975. Accessed 20 Aug 2020
7. Leonardo and Mathematics: https://www.monalisa.org/2012/09/12/leonardo-and-mathematics-in-his-paintings. Accessed 20 Aug 2020
8. Victoria and Albert Museum: Online Museum, A History of Computer Art. www.vam.ac.uk/content/articles/a/computer-art-history. Accessed 21 May 2021

An Approach to Monitoring and Guiding Manual Assembly Processes

Benjamin Standfield(✉) and Denis Gračanin(✉)

Virginia Tech, Blacksburg, VA 24060, USA
{bsta7599,gracanin}@vt.edu

Abstract. With the dawn of Industry 4.0, companies are constantly looking for ways to digitize their work flows in order to quantify, monitor, and improve work in industrial settings. While some processes, such as those using computer numerical control machinery, are either easy to embed sensors into or already have sensors embedded that are providing information, there still are core processes taking place in industrial settings that do not have easy ways to retrieve data from. One such process is the manual assembly process. In addition to the difficulty in retrieving data from assembly processes, the assemblies that rely on human operation with simple tools rather than machining centers are more difficult to immerse in Industry 4.0 practices due to its primarily offline nature. To better address this issue, we propose an approach and describe implementation of the corresponding system that is capable of providing information to assemblers based on data received during an active process. Specifically, the system informs the assembler of the next steps in the assembly process based on what the platform determines has already been done. In order to accomplish this, a convolutional neural network is used to analyze images on a camera that will be overseeing the physical assembly process. In this way, there will be a live digital record of the assembly process taking place as well as some, albeit basic, interaction between the assembler and the overarching system monitoring the process.

Keywords: Human computer interaction · Internet of Things · Industrial Internet of Things · 3D printing · Assembly · Machine learning · Convolutional neural network

1 Introduction

Human computer interaction (HCI) brings together a number of disciplines. One such discipline is industrial engineering that includes a number of processes and technologies than can benefit from HCI. HCI research is primarily focused on humans and how computers and electronic systems can best serve their needs [14] in a way that is as seamless as possible [10]. Stephanidis et al. [14] further identify that seven major topics of focus in HCI include human-technology symbiosis; human-environment interaction; ethics, privacy and security; well-being, health,

© Springer Nature Switzerland AG 2021
C. Stephanidis et al. (Eds.): HCII 2021, CCIS 1498, pp. 165–176, 2021.
https://doi.org/10.1007/978-3-030-90176-9_23

and eudaimonia; accessibility and universal access; learning and creativity; and social organization and democracy. Our research addresses mostly the first two topics.

There is a large push for using data analysis techniques for quantifying processes, improving processes, or even scheduling tasks. While this is simple in the cases of many processes utilizing computer numerical control machinery as such machines generate and log their own data, this becomes more complicated in situation where such data collecting machines are either absent, in part or entirely, from the process. One example of such a process are assembly operations where, in some cases, the assembly procedure is too complicated to completely automate using robots within a cost effective budget.

Acceptance of the use of augmented reality (AR) in manual assembly processes has been studied and shown to be both desired and effective [4,9,11,12,16]. Furthermore, the use of AR for presenting instructions, even for those with cognitive abilities, makes tasks easier to perceive and understand [18]. Outside of assembly processes, AR is also being researched for improving other human involved processes such as those belonging to the maintenance category which are similar in nature to assembly [3].

While AR-based approaches mostly use head mounted displays such as Microsoft's HoloLens [7], we use a simple monitor for information display. This has the benefit of cheaper deployment with the trade off of requiring more work for the assembler to view the information, for example, head turning. Also, AR has been shown to increase mental strain with long exposure [5]. As a result, by using a monitor instead of a head mounted display, the assembler can reduce AR exposure by looking away from the display when information is not necessary.

2   Related Work

The use of AR in assembly processes is a currently a trending research area. From 2017 to 2020, on average over hundred papers were published per year showing a clear rising interest in the topic. To this point, Agati et al. [1] provide a set a guidelines, with respect for usability, cognitive load, economy, and the corporation, for using AR in manual assembly processes in the context of Industry 4.0. A key performance indicator of assembly processes, especially in industrial settings, is the speed at which the process completes. Generally speaking, the faster the process, the more profitable the process is for corporations. A study by Wang et al. [19] shows that AR has a positive benefit to assembly speed.

One such example is Tsai et al.'s work [17] where an AR system composed of a multi-template AR unit, 3D model assembly unit, and a hand gesture interaction unit is used in order to teach a simple assembly processes to a group of participants who generally had a good background in mechanical design. The students found the teaching method to be both useful and usable according to a survey participants took after participating in an assembly using the system.

More on the side of information portrayal, Petrone et al. [9] performed a study in which it was found that video instructions generally made its easier for assemblers to complete assemblies than AR in low-complexity tasks. However, AR tended to perform better for conveying instructions in higher complexity tasks than video.

Tainaka et al.'s [16] work also sheds some light on this double edged bladed nature of AR for presentation where it is shown that some participants in an assembly process struggled due to information overload, specifically, the display sometimes blocked important information the participants were trying to look at. This is further supported by Schuster et al. [12] work where it was determined that AR lead to decreased mean assembly time when compared to not using AR. In addition to AR for providing instructions in a easy and readable manner, it has also been used with the goal of increasing part quality [3].

While AR dominates assembly process monitoring, it has clear drawbacks, such as in the reliability domain, as it is a relatively new technology compared to some of the older methods such as image recognition. For example, Gogolák et al. used wireless sensor networks [6] for assembly process monitoring in the context of Industry 4.0. They consider this to be a general solution to assembly supervision after a study was performed under both simulated and live conditions.

On a larger scale, Aoyama et al. [2] extended the monitoring concept to ship building cutting and sub-assembly by designing a system in order visualize the processes taking place. This monitoring took place by running image analysis algorithms on video captured in several locations though out the shipbuilding factory. Obinata et al. [8] created a assembly processes guidance system that aims to reduce error by tracking human movements and warn of an approaching error before it occurs by using a RGB-D camera. The system itself has high, 98%, accuracy for detection within the workspace itself, but errors are currently limited to skipped procedures and misplaced parts.

3   Problem Definition

The problems to be addressed can be grouped into three categories:

1. Manual assembly process can't effectively quantify or summarize work done and work in progress.
2. Image processing enabled by machine learning has high accuracy, but training can take a long time when data collection and labeling is included in the process.
3. Assembly instructions are static, and in some cases, hard to read.

For the first category of problems, while one could quantify statistics regarding the manual process, there are two options: either assemblers record what they are doing or another person must watch and record what happens. For the first option, the time taken out of assembling parts and put into recording would, over time, lead to reduced productivity. The second option would increase the total cost of the process as another person would need to be hired.

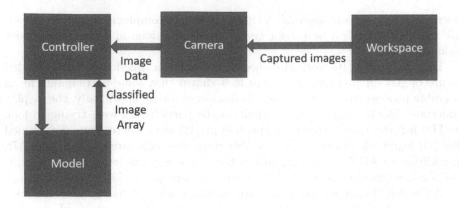

Fig. 1. An illustration of the proposed approach.

For the second category of problems, when using machine learning for image classification, prediction is relatively fast, training the model is typically exponentially more time consuming, but most of the time goes into the data collection and processing for training. Furthermore, when introducing new assembly process, data needs to collected and models need to be retrained leading to downtime of the machine learning solution.

The third category of problems refers to a key issue that arises when there are a set of instructions for the assembler to follow and the assembler needs to find out how to move to the next step. If the instructions are written in such a way where they are hard to read at a glance, the assembler would need to jump through large amounts of text in order to reach the instructions relevant to the stage of assembly the assembler is currently performing. This results in wasted time, and in the worse case, a wasted part if the assembler were to mistakenly jump to the wrong step in the instructions.

4   Proposed Approach

Figure 1 illustrates the proposed approach that addresses the three categories of problems.

Controller is responsible for processing video stream from the camera recording the assembly process and sending the results to the machine learning *Model*. Afterwards, the controller will be responsible for interpreting information from the model to determine the assembly stage and present relevant information to the assembler.

Model is responsible for determining what objects relevant to the assembly are currently within view. When relevant objects are sent to the controller, the controller should be capable of determining what the assembler should do next.

An alternative consideration is using a mobile platform [13,15], but the additional complexity introduced with different camera positions and changing backgrounds isn't necessary for a static workspace.

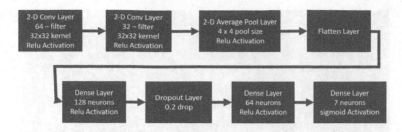

Fig. 2. Neural network architecture.

The controller of the process is responsible for first reading an image captured from the camera and splitting it into 64 images of equal sizes. The camera overseeing the process is capturing images at 1920×1080 resolution and each image is split 8 times on each axis of the images. This results in 64 sub-images with 240×135 resolution. Each of these images is then fed into neural network to determine what, if any, relevant objects are within the sub-images. After classification of each sub-image, the images is reassembled and boxes are drawn around relevant objects of the complete image.

Additionally, the controller keeps track of which objects, if any has been detected throughout the process. As for the determination of the current stage of assembly, the model works off the assumption that one will not go backwards in the during the assembly process that consist of stages. With respect to this, when the model determines that a new stage of the assembly has been reached, it will, regardless of probability, assume that any objects detected can not belong to previous stages.

When presenting the fully classified image to the assembler, the controller merges classified boxes to present the part that is furthermost along the process. This means that if, for example, there is an object in stage 2 next to and object in stage 1, the box will surround both objects and present it as stage 2. At a higher level, the model assumes that every time a stage is reached, if the basic components composing that object are seen, the object must be the object created by that stage.

The machine learning model for classifying assembly stages is a convolutional neural network (CNN) training to detect each of the individual parts of the assembly as well as the part combinations leading to the fully assembled product. The architecture for the model is shown in Fig. 2, and is based on Tensorflow's recommended CNN architecture for image classification.

The model is trained to take in 240×135 resolution images and determine the likelihood that the image falls under any part of the assembly with a probability from 1 (certain to be a specific part) to 0 (certain not to be a specific part). The probabilities of each class is determined with an output 10-dense layer using a Sigmoid activation function where the parameter is however many classes the model is trained to detect. A Sigmoid output was layer was used in place of a soft

Fig. 3. 3D assembly.

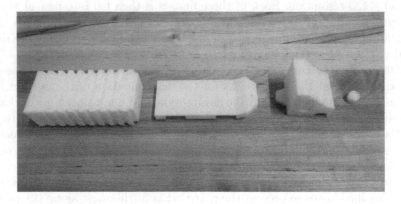

Fig. 4. Assembly components (from left to right): cargo, cargo base, cabin, and wheel.

max layer due to the high probability of unknown objects coming into camera view during actual usage.

Should an unknown object come into view, a soft max layer would attempt to classify it as one of the known objects without any indication that it doesn't fit any of the classes. In order to function correctly, the model is trained to detect four things, the area in which the assembly takes place, limbs (arms and hands), the basic parts of the assembly, and the sub assemblies of the completed part.

5   Experiment

In order to quantify the reliability of the system, an experiment was designed using a 3D printed assembly. The assembly to be created is a static toy truck without any moving parts (Fig. 3). The assembly possesses nine total parts and

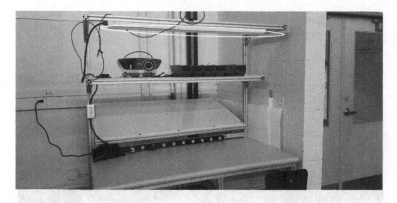

Fig. 5. Experiment work space, light (red), and camera (blue). (Color figure online)

four unique parts (Fig. 4). These parts include the cabin, cargo base, cargo, and wheels.

In order to complete the assembly, the assembly will need to attach two wheel to the cabin (stage 1), four wheels to the cargo base (stage 2), place the cargo onto the cargo base (stage 3), and attach the cargo base to the cabin (stage 4).

Each of these parts were placed within the assembly area and the training data was collected by taking sub images of the work space in 240 × 135 resolution as required by the model. Each of the sub-images was manually labelled according what object was in the camera window.

Initial training was done by generating 576 training images of each class by rotating the STL file in Blender, a 3-D modeling software, on two different axis at 1920 × 1080 resolution and taking 240 × 135 resolution gray scale sub images out of the total image.

Sub-images that did not contain the object were thrown away, and the rest were labelled as the object rendered object. As a result of this method of data generation, anywhere between 2000 and 5000 training samples were generated per an object with the varying factor being the size of the object. When performing the training, 2000 randomly chosen sub-images from each class was chosen in order to prevent issues arising from having an unbalanced data set. Each of these images had their pixels divided by 255 in order to scale them between 0 and 1, and then gamma corrected in order to reduce the difference between the 3D generated training data and the live data.

The generated images were rotated 180° in order to double the training image count. As a result, a total of 14000 images were used to train the basic model, before considering sub assemblies, after including the training data for the work space.

The experiment takes place at a white worktable with shelves for holding parts as seen in Fig. 5. Attached to the work table is a spotlight along with a camera overseeing the work space. The spotlight and the camera both are looking down on the table which provides a somewhat orthogonal view of the

Fig. 6. Pre-processed image.

Fig. 7. Table versus assembly object after processing.

assembly process. Next to the working table, there is a second small table with a monitor on top showing the camera's point of view of the process. This monitor is connected to a laptop and used for displaying guidance to the assembler during the experiment.

Because the parts for assembly came from 3D printing and is the color white which happens to be the same color as the table on which the assembly takes place (Fig. 6), some image processing techniques were used on the images in order to help the model differentiate the different shades of white. First, the images were converted to gray scale from their initial 3-channel RGB state.

After the application, there still wasn't a strong distinction between the table and part, however, gray scaling allowed a wider range of techniques to be applied. Afterward gray scaling, gamma correction was applied to the images in order

Table 1. Cross validation results from live data.

Predicted class	Actual class									
	Cabin	Cargo	Cargo base	Limb	Stage 1	Stage 2	Stage 3	Stage 4	Table	Wheel
Cabin	72.7	2.5	4.2	2.5	5.1	2.7	3.4	3.0	0.1	3.1
Cargo	2.4	80.5	6.1	0.1	3.5	1.8	2.2	1.9	0.1	0.3
Cargo base	4.4	3.9	62.6	2.2	5.3	4.6	4.7	1.8	0.2	2.3
Limb	3.1	0.1	4.1	90.5	0.3	0.9	0.7	0.9	0.3	7.3
Stage 1	4.9	2.8	7.3	0.8	73.8	4.5	3.4	2.6	0.1	1.4
Stage 2	4.1	2.4	4.5	1.4	5.8	81.5	2.3	2.5	0.1	1.4
Stage 3	4.0	2.8	6.0	0.1	3.5	2.0	79.2	3.1	0.1	0.4
Stage 4	2.8	1.1	1.4	0.4	1.4	1.0	3.4	84.1	0.1	0.4
Table	0.4	1.1	0.7	0.6	0.2	0.1	0.0	0.0	96.9	3.3
Wheel	1.2	2.8	3.1	1.4	1.1	0.9	0.7	0.1	2.0	80.1

to differentiate the shades of white. Doing so rendered the table to be various shades of gray due to the spot light above it, but this change was satisfactory as the due to the mixed affect of the spotlight and gamma correction, an easy to pick up texture was applied to the table which is not found on the assembly parts as seen in Fig. 7.

In order to train the model for use in the experiment, leave two out cross validation was performed on the data where one of the outed sets was used for testing and the other for validation. Model training was initially done for 20 epochs and then reduced to five due apparent over-fitting in the model to the training data. Initial training of the model was done by taking the STL file of the printed assembly and capturing each of the individual parts at different orientations.

Training on the 3D generated data yielding good results when tested only on other 3D generated data, however, did not yield satisfactory results when tested against live data. Consequently, live data was included in training. The camera was used to create a set of training data from a preliminary run of the assembly. The results of performing cross validation are displayed in Table 1.

In order to capture the data, 1000 subsequent images was taken of the work space when the space was empty, then again with each stage of the assembly at a time. Image subtraction was used in order to reduce the amount of useless training images in the image sets that consisted of parts by subtracting a single image from the empty work space set.

6 Discussion

There are two key observations to be made from the cross validation are that the cargo base has the lowest accuracy and the cabin is often confused with the stage 1 assembly. Since the cargo base is one of the largest pieces and the piece with the lowest amount of features, it is not a surprise that it get confused with the most of all of the pieces. As for the cabin, the only difference between the

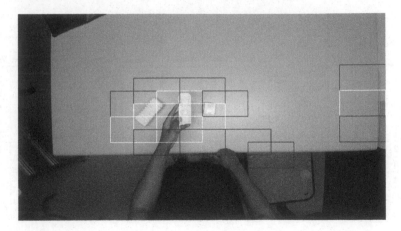

Fig. 8. Simplified classified image with simple parts (blue) and sub assemblies (green). (Color figure online)

cabin and the stage 1 assembly are two wheels attached to the cabin. Because the cabin is the smallest of the main components, save for the wheels, this is to be expected.

Results form testing the model's classification on live data were mixed. As seen in Fig. 8, the model tends to consider lone basic parts as singular basic parts as they should, however parts in close proximity, specifically when two different objects are in the same sub-image, seem to be labeled as sub-assemblies despite the parts not being physically attached to one another.

There are several ways to address this issue. First, one can incorporate a rule based system that works in tandem with the model. This rule based system would look at all the classifications in the image and rule out any classifications that should not logically exist. For example, stages 2, 3, and 4 should not exist if stage 1 does not exist. Additionally, if stage 1 exists, anyway where the cabin is found from then on, it should be labelled as stage 1.

Second, one can reduce the size of the input shape of the model. This will reduce the probability of this event occurring, but at the trade off of potentially not picking up enough feature to make reasonable make accurate predictions.

Third, one can introduce pre-processing techniques in order to remove sub-images from the pool to be processed before being fed into the mode. The trade off for this approach is the it can make the boxes in accurate and this may not work for objects with irregular shapes. In addition to these changes, one could also limit the sub-images selected for classification to one within the work area. By doing so, the probability of running into a scenario where objects within frame are misclassified is reduced.

7 Conclusion

We proposed an approach that uses real-time video processing and machine learning to provide information to assemblers during an active assembly process. Individual parts of the assembly, as well as the part combinations, are identified using a CNN and the results are provided to the assembler (on a monitor) to guide the assembly process, eventually leading to the fully assembled product.

CNN is trained on the 3D generated data (from 3D models of the components) and live data (from camera). Live data was to train for the experiment. Four groups of objects are recognized, the area in which the assembly takes place, limbs (arms and hands), the basic parts of the assembly, and the sub assemblies of the completed part.

Results were mixed since when basic parts are in close proximity, they can be labeled as sub-assemblies despite the parts not being physically attached to one another.

There are three main directions for future research. The first direction is improving the results and capabilities of the developed system. The accuracy is satisfactory, but the performance in live scenarios needs improvement. The second direction is reducing the work involved in setting up the system to work for new assemblies. Specifically, the goal is to be able to train the model using the STL file that was used for printing. The third direction is on the linkage between this system and the process monitoring system in-place within the room. While our goal was to, based on the proposed approach, develop and implement a system for monitoring and advising assemblers mid-process, we could leverage additional data from observing manual assembly processes.

References

1. Agati, S.S., Bauer, R.D., d. S. Hounsell, M., Paterno, A.S.: Augmented reality for manual assembly in industry 4.0: gathering guidelines. In: Proceedings of the 22nd Symposium on Virtual and Augmented Reality (SVR), pp. 179–188, 7–10 November 2020
2. Aoyama, K., Yotsuzuka, T., Tanaka, Y., Tanabe, Y.: "Monitoring platform" of monitoring and visualizing system for shipyard: application to cutting and sub-assembly processes. In: Okada, T., Suzuki, K., Kawamura, Y. (eds.) PRADS 2019. LNCE, vol. 65, pp. 321–337. Springer, Singapore (2021). https://doi.org/10.1007/978-981-15-4680-8_23
3. Bauer, R.D., Agati, S.S., da Silva Hounsell, M., da Silva, A.T.: Manual PCB assembly using augmented reality towards total quality. In: Proceedings of the 22nd Symposium on Virtual and Augmented Reality (SVR), pp. 189–198, 7–10 November 2020
4. Dasgupta, A., Manuel, M., Mansur, R., Nowak, N., Gračanin, D.: Towards real time object recognition for context awareness in mixed reality: a machine learning approach. In: Proceedings of the 2020 IEEE Conference on Virtual Reality and 3D User Interfaces Abstracts and Workshops (VRW), pp. 262–268. IEEE, 22–26 March 2020

5. Drouot, M., Le Bigot, N., Bolloc'h, J., Bricard, E., de Bougrenet, J.L., Nourrit, V.: The visual impact of augmented reality during an assembly task. Displays **66**, 101987 (2021)
6. Gogolák, L., Fürstner, I.: Wireless sensor network aided assembly line monitoring according to expectations of industry 4.0. Appl. Sci. (Switzerland) **11**(1), 1–18 (2021)
7. Hoover, M., Miller, J., Gilbert, S., Winer, E.: Measuring the performance impact of using the Microsoft HoloLens 1 to provide guided assembly work instruction. J. Comput. Inf. Sci. Eng. **20**(6), 061001-1-061001-7 (2020)
8. Obinata, T., Kawamoto, H., Sankai, Y.: Development of real-time assembly work monitoring system based on 3D skeletal model of arms and fingers. IEEE Trans. Syst. Man Cybern. Syst. **2020**, 363–368 (2020)
9. Petrone, K., Hanna, R., Shankaranarayanan, G.: A comparative examination of AR and video in delivering assembly instructions. In: Auer, M.E., Tsiatsos, T. (eds.) IMCL 2019. AISC, vol. 1192, pp. 445–456. Springer, Cham (2021). https://doi.org/10.1007/978-3-030-49932-7_43
10. Qian, C., Zhang, Y., Jiang, C., Pan, S., Rong, Y.: A real-time data-driven collaborative mechanism in fixed-position assembly systems for smart manufacturing. Robot. Comput. Integrated Manuf. **61**, 101841 (2020)
11. Schuster, F., Engelmann, B., Sponholz, U., Schmitt, J.: Human acceptance evaluation of AR-assisted assembly scenarios. J. Manuf. Syst. (2021)
12. Schuster, F., Sponholz, U., Engelmann, B., Schmitt, J.: A user study on AR-assisted industrial assembly. In: Proceedings of the 2020 IEEE International Symposium on Mixed and Augmented Reality Adjunct (ISMAR-Adjunct), pp. 135–140, 9–13 November 2020
13. de Souza Cardoso, L.F., Mariano, F.C.M.Q., Zorzal, E.R.: Mobile augmented reality to support fuselage assembly. Comput. Ind. Eng. **148**, 106712 (2020)
14. Stephanidis, C., et al.: Seven HCI grand challenges. Int. J. Hum. Comput. Interaction **35**(14), 1229–1269 (2019)
15. Szajna, A., Stryjski, R., Woźniak, W., Chamier-Gliszczyński, N., Kostrzewski, M.: Assessment of augmented reality in manual wiring production process with use of mobile AR glasses. Sensors **20**(17), 1–26 (2020)
16. Tainaka, K., et al.: Guideline and tool for designing an assembly task support system using augmented reality. In: Proceedings of the 2020 IEEE International Symposium on Mixed and Augmented Reality (ISMAR), pp. 486–497, 9–13 November 2020
17. Tsai, C.-Y., Liu, T.-Y., Lu, Y.-H., Nisar, H.: A novel interactive assembly teaching aid using multi-template augmented reality. Multimedia Tools Appl. 31981–32009 (2020). https://doi.org/10.1007/s11042-020-09584-0
18. Vanneste, P., Huang, Y., Park, J.Y., Cornillie, F., Decloedt, B., Van den Noortgate, W.: Cognitive support for assembly operations by means of augmented reality: an exploratory study. Int. J. Hum. Comput. Stud. **143** (2020)
19. Wang, Z., et al.: User-oriented AR assembly guideline: a new classification method of assembly instruction for user cognition. The Int. J. Adv. Manuf. Technol. 41–59 (2020). https://doi.org/10.1007/s00170-020-06291-w

Deep Learning Methods as a Detection Tools for Forest Fire Decision Making Process Fire Prevention in Indonesia

Dia Meirina Suri[1,3] [iD] and Achmad Nurmandi[2(✉)] [iD]

[1] Department of Islamic Politics-Political Science, Universitas Muhammadiyah Yogyakarta, Yogyakarta, Indonesia
[2] Department of Government Affairs and Administration, JK School of Government, Universitas Muhammdiyah Yogyakarta, Yogyakarta, Indonesia
nurmandi_achmad@umy.ac.id
[3] Public Administration, Universitas Islam Riau, Pekanbaru, Indonesia

Abstract. This research examines the collaboration between agencies in policy-making based on hotspot monitoring from satellites. Valid data regarding the number of hotspots from the satellite is needed in decision making because it provides information used to control forest and land fires in Indonesia. For instance, the Ministry of Forestry uses data from the NOAA-18 satellite for analysis, while the BMKG utilizes those from the Agua/Terra. However, the data generated by each satellite has differences in the number of hotspots. Therefore, this research aims to determine the collaboration between the Ministry of Forestry and BMKG in the use of satellite data for decision-makers to determine disaster alert status. This research uses a qualitative approach to analyze secondary data from two popular media sources collected using the Nvivo 12 plus application. The result showed that agencies involved in fire prevention lack collaboration due to institutional designs that lead to a lack of communication and unclear roles for each institution during the decision making process.

1 Introduction

The impact of forest and land fires deteriorates the quality of air in the surrounding area and leads to loss of crops, resources, animal, people, etc. [1]. Due to Indonesia's vast forest area, detecting the fire source or location is quite difficult [2]. Therefore, one of the methods used to detect the source of forest fires is satellite sensing [3]. The data from the satellite provides the ability for forest and land fires to be easily detected. In controlling forest and land fires, collaboration is carried out between BPBD and KLHK as the institution responsible for preventing forest and land fires.

The collaboration of various actors and institutions is essential in making discussions on forest and land fire management. Furthermore, collaboration is also needed to solve arrangements problems to achieve the desired output [4, 5]. Deals regarding the communication interaction between various institutions are significant and need to be carried out for the creation of better results [6]. This discussion is particularly relevant

© Springer Nature Switzerland AG 2021
C. Stephanidis et al. (Eds.): HCII 2021, CCIS 1498, pp. 177–182, 2021.
https://doi.org/10.1007/978-3-030-90176-9_24

because it contributes to understanding institutions' role in forest and land fire management. Besides, the collaborative arrangements created and implemented answer critical questions related to authorities in the forest and land fire governance, such as how the various agencies involved make arrangements designed to work together. Therefore, it is important to determine the capacity needed to reach joint decisions on forest and land fire management [7].

This research aims to analyze the collaboration between the Ministry of Environment and Forestry and BMKG in controlling forest and land fires in Riau Province, especially in determining disaster emergency alert status, based on the number of hotspots from satellite monitoring. This study focuses on making a collaborative decision between initial conditions, institutional design, leadership, and processes.

2   Literature Review

Currently, smokes due to forest fires are being detected by applying deep learning methods to produce satellite-generated images [8]. The use of deep learning methods is due to the numerous disadvantages of traditional methods, such as the time-consuming process and low feature performance analysis in fire detection [9]. It is also used to detect shadows, lighting, and objects that are coloured like fire, thereby leading to false detection [10]. [11] uses deep learning methods for early detection by classifying and extracting fire and non-fire areas simultaneously to resolve the issue. This method also has a high detection rate, which increases the smoke detection speed [12]. Furthermore, the deep learning method used on satellites as a data source in monitoring hotspot produces valid data [12].

Deep learning methods have also been applied to detect fire and smoke from multispectral satellite imagery [12]. The process of detecting hotspots using deep learning methods and MODIS instrument data from the Tera-Aqua satellite easily distinguishes fire and non-fire objects to produce more valid data. [12] also evaluated fire and non-fire imagery to determine the accuracy of the proposed fire detection method. Deep learning methods have better performance and easily used to determine the right fire area, which is extracted based on the thresholding pattern and local binary. [13] generated data for predicting fire smoke in satellite images in fast time using data from the Himawari-8/HI sensor. Every hotspot detected by a satellite is not necessarily valid. Therefore deep learning methods on satellites are needed to prevent errors in decision making.

3   Research Method

Data were first collected from articles related to forest and land fires in three media, namely Kompas, Tribun Pekanbaru, and media indonesia, using the Ncapture feature in the Nvivo 12 plus data processing application. The articles were freely obtained from accessible newspaper archives from january 1, 2014, to December 201, using the keywords "hotspot monitoring," "forest fire," "land fire," "determination of emergency alert status," and "haze." for 564, 435, and 323 articles met the search criteria for kompas.com, pekanbaru.tribunnews.com, and mediaindonesia.com, respectively. Fifty articles were selected per newspaper culminating in 150 articles. The articles were reviewed to ensure they included a substantial section that uses satellites in hotspot detection by removing those not related to news and replacing them with other randomly selected articles. Also, study documents, including policy papers, reports, and updates from provincial governments and interest groups, helped consolidate the study.

4 Result

This study found a lack of collaboration between institutions due to institutional design, which led to inadequate communication in determining the time to choose the alert status for forest and land fires. The emergency alert policy is critical in decision-making because it deals with the increasingly widespread threat of fire hazards. Early warning is part of the collaboration, which focuses on communicating individuals and institutional actors in negotiating interests and concerns on risk assessment and management [6]. This communication encourages exchanging evaluations, estimates and opinions on hazards and risks among the various stakeholders involved. As such, communication governance needs collaboration between multiple agencies involved in forest and land fire prevention.

Collaboration on institutional designs only occurs in 5% of BMKG and 4% of KLHK, as shown in Fig. 1.

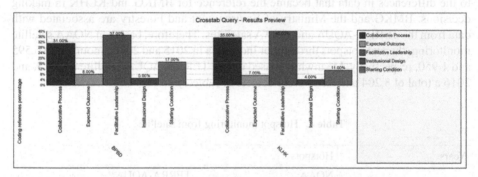

Fig. 1. Collaboration between KLHK and BMKG

Figure 1 shows that KLHK and BMKG collaborate in using satellite data to determine the number of hotspots for policy-making by 5% and 4%, respectively. The institutional design means that the two essential decision-making institutions do not collaborate properly in determining the disaster preparedness status. Lack of communication among stakeholders leads to an inadequate institutional effort to collect and interpret risk signs [6, 14].

BMKG conducts early warning by anticipating forest and land fires when entering the dry season because people in fire-prone areas need to be vigilant. According to information provided by BMKG, the early warning process is carried out in three stages, namely (1) warning to districts/cities whose areas are predicted to experience dry season, (2) 10-day rainfall analysis maps that is analyzed and classified into low, medium and high rainfall, and (3) provides initial information as a basis for determining the status of Emergency Alert in an area [6]. The Ministry of Environment and Forestry, based on satellite data, also provided BPBD with information on the number of hotspots monitored to carry out extinguishing actions at the fire location. However, due to differences in data regarding the number of hotspots, decision making is constrained. Therefore, it is necessary and unnecessary to determine the emergency alert status of BMKG and KLHK, respectively. Early detection activities in preventing forest and land fires are important factors to conduct because it is an effort to obtain very early information on forest fires by applying simple to advanced technology [15]. Furthermore, early detection can determine the decision-making process used to assess forest and land fire preparedness [15]. Accurate detection can assist the fire fighting stage and the sound post-fire handling stage [6]. Also, at the implementation stage, the detection process's accuracy tends to affect the allocation of funds, smooth operation of blackouts, and the need for investigation in cases of violations of environmental law [16]. Early detection is processed by land through patrols, tower observation and guarding in fire-prone areas, while by air, it is carried out by helicopter, aeroplane and satellite [6].

The Ministry of Environment and Forestry and BMKG used information from two different satellites to reference forest and land fires. The data generated by each satellite has a different number of hotspots, which shows that there are obstacles in making emergency alert status decisions, especially in taking essential steps before the fire spreads [6]. The prevention system relies on data used as a reference on the hotspot detection produced by the Terra-Aqua and NOAA satellites. The problem occurred due to the differences in data that became the reference for BMKG and KLHK in making decisions. BMKG and the Ministry of Environment and Forestry are associated with data from the TERRA-AQUA and NOAA satellites. Therefore, based on NOAA satellite monitoring, the real hotspots throughout Indonesia in 2015 and 2016 amounted to 6,595 and 1,950, respectively. Meanwhile, based on the TERRA-AQUA satellite in 2015, and 2016 a total of 8,204 and 2,544 were detected (Table 1).

Table 1. Hotspot monitoring from satellite

Years	Hotspots	
	NOAA	TERRA-AQUA
2015	6.595	8.204
2016	1.950	2.544

In Riau Province, the number of hotspots observed on the NOAA satellite was 1,208 in 2015 and 297 in 2016. On the Terra-Aqua satellite, the number of hotspots was 1,537 and 499 in 2015 and 2016. Data from satellites using the deep learning method is more accurate than those that do not use these methods. This is because the use of deep learning methods is useful for avoiding large-scale fires. Furthermore, effective fire detection from the visual scene is essential [12]. Due to the severe and dangerous consequences that forest fires have on human, animal and plant life worldwide, traditional methods, rapid response, and large detection areas do not apply to detect fires [9]. Therefore, to improve the accuracy of fire detection, the deep learning method is used to classify the data set into the fire and non-fire images, create a matrix to determine the efficiency of the framework, and extract the area where fires occur in satellite imagery which aims to reduce the false detection rate [12].

The NOAA satellites' image resolution is very coarse and allows the location description to be distorted, making it less accurate in identifying forest fires [17]. It provides information from hotspot detection satellites in data on the location and direction of smoke spread [17]. Hotspot information, which is the basis for a fire warning system, sometimes produces an error in decision-making when there is no fire incident in the field [18]. It is common evidence that the absence of acknowledged exchange on information between ministries in forest management is due to a combination of institutions [19]. Organizational weaknesses are caused by various factors, such as the unclear role in organizing [2], the relationship between the organizations involved [1], and their ineffectiveness [20].

5 Conclusion

In conclusion, the use of different satellites results in a varying number of hotspots, thereby leading to various references when making decisions, which can confuse local governments in determining disaster emergency alert status. Furthermore, its use shows a lack of collaboration between institutions due to the institutional design, which causes a lack of communication and unclear roles for each institution in decision making. This collaboration's failure shows that the policy-making process in dealing with forest fires faces significant challenges in strengthening collaboration between government agencies at the national and local levels.

References

1. Sukrismanto, E.: Sistem Pengorganisasian Pengendalian Kebakaran Hutan dan Lahan di Indonesia (2012)
2. Sukrismanto, E., Alikodra, H.S., Saharjo, B.H., Kardono, P.: Hubungan Antar Organisasi Dalam Sistem Pengorganisasian Pengendalian Kebakaran Hutan/Lahan Di Indonesia. J. Penelit. Hutan Tanam. 8(3), 169–177 (2011)
3. Yabueng, N., Wiriya, W., Chantara, S.: Influence of zero-burning policy and climate phenomena on ambient PM2.5 patterns and PAHs inhalation cancer risk during episodes of smoke haze in Northern Thailand. Atmos. Environ. 232, 117485 (2020)
4. Ansell, C., Gash, A.: Collaborative governance in theory and practice. J. Public Adm. Res. Theory 18(4), 543–571 (2008)
5. Fish, R.D., Ioris, A.A.R., Watson, N.M.: Integrating water and agricultural management: collaborative governance for a complex policy problem. Sci. Total Environ. 408(23), 5623–5630 (2010)
6. Badri, M., Lubis, D.P., Susanto, D., Suharjito, D.: Sistem Komunikasi Peringatan Dini Pencegahan Kebakaran Hutan Dan Lahan Di Provinsi Riau. J. Penelit. Komun. dan Pembang. 19(1), 1 (2018)
7. Dressel, S., Ericsson, G., Johansson, M., Kalén, C., Pfeffer, S.E., Sandström, C.: Evaluating the outcomes of collaborative wildlife governance: the role of social-ecological system context and collaboration dynamics. Land Use Policy 99, 105028 (2020)

8. Barmpoutis, P., Papaioannou, P., Dimitropoulos, K., Grammalidis, N.: A review on early forest fire detection systems using optical remote sensing. Sensors (Switzerland) **20**(22), 1–26 (2020)
9. Maier, M., Chowdhury, M., Rimal, B.P., Van, D.P.: The tactile internet: vision, recent progress, and open challenges. IEEE Commun. Mag. **54**(5), 138–145 (2016)
10. Muhammad, K., Ahmad, J., Mehmood, I., Rho, S., Baik, S.W.: Convolutional neural networks based fire detection in surveillance videos. IEEE Access **6**, 18174–18183 (2018)
11. Kaabi, R., Frizzi, S., Bouchouicha, M., Fnaiech, F., Moreau, E.: Video smoke detection review: state of the art of smoke detection in visible and IR range. In: 2017 International Conference on Smart, Monitored and Controlled Cities, SM2C 2017, pp. 81–86 (2017)
12. Priya, R.S., Vani, K.: Deep learning based forest fire classification and detection in satellite images. In: Proceedings of the 11th International Conference on Advanced Computing, ICoAC 2019, pp. 61–65 (2019)
13. Larsen, A., et al.: A deep learning approach to identify smoke plumes in satellite imagery in near-real time for health risk communication. J. Expo. Sci. Environ. Epidemiol. **31**(1), 170–176 (2021)
14. Pascasarjana, S.: Komunikasi risiko dalam pencegahan kebakaran hutan dan lahan di provinsi riau muhammad badri (2018)
15. Zhang, J., Li, W., Han, N., Kan, J.: Forest fire detection system based on a ZigBee wireless sensor network. Front. For. China **3**(3), 369–374 (2008)
16. Syaufina, L., Siwi, R., Nurhayati, A.D.: Perbandingan Sumber Hotspot sebagai Indikator Kebakaran Hutan dan Lahan Gambut dan Korelasinya dengan Curah Hujan di Desa Sepahat, Kabupaten Bengkalis. Riau. J. Silvikultur Trop. **05**(2), 113–118 (2014)
17. Indradjad, A., Purwanto, J., Sunarmodo, W.: Analisis Tingkat Akurasi Titik Hotspot Dari S-Npp Viirs Dan Terra/Aqua Modis Terhadap Kejadian Kebakaran. J. Penginderaan Jauh dan Pengolah. Data Citra Digit. **16**(1), 53–60 (2019)
18. Cuomo, V., Lasaponara, R., Tramutoli, V.: Evaluation of a new satellite-based method for forest fire detection. Int. J. Remote Sens. **22**(9), 1799–1826 (2001)
19. Moeliono, M., Santoso, L., Gallemore, C.: REDD + policy networks in Indonesia. no. 63, pp. 1–8 (2013)
20. Rothe, P., Lindholm, A.L., Hyvönen, A., Nenonen, S.: Work environment preferences - does age make a difference? Facilities **30**(1), 78–95 (2012)

Intelligent Music Lamp Design Based on Arduino

Yuanlu Wang and Xiaofang Li[✉]

USC-SJTU Institute of Cultural and Creative Industry,
Shanghai Jiao Tong University, Shanghai, China
{wangyuanlu,maggieli}@sjtu.edu.cn

Abstract. With the rapid development of science and technology, people's lives are becoming more and more intelligent. As a necessities of home life, desk lamps have always been the focus of smart home research. The current research on smart lamps is mostly concentrated on realizing the automatic adjustment of lights with environmental changes, improving the energy efficiency of the desk lamps, and enriching the auxiliary functions of the lamps. There is a lack of research on home entertainment lamps. This article proposes a design scheme of an intelligent music light based on Arduino UNO MCU. The device integrates apart from the colored lamp itself, a music player and a Bluetooth speaker that can be used to play music. We also designed an Android APP, Yin. Users can use the APP on their mobile phones to change the color of the light and control the music playback function. Practice has shown that this design is rich in functions, convenient and interesting, combines technical and artistic features, and can be widely used in daily life.

Keywords: Internet of Things · Smart home · Intelligent music lamp

1 Introduction

New technologies represented by Internet of Things (IOT) have gradually changed people's lives. Smart refrigerators, smart washing machines, smart door locks and other smart products have begun to enter the family life. Under the background of continuous technological innovation, the public has formed a better pursuit of quality of life and paid more attention to the satisfaction of spiritual needs. Therefore, traditional single-function home appliances can no longer meet the needs and scenarios of consumers, the smart home has begun to become a new field of mass consumption.

A home, which is smart, must contain three elements, which are internal network, intelligent control and home automation. Internal network is the basis of a smart home, and it can be wire and wireless. Intelligent control means gateways to manage the systems. Home automation refers to products within the home, as well as links to out-of-home services and systems [1]. Compared with ordinary home, smart home not only has the traditional living functions, but also can provide information interaction function, so that people can control the related devices of the home outside, making home life

© Springer Nature Switzerland AG 2021
C. Stephanidis et al. (Eds.): HCII 2021, CCIS 1498, pp. 183–190, 2021.
https://doi.org/10.1007/978-3-030-90176-9_25

more safe and comfortable. In addition, the smart home can also provide personalized services for consumers based on the home environment, and further improve the overall use experience of the smart home. With the improvement of living standards, people are more willing to accept more convenient and comfortable home devices.

Desk lamp is the most frequently used in household lighting, which has become a necessity in modern home life. Due to the lack of intelligent control, the original desk lamp is only used as a general lighting equipment. With a single functional structure, the value of desk lamp in family life needs to be improved [2]. At present, the research of intelligent lamp mainly concentrates on three aspects. First, focus on realizing automatic perception with the environment, making the desk lamp light adjustment more intelligent. Qin, Z. [3] pointed out that compared with the intelligent lamp, the original desk lamp has obvious disadvantages in the brightness adjustment. It cannot be adjusted intelligently according to the environmental change, and users need to manually adjust the brightness of the light, which affects the experience of the lamp to a certain extent. The intelligent improvement of lamp is carried out by using single chip microcomputer, and various sensors are embedded. The processed desk lamp can detect the external environmental factors, such as light intensity, so as to realize the intelligent adjustment of brightness. Chen, J. [4] designed an intelligent LED lamp based on Arduino to solve the problem that traditional desk lamp cannot dimmer automatically. This design can meet the dynamic needs of human eyes, realize automatic dimming, and ensure the health of people's eyes. Riyadi, G. A. et al. [5] added ultrasonic sensor and optical sensor into the design of intelligent lamp to realize automatic brightness adjustment. Second, improve the energy efficiency of desk lamp. Energy conservation and sustainable economic development is always an important issue. Thus, to improve the energy saving and efficiency of desk lamp is one of the important directions of intelligent lamp design. Zhang, L. et al. [6] designed an intelligent voice control lighting device based on Arduino Uno Microcontroller. Users can use voice to switch on and off the lamp and adjust the light brightness. The intelligent lamp designed by Dai, Z. [7] puts forward a new idea of automatically adjusting the light intensity of the lamp. He used the photosensitive resistance sensor as an auxiliary device to set and adjust the light intensity signal directly through software to achieve the purpose of automatic dimming and achieve the high efficiency of the desk lamp. Third, enrich the auxiliary function of desk lamp. Desk lamp, as a necessary electrical appliance for family and work, is indispensable in life. Using advanced technology and people-oriented concept to design intelligent desk lamp and improve the practicability and versatility of desk lamp is another main direction of intelligent desk lamp research [8]. The intelligent lamp designed by Chen, X. et al. [9] realizes the convenience and humanization of the desk lamp, and has the functions of preventing hunchback, myopia, voice interaction and camera monitoring. Medica's Sleepace brand is dedicated to the development of intelligent sleep-aid products, including NOX intelligent sleeping lamp, NOX sleeping music lamp and NOX children's company lamp. Based on lighting technology and integrating a variety of new technologies, Sengled is committed to providing global consumers with a brand new smart lifestyle, launching products such as smart light for security monitoring and smart wireless security light for early education.

However, at present, smart home products mainly focus on two aspects: one is home infrastructure, the other is practical home life products, and there is less application in the research of entertainment home products [10]. Globally, "security and control" and "energy or lighting" (respectively 55% and 53%) are the top choices for smart home applications, while "entertainment and smart interconnection" ranks third (48%). In addition to providing lighting function, desk lamp can also play an important role in setting off the atmosphere. Therefore, this paper aims to design an intelligent music lamp, which combines music with light effect, enhances the entertainment and interest of intelligent lamp, and provides a unique product experience.

2 Design Concept

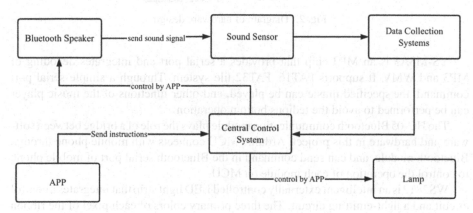

Fig. 1. Diagram of design scheme

This design aims to produce an intelligent and entertaining household lamp. The design of the intelligent music lamp includes two parts: hardware design and software design (Fig. 1).

The hardware design is based on Arduino MCU. Its purpose is to transform the original lamp, improve the lighting effect, and add music playing function.

The software design is developed based on Android, and the software functions are divided into two parts: software functions and interactive functions between software and hardware.

Hardware Design

The hardware design of intelligent music lamp is based on Arduino UNO MCU. Arduino UNO MCU is easy to operate and has strong encapsulation. Combine Arduino MCU with HC-05 Bluetooth module, YS-M3A3 music player module, WS2812 color lamp strip and speaker module, the three functions of music payback, Bluetooth communication and light color change are realized (Fig. 2).

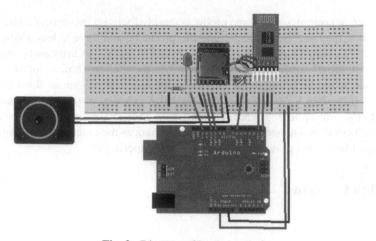

Fig. 2. Diagram of hardware design

YS-M3A3 is an MP3 chip that provides a serial port and integrates decoding of MP3 and WMV. It supports FAT16, FAT32 file system. Through a simple serial port command, the specified music can be played, and other functions of the music player can be performed to avoid the tedious bottom operation.

The HC-05 Bluetooth communication module plays the role of a bridge between software and hardware in this project. Arduino MCU connects with mobile phone through Bluetooth module, and can send command in the Bluetooth serial port of mobile phone to control the operation of each module on MCU.

WS2812 is an intelligent externally controlled LED light strip that integrates a control circuit and a light-emitting circuit. The three primary colors of each pixel of the ribbon can realize 256-level brightness display. The ribbon has a serial cascade interface, which can receive and decode data through a signal line. By changing the color of each lamp bead, this design can achieve different color effects of light, which can be applied to different scenarios.

Software Design

The software design adopts Android Studio development environment, which aims to make an android app that can remotely control intelligent music lights. The software design involves SQLite database, media player and several related subclasses of Bluetooth serial port.

QLite is a lightweight database, a relational database management system that complies with ACID. Its design goal is embedded, and it has been used in many embedded products. This design uses the QLite database to store user information to realize new user registration and login functions.

The app music player is implemented by instantiating Android media player. Users can select a song to play in the music list, get the playing progress of the song in real time, and drag the slider to change the progress of the current music.

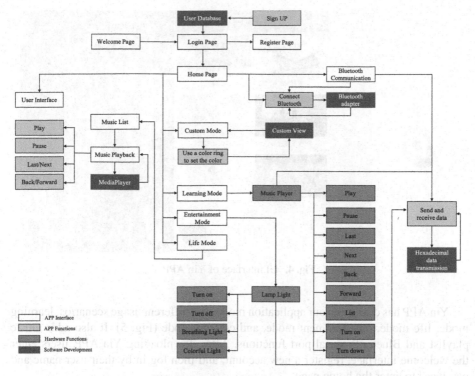

Fig. 3. Diagram of software design

Software development also realizes the function of Bluetooth serial port. Through Bluetooth data transmission, the remote control of the lamp by the mobile phone can be realized, the lighting effect can be automatically adjusted, and the Bluetooth speaker can be used to play music (Fig. 3).

3 Result

This paper presents a design of intelligent music lamp based on Arduino. The design combines hardware development with mobile application development. The hardware development uses C language, and the software development uses Java. It is developed on Arduino and Android studio platform. The overall design scheme mainly uses HC-05 Bluetooth module, WS2812 color lamp strip and YS-M3A3 music player module to realize the functions of lamp lighting, music playing, remote control of mobile app and voice control of light color. We have specially designed an APP, Yin, for the intelligent music lamp (Fig. 4). Users can log in their accounts on mobile phones to enter the APP, and experience the different lighting styles through four different modes. Meanwhile, users can also use their mobile phones to control the built-in Bluetooth speaker to play songs. Intelligent music lamp combines music and lighting effect, realizes the integration of technology and art, and can be widely used in life.

Fig. 4. UI interface of Yin APP

Yin APP has designed four application modes for different usage scenarios: learning mode, life mode, entertainment mode, and custom mode (Fig. 5). It also adds music playlist and Bluetooth serial port functions. After downloading Yin APP, users enter the welcome interface, register a new account, and then log in by their user name and password to enter the home page.

The learning mode realizes the basic lighting function of the lamp. Click the light on button, the music light turns on white light, and click the light off button to turn off the light. The intelligent music light is equipped with the function of light intensity perception, and automatically adjust the brightness according to the ambient light effect.

The life mode has a warm light function, supports music playback. Click the light on button, the music light flashes with warm yellow light, and click the light off button to turn off the light. Click the play/pause button to control the playback of the music.

In the entertainment mode, the lights can be rhythmically moved with the music. Click the light on button, each small lamp bead flashes a different color of light, and click the light off button to turn off the light. Click the play/pause, up/next, fast forward/back button on the interface to control the playback of the music.

In the custom mode, the user can set the color and rhythm of the lamp light to meet the user's customization needs.

(a) Learning mode   (b) Life Mode

(c) Entertainment Mode   (d) Custom Mode

Fig. 5. Light effects of intelligent music lamp

4 Conclusion

This paper proposes a design scheme of intelligent music lamp based on Arduino. The device integrates apart from the colored lamp itself, a music player and a Bluetooth speaker that can be used to play music from. It makes up for the shortage of research on entertainment smart lamps. Also, this intelligent music lamp gathers a variety of different modes, which can meet the requirements of different user groups and different scenes. Through soothing music and soft lighting, it creates a very relaxed atmosphere, which can relieve the increasing pressure of life and work of modern people. Colored lights with cheerful music, can quickly arouse people's emotions, play the role of entertainment and leisure. This design can also be developed for larger commercial use, in some special public places, such as bookstores, cafes, gyms, etc. Facing the huge commercial development potential of the smart home market, we believe that in the future, such products will be more and more needed by the market.

References

1. Jiang, L., Liu, D., Yang, B.: Smart home research. In: Proceedings of 2004 International Conference on Machine Learning and Cybernetics, vol. 2, pp. 659–663 (2004). https://doi.org/10.1109/ICMLC.2004.1382266
2. Cao, S.: Research on the application of single chip microcomputer in the field of smart home appliance. Policy Res. Explor. (09), 59 (2020)

3. Qin, Z.: Application analysis of single chip microcomputer in the field of smart home appliances. China Plant Eng. **03**, 31–33 (2020)
4. Chen, J., Wu, Z., Song, K.: Design of smart LED desk lamp based on Arduino. China's New Technol. New Prod. **01**, 21–23 (2020). https://doi.org/10.13612/j.cnki.cntp.2020.01.010
5. Riyadi, G.A., Sussi, R.M.: Implementation and analysis of smart lamp using android application based on Internet of Things. In: Proceedings of the International Seminar of Science and Applied Technology (2020). doi:https://doi.org/10.2991/aer.k.201221.072
6. Zhang, L., et al.: Intelligent voice control lighting device based on arduino UNO microcontroller. In: IOP Conference Series: Earth and Environmental Science, vol. 252, p. 032188 (2019). https://doi.org/10.1088/1755-1315/252/3/032188
7. Dai, Z.: Design of intelligent desk lamp for eyesight protection based on single chip microcomputer system. Pract. Electron. **07**, 89–91 (2021). https://doi.org/10.16589/j.cnki.cn11-3571/tn.2021.07.029
8. Chai, J.: Design of LED intelligent learning lamp system based on the STM32 (2016)
9. Chen, X., Pan, Si., Yi, W., Liao, W.. Design of intelligent table lamp based on single chip computer. Electron. Test (04), 34–46 (2020). https://doi.org/10.16520/j.cnki.1000-8519.2020.04.013
10. Luo, X., Gao, W.: Current status and development status of smart home research based on Arduino technology. Furniture **02**, 7–11 (2020). https://doi.org/10.16610/j.cnki.jiaju.2020.02.002

Exploring Drag-and-Drop User Interfaces for Programming Drone Flights

Joshua Webb[✉] [iD] and Dante Tezza[✉] [iD]

St. Mary's University, San Antonio, TX 78228, USA
jwebb@mail.stmarytx.edu, dtezza@stmarytx.edu

Abstract. Drones are commonly seen in today's society, however, applications for drone swarms are still relatively new and emerging. As these applications grow in popularity, it becomes important to research new methods to control drone swarms while providing a better user experience to pilots and safer flights. In this paper, we present the design of a drag-and-drop user interface that allows both novice and experienced pilots to control drone swarms. Among its advantages, this type of interface can be easy-to-use, provide flexibility for flight modes and platforms, constant visual feedback, and accurate control. The user-interface design presented is based on the results of a focus group study conducted with seven participants divided into three sessions. Discussions and common characteristics found in participants' drawings during the focus group sessions enabled the design of the high-fidelity wireframe presented in this work. Following, the benefits a drag-and-drop interface provides to human-drone interaction and future research directions are discussed.

Keywords: Drones · Human-drone interaction · Unmanned-aerial vehicles · UAV

1 Introduction

Human-Drone Interaction is the field of study dedicated to understanding, designing, and evaluating drone systems for use by or with humans [12]. A major focuses for HDI researchers is to develop natural user interfaces [10] and new control modalities, such as gesture [11], speech [4], touch [1], brain-computer interfaces [9], first-person view control [13] and multi-modal interaction [5]. One control modality previously employed with ground robots [6] that has not been explored to control multiple drones simultaneously (a swarm of drones) is the use of drag-and-drop interfaces. This type of interface is widely used for different software (e.g. CAD, games, mobile applications, etc.) and is becoming ubiquitous in modern technologies. The hypothesis is that a drag-and-drop interface will allow both novice and experienced pilots to quickly and easily control a swarm of drones.

Supported by Connect-The Consortium on Nuclear Security Admin – National Nuclear Safety Administration (NNSA) Minority Serving Institutions (MSI) Program – Dr. Juan Ocampo, StMU PI.

© Springer Nature Switzerland AG 2021
C. Stephanidis et al. (Eds.): HCII 2021, CCIS 1498, pp. 191–196, 2021.
https://doi.org/10.1007/978-3-030-90176-9_26

To explore this type of interface for drone control, a focus group study was first conducted to elicit requirements and an initial application design. A focus group study design was chosen as it is a widely accepted method among research communities [8] to collect data on a specific topic through group interaction and discussion among participants [2,3,7]. The main advantage versus one-on-one interviews is the ability to collect data not accessible without the participants interacting as a group [8]. The results of this study enabled the design of a high-fidelity wireframe for a drag-and-drop mission control software for a drone swarm. In following studies, this design will be implemented and evaluated through a usability user study.

2   Methodology

The study design consists of a focus group with seven participants divided into three sessions (n = two, three, two). Each participant attended one session, which lasted between 30 and 60 min. The study was conducted remotely through Zoom for conference calls and Microsoft Whiteboard for sketch-designing. Recruitment was performed solely online, and each session was recorded by audio and video.

2.1   Procedures

In this study, each participant was given and referred to by a unique research ID number. Before the focus group session, participants were emailed a pre-experiment survey related to demographics and previous experience, the informed consent form, and download links for the software tools needed for the focus group (Zoom Meetings and Microsoft Whiteboard). The session began with verbal confirmation of consent and participants were reminded that the session being recorded and that their video was optional. Following this, a member of the research team moderated the session. Participants were introduced to the necessary features of the program, followed by questions regarding these features such as how to select drones for programming, activate and deactivate drones during a flight, turning drones on and off, toggling between control methods, and controlling drones in the drag-and-drop method.

2.2   Participants

A total of seven participants were recruited from a local university to participate in the study, four of them being males and three females. Out of these, six were between the ages of 18 and 24 and one was between 25 and 34 years old. Additionally, three participants declared no previous experience with drones, three declared beginner and one declared intermediate experience. Participants were divided into three different sessions (n = two, three, and two).

3   Results

This study explored a new control modality for drones, based on a drag-and-drop user interface. During three focus group sessions, the majority (six out of seven) participants agreed that a 3-D drag-and-drop user interface is an adequate control modality for drones, and provided insights on how the interface should look like and which features it should contain. During these sessions, participants also designed low-fidelity wireframes they believed to be easy-to-use and natural for interaction. These low-fidelity designs can be seen in Fig. 1.

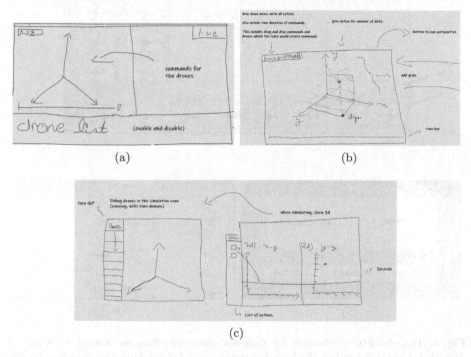

Fig. 1. Low-fidelity wireframes designed by participants during focus group sessions.

Participants' discussions during the study and common characteristics found in the low-fidelity wireframes (above) enabled the design of a high-fidelity wireframe, presented in Fig. 2a. This main user interface window is divided into four areas (marked in red). Area one is the main control area, where users can drag and drop each drone to the desired location. Additionally, users can manipulate this area with commands such as zoom (in and out), and plan rotations. The software also allows two control methods, (1) a live method will control drone movements as soon as the user drags and drops drone icons on the screen, and (2) a pre-planned flight will allow the user to plan the entire flight before it begins. The slide demonstrated in area two allows the user to control the time dimension when pre-planning flights. Additionally, area three presents the drone's telemetry screen, and area four each drone configuration tab. Lastly, Figs. 2b and c presents the initial menu to start the application, and a configuration window to allow further configuration options.

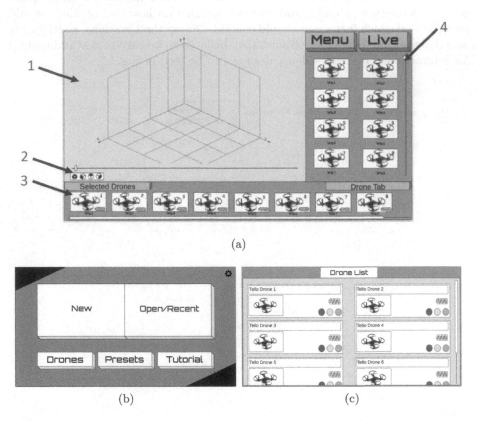

Fig. 2. High-fidelity wireframes for drag-and-drop interface to control a swarm of drones: (a) control window (b) launch window, and (c) configuration window. (Color figure online)

3.1   Discussion

The use of drag-and-drop style interfaces became popular in many applications, including video games, design software, block-based programming, robotics, and others. This type of interface has the potential to enhance the user experience in human-drone interaction. The advantages of controlling drone swarms through a drag-and-drop interface like the one presented in this work are summarized below.

- **Easiness of use** - Drag-and-drop user interfaces are easy-to-use in nature, and as mentioned, various applications already employ this approach.

For instance, modern smartphones are heavily based on drag-and-drop characteristics. Therefore, it becomes easy even for pilots without any previous experience to program drone flights. Additionally, they can potentially decrease the pilot's training period when compared to other control modalities, which also decreases the cost for commercial use of drones.
- **Flexibility** - another advantage is the flexibility provided in various aspects. First, dragging-and-drop drone icons on the screen can be used for different flight modes. For instance, the application presented in this work allows pilots to control the swarm in live (real-time) mode or pre-programmed flights without the need for training in a different control modality. Additionally, it allows different drones to be controlled in the same manner independently of their characteristics (i.e. cinematography vs racing drones). Lastly, it also allows pilots to control the drones from different hardware platforms using the same skill set. For example, the application presented above can be implemented for desktop computers and mobile applications in smartphones, from the pilot's perspective, the skills necessary to control the drone swarm are the same.
- **Control advantages** - there are also advantages directly related to the control of the drone swarm. The continuous visual feedback enables the pilot to precisely control each drone while monitoring the overall swarm flight. A potential drawback of this type of interface is that to make use of its advantages, it is required a modeled area of the flight zone. However, once the area has been modeled, it allows the pilot to control each drone to specific locations and enforce obstacle avoidance.

4   Conclusion and Future Work

Drag-and-drop interfaces are used on various software applications. Nonetheless, they have not been used to control drone swarms. This work's contribution to the human-drone interaction research field is the design of a drag-and-drop user interface for drone control. The design is based on the results of a focus group research conducted with seven participants and can be extended both for desktop and mobile applications. Novice and experienced pilots can control a drone or a swarm of drones by dragging and dropping their respective icons on the application screen.

This paper presents the initial design of a multi-study project. Following, this design will be individually presented to both novice and experienced pilots during interviews to collect feedback and further improve the design. After finalized, the design will be implemented and the system evaluated and compared to other control modalities through a usability study.

References

1. Abtahi, P., Zhao, D.Y., E, J.L., Landay, J.A.: Drone near me: exploring touch-based human-drone interaction. In: Proceedings of the ACM on Interactive, Mobile, Wearable and Ubiquitous Technologies, vol. 1, no. 3, pp. 1–8 (2017)

2. Asbury, J.E.: Overview of focus group research. Qual. Health Res. **5**(4), 414–420 (1995)
3. Beck, L.C., Trombetta, W.L., Share, S.: Using focus group sessions before decisions are made. N. C. Med. J. **47**(2), 73–74 (1986)
4. Cauchard, J.R., Janel, E., Zhai, K.Y., Landay, J.A.: Drone & me: an exploration into natural human-drone interaction. In: Proceedings of the 2015 ACM International Joint Conference on Pervasive and Ubiquitous Computing, pp. 361–365 (2015)
5. Fernandez, R.A.S., Sanchez-Lopez, J.L., Sampedro, C., Bavle, H., Molina, M., Campoy, P.: Natural user interfaces for human-drone multi-modal interaction. In: 2016 International Conference on Unmanned Aircraft Systems (ICUAS), pp. 1013–1022. IEEE (2016)
6. Ishii, K., Takeoka, Y., Inami, M., Igarashi, T.: Drag-and-drop interface for registration-free object delivery. In: 19th International Symposium in Robot and Human Interactive Communication, pp. 228–233. IEEE (2010)
7. Morgan, D.L.: Focus Groups as Qualitative Research, vol. 16. Sage Publications, Beverly Hills (1996)
8. Morgan, D.L.: Focus group interviewing. Handbook of interview research: context and method, pp. 141–159 (2002)
9. Nourmohammadi, A., Jafari, M., Zander, T.O.: A survey on unmanned aerial vehicle remote control using brain-computer interface. IEEE Trans. Hum.-Mach. Syst. **48**(4), 337–348 (2018)
10. Peshkova, E., Hitz, M., Kaufmann, B.: Natural interaction techniques for an unmanned aerial vehicle system. IEEE Perv. Comput. **16**(1), 34–42 (2017)
11. Sun, T., Nie, S., Yeung, D.Y., Shen, S.: Gesture-based piloting of an aerial robot using monocular vision. In: 2017 IEEE International Conference on Robotics and Automation (ICRA), pp. 5913–5920. IEEE (2017)
12. Tezza, D., Andujar, M.: The state-of-the-art of human-drone interaction: a survey. IEEE Access **7**, 167438–167454 (2019)
13. Tezza, D., Laesker, D., Andujar, M.: The learning experience of becoming a FPV drone pilot. In: Companion of the 2021 ACM/IEEE International Conference on Human-Robot Interaction, pp. 239–241 (2021)

Research on the Logical Levels and Roles of Human Interaction with Intelligent Creatures Under the Trend of Human-Computer Intelligence Integration

Wei Yu[✉] and Xiaoju Wang

School of Art Design and Media, East China University of Science and Technology,
Shanghai, China
weiyu@ecust.edu.cn

Abstract. At present, the combination of computers and humans in the field of artificial intelligence is getting closer and closer, which is not only reflected in the physical level, but also in the psychological level. Such a combination of computer and human is more like the birth of a new life form, which contains both the characteristics of natural life and the characteristics of non-life. In this paper, the interactive roles that will be generated under the premise of completing tasks in the "human-computer intelligent fusion" are divided into three categories: "smart creatures", biological humans and smart pieces. At the same time, these three types of roles will alternately produce three different types. The interactive relationship between "intelligent creatures" and "intelligent creatures", biological humans and "intelligent creatures", and biological humans and smart devices. After dividing the interactive relationship in the horizontal dimension, this article uses Donald Norman's "Three Designs" Each level" divides all kinds of interactions vertically. Then use Donald Norman's "Seven Stages of Action" to refine the design elements required for the three-tier interaction. Donald Norman's "Three Levels of Design" and "Seven Stages of Action" have been verified to help guide interaction design and human action design, and provide a useful framework for design activities. By expounding the interaction characteristics of each role and level, a more detailed discussion of the effectiveness of this new interaction is made, which provides usability reference for the upcoming human-machine intelligent integration interaction.

Keywords: Human-computer integration · Intelligent creatures · Smart pieces · Instinct · Behavior · Reflection

1 Introduction

1.1 Research Background

Modern human-computer interaction research has made considerable progress since its inception during the Second World War. The relationship between humans and machines and the division of roles have gone from the initial adaptation of machines to humans and now that humans cooperate with machines to make decisions. A profound transformation has taken place. With the maturity of big data, blockchain, biotechnology, and artificial intelligence technology, the relationship between man and machine is evolving increasingly fierce. With the continuous optimization and improvement of human-machine link bandwidth, the machine will gradually change from "other things" to "self-things" at the physical level. When artificial intelligence begins to gain a deeper grasp of situational awareness and decision analysis theoretical models, the machine will fully Qin into the human body and mind. At first, as an extension of human physical ability, the machine began to include the extension of emotion and mind. This will be the birth of a "new species" different from other creatures on the earth, which integrates the first natural life. The characteristics of (humans) and second natural life (robots) blur the boundaries between them. Before this new life form becomes the new normal, how should we examine the evolution of its role from the original physical and mechanical level to the spiritual level and even the ethical and philosophical level? How can we effectively interact with it and maintain a virtuous circle of communication and interaction?

Development of Artificial Intelligence Technology. Artificial intelligence has undergone more than 60 years of evolution since it was first proposed in 1956, from the initial development that was mainly used to prove formulas and theories to the current general artificial intelligence research that integrates various perceptions and different tasks [1]. Artificial intelligence is gradually transforming from a single field of task solution to providing multi-field task solutions, trying to solve more diverse problems. People are increasingly discovering that the bottleneck of artificial intelligence lies in the gap between it and human thinking, so simulation The neural network thinking mode of the human brain has become a hot topic in artificial intelligence research, and it has also become a breakthrough in breaking through the technical problems of artificial intelligence. Such as: natural semantic recognition processing, computer vision and complex environment situation awareness, analysis and decision-making, etc. The latest research in this area: Zhou et al. studied the temporal neural dynamics of different grammatical levels in reading Chinese and brain image processing [2] For vision, Orlov and Zohari [3] aimed to study the temporal combination of shape extraction using continuous partial shape views. Li and Zhong [4] proposed an innovative context-aware brain-computer interface system. Kumarasing et al. [5] proposed a brain-driven spiking neural network framework that can be used to learn and reveal the deep-level spatio-temporal functions and structural patterns in spatiotemporal data. Fincham et al. proposed a hidden semi-Markov model-multi-voxel mode-analysis method to infer the brain state sequence experienced by a person when performing tasks [6]. In terms of predicting personal response decision-making, Si et al. proposed an EEG driven computational intelligence method, which uses a supervised learning method to extract distinctive spatial network patterns from the brain network of a single experiment to predict different people's decision-making for the situation [7]. We can see that today's artificial intelligence has tried to imitate human thinking to solve problems, but there are already bottlenecks. For example, human thinking's unique emotions, motivations, subconsciousness, emotions and other factors are caused by artificial intelligence. What is not available, and these often play a very important role in decision-making. So at present, the best solution that people can see is the combination of computer intelligence and humans. Computers rely on big data and high efficiency to assist humans in making decisions, and they already have the thinking characteristics of some people, so in When the computer already has some human intelligence, we should handle our new interactive relationship with it.

Smart Devices and Smart Creatures. The smart device defined here refers to a device that has certain intelligence and participates in the decision-making process of human activities. The way of participation can be to participate in decision-making, which of course depends on the choice of the person interacting with it and the degree of trust in the device, or it can be an activity Presentation of data in the process. In this respect, smartphones are representative, which have become an extension of human beings. What humans see, think and make decisions to a large extent depend on the presentation of their respective smartphones and social media. They can resonate with our emotions. , Which also serves as a mental extension of human beings, but this extension has bandwidth problems with artificial intelligence [8]. Therefore, smart devices refer to devices that can cooperate for human activities. It is not limited to whether it is independent of the physical structure of the human body. At present, it seems that people are no longer satisfied with the coordination of the device outside the body, or not just limited to conventional touch. Simple interactions such as actions, and deeper interactions will produce more efficient and precise results, thereby exerting the capabilities of hardware and human potential to a greater extent. Wearable devices have become a popular research direction for the combination of humans and smart devices. [9–11] et al. proposed a new framework that can be used to develop new wearable systems in a cyber-physical universal computing environment. Chen Min et al. proposed The BioMan bionic robot can collect the user's physiological signals and design algorithms according to the human cognitive process [12]. The brain-computer interface (BCI) allows users to communicate with an external computer by means of brain signals to control the computer. In recent years, the decoding of brain information to control equipment has developed rapidly [13]. In the latest research, the intelligent living environment automatic adjustment control system (BSLEACS) based on the brain-computer interface will be automated to a new level [14]. Intelligent creatures are defined here as a combination of biological humans and smart devices. It is like a brand-new creature. This new creature manifests as a combination of equipment and humans at the physical level, and the deeper level is the birth of a new system. This new system includes the intelligent characteristics of machines and the physiological characteristics of normal people, but the two will participate in activities as a whole.

Human-Computer Intelligent Integration. Human-machine intelligence integration is to make full use of the strengths of any machine to form a new form of intelligence [1]. At present, there are still barriers to the process of artificial intelligence imitating human thinking, mainly because human cognition contains subjective factors, and computers are still extremely objective. Therefore, how to combine supervisory parameters with objective data is a difficult problem. People's decision-making is also affected by higher levels of emotions and consciousness, all of which make machines have limitations in imitating human thinking. Therefore, the best outcome for humans and machines will be to take their own strengths. Humans and machines do what they are good at. Humans use cognition to control machines in multiple dimensions. What we have to do is to achieve more of humans and machines. Interfaces and higher bandwidth make human-machine collaboration faster and more precise. To achieve a harmonious human-machine can only integrate and cooperate.

2 Theoretical Background and Methods

2.1 Theoretical Background

This article uses the "three levels of design" model proposed by Donald Norman in the book "Emotional Design" and the "seven stages of action" model he proposed in the book "Daily Design". Analyze the interaction mode between different roles, so as to get the paradigm characteristics that each level should have. The "three levels of design" proposed by Donald Norman include: "instinct level", "behavior level" and "reflection level". Norman and Northwestern University professors Andrew Otoni and William Revell found that the characteristics of human brain activity can be divided into three levels: the innate part, the instinct level; the level of controlling the body's daily behavior, the behavior level; the brain The thinking part, the level of reflection. These three levels reflect the original characteristics of the brain and play different roles in the human brain [15]. The three different levels of thinking correspond to different design levels, and each plays an important role in the user experience [15]. The "seven stages of action" are divided into: goal (determining the intention), plan (determining the plan), confirmation (action sequence), execution (implementation of action), perception (state of the external world), interpretation (perception effect) and comparison (Goals and results). The seven stages of action provide a useful basic framework for understanding human actions and guide design. It has also proven to be helpful in interaction design [16]. The seven stages of action provide guidance for the development of new products or services [16].

2.2 Method

In this paper, the "intelligent creatures" after the integration of human-computer intelligence are divided into three categories: "intelligent creatures", biological humans, and smart devices based on the completion of tasks. At the same time, these three types of roles will be produced alternately. There are three different effective interaction relationships, and the relationship with human participation is the effective relationship: the interactive relationship between "intelligent creatures" and "intelligent creatures", the interactive relationship between biological humans and "intelligent creatures", and the interactive relationship between biological humans and smart pieces, such as Shown in Fig. 1. After dividing the interaction relationship in the horizontal dimension, this article uses Donald Norman's "Three Levels of Design" in the book "Emotional Design" to divide the various interaction relationships vertically, including: the interaction of the instinct level. Relationships, emotional interactions, and reflective interactions, followed by Donald Norman's "Seven Stages of Action" in the book "Daily Design" to define what each interaction layer should have in each interaction relationship Interactive mode. This horizontal and vertical division method refines the possible range of human-machine fusion intelligent biological interaction, and then combines the action mode framework to fill in the content of each subdivided part, thereby making a more subdivided definition of the effectiveness of the new interaction.

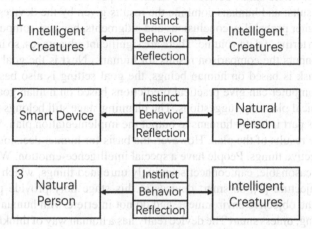

Fig. 1. Interaction and hierarchy

3   Conclusion

3.1   Interaction Between Biological Humans and Smart Devices

Biological people are normal people. If normal people and smart devices want to interact smoothly, they must include three levels of logic: instinct, behavior, and reflection. As the smallest unit of intelligent interaction relations, normal people play one of the roles, so they are in the interaction relationship. The source of this must be people-oriented, and smart devices assist humans in decision-making activities. In the process of smart devices assisting humans in completing tasks, humans will still lead the completion of seven steps: perception, interpretation, comparison, planning, confirmation and execution. Of these seven steps, execution and perception belong to the instinct level, and confirmation and interpretation belong to the behavior level., Planning and comparison belong to the level of reflection. Smart devices need to give humans assistance and feedback at every step, and there are precautions based on the existing interaction level. As shown in Fig. 2, perception is the first step to complete action. Biological humans instinctively perceive the external world to obtain information, thereby judging the situation, and producing instinctive physiological responses. Here, smart devices can be more sensitive than humans. Perception ability can be in the part that humans are not good at, or in the part that humans are good at. Smart devices can be used as an amplification of human perception. But because at this step, humans are often in sudden and passive acceptance. Because it belongs to the instinct level, humans are often in This step does not envisage the perception of smart devices, so the device needs default perception in the background, and after detecting that the human physiological response reaches the set warning value, it is based on the warning reminder to supplement the device's perception information. The interpretation step belongs to the behavioral level. Humans will map contact information with memory. At this time, smart devices can take advantage of their memory and big data based on a more precise interpretation of humans. The comparison step enters the reflection layer, where smart devices are needed to provide humans with more sample comparison results, and humans combine the results given by the devices to reflect, so as to obtain higher probability conclusions and judgments, because computers are better than humans in terms of data volume. There are significant advantages, so in this step, the smart device inputs the comparison results for humans. Next is the goal setting stage. Because the task is based on human beings, the goal setting is also based on human beings. The computer can give practical predictions based on human goals, as well as target hierarchical planning suggestions. The planning stage still belongs to the level of reflection. This part is led by humans to output the implementation plan. Smart devices can predict the results of the plan. However, the basis for human decisions is often not limited to objective things. People have a special intelligence-emotion. Wisdom, which means being reasonable, can connect seemingly unrelated things, which also includes subjective conjecture [1], so smart devices at this stage only provide predictions of the results of the objective environment, and do not interfere with human planning and decision-making, unless smart The device really has a human way of thinking, otherwise it will only make people offensive, just do what you are good at. Immediately after entering the confirmation stage, the action sequence is formulated in this stage, which belongs to the action stage, but the determination that the action sequence is still related to the plan will be carried out by humans, and the actual action steps can be selectively handed over to the smart device, and the smart device only confirms to the human at this step Action steps and accept whether to dispatch the action. The last step is execution. This part can be completed by humans choosing whether to deliver the device or not. If it is completed by a smart device, it requires immediate feedback of the execution result, in a way that humans can understand, and provide a way that humans can modify, terminate, and intervene.

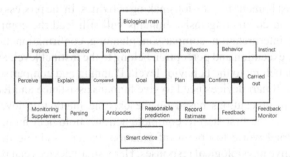

Fig. 2. Interaction between biological humans and smart devices

3.2 Interaction Between Biological Humans and Intelligent Creatures

There are still three levels of logic in the interaction between normal people and intelligent creatures, because one of the characters is still a biological person. There may be two situations when a normal person interacts with a smart creature. One is to interact with the biological part of the smart creature, and the other is to interact with the smart device when the biological person is on standby. But in either case, the way of interaction should be made more like human relations, because normal biological humans will not use intelligent creatures as real devices to communicate. Whatever interacts with him in real time is only the device, but he will also understand it. The person represented by the device. As shown in Fig. 3, when a biological person and an intelligent organism complete a task together, the biological person needs to perceive the state of the intelligent organism at the perceptual level. The intelligent device can provide a display of the state of the intelligent organism at this time, so that the biological person can obtain it intuitively. information. In the interpretation and comparison stage, biological humans can participate in the interpretation and comparison of smart devices in smart creatures, which means that smart devices need to have the ability to display to the outside world. In the goal and planning stage, intelligent creatures should use equipment to give data feedback based on the language, movement and emotions of the biological person interacting with it, and the feedback must be directly observed. Ultimately, intelligent creatures decide goals, plans, and sequence of actions. In the final execution stage, intelligent creatures need programs that can be intervened by others, which serve as repairs and maintenance, mainly physical-level interactions. At the same time, they need to display execution status and instant feedback information when collaborating with normal people.

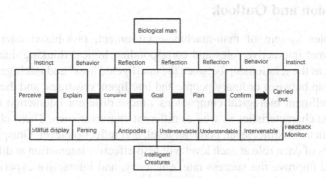

Fig. 3. Interaction between biological humans and intelligent creatures

3.3 Interaction Between Smart Creatures and Smart Creatures

Intelligent organisms and intelligent organisms have intelligent devices in the process of performing tasks, so the information aggregation at each step can be shared through wireless communication, so that both hosts can receive information. Human members of intelligent creatures can communicate with each other under higher-level interaction conditions. In this case, the communication between smart organisms is based on smart devices as an intermediary, which brings higher efficiency and accuracy. As shown in Fig. 4, in the perception, interpretation, and comparison stages, intelligent creatures use their own smart devices to display information and then complete the interaction logic with smart devices and biological humans. In the goal and planning stage, interpersonal communication and decision-making are still maintained, and computers are provided as information. In the confirmation and execution stage, it is necessary for intelligent creatures to choose to switch the host operating the intelligent hardware to transfer the task to the intelligent biological host with operational capabilities. In the case of normal cooperative execution, except for actively transferring status to other intelligent creatures In addition to information, intelligent creatures need to understand each other's operational capabilities.

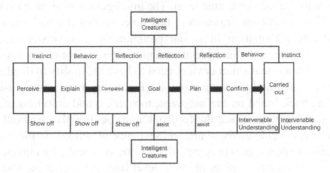

Fig. 4. The interaction between smart creatures and smart creatures

4   Discussion and Outlook

In the complex system of man-machine-environment, task-based interaction often derives different interactive roles and corresponding logical thinking due to position. For example, as the relationship between the intelligent "host" and intelligent machines, the relationship between ordinary people and intelligent creatures, and the relationship between "intelligent biological companions", these different interaction relationships have the same characteristics as well as different characteristics. These characteristics are reflected in the instinct level, behavior level, and reflection level. Grasping the interactive features of each role at each level will help effective interaction at different levels of needs, and improve the success rate, efficiency, and interactive experience of task completion. People also You can redesign and define functions, adjust operating specifications and parameter settings, and change the background management mode and software and hardware maintenance based on requirements. At the same time, what problems will the emergence of this new thing bring about social ethics and morality? The next research can consider positioning the role and meaning of the new "human-machine fusion intelligent creature" in society, examining its impact on the social level from different roles and different levels, and how we should deal with this situation, so as to promote the new The interaction between humans and AI of a generation is developing in the direction of a more harmonious "new interpersonal relationship", helping to compose a new collaborative model of a new "community of wisdom and destiny".

References

1. Liu, W.: Ask Artificial Intelligence-From Cambridge to Beijing. Science Press, Beijing (2019)
2. Zhou, X., Jiang, X., Ye, Z., Zhang, Y., Lou, K., Zhan, W.: Semantic integration processes at different levels of syntactic hierarchy during sentence comprehension: an ERP study. Neuropsychologia 48(6), 1551–1562 (2010)
3. Orlov, T., Zohary, E.: Object representations in human visual cortex formed through temporal integration of dynamic partial shape views. J. Neurosci. 38(3), 659–678 (2018)
4. Li, G., Chung, W.-Y.: A context-aware EEG headset system for early detection of driver drowsiness. Sensors 15(8), 20873–20893 (2015)
5. Kumarasinghe, K., Kasabov, N., Taylor, D.: Deep learning and deep knowledge representation in spiking neural networks for brain-computer interfaces. Neural Netw. 121, 169–185 (2020)
6. Fincham, J.M., Lee, H.S., Anderson, J.R.: Spatiotemporal analysis of event-related fMRI to reveal cognitivestates. Hum. Brain Mapp. 41(3), 666–683 (2020)
7. Si, Y., Li, F., Duan, K., Tao, Q., Li, C., Cao, Z., et al.: Predicting individual decision-making responses based on single-trial EEG. Neuroimage 206, 116333 (2020)
8. Kunlun Academy: Tech madman Musk: Human beings live in a more civilized game? Turn AI into a weapon! https://mp.weixin.qq.com/s/9JCyizTpfcmzGu_k4B5dRQ. Accessed 19 Sept 2018
9. Fortino, G., Galzarano, S., Gravina, R., et al.: A framework for collaborative computing and multi-sensor data fusion in body sensor networks. Inf. Fusion 22, 50–70 (2015)
10. Gravina, R., Alinia, P., Ghasemzadeh, H., et al.: Multi-sensor fusion in body sensor networks: state-of-the-art and research challenges. Inf. Fusion 35, 68–80 (2017)
11. Fortino, G., Giannantonio, R., Gravina, R., et al.: Enabling effective programming and flexible management of efficient body sensor network applications. IEEE Trans. Hum. Mach. Syst. 43(1), 115–133 (2013)
12. Chen, M., Jiang, Y., Cao, Y., Zomaya, A.Y.: CreativeBioMan: a brain- and body-wearable, computing-based, creative gaming system. IEEE Syst. Man Cybern. Mag. 6(1), 14–22 (2020)
13. Kamble, S.J., Kounte, M.R.: Enabling technologies for internet of vehicles. In: Pandian, A.P., Senjyu, T., Islam, S.M.S., Wang, H. (eds.) ICCBI 2018. LNDECT, vol. 31, pp. 257–268. Springer, Cham (2020). https://doi.org/10.1007/978-3-030-24643-3_31
14. Kounte, M.R., Tripathy, P.K., Pramod, P., Bajpai, H.: Implementation of brain machine interface using mind wave sensor. Procedia Comput. Sci. 171, 244–252 (2020)
15. Norman, D.: Design Psychology- Emotional design. CITIC Publishing House, Beijing (2015)
16. Norman, D.: Design Psychology- Everyday design. CITIC Publishing House, Beijing (2015)

An AR-Enabled See-Through System for Vision Blind Areas

Shaohua Zhang, Weiping He$^{(\boxtimes)}$, Shuxia Wang, Shuo Feng, Zhenghang Hou,
and Yupeng Hu

Cyber-Physical Interaction Lab, Northwestern Polytechnical University,
Xi'an 710072, People's Republic of China
weiping@nwpu.edu.cn

Abstract. The manual assembly has a high proportion in industry. However, in many industrial scenarios, manual assembly in the Vision Blind Areas (VBAs) is time-consuming and challenging due to the lack of necessary visual information. This study presented a see-through Augmented Reality (AR) system to solve the problems during manual assembly in the vision blind area. This system enabled users to see the inner components of the VBAs cross the surface of mechanical products. The human hand and the mechanical part in a VBA were tracked and rendered in an AR HMD. We developed a prototype system and conducted a user study to evaluate the system usability, users' performance and workload. The results indicated that this system was well integrated and easy to use. Moreover, participants worked with this system had a lower workload with improved performance.

Keywords: Vision blind area · Augmented reality · Hand tracking

1 Introduction

AR has been a popular technology, which provides a seamless interface that bridges the gap between the real and virtual worlds [1]. In recent years, AR has been applied to training scenarios in different fields, such as industry [2], healthcare [3], military [4], and education [5].

One of the most promising application areas of the technique is the manual assembly of mechanical products since it provides real-time onscreen instructions for users. However, there are many practical assembly scenarios with an invisible and narrow space, which leads to Vision Blind Areas (VBAs). For VBAs, workers take the parts and machine tools into the invisible space and understand the inner structures of mechanical products by directly touching the surfaces. The invisibility of hands, parts and inner structures of the product results in lower efficiency, higher error rate, and a heavier workload. Workers have to perceive the assembly condition greatly based on their experiences, and the mechanical parts may even hurt their hands.

In this work, we present a prototype AR system to enable users to see the inner components of the VBAs cross the surface of mechanical products. We tracked the

C. Stephanidis et al. (Eds.): HCII 2021, CCIS 1498, pp. 206–213, 2021.
https://doi.org/10.1007/978-3-030-90176-9_28

user's hand and the handheld part and rendered them in AR HMD. The inner structure of the VBA was also rendered to help users quickly understand and find the location for the part to be assembled. With this prototype, we conducted a user study to explore the effect of this system, including users' mental effort, system usability, and efficiency in a controlled part assembly task.

2 Related Works

2.1 AR-Assisted Assembly Systems

AR-assisted systems have been developed generally to augment virtual instructions onto a user's view to facilitate assembly processes [6]. It enables operators to perform tasks that require a higher level of qualification. Mizell et al. [7] proposed the first implementation of a classic AR assembly guidance system by combining head position sensing and real-world registration with a head-mounted display (HMD). Henderson et al. [8] developed an AR prototype that supports military mechanics conducting routine maintenance tasks inside an armored vehicle turret. Yin et al. [9] proposed a synchronous AR assembly assistance and monitoring system, which monitors the operator's hand activity and process completeness to recognize the assembly state and then display the AR contents contextually.

Some of the AR assembly guiding systems focus solely on providing step-based instructions for the users and add virtual instructions directly on the real object in the view. In these scenarios, the components that need to be tracked are within the user's view to be tracked easily by optical sensors. In contrast, once the assembly task is in the VBAs, the components are difficult to be tracked by traditional methods. Therefore, this work focuses on the tracking of the components in the VBAs.

Vision is an important channel for perceiving the world [10]. If users visualize their own hands' movement while performing the task, they could accelerate the learning process. Therefore, we speculate that the visualization of hand and other components in VBAs may enhance users' spatial perception ability and help users to operate efficiently. The virtual 3D models of the inner structure can be easily superimposed on the real products to help workers understand. For parts grabbed in hand, their locations are obtained indirectly by specific gestures. Therefore, tracking hand movements is a crucial portion and most difficult for VBAs.

2.2 Hand Tracking Technology

In general, we fall into two categories to track the user's hand movements: through optical sensors, such as the Microsoft Kinect or the Leap Motion, or by using inertial sensors or data-gloves [11]. Optical sensors are usually installed on HMDs during interactions in AR systems. However, if the hand holds a tool or the hand is obstructed by other structure, the hand movements will not be tracked. In terms of data-gloves, they are more expensive than optical trackers and require proper calibration to obtain acceptable tracking performance. However, they are robust to occlusion issues when the user holds a tool.

Hung et al. [12] developed an AR system to assisted manual assembly with occluded components. In their system, a Leap Motion was placed in the occluded region of assembly products to track the operator's hand movement in real time. The limitation of this system is that the Leap Motion's location in real industrial scenarios is random, because there is no special structure to fix it. Moreover, in many precise equipment, the redundant devices are not allowed to intrude into the inner structure. In this case, data-gloves are more appropriate, because data-gloves are fixed on the users' real hand, not on the mechanical products. For our prototype, we expected to install less auxiliary sensors on the inner structure of mechanical products. Therefore, we used data-gloves to track users' hand in VBAs.

3   Methodology

3.1   System Implementation and Setup

In this work, we implemented an AR prototype to visualize inner components in VBAs (ARVBA). The inner components include the users' hand, the parts grabbed in hand and the inner structure of mechanical products. The participants wore a 2nd generation HoloLens, served as the AR HMD to render the inner components, and a data-glove consisted of seven bending sensors and three positioning sensors.

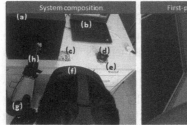

Fig. 1. System composition: (a) a black box, (b) server, (c) first picture from Vuforia library, (d) first VIVE Tracker, (e) second picture from Vuforia library, (f) HoloLens, (g) second VIVE Tracker, (h) data-glove; First-person perspective in HoloLens: (i) virtual hand, (j) part to be assembled, (k) the location for the part to be assembled; First-person perspective without HoloLens: (l) real hand.

We integrated a data-glove, two VIVE trackers, and two pictures from the Vuforia tracking library (see Fig. 1). Through the data-glove, we obtained the hand gestures and arm gestures, which were associated with the shoulder. Then, we fixed the first VIVE Tracker to the shoulder, and their centers were coincident. At the same time, we placed the second VIVE Tracker on the desk, whose center was coincident with the first picture's center. Then, we calculated the relative location matrix (M_1) of the first VIVE Tracker to the second VIVE Tracker with a calibration algorithm. We found that M_1 was also the relative location matrix of the shoulder to the first picture through the coincident centers. In the AR world, we set the first picture's center as the world center, and we got the location matrix (M_2) of the first picture. Therefore, we calculated the shoulder location matrix (M_3) in real-time through Eq. (1). Then, we analyzed hand movements by the shoulder location and gestures.

$$M_3 = M_1 \cdot M_2 \tag{1}$$

For the parts grabbed in hand, we indirectly obtained their locations by specific hand gestures. We stipulated participants to grab the parts with index and thumb fingers. Thus, we calculated part's location through the specific fingertip locations. Finally, to render the inner structure of mechanical products, the virtual inner structure was superimposed on the real products directly.

This prototype was developed by Unity3D (version 2019.3.13f1) with a client-server mechanism. The server side was on a Windows 10 PC (AMD 3700X, 16 GB of RAM, and an NVIDIA GTX 1650S). The data-glove and trackers were connected to it. The client side was HoloLens, which communicated with the PC by UDP. The server analyzed the sensors' data and calculated matrixes, and sent them to the client. The client received the datum and calculated hand location and hand gestures, and rendered the hand and part in the real world.

3.2 Hypotheses

According to the literature review and analyses, we found that visual perception influences operation and training. Therefore, we conducted a user study to explore the effect of visualizing components in VBAs. Our study set the ARVBA as the experimental group, while operation in VBAs with paper instructions (PIVBA) was set as the control group. Then, we defined the following hypotheses for our study:

H1) The users' performance will be improved by visualizing inner components in VBAs during operation.
H2) Users will have a lower mental workload by visualizing inner components in VBAs during operation.

3.3 Participants

The experiment involved a total of 20 participants (12 males and 8 females) from the university aging from 23 to 30 (M = 24.3; SD = 1.5). All of them came from the school of mechanical engineering, majoring in mechanical engineering or industrial design. Fifteen of them are right-hand, 4 left-hand, and 1 ambidextrous. Eighteen of them have experience of using AR applications, with 8 of them usually developing AR applications. Six participants have the experience of data-glove.

3.4 Experimental Procedure

The task was installing bolts to the bolt holes and square plugs to the sockets. The bolt holes and sockets were inside a black box. All participants performed the task in two conditions (one time for each condition). The order of the condition sets was randomized based on a Latin Square design to avoid ordering effects in the within-subject design. In terms of PIVBA, participants operated the assembly task with the paper instructions, which described mechanical and key dimensions in detail (see Fig. 2a). Regarding ARMBS, participants wore a HoloLens and a data-glove, observing the inner components through HoloLens in real time (see Fig. 2b).

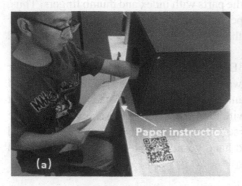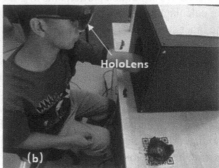

Fig. 2. (a) Operation with PIVBA; (b) Operation with ARVBA.

As dependent variables, we measured the mental effort of participants and the usability and efficiency of the system to evaluate how the participants performed differently in VBAs in different conditions. For the mental effort, a Subjective Mental Effort Questionnaire (SMEQ) [13] was evaluated to observed whether the different conditions affect the users' workload. For system usability, we utilized the System Usability Scale (SUS) questionnaire [14], a commonly adopted method, to evaluate the usability of the system being tested. The SMEQ was rated between 0 to 150 (0 = no effort; 150 = amount of effort), and the SUS was rate on a five-point Likert scale (1 = strongly disagree; 5 = strongly agree). The task completion time was recorded and measured during the task. In addition, we also recorded the time of installing bolts and the time of installing plugs.

4 Results

4.1 Objective Measures

The results for objective measures are detailed in Fig. 3a. ARVBA helped users save more time than PIVBA on total time ($t_1 = 164.3$ s, $t_2 = 201.8$ s), on bolts ($t_1 = 66.3$ s , $t_2 = 80.5$ s), on plugs ($t_1 = 98.0$ s , $t_2 = 121.3$ s). Then, we checked the normality assumption of the data through the Shapiro-Wilk test, which indicated that they all follow a normal distribution. Finally, the paired samples t-test was used for these variables data to compare the mean values for the two conditions. The test showed significant difference on the condition on the mean total time [$t = -3.24$; $p = 0.004$] and on the mean time of installing plugs [$t = -3.97$; $p = 0.001$], while shows no significant effect of the condition on the mean time of installing bolts [$t = -2.33$; $p = 0.031$].

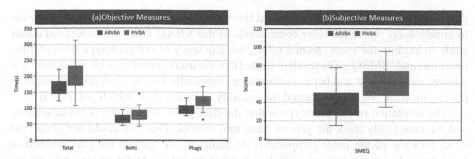

Fig. 3. (a) Time measures; (b) Score of subjective mental effort questionnaire (SMEQ)

4.2 Subjective Measures

The results for SMEQ are detailed in Fig. 3b. We found that the scores of SMEQ are normally distributed. We also used paired-samples t-test to compare the means scores of SMEQ. The test shows a significant effect of the condition on the participant's mean scores of SMEQ [t = −4.52; p < 0.001]. In addition, the SUS score reports a mean value of 77.35 (SD = 9.32), which stands for a grade B$^+$ on the usability scale.

5 Discussion

Based on the analyzes of the results, we verify our hypotheses H1 and H2. Firstly, users operated in VBAs with ARVBA would have great efficiency, especially for a complex task. For a more manageable task, such as installing the bolts, users only need to find the general location of the bolt holes through vision. Then, they would find the precise location with tactile sensation. For a complex task, such as installing the plugs, the workers need to find the location and spatial poses of the sockets. In this case, vision is predominant. The ARVBA provided users with abundant vision information in VBAs. Therefore, the users could work with enhanced performance.

Secondly, the analysis of SMEQ showed that users operating in VBAs with ARVBA would have a lower mental workload than the traditional approach. For ARVBA, users could observe the hands, parts, and inner structure of mechanical products. They did not need to guess the location of the inner structure with just tactile sensation. In addition, they did not need to analyze the inner structure by abstract paper. Therefore, they had little stress on the task.

Finally, in terms of usability, the SUS questionnaire reports an above-average value (77.35), verifying that ARVBA is suitable for operation in VBAs and easy to use for users.

6 Conclusion and Future Work

Mechanical assembly is one of the most promising application domains of AR that provides real-time guidance for users. However, there are many practical assembly scenarios with an invisible and narrow space, which leads to vision blind areas. In this work, we developed a prototype system, integrated HoloLens and data-glove with tracking sensors to enable users to see the inner components of the VBAs. Then, we conducted a user study to explore the users' mental effort, the efficiency of our prototype through time measures and "SMEQ". The result indicated that the users operating with this system had a lower mental effort and better performance, especially for the complex task required precise location. We also evaluated the usability of this system, which got level B^+.

The limitation of our prototype is that the data-glove only contains seven sensors, and we could only track the general hand movements. Thus, we could not obtain the exact location of the inner components. In addition, we tracked the part grabbed in hand through specific gestures, which is another limitation. In future research, we are planning to explore more precise tracking technology suitable for operation in VBAs. Furthermore, we will conduct more comprehensive user studies with a more improved system.

Acknowledgement. This work is partially supported by the National Key R&D Program of China (Grant No. 2019YFB1703800), Natural Science Basic Research Plan in Shaanxi Province of China (Grant No. 2016JM6054), the Programme of Introducing Talents of Discipline to Universities (111 Project), China (Grant No. B13044).

References

1. Behzadan, A.H., Timm, B.W., Kamat, V.R.: General purpose modular hardware and software framework for mobile outdoor augmented reality applications in engineering. Adv. Eng. Inform. **22**(1), 90–105 (2008)
2. Lorenz, M., Knopp, S., Kim, J., et al.: Industrial augmented reality: 3D-content editor for augmented reality maintenance worker support system. In: 2020 IEEE International Symposium on Mixed and Augmented Reality Adjunct (ISMAR-Adjunct). IEEE, Brazil (2020)
3. Heinrich, F., Joeres, F., Kai, L., et al.: Comparison of projective augmented reality concepts to support medical needle insertion. IEEE Trans. Vis. Comput. Graph. **25**, 2157–2167 (2019)
4. Livingston. M.A., Rosenblum, L.J., Julier, S.J., et al.: An augmented reality system for military operations in urban terrain. In: Proceedings of Interservice/Industry Training, Simulation & Education Conference 2002, Orlando (2008)
5. Köse, H., Güner-Yildiz, N.: Augmented reality (AR) as a learning material in special needs education. Educ. Inf. Technol. **26**(2), 1921–1936 (2020). https://doi.org/10.1007/s10639-020-10326-w
6. Wang, X., Ong, S.K., Nee, A.: Multi-modal augmented-reality assembly guidance based on bare-hand interface. Adv. Eng. Inform. **30**(3), 406–421 (2016)
7. Caudell, T.P., Mizell, D.W.: Augmented reality: an application of heads-up display technology to manual manufacturing processes. In: Hawaii International Conference on System Sciences. IEEE (1992)
8. Henderson, S., Feiner, S.: Exploring the benefits of augmented reality documentation for maintenance and repair. IEEE Trans. Vis. Comput. Graph. **17**(10), 1355–1368 (2011)
9. Yin, X., Fan, X., Zhu, W., et al.: Synchronous AR assembly assistance and monitoring system based on ego-centric vision. Assem. Autom. **39**(1), 1–16 (2019)
10. Jung, S., Bruder, G., Wisniewski, P.J., et al.: Over my hand: using a personalized hand in VR to improve object size estimation, body ownership, and presence. In: The Symposium. ACM, Berlin (2018)

11. Saurabh, Dargar, Rebecca, et al.: Haptic technology Immersive virtual reality surgical learning Surgical simulations. J, Comput. Surg. **2**(2), 1–26 (2015)
12. Chu, C.H., Ko, C.H.: An experimental study on augmented reality assisted manual assembly with occluded components. J. Manuf. Syst. (2021)
13. Grochola, L.F., Soll, C., Zehnder, A., et al.: Robot-assisted single-site compared with laparoscopic single-incision cholecystectomy for benign gallbladder disease: protocol for a randomized controlled trial. BMC Surg. **17**(1), 13 (2017)
14. Brooke, J.: SUS: a quick dirty usability scale. Usability Eval. Ind. **189**(1), 15 (1996)

IMGDS - Intelligent Multi-dimensional Generative Design System for Industrial SCADA

Wei Zhao[✉], Ruihang Tian, Nan Zhao, Jiachun Du, and Hanyue Duan

Alibaba Cloud, Hangzhou, People's Republic of China
{ruihang.tianrh,jiachun.djc,hanyue.dhy}@alibaba-inc.com

Abstract. Through design and implementation of IMGDS in SCADA, we are able to create a more user-friendly information display system for industries. We offer comprehensive and high quality pre-designed industrial component system to use improve conventional industry design. Such a system can switch intelligently between monitoring mode and key information mode. In the meantime, to meet industrial needs, multi-dimensional display system with 2D and 3D switch mode is developed. Also, a theme switching mode is presented to meet brand need, nighttime operation and other purposes.

Keywords: SCADA · IMGDS · User experience design · Generative design system · IoT

1 Background

SCADA (Supervisory Control and Data Acquisition) is a computer system for gathering and analyzing real time data, which is widely used in factories. For lack of use experience design consideration, traditional SCADA system have multiple drawbacks, such as poor user experience design (both bad interface visual and user interaction), lack of standard and high-quality industry component, inefficient key information display, restricted operation mode (no 2D and 3D mutual switch), lack of remote operation abilities, etc. But with continuous more application of cloud computing and IoT (Internet of things) in the field, opportunities are opened for solving aforementioned problems.

In this poster, we present IMGDS – Intelligent Multi-Dimensional Generative Design System to improve the existing user experience of traditional SCADA, which is formed with user experience consciousness, industry knowledge, design guidelines and technological tools developed by Alibaba Cloud IoT. Compared with traditional SCADA design, what improvements in user experience IMGDS can bring about are listed as follows.

2 IMGDS Advantages

2.1 A More User-Friendly Information Display Design

In IMGDS, we bring consumer-level interface design standard into SCADA. What we provide to application users are information display guidelines and pre-designed solution templates. Therefore, users can design applications by following the guidelines to

C. Stephanidis et al. (Eds.): HCII 2021, CCIS 1498, pp. 214–219, 2021.
https://doi.org/10.1007/978-3-030-90176-9_29

meet their specific needs, or use pre-designed templates to create deliverable solutions faster and easier. To make sure these pre-designed solution templates meet the needs of real scenarios in the industry, during the process of designing, not only do we pursue better user experience, but also we take into account industry expertise and customer actual cases. Until the end of March 2021, we will have launched 25 new high-quality official templates in IoT Studio. On the one hand, the number of calls to use this solution template has increased by more than 15% compared to the old solution templates, and every new solution template has been used. On the other hand, we have also received positive compliments from corporate users for using templates, including Shanghai Kinco Automation Co., Ltd. Customers highly praised the fresh new visuals and better interaction experience of the new information display system. Based on these, we can see the new information display system we launched has been accepted by customers.

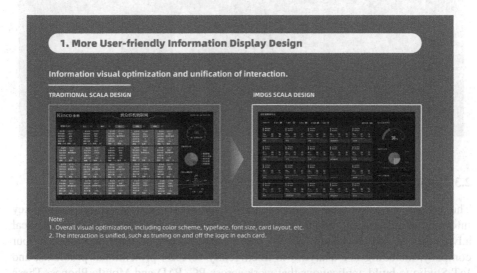

2.2 Comprehensive and High Quality Industrial Component System

Firstly, we formulated explicit design specifications for industrial components. Then, we have cooperated with our third-party partners to produce more than 140 high-quality industrial component systems. These components were recently used in an actual delivery project and received positive reviews from clients. We expect that as the number of component systems gradually increases and meet the needs of more industrial scenarios, more enterprise users or individual developer users will use these high-quality component systems for project delivery to their clients.

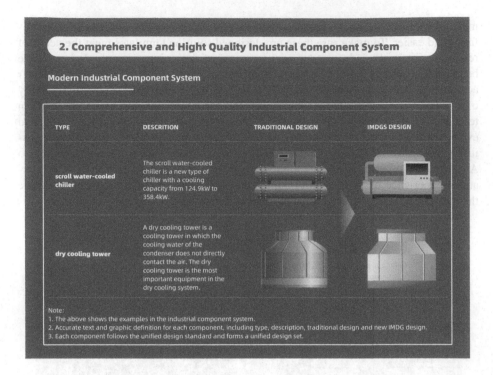

2.3 Monitoring Information Mode and Key Information Mode

The system can detect what is abnormal and intelligently generate corresponding key information mode at the right time. During this process, we make use of the ecological advantages of Alibaba Cloud IoT. We make use of combined tools developed by our company, including IoT analytics to intelligently forecast protentional problems, and IoT Studio to build applications that work across PC, PAD and Mobile Phones. These alarm information and interface windows can not only be created with ease but can also work across on all plat-forms, especially in the scenarios of remote monitoring, which not only saves R&D expense for companies but makes remote control possible. As we know from user research, remote control with explicit alarm information can save a large number of maintenance cost of different companies.

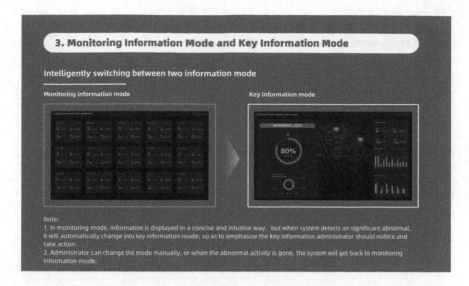

2.4 Multi-dimensional Information Display (2D 3D Mutual Conversion Information Display System)

Through a demo demonstration to beta test users, they showed a strong interest for the new 3D digital space workbench. The 3D workbench is currently in the internal test development stage and will be open to more users at the end of March. Users can create 2D and 3D application on one application and they can switch to one another seamlessly with just one-click. From user research, we know that many users encounter difficulties in obtaining high-quality 3D models, which cause direct troubles in creating 3D applications. To solve this, we will launch an official 3D model library in the 3D workbench, and in the future, we are planning to open an online 3D model store in it to bring more and diverse models to users. Now, we have offered more than a hundred 3D prefabricated models, and the number just keeps growing. Also, there is a way for users to upload 3D models to meet their own needs.

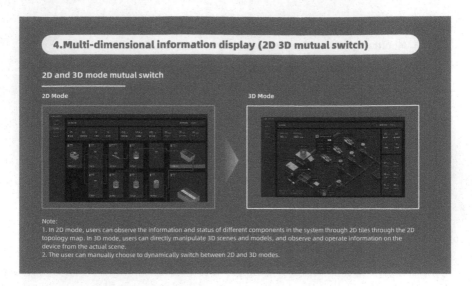

2.5   Theme Switching: Light Mode, Dark Mode, and User-Defined Color Mode

Dark mode is really helpful for users when they perform tasks under low light, and it is a good way for users to focus on the information. Also, we provide theme managed system to better meet user needs in personalizing with their own brand color (red, blue, yellow, etc.). In the near future, we are going to introduce intelligent control into theme management, so that the them color can not only change according to light condition, but also can adjust by uploading a picture from users.

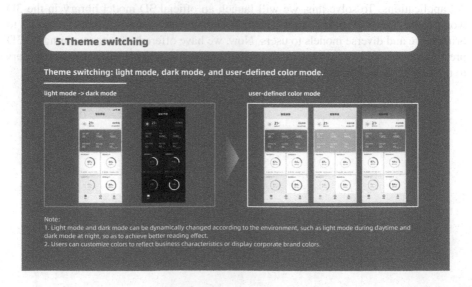

3 IMGDS Limitations

We clearly understand that IMGDS, as a design system that is aimed to serve industrial scenarios, still has a number of limitations, especially the understanding of industry expertise. IMGDS should provide a set of designs guidelines, design materials and design tools that truly meet the real needs of the industry. To solve this problem, we are also conducting in-depth communication with industry experts in order to improve this system from a deeper level.

4 Conclusion

With IMGDS, existing SCADA user experience has been improved dramatically in multiple ways. After we implement this system in IoT Studio, we have produced 25 sets of high-quality solution templates, 140+ 2D modern industrial components and 100+ 3D models that meet the needs of the industry. Meanwhile, the number of these design materials is still increasing. More than 3 partners have used our solution and materials to design and deliver on-site solutions, and clients have highly praised the freshly new visuals and better interaction experience with the help of IMGDS. Until now, we have received multiple positive recognition and affirmation from customers.

Design Team: Alibaba Cloud IoT DESIGN.

Tools: IoT Studio/Xconsole Studio/Link UI/IoT analytics/IoT Link Platform.

References

1. Bailey, D., Wright, E.: Practical SCADA for Industry. Elsevier (2003)
2. Sajid, A., Abbas, H., Saleem, K.: Cloud-assisted IoT-based SCADA systems security: a review of the state of the art and future challenges. IEEE Access **4**, 1375–1384 (2016)
3. Igure, V.M., Laughter, S.A., Williams, R.D.: Security issues in SCADA networks. Comput. Secur. **25**(7), 498–506 (2006)
4. Carlson, R.: Sandia SCADA program high-security SCADA LDRD final report. SANDIA Rep. SAND **729**, 2002 (2002)
5. Tom, R.J., Sankaranarayanan, S.: IoT based SCADA integrated with fog for power distribution automation. In: 2017 12th Iberian Conference on Information Systems and Technologies (CISTI), pp. 1–4. IEEE, June 2017
6. Aghenta, L.O., Iqbal, M.T.: Low-cost, open source IoT-based SCADA system design using thinger. IO and ESP32 thing. Electronics **8**(8), 822 (2019)
7. Saravanan, K., Anusuya, E., Kumar, R.: Real-time water quality monitoring using Internet of Things in SCADA. Environ. Monit. Assess. **190**(9), 1–16 (2018)
8. Nasr, M.S., Abdullah, A.N.: Design and Implementation of IoT cloud moveable SCADA supported by GSM for industrial applications. J. Babylon Univ./Eng. Sci. **2**, 409–424 (2017)
9. Aghenta, L.O., Iqbal, M.T.: Design and implementation of a low-cost, open source IoT-based SCADA system using ESP32 with OLED, ThingsBoard and MQTT protocol. AIMS Electron. Electr. Eng. **4**(1), 57 (2020)
10. Zhou, T., Zhang, J.: Design and implementation of agricultural Internet of Things system based on Aliyun IoT platform and STM32. In: Journal of Physics: Conference Series, vol. 1574, no. 1, pp. 012159. IOP Publishing, June 2020

Interaction with Robots, Chatbots, and Agents

Storytelling Robots for Training of Emotion Recognition in Children with Autism; Opinions from Experts

Maryam Alimardani[✉] [iD], Lisa Neve, and Anouk Verkaart

Tilburg University, 5037 AB Tilburg, The Netherlands
m.alimardani@tilburguniversity.edu

Abstract. Social robots are being increasingly used in the therapy of children with autism spectrum disorder (ASD). However, robot interaction is often designed by HRI researchers who are not fully familiar with cognitive challenges faced by children with autism. This study aimed to validate a social robot interaction designed for emotion recognition training for children with autism by seeking opinions from ASD educators and experts. A total of 26 participants (13 ASD experts and 13 non-experts) filled out a survey in which they watched videos of six emotional gestures performed by a NAO-robot. The emotional gestures were prepared with and without situational context presented in form of storytelling by the robot. Participants first made a recognition of the robot emotion in each gesture and then evaluated the feasibility of gesture recognition for children with ASD. Results showed that for almost all emotions, addition of context by storytelling significantly increased the feasibility of gesture recognition. Gestures were considered as not feasible for children with ASD when storytelling was missing and that in general, experts gave a significantly lower feasibility score to robot gestures as compared to non-experts. Our findings suggest that creation of context play an important role in the design of robot gestures which can make the training of social skills in children with ASD more effective. Additionally, the observed difference in the evaluation of the two groups suggests that social robot interventions should be validated by professionals who are more knowledgeable about social and cognitive difficulties experienced by these children.

Keywords: Autism (ASD) · Social robots · Child-robot interaction · Emotional gestures · Facial Emotion Recognition (FER) · Situational context · Experts

1 Introduction

Children acquire social skills when growing up and use these skills to create relationships with others. However, for children diagnosed with Autism Spectrum Disorder (ASD), learning and developing social skills is not self-evident. For example, they find it difficult to identify human emotions from verbal and facial expressions [1]. Emotions are an important aspect of human-human interaction [1], and therefore such impairment in the development of Facial Emotion Recognition (FER) skills can have negative effects on

© Springer Nature Switzerland AG 2021
C. Stephanidis et al. (Eds.): HCII 2021, CCIS 1498, pp. 223–233, 2021.
https://doi.org/10.1007/978-3-030-90176-9_30

the future relationships and social interactions of these children [2]. Research shows that early life interventions can help children with ASD acquire these skills, which in return can positively impact their quality of life [3] and prevent negative consequences in their adulthood such as loneliness and depression [4].

In recent years, more emphasis has been placed on employment of social robots in teaching of social skills to children with autism [2, 5, 6]. Social robots are useful in these training programs, because compared to humans, robots can create a more predictable and safe environment for these children and hence are preferred by them [5]. Additionally, social robots have benefits over other existing technologies such as computer-generated characters or tablets. Computer-generated animations lack spatial interaction, which is quite important to keep children with low-functioning autism interested and engaged in the training [7]. On the other hand, tablets can evoke outbursts in children with autism or even cause obsessive behavior [8]. Therefore, social robots are generally preferred over other assistive technologies.

Within the terrain of affect recognition training for children with ASD, two types of robot interaction are common: robots that teach emotions through expressive faces (e.g. ZECA-robot [9] or QT-robot [10]) and robots that teach emotions through gestures, such as the NAO-robot [1, 6, 11]. Most gestures of the NAO-robot are accompanied by sounds and changing LED colors, and are derived from real-life human movements [11]. The robot's mimicking of the human emotions is considered helpful in generalizing acquired skills to other human encounters outside of the training setup [11, 12].

While some studies only focus on emotion training by focusing on gestures and imitation [6, 11], others have gone a step further and included FER in the training [1, 9, 13] to establish a relationship between emotions, gestures and facial expressions. A recent case study by Conti et al. [1] showed positive impact of a NAO-robot in FER training of a single child with ASD over four weeks. Soares et al. [9] used a ZECA-robot to improve FER skills of children with high-functioning ASD by combining robot gestures, robot facial expression and storytelling. Although an improvement in FER skills was found, the contribution of each employed factor remained unclear. It has been demonstrated in the past that adding situational context through stories can improve recognition of robot gestures among normal individuals [14]. Also storytelling robots [15] and avatars [16] have been shown useful in increasing social performance and safety awareness in children with autism. However, it still remains unclear how creation of situational context through storytelling can enhance emotional gesture recognition and feasibility of FER training for children with ASD.

In this study, we developed an emotion recognition training using robot gestures and storytelling and validated the training design by seeking opinions from two groups of ASD experts and non-experts. Both groups watched the robot gestures with and without created stories and evaluated the training for children with ASD. Consequently, the following research questions were formulated:

RQ1: Does the addition of situational context to robot gestures influence emotion recognition accuracy?

RQ2: Is the recognition of the robot emotional gestures evaluated as feasible for children with ASD by experts and non-experts?

Given that situational context had a positive effect on emotion recognition of healthy individuals in earlier research [14], we hypothesized that participants would recognize emotions more accurately when the robot gestures were accompanied by stories. Additionally, it was expected that both groups would evaluate robot gestures more feasible for children with ASD when the gestures were accompanied by stories. Furthermore, we hypothesized a difference of feasibility assessment between the two groups as experts were expected to know better the challenges faced by children with autism [13].

2 Experimental Setup

2.1 Preparation of Robot Gestures and Stories

The humanoid NAO-robot (version 6, SoftBank Robotics) was used in this research. This robot is particularly popular for child-robot interaction because its human-like appearance can prompt social responses in children with autism [1]. The robot movements were programmed in Choregraphe 2.8.6.23. The gestures were accompanied by LED colors and sounds depending on the emotion. The emotional gestures Happiness and Anger were adopted from the research of Miskam et al. [11] and the gestures representing Sadness, Surprise, Fear and Disgust were taken from the research of Monceaux et al. [12]. The gestures were based on human movements and should therefore be more educational and possibly recognizable [16]. Figure 1a shows the envisioned FER training with the NAO-robot. The child watches a robot gesture and selects the corresponding facial expression from the available cards that would best match the portrayed emotion by the robot. Figure 1b provides images of the developed robot movements when gesturing each emotion. The association of the robot eyes LED color with each emotion was based on the research of Johnson et al. [17].

Situational context was created by one-sentence short stories that were told by the robot. A total of 48 sentences were prepared by the researchers and validated beforehand by 20 people (other than the two subject groups of this study) who were recruited through convenience sampling. If a story was an insufficient representation of an emotion (inter-rater reliability below 0.5), it was removed from the list. Table 1 includes examples of the approved stories for which the inter-rater reliability was the highest.

2.2 Participants

A total of 26 Dutch participants took part in this study. None of them had any deficits in emotion recognition. All participants reported their knowledge of autism on a 5-point Likert scale (1 = very little, 5 = very much). Thirteen participants (4M/9F, M (age) = 34.85, SD (age) = 12.88) had extensive knowledge of autism (Knowledge score 4 or 5) and were considered as the Expert group (e.g. they were teachers, parents or supervisors of children with ASD). The rest (4M/9F, M (age) = 47.46, SD (age) = 15.67) had little knowledge of autism and were seen as Non-Experts in this study.

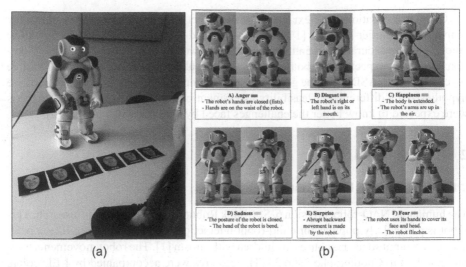

Fig. 1. The emotion training setup with the NAO-robot. (a) The child watches robot's emotional gestures and selects the best matching facial expression. (b) Six emotional gestures were developed. The movement description is given below each image. The color bar illustrates the robot eyes LED color during the gesture. (Colour figure online)

Table 1. Stories told by the robot during emotional gestures to create situational context

Sentence	Target emotion	Inter-rater reliability
Today, I am going to the amusment park.	Happiness	1
The teacher gives me a compliment.	Happiness	1
It's dark in my room.	Fear	0.95
There is a thunderstorm outside.	Fear	0.90
My boyfriend does not like chocoloate.	Surprise	0.95
It is snowing in summer.	Surprise	0.95
I lost my cuddly bear.	Sadness	1
My rabbit died.	Sadess	1
My friend cheats in the game.	Anger	0.80
My brother broke my cuddly bear.	Anger	0.85
My brother picks his nose.	Disgust	0.95
I stepped on dog poop.	Disgust	0.85

2.3 Questionnaire and Procedure

Due to COVID-19 pandemic, an online questionnaire was prepared in Qualtrics and sent to the participants for digital participation. After signing the consent form and responding to demographic questions, participants saw videos in which the robot gestured an emotion. First, they saw all gestures without situational context (Gesture-only condition). Then, they saw the gestures accompanied by stories told by the robot (Gesture-with-Story condition). In each video, participants were given six choices (Happiness, Fear, Surprise, Sadness, Anger, and Disgust) from which they had to choose the emotion that they thought was portrayed by the robot. Additionally, they rated the feasibility of emotion recognition for children with autism on a Likert scale (1 = Not feasible at all, 7 = Extremely feasible). Participants were instructed to assume children with a mental age between 6 and 9 years old, and a chronological age between 12 and 14 years old.

2.4 Data Analysis

To answer RQ1, recognition accuracies were obtained per emotion and compared between the two gesture conditions. Since emotion recognition is independent from ASD knowledge level, experts and non-experts were considered as one group (N = 26) in this comparison. To answer RQ2, the obtained Likert scores pertaining to feasibility of gesture recognition were compared across emotions, conditions and groups using a mixed ANOVA.

3 Results

3.1 Gesture Recognition Accuracy

First, the data was converted into a binomial distribution with values "1" if the participant recognized the emotion portrayed by the robot correctly and "0" if the selected emotion was wrong. For each emotion in each gesture condition, the total number of correct responses was obtained as a percentage of all participants' responses and was assigned as the overall recognition accuracy for that emotion (Fig. 2).

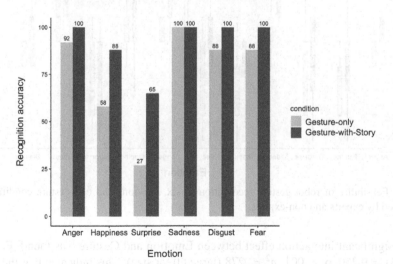

Fig. 2. Recognition accuracy of the robot gestures in six emotions and two gesture conditions as evaluated by all participants.

To statistically analyze the pattern in responses, a binary logistic regression analysis was conducted with Emotion and Gesture as predictors. Results showed that both Emotion ($\chi^2(5) = 79.428$, p $< .001$) and Gesture ($\chi^2(1) = 23.361$, p $< .001$) were significant predictors of the participants' responses. Emotions Happiness ($\beta = -2.385$, $Z = -2.962$, p $= .003$) and Surprise ($\beta = -3.792$, $Z = -4.673$, p $< .001$) as well as condition Gestures-Only ($\beta = -1.918$, $Z = -4.389$, p $< .001$) had significant negative coefficients in the model, which indicated that the likelihood that participants could recognize the robot gesture correctly significantly decreased in these three conditions.

3.2 Gesture Recognition Feasibility

Figure 3 displays the obtained feasibility scores for all emotions from Expert and Non-Expert groups in Gesture-only and Gesture-with-Story conditions. To examine if the gestures were evaluated as feasible for children with ASD by experts and non-experts, a mixed ANOVA was conducted with three factors: Emotion (within-subjects; 6 levels), Group (between-subjects; 2 levels), and Gesture (within-subjects; 2 levels). The feasibility score given to each emotion (Likert score between 1 and 7) was the dependent variable. Mauchly's test indicated that the assumption of sphericity was violated, $\chi^2(14) = 31.398$, p $= .005$. Therefore, degrees of freedom were corrected using Greenhouse-Geisser estimates of sphericity ($\varepsilon = .663$).

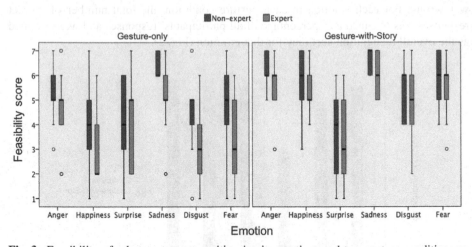

Fig. 3. Feasibility of robot gesture recognition in six emotions and two gesture conditions as evaluated by experts and non-experts.

A significant interaction effect between Emotion and Gesture was found, $F(3.316, 79.593) = 9.250$, p $< .001$, $\eta^2 = .278$ (large effect size). This indicated that the effect of Emotion on feasibility scores was mediated by Gesture type. Therefore, simple main effect analyses were conducted followed by pairwise comparisons with Bonferroni adjustment.

Results of analysis between Gesture conditions showed that feasibility scores were significantly higher for Anger (Mean Difference = .923, p $< .01$), Happiness (MD =

1.846, p < .001), Sadness (MD = .615, p < .01), Disgust (MD = 1.308, p < .01) and Fear (MD = 1.692, p < .001) in the Gesture-with-Story condition compared to the Gesture-only condition. No significant difference between the two Gesture conditions was found for emotion Surprise.

Results of pairwise comparisons between Emotions in each Gesture condition are summarized in Table 2 (MD and p-values). The feasibility scores were significantly higher for emotion Sadness than all other emotions except Anger in both Gesture conditions. The feasibility scores for Surprise were significantly lower than all other emotions in the Gesture-with-Story condition. Furthermore, emotion Anger was evaluated as significantly more feasible compared to Happiness and Disgust in the Gesture-only condition.

Table 2. Pairwise comparison between emotions in each gesture condition using gesture recognition feasibility scores

		Anger	Happiness	Surprise	Sadness	Disgust	Fear
Gesture-only	Anger	NA					
	Happiness	**-1.346***	NA				
	Surprise	-.923	.423	NA			
	Sadness	.769	**2.115***	**1.692***	NA		
	Disgust	**-1.192**	.154	-.269	**-1.962***	NA	
	Fear	-.885	.462	.038	**-1.654***	.308	NA
Gesture-with-Story	Anger	NA					
	Happiness	-.423	NA				
	Surprise	**-2.385***	**-1.962***	NA			
	Sadness	.462	**.885**	**2.846***	NA		
	Disgust	-.808	-.385	**1.577***	**-1.269***	NA	
	Fear	-.115	.308	**2.269***	**-.577***	.692	NA

Note. Bold = significant value ($* p < .05$, $** p < .01$, $*** p < .001$)

Finally, there was a significant main effect of between-subjects factor Group, $F(1, 24) = 4.980$, p = .035. No significant interaction effect was found between Group and other factors. A post-hoc analysis with Bonferroni adjustment indicated that the Expert group rated the gestures significantly less feasible than Non-Expert group (Mean difference = .654, SD = .293, p = .035).

4   Discussion

The goal of the current study was to design and validate emotional gestures for a NAO-robot with the purpose of emotion training in children with autism. A group of ASD experts and non-experts watched videos of the developed robot emotional gestures with and without situational context and evaluated the emotion recognition feasibility for these children. We hypothesized that creation of situational context through short stories told by the robot would increase the accuracy and feasibility of gesture recognition in participants' responses.

Our results supported our first hypothesis, indicating that Gesture type was a predictor of participants' recognition and that robot gestures could be recognized more correctly when they were accompanied by stories (except for Sadness, which had 100% accuracy in both conditions). These results are in line with Li and Chignell [14] who found that emotional gestures of a bear robot were recognized more accurately when an imaginary scenario was told to the participants before the bear executed the emotion. The improvement of accuracy was the largest for emotions Happiness and Surprise (see Fig. 2). These two emotions, particularly Surprise, had very low recognition accuracy in the Gesture-only condition and were associated with a significant decrease in the likelihood of participants' recognition accuracy, which is indicative of their complexity. Both emotions have been shown to be confusing and difficult to recognize without context in previous research as well [18].

Further inspection of participants' responses showed that the gesture portraying Surprise was mostly mistaken with Fear. The backward movement made by the robot and high movement dynamics, which are seen as characteristics of surprise in human body language [12], has previously been reported to have 82% recognition accuracy when executed by another robot, named Brian 2.0 [20]. However participants in our study saw this gesture on the NAO-robot as a sign of fear, which could be due to a difference of shape, size and degrees of freedom between the two robots. Among all gestures, Sadness could obtain maximum recognition accuracy (100%) even in the absence of situational context. This is consistent with the results of English et al. [19] in which Sadness among five emotions achieved maximum recognition accuracy of 96% with the NAO-robot. Sadness seems to be a simpler emotion, which can be identified with a few movements of closed posture and lowered head.

Regarding our second research question, results showed that in general robot gestures were not evaluated as feasible for children with ASD when situational context was missing, however, the feasibility scores increased significantly for almost all emotions when stories were added to the gestures. Context seems to play a critical role in both recognition accuracy as well as the recognition feasibility of emotional gestures and it is not specific to children with autism [14]. The advantage of adding situational context is that not only it makes the gesture recognition task more reliable and feasible for children, but also it creates a persona illusion for the robot, which in return makes the training more engaging [20].

An important finding in this study was the significant difference of feasibility assessment between Expert and Non-Expert groups. Although all participants were instructed to imagine a certain mental age for the target children group, experts evaluated gestures less feasible to be recognized by children with autism. This difference of perception between experts and non-expert individuals is an evidence for the fact that ASD professionals who have the experience of working with these children are more informed about their cognitive challenges and educational needs and hence should closely collaborate with HRI scientists to provide feedback regarding stimuli appropriateness and optimization of robot training paradigms [13, 21].

One of the limitations of this study was that due to the time restrictions of the survey, participants could not evaluate all variations of the designed gestures. Multiple emotional gestures per emotion were created for this study but a choice had to be made.

Another gesture for emotion Surprise was available, which involved more hand movements [12]. This gesture might have been evaluated more positively, had it been included in the survey. Future research should focus on the ambivalent emotion Surprise by examining the recognition feasibility of other movements for children with ASD. It is also recommended to add other emotional signals such as a sound effect (e.g. gasp) [22].

Another limitation of the current study was the number of recruited participants in each group (particularly ASD experts), which could have led to an insufficient statistical power in some parts of the analysis. ASD professionals often have a very busy schedule, making it difficult for them to participate in surveys. Future research should attempt to recruit a larger expert group to confirm the reported results of this paper.

It is expected that adoption of social robots in affect training of children with ASD will prevail in the future. Our findings suggest that robot gestures in combination with social context are generally considered feasible and useful in these interventions, however, professionals and practitioners in the domain of autism should be consulted during design and implementation of these studies to ensure the successful application of social robots in practical interventions.

5 Conclusion

Two research questions were central to this study: 1) whether addition of situational context to robot gestures improves recognition accuracy of emotions and 2) whether ASD experts evaluate emotional gestures developed in this study as feasible for emotion training of children with autism. Our findings showed that robot gestures were recognized more accurately and were assessed as more feasible for children when they were accompanied by context-related stories. Another important finding was that ASD experts had a significantly lower estimation of gesture recognition feasibility for children with ASD compared to non-experts, which shows that challenges faced by these children are not fully understood by people who have not worked with them. Overall, our results confirm that social and situational context play an important role in robot training programs designed to increase social skills of children with developmental disability and that these programs should be validated by professionals who have a better knowledge of cognitive and social capacities of the target population.

References

1. Conti, D., Trubia, G., Buono, S., Di Nuovo, S., Di Nuovo, A.: Affect recognition in autism: a single case study on integrating a humanoid robot in a standard therapy. Qwerty-Open Interdiscipl. J. Technol. Cult. Edu. **14**(2), 66–87 (2020)
2. Cabibihan, J.J., Javed, H., Ang, M., Aljunied, S.M.: Why robots? A survey on the roles and benefits of social robots in the therapy of children with autism. Int. J. Soc. Robot. **5**(4), 593–618 (2013)
3. Ntaountaki, P., Lorentzou, G., Lykothanasi, A., Anagnostopoulou, P., Alexandropoulou, V., Drigas, A.: Robotics in autism intervention. Int. J. Recent Contrib. Eng. Sci. IT (iJES) **7**(4), 4–17 (2019)

4. Test, D., Smith, L.E., Carter, E.W.: Equipping youth with autism spectrum disorders for adulthood: promoting rigor, relevance, and relationships. Remed. Special Educ. **35**(2), 80–90 (2014)
5. Robins, B., Dautenhahn, K., Te Boekhorst, R., Billard, A.: Robotic assistants in therapy and education of children with autism: can a small humanoid robot help encourage social interaction skills? Univ. Access Inf. Soc. **4**(2), 105–120 (2005)
6. Shamsuddin, S., Yussof, H., Miskam, M.A., Hamid, A.C., Malik, N.A., Hashim, H.: Humanoid robot NAO as HRI mediator to teach emotions using game-centered approach for children with autism. In: HRI 2013 Workshop on Applications for Emotional Robots (2013)
7. So, W.C., Wong, M.Y., Cabibihan, J.J., Lam, C.Y., Chan, R.Y., Qian, H.H.: Using robot animation to promote gestural skills in children with autism spectrum disorders. J. Comput. Assist. Learn. **32**(6), 632–646 (2016)
8. Yavich, R., Davidovich, N.: Use of iPads in the education of children with autism-spectrum disorder. High. Educ. **9**(4), 214–225 (2019)
9. Soares, F.O., Costa, S.C., Santos, C.P., Pereira, A.P.S., Hiolle, A.R., Silva, V.: Socio-emotional development in high functioning children with autism spectrum disorders using a humanoid robot. Interact. Stud. **20**(2), 205–233 (2019)
10. Costa, A.P., Steffgen, G., Lera, F.R., Nazarikhorram, A., Ziafati, P.: Socially assistive robots for teaching emotional abilities to children with autism spectrum disorder. In: 3rd Workshop on Child-Robot Interaction at HRI, March, 2017
11. Miskam, M.A., Shamsuddin, S., Samat, M.R.A., Yussof, H., Ainudin, H.A., Omar, A.: R.: Humanoid robot NAO as a teaching tool of emotion recognition for children with autism using the Android app. In: IEEE 2014 International Symposium on Micro-Nano Mechatronics and Human Science, pp. 1–5 (2014)
12. Monceaux, J., Becker, J., Boudier, C., Mazel, A.: First steps in emotional expression of the humanoid robot NAO. In: Proceedings of the 2009 International Conference on Multimodal Interfaces, pp. 235–236 (2009)
13. Wang, H., Hsiao, P.-Y., Min, B.-C.: Examine the potential of robots to teach autistic children emotional concepts: a preliminary study. In: Agah, A., Cabibihan, J.-J., Howard, A.M., Salichs, M.A., He, H. (eds.) ICSR 2016. LNCS (LNAI), vol. 9979, pp. 571–580. Springer, Cham (2016). https://doi.org/10.1007/978-3-319-47437-3_56
14. Li, J., Chignell, M.: Communication of emotion in social robots through simple head and arm movements. Int. J. Soc. Robot. **3**(2), 125–142 (2011)
15. Vanderborght, B., et al.: Using the social robot probo as a social story telling agent for children with ASD. Interact. Stud. **13**(3), 348–372 (2012)
16. Ying, K.T., Sah, S.B.M., Abdullah, M.H.L.: Personalised avatar on social stories and digital storytelling: fostering positive behavioural skills for children with autism spectrum disorder. In: 2016 4th International Conference on User Science and Engineering (i-USEr), pp. 253–258. IEEE, August, 2016
17. Gunes, H., Shan, C., Chen, S., Tian, Y.: Bodily expression for automatic affect recognition. In: Konar, A., Chakraborty, A. (eds.) Emotion Recognition: A Pattern Analysis Approach, 1st edn, pp. 343–377. John Wiley & Sons, Inc (2015)
18. Johnson, D.O., Cuijpers, R.H., van der Pol, D.: Imitating human emotions with artificial facial expressions. Int. J. Soc. Robot. **5**(4), 503–513 (2013)
19. English, B.A., Coates, A., Howard, A.: Recognition of gestural behaviors expressed by humanoid robotic platforms for teaching affect recognition to children with autism - a healthy subjects pilot study. In: Kheddar, A., et al. (eds.) Social Robotics. ICSR 2017. LNCS, vol. 10652, pp. 567–576. Springer, Cham (2017). https://doi.org/10.1007/978-3-319-70022-9_56
20. McColl, D., Nejat, G.: Recognizing emotional body language displayed by a human-like social robot. Int. J. Soc. Robot. **6**(2), 261–280 (2014)

21. Niculescu, A., van Dijk, B., Nijholt, A., Li, H., See, S.L.: Making social robots more attractive: the effects of voice pitch, humor and empathy. Int. J. Soc. Robot. **5**(2), 171–191 (2013)
22. Huijnen, C.A., Lexis, M.A., de Witte, L.P.: Matching robot KASPAR to autism spectrum disorder (ASD) therapy and educational goals. Int. J. Soc. Robot. **8**(4), 445–455 (2016)
23. Tsiourti, C., Weiss, A., Wac, K., Vincze, M.: Multimodal integration of emotional signals from voice, body, and context: effects of (in) congruence on emotion recognition and attitudes towards robots. Int. J. Soc. Robot. **11**(4), 555–573 (2019)

A Study on the Usability Evaluation of Teaching Pendant for Manipulator of Collaborative Robot

Jeyoun Dong[✉], Wookyong Kwon, Dongyeop Kang, and Seung Woo Nam

Electronics and Telecommunications Research Institute (ETRI), Daegu, South Korea
jydong@etri.re.kr

Abstract. Nowadays, a collaborative robot, known as a cobot, is a robot that can learn multiple tasks and assist alongside human workers. Thus, it plays a key role in the usage of a teaching pendant controlling the collaborative robot. However, it is gap to control a cobot and a teaching pendant proficiently between beginners and skilled engineer. Programming for teaching requires coding knowledge by line and it takes time to understand the instruction of existing teaching pendants.

The teaching pendant controlling a cobot requires intuitive interfaces, not only for ease of use, but also for modifying existing execution programs. However, there is no standard or guideline for an intuitive teaching pendant controlling cobot, and it can be noticed that the usability of the teaching pendant's interface is rather poor.

This paper shows the result of usability evaluation concerning evaluation items of usability and measurement indications. We conducted a study based on performing several steps of teaching tasks.

We recruited 30 participants consisting of beginners, intermediates, and advanced participants (F = 10, M = 20, 34.75 ± 2.50 years). Half of beginners are engineering majors and the rest are non-engineering majors. In this experiment, Indy 7 (Neuromeka) and Conty, or a teaching pendant, were used, and each participant conducted the experiment for 30 min, consisting of basic tasks and advanced tasks. Before the experiment, the coordinator explained the experimental method to the participants, After the experiment was over, after 10 min break, the interview, questionnaire and SUS about the experiment was performed.

In the result, the average of SUS is 57.86 that means the teaching pendant is not easy to use and complicate. After analysis of the result, we found that the function of the teaching pendant was so complex and the participants needed help. In the future work, we plan to propose an improved teaching pendant reflecting the usability result.

Keywords: Usability evaluation · Teaching device · Collaborative robot

1 Introduction

A collaborative robot is a robot that meets the conditions for collaborative operation (ISO 10218) while performing various tasks in the same space with field workers. Collaborative robots have less fatal risk in case of a physical collision between a human

© Springer Nature Switzerland AG 2021
C. Stephanidis et al. (Eds.): HCII 2021, CCIS 1498, pp. 234–238, 2021.
https://doi.org/10.1007/978-3-030-90176-9_31

and a robot with a payload of less than 20 kg, and they have the advantage of being able to perform the same task efficiently and repeatedly [1]. A teaching pendant refers to a portable device that inputs a program necessary for robot operation.

In order to utilize collaborative robot, it is necessary to implement the intention of the task to be performed so that the robot can understand them. It is called robot teaching. Teaching techniques include direct teaching, programming, and input of waypoint using a teaching pendant. However, the teaching pendant currently used in the field is mostly used by professional engineers because it is required to learn the actual process method and how to use it. Therefore, the UX (User Experience) of the teaching pendant is important so that field workers can understand the robot's status and respond according to the process situation [2, 3]. The teaching pendant should provide an intuitive interface and should be easy to execute and modify the program.

In this paper, we designed an evaluation process for usability improvement and performed usability evaluation. As a result, the results on the usability of the teaching pendant for collaborative robot were analyzed.

2 Experiments

There were differences in collaborative robots and teaching pendants according to the characteristic of the manufacturer. Also, they have something in common of the functions. The robots are generally made up of programming mode for teaching, execution mode and setting mode for robot's status. Teaching pendants usually have a main page and are composed of sub menus providing each function.

Teaching pendants support the waypoint for robot teaching in common. In the programming method, it can be divided into pendants that provide text-based programming for experts and pendants that provide block programming for beginners.

As such, the teaching pendants of each manufacturer tend to reflect an intuitive user interface (UI). However, there are few teaching pendants that have performed usability evaluation and reflected the results.

2.1 Subjects

In this paper, we designed a usability evaluation process for usability improvement using Neuromeka's Indy7 and a teaching pendant, Conty, and performed usability evaluation. Conty provides ease of use in the form of a wireless app, but has relatively complex teaching steps.

The purpose of the usability evaluation is to conduct a usability test for beginners who are using the product for the first time, and for intermediate and advanced users who have used collaborative robots. And we measure the usability of teaching pendant interface by performing various tasks. Based on the evaluation results, we intend to discover the current problems and suggest improvements.

In this evaluation test, 30 participants with beginners, intermediates, and advanced participants (F = 10, M = 20, 34.75 ± 2.50 years) were recruited. It consisted of 13 beginners in the engineering major and non-engineer majors who had never used collaborative robots and similar products, and 17 intermediate and advanced users who had experience using collaborative robots and similar products.

2.2 Procedure

We informed consent of participants and conducted the experiments after explaining the purpose, procedure, and method of the experiments.

The usability evaluation process consists of three steps as follows; in the first step, the main functions required for the test are explained along with images, text, and video data. The coordinator explained the experimental method to the participants for 30 min. The main training items include basic posture movement, program mode, and process introduction.

In the second stage, tasks were provided by dividing the steps by difficulty and function in the experimental environment as shown in Fig. 1. It was measured how many tasks the participants completed within 1 h.

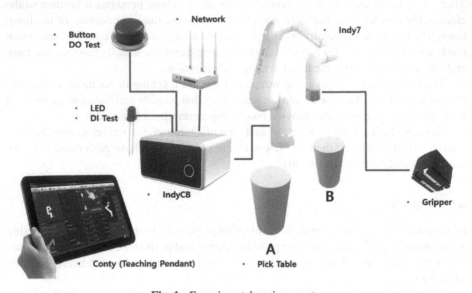

Fig. 1. Experimental environments

After the experiment was over, the participants had 10 min break. In the final third step, the operator asked questions related to usability evaluation items and measurement metrics as shown in Table 1. In addition, questions about the specifics observed during the experiment, questionnaires and SUS evaluation were conducted [4].

Table 1. Usability evaluation items and measurement metrics

Evaluation item	Measurement metrics	Evaluation item	Measurement metrics
Time	Time for task completion	Consistency	Visual consistency
Usage pattern	Frequency of use	Usability	SUS test
Accuracy	Error rate	Effectiveness	Accessibility to features
Completeness	Success/failure ratio	Efficiency	Interaction
Ease of learning	Ease of memory	Satisfaction	Satisfaction with use

3   Results

As a result of collecting and analyzing the results of the usability evaluation of all stages, we acquired results not only on quantitative but also on qualitative findings.

The average success rate of overall task execution was 63.2%. In more detail, the success rate of basic tasks was 70.3% and the success rate of advances tasks was 45.2%.

Also, the usability of SUS was obtained as shown in Fig. 2. Usually, a usability score of 68 or higher is considered average usability. However, a usability score of 57.86, which is below the average, was calculated in this evaluation. This score means that the teaching pendant is not easy to use.

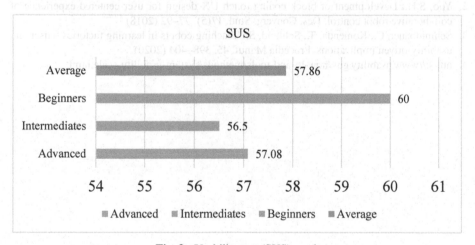

Fig. 2. Usability test (SUS) result

In addition, the results of qualitative analysis of the collected results are as follows; Improvements such as the need for a guide for easy use of the teaching pendant and for an intuitive jog button, templates for frequent use, the need to improve programming method, and deletion of unnecessary work steps were derived.

4 Conclusion

In this paper, we designed an evaluation process for usability improvement for collaborative robots and teaching pendants, and performed usability evaluation. Participants performed various tasks in the basic and advanced stages, and after performing the tasks, they left feedback through questionnaires, SUS evaluation, and interviews on specific matters during the tasks.

As a result, we analyzed the results on the usability of the current teaching pendant for collaborative robot and came up with an improvement point. If the results derived in the future work are applied to the improvement of the teaching pendant, it will help not only experts but also all workers to use the teaching pendant easily.

Acknowledgement. This work was supported by Electronics and Telecommunications Research Institute (ETRI) grant funded by the Korean government. [21ZD1130, Development of smart machine and robot technology based on intelligent control].

References

1. Wanga, X.V., Keményb, Z., Váncza, J., Wang, L.: Human–robot collaborative assembly in cyber-physical production: classification framework and implementation, CIRP Ann. Manuf. Technol. **66**(1), 5–8 (2017)
2. Yoo, S.H.: Development of block coding touch UX design for user centered experience of collaborative robot control. Des. Converg. Stud. **17**(5), 77–92 (2018)
3. Schmidbauer, C., Komenda, T., Schlund, S.: Teaching cobots in learning factories – user and usability-driven implications. Procedia Manuf. **45**, 398–404 (2020)
4. https://www.usability.gov/how-to-and-tools/methods/system-usability-scale.html

The Design and Evaluation of a Chatbot for Human Resources

Jaimie Drozdal[1]([✉]) [iD], Albert Chang[1], Will Fahey[1], Nikhilas Murthy[1], Lehar Mogilisetty[1], Jody Sunray[1], Curtis Powell[1], and Hui Su[1,2]

[1] Rensselaer Polytechnic Institute, Troy, NY 12180, USA
drozdj3@rpi.edu
[2] IBM T.J. Watson Research Center, Yorktown Heights, New York, USA
https://cisl.rpi.edu

Abstract. Technological innovations in artificial intelligence and machine learning enable business operators to engage with their customers 24/7 through chatbots. Many customers expect around-the-clock support which puts a strain on human resources; augmenting human resources with a chatbot can reduce costs for an organization and increase customer satisfaction. This work presents the HR Chatbot: a chatbot that answers general questions about human resource topics (i.e. payroll, benefits) for a private university. The research involves a collaboration between computer scientists, user experience researchers, and human resource administration. This work addresses two research questions: What are employees at a private university looking for from a chatbot for human resources?; and what are the appropriate methods to evaluate and measure the success of a chatbot for human resources? The HR Chatbot uses IBM Watson Assistant services, and an initial prototype was designed from a document of 31 frequently asked questions. Three rounds of user testing were conducted with employees of the university. The initial tests revealed that the chatbot was perceived as useful, but many were dissatisfied with the responses, specifically the lack of responses. Errors in the chatbot were classified into different categories; the most common being that the question was not in the content scope for the chatbot. Thus, data from the initial studies informed the scope of the chatbot; the number of unique questions grew to 157 and the total number of questions increased to 463. The HR Chatbot has 90% accuracy and an average sustained usability score of 69.5, surpassing the benchmark score. Following the initial tests, the HR Chatbot was deployed in real-time on the human resources website. This work describes how a chatbot was created, evaluated, and deployed online. We hope that this work inspires and informs others to explore similar use cases with chatbot technologies.

Keywords: Chatbots · Evaluation · Human-chatbot interaction

1 Introduction

Chatbots, "text messaging-based conversational agents", can provide a means for direct user engagement, improving business processes through relatively simple

C. Stephanidis et al. (Eds.): HCII 2021, CCIS 1498, pp. 239–248, 2021.
https://doi.org/10.1007/978-3-030-90176-9_32

interactions [10]. They are increasingly popular for customer service [5,20], and it is suspected that the usage of chatbots will continue to grow [6,7]. Brandtzaeg and Følstad say "chatbots represent a potential shift in how people interact with data and services online" [6]. Human resource (HR) departments that leverage this shift can transform their operations. HR departments are tasked with a lot of responsibilities such as ensuring employees are happy, healthy, productive, etc. Chatbots can help automate processes, reinforce the culture of the organization, and can free up time for the HR department to handle more complex needs [19]. Currently relatively few institutions have published on the use of a chatbot for HR. Jitgosol et al. created a chatbot for HR at a Spa Resort in Thailand [11]. Spot is a chatbot solution to tackle harassment and discrimination in the workplace [1]. The chatbot allows employees to document inappropriate behavior. Ivy.ai is a company that works with private universities to create chatbots for their needs [2]. Their case study page does not list any HR departments, but many universities have reported a reduction in calls from students and a better understanding of student needs with the use of Ivy.ai. AdmitHub [4] and VirtualSpirits [3] are also chatbots for universities, but they focus on student needs as opposed to the HR needs of staff and faculty.

This research focuses on the design and evaluation of a chatbot for HR at Rensselaer Polytechnic Institute (RPI). The HR Chatbot is a simple tool that answers general queries about HR topics (Fig. 1). This work provides an overview of the technology used for the chatbot and a description of how the HR Chatbot was initially implemented. As little is still understood regarding why people use chatbots [6,14], we outline four pilot tests that reveal user intentions and needs for the chatbot. We discuss how the chatbot is refined as new data is collected and describe our process for deployment. This work is carried out by a multidisciplinary team composed of a computer scientist, an AI researcher, a user experience researcher, HR administration, and undergraduate researchers. We hope others are inspired to explore why and how chatbots can enhance human resource experiences and we hope that our research can provide guidance or a shared experience for those who wish to create their own chatbot using online services.

2   Background

The increase in chatbot popularity is often attributed to advancements in artificial intelligence (AI) and machine learning [6,7]. Chatbots can be categorized into three different types: rule-based, retrieval based, and self-learning [15]. The main difference lies in how the chatbot generates responses. Rule-based chatbots, respective to their name, follow rules that are predefined with information and responses that are stored locally. Retrieval-based chatbots usually follow the same guidelines at rules-based ones but obtain information from outside sources and are able to provide up-to-date responses. Finally, self-learning chatbots generate their own responses and may partly use rule-based and retrieval-based components.

This work leverages IBM's Watson Assistant Services[1] to create a rule-based chatbot. da Silva Oliveira et al. compared eight platforms for creating chatbots and ultimately chose IBM's Watson Assistant based on its capabilities and cost [21]. Intents and entities comprise the defining linguistic structures of Watson Assistant. As defined in Watson Assistant's documentation[2], an intent represents a task or action the user wants to perform. It is a purpose or goal expressed in a user's utterance. An entity modifies an intent and represent information in the user input that is relevant to the user's purpose. Both of these items are used by Watson Assistant to evaluate dialogues.

Watson Assistant organizes chatbot responses into a dialogue tree, which contains dialogue nodes for specific responses to user inputs. The dialogue tree is evaluated from top to bottom, and dialogue nodes may have subsequent child nodes. An additional feature called context variables, similar to variables in programming, can be defined in Watson Assistant to store information to be used later in the conversation. Intents, entities, and context variables can all be used as evaluation criteria in the dialogue tree. Additionally, machine learning is used for intent and entity recognition. Intent recognition can be adjusted in real time by user feedback using a disambiguation feature that allows users to choose the response that best fits their input. In addition, Watson Assistant supports webhooks that allow calling external API's to get information or responses to be used in dialogue nodes.

2.1 Evaluating Chatbots

While research on chatbots has been ongoing for decades, the rapidly evolving world of AI makes it difficult for researchers to agree on standard evaluation methods [9,16,17]. Evaluations can be automated, performed by humans, or a combination of both [12]. Furthermore, evaluations can be made from different perspectives.

Dijana Peras [16] analyzes 15 relevant papers to create a chatbot evaluation framework. The work identifies chatbot attributes, groups the attributes into 14 categories, and organizes the categories into 5 perspectives. The user experience, information retrieval, linguistic, technology perspectives are inspired by Russell-Rose [18]. A business perspective was included in Peras's framework based on the findings. Similarly, Radziwill and Benton performed an analysis to create the Analytic Hierarchy Process. The process compares two or more conversational systems by selecting the most significant quality attributes or compares a system at two points in time to measure changes or improvements. However, because chatbots vary based on platforms and concepts there is no one-fit-all evaluation method. The System Usability Scale (SUS) is designed to measure and quantify the perception of usability through 10 validated statements [13]. Participants score each question out of five and final scores are out of 100. The benchmark score is 68.0. Recently, researchers have used the SUS to

---

[1] https://www.ibm.com/cloud/watson-assistant.
[2] https://cloud.ibm.com/docs/assistant.

measure chatbot usability [8]. Because chatbot development is multi-disciplinary research, it is challenging to find the correct marriage between technical and user experience evaluations.

3   Creating the HR Chatbot

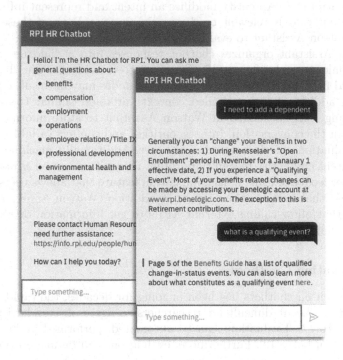

Fig. 1. A screenshot of the HR Chatbot.

3.1   Implementing the Initial Q&A Set in Watson Assistant

The Department of Human Resources at RPI initially supplied a document of 31 unique, frequently asked questions (FAQs) with correct answers. The questions were organized into seven different categories based on their respective HR department (i.e. benefits, compensation, employment, operations, employee relations/title IX, professional development, environmental health and safety and risk management). In the beginning the implementation process went as follows:

1. Create a new intent
2. Name the intent based on the intention of the question (i.e. #ask_"subject")
3. Use the HR provided question as an example for the intent
4. Create a new dialogue node for the intent
5. Use the HR provided answer as a response to the intent if recognized.

4   Testing the HR Chatbot

Four pilot tests were run to evaluate the performance of the HR chatbot and to understand user needs. Participants for the studies were recruited via email from staff and faculty in different departments at the university. Overall, there were 32 participants (16 female, 14 male, 2 unknown). This study was approved by the Institutional Review Board at RPI. Upon consenting to the study online, participants were given a link to access the HR chatbot. They were advised to ask the chatbot questions about human resource topics for a few minutes and were shown a list of five example questions. Participants were informed that after interacting with the chatbot they should return to the form to complete a voluntary survey. This survey included the 10 SUS questions, two Likert-scale questions asking about user satisfaction and expectations being met, and demographic questions.

4.1   Pilot Tests I–III

In total, 16 participants participated in Pilot Tests I–III. These conversations with the HR Chatbot resulted in 114 inputs. As the HR Chatbot engages in one-round dialogue, a single input in a conversation almost always represents a question to the chatbot. It should be noted that occasionally participants refreshed the web page which started a new dialogue with the HR Chatbot, resulting in more conversations than participants.

Table 1. Analysis of conversations collected from Pilot Tests I–III.

Pilot test	Number of conversations	Number of inputs	Correct responses	Incorrect responses	Somewhat correct responses
I	6	52	13%	79%	8%
I	7	46	18%	80%	2%
III	4	16	13%	81%	6%

Similar to da Silva Oliveira et al., user inputs were classified into three categories based on whether the chatbot's response to the input was correct, somewhat correct, or incorrect (see Table 1) [21]. Somewhat correct responses included cases when the intent classification was incorrect but the response given handled the users query.

Many of the questions from Pilot Tests I–III were out of scope from the original FAQ document supplied by HR, and it was not uncommon for a single conversation to contain questions on different topics. Thus a majority of the responses were incorrect because the question and its answer were not implemented in the chatbot.

When new questions do not have answers we first search online to see if there is an available answer on the HR website. If there is no clear answer then the questions are shared with the Human Resource department at the university to get answers. The new questions also inspired the design team to brainstorm more questions and answers. After the first three pilot tests, 98 questions received new answers from HR.

As mentioned, many new question themes arose from the pilot study. Initially, the most common action was to create new intents and dialogue nodes for the new questions as they came in from the pilot studies, as described in Sect. 3.1. This process changed after a fourth pilot study was performed.

4.2   Pilot Test IV

The fourth pilot test resulted in 20 conversations from 16 participants. Out of the 162 inputs to the chatbot, 43 (27%) of responses were deemed correct.

Due to the increasing scope of the chatbot questions it became more difficult to define and sort out new errors. Unlike Pilot Tests I–III, the reason(s) a response was incorrect or somewhat correct were complicated because not every input was an unknown topic. While 71 (44%) of the inputs required new or updated answers from HR, over 40 inputs still had incorrect responses. To better understand the issues a user experience researcher and a computer science researcher went through the conversation logs line by line. Based on the incorrect response at hand an action was created to resolve the issue. After analyzing a few conversations some common categories emerged and inputs and chatbot responses became categorized and edited based on the following list:

- get a chatbot response from HR
- question correctly answered
- add example to intent or entity
- split intent into multiple intents
- create new intent or entity
- change name of intent or entity
- change response
- combine intents.

4.3   User Experience Evaluation

The user experience survey was fully completed by 30 participants (15 female, 14 male, 1 unknown). Twelve of the participants were 45 years of age or older and eight indicated that they have never used a chatbot before. The average SUS score for all of the pilot tests is 69.5 ± 15, surpassing the benchmark score. When asked what they would like to use the HR chatbot for, 12 participants (40%) expressed that they want to use the chatbot for general questions and six participants specifically mentioned that they want to use the chatbot for benefits questions. In an open ended response, participants revealed that they most enjoyed the chatbot's quick responses and ease of use. Most participants said that the chatbot could not answer their questions, but overall the feedback was positive.

5   Refining the HR Chatbot

A major takeaway from the pilot tests is that the users of the HR Chatbot want a quick, easy tool to get information. Only one participant mentioned an interest in a personalized, conversational experience. Thus we focus on refining the chatbot responses to be concise and contain accurate, specific hyperlinks to appropriate sources of information.

After collecting questions from the pilot tests and manually pulling questions and answers from the human resource website, the total number of unique questions and answers programmed in the HR Chatbot has reached 157. Including questions that cover the same topic, there are 463 questions that the HR Chatbot has an answer for.

5.1 Creating a Test Set

Outside of user testing, it is useful and common to test the accuracy of the chatbot with the questions and answers that are expected to be handled. However, Watson Assistant currently does not provide an interface for automatically testing the chatbot with existing examples and expected responses. One can manually ask the chatbot a question and record the response or use API calls to send inputs and log outputs. Furthermore, there is no interface connecting an intent and its examples directly to its response in the dialogue node. This makes it difficult to understand what the accurate responses are for each intent.

Therefore, we created a spreadsheet that allows us to organize example inputs based on their intents and responses, called golden intents and ground truth responses, respectively. The spreadsheet also includes information from Watson Assistant about the example input including the predicted intent and the response from the chatbot. Example inputs are organized into categories and subcategories so that the spreadsheet can be sorted based on the category of a question. See Fig. 2. All of this information allows us to better understand the different user questions and topics. Looking at the spreadsheet, one can easily identify when the response from the chatbot does not match the ground truth response. This issue can be worked through by evaluating the predicted intent compared to its golden intent and the golden intents for related topics. This spreadsheet has been critical to designing the chatbot and creating a bridge in understanding between the designers and the developers. When the HR chatbot is deployed online this spreadsheet will continue to help the design team organize information to make decisions.

Golden Intent	High level topic	Context / Sub-topic	User Input Examples	Ground Truth Response	Dialogue Response
401k	Benefits	retirement, 401k	401k	Rensselaer offers two	Rensselaer offers two
401k	Benefits	retirement, 401k	What is your 401k plan?	Rensselaer offers two	Rensselaer offers two
401k	Benefits	retirement, 401k	What's the link for my 401k	Rensselaer offers two	Rensselaer offers two
403b	Benefits	retirement, 403b	What options to I have for my 403 b.	Rensselaer sponsors a 403(b)	Rensselaer offers
about_sodexo	Services	Sodexo, ordering food	How do I order food through sedexo?	Your dining and catering	Your dining and catering
absence_and_pto	PTO	absence policy	Absence policy	Rensselaer combines vacation,	When an employee is

Fig. 2. This spreadsheet allows the chatbot designers and developers to understand the intended and the actual behaviors of the chatbot.

6   Deploying the HR Chatbot

6.1   Online Deployment

The HR chatbot is in the process of being deployed online using IBM services. Watson Assistant provides a copy-paste format that allows embedding of the service into web pages using its API. This allows for an interactive chat bubble that can expand into the HR Chatbot interface. The HR Chatbot will be available on the HR website[3].

6.2   Evaluating the Chatbot

After users interact with the HR Chatbot, they will be asked to participate in a voluntary survey. Similar to the pilot tests, the SUS survey will be utilized. However, more refined user experience questions will be added in correspondence with the Chatbot Usability Questionnaire [8]. It is imperative to consistently review user needs and expectations and evaluate if they are being met.

6.3   Creating a Dashboard

Even with new features being released, using a third-party service to create a chatbot can be challenging based on the design and the capabilities of the given interface. We created a spreadsheet to act as a dashboard that can provide a report on the current status of the HR Chatbot. The dashboard pulls information from logs stored internally by Watson Assistant. The dashboard organizes information into an overview (i.e. total messages, total conversations, total covered messages), a section of uncovered messages, top intents, top entities, and top questions that require disambiguation. We hope to work with the HR department to create a dashboard that can be understood by the lead AI researcher as well as the head of HR so that the entire team can have a mutual understanding of the HR Chatbot's performance.

7   Discussion and Future Work

This research presents the design and development of a chatbot for human resources at a university. User testing suggests users want a chatbot that provides quick and easy information in response to a user query. Future work and design directions will be determined as more conversation data and user feedback is collected. Through the real-world deployment of the HR chatbot we hope to better understand and to meet the needs of staff and faculty at Rensselaer Polytechnic Institute. Findings from the real world use of the HR Chatbot will be published in the future. We hope that our current and future research forages the bridge between technical research and real world users.

---

[3] https://hr.rpi.edu/.

References

1. https://talktospot.com/index
2. Bot-ify your campus. https://ivy.ai/
3. Get more student leads and registrations automatically 24/7. https://www.virtualspirits.com/chatbot-for-university.aspx
4. AI-powered conversational strategy for student success, October 2019. https://www.admithub.com/
5. Adam, M., Wessel, M., Benlian, A.: AI-based chatbots in customer service and their effects on user compliance. Electr. Mark. **31**, 1–19 (2020)
6. Brandtzaeg, P.B., Følstad, A., et al.: Why people use chatbots. In: Kompatsiaris, I. (ed.) INSCI 2017. LNCS, vol. 10673, pp. 377–392. Springer, Cham (2017). https://doi.org/10.1007/978-3-319-70284-1_30
7. Ho, R.C.: Chatbot for online customer service: customer engagement in the era of artificial intelligence. In: Impact of Globalization and Advanced Technologies on Online Business Models, pp. 16–31. IGI Global (2021)
8. Holmes, S., Moorhead, A., Bond, R., Zheng, H., Coates, V., McTear, M.: Usability testing of a healthcare chatbot: can we use conventional methods to assess conversational user interfaces? In: Proceedings of the 31st European Conference on Cognitive Ergonomics, pp. 207–214 (2019)
9. Io, H.H.N., Lee, C.: Chatbots and conversational agents: a bibliometric analysis, pp. 215–219, December 2017. https://doi.org/10.1109/IEEM.2017.8289883
10. Jain, M., Kumar, P., Kota, R., Patel, S.N.: Evaluating and informing the design of chatbots. In: Proceedings of the 2018 Designing Interactive Systems Conference, pp. 895–906 (2018)
11. Jitgosol, Y., Kasemvilas, S., Boonchai, P.: Designing an HR chatbot to support human resource management, pp. 165, 170, December 2019
12. Jongerius, C.: Quantifying chatbot performance by using data analytics. Ph.D. thesis, Utrecht University (2018)
13. Lewis, J.R.: The system usability scale: past, present, and future. Int. J. Hum.-Comput. Inter. **34**(7), 577–590 (2018)
14. Melián-González, S., Gutiérrez-Taño, D., Bulchand-Gidumal, J.: Predicting the intentions to use chatbots for travel and tourism. Curr. Issue Tour. **24**(2), 192–210 (2021)
15. Madana Mohana, R., Pitty, N., Lalitha Surya Kumari, P.: Customer support chatbot using machine learning. In: Satapathy, S.C., Zhang, Y.-D., Bhateja, V., Majhi, R. (eds.) Intelligent Data Engineering and Analytics. AISC, vol. 1177, pp. 445–451. Springer, Singapore (2021). https://doi.org/10.1007/978-981-15-5679-1_42
16. Peras, D.: Chatbot evaluation metrics. In: Economic and Social Development: Book of Proceedings, pp. 89–97 (2018)
17. Radziwill, N.M., Benton, M.C.: Evaluating quality of chatbots and intelligent conversational agents. arXiv preprint arXiv:1704.04579 (2017)
18. Russell-Rose, T.: A framework for chatbot evaluation, February 2017. https://chatbotnewsdaily.com/a-framework-for-chatbot-evaluation-15d236557ad5
19. Sheth, B.: Want to use chatbots to automate the majority of HR services? June 2019. www.thebalancecareers.com/use-chatbots-to-automate-hr-many-services-4171964#::text=Chatbots%20enable%20HR%20teams%20to,need%20escalation%20for%20human%20engagement

20. Shumanov, M., Johnson, L.: Making conversations with chatbots more personalized. Comput. Hum. Behav. **117**, 106627 (2021)
21. da Silva Oliveira, J., Espíndola, D.B., Barwaldt, R., Ribeiro, L.M., Pias, M.: IBM Watson application as FAQ assistant about moodle. In: 2019 IEEE Frontiers in Education Conference (FIE), pp. 1–8. IEEE (2019)

Relationship Between Eating and Chatting During Mealtimes with a Robot

Ayaka Fujii[✉], Kei Okada, and Masayuki Inaba

The University of Tokyo, Tokyo, Japan
{a-fujii,k-okada,inaba}@jsk.imi.i.u-tokyo.ac.jp

Abstract. Eating with someone makes mealtimes more enjoyable and enriches our lives. However, lifestyle changes and the current COVID-19 pandemic have forced many people to frequently eat alone. Communication robots can be good mealtime partners. People would not worry about matching their mealtime schedules with robots, and they present no risk of disease transmission. Chatting is an important component of mealtime interaction. Thus, we developed a chatting system that can respond with natural timing and investigated the relationship between eating and talking when eating with a robot. We combined the good points of speech content recognition and volume recognition. Conversation systems only based on speech-content recognition experience long response-lag times because they use complex technologies. Using volume recognition to recognize human speech, which is faster than speech-content recognition, we aimed to reduce this lag by using filler responses, such as "I see," before the speech content recognition finished. Using this system, we conducted an experiment to analyze the relationship between utterances and eating behaviors from the recorded videos and questionnaire answers of 25 participants. The results suggest that the recognition of picking-up and eating motions could support the recognition of utterances from humans but not necessary in deciding when robots should start talking.

Keywords: Co-eating · Partner robot · Human–robot interaction

1 Introduction

Eating is an indispensable activity in our daily lives. It not only plays a role of nutrition to sustain life but also enriches our lives. Co-eating with someone gives us satisfaction [1] and has many health benefits [2,3]. Despite many merits of co-eating, there are more opportunities for many people to eat alone because of changes in the social structure and the shape of the family. The outbreak of the COVID-19 pandemic has promoted solitary eating.

Though online video-meeting platforms, such as Zoom, are becoming popular and remote co-eating is becoming common, nonhuman agents are considered good solutions since we can eat with them anytime and anywhere, as long as there is the necessary equipment. Takahashi et al. developed a virtual co-eating

© Springer Nature Switzerland AG 2021
C. Stephanidis et al. (Eds.): HCII 2021, CCIS 1498, pp. 249–256, 2021.
https://doi.org/10.1007/978-3-030-90176-9_33

system with an agent projected on the screen [4]. The agent could interact with users and provide a better eating experience than eating alone. We think that communication robots that exist in the real world and interact based on observations, can be good mealtime partners. Several studies have been reported on robots that can help physically disabled people to eat [5,6], but there are limited reports on robots that can behave as meal partners.

Herein, we investigated the relationship between eating and chatting with a robot during mealtime since chatting is a very common activity while eating with others, and we often use our mouths unconsciously for both eating and talking. We designed a chatting system that gives responses with a little time lag and experimented on co-eating with a robot equipped with the chatting system. We evaluated the developed system and addressed the following research questions about co-eating with a robot:

– Are there any relationships between eating behavior and chatting?
– Do people dislike to be talked to by a robot when they have food in their mouths?

2   Chatting System with a Little Time Lag

2.1   Overview

When a robot interacts with a human, there are some time lags for the robot to recognize what the human says because it employs complex technologies, such as deep learning or cloud services. To address this issue, we combined volume recognition and speech-content recognition. First, the beginning and end of utterances are recognized by volume recognition. When the end of utterance is detected, the robot starts giving the first response, such as "Mm-hmm" and "I see." During the first response, the speech-content recognition runs in the background. We fill the time lag in speech-content recognition by showing that the robot has recognized the speech. The details of each component are described below, and the concrete flow of the program is shown in Fig. 1.

2.2   Volume Recognition

When the robot hears a sound louder than the threshold value, decided by the environmental noise, for a certain period, it considers it to be the start of a speech. When the duration of sounds above the threshold value is less than a certain amount of time within a certain period, the speech is considered to have ended. Considering the two-second rule that is widely known as the limit of the system reaction time allowed by the user [7,8] and affects the noise in the real environment, we determined that the speech is ended when a volume higher than the threshold level is heard for less than 0.3 s in the last 2.5 s.

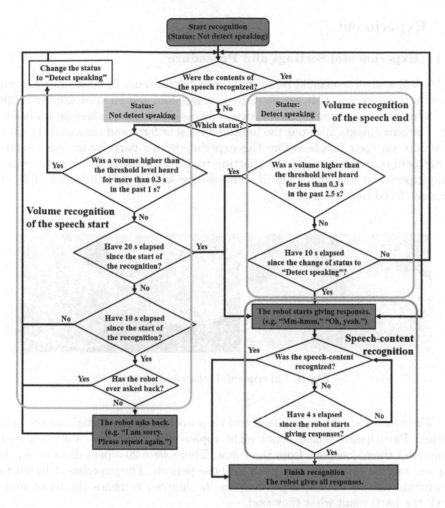

Fig. 1. Flow of the developed chatting system.

2.3 Speech-Content Recognition and Robot Response

We use Google Speech Recognition API to make human speech into text. We split the recognized text into words, and the robot can change its response according to the included words. If the speech-content recognition fails or the user gives an answer not anticipated, the robot states the comment that can match many types of user answers. To avoid interaction disruptions due to recognition failure, if the start of a speech is not recognized for 10 s, the robot asks the user to speak again more clearly, and if speech is not recognized for 20 s, the robot starts giving a response. Referring to Question-Answer-Response Dialog Model [9], the robot starts the chatting and takes control of the dialog by asking questions to the user during topics.

3 Experiment

3.1 Experimental Settings and Procedure

NAO V5, a small humanoid robot developed by Softbank Robotics Europe, was used in the experiment. It has 25 degrees of freedom and an approximate height of 58 cm. It has four microphones, two cameras, and two speakers on its heads.

The participants filled out the informed consent form and answered the questionnaire on their profile before the experiment. All participants were served potato chips and water, and the chatting topics with the robot were the same. The experiment was conducted in a one-on-one setting, and the robot and participant faced each other (Fig. 2).

Fig. 2. Experimental setup and scene.

The robot first introduced itself and then instructed the participants to start eating. Participants talked about eight topics with the robot, and each topic contained three questions from the robot. There were 20-s periods between the topics, and the robot did not speak in those periods. The experiment lasted for approximately 10–15 min, depending on the number of times the robot asked back the participant what they said.

3.2 Measurements

The experiments were video-recorded from diagonally in front of and behind the participants. We analyzed the eating behavior of the participants, focusing on the periods the participants responded to the questions from the robot and the 2.1 s after the utterances were over. We determined the analysis period according to the previous research of human–human interaction [10] that analyzed the relationship between utterances and eating actions and defined eating within 2.1 s after the utterance as "related eating."

After eating with the robot, the participants answered the questionnaire that contained the following items. Each question was first answered with "yes," "no," or "neither." Only those who answered "yes" to the question answered the additional question, "How much did you mind it?" on a five-point scale: from one ("I did not mind it at all.") to five ("I minded it very much.").

Q1 Were you talked to while you had something in your mouth?
Q2 Was your speech interrupted by the robot?
Q3 Did you have a problem with the speech contents of the robot?
Q4 Did you both have time to be silent?
Q5 Did you think that the robot was talking too much?

3.3 Participants

The participants were recruited at a science museum. A total of 25 participants (14 women and 11 men, within the age of 9–51 years) were included in the analysis.

4 Results

4.1 Total Experiment

The robot asked back once 141 times (23.5%) out of 600 response opportunities in total (8 topics × 3 questions × 25 participants) because it could not recognize the utterance of the participant due to volume-recognition failure or the participant did not answer while the robot was awaiting a response. Therefore, the total number of utterance opportunities was 741. Among the 718 times, excluding the 23 times when there was no speech from the participant, the robot interrupted the speech of participants by starting response 143 times (19.3%).

4.2 Results of Video Analysis

Figure 3 shows the relationships between utterances and eating behavior when eating with the robot. The chatting topic number on the horizontal axis indicates the order of chatting. Number one was the first topic and eight was the last during the experiment. From all utterance opportunities (741 times), 714 were included in the video analysis, excluding the occasions when there was no speech from the participant (23 times), or the participant had finished eating the potato chips (4 times). Averaged over the entire experiment, 4.90% of the participants picked up food or drink, 1.26% put food or drink in their mouth, and 23.9% held food or drink in their hand while responding to questions from the robot. After their response, 14.3% picked up food or drink, 18.8% put food or drink in their mouth, and 7.70% held food or drink in their hand.

4.3 Results of Questionnaires

Figure 4 shows the answers to the questionnaire. In Q1, 84% of the participants answered "Yes" and 24% answered more than three in the additional question, "Do you mind it?". Further, 80% answered "Yes," 64% answered more than three in Q2, 76% participants answered "Yes," and 64% answered more than three in Q3. All participants answered "Yes" and 48% answered more than three in Q4. In Q5, 12% answered "Yes" and 8% answered more than 3.

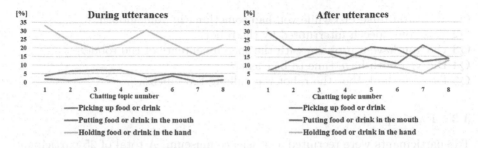

Fig. 3. Relationships between utterances and eating behaviors analyzed from the recorded videos.

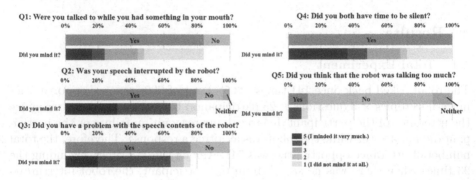

Fig. 4. Results of questionnaires about chatting with a robot during eating.

5   Discussion

5.1   Relationship Between Chatting and Eating Behavior

A few participants picked up or ate any food or drink during their utterances, and approximately 14% picked up and 19% ate after the utterances ended. When they were holding the food or drink in their hands while speaking, approximately two-thirds of them ate it immediately after speaking. These results suggest that recognizing the eating and picking-up motions of humans could improve the recognition of the end of utterances.

Focusing on the time course of the meal, the number of people who brought food or drink to their mouths after utterances decreased with time, whereas the number of people who kept it in their hands increased. This may indicate that the pace of eating decreased over time.

Considering the contents of the conversation topics, Topic 7 involved talking about the greasiness of potato chips. The number of people who picked up food or drink after the utterance increased a little in Topic 7, which implies that the content of communication with a robot could influence the eating behavior of humans.

5.2   Chatting with a Robot During Eating

From the results of the questionnaire in Q1, a few participants were bothered by the robot's questions when they had food in their mouths, suggesting that motion recognition is not necessary for the robot to decide when it should start talking. Previous studies on human–human interaction have shown that people often speak during mealtime even when there is some food in their mouths by putting the food to one side of the mouth or covering the mouth with their hands [11]. Similar behaviors were observed herein during human–robot interaction. However, when the robot was unable to recognize the participant's speech and asked back, the behavior of trying to speak clearly after cleaning the mouth was observed.

Considering the amount of conversation, few people thought that the robot talked too much under the conditions of this experiment according to Q5. We set up a time between topics when neither humans nor robots spoke, just like our daily mealtime conversation. From the results of Q4, some participants minded about the silent time and some did not. Some participants who minded the silence said "I wanted to continue the conversation on the same topic longer" and "I felt like I had to do something for the robot." Others were not bothered because it was the same as a normal conversation while eating with humans. These results show that people expect robots to have the same or higher amount of conversation than humans during mealtimes.

According to Q2 and Q3, more than half of the participants were bothered by the robot starting to talk in the middle of their utterance due to the failure of volume recognition and the breakdown of dialog due to responses that did not fit the expected scenario. When the robot frequently started talking before the participants finished their utterances, some participants felt compelled to respond quickly, which disrupted the pace of their meal. There is a need to improve the chatting system to improve the dining experience with robots.

5.3   Limitation

Since only NAO V5 was used as the meal partner robots and participants only ate potato chips in the experiment, there is a possibility of having different results in different situations. There is a need for further experiments with other robots and other dining conditions, such as using knives and forks. Furthermore, the experiment was conducted only in Japan, and different food cultures may have different results. Nevertheless, this study provides useful insights to the research on meal partner robots, which is not widely studied.

6   Conclusion

In this study, we developed a chatting system to reduce the time lag and realize natural response timing and conducted an experiment to investigate the relationship between eating and chatting during mealtimes with a robot. Although most people did not mind being talked to by the robot while there was food in their mouths, the chatting system failures, such as the robot starting to talk before the human finished their answers or mismatch of the context of the dialog, could impair the eating experience with a robot. In future studies, considering that participants tended to pick up and eat food or drink after their utterances than during the utterances, we assume that the multimodal chatting system that recognizes not only sounds but also eating motions could improve meal experience.

References

1. Kim, S.: Solitary eating, an inferior alternative? An examination of time-use data in South Korea. Int. Sociol. **35**(4), 415–432 (2020)
2. Tani, Y., Sasaki, Y., Haseda, M., Kondo, K., Kondo, N.: Eating alone and depression in older men and women by cohabitation status: the JAGES longitudinal survey. Age Ageing **44**(6), 1019–1026 (2015)
3. Kwon, A.R., Yoon, Y.S., Min, K.P., Lee, Y.K., Jeon, J.H.: Eating alone and metabolic syndrome: a population-based Korean National Health and Nutrition Examination Survey 2013–2014. Obesity Res. Clin. Pract. **12**(2), 146–157 (2018)
4. Takahashi, M., Tanaka, H., Yamana, H., Nakajima, T.: Virtual co-eating: making solitary eating experience more enjoyable. In: Proceedings of International Conference on Entertainment Computing, pp. 460–464, February 2017
5. Guo, M., Shi, P., Yu, H.: Development a feeding assistive robot for eating assist. In: Proceedings of 2017 2nd Asia-Pacific Conference on Intelligent Robot Systems, pp. 299–304 (2017)
6. Ikeda, T., Makino, T., Furuno, S., Nagata, F.: Wiping the mouth using the robot arm with information of RGB-D sensor. Artif. Life Robot. **24**(3), 360–367 (2019). https://doi.org/10.1007/s10015-019-00533-1
7. Miller, R.B.: Response time in man-computer conversational transactions. In: Proceedings of the December 9–11, 1968, Fall Joint Computer Conference, Part I, pp. 267–277 (1968)
8. Shiwa, T., Kanda, T., Imai, M., Ishiguro, H., Hagita, N.: How quickly should a communication robot respond? Delaying strategies and habituation effects. Int. J. Soc. Robot. **1**(2), 141–155 (2009)
9. Iio, T., Yoshikawa, Y., Chiba, M., Asami, T., Isoda, Y., Ishiguro, H.: Twin-robot dialogue system mismatch in with robustness against speech recognition failure in human-robot dialogue with elderly people. Appl. Sci. **10**(4), 1522 (2020)
10. Tokunaga, H., Mukawa, N., Kimura, A.: Structure of cooperative communication behavior during table talk: when do hearers eat and when do they respond. J. Jpn. Soc. Fuzzy Theory Intell. Inform. **26**(4), 793–801 (2014). (in Japanese)
11. Mukawa, N., Tokunaga, H., Yuasa, M., Tsuda, Y., Tateyama, K., Kasamatsu, C.: Analysis on utterance behaviors embedded in eating actions: how are conversations and hand-mouth-motions controlled in three-party table talk? Trans. Inst. Electron. Inf. Commun. Eng. A **94**(7), 500–508 (2011). (in Japanese)

When in Doubt, Agree with the Robot? Effects of Team Size and Agent Teammate Influence on Team Decision-Making in a Gambling Task

Gregory J. Funke[1]([✉]), Michael T. Tolston[1], Brent Miller[1], Margaret A. Bowers[2], and August Capiola[1]

[1] Air Force Research Laboratory, Wright-Patterson AFB, OH 45433, USA
gregory.funke.1@us.af.mil
[2] Ball Aerospace and Technologies Corporation, Dayton, OH 45324, USA

Abstract. Human-machine teaming is expected to provide substantive benefits to team performance; however, introduction of machine agents will also impact teamwork. Agents are likely to exert substantial influence on team dynamics, even if they possess only limited abilities to engage in teamwork processes. This influence may be mitigated by team size and experience with the agent. The purpose of this experiment was to investigate the influence of an agent on team processes in a team consensus gambling task. Teams were either two or three humans and a machine agent. Participants completed fifty rounds of a gambling task, similar to the game roulette. In each round, team members entered their belief about what the next round outcome would be, a proposed wager, and how confident they were. The machine agent also made a suggestion regarding outcome and wager, but its accuracy was fairly low. The human team members then had to come to a consensus regarding outcome and wager. Overall, the agent exerted significant influence on team decision making, wagering, and confidence. Contrary to initial predictions, team size had only a modest effect, mostly on confidence ratings. Experience with the agent also did not have much effect on the agent's influence, even as the team was able to observe that the agent's accuracy was low. These results suggest that machine agents are likely to exert significant influence on team processes, even when they possess limited abilities to engage in teamwork.

Keywords: Human-machine teaming · Agent influence · Consensus decision making

1 Introduction

In the future, human-machine teaming (HMT) is expected to play an important role in a number of environments, including aviation [8], healthcare [25], and national defense [28]. Inclusion of these agent teammates will provide substantive benefits, including personnel augmentation (or replacement), access to sophisticated computational abilities, and decision support, among other possibilities [7]. Here, we use the term "agent" in

C. Stephanidis et al. (Eds.): HCII 2021, CCIS 1498, pp. 257–270, 2021.
https://doi.org/10.1007/978-3-030-90176-9_34

the same sense as Chen and Barnes [4], to refer to intelligent systems (with or without physical embodiment) that possess autonomy, the ability to observe and act upon the environment, and direct their activity toward achieving certain goals.

The incorporation of these agents into team settings will also have a profound effect on the dynamics of teamwork [24]. In the short- to medium-term, constraints in machine agents' abilities to engage in teamwork behaviors, due to limitations in their sensors and ability to communicate, for example, means that human teammates will be largely responsible for adapting to fit the capabilities of those agents to enable successful team-work to occur. Nonetheless, humans tend to anthropomorphize agents and infer social affordances, even when agents are not designed to support those expectations [11]; as such, agents may be expected to influence team processes and team decision making [3] despite their limited capacity for teamwork.

This is potentially concerning because a large body of research suggests that humans have a tendency to over-rely on automation, particularly when they are under cognitive load [14]. The potential activation of social cues and norms by agents in team settings is likely to further increase the propensity for humans to rely on their agent teammates, since factors such as previous experience and liking indirectly influence trust [20], and trust influences reliance [13]. In fact, simply presenting an agent as a teammate, rather than a tool, can significantly change human affective evaluation and communication with an agent [24].

The predisposition to over-rely on agents may be moderated, to some extent, by the size of the team. Provided that the team's task and goals are unchanged, increasing team size typically increases team productivity and performance [15, 27]. Greater team size also serves to diffuse responsibility for decision making across more team members [2], potentially reducing the influence of individual teammates. Increasing team size may also distribute task-related cognitive load across more team members, thereby reducing the likelihood that team members will experience overload, a critical factor in determining over-reliance on automation [14]. As such, increasing team size may be expected to reduce the influence of an agent on team processes and decision making.

An additional factor that will likely affect agent influence is team experience with the agent. Research suggests that perceptions of a machine agent are likely to change in complex ways with greater experience, including both positive (e.g., increases in liking [12]) and negative (e.g., reductions in trust following errors [5]) reevaluations. While initial interactions may result in human teammates' over-reliance on an agent, followed by under-reliance if the agent makes errors [5], greater experience with an agent provides opportunities for human teammates to better estimate agent abilities and reliability, and to accurately calibrate their trust and reliance. As such, agent influence on team processes and decision making may be expected to be at its peak in early team interactions, and then to wane as human team members gain further experience with it, until it stabilizes at some point that is approximately commensurate with human team members' perceptions of the agent's reliability.

The purpose of the current experiment was to investigate the influence of a machine agent with limited ability to communicate and engage in teamwork processes, presented as a teammate, on team decision making in a consensus-building task. Teams were either triads (two humans and an agent) or tetrads (three humans and an agent). As we also expected that experience with the task and agent would influence team decision making, we also examined data in the first and second halves of the task. We hypothesized that, consistent with previous research on automation reliance, the agent would exert significant influence on team decision making in this task. However, we hypothesized this influence would be moderated by team size, as we expected tetrads to be less influenced by the agent. In addition, we hypothesized that the influence of the agent would be reduced from the first to second half of the task, as participants learned that the agent's task performance was imperfect.

2   Method

2.1   Participants and Design

Ninety-two participants recruited from the campus of a midwestern university in the U.S. took part in this study. However, the data of two teams were excluded from our analyses because they adopted a strategy of exclusively following the agent teammate's answer suggestion in each round for the majority of the experiment. The final sample included 88 participants (30 men and 58 women). Participants' ages ranged from 18 to 42 ($M = 22, SD = 5.48$).

The experiment utilized a 2 (team size) $\times$ 2 (game half) mixed design. Team size was either a triad (two human participants and a machine agent) or a tetrad (three human participants and a machine agent). Game half was included to allow us to compare team behavior and decision making in the first and second halves of the game as participants gained experience with the task and the agent (see below for further details). A final factor that we considered in several analyses was whether or not the team's consensus answer in each round agreed with the agent teammate's suggestion. Inclusion of this factor allowed us to explore the influence of the agent teammate on team outcomes.

2.2   Materials and Apparatus

This experiment included two serially-presented tasks: first, a "roulette-like" task, further described below, and second, a resource gathering task (the Checkmate task [1]). However, due to space limitations, this manuscript will focus exclusively on data from the roulette task; data from the resource gathering task have been presented in Tolston et al. [23].

The agent teammate in this experiment was an interactive humanoid "Nao" robot (Softbank Robotics, San Francisco, CA).

During the experiment, participants sat at individual workstation desks in padded chairs approximately 95 cm from separate Samsung Syncmaster 2443 60.96 cm LCD monitors with 1280 $\times$ 1024 pixel displays.

Roulette Task. In the first of the two tasks, participants were asked to make a series of consensus wagers from a shared pool of resources regarding the outcome of a custom roulette-type guessing game [6] (see Fig. 1), where outcomes were drawn from a static distribution initially unknown to participants. The game included five possible outcomes, presented to participants as the letters "A" through "E." Out of 50 rounds, 22 outcomes were mapped to one value (i.e., the dominant outcome, e.g., "A"), and seven were mapped to each of the remaining four possibilities (i.e., the infrequent outcomes, e.g., B–E). This distribution was generated in advance, randomized, and then saved to a file. Five versions of the file were made, so that each of the five letters presented in the roulette game was the dominant outcome in one of the files. These equivalent outcome distributions were then approximately counterbalanced across groups.

During each round of the roulette task, each participant first individually indicated which letter they thought would be the next roulette outcome (i.e., their individual answer) and their desired wager (from 20 to 100 in 20-point increments), along with an assessment of confidence in their proposal on a scale of 1 ("no confidence") to 5 ("certain"). Participants then entered a collaborative consensus-building phase, during which the team deliberated and chose a single outcome (i.e., the team's consensus answer) and wager, again with separate ratings of confidence. Participants interacted with each other during the consensus-building phase using a chat interface. The agent also interacted with teammates in each round via the chat interface by giving a pre-established suggestion regarding the correct answer and a recommended wager, but it did not give a confidence rating. The agent gave its answer and wager suggestion to the team at the outset of each consensus-building phase; however, it was not capable of further communication with the team, and remained silent for the remainder of each consensus-building phase.

The recommendations from the agent were determined in advance as the per-round modal responses from a sample of human participants in a pilot study we conducted of the roulette task. The agent's suggestions across rounds strongly favored the dominant outcome from the underlying non-uniform distribution. It suggested the dominant outcome on 33 of 50 rounds (13 rounds in the first half of the game, and 20 rounds in the second half). The agent's answer suggestions were "correct" (i.e., they matched the roulette outcome of the round) on 17 of 50 rounds (10 rounds in the first half of the game, and 7 rounds in the second half). Of its correct answer suggestions, 14 were the dominant outcome, meaning that when the agent's suggestion was correct (which was fairly infrequent), it was almost always the dominant outcome. With regard to the agent's wager recommendations, it suggested a wager of 20 points on 36 rounds (15 rounds in the first half and 21 rounds in the second half), and the other four wager values approximately equally across the remaining 14 rounds.

After the team's consensus answer and wager were made, and all human participants entered their confidence rating for that answer, an indicator would cycle through all options for a preset number of iterations (broadly imitating the "spin" of a roulette wheel) and stop on the predetermined outcome for the round. If the group guessed incorrectly, they lost the amount they wagered; if they guessed correctly, they won back 3 times the wager (the initial amount plus the wager multiplied by a payoff factor of 2). The outcome was displayed at each individual workstation, and the task continued to the next round, until all 50 rounds were completed. The resource pool used for wagering in each round was initially set to 5000 points so that, in the worst-case scenario, participants could make the maximum 100-point wager over all 50 rounds, losing each time, and end the task with 0 points.

Checkmate Task. Following completion of the roulette task, participants advanced to the Checkmate task. In brief, participants were instructed before this task that they

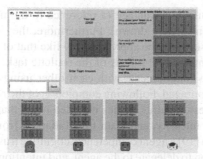

Fig. 1. A screen capture of the roulette task environment from a tetrad team during the consensus phase of a round. The upper left panel of the display was the chat environment participants and the agent used to communicate. The upper middle panel displayed the team's point total and the roulette "wheel" display, which animated to reveal the winning letter in each round. In the upper right panel, participants would enter their letter and wager selections, and confidence ratings, first in the individual phase, and again following the consensus phase. The bottom four panels displayed the individual round letter, wager, and confidence ratings of the human team members and the letter and wager suggestion of the agent teammate in red (all four were blank during the individual phase). In this experiment, the agent teammate's suggested outcome and wager always appeared in the bottom-right position (above the Nao robot face icon). The images displayed below each of the human team members' panels were selected individually by participants before starting the roulette game from a library of colored, geometric face icons.

would be able to wager the resources they had remaining after the roulette task on the performance of the agent teammate during its execution of the Checkmate task. Further information regarding this task is presented in Tolston et al. [23].

2.3 Procedure

Prior to the experiment, informed consents were obtained from all participants. Next participants were fitted with a Zephyr BioHarness 3 (Zephyr Technology Corporation, Annapolis, MD) to record their heart rate during the experiment (for more information about how this data was used, please see [23]). Participants were then introduced to the Nao robot (who was referred to as "Rufus" during the experiment), who executed a simple choreographed greeting by waving to participants and "speaking" a short greeting message. Participants were then informed that the agent would be acting as a member of their team during the experiment.

Next, participants were seated at their workstations, from which they engaged in both the roulette and Checkmate tasks. Each workstation was equipped with a computer, monitor, mouse, and keyboard. The Nao robot occupied its own separate workstation. Baseline physiological recordings were collected from all participants during a seated period while participants watched a video recording of a Windows screen saver that was 10 min long.

Computer-based instructions for the experimental task were presented after baseline recordings. Participants were instructed that the outcomes of the roulette game did not have a specific pattern that they could take advantage of, but if they paid close attention, they could find an exploitable advantage (a reference to the non-uniform distribution from which round outcomes were drawn). Furthermore, they were instructed that the agent's abilities at the task would be approximately like that of any other human's.

Participants then completed 50 rounds of the roulette task. During the experiment, participants were able to communicate with each other using a chat interface; verbal communication was discouraged. Following completion of the roulette task, participants completed a series of questionnaires. Scales included items that measured team ability, team benevolence, team integrity, and team trust (adapted from [16]); trust in human teammates (adapted from [19]); agent competence, cognitive trust in the agent, emotional trust in the agent, intention to delegate to the agent, and intention to adopt the agent as an aide (adapted from [9]); and collective efficacy (adapted from [22]). Results regarding questionnaire data are reported in Tolston et al. [23]. After this, participants were offered a short break – during which any discussion of the task was prohibited – and then received instructions on the Checkmate task. Following the Checkmate task, participants again completed all previously mentioned questionnaires.

Time to completion for this study was approximately 2 h. This included 20 min for pre-experimental setup (including donning physiological monitoring equipment), 55 min for the first-round task, 15 min for the second-round task, 20 min for surveys, and 10 min for cleanup and debriefing. Participants were told that they would receive a base pay of $20 for completing the study. In addition to their base pay, participants were informed that they could win a "bonus" of up to $10 across the first and second-round tasks by earning points. However, following the experiment, all participants received a payment of $30 regardless of performance in the two tasks.

3   Results

3.1   Team Performance

Overall, teams in this experiment tended to lose points across the 50 rounds of the roulette game. The mean team point loss was -343.43 points ($SE = 76.23$ points), approximately 7% of their starting points. To determine if change in score was influenced by team size or game half, we computed a 2 (team size) $\times$ 2 (game half) mixed ANOVA. The results of that analysis indicated there were no statistically significant main effects or interactions (all $ps > .05$).

3.2   Agent Influence

In general, teams' consensus answers were frequently in agreement with the answer suggested by the agent teammate. Across teams, on average, the consensus answer was the same as the agent's suggestion on 28.57 rounds ($SE = .86$). This is higher than the degree of agreement that would be expected to occur simply by chance (i.e., 10 rounds), $t(34) = 21.54, p < .001$, suggesting that team consensus answers were likely influenced by the agent teammate's suggestions.

Beyond simply choosing an answer in common with the agent, we examined the number of rounds in which none of the human teammates' individual answers matched the team's consensus answer, but the consensus answer did match the agent's suggested answer. In other words, in such rounds, the human teammates disregarded their own individual answers and selected a consensus answer in common with the agent's suggestion. On average, triad teams had 10.48 rounds and tetrad teams had 7.94 rounds that matched these criteria. Such outcomes are further evidence that the agent influenced team decision making.

It is important to acknowledge here that agreement in the team's consensus answer and the agent's suggestion does not necessarily indicate that the team selected a particular answer because of the agent's suggestion (though that could be true), but rather that the agent teammate's suggestion may have influenced team decision making in some way, systematically resulting in greater agreement than would be expected exclusively by chance.

3.3 Multinomial Regression

As a further examination of the agent's influence on team dynamics, we conducted a multinomial regression in two steps. Our goal was to determine the influence of human team members on the team's final answer selection in each round, without the machine agent (first step), and to compare the fit of that outcome with a model that did include the agent (second step). A statistically significant increase in model fit from the first to the second step of the regression would indicate that the agent exerted a significant influence on team answer per round. We also evaluated the effects of game half and the interaction between game half and the agent's suggestion on team consensus decisions.

To conduct these analyses, we predicted team consensus decisions using multilevel multinomial logistic regression models [10] fitted using *Rstan* and *rethinking* packages in R [18, 21]. To make sure there were sufficient observations of each outcome to effectively fit multinomial models, the data were condensed from five outcomes to three (the most likely answer from the distribution as one category and two more categories that most evenly balanced the four other outcomes). Prior to fitting the full model, individual multinomial regressions were conducted for each team in the tetrad condition to determine the first- and second-most influential human teammates (determined by comparing model improvement over an intercept only model). These two individuals were then included in the multilevel models so that all teams had two human inputs regardless of team size. The multilevel models were fit with random intercepts and the following predictors were entered sequentially: 1) the most influential human teammate's suggested answer; 2) the next most influential teammate's suggested answer; 3) the agent's suggested answer; 4) game half; and 5) the interaction between the agent's suggested answer and game half. To guide model selection, we used the Widely Applicable Information Criterion (WAIC) [18].

Outcomes from the regression analyses can be seen in Fig. 2. Results show that the model that includes suggestions from the two most influential humans and the agent, game half, and an agent by game half interaction provides the best absolute fit. However, the standard errors in the differences in WAIC between this model and the other two less complicated models that include the agent's suggestions are bigger than the differences in WAIC values themselves. In other words, the model that includes the agent's suggestions is similar in fit to the more complicated models that include half and interactions of half

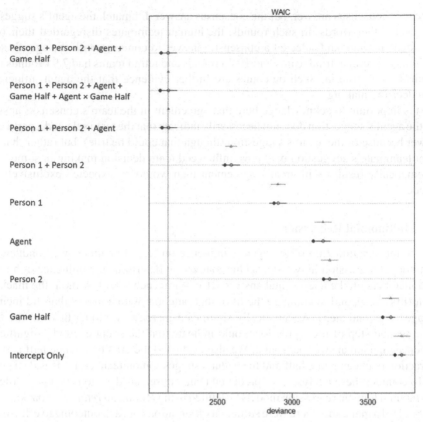

Fig. 2. Outcomes of model selection showing deviance (filled circles), Widely Applicable Information Criterion (WAIC; open circles), standard error of the difference in WAIC (triangles), and standard errors (line segments) of fitted models. The analyses show that the model including suggestions from the two most influential humans and the agent are similar in fit to the more complicated models that include half and interactions of half with the agent, and are better in fit compared to the other, less complicated, models.

with the agent, and is a better fit compared to the other, less complicated, models. These results show that the agent's suggestions influence team consensus decisions even after taking into account other team members preferences and learning (i.e., game half).

3.4   Agent Influence on Consensus Answers and Wagers

To further explore the influence of team size and the agent teammate on human teammate decision making, we examined the number of rounds that teams' consensus answer for the round was the same as the one suggested by the agent using a 2 (team size) × 2 (game half) mixed ANOVA. The results of this analysis indicated a statistically significant main effect of game half, $F(1, 35) = 7.98$, $p = .008$, $\eta_p^2 = .186$; no other effects in the analysis were statistically significant (all $p > .05$). Teams' consensus answer selections were in agreement with the agent's suggestion on fewer rounds in the first half of the game (M = 14.05 rounds, SE = .59) compared to the second half (M = 15.51 rounds, SE = .60).

We further examined the influence of the agent by comparing team wagering behavior during rounds when they did and did not select a consensus answer in agreement with the agent's suggestion by computing a 2 (team size) × 2 (game half) × agreement (final answer agreed or disagreed with the agent's suggestion) mixed ANOVA. The results of this analysis indicated a statistically significant main effect of agreement with the agent, $F(1, 33) = 20.06$, $p < .001$, $\eta_p^2 = .378$; no other effects in the analysis were statistically significant ($p > .05$). Teams wagered significantly more points during rounds where their answer agreed with the agent's answer ($M = 51.62$, $SE = 2.91$) than in rounds when it did not ($M = 43.78$, $SE = 2.98$).

3.5 Team Confidence

As mentioned above, participants rated their confidence first during the individual phase and again during the consensus phase. In general, team member confidence ratings increased from the individual phase ($M = 2.19$, $SE = .09$) to the consensus phase ($M = 2.47$, $SE = .11$), $t(87) = -4.28$, $p < .001$, a phenomenon frequently referred to as the "risky shift" (e.g., Dion, Baron, & Miller, 1970).

To explore the influence of the agent on ratings of confidence in the team's consensus answer, we first calculated the change in confidence ratings for each team member from their individual phase rating to their consensus phase rating, and then averaged across team members to create a team-level estimate of confidence change. We then examined the team confidence change scores for influence from the agent by comparing confidence change scores during rounds when the team did and did not select a consensus answer in agreement with the agent's suggestion using a 2 (team size) × 2 (game half) × agreement (consensus answer agreed or disagreed with agent's suggestion) mixed ANOVA. The results of the analysis indicated a statistically significant main effect of game half, $F(1, 33) = 5.05$, $p = .031$, $\eta_p^2 = .133$, such that the average increase in team confidence was greater in the second half of the game ($M = .34$, $SE = .07$) compared to the first ($M = .26$, $SE = .08$).

The ANOVA results also indicated a statistically significant team size by game half interaction, $F(1, 33) = 5.36$, $p = .027$, $\eta_p^2 = .140$. Follow up simple main effect tests indicated that, for triad teams, confidence increased similarly in the first and second halves of the game, but for tetrad teams, confidence change scores were greater in the second half of the game compared to the first. These effects are depicted in Fig. 3.

Finally, the ANOVA results indicated a statistically significant game half by agreement interaction, $F(1, 33) = 5.71$, $p = .023$, $\eta_p^2 = .148$. Follow up simple main effect tests indicated that there were no differences in team confidence change scores based on agreement with the agent in the second half of the game, but in the first half there was a trend (Bonferroni corrected $p = .056$) for teams to rate their confidence as higher in rounds where they agreed with the agent's answer suggestion compared to those where they did not. These effects are also depicted in Fig. 2.

No other sources of variance in this analysis were statistically significant (all $ps > .05$).

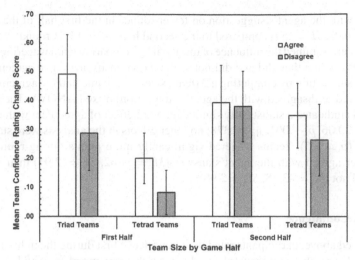

Fig. 3. Mean team confidence rating change scores as a function of team size and game half during trials when the team's consensus answer agreed or disagreed with the agent's suggested answer.

4 Discussion

The purpose of the current experiment was to investigate the influence of a machine agent with limited ability to communicate and engage in teamwork processes, presented as a teammate, on team decision making in a consensus-building task. We manipulated team size, as triads (two humans and an agent) or tetrads (three humans and an agent), and examined the agent's influence in the first and second halves of the experiment to see if its influence changed as participants gained more experience with the game and said agent.

We hypothesized that, consistent with previous research on automation reliance, the agent would exert significant influence on team decision making in this task. This hypothesis was strongly supported, as the agent appears to have influenced teams' consensus answers, wagers, and confidence during the game. We also hypothesized that the agent's influence would be moderated by team size, as the additional teammate in tetrads was expected to decrease each members' influence. This hypothesis was not well supported, as team size was only found to influence team confidence ratings. Finally, we hypothesized that the agent's influence would be reduced from the first to second half of the task as participants gained greater experience with the agent and understood that its performance was imperfect. This hypothesis was not supported, however; the agents' influence was approximately the same throughout the game.

4.1 Agent Influence

The agent teammate had a fairly pronounced effect on team decision making in the roulette task, influencing team consensus answer selection, wagering, and a marginal influence on team confidence. The multinomial regression analysis also supported the strong influence the agent had on team decisions. Interestingly, though the agent's suggestions were less influential than those from the most-influential human teammate, the regression indicated that the agent's suggestions influenced team decision making to a degree that is commensurate with the influence of the second-most influential human teammate. Furthermore, this effect was not moderated by experience, as the agent's influence remained approximately the same across the fifty roulette rounds, despite accumulating evidence for participants across those rounds that the agent's performance was far from perfect. These results confirm that even machine agents with low abilities to engage in teamwork processes, such as consensus formation, may still exert a strong influence on them.

The agent's influence in the current experiment may be due to several factors (or a combination of them). First, the agent was presented as teammate, rather than a tool [24], potentially activating social and behavioral norms regarding consideration of its suggestions in team processes.

Second, though the agent's overall accuracy (34% across all trials) was quite low, and considerably less than the minimum accuracy of 70% suggested in the automation reliability literature to engender use [26], it was still considerably higher than the accuracy teams might have expected by chance if they believed the underlying distribution was uniform. As such, routinely defaulting to the agent's suggestion represents a rational strategy in a situation of high uncertainty.

Third, and perhaps more importantly, the underlying distribution of outcomes in the roulette game *was not* uniform, and the agent's behavior strongly modeled the strategy most likely to produce gains, i.e., probability maximizing, whereby players select the dominant outcome as their response for all trials [6]. This was particularly true in the second half of the game, where the agent suggested the dominant outcome on 80% of trials. Though no teams fully adopted a probability maximizing strategy by the end of the experiment (it usually takes 100–200 trials for participants to adopt this strategy in similar experiments [6]), the agent's influence and modeling may have permitted teams to adopt the strategy more quickly than typical if more rounds had been included in the current experiment.

This raises an interesting potential application for utilizing agent influence in teams, if the agent is specifically modeling behaviors that are desirable for team members to adopt. Observational learning research suggests that team members will learn behaviors and attitudes from those they observe, particularly if the person being modeled is believed to be high in status or influence [17] – as agents may be. This goal need not be explicitly stated to participants; instead, the natural influence of an agent may be sufficient to bias participants to adopt desired outcomes. For example, in the current experiment the agent's suggestion in each round of roulette was based on the modal answer of our pilot participants, but in future studies its behavior could be modified to more strongly demonstrate a probability maximization strategy, potentially causing participants to adopt this more effective strategy earlier in the experiment.

4.2 Effects of Team Size

Contrary to initial hypotheses, team size had a relatively small effect, mostly on confidence ratings. There may be several explanations for this in the current experiment. First, increasing team size in the roulette game did not yield the performance benefits observed in some tasks, particularly those where performance is related to task directed effort [15]. In the current experiment, increases in team size did not increase team accuracy, most likely because the random nature of outcomes in the roulette game could not be influenced by team effort, undercutting the utility of an additional team member. In fact, from this perspective, it is possible that increases in team size could have potentially impeded development of more effective strategies, such as probability maximization, due to increased diffusion of responsibility in larger teams.

Second, task load in the current experiment was likely quite low, as the process of consensus-building did not require participants to engage in complex mental computations and temporal pressure was minimal. As mentioned previously, cognitive overload is a critical factor in determining reliance on automation [14], and though there presumably was some pressure to maximize performance and thereby fiscal gain, that pressure was likely insufficient to result in overload and greater reliance on the agent's suggestions.

4.3 Conclusions and Directions for Future Research

The current experiment was designed to explore the influence of a machine agent with minimal ability to engage in teamwork on team decision making processes. Our results suggest that agents, even those with minimal teamwork capabilities, are likely to exert a strong influence on teams, though this could be used advantageously if the agent models behaviors, attitudes, or strategies that are desirable for human teammates to adopt.

Though the results of the current experiment support that agents are likely to exert influence, further research is necessary to determine the relative contribution of several potential causes of that influence, such as presentation of an agent as a teammate, rather than a tool; agent accuracy, relative both to expected accuracy and to human team member accuracy; and agent strategy modeling. In addition, further exploration of the effects of team size on agent influence is warranted, particularly in tasks where increases in team size may be expected to yield greater task-directed effort and improved team performance.

References

1. Alarcon, G.M., et al.: The effect of propensity to trust and perceptions of trustworthiness on trust behaviors in dyads. Behav. Res. Methods **50**(5), 1906–1920 (2017). https://doi.org/10.3758/s13428-017-0959-6
2. Alnuaimi, O.A., et al.: Team size, dispersion, and social loafing in technology-supported teams: a perspective on the theory of moral disengagement. J. Manage. Inf. Syst. **27**(1), 203–230 (2010). https://doi.org/10.2753/MIS0742-1222270109
3. Berberian, B.: Man-machine teaming: a problem of agency. IFAC-PapersOnLine **51**(34), 118–123 (2019). https://doi.org/10.1016/j.ifacol.2019.01.049
4. Chen, J.Y.C., Barnes, M.J.: Human-agent teaming for multirobot control: a review of human factors issues. IEEE Trans. Hum.-Mach. Syst. **44**(1), 13–29 (2014). https://doi.org/10.1109/THMS.2013.2293535
5. Dzindolet, M.T., et al.: The role of trust in automation reliance. Int. J. Hum. Comput. Stud. **58**(6), 697–718 (2003). https://doi.org/10.1016/S1071-5819(03)00038-7

6. Green, C.S., et al.: Alterations in choice behavior by manipulations of world model. Proc. Natl. Acad. Sci. U.S.A. **107**(37), 16401–16406 (2010). https://doi.org/10.1073/pnas.100170 9107

7. Grigsby, S.S.: Artificial intelligence for advanced human-machine symbiosis. In: Schmorrow, D.D., Fidopiastis, C.M. (eds.) AC 2018. LNCS (LNAI), vol. 10915, pp. 255–266. Springer, Cham (2018). https://doi.org/10.1007/978-3-319-91470-1_22

8. Holbrook, J.B., et al.: Enabling urban air mobility: human-autonomy teaming research challenges and recommendations. In: AIAA Aviation 2020 Forum. American Institute of Aeronautics and Astronautics Inc, AIAA (2020). https://doi.org/10.2514/6.2020-3250

9. Komiak, S.Y.X., Benbasat, I.: The effects of personalization and familiarity on trust and adoption of recommendation agents. MIS Q. **30**(4), 941–960 (2006). https://doi.org/10.2307/25148760

10. Koster, J., McElreath, R.: Multinomial analysis of behavior: statistical methods. Behav. Ecol. Sociobiol. **71**(9), 1–14 (2017). https://doi.org/10.1007/s00265-017-2363-8

11. Kwon, M., et al.: Human expectations of social robots. In: 2016 11th ACM/IEEE International Conference on Human-Robot Interaction (HRI), pp. 463–464. IEEE Press, New York (2016). https://doi.org/10.1109/HRI.2016.7451807

12. Lee, M.K., et al.: Personalization in HRI: a longitudinal field experiment. In: 2012 7th ACM/IEEE International Conference on Human-Robot Interaction (HRI), pp. 319–326. IEEE Press, New York (2012). https://www.ri.cmu.edu/pub_files/2012/3/HRI12_Personalization_camready_final.pdf

13. Lee, J.D., See, K.A.: Trust in automation: designing for appropriate reliance. Hum. Factors **46**(1), 50–80 (2004). https://doi.org/10.1518/hfes.46.1.50_30392

14. Lyell, D., Coiera, E.: Automation bias and verification complexity: a systematic review. J. Am. Med. Inform. Assoc. **24**(2), 423–431 (2017). https://doi.org/10.1093/jamia/ocw105

15. Mao, A., et al.: An experimental study of team size and performance on a complex task. PLoS ONE **11**, 4 (2016). https://doi.org/10.1371/journal.pone.0153048

16. Mayer, R.C., Davis, J.H.: The effect of the performance appraisal system on trust for management: a field quasi-experiment. J. Appl. Psychol. **84**(1), 123–136 (1999). https://doi.org/10.1037/0021-9010.84.1.123

17. McCullagh, P.: Model status as a determinant of observational learning and performance. J. Sport Psychol. **8**(4), 319–331 (1986). https://doi.org/10.1123/jsp.8.4.319

18. McElreath, R.: Statistical Rethinking: A Bayesian Course with Examples in R and STAN. 2nd edn. CRC Press, New York (2020). https://www.routledge.com/Statistical-Rethinking-A-Bayesian-Course-with-Examples-in-R-and-STAN/McElreath/p/book/9780367139919

19. Naquin, C.E., Paulson, G.D.: Online bargaining and interpersonal trust. J. Appl. Psychol. **88**(1), 113–120 (2003). https://doi.org/10.1037/0021-9010.88.1.113

20. Nicholson, C.Y., et al.: The role of interpersonal liking in building trust in long-term channel relationships. J. Acad. Mark. Sci. **29**(3), 3–15 (2001). https://doi.org/10.1177/009207030129 1001

21. R Core Team: R: a language and environment for statistical computing. R Foundation for Statistical Computing, Vienna, Austria. https://www.R-project.org/

22. Riggs, M.L., Knight, P.A.: The impact of perceived group success-failure on motivational beliefs and attitudes: a causal model. J. Appl. Psychol. **79**(5), 755–766 (1994). https://doi.org/10.1037/0021-9010.79.5.755

23. Tolston, M.T., et al.: Have a heart: predictability of trust in an autonomous agent teammate through team-level measures of heart rate synchrony and arousal. Proc. Hum. Fact. Ergon. Soc. Ann. Meet. **62**(1), 714–715 (2018). https://doi.org/10.1177/1541931218621162

24. Walliser, J.C., et al.: Team structure and team building improve human–machine teaming with autonomous agents. J. Cogn. Eng. Decis. Mak. **13**(4), 258–278 (2019). https://doi.org/10.1177/1555343419867563

25. Warden, T., et al.: The national academies board on human system integration (BOHSI) panel: promise, progress and challenges of leveraging AI technology in healthcare. Proc. Hum. Fact. Ergon. Soc. Ann. Meet. **64**(1), 2124–2128 (2020). https://doi.org/10.1177/107 1181320641515
26. Wickens, C.D., et al.: Workload and automation reliability in unmanned air vehicles. In: Cooke, N.J., et al. (eds.) Advances in Human Performance and Cognitive Engineering Research: Vol. 7. Human Factors of Remotely Operated Vehicles, pp. 209–222. Elsevier, Amsterdam (2006). https://doi.org/10.1016/S1479-3601(05)07015-3
27. Wolfe, J., Chacko, T.: The effects of different team sizes on business game performance. Dev. Bus. Simul. Exp. Exerc. **9**, 232–235 (1982). https://absel-ojs-ttu.tdl.org/absel/index.php/absel/article/view/2372/2341
28. Zacharias, G.L.: Autonomous Horizons: The Way Forward. Air University Press, Maxwell AFB (2015). https://www.airuniversity.af.edu/Portals/10/AUPress/Books/b_0155_zacharias_autonomous_horizons.pdf

Modeling Salesclerks' Utterances in Bespoke Scenes and Evaluating Them Using a Communication Robot

Fumiya Kobayashi[1]([⊠]), Masashi Sugimoto[2], Saizo Aoyagi[3], Michiya Yamamoto[2], and Noriko Nagata[2]

[1] Graduate School of Science and Technologies, Kwansei Gakuin University, Sanda, Japan
kobayashi-fumiya@kwansei.ac.jp
[2] School of Engineering, Kwansei Gakuin University, Sanda, Japan
[3] Faculty of Global Media Studies, Komazawa University, Setagaya-ku, Tokyo, Japan

Abstract. A paradigm shift is taking place, from the era of common off-the-shelf products to that of personalized products. In this study, we developed a communication robot that could improve customers' satisfaction in bespoke scenes, which is a sales method of personalized products. First, we extracted the model of the salesclerks' utterances that would be useful for improving satisfaction in bespoke tailoring. We modeled the salesclerks' utterances based on the utterance content. Next, we designed a bespoke origami task by communicating with a robot, which worked based on the salesclerks' utterance model. Then, we analyzed how the robot's utterances evoked customers' emotions and improved satisfaction. As a result, we revealed that the utterances that encouraged customers' decisions improved customer satisfaction.

Keywords: Bespoke · Communication robot · Expert salesclerk model

1 Introduction

A paradigm shift is taking place, from the era of common off-the-shelf products to that of personalized products [1]. Customers who have a certain level of knowledge can make customized products by themselves. On the other hand, customers who do not have a certain level of knowledge about products cannot make customized products by themselves and need support from salesclerks.

In our study, we focus on bespoke tailoring, which is a sales method for customized products. In bespoke scenes, customers communicate with salesclerks to tailor products. When salesclerks serve customers in actual stores, the salesclerks try to understand the customers' needs and what customers feel through communication, and they provide feedback such as appropriate suggestions and assistance accordingly, thereby improving customers' satisfaction. Sugimoto [2] conducted a study on the customer service of expert salesclerks who improve customers' satisfaction. In the study, Sugimoto investigated the behavior of salesclerks in suit bespoke. They found that expert salesclerks limited the number of choices and reassured the customers of their decisions. In this study,

© Springer Nature Switzerland AG 2021
C. Stephanidis et al. (Eds.): HCII 2021, CCIS 1498, pp. 271–278, 2021.
https://doi.org/10.1007/978-3-030-90176-9_35

we modeled the salesclerks' utterances, which were useful for improving customers' satisfaction.

In addition, because of the spread of COVID-19, people need non-contact customer service to prevent infection. The number of opportunities robots to serve customers is increasing. There have been many studies about impressions of robots working in stores. Kubota [3] conducted an experiment in which androids spoke in an actual store. However, there were predetermined scenarios of utterances in Kubota's experiment, and androids could not communicate with customers flexibly. Thus, we oriented service robots that could communicate with customers based on an utterance model that could improve customers' satisfaction.

In this study, we first analyzed the utterances of salesclerks from videos of suit bespoke in an actual store, and we created an utterance model that improves customers satisfaction. Next, we designed an origami bespoke task in which a robot acts as a salesclerk and speaks according to our utterance model. Through the task we revealed that salesclerks' utterance model could improve customers' satisfaction.

2 Modeling Salesclerks' Utterances and Emotions in Bespoke Scenarios

2.1 Modeling Salesclerks' Utterances

In this study, we modeled the utterances of salesclerks from videos [4] of suit bespoke at the Family Bazaar (9/15–17/2018) held by a suit manufacturing and sales company. We referred to Sugimoto's study [2] and divided the videos into two types: ones with expert salesclerks serving the customers, and ones with novice salesclerks serving the customers. There were five videos in each category. The expert salesclerks' videos were totaled 90 min (mean 18 min, $SD = 11.85$ min), and the novice salesclerks' videos were totaled 105 min (mean 21 min, $SD = 9.85$ min).

Fig. 1. An example of actual bespoke tailoring consisting of three typical steps. A customer defines requirement and selects material and designs with a salesclerk.

In the analysis, we first divided the suit bespoke into three steps: In the first step, salesclerks listened to the customers' needs and usage of the suit (defining requirements). In the second step, customers selected the materials for the suit (selecting a material). In the third step, customers selected the designs, such as buttons and tucks (selecting design) (Fig. 1). Next, we tagged each salesclerk's utterances using the video analysis tool ELAN (Fig. 2). To analyze salesclerks' utterances, we compared expert and novice salesclerks in terms of the amount of utterances, the kinds of utterances, and the transition of utterances. In the tagging process, the salesclerks' utterances were classified into six categories: "suggestion," "closed question (CQ)," "open question (OQ)," "explanation," "encouragement," and "other" (Table 1).

Fig. 2. Analyzing salesclerks' utterances using ELAN (annotation tool)

Table 1. Six categories of salesclerks' utterances

Category	Content	Example	Percentage
Suggestion	Suggest specific something	How about ~?	11%
CQ	Closed Question	Do you like bright one?	9%
OQ	Open Question	What color do you like? What do you want something?	3%
Explanation	Explanation about materials and designs	This material is ~. ~ is popular.	48%
Encouragement	Agree with customers' decisions	That' good I think that is good ,too.	5%
Other	Other sentences		24%

To compare the amount of utterances between expert and novice salesclerks, we conducted a t-test on the percentage of utterance time per minute for expert and novice salesclerks. It showed that the experts spoke longer than the novices did (Fig. 3 left). To compare the kinds of utterance between expert and novice salesclerks, we conducted a t-test on the number of utterances per minute for each of the five types of utterances. It showed that there was a significant difference between the expert and novice salesclerks in terms of the "suggestion" and "encouragement" utterances, indicating that the expert salesclerks used the "suggestion" and "encouragement" utterances more frequently than did the novice salesclerks (Fig. 3 right).

Next, to compare the transition of the five types of utterances, we made diagrams. The probability transitions of the five types of utterances of the expert and novice salesclerks in the material selection and design selection were calculated (Fig. 4). In the material selection, the experts offered repeated suggestions and explanations, and then multiple encouragement. On the other hand, the novices tended to repeat the explanations. In the design selection, the experts asked questions and made suggestions, and then they explained and gave encouragement. On the other hand, the novices tended to repeat questions and explanations, with little encouragement.

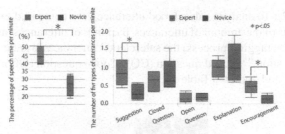

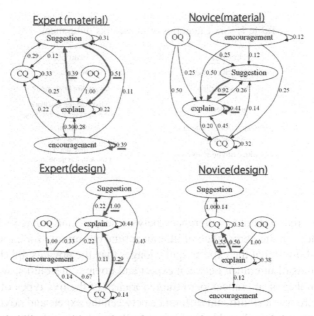

Fig. 3. The percentage of utterance time (left) and the number of the five types of utterances: suggestion, closed question, open question, explanation, and encouragement (right). The expert salesclerks spoke longer than did the novice salesclerks in bespoke. The experts' utterances contained more suggestions and encouragements than those of novices. (Bars indicate maximum and minimum. The line on the surface, bottom, and between them indicate upper quartile, lower quartile, and median, respectively.)

Fig. 4. The probability transitions of the five types of utterances of the expert and novice salesclerks in the material selection and design selection

2.2 Modeling Emotions in Bespoke Scenarios

To model emotions customers feel in bespoke scenarios, we extracted emotion words that were evoked in the suit bespoke from the study by Obata et al. [4]. We chose twenty-five emotion words. Forty-six students answered a questionnaire about the characteristics of these emotion words. The characteristics of the emotions here refer to where the emotions are located on Russell's core-affect model plane [5]. Each emotion word was evaluated in two dimensions: pleasure-displeasure and arousal-sleep. Each evaluation was made on a 5-point scale. The results of the questionnaire were transformed so that the maximum value was +2 and the minimum value was 2, and the emotion words were distributed on Russell's core-affect model plane. After that, we determined representative and valid emotions of the eight domains on Russell's core-affect model through discussion. Thereby, we created the bespoke version of the core-affect model (Fig. 5).

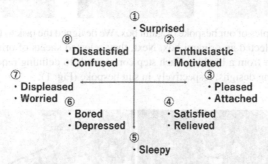

Fig. 5. A core-affect model of bespoke tailoring. We identified 13 emotions in eight categories.

3 Verifying the Effect of Robots' Utterances

3.1 Bespoke Origami

We analyzed salesclerks' utterances and made a bespoke utterance model. However, it is uncertain if robots can improve customer satisfaction. To evaluate if the robot's utterance could improve customer satisfaction, we designed the task of customizing an origami[1] box while participants communicated with a robot (origami task). The origami task consisted of three steps, as the suit bespoke did (Fig. 6): In the first step, participants reviewed six samples of origami boxes and selected one. In the second step, they selected sheets of origami. Eighty-three sheets of origami paper (5 cm squared) were regularly lined up on a rack, and participants selected the number of sheets they needed to make the box freely. In the third step, they selected designs for optional decorations on the box. Participants chose stickers and tape to decorate the box from a booklet with samples of stickers and tape. In this way, we created a situation in which the participants felt the same emotions as in suit bespoke.

3.2 A Robot Plays the Role of Supporter in Bespoke

In the origami task, a robot played the role of a salesclerk in the bespoke scenario. We used SHARP's RoBoHoN (Fig. 7). We developed an Android application that allowed the RoBoHoN to speak the sentences the experimenter entered on the remote PC. Using this application, we could communicate with the participants using the WOZ (Wizard of Oz) method [6]. The experimenter watched the participants on a monitor and operated RoBoHoN. Based on the expert salesclerks' utterances model, RoBoHoN spoke encouraging utterances when participants made choices and spoke suggestion utterances when they were troubled.

---

[1] Origami: Japanese traditional paper craft.

Selecting a product   Selecting sheets of origami   Selecting designs

  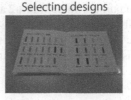

Fig. 6. Product samples of our bespoke origami box. We designed the task to fit with suit bespoke. First, participants selected an origami box. Next, they selected sheets of origami paper. Finally, they selected options from a booklet. Each step corresponds to defining requirements, selecting material, and selecting designs, respectively, in suit bespoke (Fig. 1).

Fig. 7. The experimenter operated the service robot (RoBoHoN) through monitors.

3.3 Experiment Processes

Participants conducted an origami bespoke tasked with the help of RoBoHoN. Participants first chose one of the six products and selected sheets of origami paper from the rack. After that, they decided on the design by looking at the booklet (Fig. 8). After they had completed the task, we conducted an interview survey. The participants watched videos of their own bespoke activity and reported the changes in their emotions and satisfaction levels during the task. The participants reported the time when their emotions or satisfaction levels changed during the task and selected one from the emotion groups as the most appropriate emotion they felt at that time. At the same time, participants selected one of the following three options: "satisfied," "dissatisfied," and "neither." If participants answered "satisfied" or "dissatisfied," they recorded the degree to which they felt it on a 5-point scale ("1: not at all" to "5: very much so"). The degree of satisfaction (satisfaction level) was evaluated on an 11-point scale (from –5 to +5), with "satisfied" on a scale of +1 to +5, "dissatisfied" on a scale of –1 to –5, and "neither" as 0. Participants were 26 students (12 males and 14 females).

3.4 Result of the Experiment and Discussion

The total duration of the experiment was 551 min (average: 21 min per participant), and the total number of RoBoHoN utterances was 724 (average: 27.9 utterances per participant, 1.3 utterances per minute). Of these, the suggestion utterances were spoken a total of 66 times to 23 participants, and the encouraging utterances were spoken a total of 148 times to all participants.

Selecting a product   Selecting sheets of origami   Selecting designs

Fig. 8. An example of the origami box bespoke task. The red circles show the robot, which serves customers just like a bespoke tailor.

We compared the percentage of evoked emotions in the 20 s before and after the suggested utterances (before: −20 to 0 s, after: 0 to 20 s) for 23 participants. Participants felt more "enthusiastic" after the utterances than before the utterances ($t(22) = 2.25$, $p = .035, d = .23$) and felt less "satisfied" after the utterances than before the utterances ($t(22) = 2.56, p = .018, d = .36$). Similarly, when comparing the mean values of satisfaction for 20 s before and after the utterances, there was no change in satisfaction level before and after the utterances (Fig. 9).

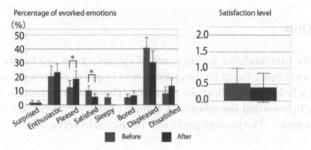

Fig. 9. Participants felt less "pleased" after "suggestion" utterances than before the utterances significantly. Participants felt more "satisfied" after the utterances and after the utterances, but satisfaction level didn't change.

Next, we compared the percentage of evoked emotions in the 20 s before and after the encouraged utterances for 26 participants. Participants felt more "satisfied" after utterances than before utterances ($t(25) = 2.96, p = .004, d = .43$) and felt less "displeased" after utterances than before utterances ($t(25) = 2.39, p = .018, d = .30$). Similarly, comparing the mean values of the satisfaction levels for 20 s before and after the utterances, the satisfaction level after the utterances was higher than before the utterances ($t(25) = 3.39, p = .002, d = .33$) (Fig. 10).

The satisfaction levels after the encouraging utterances were higher than before the utterances. However, the participants' satisfaction levels might have increased simply because of participants making choices (e.g., deciding which suit materials to choose). This is because the RoBoHoN spoke encouraging utterances when the participants were selecting their origami and designs. Here, to prove that the encouraging utterances were the factor that increased the satisfaction level, we compared the satisfaction levels in the 20 s before and after the "choice" scene, in which there was no utterance by RoBoHoN. Such "choice" situations were found in 16 of the 26 participants. There was no change

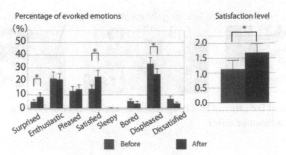

Fig. 10. Participants felt significantly more "satisfied" after encouraging utterances than before them. Participants felt less "displeased" after the utterances, and satisfaction level also increased significantly.

in satisfaction levels 20 s before and after the "choice" scene ($t\,(15) = 0.32, p = .751$). Therefore, we proved that the participants' satisfaction levels did not increase due to the "choice" but due to RoBoHoN's encouraging utterances.

4   Conclusion

In this study, we first modeled the utterance of salesclerks in suit bespoke and revealed that the robot's utterance based on the model could improve customers' satisfaction. The origami task included typical bespoke elements: There were communication and steps. Therefore, we believe that the robots can improve customer satisfaction in other types of bespoke scenarios. The present study will be useful to serve also in the VR space.

References

1. Tsuhan Shimbun Digest, Farewell to the age of mass consumption and mass production. Personalization and experiences through products are the keys to winning in the age of diversified consumption. https://netshop.impress.co.jp/node/7232. Accessed 22 Apr 2021. (in Japanese)
2. Sugimoto, M., et al.: Differences in customers' interactions with expert/novice salesclerks in a bespoke tailoring situation: a case study on the utterances of salesclerks. In: International Conference on Human-Computer Interaction, pp. 131–137 (2019)
3. Kubota, T., Isowa, T., Ogawa, K., Ishiguro, H.: Development and verification of an onsite-operated android robot working cooperatively with humans in a real store. In: Proceedings of the Human Interface Society, vol. 22, no. 3, pp. 275–290 (2020). (in Japanese)
4. Obata, K., et al.: Construction of customers 'emotion model in the bespoke tailoring using evaluation grid method. In: 2020 IEEE International Conference on Consumer Electronics, pp. 1–4 (2020)
5. Russell, J.A.: A circumplex model of affect. J. Pers. Soc. Psychol. **39**, 1161–1178 (1980)
6. Kelley, J.F.: An iterative design methodology for user-friendly natural language office information applications. ACM Trans. Inf. Syst. (TOIS) **2**(1), 26–41 (1984)

User Satisfaction with an AI-Enabled Customer Relationship Management Chatbot

Maarif Sohail[1(✉)], Zehra Mohsin[2], and Sehar Khaliq[3]

[1] DeGroote School of Business, McMaster University, Hamilton, ON, Canada
sohaim9@mcmaster.edu
[2] Lahore College for Women University, Lahore, Pakistan
[3] Foundation University Islamabad, Islamabad, Pakistan

Abstract. Chatbots' ability to carry out focused, result-oriented online conversations with human end-users impacts user experience and user satisfaction. Using "Chatbots" as key identifiable examples utilized by Electronic Commerce (E-Commerce) firms in Customer Relationship Management (CRM), this study offers a user satisfaction model in the context of Artificial Intelligence (AI) enabled CRM in E-Commerce. The model is based on Expectation Confirmation Theory (ECT) and Uncertainty Reduction Theory (URT) within the Chatbot context. This model will allow us to investigate if chatbots can provide both businesses and consumers the opportunity to complete a journey from normal through abnormal to the new normal in situations similar to a covid pandemic.

Keywords: Artificial Intelligence (AI) · Customer Relationship Management (CRM) · Electronic Commerce (E-Commerce) · Expectation Confirmation Theory (ECT) · Uncertainty Reduction Theory (URT)

1 Introduction

Businesses today originate, operate, sustain, and eventually die out in complex environments. As businesses across the world abruptly closed their doors to stop the spread of COVID-19, an entire spectrum of industries sputtered to a halt in some countries. Retailers, restaurants, coffee shops, bars, malls, theaters, cinemas, and stadiums—places that normally housed gatherings of people ended up becoming empty. In covid times, or for that matter, in any normal, though abnormal to the new normal life cycle, the businesses will face uncertainty. Information Systems over the years have faced a state of uncertainty that may decrease the quality of the decision process and result in a negative impact in terms of efficiency and welfare for the society (Osório and Pinto 2019).

Chatbots are recognized as a software systems, which can chat or interact with a human user in a natural language such as English (Shawar and Atwell 2007). It is a computer program or an artificial intelligence which conducts a conversation via auditory or textual methods (Bilange 1991; Vassos et al. 2016; Følstad and Brandtzaeg 2017; Valtolina et al. 2018; Varitimiadis et al. 2020). A chatbot is also known as a chatterbot, bot, smart bot, conversational interface, or artificial conversational entity. While working

© Springer Nature Switzerland AG 2021
C. Stephanidis et al. (Eds.): HCII 2021, CCIS 1498, pp. 279–287, 2021.
https://doi.org/10.1007/978-3-030-90176-9_36

for the CRM function, a chatbot assists human agents and answers users' queries. End users are observed to receive a pleasant or acceptable experience if chatbots succeed in delivering appropriate information, maintaining high system availability, and providing personalized solutions. Thus, Chatbot improves user experience and user satisfaction. Chatbots are noted to redirect queries to proper authorities in the organization to answer customer queries (Bernazzani 2018). In covid times use of Chatbot transcend into basic activities like food delivery services (De Cicco et al. 2020). Thus, the motivation for AI-enabled CRM is identified in terms of the cost of interaction with customers in E-commerce.

The remainder of the paper is structured as follows: In Sect. 2, we present the literature review that focuses on AI, E-commerce, Chatbots. We illustrate and discuss the proposed research model and hypotheses in Sect. 3. Similarly, we furnish the research methodology and the theoretical and practical contributions in Sect. 4. Future Research and Limitations follow this in Sect. 5. We then conclude the research paper in Sect. 6.

2   Literature Review

Conversational User Interface (CUI) is one of the more popular forms of Human-Computer Interaction. A CUI allows users to communicate with computers using a spoken dialogue or text for information access and processing (Zue and Glass 2000). Researchers identify Chatbots as one of the popular types of CUI. Researchers define Chatbot as an AI application that uses NLP to understand and enable a conversation between a human and a machine (Abdul-Kader and Woods 2015). Others view a chatbot as a unique application system that uses artificial intelligence technologies to provide a natural language user interface (Meyer von Wolff et al. 2019). Chatbots are designed to convincingly replicate how a human would interact as a conversational partner and, in turn, pass the Turing test (McDonnell and Baxter 2019). Turing test relates to is an experiment developed to test a machine's capability to exhibit intelligent behavior equivalent (Turing 1950). User expectations within the context of AI-enabled CRM in E-Commerce pivots on completing essential and gigantic multifaceted tasks, such as coordinating and performing same-day delivery to customers and placing voice-enabled orders to complete individual orders from individual stores (Kawa et al. 2018). E-Commerce thus can sustain lean supply chains using AI (Kawa and Maryniak 2019). E-Commerce uses a dynamic pricing strategy, allowing businesses to change prices for products or services in real-time based on the current market demand. This strategy is pragmatic because AI models employ automatic algorithms to compute prices, whereas decisions made by humans can not possibly keep up with the volume of data (Weber and Schütte 2019).

User Experiences within the context of AI-enabled CRM in E-Commerce hinges on accepting improved customer service and is often measured through chatbots (Skjuve and Brandzaeg 2018) using large-scale and publicly available E-Commerce data. The interest in end users is that this type of Chatbot can take advantage of data from in-page product descriptions and user-generated content from E-Commerce websites (Cui et al. 2017). The use of chatbots is also attributed to the surge in the burden on call centers. The feasibility of using chatbots in call centers has started to be studied. The call centers strive to cut operating and training expenses (Toader et al. 2020). End user's expectations and experience about call center chatbots vary from industry to industry. According to research, end-users feel more at ease communicating and interacting with anthropomorphic recommendation agents than with human-like interfaces (avatars) that are ethnically and gender compatible with end-users (Benbasat et al. 2020). The third important part of our literature review centers on factors that satisfy the end-user while using chatbots. Acceptance of hedonistic technology is attributed intrinsically to cognitive absorption (Agarwal and Karahanna 2000; Lowry et al. 2013); we can apply the same concept to the acceptance of Chatbot, e.g., Acceptance of Xiaoice Chatbot by Chinese users (Zhou et al., Zhou et al. 2020). We also consider the essential concept of Trust in E-Commerce, as Trust is especially critical in the early phases of interactions, which is the situation with new technology adoption when the situation is vague. Also, consequences are indeterminate (Ostrom et al. 2019). Trust acts as a bridge between an individual's beliefs about the characteristics and capabilities of automation and the individual's intention to use and rely on automation (Lee and See 2004). When we explore E-Commerce, we need to differentiate between trust in the provider and trust in the transaction medium (Pavlou 2003). This differentiation will also apply in the context of AI-enabled service encounters, where both trust in the service provider and trust in the specific AI technology will contribute to customers' trust toward the AI-enabled service. An organization's trustworthiness is determined through ability, integrity, and benevolence (Mayer et al. 1995). The literature also exemplifies that AI-enabled services lead to a lack of privacy that may result from an even greater trove of detailed information about us continually being gathered and analyzed. AI virtual assistants will have extensive knowledge about what we like, the trade-offs we are willing to make, likely at a level we do not know ourselves (Dawar 2018). Extant literature also provides the concept of reliability. It is defined as the degree to which a consumer believes new technology will perform a job consistently and accurately (Lee et al. 2003).

Similarly, it is also identified as the quality of a service outcome (Shamdasani et al. 2008) and the ability to deliver an expected standard at any given time (Iberahim et al. 2016). We substantiate these definitions by referring to the reliability concept presented in TAM3 Model, which is the perceived output quality (Venkatesh and Bala 2008). Since chatbots are supposed to address the dynamic needs of the customers, we also focus on the fact that 'the reliability dimension is critical because it embeds the dynamic capability to perform the promised service dependably and accurately (Narteh 2015). Hence reliability aspect will help our understanding of whether the customer would use the Chatbot again in the future or not. The dearth of articles discusses the positioning of chatbots in e-commerce (Vinodhini and Chandrasekaran 2016) and examines the factors influencing the adoption of Chatbots in e-commerce (Lucente 2002). The literature has started to discuss and inspect the reasons influencing the adoption of Chatbots from the perspective of e-commerce (Araújo and Casais 2020). Chatbots also feature as context-specific internal communication processes (Saenz et al. 2017).

3 Proposed Research Model and Hypotheses

We present our model in Fig. 1, developed to study end users' behavior in the three stages of engagement with a chatbot. The three stages represent the normal phase, abnormal phase, and the new normal phase. The model combines several significant antecedents that may influence users' decisions and actions at each stage. We present the constructs for our model based on studies using an expectancy-confirmation (or disconfirmation) archetype while theorizing those expectations influence the satisfaction with a product or service and showing the intention to use (Oliver 1977; Bhattacherjee Bhattacherjee 2001).

Privacy Concerns: We base our understanding of privacy concerns on the work of Han and Yang (2018). Intelligent Personal Assistants (IPA) observed privacy concerns as an important barrier to continuance intention. We extend the IPA concept to chatbots; therefore, we assume the relationship:

H1: Privacy concerns about the Chatbot will be negatively related to chatbot performance expectations.

Perceived Trust: Perceived Trust is defined as the extent to which a person feels about their ability to control their tasks freely. The successful adoption of Chatbots would rely to a large extent upon the ability of the dialogue systems to digitalize the human capacity to build trust by imitating the linguistic communication in human-agent interactions through NLP (Rodríguez Cardona 2019). Chatbot technology is trusted as a supporting tool in the decision-making process and may provide suggestions to act, but the decisions to be made are always a human responsibility. To increase the Chatbot's ability to help and increase trust, the users need the training to phrase themselves for better mutual comprehension. Hence, we suggest H2, H3, and H4 as follows:

H2: Perceived Trust about the Chatbot will be positively related to the chatbot performance expectations.

H3: Perceived Trust in the Chatbot will be positively related to the user satisfaction with the Chatbot.

H4: Perceived Trust about the Chatbot will be positively related to the confirmation about the chatbot performance expectations.

Perceived Reliability: Confirmation about the chatbot performance will increase if the Chatbot can provide appropriate responses to most questions over time. Ideally, the Chatbot should admit its limitations as opposed to giving a wrong response. When faced with ambiguous questions, the Chatbot should ask follow-up questions to identify the desired response. The absence of reliability may waste the time of customers (Demoulin and Djelassi 2016). We also observe that reliability is one of the strong determinants of customer satisfaction (Gunawardana et al. 2015; Narteh 2015). Therefore, we hypothesize

H5: Perceived Reliability about the Chatbot will be positively related to the confirmation about the chatbot performance expectations.

Expectation Confirmation Theory: The Expectation Confirmation Theory (ECT) is prevalent in the marketing research circles and has been used extensively in Information Systems. ECT captures the relationship that Expectation influences Satisfaction directly and is mediated through Disconfirmation (Oliver 1977,1980). Keeping in view the Information Systems perspective, this theory was modified to include the environmental effect of social influence and marketing campaign due to possible changes in the end-user's perception about the product or service (Bhattacharjee 2001). We make use of ECT theory to hypothesize the relationship for our model as follows:

H6: Chatbot Performance confirmation of Expectation will be positively related to User Satisfaction.

H7: Chatbot Performance Expectation will be positively related to User Satisfaction.

H8: Chatbot Performance confirmation of Expectation will be positively related to User Satisfaction.

Also, we use Uncertainty Reduction Theory suggests that communication removes uncertainty through interpersonal interaction (Berger and Calabrese 1974). The chatbots, as communicators, engage the end-user by interaction in this manner. The chatbot end user will perceive the environment is identified as the new normal. In this stage, the end-user has more clarity and a fair evaluation of certainty about the Chatbot's performance. The end-user can decide whether to continue to use the Chatbot for ordering or inquiring information. Thus, we propose.

H9: Higher the end users' satisfaction with the Chatbots, higher will be end users' behavioral intentions to continue to use it.

4 Research Methodology and Contribution

This research applies ECT theory, in conjunction with HCI, AI, and E-Commerce streams of literature, to understand the factors influencing user satisfaction with AI-enabled CRM in E-Commerce. We will use the quantitative analysis approach and operationalize the research using pre-validated scales from the extant literature to maximize the validity and reliability of the measurement model. The study has the potential to contribute to the theoretical as well as practical levels. Findings can back managers on preparing, persuading, and urging individual users in call centers and help desks to use chatbots.

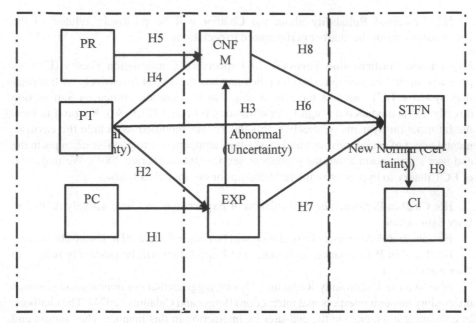

Fig. 1. Proposed research model

5 Limitations and Future Research

It is important to be aware of several limitations. First, the scope of the research study is limited to a single Chatbot, and subsequently, the consequences may not be generalizable to other types of chatbot applications. Second, the self-reported survey submitted may not accurately represent how average users state their satisfaction with their interactions with the Chatbot.

6 Conclusion

In this study, we take a modest view of AI-enabled CRM in E-Commerce by endeavoring to understand user satisfaction in the context of service encounters.

References

Abdul-Kader, S.A., Woods, J.C.: Survey on chatbot design techniques in speech conversation systems. Int. J. Adv. Comput. Sci. Appl. **6**(7) (2015)

Agarwal, R., Karahanna, E.: Time flies when you're having fun: cognitive absorption and beliefs about information technology usage. MIS q. **24**(4), 665 (2000)

Alan, M.T.: Computing machinery and intelligence. Mind **59**(236), 433 (1950)

Araújo, T., Casais, B.: Customer Acceptance of Shopping-Assistant Chatbots. Mark. Smart Technol., 278–287 (2020)

Berger, C.R., Calabrese, R.J.: Some explorations in initial interaction and beyond: toward a developmental theory of interpersonal communication. Hum. Commun. Res. 1(2), 99–112 (1974)

Benbasat, I., Dimoka, A., Pavlou, P.A., Qiu, L.: The role of demographic similarity in people's decision to interact with online anthropomorphic recommendation agents: evidence from a functional magnetic resonance imaging (fMRI) study. Int. J. Hum Comput Stud. 133, 56–70 (2020)

Bernazzani, S.: How Chatbots Can Improve User Experience, https://blog.hubspot.com/service/chatbots-user-experience. Last accessed 6 June 2020

Bhattacherjee, A.: Understanding information systems continuance: an expectation-confirmation model. MIS Q. 351–370 (2001)

Bilange, E.: A task independent oral dialogue model. In: Proceedings of the fifth conference on European chapter of the Association for Computational Linguistics, pp. 83–88. Association for Computational Linguistics, April 1991

Brandtzaeg, P.B., Følstad, A.: Why people use chatbots. In: Kompatsiaris, I., Cave, J., Satsiou, A., Carle, G., Passani, A., Kontopoulos, E., Diplaris, S., McMillan, D. (eds.) INSCI 2017. LNCS, vol. 10673, pp. 377–392. Springer, Cham (2017). https://doi.org/10.1007/978-3-319-70284-1_30

Castellanos, S.: What's next for company chatbots. Wall Street J. (2019). www.wsj.com/articles/whats-next-for-company-chatbots-11569317402?mod=djemCIO. Accessed 22 Mar 2020

Cui, L., Huang, S., Wei, F., Tan, C., Duan, C., Zhou, M.: SuperAgent: a customer service chatbot for e-commerce websites. In: Proceedings of ACL 2017, System Demonstrations, pp. 97–102, July 2017

Dale, R.: The return of the chatbots. Nat. Lang. Eng. 22(5), 811–817 (2016)

Dawar, N., Bendle, N.: Marketing in the Age of Alexa. Harv. Bus. Rev. 96, 80–86 (2019)

De Cicco, R., Silva, S.C.L.D.C.E., Alparone, F.R.: "It's on its way": Chatbots applied for online food delivery services, social or task-oriented interaction style? J. Foodservice Bus. Res. 1–25 (2020)

Demoulin, N.T., Djelassi, S.: An integrated model of self-service technology (SST) usage in a retail context. Int. J. Retail Distrib. Manage. 44(5), 540–559 (2016)

Duffy, B.R.: Anthropomorphism and the social robot. Robot. Auton. Syst. 42(3–4), 177–190 (2003)

Graham, B.S.: An empirical model of network formation: detecting homophily when agents are heterogenous (2014)

Gunawardana, H.M.R.S.S., Kulathunga, D., Perera, W.L.M.: Impact of Self-Service Technology Quality on Customer Satisfaction; A Case of Retail Banks in Western Province in Sri Lanka (2015)

Han, S., Yang, H.: Understanding adoption of intelligent personal assistants: a parasocial relationship perspective. Ind. Manage. Data Syst. 118(3), 618–636 (2018)

Iberahim, H., Taufik, N.M., Adzmir, A.M., Saharuddin, H.: Customer satisfaction on reliability and responsiveness of self-service technology for retail banking services. Procedia Econ. Finan. 37, 13–20 (2016)

Kawa, A., Maryniak, A.: Lean and agile supply chains of e-commerce: empirical research. J. Inf. Telecommun. 3(2), 235–247 (2019)

Kawa, A., Pieranski, B., Zdrenka, W.: Dynamic configuration of same-day delivery in E-commerce. In: Sieminski, A., Kozierkiewicz, A., Nunez, M., Ha, Q.T. (eds.) Modern Approaches for Intelligent Information and Database Systems. SCI, vol. 769, pp. 305–315. Springer, Cham (2018). https://doi.org/10.1007/978-3-319-76081-0_26

Lee, E.J., Lee, J., Eastwood, D.: A two-step estimation of consumer adoption of technology-based service innovations. J. Consum. Affairs 37(2), 256–282 (2003)

Lee, J.D., See, K.A.: Trust in automation: designing for appropriate reliance. Hum. Factors 46(1), 50–80 (2004)

Lee, J.M., Rha, J.Y.: Personalization–privacy paradox and consumer conflict with the use of location-based mobilE-Commerce. Comput. Hum. Behav. 63, 453–462 (2016)

Lowry, P.B., Gaskin, J.E., Twyman, N.W., Hammer, B., Roberts, T.L.: Taking "fun and games" seriously: proposing the hedonic-motivation system adoption model (HMSAM). J. Assoc. Inf. Syst. 14(11), 617–671 (2013)

Lucente, M.: Conversational interfaces for e-commerce applications. Commun. ACM 43(9), 59–61 (2002)

Mayer, R.C., Davis, J.H., Schoorman, F.D.: An integrative model of organizational trust. Acad. Manag. Rev. 20(3), 709–734 (1995)

McDonnell, M., Baxter, D.: Chatbots and gender stereotyping. Interact. Comput. 31(2), 116–121 (2019)

Meyer von Wolff, R., Masuch, K., Hobert, S., Schumann, M.: What Do You Need Today? -An Empirical Systematization of Application Areas for Chatbots at Digital Workplaces (2019)

Narteh, B.: Perceived service quality and satisfaction of self-service technology: the case of automated teller machines. Int. J. Qual. Reliab. Manage. 32(4), 361–380 (2015)

Oliver, R.L.: Effect of expectation and disconfirmation on postexposure product evaluations: an alternative interpretation. J. Appl. Psychol. 62(4), 480–486 (1977)

Oliver, R.L.: A cognitive model of the antecedents and consequences of satisfaction decisions. J. Mark. Res. 17(4), 460–469 (1980)

Osório, A., Pinto, A.: Information, uncertainty and the manipulability of artificial intelligence autonomous vehicles systems. Int. J. Hum Comput Stud. 130, 40–46 (2019)

Ostrom, A.L., Fotheringham, D., Bitner, M.J.: Customer acceptance of AI in service encounters: understanding antecedents and consequences. In: Maglio, P.P., Kieliszewski, C.A., Spohrer, J.C., Lyons, K., Patrício, L., Sawatani, Y. (eds.) Handbook of Service Science, Volume II. SSRISE, pp. 77–103. Springer, Cham (2019). https://doi.org/10.1007/978-3-319-98512-1_5

Pavlou, P.A.: Consumer acceptance of electronic commerce: integrating trust and risk with the technology acceptance model. Int. J. Electron. Commer. 7(3), 101–134 (2003)

Rodríguez Cardona, D., Werth, O., Schönborn, S., Breitner, M.H.: A Mixed Methods Analysis of the Adoption and Diffusion of Chatbot Technology in the German Insurance Sector (2019)

Saenz, J., Burgess, W., Gustitis, E., Mena, A., Sasangohar, F.: The usability analysis of chatbot technologies for internal personnel communications. In: IIE Annual Conference Proceedings, pp. 1357–1362 (2017)

Shamdasani, P., Mukherjee, A., Malhotra, N.: Antecedents and consequences of service quality in consumer evaluation of self-service internet technologies. Serv. Ind. J. 28(1), 117–138 (2008)

Shawar, B.A., Atwell, E.: Chatbots: are they really useful? LDV-Forum Zeitschrift für Comput. und Sprachtechnologie. 22, 29–49 (2007)

Skjuve, M., Brandzaeg, P.B.: Measuring user experience in chatbots: an approach to interpersonal communication competence. In: Bodrunova, S.S., Koltsova, O., Følstad, A., Halpin, H., Kolozaridi, P., Yuldashev, L., Smoliarova, A., Niedermayer, H. (eds.) INSCI 2018. LNCS, vol. 11551, pp. 113–120. Springer, Cham (2019). https://doi.org/10.1007/978-3-030-17705-8_10

Toader, D.C., et al.: The effect of social presence and chatbot errors on trust. Sustainability 12(1), 256 (2020)

Turing, A.M.: Imported from https://academic.oup.com/mind/pages/emotions. Mind. LIX, 433–460 (1950). https://doi.org/10.1093/MIND

Valtolina, S., Barricelli, B.R., Di Gaetano, S., Diliberto, P.: Chatbots and conversational interfaces: three domains of use. In: CEUR Workshop Proceedings, vol. 2101, pp. 62–70 (2018)

Varitimiadis, S., Kotis, K., Skamagis, A., Tzortzakakis, A., Tsekouras, G., Spiliotopoulos, D.: Towards implementing an AI chatbot platform for museums. In: International Conference on Cultural Informatics, Communication & Media Studies, vol. 1, no. 1 (2020)

Vassos, S., Malliaraki, E., Falco, F.D., Di Maggio, J., Massimetti, M., Nocentini, M.G., Testa, A.: Art-bots: Toward chat-based conversational experiences in museums. In: Nack, F., Gordon, A.S. (eds.) ICIDS 2016. LNCS, vol. 10045, pp. 433–437. Springer, Cham (2016). https://doi.org/10.1007/978-3-319-48279-8_43

Venkatesh, V., Bala, H.: Technology acceptance model 3 and a research agenda on interventions. Decis. Sci. **39**(2), 273–315 (2008)

Vinodhini, G., Chandrasekaran, R.M.: Conversational interfaces for e-commerce applications. Inf. Process. Manage. **9**(1), 1–14 (2016)

Weber, F., Schütte, R.: A domain-oriented analysis of the impact of machine learning—the case of retailing. Big Data Cogn. Comput. **3**(1), 11 (2019)

Xu, H., Dinev, T., Smith, J., Hart, P.: Information privacy concerns: linking individual perceptions with institutional privacy assurances. J. Assoc. Inf. Syst. **12**(12), 798–824 (2011)

Zhou, L., Gao, J., Li, D., Shum, H.Y.: The design and implementation of xiaoice, an empathetic social chatbot. Comput. Linguist. **46**(1), 53–93 (2020)

Zue, V.W., Glass, J.R.: Conversational interfaces: advances and challenges. Proc. IEEE **88**(8), 1166–1180 (2000)

Evaluation of a NUI Interface for an Explosives Deactivator Robotic Arm to Improve the User Experience

Denilson Vilcapaza Goyzueta$^{(\boxtimes)}$ (D), Joseph Guevara Mamani (D),
Erasmo Sulla Espinoza (D), Elvis Supo Colquehuanca (D), Yuri Silva Vidal (D),
and Pablo Pari Pinto (D)

Universidad Nacional de San Agustín de Arequipa, Arequipa, Peru
{dvilcapazag,jguevaram,esullae,esupo,ysilvav,pparip}@unsa.edu.pe

Abstract. TEDAX agents performe explosives handling tasks that require good assistance in handling EOD robotic arms. The interface used for handling explosive devices is relevant for explosive deactivating agents due to the fact that it can ensure greater immersion and performance in their operations. Generally, robotic arms are manipulated by joysticks, keyboard or buttons that are not very intuitive. NUI interfaces are intuitive and provide assistance in robotic arm manipulation. In this study, it is proposed to verify the feasibility of a NUI interface to manipulate EOD robotic arms. The degree of assistance provided by the interfaces through the NASA-TLX method in TEDAX agents of the UDEX-AQP (Unidad de Desactivación de Explosivos de Arequipa) is compared. The compared interfaces are: a MK-2 commercial robot from Allen Vanguard and a NUI interface based on specular Imitation. The tests show that the NUI interface evaluated can be applied in explosives disposal interventions.

Keywords: UX (User experience) · EOD (Explosive Ordnance Disposal) · NUI (Natural User Experience) · TEDAX · Specular Imitation

1 Introduction

EOD (Explosive Ordnance Disposal) robots are used worldwide to deactivate explosives in order to support TEDAX agents (Technician Specialist in Deactivation of Explosive Artifacts). As a result of the terrorist attacks that took place in the 1980s in southern Peru, the explosives disposal unit was created in the Arequipa region (UDEX-AQP), which is one of the oldest explosives disposal institutions in south America. The studies carried out on the interventions of the UDEX - AQP in the period 2013 to 2020, show that an EOD robot would have had a more efficient participation in 91% of the cases. Likewise, 47% of the most recurrent explosive devices were grenades and dynamites [1]. Due to

© Springer Nature Switzerland AG 2021
C. Stephanidis et al. (Eds.): HCII 2021, CCIS 1498, pp. 288–293, 2021.
https://doi.org/10.1007/978-3-030-90176-9_37

the size of these objects, it is difficult to manipulate them with an EOD robot; therefore, they require an intuitive and easy-to-use interface.

The importance of control interfaces is due to the fact that the operator must be more focused on handling tasks than on handling the control interface, therefore, it is not advisable to use keyboard interfaces or control buttons [2]. In several cases, only the sporadic use of robots is required (e.g. search and rescue), therefore, the agents do not have sufficient training and experience in the manipulation of control interfaces for a correct operation [5]. For these reasons, it is recommended to use easy and intuitive interfaces instead of using keyboard interfaces or control buttons.

NUI (Natural User Interface) can imitate the way a person expresses itself, providing the possibility that human-robot interaction is by direct command and interaction through gestures such as mirroring [3]. Leap Motion is a sensor that recognizes the gestures of the human hand with precision, especially the movement of the thumb [6]. This sensor serves as an intuitive interface that can be used to manipulate robotic arms by being able to replicate the movements of the hand to the robotic arm, for this reason this sensor can be applied as a NUI [7,8].

In this research, the feasibility of using a NUI, which is based on the recognition of hand gestures, is evaluated in order to it can be applied in EOD robotic arms. NUI and MK-2 interface were tested and compared with explosives handling tasks. NASA-TLX method (National Aeronautics and Space Administration Task Load index) was applied to measure the user experience and determine the possibility of use for this type of operation.

2   Methodology

To determine the feasibility of using our gestural NUI, which is called the DL01 interface, an elementary open-loop control algorithm was developed that does not present filtering processing algorithms, on the Leap Motion and the Dobot Magician with the aim of evaluate its possible application in an EOD robotic arm.

The MK-2 robot from the Allen Vanguard company that is based on keyboard manipulation and the DL01 interface were compared testing explosives manipulation tasks, applying the NASA-TLX method [4,9] to measure user experience.

2.1   Evaluation Procedure

10 UDEX-AQP agents (24 to 52 years old, 10 men) were taken for the 120-min study. A brief information was given to the TEDAX agents on the general description of the study and manipulation of the robotic arm: the movements of the robot arm and gripper were described and the tasks they had to perform were presented.

Before starting the task, participants were given a description of the user interface and the commands. To ensure understanding of the interface, each participant was instructed for 10 min, then a test assisted by the experimenter in which they manipulated the robotic arm in various positions, for example, movement of each degree of freedom, extended arm, bent). After completing this training, the explosives handling tests were carried out. After performing the manipulation tasks with an interface, they were given a NASA-TLX sheet. After each agent took a 10-min break, they continued with the next interface and finish with the total evaluation test, in Fig. 1 the block diagram of this study is shown to evaluate the user experience.

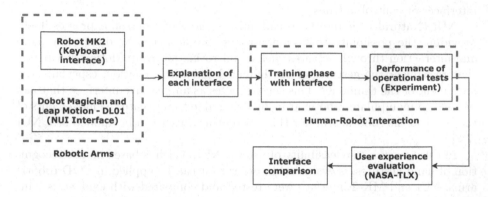

Fig. 1. Block diagram for the user experience evaluation.

3   Study Tasks

TEDAX agents performed a task that required proper monitoring. More recurrent explosives, grenade and dynamite, were manipulated with the MK2 robot, the participants moved these explosive devices from a table to a container, simulating a real situation of deactivating explosives, in addition to ensuring that the participants took the object correctly. Figure 2 shows the operating procedure.

Fig. 2. Operation procedure.

The same tests were carried out with the DL01 interface in scale, considering the ratio of proportion between the Dobot Magician and commercial robot MK2 to be able to scale the explosive devices in a proportional way through the 3D printing of a grenade and a dynamite. Only the movement of the robotic arm with the MK-2 chassis in a fixed place was considered for the tests, in addition the tests were taken without the use of assistive cameras. Figure 3 shows the tests with the DL01 interface and the MK2 robot.

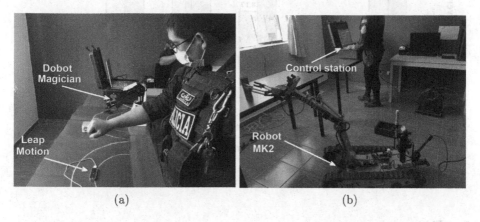

(a)   (b)

Fig. 3. Field tests. (a) With the DL01 interface. (b) With the MK2 robot keyboard interface.

4 Results and Conclusions

Figure 4 shows the mean of the categories of the NASA-TLX method, it is observed that the mental demand for the DL01 interface is greater compared to the MK2 due to the need for a greater degree of concentration and immersion on the tests. The average total workload of the MK2 interface is 72.33 and the DL01 interface is 60.3. The total workload and temporal demands of the DL01 interface got important improvements, for that reason the gestural interface can be of great help in manipulating EOD arms for these operations. Future work will try to reduce effort and frustration, as well as to improve the total workload by applying special filters and control strategies for the robotic arm.

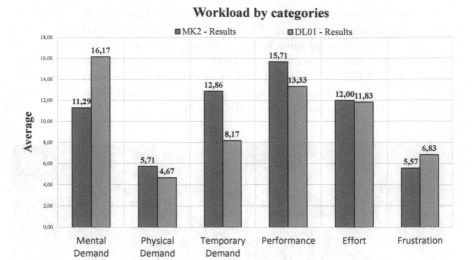

Fig. 4. Graph of results using the NASA-TLX index.

5   Discussion

The results of this experiments show that the proposed interface has good results in assisting TEDAX agents, as well as being a natural interface according to the operator's movements.

It is considered that the DL01 interface has good results because the movements of the robotic arm have a natural relationship with the movements of the person's arm, in addition to integrating similar workspaces for the operator and the robot. These novel applications of established HCI design principles can improve the ease of use and efficiency of remote control robotic interfaces for field control.

References

1. Guevara Mamani, J., Pinto, P.P., Vilcapaza Goyzueta, D., Supo Colquehuanca, E., Sulla Espinoza, E., Silva Vidal, Y.: Compilation and analysis of requirements for the design of an explosive ordnance disposal robot prototype applied in UDEX-arequipa. In: Stephanidis, C., Antona, M., Ntoa, S. (eds.) HCII 2021. CCIS, vol. 1420, pp. 131–138. Springer, Cham (2021). https://doi.org/10.1007/978-3-030-78642-7_18
2. Cio, Y.-S.L.-K., Raison, M., Leblond Ménard, C., Achiche, S.: Proof of concept of an assistive robotic arm control using artificial stereovision and eye-tracking. IEEE Trans. Neural Syst. Rehabil. Eng. **27**(12), 2344–2352 (2019). https://doi.org/10.1109/TNSRE.2019.2950619

3. Gîrbacia, F., Postelnicu, C., Voinea, G.-D.: Towards using natural user interfaces for robotic arm manipulation. In: Berns, K., Görges, D. (eds.) RAAD 2019. AISC, vol. 980, pp. 188–193. Springer, Cham (2020). https://doi.org/10.1007/978-3-030-19648-6_22

4. Hart, S.G., Staveland, L.E.: Development of NASA-TLX (Task Load Index): results of empirical and theoretical research. In: Advances in Psychology, vol. 52, pp. 139–183. North-Holland (1988)

5. Singh, A., Seo, S.H., Hashish, Y., Nakane, M., Young, J.E., Bunt, A.: An interface for remote robotic manipulator control that reduces task load and fatigue. In: 2013 IEEE RO-MAN, pp. 738–743 (2013). https://doi.org/10.1109/ROMAN.2013.6628401

6. Mizera, C., Delrieu, T., Weistroffer, V., Andriot, C., Decatoire, A., Gazeau, J.: Evaluation of Hand-tracking systems in teleoperation and virtual dexterous manipulation. IEEE Sens. J. 20(3), 1642–1655 (2020). https://doi.org/10.1109/JSEN.2019.2947612

7. Artal-Sevil, J.S., Montañés, J.L.: Development of a robotic arm and implementation of a control strategy for gesture recognition through Leap Motion device. In: 2016 Technologies Applied to Electronics Teaching (TAEE), pp. 1–9 (2016). https://doi.org/10.1109/TAEE.2016.7528373

8. Marin, G., Dominio, F., Zanuttigh, P.: Hand gesture recognition with leap motion and kinect devices. In: IEEE International Conference on Image Processing (ICIP) 2014, pp. 1565–1569 (2014). https://doi.org/10.1109/ICIP.2014.7025313

9. Mendes, V., et al.: Experience implication in subjective surgical ergonomics comparison between laparoscopic and robot-assisted surgeries. J. Robot. Surg. 14(1), 115–121 (2019). https://doi.org/10.1007/s11701-019-00933-2

Attitudes Towards Human-Robot Collaboration and the Impact of the COVID-19 Pandemic

Verena Wagner-Hartl$^{(\boxtimes)}$ (ID), Kevin Pohling, Marc Rössler, Simon Strobel, and Simone Maag

Faculty Industrial Technologies, Furtwangen University, Campus Tuttlingen, Kronenstraße 16, 78532 Tuttlingen, Germany
`verena.wagner-hartl@hs-furtwangen.de`

Abstract. It is expected that human-robot collaboration will increase in the future. Some people are already experiencing this in their working life, but other people are still skeptical about it. The COVID-19 pandemic has brought new challenges to the world's population and has a strong impact on our everyday working life. The question arises, whether the perceived involvement in the current situation as well as the occupational field influence the attitudes towards human-robot collaboration. Overall, 54 men, 45 women and 1 non-binary ($N = 100$) aged between 18 and 71 years ($M = 29.87, SD = 14.00$) participated in an exploratory online study. The results of the study show that the participants' attitudes towards the use of collaborative robots in the three different categories assembly, logistics and cleaning were rather positive. Furthermore, assembly and logistics tasks were assessed as significant more conceivable for human-robot collaboration than cleaning tasks. Interestingly, participants that were more concerned about the COVID-19 pandemic assessed the use of collaborative robots overall significant more positive than other participants did. Attitude differences due to the different occupational fields of the participants did not reach the level of significance. In addition, the participants described different functions in which they could imagine collaborative robots in the three categories assembly, logistics and cleaning. The results of the presented exploratory study shall help to get more insight in this important future field.

Keywords: Human-robot collaboration · COVID-19 pandemic · Occupational fields

1 Introduction

It is expected that human-robot collaboration will increase in the future [1]. Some people are already experiencing this in their working life, especially in manufacturing [2]. On the other hand, some people are still skeptical about human-robot collaboration [3].

Former research [4] has shown that participants with a higher affinity for technology or communicating via technology are more worried about possible negative effects on society when integrating robots into it. This might be because they know the limitations to this technology better than others do. Following Takayama, Ju and Nass [5] the

© Springer Nature Switzerland AG 2021
C. Stephanidis et al. (Eds.): HCII 2021, CCIS 1498, pp. 294–299, 2021.
https://doi.org/10.1007/978-3-030-90176-9_38

attitude of people towards robots in the working environment is dependent on the kind of occupational field robots are used in. It was found that jobs that include memorizing, perceptual skills and service orientation are preferred jobs for robots. An example therefore could be that a robot is seen as very capable to work in a place where very controlled movements are necessary. In addition, a working environment where robots do the job together with people but not instead of them seemed to increase a positive attitude towards robots.

The COVID-19 pandemic has brought new challenges to the world's population and has a strong impact on our everyday working life. Furthermore, the COVID-19 pandemic has strengthened the trend towards digitalization that was shown in the last years [6–9]. In addition, the results of the experiments with service robots in hotels conducted during the COVID-pandemic (May–Sept 2020) of Kim et al. [10] showed that people may be more open to services of robots than before the pandemic. Following the authors, "(…) the current COVID-19 pandemic may accelerate acceptance of service robots providing contactless services, which are beneficial for maintaining social distancing and reducing anxiety regarding contagion through human interaction." (ibid., p. 9). Furthermore, it is suggested that the pandemic could act as a driver for robot adoption in different areas [11, 12].

Also, Savela, Turja and Oksanen [13] reported in their literature review regarding the social acceptance of robots in different occupational fields a lack of research concerning other occupational fields than health care or social care. Therefore, an exploratory online study was conducted to get more insight in this important field.

The research questions that should be investigated within this study were: (1) Do the perceived involvement in the current situation as well as the occupational field have an influence on the attitudes towards human-robot collaboration? (2) What different functions of collaborative robots would be imaginable in the three different areas of application assembly, logistics and cleaning?

2   Method and Materials

2.1   Participants

Overall, 54 men, 45 women and 1 non-binary ($N = 100$) aged between 18 and 71 years ($M = 29.87$, SD $= 14.00$) participated in an online survey. Regarding the occupational field, the sample consists of 24.00% employees and workers that work in the technical area, 40.00% that work in a non-technical field and 36.00% students from a wide variety of different studies. All participants provided their informed consent at the beginning of the online study.

2.2   Study Design and Materials

The exploratory study consists of different parts and scenarios of human-robot collaboration. Overall, the participants needed about 15–20 min to complete the whole questionnaire. To answer the research question presented in this paper only the part regarding attitudes towards human-robot collaboration will be presented in detail. A repeated measurement design was chosen for the study. The independent variables were perceived involvement in the current situation (COVID-19 pandemic; two groups: participants that think about it more often, more concerned/less often, less concerned) and the occupational field (three groups: employees and workers that work in the technical area/employees and workers that work in a non-technical field/students). The measurement repetition factor represents three different possible areas of application of human-robot collaboration (assembly, logistics and cleaning). Each function was assessed by each participant regarding whether participants could imagine human-robot collaboration within this area of application using a 5-point scale [no (1) – rather no – partly – rather yes – yes (5)]. In addition, the participants were asked to describe different functions in which they could imagine collaborative robots in the three different areas of application assembly, logistics and cleaning.

2.3 Statistical Analyses

The statistical analyses of the data were conducted using the software IBM SPSS Statistics. The analyses were based on a significance level of 5%. Open responses of the participants were analyzed using the method of qualitative content analyses by Mayring [14].

3 Results

3.1 Attitudes Towards Human-Robot Collaboration

Following the results of an analysis of variance with repeated measures, significant differences regarding the assessment of the different possible areas of application of human-robot collaboration can be shown, $F_{HF}(2.00, 188.00) = 6.62, p = .002, \eta_{part.}^2 = .066$. Post-hoc analyses (Sidak) showed that assembly ($p = .001$) and logistics ($p = .048$) tasks were assessed as significant more conceivable for human-robot collaboration than cleaning tasks. Furthermore a significant effect of the perceived involvement in the current COVID-19 pandemic-situation can be shown, $F(1, 94) = 6.83, p = .010, \eta_{part.}^2 = .068$ (see Fig. 1). Participants that were more concerned about the COVID-19 pandemic assessed the use of collaborative robots overall significant more positive than other participants did ($p = .010$). All other effects did not reach the level of significance.

3.2 Possible Functions of Collaborative Robots

The answers of the open responses of the participants when they were asked to describe the functions which they could imagine for collaborative robots in the three different areas of application assembly, logistics and cleaning were analyzed using the method of qualitative content analyses by Mayring [14].

First, for the application assembly, overall, 75 responses of 70 participants were categorized (multiple answers possible). The results show that most participants think about collaborative robots that support the assembling of different parts and products

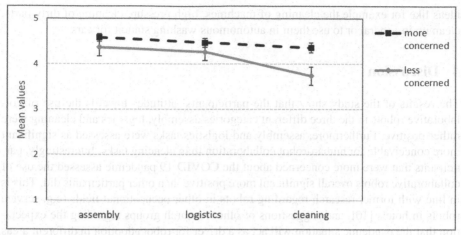

Note. 5-point scale: no (1) – rather no – partly – rather yes – yes (5);
    I ... standard error of mean

Fig. 1. Attitudes towards human-robot collaboration - perceived involvement in the current COVID-19 pandemic-situation.

(48.00%). Also, 13.33% of the participants could imagine that a robot can execute heavy, non-ergonomic and/or dangerous work for humans, 8.00% think about functions like holding or fixing of parts and 4.00% of the transport of different parts. 26.67% of the participants reported other ideas like for example "a robot would be able to work 24 h a day", "a collaborative robot should support humans in all aspects of assembly" or "assembly line work in general" and "functions within an automotive manufacturing line".

For the second application logistics, 66 participants responded on the open question (79 categorized answers; multiple answers possible). The results show that collaborative robots are conceivable in warehouse logistics or intelligent warehouses for 25.32% of the participants. In addition, 17.72% reported that collaborative robots could be used to carry heavy load and products or retrieve them from storage racks. Furthermore, it was imaginable that they can support the sorting (16.46%), transport (11.39%), packing (7.59%) and picking (6.33%) of products. 15.19% of the participants reported other ideas like for example work preparation, container distribution (e.g., port, rail, truck), or supporting the creation of efficient time tables.

Regarding the third application cleaning, 76 responses of 63 participants were categorized (multiple answers possible). Most participants reported that they could imagine the use of collaborative robots for relatively simple cleaning tasks such as vacuuming or mopping (30.27%) and/or to use them for the cleaning of large areas, large surfaces or floors (26.32%). In addition, 11.84% would use them in different settings like in industrial buildings, household, manufacturing facilities and there for a wide variety of areas. Also, collaborative robots should clean windows (9.21%), and/or other hard to reach (5.26%) and dangerous (5.26%) areas. 11.84% of the participants reported other ideas like for example the cleaning of machines, high pressure cleaning of dirty parts, clean up in general or to use them in autonomous washing station for cars.

4 Discussion

The results of the study show that the participants' attitudes towards the use of collaborative robots in the three different categories assembly, logistics and cleaning were rather positive. Furthermore, assembly and logistics tasks were assessed as significant more conceivable for human-robot collaboration than cleaning tasks. Interestingly, participants that were more concerned about the COVID-19 pandemic assessed the use of collaborative robots overall significant more positive than other participants did. This is in line with former research regarding robots in other occupational fields (e.g. service robots in hotels [10]) and suggestions of other research groups regarding the expectation that the pandemic situation will act as a driver for robot adoption in different areas [11, 12]. Attitude differences due to the different occupational fields of the participants did not reach the level of significance. Therefore, to answer the first research question, the perceived involvement in the current pandemic situation seems to have a significant effect on the attitudes towards human-robot collaboration. On the other hand, no significant effects can be shown regarding the occupational field or for the interaction involvement x occupational field within this study.

In addition, the participants described different functions in which they could imagine collaborative robots in the three categories assembly, logistics and cleaning (second research question). Future research should consider these ideas and provide employees of the different occupational fields opportunities to work with collaborative robots. This should help to develop and evaluate new possible working environments where collaborative robots can be used to support human beings.

To sum it up, the results of the presented exploratory study can help to understand how human-robot collaboration is seen today, show that the COVID-19 pandemic may have an impact on the attitudes towards human-robot collaboration and shall help to get more insight in this important future field.

Acknowledgements. The authors would like to thank Klara Faitsch for her support in conducting the study, and all participants who participated. **Author's Statement.** The authors state no conflict of interest. Informed consent has been provided from all participants of the online study. The study was approved by the ethics committee of the Furtwangen University.

References

1. Ajoudani, A., Zanchettin, A.M., Ivaldi, S., Albu-Schäffer, A., Kosuge, K., Khatib, O.: Progress and prospects of the human–robot collaboration. Auton. Robots **42**(5), 957–975 (2017). https://doi.org/10.1007/s10514-017-9677-2
2. Vanderborght, B.: Unlocking the potential of industrial human–robot collaboration. A vision on industrial collaborative robots for economy and society. European Commission, Brussels (2019)

3. European Commission: Public attitudes towards robots. Special Eurobarometer 382, report (2012). 97 pp.
4. Katz, J.E., Halpern, D.: Attitudes towards robots suitability for various jobs as affected robot appearance. Behav. Inf. Technol. **33**(9), 941–953 (2014)
5. Takayama, L., Ju, W., Nass, C.: Beyond dirty, dangerous and dull: what everyday people think robots should do. In: Proceedings 2008 3rd ACM/IEEE International Conference on Human-Robot Interaction (HRI), Amsterdam, pp. 25–32 (2008)
6. Kravchenko, O., Leshchenko, M., Marushchak, D., Vdovychenko, Y., Boguslavska, S.: The digitalization as a global trend and growth factor of the modern economy. SHS Web Conf. **65**, 1–5 (2019)
7. Faraj, S., Renno, W., Bhardwaj, A.: Unto the breach: what the COVID-19 pandemic exposes about digitalization. Inf. Organ. **31**, 1–7 (2021)
8. Mumm, J.-N., Rodler, S., Mumm, M.-L., Bauer, R.M., Stief, C.G.: Digitale Innovation in der Medizin – die COVID-19-Pandemie als Akzelerator von "digital health" [Digital innovation in medicine - the COVID 19 pandemic as an accelerator of "digital health"]. J. Urol. Urogynäkol. AT. 1–5 (2020)
9. Humphreys, G.: Digital health and COVID-19. Bull. World Health Organ. **98**, 731–732 (2020)
10. Kim, S., Kim, J., Badu-Baiden, F., et al.: Preference for robot service or human service in hotels? Impacts of the COVID-19 pandemic. Int. J. Hosp. Manage. **93**, 102795 (2021)
11. Zeng, Z., Chen, P.-J., Lew, A.A.: From high-touch to high-tech: COVID-19 drives robotics adoption. Tourism Geographies. Int. J. Tour. Space Place Environ. **22**(3), 724–734 (2020)
12. Zhang, Y.: A big data analyses of public perception of service robots amid COVID-19. Adv. Hosp. Tour. Res. **9**(1), 234–242 (2021)
13. Savela, N., Turja, T., Oksanen, A.: Social acceptance of robots in different occupational fields: a systematic literature review. Int. J. Soc. Robot. **10**(4), 493–502 (2017). https://doi.org/10.1007/s12369-017-0452-5
14. Mayring, P.: Qualitative Inhaltsanalyse: Grundlagen und Techniken [Qualitative content analysis: basics and techniques]. Beltz, Weinheim and Basel (2010)

Older Adults' Voice Search through the Human-Engaged Computing Perspective

Xiaojun (Jenny) Yuan[1](✉) and Xiangshi Ren[2]

[1] University at Albany, State University of New York, Albany, NY 12222 , USA
xyuan@albany.edu
[2] Kochi University of Technology, Kochi, Japan
xsren@acm.org

Abstract. Human-Engaged Computing (HEC) is a framework that addresses "synergized interaction" sustaining both humans and computers in the right balance, a relationship that consciously honors human inner capabilities over device creativity. Due to the growing interest and demand on voice search for older adults, it is critical to research on how to engage older adults with voice search to improve their healthiness and wellbeing. This paper presents two case studies to discuss the approaches and thoughts about applying HEC to the current voice search systems, in particular, how HEC can engage older adults with interaction of voice search systems and how we can measure older adults' engagement with such systems.

Keywords: Human-engaged computing · Synergized interaction · Dialogue structure · Voice search · Older adults

1 Introduction

With the fast development of various voice assistants on mobile device platforms as well as stand-alone instruments, for example Siri, Google Now, Cortana, and Amazon Echo, research on voice search has been drawing much attention [6]. In a survey by Sa and Yuan [17] on users' voice search behavior, the general usage of voice search and user perception about voice search systems were examined. Results indicate that users performed voice search much less frequently than keyboard search, and could give up voice search easily or simply switch to keyboard search. However, users thought voice search is convenient.

According to the Census Bureau, all baby boomers will be age 65 or older by 2030 [2]. This has increased the demand for applying artificial intelligence (AI) technologies into automated systems to lighten the load on health professionals and caregivers. Therefore, voice search is becoming an important and acceptable way for older adults to access online information. Through a pilot study with Google Home, Kowalski et al. [8] reported that the natural language interaction frees older adults from inputting using a small screen and/or keyboard. Furthermore, they found that voice interaction gives older adults a chance to multi-tasking when they are otherwise occupied.

© Springer Nature Switzerland AG 2021
C. Stephanidis et al. (Eds.): HCII 2021, CCIS 1498, pp. 300–307, 2021.
https://doi.org/10.1007/978-3-030-90176-9_39

Research has shown that older adults prefer to search for information through interpersonal relations in human language, particularly when they need health-related information, which fits for the nature of the natural communication of human beings [3].

In [22], we proposed to employ Human-Engaged Computing (HEC) to "ensure our interaction design processes consciously engage and enhance inner human capacities (e.g., wisdom, intuitive skills, and personal integrity) to help users face future challenges with a sense of personal responsibility, rather than merely developing conventional technologies for functional needs or potentially diminishing their skills and responsibilities through the use of our technologies." In this paper, we explore ways to apply the concept and framework of HEC to the current voice search systems, with the focus on how HEC can engage older adults with interaction of voice search systems. Meanwhile, how we can measure older adults' engagement with voice systems is discussed.

In the following, we first introduce the background of HEC, and the difference between HEC and HCI, followed by voice search and older adults. Next, we present two case studies about how to apply HEC to improve the engagement of older adults with voice search systems. At the end, we conclude the paper with future directions.

2 Background

2.1 HEC

As can be seen from Fig. 1, HEC is composed of three elements, that is, engaged human, engaging computers and synergized interaction [14]. When both human and technology capabilities are fully engaged and enhanced together, synergized interaction will be achieved [14].

The idea of HEC has been incorporated into some professional practices, such as Human-Engaged AI (HEAI) [10]. What are the major differences between HEC and HCI? What are the aspects that HEC be differentiated from HCI? Table 1 lists the difference of HEC and traditional Human Computer Interaction (HCI).

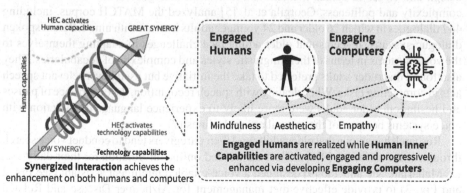

Fig. 1. Human-engaged computing framework [14]

Table 1. HEC vs. HCI [22]

	HEC	HCI
Scope	HEC is positioned as a conception, theory, and value to offer a framework, components, and related principles for guiding researchers and future practices	HCI is a field of designing computing systems and interactions by understanding wider factors
Focus	HEC focuses on developing human inner capacities via technologies and aims to enhance both sides finally	HCI mainly focuses on exploring factors of systems, users, experience for designing interface, and interactions, without focusing on improving human inner capacities
Perspective-evaluation	HEC seeks to evaluate technologies by facilitating human engagement, human enhancement, or human potential	HCI tends to evaluate technologies by measuring interaction performance, e.g., efficiency and speed

2.2 Voice Search and Older Adults/caregivers

Research has shown that older adults perceived positively with voice search interfaces [4, 20]. Specifically, [4] found that voice is the main reason that elders accept virtual humanoid agents, and elders would like to communicate with speaking agents, even if it is voice only, instead of communicating with mute agent.

When older adults interact with voice interface systems to conduct voice search, their age differences matter. Through a corpus analysis of spoken smart-home interactions of older adults, [11] found that in comparison to younger adults, older adults employed a different conversational style with the system, which was less adaptive to the system's design and closer to human-human communication dialogue on the basis of sentence complexity and politeness. Georgila et al. [5] analyzed the MATCH corpus, including 447 dialogues in which 26 older and 24 younger adults interact with nine different spoken dialogue systems. It seems that older adults face challenges in adapting themselves to the voice systems in terms of their linguistic styles and complexity of vocabularies. They also found that older adults preferred to take the initiative but used fewer relevant speech acts in completing tasks. When dealing with speech recognition, the occurrence of pauses and hesitation, older adults were more likely to experience language dysfunction with voice systems because of the general aging declines [7].

Research has shown that older adults and their caregivers tend to conduct voice search through voice assistants [9] to collect the needed online information for their daily use. Li, Maharjan, Xie and Tao [9] designed a voice-enabled intelligent assistant (see Fig. 2 and Fig. 3) to provide effective diet management for Alzheimer Disease and Related Dementias (ADRD) caregivers. The evaluation of this voice agent shows appropriate rates of dialogue success and recommendation correctness, demonstrating the feasibility and effectiveness of employing the intelligent voice assistant to help caregivers manage patients with ADRD's diet.

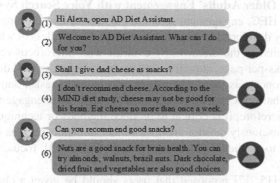

(1) Hi Alexa, open AD Diet Assistant.

(2) Welcome to AD Diet Assistant. What can I do for you?

(3) Shall I give dad cheese as snacks?

(4) I don't recommend cheese. According to the MIND diet study, cheese may not be good for his brain. Eat cheese no more than once a week.

(5) Can you recommend good snacks?

(6) Nuts are a good snack for brain health. You can try almonds, walnuts, brazil nuts. Dark chocolate, dried fruit and vegetables are also good choices.

Fig. 2. An example of a conversation between the user and the voice assistant about food and nutrition education, and meal suggestion. AD: Alzheimer disease; MIND: Mediterranean–Dietary Approaches to Stop Hypertension Intervention for Neurodegenerative Delay [9].

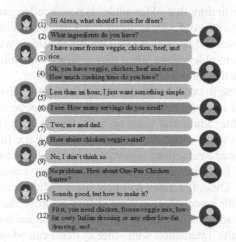

(1) Hi Alexa, what should I cook for diner?

(2) What ingredients do you have?

(3) I have some frozen veggie, chicken, beef, and rice.

(4) Ok, you have veggie, chicken, beef and rice. How much cooking time do you have?

(5) Less than an hour, I just want something simple.

(6) I see. How many servings do you need?

(7) Two, me and dad.

(8) How about chicken veggie salad?

(9) No, I don't think so.

(10) No problem. How about One-Pan Chicken Sautee?

(11) Sounds good, but how to make it?

(12) First, you need chicken, frozen veggie mix, low-fat zesty Italian dressing or any other low-fat dressing, and …

Fig. 3. An example fragment of a conversation between the user and the voice assistant about meal recipe suggestion [9].

3 HEC and Older Adults' Voice Search

According to Sidner et al., engagement is "the process by which interactors start, maintain, and end their perceived connections to each other during an interaction" [19]. Later on, Attfield, Kazai, Lalmas and Piwowarski elaborated it and proposed a new definition that details the dimensions of engagement – considering it as "the emotional, cognitive and behavioural connection that exists, at any point in time and possibly over time, between a user and a resource" [1]. In the following, we use two case studies to study HEC and older adults' voice search.

Case 1: Increase Older Adults' Engagement with Voice Search Systems

In the context of HEC, engagement refers to "a state of consciousness where human capacities are fully developed, engaged, and exploited, regardless of what tasks or activities are encountered in the moment, by contrast with microfocus on details such as time-on-task, clicks-per-page, attractiveness, positive effects, or task-dependence" [22]. The underlying concept is that "all functions, techniques, tasks, and microtasks find optimal integrity, harmony, and efficiency through the mindful engagement of the attentive use" [22]. Therefore, it is critical to produce methods or techniques to encourage older adults to consciously develop their own inner human capacities of awareness via mindful attention to aesthetics [21], interactive tasks [12, 13], focus, trust, sensitivity, and empathy [22].

Sa and Yuan [15, 17] proposed that users should be given a chance to partially modify their voice queries during their interaction with voice search systems. They proved that the system incorporating partial query modification feature was tested to be more effective than the baseline system without such a feature [18]. We want to take this result into consideration in the studies of older adults' interaction with voice systems, based on the research finding that older adults experience language dysfunction with voice systems because of the ordinary aging declines in coping with speech recognition, the occurrence of pauses and hesitation [7]. That being said, if we only request partial query modification from older adults when they interact with voice systems or agents, it may release their burden on memorizing the entire query.

In addition, it is time to consider how to design interactive tasks in user experiment with older adults, and how to provide an appropriate dialogue structure to guide the interaction between older adults and voice systems. Sa and Yuan [16] designed a prototype of voice search systems which implements proposed basic functions (see Table 2) and supports the required interactions. They proposed the basic functions based on the assumption that users have the need to switch between two communication channels, that is text and voice. These functions will help users switch communication channels when they interact with voice systems, thus in turn improve the quality of their dialogues between users and voice systems. The design of interactive tasks and dialogue structure for older adults' interaction with voice systems can adopt this idea, and adapt it to accommodate the needs of older adults.

Case 2: Evaluate Older Adults' Engagement with Voice Search Systems

In the context of HEC, "the facilitation of deep human engagement with technologies is significantly affected by the corresponding engaging qualities of technologies, which are, in turn, dependent on the researcher/developer's own capacity to fully engage in the development process"; and "harmonious engagement and its consequent efficiencies cannot be optimized in the end user if the tools adopted do not bear the qualities of researchers/developers who are mindfully engaged." [22]. In other words, "engagement is not something experts can impose on their "subjects"; it is organic throughout and, thus, it is an expression of the interdependence of all things." [22]. Hence, when designing voice systems or voice agents for older adults, how to design interactive tasks, and how

Table 2. Basic functions of a voice search system [16]

Phase in search process	Basic functions
Query formation and reformulation	Enable the user to input new query; Enable the user to modify the previous query; Remind the user of the previous query (queries); Provide query clarification; Provide suggestion/expansion
Result presentation	Show quick answer (when available); Refine the results by category (news, image, shopping, etc.); List results; Enable the user to visit individual webpages; Track the browsing history
Interaction	Switch the primary communication channel Mixed initiative; Interrupt; Understand

to measure their human engagement and interaction need to be considered at the very beginning of the design process.

Ma [10] proposed various ways to measure the four dimensions of user engagement, which give us a chance to quantitatively evaluate the level of engagement of older adults during their interaction with voice systems. This initiative and the relevant findings provided a solid foundation for the proposed case study. In particular, the data-driven human-engaged AI framework by [10] is composed of five main components, including 1) construction of computational model of human engagement; 2) real-time holistic and analytical inference of human engagement; 3) management of human engagement; 4) expression of AI engagement; and 5) engagement-based applications. Each component works together to create the harmonious engagement of older adults with voice systems.

As mentioned in Sect. 2.2, age differences play significant roles in older adults' interaction with voice systems. This factor should be taken into consideration in the relevant research. It would be interesting to compare human engagement with voice systems or agents across different age groups of older adults. The results will provide practical guidance for the design of voice systems for older adults.

4   Conclusion

This paper proposes to apply HEC to design voice search systems for older adults. It presents two case studies to discuss the approaches and thoughts about how HEC can engage older adults with voice search systems and how we can measure their engagement with such systems. Our next step is to design user studies to examine the interaction and engagement of older adults with voice search systems.

Acknowledgments. We thank the Initiative for Women (IFW) Endowment Award.

References

1. Attfield, S., Kazai, G., Lalmas, M., Piwowarski, B.: Towards a science of user engagement (position paper). In: WSDM Workshop on User Modelling for Web Applications, pp. 9–12 (2011)
2. Census: By 2030, All Baby Boomers Will Be Age 65 or Older (2019). https://www.census.gov/library/stories/2019/12/by-2030-all-baby-boomers-will-be-age-65-or-older.html#:~:text=Since%20then%2C%20about%2010%2C000%20a,of%20the%20U.S.%20Census%20Bureau. Accessed 30 Apr 2021
3. Chaudhuri, S., Le, T., White, C., Thompson, H., Demiris, G.: Examining health information–seeking behaviors of older adults. Comput. Informat. Nurs. CIN. **31**(11), 547–553 (2013)
4. Esposito, A., et al.: The dependability of voice on elders' acceptance of humanoid agents. In: INTERSPEECH, pp. 31–35 (2019)
5. Georgila, K., Wolters, M., Moore, J.D., Logie, R.H.: The MATCH corpus: a corpus of older and younger users' interactions with spoken dialogue systems. Lang. Resour. Eval. **44**(3), 221–261 (2010)
6. Guy, I.: Searching by talking: Analysis of voice queries on mobile web search. In: Proceedings of the 39th International ACM SIGIR conference on Research and Development in Information Retrieval, pp. 35–44, July, 2016
7. Kobayashi, M., et al.: Effects of age-related cognitive decline on elderly user interactions with voice-based dialogue systems. In: Lamas, D., Loizides, F., Nacke, L., Petrie, H., Winckler, M., Zaphiris, P. (eds.) INTERACT 2019. LNCS, vol. 11749, pp. 53–74. Springer, Cham (2019). https://doi.org/10.1007/978-3-030-29390-1_4
8. Kowalski, J., et al.: Older adults and voice interaction: a pilot study with google home. In: Extended Abstracts of the 2019 CHI Conference on human factors in computing systems, pp. 1–6 (2019)
9. Li, J., Maharjan, B., Xie, B., Tao, C.: A personalized voice-based diet assistant for caregivers of Alzheimer disease and related dementias: system development and validation. J. Med. Internet Res. **22**(9), e19897 (2020)
10. Ma, X.: Towards human-engaged AI. In: IJCAI, pp. 5682–5686 (2018)
11. Möller, S., Gödde, F., Wolters, M.: A corpus analysis of spoken smart-home interactions with older users. In: Proceedings of the 6th International Conference on Language Resources and Evaluation (LREC), Marrakech, Morocco, pp. 735–740 (2008)
12. Niksirat, K.S., Silpasuwanchai, C., Cheng, P., Ren, X.: Attention regulation framework: designing self-regulated mindfulness technologies. ACM Trans. Comput. Hum. Inter. (TOCHI) **26**(6), 1–44 (2019). https://doi.org/10.1145/3359593
13. Niksirat, K.S., Silpasuwanchai, C., Mohamed Hussien Ahmed, M., Cheng, P., Ren, X.: A framework for interactive mindfulness meditation using attention-regulation process. In: Twelve Agendas on Interacting with Information: A Human-Engaged Computing Perspective 199 Proceedings of the 2017 CHI Conference on Human Factors in Computing Systems, pp. 2672–2684. Association for Computing Machinery, New York (2017). https://doi.org/10.1145/3025453.3025914
14. Ren, X., Silpasuwanchai, C., Cahill, J.: Human-engaged computing: the future of human–computer interaction. CCF Trans. Perv. Comput. Inter. **1**(1), 47–68 (2019). https://doi.org/10.1007/s42486-019-00007-0
15. Sa, N., Yuan, X.-J.: Examining users' partial query modification patterns in voice search. J. Am. Soc. Inf. Sci. Technol. **71**(3), 251–263 (2020) (cover article). First published on 29 April 2019. https://doi.org/10.1002/asi.24238
16. Sa, N., Yuan, X.-J.: Challenges in conversational search: improving the system capabilities and guiding the search process. In: Proceedings of the 24th World Multi-Conference on Systemics, Cybernetics and Informatics (WMSCI 2020), pp. 37–42 (2020)

17. Sa, N., Yuan, X.-J.: Examining user perception and usage of voice search. J. Data Inf. Manag. **5**(1), 1–14 (2021)
18. Sa, N., Yuan, X.-J.: Improving voice search system effectiveness through partial query modification. J. Am. Soc. Inform. Sci. Technol. (JASIST), (2021) (under review, major revision)
19. Sidner, C.L., Lee, C., Kidd, C.D., Lesh, N., Rich, C.: Explorations in engagement for humans and robots. Artif. Intell. **166**(1–2), 140–164 (2005). https://doi.org/10.1016/j.artint.2005.03.005
20. Vandemeulebroucke, T., de Casterlé, B.D., Gastmans, C.: How do older adults experience and perceive socially assistive robots in aged care: a systematic review of qualitative evidence. Aging Ment. Health **22**(2), 149–167 (2018)
21. Wang, C., et al.: Approaching aesthetics on user interface and interaction design. In: Proceedings of the 2018 ACM International Conference on Interactive Surfaces and Spaces, pp. 481–484. Association for Computing Machinery, New York, November 2018. https://doi.org/10.1145/3279778.3279809
22. Wang, C., Yuan, X.J., Ren, X.: Twelve agendas on interacting with information: a human-engaged computing perspective. Data Inf. Manag. **4**(3), 191–199 (2020)

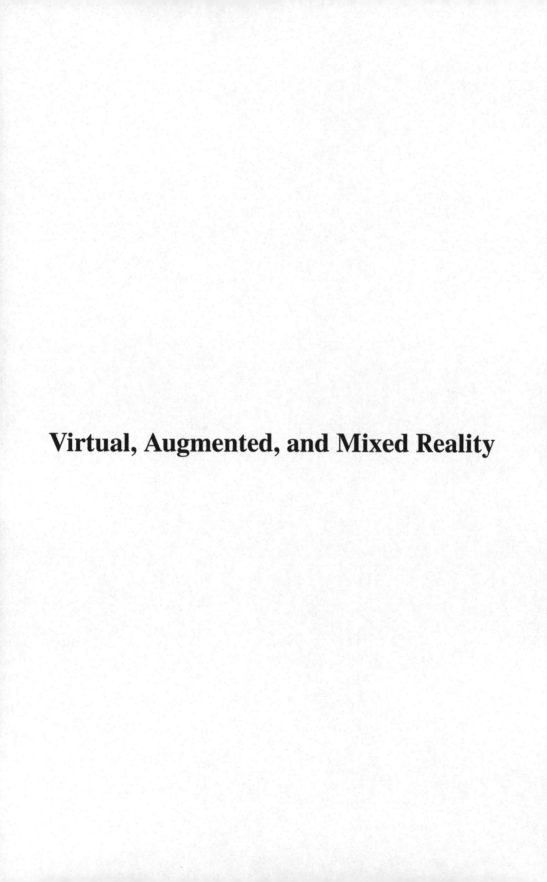

Virtual, Augmented, and Mixed Reality

Research on Projection Interaction Based on Gesture Recognition

Zhiwei Cao, Weiping He[✉], Shuxia Wang, Jie Zhang, Bingzhao Wei, and Jianghong Li

Northwestern Polytechnical University, Xi'an 710072, Shaanxi, People's Republic of China
2019201232@mail.nwpu.edu.cn

Abstract. With the continuous emergence and vigorous development of various new technologies in the information age, human-computer interaction is also changing constantly. People are increasingly connected with the virtual world, so it is necessary to study more natural ways of human-computer interaction. Projection interaction is one of the most important interaction methods. The purpose of this paper is to study how to overcome the misoperation problem caused by foreign objects (interferers) in the environment of projection interaction (Fig. 1c). The method (named after FDGR) adopted is to use the fingertip detection algorithm based on user habits in image processing and the gesture recognition algorithm based on Leap Motion to complete the accurate and convenient natural human-computer interaction. Through user experiments, the experiences of completing the fixed assembly task in the mode of projection (P), gesture (G) and FDGR (PG) were compared, and the data was processed and analyzed. The experimental results showed that FDGR could effectively overcome the misoperation caused by foreign objects (interferers) and the non-intuitiveness of simple gestures, and effectively improved the user's operating experience.

Keywords: Projection interaction · Gesture recognition · Picture processing

1 Introduction

With the development of computer vision and machine learning and other related disciplines, human-computer interaction technology is gradually changing from "computer-centered" to "human-centered" [1]. The new human-computer interaction will no longer rely solely on machine language, but can realize natural human-computer communication without intermediate devices such as keyboard, mouse and touch screen, so as to realize the deep integration of the physical world and the virtual world [2]. Virtual reality (VR), augmented reality (AR) and mixed reality (MR) technologies expand the space scope of human-computer interaction. Gesture interaction, speech interaction and spatial enhanced interaction (SAR) give people a more natural interactive experience. The traditional interaction mode mainly used in the actual assembly process is gradually unable to meet the needs of development. Therefore, it is necessary to study the application of new interaction mode in the actual assembly.

© Springer Nature Switzerland AG 2021
C. Stephanidis et al. (Eds.): HCII 2021, CCIS 1498, pp. 311–317, 2021.
https://doi.org/10.1007/978-3-030-90176-9_40

AR is a technology that superimposes computer-generated images onto the real world for medical, industrial manufacturing, military and entertainment applications. AR is divided into headset type and projection type according to device classification. Headset type can provide the most authentic user experience and deeply integrates virtual objects with real objects. However, there are also complex equipment, in the actual assembly of workers affect the operation and increase the burden of workers. On the contrary, the projection enhancement method can effectively avoid increasing the burden of workers, and project the information onto the assembly in a large range, and the cost is much lower than that of head-mounted enhancement equipment [3]. Therefore, projection enhancement has strong usability in actual assembly. However, in the human-computer interaction enhanced by projection, there is a problem of accidental touch when clicking the projected operation menu. Gesture recognition has been an active research field in the field of human-computer interaction for more than 20 years [4]. Gesture can be used to achieve more natural human-computer interaction. However, when gesture recognition is carried out by image processing, the definition of gesture is complicated, and the workers need to memorize the corresponding operation gesture, thus aggravating the workload, and the operation is not intuitive [5]. Therefore, in order to improve the user's human-computer interaction experience in projection enhancement and solve the problem of mis-touch in projection interaction, this paper proposes a new projection enhanced human-computer interaction method using FDGR.

The purpose of this paper is to solve the problem of miscontact caused by foreign objects (interferers) in projection interaction. The method adopted (FDGR) uses a fingertip recognition image processing algorithm based on user habits and a gesture recognition algorithm based on Leap Motion. In the experiment, groups of projection, gesture and FDGR were set, and the advantages and disadvantages of each interaction mode were determined by comparing the performance of users in different experimental conditions to complete the fixed assembly task.

2 Related Works

2.1 Spatial Augmented Reality

Spatial augmented reality (SAR) separates the technology from the user and integrates it into the environment, rather than a display attached to the body (such as a head-mounted display (HMD)). SAR uses data projectors to superimpose computer-generated virtual objects directly on physical surfaces. The user can then view and interact with the digital information projected directly onto the workspace surface in a natural way [6]. Doshi et al. [7] investigated the use of projector-based spatial augmented reality systems to highlight welding positions on vehicle panels for use by manual welding operators while ensuring industrial quality. The results show that visual cues enable the operators to spot weld with higher accuracy. Zhou et al. [8] used spatial augmented reality (SAR) technology to project visual data onto any surface in order to provide real-time information to users in the field within the physical unit of work. This helps operators find spot solder joints more easily. Therefore, spatial augmented reality, such as using projectors, can effectively assist assembly.

2.2 Gesture Recognition

Gesture is a way of non-verbal communication, which can be expressed through the center of the palm, the position of the finger and the shape formed by the hand. It can be used in many fields such as human-computer interaction, robot control, home automation and medical treatment [5]. Gesture interaction can be divided into contact type and non-contact type according to the contact mode. In the contact type, wearable devices such as gloves are used to obtain hand information. Non-contact method is to obtain hand information by image processing. Wearable gloves can achieve better operation accuracy, but it is inconvenient to operate and will make the operator feel constrained [9]. In addition, wearable gloves are often expensive and fragile, which is not conducive to their use in industrial production. The way of gesture recognition using image processing is to obtain the state information of the hand through depth camera, RGB camera and so on, and then process it according to the relevant knowledge of computer vision and computer graphics. Thus, the position and shape of the hand can be obtained in the background, and then the instruction information can be further determined. Parvathy et al. [9] proposed a visual-based gesture recognition system based on the online Sebastian Marcel static hand posture database, which solved the complex background problems and improved the robustness of gestures. Chen et al. [10] studied a gesture human-computer interaction model based on computer vision, which is expected to greatly improve the usability of mobile augmented reality. Bai et al. [11] added depth cameras to wearable devices for gesture recognition, thus providing a more natural human-computer interaction. Billing Hurst et al. [12] used Kinect camera for gesture recognition and defined the meaning of commonly used gestures, thus completing human-computer interaction in AR. Kim et al. [13] obtained gestures through Leap Motion and realized the natural and direct operation of 3D AR objects in handheld devices through touch and gesture interaction.Hu et al. [13] used Leap Motion to obtain hand information, and then analyzed the current gesture representation information according to multi-layer convolution to complete the gesture recognition system for UAV flight control.

2.3 Summary

This paper adopts a combination of projection enhancement (i.e., spatial augmented reality) and gesture recognition using Leap Motion. OpenCV library is used for image processing in the projection enhancement interaction, and fingertip detection is carried out according to the user's habits. At the same time, the Leap Motion is used to find the hands to eliminate the influence of foreign body interference.

3 Methodology

3.1 Proposed Method

The purpose of this paper is to study how to overcome the misoperation problem caused by foreign objects (interferers) in the environment of projection interaction (Fig. 1c). The method (named after FDGR) adopted is to use the fingertip detection algorithm based on user habits in image processing and the gesture recognition algorithm based on Leap

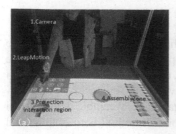

Fig. 1. a) Assembly scene (front view). b) Assembly scene (top view). c) Schematic diagram of the projection interaction based on gesture recognition.

Motion to complete the accurate and convenient natural human-computer interaction. FDGR includes two steps, the first step H is to use gesture recognition algorithm based on Leap Motion to find out user's hand. And the next step F is to use the fingertip detection algorithm based on user habits in image processing to find out user's fingertip under the precondition of finding out user's hand. α and β (Eq. 1) are the coefficients of H and F, respectively. The res (Eq. 1) is true only when both α and β are true. When the res is true, it indicates that the interactive command is triggered.

$$Res = \alpha H + \beta F \qquad (1)$$

3.2 System Implementation and Setup

The experimental interaction prototype included the following parts: simulation experiment scene and interaction module (Fig. 1a). Among them, the simulation experiment scene was selected as the assembly process of low-pressure fan rotor blades. The interaction module includes projection interaction, gesture interaction and FDGR interaction. As shown in Fig. 1a, the hardware includes computer, projector, camera, Leap Motion, etc., and the software includes Unity3D194.12F1, Visual Studio 2019, etc. In the projection augmented reality assembly, the entire assembly system was constructed in Unity3D, and then the whole assembly area and command operation area were projected by the projector. The assembly process was filmed by camera, and then the video stream information obtained by camera was transmitted to the computer end, and the projection was completed at the computer end. Set up devices such as Leap Motion and camera at appropriate locations and then analyze specific operation instructions of gesture expression according to gesture recognition algorithm.

3.3 Participants

Twelve participants (N = 12), aged between 20 and 26 years old (M = 23.42, SD = 1.66) were recruited for the experiment, including 8 males and 4 females. There were 7 employees who had experience in using augmented reality or related operations, and 5 employees who had no experience. All of them were in normal mental condition and could complete the assembly experiment tasks normally.

3.4 Experimental Design

Before the experiment, we introduced the hardware and software used in the study, including mobile AR, Leap Motion, etc. Participants were then presented with task requirements and considerations. In the experimental process, each participant was required to complete the assembly process of blades according to the guidance in the projection augmented reality environment in accordance with the required interaction modes, which were gesture interaction (G), projection interaction (P) and FDGR (PG). After completing the assembly task, participants filled out a Likert scale (1: strongly disagree, 5: strongly agree) and the time that finished the task was recorded.

4 Results

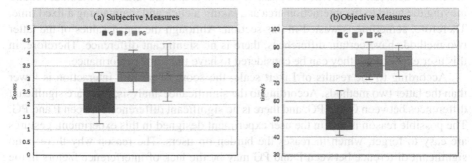

Fig. 2. (a) Likert scale data box diagram; (b) Time measures

4.1 Subjective Measures

Likert Scale was used in this paper to evaluate users' feelings. Scores were used to indicate satisfaction with the experiment. The mean was M and the standard deviation was SD. The experimental results (Fig. 2a) of each group were respectively G (M = 2.34; SD = 0.685), P (M = 3.38; SD = 0.566), PG (M = 3.19; SD = 0.728). The results of normality test were G (p = 0.192), P (p = 0.16), PG (p = 0.589). They were greater than 0.05, therefore, the data could be considered normal. To compare whether there was a significant difference between the means of each group, paired sample T test was carried out in this paper, the results were G-P (t = −3.97; p = 0.002), G-PG (t = −2.51; p = 0.029), P-PG (t = 0.739; p = 0.475). Therefore, G-P and G-PG were significant differences, while P-PG were not significant differences.

4.2 Objective Measures

The time to complete the experiment reflected the efficiency of the experiment. The experimental results (Fig. 2b) of each group were respectively G (M = 52.42s; SD =

8.9s), P (M = 80.83s; SD = 6.9s), PG (M = 86.5s; SD = 5.66s). The results of normality test were G (p = 0.337), P (p = 0.59), PG (p = 0.155). They were greater than 0.05, therefore, the data could be considered normal. The results of paired sample T test were G-P (t = −9.44; p = 0.004), G-PG (t = −10.24; p = 0.016), P-PG (t = −1.005; p = 0.336). Therefore, G-P and G-PG were significant differences, while P-PG were not significant differences.

5   Discussion

By analyzing the mean time and standard deviation of the task, it can be seen that gesture interaction can complete the task quickly and in the shortest time. Projection interaction and FDGR interaction are slower than gesture interaction. According to the significance analysis, there are significant differences between G and PG, and there is no significant difference between P and PG. The possible reason is that the latter two methods require moving the hand to the interaction area and taking a click and maintaining a fixed time. Therefore, sometime is wasted in this section. Although the mean values of the latter two methods have certain differences, there is no significant difference. Therefore, in this user experiment, they can be considered to have the same performance.

According to the results of Likert scale, the score of gesture interaction is lower than the latter two methods. According to the significance analysis, there are significant differences between G and PG, and there is no significant difference between P and PG. The possible reason is that in the user experiment designed in this experiment, gestures are easy to forget, which increases the burden on users. The reason why there is no significant difference between P and PG may be the lack of interference factors in the experiment, thus the advantage that PG can eliminate interference factors cannot be exerted.

6   Conclusion and Future Work

Human-computer interaction technology is changing quickly, and it is necessary to study the application of new interaction mode in assembly. AR is a technology that superimposes computer-generated images onto the real world for medical, industrial manufacturing, military and entertainment applications. In this paper, the problem of miscontact caused by foreign objects in projection interaction is studied. The method adopted (FDGR) uses a fingertip recognition image processing algorithm based on user habits and a gesture recognition algorithm based on Leap Motion. By comparing the experiments using FDGR method with those of gesture and projection interaction, it is found that the FDGR method overcomes the non-intuitive and instability of gesture recognition only, as well as the problem of wrong touch in projection interaction, and effectively improves the user's operating experience.

However, there are still some problems. The system is not robust enough, because the Leap Motion may not track user's hand. In the future, we will use different measures to track user's hand robustly.

Acknowledgement. This work is partly support by National Key R&D Program of China (Grant No. 2019YFB1703800), Natural Science Basic Research Plan in Shaanxi Province of China (Grant No. 2016JM6054), the Programme of Introducing Talents of Discipline to Universities (111 Project), China (Grant No. B13044).

References

1. Hongjian, C.: Research on gesture recognition method based on computer vision technology. In: 2020 International Conference on Computer Information and Big Data Applications (CIBDA), pp. 358–362. IEEE, Guiyang (2020)
2. Fengjun, Z.: A survey on human-computer interaction in virtual reality. Sci. Sinica Inf. **46**(12), 1711–1736 (2016)
3. Jin, H.: An overview of human-computer interaction in mixed reality. J. Comput. Aided Des. Graph. **28**(06), 869–880 (2016)
4. Granit, L.: A sliding window approach to natural hand gesture recognition using a custom data glove. In: 2016 IEEE Symposium on 3D User Interfaces (3DUI), pp. 81–90 (2016)
5. Munir, O.: Hand gesture recognition based on computer vision: a review of techniques. J. Imaging **6**(8), 73–102 (2020)
6. Ivan, P.: The go-go interaction technique: non-linear mapping for direct manipulation in VR. In: Proceedings of the 9th Annual ACM Symposium on User Interface Software and Technology, pp. 79–80. Association for Computing Machinery, Seattle, Washington (1996)
7. Doshi, A., Smith, R.T., Thomas, B.H., Bouras, C.: Use of projector based augmented reality to improve manual spot-welding precision and accuracy for automotive manufacturing. Int. J. Adv. Manuf. Technol. **89**(5–8), 1279–1293 (2016). https://doi.org/10.1007/s00170-016-9164-5
8. Jianlong, Z.: Applying spatial augmented reality to facilitate in-situ support for automotive spot welding inspection. In: Proceedings of the 10th International Conference on Virtual Reality Continuum and Its Applications in Industry, pp. 195–200 (2011)
9. Priyanka, P.: Development of hand gesture recognition system using machine learning. J. Amb. Intell. Hum. Comput. **12**, 6793–6800 (2020)
10. Kuen-Meau, C., Ming-Jen, W.: Using the Interactive Design of Gesture Recognition in Augmented Reality. Trans Tech Publications Ltd., Durnten-Zurich (2013)
11. Huidong, B.: Using 3D hand gestures and touch input for wearable AR interaction. In: CHI, pp. 1321–1326. ACM, Toronto (2014)
12. Mark, B.: Hands in space gesture interaction with augmented-reality interfaces. IEEE Comput. Graph. Appl. **34**(1), 77–81 (2014)
13. Kim, M., Lee, J.Y.: Touch and hand gesture-based interactions for directly manipulating 3D virtual objects in mobile augmented reality. Multimedia Tools Appl. **75**(23), 16529–16550 (2016). https://doi.org/10.1007/s11042-016-3355-9

The Effects of Social Proneness and Avatar Primes on Prosocial Behavior in Virtual and Real Worlds

Yu-chen Hsu[1]([⊠]), Siao-wei Huang[2], and Hsuan-de Huang[3]

[1] Institute of Learning Sciences and Technologies, National Tsing Hua University,
Hsinchu, Taiwan
ychsu@mx.nthu.edu.tw
[2] Information Management Center, New Taipei City Government, Taipei, Taiwan
[3] Qisda Corporation, Hsinchu, Taiwan

1 Introduction

Prosocial behavior is a stable personality trait that is developed in the process as a person grows up and is continuing to be changed by environmental factors. There are many studies exploring the phenomena of prosocial behavior, but few of them are studied in the virtual environment. Nowadays, teenagers spend a lot of time role-playing in the virtual environment. Past studies have confirmed that virtual experience will have a certain impact on their lives in the real world. If we can design avatars and tasks to change teenagers' prosocial beliefs and behaviors in the virtual world through roleplay and to achieve sustainable behavior change in the real world, it will become an alternative channel for training in educational context.

In the past, the priming researches were mostly conducted through the experimental method and the results indicated that only a short period of exposure by the stimuli in the virtual world did achieve the effect of changing beliefs and behaviors. This study intended to examine the priming effect in the virtual space to understand whether it was possible to change subjects' prosocial behavior through cues from avatar if the change existed after the experiment.

A phenomenon in virtual space is the Proteus effect. When the players enter the virtual space to play the avatar, their behaviors will naturally conform to the avatars' visual character. After following the research stream of the Proteus effect, this study examines how subjects' prosocial behaviors change when they are primed with positive or negative cues from avatars (hero and villain). Most of the Proteus effect studies observed their behaviors during the avatar role-play process. Only a few of them examined subjects' priming behaviors after the experiment. The present study observed both subjects' behaviors in and after the role play in the virtual world to see if the effect extends to real life even when they were out of the priming context. In addition, we also examined how the priming effect change the prosocial behaviors of people with high or low prosocial personality.

C. Stephanidis et al. (Eds.): HCII 2021, CCIS 1498, pp. 318–323, 2021.
https://doi.org/10.1007/978-3-030-90176-9_41

1.1 Priming Effects on Avatars

Bargh and Chartrand (2000) indicated that conceptual priming could activate the subjects' mental representation and brought out the subsequent impact on cognition and behaviors. In a series of studies, Nelson and Norton (2005) adopted situational primes (superhero vs Superman) to examine subjects' commitment to helping others in the real world. The results indicated that situational primes had an effect both on spontaneous and future behavior. The effect lasted even three months later after the exposure.

The Proteus effect was proposed by Yee and Bailenson (2006), which referred that a player developed an impression of an avatar based on its stereotyped traits and conformed to that traits as he or she played the avatar (Chan and Wallace 2008). Peña et al. (2009) conducted two studies showing that the avatars dressed in black color developed aggressive intentions and behaviors and lower group coherence than the white-cloaked avatars. The results of another study (Peña et al. 2012) indicated that the visual appearance of avatars unconsciously activated subjects' language use. Those dressed in glamorous clothes referred more to sports, entertainment, clothes, and beauty compared to people dressed in formal clothes used more words about education, books, and numbers. In addition, visual appearance plus name label elicited further words related to the stereotype of the corresponding avatar.

Yoo et al. (2015) investigated how roleplay elderly or young avatars affected subjects' attitudes and purchasing behavior. The results showed that roleplay aging avatars could significantly increase the intention of donation and volunteer for NPO supporting the elderly compared to those playing young avatars. For example, participants who play aging avatars would donate $1.41 and 1 h and 30 min of volunteer service to older non-profit organizations.

Some other studies were carried out in games to explore the effects on prosocial behaviors. Yoon and Vargas (2014) assigned subjects to the heroic, villainous, and neutral geometric-shaped avatars and asked them to play a battle game for five minutes. Then subjects were instructed to select either chocolate or chili sauce as study materials for the future participant to consume. This was to measure good or bad behaviors as a result of the previous priming procedure. The study found out that the heroic avatar subjects poured more chocolate than the other two groups, while the villain subjects poured more chili sauce than other groups.

Rosenberg et al. (2013) asked players to wear virtual helmets when playing pro-social video games. The results showed that virtual experience led to more prosocial behaviors in the real world. Those with the "superpower" of flight showed greater helping behaviors in the physical world which indicated that having the power of flight primed concepts and prototypes associated with superheroes and led to related behaviors.

The study of Pena and Chen (2017) adapted the situational priming manipulation of the study of Nelson and Norton (2005) by priming superhero, supervillain, and control condition on subjects in the real world and found that subjects primed with superhero perform faster-helping behavior than the control group.

Consistent with the concept of priming research, participants who played the role of a hero were more likely to behave in virtual space than those who played a villain. In addition, the spreading activation mechanisms (Anderson and Spellman 1995; Collins and Loftus 1975) could be adapted to predict that the appearance of the avatar may temporarily change the behavior and willingness of the player. For example, subjects who play a hero is expected to donate more money, time, and willing to help others than subjects who played the villain. The researchers propose the following hypotheses:

H1. In the virtual world, subjects who play an avatar of the superhero will be more enthusiastic to help others than subjects playing the supervillain avatar.

H2. In the real world, subjects who play an avatar of superhero will pick up more books than subjects playing the supervillain avatar.

H3. In the real world, subjects who play an avatar of superhero will perceive lower hostile perception bias than subjects playing the supervillain avatar.

H4. In the real world, subjects who play an avatar of superhero will demonstrate higher prosocial intentions than subjects playing the supervillain avatar.

1.2 Prosocial Behavior and Priming Effect

The present study aims to understand how the subject's prosocial tendencies affect their behavior after playing an avatar. Prosocial behavior refers to the actions of helping another person or group of individuals with no obvious benefit to the helper. According to Bierhoff (2005), the purpose of prosocial behavior is to improve the situation of the help-seeker. In addition, this behavior is voluntary, so behaviors such as donating, sharing, helping, assisting, and providing support to others are considered prosocial behaviors. Carlo and Randall (2002) propose PTM (Prosocial Tendencies Measure) with four dimensions to measure prosocial behavior: altruistic prosocial behaviors, compliant prosocial behaviors, emotional prosocial behaviors, and public prosocial behaviors. The prosocial tendency of a person will affect his prosocial behavior and intention. According to the priming effect, when the stimuli are consistent with the personality trait of the subject, he is more likely to have corresponding behaviors and reactions. For example, compared to the low prosocial tendency group, we expect that a high prosocial tendency group will donate more money, time, and willing to help others. The relevant assumptions are listed as follows:

H5. In the virtual world, subjects with high prosocial tendencies will be more enthusiastic to help others than those with a low prosocial tendency.

H6. In the real world, subjects with high prosocial tendencies will pick up more books than those with a low prosocial tendency.

H7. In the real world, subjects with high prosocial tendencies will perceive lower hostile perception bias than those with the low prosocial tendency.

H8. In the real world, subjects with high prosocial tendencies will demonstrate higher prosocial intentions than those with a low prosocial tendency.

2 Materials and Method

2.1 Measure

Subjects' subjective perception, prosocial intention, and prosocial behaviors were measured. Following the procedure of Happ et al. (2013), the hostile perception bias was measured to understand their hostile feeling. The measure of prosocial intention is adapting from Nelson and Norton (2005) with two items: "raising up the elder" and "offer one's seat to somebody". The prosocial behaviors in the virtual and real worlds were measured by asking subjects to perform two helping tasks in Second Life and a book pick-up task in the physical world. The method was adopted from that in Yoo et al. (2015). The researchers also interviewed some of the subjects to collect qualitative data.

2.2 Participants

Eighty-eight male subjects aged from 18 to 40 (M = 24.69, SD = 4.99) were recruited based on the median score of the prosocial personality scale (high prosocial tendencies n = 22, low prosocial tendencies n = 22). Then those with high and low prosocial tendencies were randomly divided into the hero and valiant groups.

2.3 Procedure

Subjects were told the study was testing the operation fluency and usability of two virtual environments. They then spent 5 to 10 min playing a fighting game in which the hero and villain groups play the hero and villain avatars. Then they entered Second Life playing hero and villain avatars in third-person view and were given two training rounds for 5 min to become familiar with the environment and controls. After they viewed their avatar, they were asked to list the attributes of the avatar then perform two prosocial tasks in Second Life. Then subjects performed the facial expression recognition and book pickup tasks after logging out Second Life. Finally, they filled out an online questionnaire and were told the real purpose of the study. Some of the subjects were interviewed before they were told of the study purpose.

3 Result

3.1 Hostile Perception Bias

An ANOVA test showed that only the main effect of the subject's prosocial tendency on hostile perception bias was significant $F(1,69) = 11.206$, $p = .001$, but no other significant findings were found. the subject's prosocial tendency has a greater influence on their Hostile perception bias.

3.2 Prosocial Intention

An ANOVA test showed that only the main effect of the subject prosocial tendency on "raising up the elder" was significant $F(1,88) = 10.18$, $p = .002$, but others were not significant. An ANOVA test showed that only the main effect of the subject prosocial tendency on "offer one's seat to somebody" was significant $F(1,88) = 5.79$, $p = .018$, but others were not significant. To sum up, the subject's prosocial tendency has a greater influence on their prosocial intentions.

3.3 Prosocial Behaviors in the Virtual and Real World

The results of chi-square analysis on two virtual prosocial tasks indicated that the percentage of participants who did not help was not affected by their prosocial tendency or avatar roles. The results of chi-square analysis on the real world prosocial tasks indicated that the percentage of participants who did not help was not affected by their prosocial tendency or avatar roles.

According to the aforementioned results, only H7 and H8 were supported but the others were not. it indicates that the role of the avatar is not the main factor that influences subjects' prosocial behavior.

4 Discussion

From the results of the study, the avatar's priming effect was not found in all the dependent variables, while subjects' prosocial tendencies had an impact only on their perception or prosocial intention but not on real behavior. As regards the book pick-up task, it is known from the interview that some other psychological or context factors confound the results. The researchers conducted pre-test for several times to eliminate possible confounding factors or exclude other aspects such as subject's preferences or personality influences. However, the priming effect was still not observed. From the interview, it is observed that the young generation has experience in various games. This plus some other issues like preferences would inevitably impact the roleplay effect of avatars. The past prosocial studies only measure subjects attitude changes and prosocial behavior in the real world. This study is one of the few that attempt to observe the prosocial behavior in the virtual environment. Future researchers can adopt various methods to observe prosocial behaviors in the virtual environment.

References

Abbate, C.S., Ruggieri, S., Boca, S.: The effect of prosocial priming in the presence of bystanders. J. Soc. Psychol. **153**(5), 619–622 (2013)

Anderson, M.C., Spellman, B.A.: On the status of inhibitory mechanisms in cognition: memory retrieval as a model case. Psychol. Rev. **102**(1), 68 (1995)

Bargh, J.A., Chartrand, T.L.: The mind in the middle. In: Handbook of Research Methods in Social and Personality Psychology, pp. 253–285 (2000)

Carlo, G., Randall, B.A.: The development of a measure of prosocial behaviors for late adolescents. J. Youth Adolesc. **31**(1), 31–44 (2002)

Collins, A.M., Loftus, E.F.: A spreading-activation theory of semantic processing. Psychol. Rev. **82**(6), 407 (1975)

Eagly, A.H.: The his and hers of prosocial behavior: An examination of the social psychology of gender. Am. Psychol. **64**(8), 644 (2009)

Gonzales, A.L., Hancock, J.T.: Identity shift in computer-mediated environments. Media Psychol. **11**(2), 167–185 (2008)

Kim, Y.J., Baker, J., Song, J.: An exploratory study of social factors influencing virtual community members' satisfaction with avatars. Commun. Assoc. Inf. Syst. **20**(1), 36 (2007)

Klapp, O.E.: The creation of popular heroes. Am. J. Sociol. **54**(2), 135–141 (1948)

Mackinnon, A., Jorm, A.F., Christensen, H., Korten, A.E., Jacomb, P.A., Rodgers, B.: A short form of the positive and negative affect schedule: evaluation of factorial validity and invariance across demographic variables in a community sample. Personality Individ. Differ. **27**(3), 405–416 (1999)

Nelson, L.D., Norton, M.I.: From student to superhero: situational primes shape future helping. J. Exp. Soc. Psychol. **41**(4), 423–430 (2005)

Peña, J.F.: Integrating the influence of perceiving and operating avatars under the automaticity model of priming effects. Commun. Theory **21**(2), 150–168 (2011)

Pennebaker, J.W., Boyd, R.L., Jordan, K., Blackburn, K.: The development and psychometric properties of LIWC2015, The University of Texas at Austin (2015)

Peña, J., Chen, M.: With great power comes great responsibility: superhero primes and expansive poses influence prosocial behavior after a motion-controlled game task. Comput. Hum. Behav. **76**, 378–385 (2017)

Peña, J., Hancock, J.T., Merola, N.A.: The priming effects of avatars in virtual settings. Commun. Res. **36**(6), 838–856 (2009)

Peña, J., McGlone, M.S., Sanchez, J.: The cowl makes the monk: how avatar appearance and role labels affect cognition in virtual worlds. J. Virtual Worlds Res. **5**(3) (2012)

Rosenberg, R.S., Baughman, S.L., Bailenson, J.N.: Virtual superheroes: using superpowers in virtual reality to encourage prosocial behavior. PLoS ONE **8**(1), e55003 (2013)

Van Looy, J., Courtois, C., De Vocht, M., De Marez, L.: Player identification in online games: validation of a scale for measuring identification in MMOGs. Media Psychol. **15**(2), 197–221 (2012)

Yee, N., Bailenson, J.N.: Walk a mile in digital shoes: the impact of embodied perspective-taking on the reduction of negative stereotyping in immersive virtual environments. In: Proceedings of PRESENCE, vol. 24, p. 26 (2006)

Yoo, S.C., Peña, J.F., Drumwright, M.E.: Virtual shopping and unconscious persuasion: the priming effects of avatar age and consumers' age discrimination on purchasing and prosocial behaviors. Comput. Hum. Behav. **48**, 62–71 (2015)

Yoon, G., Vargas, P.T.: Know thy avatar: the unintended effect of virtual-self representation on behavior. Psychol. Sci. **25**(4), 1043–1045 (2014)

VR-Based Interface Enabling Ad-Hoc Individualization of Information Layer Presentation

Luka Jacke[1], Michael Maurus[1(✉)], and Elsa Andrea Kirchner[1,2] [ID]

[1] German Research Center for Artificial Intelligence – Robotics Innovation Center,
Bremen, Germany
{luka.jacke,michael.maurus,elsa.kirchner}@dfki.de
[2] Robotics Lab, University of Bremen, Bremen, Germany

Abstract. Graphical user interfaces created for scientific prototypes are often designed to support only a specific and well-defined use case. They often use two-dimensional overlay buttons and panels in the view of the operator to cover needed functionalities. For potentially unpredictable and more complex tasks, such interfaces often fall short of the ability to scale properly with the larger amount of information that needs to be processed by the user. Simply transferring this approach to more complex use-cases likely introduces visual clutter and leads to an unnecessarily complicated interface navigation that reduces accessibility and potentially overwhelms users. In this paper, we present a possible solution to this problem. In our proposed concept, information layers can be accessed and displayed by placing an augmentation glass in front of the virtual camera. Depending on the placement of the glass, the viewing area can cover only parts of the view or the entire scene. This also makes it possible to use multiple glasses side by side. Furthermore, augmentation glasses can be placed into the virtual environment for collaborative work. With this, our approach is flexible and can be adapted very fast to changing demands.

Keywords: Virtual reality · CAVE · Head-mounted display · Virtual environment · Interaction · Visualization

1 Introduction

Environments, requirements, and ways to solve a task are often unpredictable and therefore cannot always be planned. Still, user interfaces (UI) created for scientific prototypes are often designed to only support a specific and well-defined use case of a very complex endeavor [1–4]. They often use a handful of classical graphical user interface (GUI) elements like buttons and panels, e.g., at the top of the field of view, to cover needed functionalities. For potentially unpredictable and more complex tasks, such interfaces are often unable to scale properly with the larger amount of information that needs to be processed by the user. Simply combining classical 2D elements and concepts would likely introduce visual clutter and lead to an unnecessarily complicated interface navigation

© Springer Nature Switzerland AG 2021
C. Stephanidis et al. (Eds.): HCII 2021, CCIS 1498, pp. 324–331, 2021.
https://doi.org/10.1007/978-3-030-90176-9_42

that reduces accessibility and potentially overwhelms users. Therefore, new methods are needed that allow users to set up their interface flexibly and appropriate to the situation at hand.

With recent developments in head-mounted display (HMD) technology, virtual reality (VR) and mixed reality applications become more relevant enabling, e.g., on-site mission planning for space and emergency services. It also has the advantage of utilizing the human capability of spatial processing, especially in combination with enriching real-world data with additional sensor data. Furthermore, VR can give the user a feeling of being on-site. This can help to understand the current environment and situation. Unfortunately, the classical way of accessing, managing, and displaying UI elements and information layers are still widely used although not very suitable for HMDs. New concepts for accessing, managing, and displaying information in VR and AR are needed.

In this work, we first give an overview on the state of the art, followed by a presentation of our concept including a general introduction to augmentation glasses, their application and possible use cases and finally a discussion of our approach.

2 State of the Art

UI design is closely linked to the characteristics of the display and its input devices. Originally, classic interaction in 2D using monitors, mouse and keyboard is based on classical GUI elements like drop-down menus or buttons which can be used efficiently for enabling and disabling the display of information and to interact with the application. Additionally, docking widgets facilitate the management of information layers and enable the user to fit the GUI to the current needs. Even in complex scenarios such as mission planning and execution for planetary exploration, these classical 2D widgets are widely being used e.g., by ESA [5, 6], displaying all the information on a wall of monitors [7] allowing multiple specialists to analyze the data at the same time.

Instead of using a wall of monitors, it is also possible to use a Cave Automatic Virtual Environment (CAVE) placing the monitors or projection surfaces in a cube, circle, or half circle to, e.g., see a virtual representation of the environment of a robot [8]. Planthaber et al. [2, 4] were able to use different input devices such as a controller, an eye tracker or even an exoskeleton [9] in their CAVE. The ability to choose the appropriate or preferred input device provides the operator with a better and more intuitive way to interact with and monitor the robot's environment. But even in their teleoperation scenario utilizing a CAVE, additional information visualization and interaction options, like setting waypoints, are managed by classical 2D widgets on different screens. This approach was appropriate for their teleoperation task, but for complex tasks like a rover exploration mission, this does not scale properly with the amount of data.

With the development of head mounted displays (HMDs) as consumer electronics mainly for gaming purposes, new use cases and approaches have been enabled. Classical UI design paradigms from 2D environments are often transferred to the immersive 3D environment provided by this new hardware. However, these design principles created specifically for constrained 2D environments limit the range of new possibilities provided by 3D. The virtual 3D environment enables new ways of interaction that can be used to solve this problem.

Many HMD and CAVE-based virtual reality applications, such as mission operations centers for rover operations [2, 4, 8] or underwater exploration [3], use UI design paradigms from classical 2D environments. Following the same approach for more complex tasks with an increased range of functions likely results in an overloaded UI making the application more difficult to use. For example, [1] and [3] are using floating 2D panels which are fixed to the field of view. They display information like a mini map, the camera view of the robot, and the robot coordinates [3] or make it possible to use a measurement tool [1]. However, this comes at the cost of covering a significant part of the main application which displays the virtual environment. Adding more functionality to the interface while retaining the same design approach would quickly overload the interface and compromise large portions of the view.

Today, even more complex implementations of a VR interface for the commercial construction sector [10, 11] still use static panels with information and UI elements to interact with the environment. As an example, [10] implemented a classic nested menu using 2D panels to control the display of routes and related information in the environment for a virtual training scenario. The virtual reality scientific collaboration tool for space exploration activities developed by García et al. [12] follows a similar design path. Various tasks like showing the rover path, selecting datasets, or creating landmarks are managed in a more structured way by using a floating menu. Even though this approach is less obtrusive by hiding unneeded information from the view, the amount and manner of presentation of information in 2D panels is static and not adaptable to changing scenarios or custom needs.

More recent concepts are being developed for mixed-reality devices that augment the real world with additional virtual data. NASA makes use of this technology in [13] to create an immersive mixed reality tool to visualize the surface of Mars. It is also possible to collaboratively inspect the environment and inform vehicle operation.

Mixed Reality applications are also being developed in the field of digital medical assistance. A review study by Kim et al. [14] discusses many practical applications for training surgeons, surgical planning, and surgery supported by VR and AR. Here, it is especially important to keep the field of view as clear as possible while augmenting it with additional information like X-ray images.

In the future, approaches will have to be developed that enable far more complex applications on the one hand, and on the other hand make even more effective use of mixed-reality approaches to enable simple, intuitive adaptation to changing, often unpredictable situations or to serve one's own preferences [15].

3 Concept Description

In the following, we present our new approach, which was designed with the aim of simplifying the interaction effort required to use the GUI and enabling efficient, ad-hoc presentation of information layers.

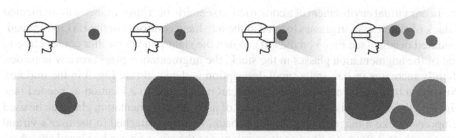

Fig. 1. Depending on the placement of the glass, the viewing area can cover only parts of the view (left, middle left) or the entire scene (middle right). This also makes it possible to use multiple glasses side by side (right).

3.1 General Idea of Augmentation Glasses

The basic idea of our design approach is to have a set of monocle-like augmentation glasses, which can be placed in front of the virtual camera or directly into the virtual scene. These augmentation glasses can display arbitrary information layers augmenting the underlying three-dimensional virtual scene with data or even depict a completely different "version" of the scene. In a construction scenario for example, this could be the representation of how the area should look like in the future.

To implement the augmentation glasses, we render a virtual sphere which can be placed with respect to the virtual camera. Depending on the distance to the virtual camera, the augmentation glass can cover anything between only a small portion of the screen and up to the full screen (see Fig. 1). The augmentation glass can also be positioned along the other two axes of the camera coordinate system which allows for placing it anywhere in the field of view. This also makes it possible to use multiple augmentation glasses side by side, enabling the user to individualize the display as needed.

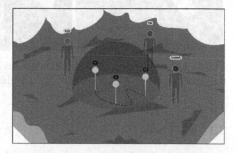

Fig. 2. Augmentation sphere (red) placed in the scene for collaborative inspection of a planned robot route (dotted line) with 3 waypoints (green) (Color figure online).

Furthermore, our concept of using such augmentation glasses allows to place the sphere directly into the virtual environment (see Fig. 2). This can facilitate collaborative work where multiple people can walk around in the virtual world looking at parts of the scene rendered with additional information through the augmentation sphere.

3.2 Accessing Information Layers

In addition to displaying layers of information, accessing, and managing information from these layers requires additional new concepts for retrieving, especially when there are many different layers to choose from.

In our virtual environment of a construction scenario on a lunar base, we implemented a stack of augmentation glasses located at the left-hand controller of the HTC Vive head-mounted display (see Fig. 3 on the left). When the right-hand controller comes close to one of the augmentation glasses in the stack, the augmentation glass preview pops out, slightly increases in size and a small description is depicted (see Fig. 3 in the middle). Pressing a button, the augmentation glass can be dragged to a location as needed (see Fig. 3 on the right). This allows for a variety of uses: The augmentation glass can be used temporarily like a magnifier and then put back, it can be attached to the user's virtual camera where it stays at a fixed position relative to the eye, or it can be placed anywhere in the scene for collaborative use in case of multiple users. The implemented solution for accessing the information layers and customizing the view was chosen with the aim of making the process of finding, selecting, and handling augmentation glasses quick and intuitive. It also enables the user to set up the interface ad hoc and as needed.

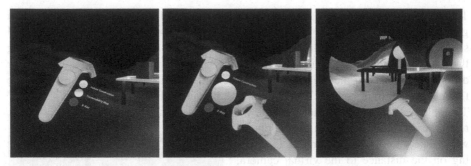

Fig. 3. Left: The stack of augmentation glasses is depicted. Middle: One glass is selected by using the right controller. Right: The user draws a glass from the stack and can use it as needed

3.3   Use Cases

As mentioned before, our prototype was developed in the context of a lunar exploration and human-robot collaboration scenario. When working with robots, it is particularly important to understand what the robot is currently doing. This is especially relevant for detecting and identifying errors when multiple error sources are possible.

In an exploration scenario, it is important to display information of the environment and the robot. This can be, e.g., the raw laser scan data, the robot map as a color-coded heightmap, images taken from the orbit, and the traversability map to see where the robot can go, and which areas may not be accessible to the robot. Mission control also needs to create new target waypoints, where the robot should explore next. Scientists, on the other hand, need to be able to annotate interesting locations such as geological rock formations or craters on-the-fly, which can later be used for mission planning. One might also be interested in the current task plan of the robot. This is especially interesting in the case of an error, but also when multiple robots or even humans must work together.

Construction site management, whether in space or on earth, can be imagined having a special display showing planned sites, buildings, or objects. This can also be easily complemented with, e.g., progress reports or a list of needed materials and assets at the specific site to be used for mission planning and task assignment.

Another very promising use case for our approach is the field of search and rescue. Here, operation centers need an overview of locations already visited, sensory information about hazards in an area such as contamination levels, the stability of buildings, fire, flooding etc.

With a very good tracking of the human on site and a virtual representation of the environment, our concept can also be implemented and used for augmented or mixed reality applications making all the features possible not only for mission control but also for humans on the moon base, the construction site or emergency services.

3.4 Implementation Details

For our concept, all the different information layers need to be in the same reference frame making it possible to overlay or exchange the views. Some features like displaying the scene as a color-coded height map or enriching it with volumetric sensor information like gas concentrations or flood levels, can be implemented using shaders. Other features, like displaying and managing a construction site or placing new buildings and objects into the scene, need a separate virtual representation. This can be implemented using render targets (render to texture). For that, we use additional virtual cameras which render other representations of the environment, e.g., one which has additional models for planned infrastructure (see Fig. 4), into a render target texture (RTT). Then, the RTT will be displayed in the corresponding augmentation glass. We implemented our prototype using the Unreal Engine [16].

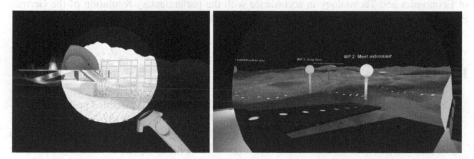

Fig. 4. Left: Example visualization of a construction view implemented using a render target. Right: An overlay with a traversability map, robot waypoints (pins) and route (dotted line) are depicted.

4   Conclusion

The concept of the augmentation glasses was developed with the goal of enabling efficient, ad-hoc individualization of information layer presentation. The augmentation glasses can be attached to the virtual camera or can be used temporarily by dragging and dropping it as needed. Depending on the placement, the augmentation glass can cover only parts of the view or even the entire scene making it possible to use multiple glasses side by side. Furthermore, augmentation glasses can be placed into the virtual environment for collaborative work. By using augmentation glasses to access and handle information layers, enabling and disabling layers only requires a single interaction that does not introduce a full change of view and does not require interacting with menu structures. Instead, it is natural and intuitive, resembling real-world interactions. However, this general concept is highly dependent on a good referencing of all the information layers and a good localization of the human.

While we believe that this concept could provide ways to simplify the workflow and provide more flexibility and individualization for users, the question on how to mix different information layers like robot maps paired with objects of future constructions has not been addressed yet. One way could be to implement an information combination feature where users can overlap different augmentation glasses with each other. When glasses overlap, their information needs to merge, and a new layer would be created.

Our approach was specifically designed for the handling of visual data. However, even numerical data, e.g., from joints of the robot, could be displayed on a placeable object that behaves similarly to the augmentation glasses and is drawable from a stack in the same way. Further, for our current interaction approach the user's hands must be free. However, using speech or eye tracking to control the accessing and handling of information layers could be a solution. For VR, we currently need an interaction device like a controller, while for AR, the control could be implemented by using gestures.

Acknowledgements. The presented work is part of the projects TransFIT and KiMMI-SF which are funded by the German Aerospace Center (DLR) with federal funds of the Federal Ministry of Economics and Technology in accordance with the parliamentary resolution of the German Parliament under grant no. 50 RA 1701 (TransFIT) and 50 RA 2021 (KiMMI-SF).

References

1. Zaker, R., Coloma, E.: Virtual reality-integrated workflow in BIM enabled projects collaboration and design review: a case study. J. Visual. Eng. **6**(4), 1–15 (2018)
2. Sonsalla, R., et al.: Field testing of a cooperative multi-robot sample return mission in Mars analogue environment. In: Proceedings of the 14th Symposium on Advanced Space Technologies in Robotics and Automation (ASTRA-2017), Leiden, the Netherlands (2017)
3. Bonin-Font, F., Massot-Campos, M., Burguera, A.: ARSEA: a virtual reality subsea exploration assistant. IFAC-PapersOnLine **51**(29), 26–31 (2018)
4. Planthaber, S., et al.: Controlling a semi-autonomous robot team from a virtual environment. In: Proceedings of the Companion of the 2017 ACM/IEEE International Conference on Human-Robot Interaction (HRI 2017), p. 417. Association for Computing Machinery, New York (2017). https://doi.org/10.1145/3029798.3036647
5. Taubert, D., et al.: METERON SUPVIS – an operations experiment to prepare for future human/robot missions on the moon and beyond. In: Proceedings of the 14th Symposium on Advanced Space Technologies in Robotics and Automation (ASTRA-2017), Leiden, The Netherlands (2017)

6. Martin, S., Rinnan, T.B., Sarkarati, M., Nergaard, K.: The surface operations Framework – transitioning from early analogue experiments to future lunar missions. In: Proceedings of the 15th Symposium on Advanced Space Technologies in Robotics and Automation (ASTRA-2019), Noordwijk, The Netherlands (2019)
7. Imhof, B., et al.: Moonwalk—human robot collaboration mission scenarios and simulations. In: Proceedings of the AIAA SPACE 2015 Conference and Exposition, Pasadena, p. 4531 (2015)
8. Kirchner, E.A., et al.: An intelligent man-machine interface—multi-robot control adapted for task engagement based on single-trial detectability of P300. Front. Hum. Neurosci. Front. **10**, 291 (2016). https://doi.org/10.3389/fnhum.2016.00291
9. Mallwitz, M., et al.: The CAPIO active upper body exoskeleton and its application for teleoperation. In: Proceedings of the 13th Symposium on Advanced Space Technologies in Robotics and Automation, (ASTRA-2015), Noordwijk, The Netherlands (2015)
10. Linde YouTube Video: Virtual Reality Training for Operators by Linde (2018). https://www.youtube.com/watch?v=KYK6wuFaES8. Accessed 24 Mar 2021
11. Vixel.no Homepage. https://www.vrex.no/vrex-information/howitworks/. Accessed 24 Mar 2021
12. García, A.S., et al.: Collaborative virtual reality platform for visualizing space data and mission planning. Multimedia Tools Appl. **78**(23), 33191–33220 (2019). https://doi.org/10.1007/s11042-019-7736-8
13. Abercrombie, S.P., et al.: OnSight: Multi-platform visualization of the surface of mars. Poster presented at the 2017 American Geophysical Union Fall Meeting, New Orleans, LA (2017). https://agu.confex.com/agu/fm17/mediafile/Handout/Paper246353/ED11C-0134-onsight-agu-web.pdf
14. Kim, Y., Kim, H., Kim, Y.O.: Virtual reality and augmented reality in plastic surgery: a review. Arch. Plast. Surg. **44**(3), 179–187 (2017). https://doi.org/10.5999/aps.2017.44.3.179
15. Kirchner, E.A., Langer, H., Beetz, M.: An interactive strategic mission management system for intuitive human-robot cooperation. In: Kirchner, F., Straube, S., Kühn, D., Hoyer, N. (eds.) AI Technology for Underwater Robots. ISCASE, vol. 96, pp. 183–193. Springer, Cham (2020). https://doi.org/10.1007/978-3-030-30683-0_16
16. Unreal Engine Website. https://www.unrealengine.com. Accessed 25 Mar 2021

Alleviate the Cybersickness in VR Teleoperation by Constructing the Reference Space in the Human-Machine Interface

Weiwei Jia[1], Xiaoling Li[1(✉)], Yueyang Shi[1], Shuai Zheng[2], Long Wang[1], Zhangyi Chen[1], and Lixia Zhang[1]

[1] School of Mechanical Engineering, Xi'an Jiaotong University, Xi'an, China
xjtulxl@mail.xjtu.edu.cn
[2] School of Software Engineering, Xi'an Jiaotong University, Xi'an, China

Abstract. The introduction of virtual reality into the teleoperation system can enhance the three-dimensional and immersive sense of visual feedback, but the serious cybersickness caused by it needs to be solved urgently. Scholars have proposed many methods proceed from the hardware or software aspect to alleviate cybersickness but increased the user's mental burden and physical exertion to some extent. Inspired by the static frame hypothesis (RFH), this research proposes a method to alleviate cybersickness by rendering virtual reference space in the virtual environment. This method aims to build a three-dimensional reference space through the rendering plane to help users establish a stable feeling on the ground of the real environment in the virtual environment, thereby alleviating cybersickness. The experiment results show that rendering the reference space in a virtual teleoperation environment can significantly alleviate the cybersickness. Specifically, the total cybersickness score (TS) of participants in the virtual environment with a reference space was significantly lower than that of a virtual environment without a reference space (0.023*), a decrease of 9%. Among them, the SSQ-D score of participants in the virtual environment with a reference space is significantly lower than the virtual environment without reference space ($p < 0.001***$), which is reduced by 19.7%.

Keywords: Teleoperation · Cybersickness · Reference space · Simulator Sickness Questionnaire (SSQ)

1 Introduction

Virtual reality (VR), is introduced into the teleoperation system to provide the operator with stereoscopic visual feedback to enhance the sense of immersion when performing tasks. With the widespread application of VR, the long-standing VR sickness problem has become more and more important [1]. Research reports have shown that in the process of experiencing VR, about 20% to 80% of participants encounter VR sickness including general discomfort, dizziness, nausea, disorientation, oculomotor, and other symptoms [2], this sickness is also called cybersickness (CS) [3]. There are currently

© Springer Nature Switzerland AG 2021
C. Stephanidis et al. (Eds.): HCII 2021, CCIS 1498, pp. 332–340, 2021.
https://doi.org/10.1007/978-3-030-90176-9_43

two mainstream theories about the etiology of CS: sensory conflict theory believes that CS is caused by the signals received by the visual and vestibular organs not necessarily causing conflict. This theory is the most common explanation of the CS [4], the postural instability theory believes that CS is caused by the individual's long-term loss of the ability to maintain and control their postural stability [5]. Around the above two theories, many scholars have made great efforts to alleviate the CS. Harvey Cash et al. try to find the best way to display stereoscopic images on VR head-mounted displays (HMD) [6, 7]. Israel Becerra et al. studied how to use trajectory planning based on human perception optimization in telepresence robots to improve the symptom of CS [8]. Kyungmin Lim et al. proposed a method of modifying the image FOV in VR based on the dynamic FOV processing to reduce the CS [9]. Zekun Cao et al. found that by rendering static or dynamic fixed visual content, CS can also be reduced [10]. Yasin Farmani et al. evaluated the effect of discrete viewpoint control in reducing the CS [11]. In addition, Da-Chung Yi et al. and others have compensated for the signal conflict between vision and vestibular organs through tactile or force feedback devices, thus ensuring the immersion [12]. However, these method increased the user's mental burden and physical exertion to some extent.

Another theory of CS is the reference frame hypothesis, which focuses on the role of reference objects when people perceive real space. This theory has been verified in some projection systems and is rarely used in VR environments. Professor David Whittinghill from the Purdue University rendered the image of the virtual human nose to the center of the VR video, which significantly reduced the discomfort caused by CS [13]. JJ-W Lin et al. have also been proven to effectively relieve the CS by rendering a fixed visual background separately as a reference, but it did not involve the exploration and application of the static frame hypothesis in the VR environment [14]. In VR teleoperation tasks, the degree of CS is often more serious due to the longer exposure time. The methods proposed by researchers based on the first two mainstream theories often increased the user's mental burden and physical exertion to some extent. Inspired by the reference frame hypothesis and based on previous work, we propose a new method for VR teleoperation system that can alleviate the CS, by rendering a reference space, it helps users in a virtual environment perceive the direction and feel standing in the real word and effectively relieve the CS.

2 Materials and Methods

2.1 Participants

25 young people (11 females, 14 males) aged between 20 and 30 (mean: 23.72, standard deviation: 2.25) volunteered to participated in this study. All of them come from the School of Mechanical Engineering, Xi'an Jiaotong University. All participants are in good health, have a normal vision or has been corrected, have no diseases related to vision and vestibular dysfunction, and are unfamiliar with the purpose and principles of the experiment. All participants gave written informed consent.

2.2 Apparatus

In this experiment, we used the ZED mini binocular camera (stereolabs) to capture images of the teleoperation environment. At the same time, we use the HTC VIVE Pro VR HMD (Taiwan, HTC company) connected to a personal computer. Through the Unity 3D development platform, the three-dimensional environment content captured by the ZED camera is created and rendered in real-time at a frequency of 90 Hz. As shown in Fig. 1, we connected the ZED binocular camera and HTC VIVE VR HMD to a computer and placed the binocular camera away from the participants through a 3 m long USB cable, and the collected real-time stereoscopic images are rendered to the VR environment to generate a virtual teleoperation environment for the subjects.

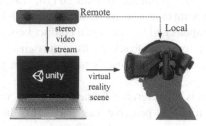

Fig. 1. Connection diagram of experimental equipment

2.3 VR Environments Construction

To alleviate the participants'CS in the VR environment, a static three-dimensional reference space was established for the virtual plane for rendering the binocular image captured by the camera so that the participants feel that they are also rendered into the virtual space. The largest virtual plane in the center rendered the binocular images captured by the remote ZED binocular camera to form stereo vision. As shown in the Fig. 2, the three planes adjacent to the largest virtual plane in the center were used to render the three-dimensional virtual wall of the participant's left and right perspectives and the ground plane of the top-down angle to provide the participant with a static reference frame. The plane content of the rendered binoculars was synchronized with the movement of the binocular camera in the remote real space, but the plane of the rendering reference space was fixed after the entire VR virtual environment is set, and will not change with the movement of any camera.

2.4 Experiment Design

This paper employed a comparative experiment design to study the effects of the reference space in VR teleoperation on the CS in humans. Before the start of the experiment, a researcher measured the inter-pupillary distances (IPD) data of each subject using a millimeter scale, then the facilitator helped the subjects adjust the IPD data to achieve the best stereo viewing effect. Once completed, the researchers began to perform Experiment 1, in which subjects watched the VR environment without a reference space for

Fig. 2. VR environment design with a fixed reference space

5 min. Then perform the Experiment 2, in which subjects watched the VR environment with a reference space. To ensure that the CS symptoms produced by the Experiment 1 would not be left in the Experiment 2 so that influences its results, the interval between each experiment of the subjects was 10 min rest. At the end of each experiment, subjects were asked to take off the VR helmets immediately and fill out the SSQ questionnaire. Finally we collected all participants' SSQ questionnaires for calculation and analysis. Figure 3 shows the details of experimental procedure of this study. The VR scene was collected at a fixed speed in a 2 m × 2 m area and following a fixed trajectory by the researcher controlling a remote control car carrying the ZED camera.

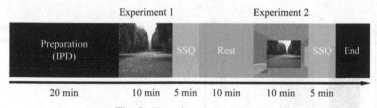

Fig. 3. Experimental procedure

2.5 Measures and Analysis Methods

We use the SSQ [26] to make a subjective assessment of their CS. SSQ mainly includes 16 symptoms for three subscores. Each symptom was divided into four-point scales: none (0), slight (1), moderate (2) and severe (3). Through adding the score of symptoms related to the nausea, oculomotor, and disorientation, we obtained the total score of the nausea (SSQ-N), oculomotor (SSQ-O), and disorientation (SSQ-D). Given the rather small sample size and the accompanying non-normal data distribution, the Wilcoxon signed-rank test method was performed to obtain the median, Z and correlation coefficient p to test whether there was a significant difference between the two matching samples. When the test result showed significance of difference, it was labeled as $* p < 0.05$, $** p < 0.01$, $*** p < 0.001$.

3 Results

The means and standard deviations of all data in each VR environment conditions are provided in Table 1.

Table 1. Characteristics of the study data for all participants

Characteristic	Experiment 1 (without reference)			Experiment 2 (with reference)		
	Mean	SD	N	Mean	SD	N
Total score	214.29	31.98	25	194.71	44.22	25
SSQ-Nausea	39.30	6.92	25	37.02	7.45	25
SSQ-Oculomotor	46.39	7.99	25	45.18	11.68	25
SSQ-Disorientation	70.71	12.00	25	56.79	16.03	25
Total score	214.29	31.98	25	194.71	44.22	25

The results of the TS are shown in Fig. 4. Subjects in the VR teleoperation environment showed a dramatically lower score of TS when rendering the reference (median = 181.84) space than no reference space (median = 223.80). Moreover, there was a significant difference in the TS under the two VR experiment conditions ($Z = 2.27$, p = $0.023 < 0.05$). Specifically, the internal comparison results of subjects showed that 76% (19 subjects) of all subjects' TS after Experiment 2 (with reference) were lower than or equal to Experiment 1 (without reference), which is shown in Fig. 5.

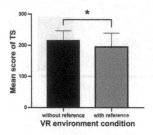

Fig. 4. Mean scores of TS

Fig. 5. Comparison of TS scores

The results of the SSQ-N are shown in Fig. 6. Subjects in the VR teleoperation environment showed a slightly lower score of SSQ-N when rendering the reference space (median = 38.16) than no reference space (median = 42.93). However, there was no significant difference in the SSQ-N under the two VR experiment conditions ($Z = 1.43$, p = $0.153 > 0.05$). Specifically, the internal comparison results of subjects showed that 68% (17 subjects) of all subjects' SSQ-N after Experiment 2 (with reference) were equal to or higher than Experiment 1 (without reference), which is shown in Fig. 7.

The results of the SSQ-O are shown in Fig. 8. Subjects in the VR teleoperation environment showed an equal score of SSQ-O when rendering the reference space (median = 38.16) than no reference space (median = 38.16). Therefore, there was no significant difference in the SSQ-O under the two VR experiment conditions, which was further proved by the Wilcoxon test results ($Z = 1.43$, p = $0.153 > 0.05$). Specifically, the internal comparison results of subjects showed that 56% (14 subjects) of all subjects'

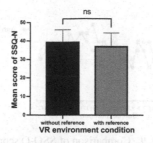

Fig. 6. Mean scores of SSQ-N

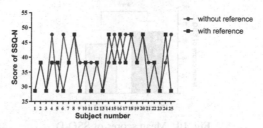

Fig. 7. Comparison of SSQ-N scores

SSQ-O after Experiment 2 (with reference) were equal to or higher than Experiment 1 (without reference), which is shown in Fig. 9.

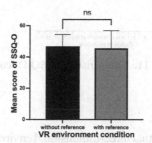

Fig. 8. Mean scores of SSQ-O

The results of the SSQ-D are shown in Fig. 10. Subjects in the VR teleoperation environment showed a dramatically lower score of SSQ-D when rendering the reference space (median = 55.68) than no reference space (median = 69.6). Moreover, there was a significant difference in the SSQ-D under the two VR experiment conditions, which was further proved by the Wilcoxon test results ($Z = 3.39$, $p = 0.0003 << 0.05$). Specifically, the internal comparison results of subjects showed that 92% (23 subjects) of all subjects' SSQ-D after Experiment 2 (with reference) were lower than or equal to Experiment 1 (without reference), which is shown in Fig. 11.

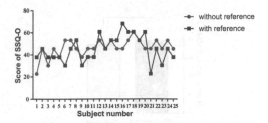

Fig. 9. Comparison of SSQ-O scores

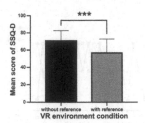

Fig. 10. Mean scores of SSQ-D

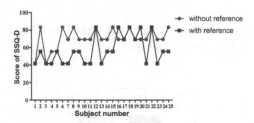

Fig. 11. Comparison of SSQ-D scores

4 Discussion

In this study, we rendered a virtual three-dimensional environment with a reference space based on a typical robot teleoperation scene, and compared the CS of VR environment with or without a reference space through the SSQ scale method. Compared with the VR environment without reference space, participants experience less CS after experiencing the VR environment with reference space, which proves that the CS of participants in teleoperation can be alleviated by rendering the reference space in the VR environment.

The degree of disorientation of participants in a VR environment with reference space is significantly less than that of participants in a VR environment without reference space, which also proves that the reference space can alleviate the disorientation by providing participants with a known reference direction and the effectiveness of this method. On the contrary, in terms of nausea and oculomotor, there is no significant difference in the SSQ scores of the participants in the VR environment with or without reference space, although the median of SSQ-N scores and SSQ-O scores in the VR environment with reference space was slightly lower than that in the VR without reference space. Therefore, we believe that the method of rendering the reference space has no significant effect on alleviating nausea and oculomotor of the participants after experiencing VR.

The advantage of this study is that the proposed CS mitigation method is inspired by human natural living habits, and the method is simple and effective. Furthermore, we can more accurately and effectively reflect the effectiveness of mitigation methods by performing the experimental environment with reference space after the experimental environment without reference space. However, we have not conducted an experimental comparison of the immersion and participation of participants in VR teleoperation environments with or without rendering space. Previous studies have shown that rendering a fixed visual background or reference frame to alleviate CS will sacrifice immersion and participation. Future research should include analysis of participants' immersion and participation, and make a better balance between immersion and the degree of CS by changing software or VR applications.

5 Conclusion

Research on VR environment construction methods to alleviate CS is of great significance to the application of VR in various human-computer interaction fields. In this research, experiments were conducted to study the mitigation effect on CS of the operator in the VR interactive teleoperation system in the reference space. Experimental results show that by rendering a fixed reference space in the virtual environment of VR teleoperation, the symptoms of CS caused by VR can be effectively alleviated, and the method has a prominent effect in alleviating disorientation. However, the method proposed in this article has less relief in nausea and eye movement, and more in-depth research on these two aspects is needed in the future.

Acknowledgments. This work is supported by the International Joint Research Center for Digital Medical Devices and Instruments.

References

1. Davis, S., Nesbitt, K., Nalivaiko, E.: A systematic review of cybersickness. In: Proceedings of the 2014 Conference on Interactive Entertainment (IE2014), pp. 1–9. Association for Computing Machinery, New York (2014)
2. Gallagher, M., Ferrè, E.R.: Cybersickness: a multisensory integration perspective. Multisens. Res. **31**(7), 645–674 (2018)
3. Palmisano, S., Mursic, R., Kim, J.: Vection and cybersickness generated by head-and-display motion in the oculus rift. Displays **46**, 1–8 (2017)
4. Johnson, D.M.: U.S. Army Research Institute for the Behavioral and Social Sciences, Fort Rucker (2005)
5. Stoffregen, T.A., Smart, L.J.: Postural instability precedes motion sickness. Brain Res. Bull. **47**(5), 437–448 (1998)
6. Cash, H., Prescott, T.J.: Improving the visual comfort of virtual reality telepresence for robotics. In: Salichs, M.A., et al. (eds.) ICSR 2019. LNCS (LNAI), vol. 11876, pp. 697–706. Springer, Cham (2019). https://doi.org/10.1007/978-3-030-35888-4_65

7. Mizukoshi, Y., et al.: A low cognitive load and reduced motion sickness inducing zoom method based on typical gaze movement for master-slave teleoperation systems with HMD. In: 2020 IEEE/SICE International Symposium on System Integration (SII), Honolulu, HI, USA, pp. 28–33. IEEE (2020)

8. Becerra, I., Suomalainen, M., Lozano, E., et al.: Human perception-optimized planning for comfortable VR-based telepresence. IEEE Robot. Autom. Lett. **5**(4), 6489–6496 (2020)

9. Lim, K., Lee, J., Won, K., et al.: A novel method for VR sickness reduction based on dynamic field of view processing. Virtual Reality **25**, 331–340 (2021)

10. Cao, Z., Jerald, J., Kopper, R.: Visually-induced motion sickness reduction via static and dynamic rest frames. In: 2018 IEEE Conference on Virtual Reality and 3D User Interfaces (VR), Tuebingen/Reutlingen, Germany, pp. 105–112. IEEE (2018)

11. Farmani, Y., Teather, R.J.: Evaluating discrete viewpoint control to reduce cybersickness in virtual reality. Virtual Reality **24**, 645–664 (2020)

12. Yi, D., Chang, K., Tai, Y, Chen, I., Hung, Y.: Elastic-move: passive force feedback devices for virtual reality locomotion. In: 2020 IEEE Conference on Virtual Reality and 3D User Interfaces Abstracts and Workshops (VRW), Atlanta, GA, USA, pp. 766–767. IEEE (2020)

13. Wittinghinll, D.M., Ziegler, B., Moore, J., Case, T.: Nasum virtualis: a simple technique for reducing simulator sickness. In: Game Developers Conference (2015)

14. Lin, J.J.-W., Abi-Rached, H., Kim, D.-H., Parker, D.E., Furness, T.A.: A "natural" independent visual background reduced simulator sickness. In: Proceedings of the Human Factors and Ergonomics Society Annual Meeting, pp. 2124–2128 (2002)

Translating Virtual Reality Research into Practice as a Way to Combat Misinformation: The DOVE Website

Chidinma U. Kalu(✉)(iD), Stephen B. Gilbert(✉)(iD), Jonathan W. Kelly(✉)(iD), and Melynda Hoover(iD)

Iowa State University, Ames, IA 50011, USA
{kalu,gilbert,jonkelly,mthoover}@iastate.edu

Abstract. There are several barriers to research translation from academia to the broader HCI/UX community and specifically for the design of virtual reality applications. Because of the inaccessibility of evidence-based VR research to industry practitioners, freely-available blog-style media on platforms like Medium, where there is no moderation, is more available, leading to the spread of misinformation. The Design of Virtual Environments (DOVE) website, attempts to address this challenge by offering peer reviewed unbiased VR research, translating it for the layperson, and opening it up to contribution, synthesis and discussion through forums. This paper describes the initial user centered design process for the DOVE website through informal expert interviews, competitive analysis and heuristic review to redesign the site navigation, translation content, and incentivized forms for submission of research. When completed, the DOVE website will aid the translation of AR/VR research to practice.

Keywords: Research translation · Virtual reality · Misinformation

1 Introduction

The challenge of translating academic research about VR to industry best practices is a part of the overall challenge of translating HCI research to the UX (User Experience) industry. The transfer of knowledge from theory to practice can be a tedious process that requires iteration and faces resistance because it requires collaboration from among stakeholders who may be required to adapt as context and tools change. A three-sided relationship between researchers, educators, and practitioners is the most critical requirement for knowledge translation [1]. In the medical field, this is a major challenge; the adoption of clinical practice guidelines (evidence-based medical techniques) into actual practice has been severely lacking [3].

There are several barriers to this translation. First, academic research often uses highly specialized language and formatting that may be unfamiliar to industry readers, even in the same work area. For example, only 7% of CHI 2011

© Springer Nature Switzerland AG 2021
C. Stephanidis et al. (Eds.): HCII 2021, CCIS 1498, pp. 341–348, 2021.
https://doi.org/10.1007/978-3-030-90176-9_44

papers were formatted to support design practice [2]. Second, the storyline or process of academic work often unfolds over multiple years, a much slower pace than in industry, making it difficult for industry practitioners to follow the academic story closely. This slower pace can be partially explained by challenges in university patent processes [6], but it nevertheless creates a gap. Third, academic research results often provide narrow, specific contributions to knowledge that may not be immediately generalizable to the practitioner's problem being solved today. Without a large frame of reference over multiple years, it can be difficult for the practitioner to assemble the relevant contributions to knowledge into something usable. Lastly, academic research is often held behind paywalls that place barriers between practitioners and researchers. The open-access movement is helping reduce these barriers [4]. However, the large profit margins of the academic publishing industry [2] will continue to pose a challenge to knowledge translation. Academic journals have a high bar to entry. All papers must be peer-reviewed and edited and few papers will make it to publishing. These protocols, although necessary, create a challenge for the rapid dissemination of research results in the UX community. As a result, evidence-based research is pitted against a variety of freely written media articles on platforms like Medium where there is no moderation, raising the potential for the spread of misinformation. The challenge of misinformation is significant enough that researchers have offered specific cognitive tools to enhance people's digital agency by boosting reasoning and resilience against manipulation by the media [8].

One example of successful research-to-practice translation is the user-centered design process and concept of usability. The user-centered design process, made famous by Don Norman and Stephen Draper in 1986 [9], has made its way into popular culture and is being adopted by the more extensive industry professionals and studied by those looking to join the craft [12]. But industry practitioners would like to find strong results sooner than waiting 30+ years. Research on the best practices for virtual environment (VE) design faces this translation challenge. While virtual reality (VR) work began in the 1960s, it has grown significantly since the introduction of the consumer grade Oculus headset in 2016 and VE freely available authoring tools such as Blender, Unity, and Unreal Engine. While the number of VEs and 3D games has grown, there is not a strong consensus of how best to design the VE experience. The "Locomotion Vault" [5], for example, documents over 100 user interface methods of simply moving within a VE. Whereas guidelines for 2D user interfaces such as mobile apps and websites are more mature, e.g., Google Material and Tidwell et al.'s design patterns [11], they do not translate easily into design guidelines for 3D virtual environments (VEs).

2   Translating VR Research into Practice: Goals for the DOVE Website

The Design of Virtual Environments (DOVE) website was envisioned to fill this gap by being an open-source unified reference that describes how VR research results lead to practical VE design advice. DOVE was intended to be a Wikipedia-style moderated site for evidence-based results of VR research contributed by the broader R&D community. The authors will create the initial structure for the DOVE site and populate it with content based on an initial literature review of VE research and the results of the proposed studies, including available code and 3D assets. One particular goal is to offer benchmarks for assessing the usability of VEs. The Oculus Developer Guide, a website for consumers and developers of VR software, provides similar design advice to what DOVE aspires to, but Oculus does not ground the advice in research. In the DOVE website we hope to extend the research gatekeeper model by offering peer reviewed unbiased VR research, translating it for the layperson, and opening it up to contribution, synthesis and discussion through forums. Eventually, the authors hope to attract broad industry and academic interest that will sustain such a site and eventually provide industry partnership.

3   Approach

The tool's software development process follows the interaction design method [7]. First, an effort was made to understand where industry VR practitioners currently get design information. By speaking initially with VR stakeholders we learned about popular self-help guides from conferences, podcasts, YouTube videos, Medium articles and UX organizational websites demonstrating how to design virtual environments. These serve as competing sources of design advice, which may or may not be grounded in rigorous research.

We then discussed the vision for DOVE with several researchers. It seems that convincing researchers to submit a layperson-translation of their research could prove to be a challenge. Based on the standard academic publishing model (which is admittedly evolving through a growing use of preprints [10]), researchers may be wary of publishing their research in layperson form. As a result, one challenge of the DOVE website was to look and feel like a credible source of evidence-based information. The second challenge was motivating and guiding the researcher in converting their academic writing into simple, easy-to-read, and applied language. To measure our team's success in addressing these challenges, the authors are establishing benchmarks based on the style of writing, and the ease of use of the DOVE website for its key stakeholders.

Initially, undergraduate colleagues implemented a framework and foundation for the DOVE website using UX techniques such as wire-framing, heuristic analysis, and user journey mapping (see Fig. 1) and the Wordpress content management system. The DOVE website aims to cover VR topics such as locomotion, 3D object interaction, presence, and VR menu design. Although the undergraduate researchers had laid the foundations for the knowledge translation for the DOVE website, it was still missing actual content contributed by researchers. It did contain one page of content regarding VR location to facilitate further feedback.

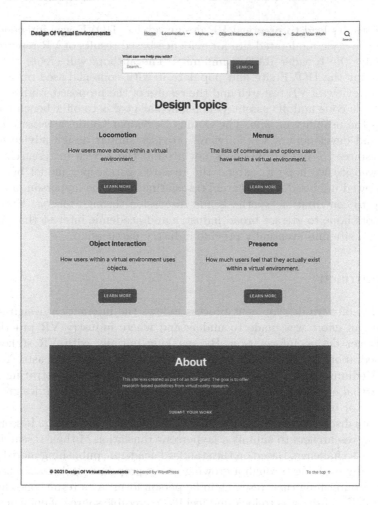

Fig. 1. First prototype of the DOVE website.

The first prototype was then reviewed with the authors and their students using a heuristic analysis. While this initial feedback was useful, it was imperative to broaden the participant pool to include a diverse group of stakeholders including website consumers and contributors. The assumption was that there are three kinds of stakeholders with three main tasks flows on the website:

– The designer: The designer will use the DOVE website as a guideline to determine the appropriate way to develop VE interactions. The designer builds 3D models, characters, and user interfaces to create an appropriate virtual environment.
– The developer: The developers will also use DOVE best practices to collaborate with designers, as well as the development platform (e.g., Unity or Unreal Engine) to build the functionality of VEs.

– The researcher: Academic researchers will use DOVE as a preliminary research source to understand topics and concepts surrounding the virtual environment. Also, expert researchers will be contributing their peer-reviewed academic research to be easily applicable for the prospective designer and researcher.

Using affinity mapping software called Miro, we could gather some initial pilot feedback on the first DOVE prototype's web page regarding best design practices on teleport locomotion (Fig. 2).

Initial informal pilot interviews with several stakeholders of each type suggested that the following themes will be important in future design iterations.

– Create a better way to submit research articles.
– Link the best practices into different pages.
– Improve discoverability - How will DOVE be found? What search terms will be used?
– Create a template with an improved information architecture to break research synthesis into digestible pieces.
– Identify VR usability testing results from the past.
– Make it clear how researchers can submit their work and rate the information they find.

The interviews also suggested that the list of stakeholder users for DOVE might differ from what was assumed. Rather than designer, developer, and researcher, a better list of stakeholders might be expert researchers, novice researchers (e.g., students), artifact designers, VR developers/designers, and product managers. In a future investigation, detailed feedback will be categorized into focus areas around navigation, content, and forms. The broader feedback will be prioritized into critical, medium, and low priority areas.

Based on the initial feedback, we were able to create an initial redesign (Fig. 3). We will focus on collecting research articles to populate and eventually publish DOVE v1.0. Therefore, we will design the submission process in a way that encourages expert researchers to submit their work and minimizes the burden of ownership for the moderators of the site.

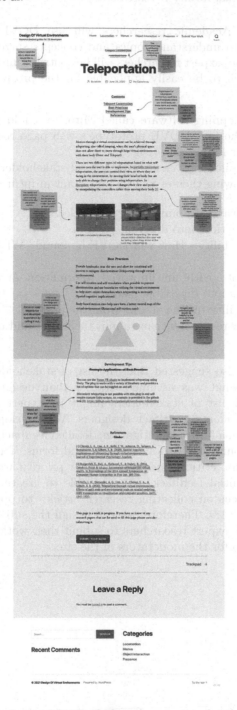

Fig. 2. A screenshot of using Miro to explore the process of gathering initial feedback on the contents page's interface design.

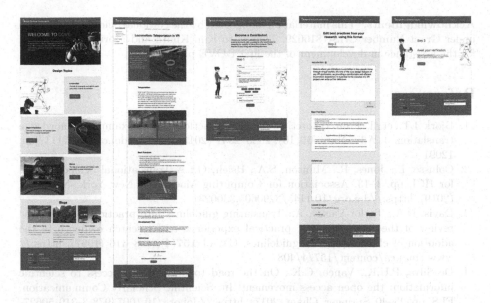

Fig. 3. A screenshot of the DOVE interface redesign based on feedback.

4   Conclusion

Our solution could be a great first step in the direction of translating research into practice. The literature review has provided some more examples of ways to adequately transform VR research into best practices. We hope to implement these changes and discover a way to test if the existence of such a site would help curtail misinformation. We conclude that translating research, although tedious, is achievable and relevant for the Design of Virtual Environments. The literature review has shown that the steps we have taken thus far are valid and could use some more iterative human-centered design methods. It also solidifies the need for collaboration of the broader HCI community, including industrial designers and usability engineering teams in fast-paced and competitive industries, to start adopting evidence-based research.

5   Future Work

After the full iteration and launching of the new DOVE website, the content format will be tested again for clarity. The DOVE initiative will also be promoted at academic conferences like IEEEVR, ACM and CHI to boost further collaboration. Once we have a good start at covering design-research translation in VR, the site could expand to encompass research for the design of augmented reality interfaces.

Acknowledgments. This material was supported by the National Science Foundation under Grant Number CHS-1816029. Thanks to Kim Knuth and Moriah Zimmerman for the assistance in development of the first DOVE prototype.

References

1. Bjørk, I.T., et al.: From theoretical model to practical use: an example of knowledge translation. J. Adv. Nurs. **69**(10), 2336–2347 (2013). https://doi.org/10.1111/jan.12091
2. Colusso, L., Jones, R., Munson, S.A., Hsieh, G.: A Translational Science Model for HCI, pp. 1–13. Association for Computing Machinery, New York, NY, USA (2019). https://doi.org/10.1145/3290605.3300231
3. Davis, D.A., Taylor-Vaisey, A.: Translating guidelines into practice: a systematic review of theoretic concepts, practical experience and research evidence in the adoption of clinical practice guidelines. CMAJ **157**(4), 408–416 (1997). https://www.cmaj.ca/content/157/4/408
4. De Silva, P.U.K., Vance, C.K.: On the road to unrestricted access to scientific information: the open access movement. In: Scientific Scholarly Communication. FLS, pp. 25–40. Springer, Cham (2017). https://doi.org/10.1007/978-3-319-50627-2_3
5. Di Luca, M., Seifi, H., Egan, S., Gonzalez-Franco, M.: Locomotion vault: The extra mile in analyzing VR locomotion techniques. Association for Computing Machinery, New York, NY, USA (2021). https://doi.org/10.1145/3411764.3445319
6. Fabrizio, K.R.: University patenting and the pace of industrial innovation. Ind. Corporate Change **16**(4), 505–534 (2007). https://doi.org/10.1093/icc/dtm016
7. Kolko, J.: Thoughts on Interaction Design. Morgan Kaufmann, Burlington (2010)
8. Kozyreva, A., Lewandowsky, S., Hertwig, R.: Citizens versus the internet: confronting digital challenges with cognitive tools. Psychol. Sci. Public Interest **21**(3), 103–156 (2020). https://doi.org/10.1177/1529100620946707, pMID: 33325331
9. Norman, D.A., Draper, S.W.: User Centered System Design. New Perspectives on Human-Computer Interaction. L. Erlbaum Associates Inc., Mahwah (1986)
10. Sarabipour, S., Debat, H.J., Emmott, E., Burgess, S.J., Schwessinger, B., Hensel, Z.: On the value of preprints: an early career researcher perspective. PLoS Biol. **17**, e3000151 (2019). https://doi.org/10.1371/journal.pbio.3000151
11. Tidwell, J., Brewer, C., Valencia, A.: Designing Interfaces. O'Reilly Media Inc., Newton (2020)
12. Velt, R., Benford, S., Reeves, S.: Translations and boundaries in the gap between HCI theory and design practice. ACM Trans. Comput. Hum. Interaction **27**(4), 1–28 (2020). https://doi.org/10.1145/3386247

Software Usability Evaluation for Augmented Reality Through User Tests

Guto Kawakami[1], Aasim Khurshid[2(✉)], and Mikhail R. Gadelha[3]

[1] Bemol, Manaus, Brazil
[2] Sidia Institute of Science and Technology, Manaus, Brazil
aasim.khurshid@sidia.com
[3] Igalia, A Coruña, Spain
mikhail@igalia.com

Abstract. Augmented Reality (AR) is becoming increasingly prominent in the market and society because it is a technology that provides new forms of interaction to users, and thus new experiences. However, with the advancement of AR interfaces, methods for assessing the usability of traditional (2D) software need to adapt to become effective when applied to software for 3D environments. This research aims to present an experimental study where tests were carried out with users to measure the usability of software for Augmented Reality glasses. Moreover, we model testing methodology to conduct user-based tests and propose improvements for software testing to evaluate 3D interfaces based on our experiments.

Keywords: Usability · Augmented reality · Human computer interaction · User testing

1 Introduction

Technology has become an integral part of our daily life. Most of the activities that were only possible in the past by leaving our houses, can now be carried out through applications embedded in smartphones. However, to make such relevant applications, the ease of use of these applications is one of the most important aspect of its usability [6], Therefore, it is essential to take great care to achieve good quality in the development of software products services and experiences.

Recently, Augmented Reality (AR) has gathered a lot of attention from the research community [1], due to its advanced computational interface, which allows the user to see the real world, with virtual objects superimposed upon the real world. This approach allows new form of user interaction and has been explored by several companies such as Apple, Google, and Microsoft through their products such as smartphones and wearable devices (glasses).

This work is partially supported by Sidia institute of science and technology, and Samsung Eletrônica da Amazônia Ltda, under the auspice of the Brazilian informatics law no 8.387/91.

© Springer Nature Switzerland AG 2021
C. Stephanidis et al. (Eds.): HCII 2021, CCIS 1498, pp. 349–356, 2021.
https://doi.org/10.1007/978-3-030-90176-9_45

In order to ensure the usability of applications in augmented reality, a series of guidelines have been created, since the cost of failure of improperly designed AR applications can be significant, resulting in loss of awareness of the situation, cognitive overload, interruption of workflows, leading to poor performance, and higher levels of human error [2].

In this context, we sought to evaluate the usability issue of an augmented reality **internet explorer software** implemented for Microsoft Hololens glasses[1]. The issues were pointed out through user tests to improve the quality of the tested application. Furthermore, efficient practices for conducting tests with users are explored for Head Mounted Display (HMD) devices.

The rest of the paper is organized as follows: the proposed methodology for software usability evaluation is detailed in Sect. 2, followed by experimental results in Sect. 3. Finally, Sect. 4 provides conclusions and some insights to the future work.

2   Methodology

In this work, the user testing approach is to measure the usability of an application. This decision was supported by the fact that part of the software is developed and ready to use. Also, this analysis may improve the software in the upcoming version.

2.1   AR Internet Browser

Figure 1 shows an internet browser for Microsoft Hololens AR glasses to validate interaction concepts for 3D environments. This browser allows the user to perform a series of tasks such as: navigating between internet pages, interacting with the page using a virtual keyboard, moving and resizing pages around the environment, closing, and minimizing pages, among other features that are possible to perform in one traditional internet browser.

2.2   Users Profiles

Defining the user's profile is the first thing to do to achieve the research objectives in Human-Computer-Interaction [3]. The definition of user-profiles of AR glasses is something intangible at the moment since a large part of the public that uses this equipment are developers and not end-users. In this case, it was defined that the test participants would be recruited through more generic variables, such as gender and experience with the platform.

Based on these criteria, two types of participant profiles were modeled: (Little Experienced) participants with little experience using HMD and (Experienced) participants with a long time of experience using HMD devices. The profile

---

[1] https://www.microsoft.com/en-us/hololens/hardware.

Fig. 1. AR internet browser (Home page).

being inexperienced, people who used HMD at least once in the last 6 months, and Experienced, people who usually use HMD more than once a month. We chose to recruit two types of profiles because it is understood that people with different profiles can provide more diverse opinions, which could contribute to the software.

2.3   Recruitment

To obtain participants with the two types of desired profiles, a questionnaire was prepared. The objective of this was to filter the profiles of the participants, helping selection for researchers. The questionnaire contained questions about the usage frequency of internet browsers, usage frequency of browser with HMD, contact details, and participation interest in the test.

The questionnaire was shared on social networks, was available for a week, and was designed on the Google Forms platform. In total, 116 responses were obtained, which were tabulated so that the researchers could select the candidates who best suited the desired profiles.

2.4   Usability Tests

This experimental study has two main objectives: (a) to evaluate the interface of an internet browser for HMD devices, and (b) identify good practices for carrying out usability tests in 3D environments. To achieve these objectives, usability tests were carried out with participants from two different profiles: Experienced and inexperienced with the use of HMD, through qualitative approaches it was possible to obtain their opinions and suggestions on the tested software.

The experience of carrying out the tests allowed us to observe each participant and understand some good practices for performing tests in 3D environments.

The tests were carried out with 14 participants, half of them belonging to the experienced profile and the other half to the less experienced. These participants were chosen through the analysis of their responses to the questionnaire, where the variables of gender and experience with the HMD platform were analyzed. Participants were contacted to set a date for holding the sections.

The division of the participants was essential for the planning of the tests since the participants with little experience of use would need special care, mainly to explain some native functions of the device, such as gestures and basic interactions. For the sessions, a facilitator participated, a person who would conduct the tests, two observers, who would be the ones who would take note of everything the participant would be doing and a person to control the infrastructure (room, cameras, and sound).

Materials and Procedures. Performing tests with users require equipment and an appropriate location, as the test performed would evaluate augmented reality software, the environment in which the user would perform interactions would be the 3D environment. In this context, access to two Microsoft Hololens glasses was obtained, a room with adequate space and equipment for testing in 3D environments, confidentiality terms, computers, cameras, and sound recorders were also provided.

Before starting the test, all participants signed a confidentiality term and authorized the use of their images for research purposes. Then, the participant was introduced with the project and questions were asked to validate the participant's profile. Then, the device was adjusted to start the software test sessions that lasted an average of one hour.

The script for carrying out the activities consisted of performing 11 tasks within the internet browser, 1) Open the internet browser by the application icon; 2) Opening a Facebook page in the browser; 3) Use the keyboard to enter a URL; 4) Move the page to another position; 5) Scale the page; 6) Close editing mode; 7) Open a new page; 8) Access the previous page; 9) Detach the page; 10) Close one of the pages; and 11) Minimize the application. As the tested software did not have any functionality over voice commands, the Thinking Aloud technique was used (think out loud). Then, every interaction that the participant performed, he described it out loud [5] so that it was possible to take notes.

The room where the tests were carried out contained an appropriate space so that the participant could move and interact with the elements of the 3D environment. The activities were carried out sequentially. After the end of the last activity, a post-test interview was conducted, to understand the degree of satisfaction of the participant with the internet browser. In this post-test session, the following questions were asked: 1) From 0 to 10, how satisfied are you with the application? Why? 2) What are the strengths and weaknesses that you highlight from the experience? 3) Was the feedback for creating a new page understandable? 4) Were you able to understand the difference between a group of pages and a single page alone? 5) Were the clickable areas comfortable for you? 6) Were you able to identify the difference between a favorites page and a recent page? 7) Was the navigation flow of the interface clear? 8 Were the editing mode interactions intuitive? All the responses were recorded for later analysis.

Data Collection. At the end of the sessions, materials were obtained from the tests, such as the signed confidentiality term, notes on the users' descriptions of the software while they were carrying out the tests, and their opinions after the experience. One of the authors acted as a moderator of the experimental study and was responsible for data tabulation, verification, and analysis of information. During the analysis, the moderator classified the issues pointed out by the participants as duplicates or not. In this context, duplicates are issues pointed out more than once in the same software by different users [6]. After this activity, the moderator generated a table that contained all the discrepancies but without duplicates. It is worth mentioning that if there was any doubt when judging whether a discrepancy was duplicate or not, this was resolved by consulting the other researchers involved in the study. In the end, a table was generated with all the problems pointed out by the participants about the internet browser.

After collecting and refining the gathered data, there was a meeting with 3 experienced researchers in usability. At this meeting, the classification of the tabled problems was carried out based on three factors: a) Frequency: how often the problem occurs; b) Impact: it will be easy or difficult for the user to overcome the problem and continue the experience; c) Persistence: it is a unique problem or it happens repeatedly. Finally, it is necessary to assess the impact of the problem on the market as certain usability problems can have a devastating effect on the product's popularity, even if they are easy to overcome [4]. Although gravity has several components, it is common to combine all aspects into a single severity classification as a general assessment of each usability problem, to facilitate prioritization and decision making. The severity rating of the problem was carried on scale of 0 to 4 for: i) I do not agree that it is a usability problem; ii) Cosmetic problem only: does not need to be corrected, unless extra time is available in the project; iii) Minor usability problem: fixing this should be given low priority; iv) Serious usability problem: important to correct, therefore high priority must be given; v) Usability catastrophe: it is imperative to correct this before the product can be launched.

The classification of the problems was carried out with 3 researchers to ensure rating quality which is satisfactory for practical purposes [4].

3   Experimental Evaluation

A qualitative analysis of the collected data was carried out, to better understand the users' opinions regarding the functionalities of the internet browser and satisfaction about the experience in general.

3.1   Qualitative Analysis

Table 1 presents the results of the usability problems pointed out by the users, by how many users the problem was pointed out, and user classification.

Table 1. Indicated usability problems.

Problem	Rating
Difficulty using the keyboard	3
Lack of visual feedback when opening a new window	2
Difficulty finding the page detach function	2
The editing mode actions are not intuitive and difficult to learn	3
Lack of tips and tutorials to assist in learning the software	2
Some classifications are not appropriate	1
The group of screens is confusing, and difficult to understand	3
The difference between the favorite pages and the most visited ones are unclear	2
Some icons are not intuitive	2
Frequently used options are not prominent	2

When comparing the notes on user satisfaction with the browser, the participants in the "less experienced" profile category is 7.5, while the experienced ones gave 6. One of the reasons for the less experienced users' rating to be higher is the innovation factor. Many of the participants were impacted by the technology and felt that it opens doors to new means of interaction. Although these users do not have as much contact with the technology, they managed to highlight what they liked, such as the feedback from clickable areas and the use of depth. Experienced users were punctual in saying that the use of the 2D mental model facilitated the learning of interactions in 3D environments.

Table 2. Indicated usability problems.

Positives	Negatives
The interface is similar to what you are used to, which facilitates learning	The visual feedback when creating a new page needs improvement. Also, it is not possible to clearly differentiate the windows in the navigation flow
Keyboard: shortcuts available like ".com" and ".net" help a lot	The editing mode is not intuitive, it is confused with moving the window in the menu of more options, the sizing was difficult
In the editing mode, the scale option is similar to that of editing software, facilitating handling	The 3D icon does not instantly communicate the intuition of the button, the fluctuation on the screen irritates users

As for the negative points, part of them is about the hardware, such as the limited field of view and physical tiredness due to the weight of the equipment. Some features were also criticized by both profiles, such as the editing mode, the keyboard, some visual feedbacks, and icons that are not intuitive.

However, the survey of the positive and negative points of the participants' experience and the analysis of usability problems provide arguments for modifying parts of the software interface. Therefore, proving the need for research even on the early level of AR adoption from the market and society to foreshadow future test practices and experiment layout.

3.2 Recommended Practices

Based on the observation made through the tests, the qualitative analysis regarding user satisfaction, and the theoretical understanding of usability assessments, we achieved a set of good practices for usability testing in 3D environments:

1. It is necessary a place with adequate space for the user to walk and interact with the elements of the interface;
2. Care must be taken when defining the test script so that there are no conflicts between the system and the activity;
3. If you choose not to use the Thinking Aloud technique (think out loud), appropriate software is required to view user interactions in real-time;
4. Take care that the software interactions do not cause motion sickness in the participants;

It is understood that a good part of the usability evaluation methods for traditional models is maintained when used in 3D models. However, since the interaction environment is different, adaptation to the context of use is needed.

4 Conclusions and Future Work

In this article, user tests were carried out to measure the usability of an internet browser for Microsoft Hololens glasses. Through the questionnaires, it was possible to recruit participants according to the established profiles. The tests provided inputs for conducting a qualitative analysis that resulted in a table of usability problems and their classifications. The analysis also made it possible to understand the participants' satisfaction with the experience provided by the software and the understanding of good practices for usability tests for 3D environments.

As future work, it is intended to make changes to the browser interface based on the problems encountered. It is also necessary to conduct idea development sessions for the emergence of new approaches to some criticized features. Finally, this study is expected to contribute to the academy and the market with new models for usability assessments and allow discussion over its good practices.

References

1. Azuma, R.T.: A survey of augmented reality. Presence Teleoperators Virtual Environ. **6**(4), 355–385 (1997)
2. Endsley, T., Sprehn, K., Brill, R., Ryan, K., Vincent, E., Martin, J.: Augmented reality design heuristics: designing for dynamic interactions. In: Proceedings of the Human Factors and Ergonomics Society Annual Meeting, vol. 61, pp. 2100–2104 (2017)
3. Mayhew, D.J.: The Usability Engineering Lifecycle: A Practitioner's Handbook for User Interface Design, 1st edn. Morgan Kaufmann Publishers Inc., Burlington (1999)
4. Nielsen, J.: Severity ratings for usability problems. In: Papers and Essays, vol. 54, pp. 1–2 (1995)
5. Nielsen, J., Yssing, C.: Getting access to what goes on in people's heads?: reflections on the think-aloud technique. In: Proceedings of the Second Nordic Conference on Human-Computer Interaction, vol. 31, pp. 101–110 (2002)
6. Rivero, L., Kawakami, G., Conte, T.: Using a controlled experiment to evaluate usability inspection technologies for improving the quality of mobile web applications earlier in their design. In: 2014 Brazilian Symposium on Software Engineering, pp. 161–170 (2014)

Virtual Reality to Mixed Reality Graphic Conversion in Unity
Preliminary Guidelines and Graphic User Interface

Ramy Kirollos[1](✉) and Martin Harriott[1,2]

[1] Defence Research and Development Canada, Toronto Research Centre, 1133 Sheppard Avenue W, Toronto, ON M3K 2C9, Canada
ramy.kirollos@drdc-rddc.gc.ca

[2] York University, Keele Campus, 4700 Keele Street, Toronto, ON M3J 1P3, Canada

Abstract. To date in the defence industry, virtual reality (VR) headsets are used primarily for training and simulation, while mixed reality (MR) headsets can be used in military operations. However, technological hardware advancements that blend VR and MR headset capabilities will result in increasing convergence of VR and MR applications. Accordingly, our primary objective in the current work was to present guidelines for Unity developers to convert graphical VR content to MR content in the Unity game engine. Guidelines herein address how to change camera settings to adapt from VR to MR applications, how to convert graphical user interfaces (GUIs) from VR to MR, and how to place graphical objects in MR environments. Another important objective of this work was to describe a user-controlled GUI we developed that allows real-time, progressive conversion of graphics from full VR to various levels of MR in a MR headset. This GUI provides end-users flexibility to customize their environment for gaming, training, and operational applications along an extended reality spectrum. In our future work, we are developing a tool that automates the VR to MR graphic conversion process. This tool, the guidelines, and the GUI will help researchers compare different levels of graphic content displayed in the scene and investigate the user-centered challenges that arise. It will also help Unity developers in defence, gaming, and commercial industries generate a scene in VR and quickly convert it to MR, saving the cost associated with generating separate MR scenes from scratch for multiple applications.

Keywords: Virtual reality headsets · Mixed reality headsets · Graphic conversion software · Graphic user interface · Extended reality · Training · Simulation

1 Introduction

Mixed reality (MR) and virtual reality (VR) are perceived as distinct capabilities in the defence industry. But as these technologies and the software that support them develop, the characteristics separating VR from MR headsets will diminish. To date, VR headsets are a more mature technology, more rigorously studied and more widely used than MR

© Her Majesty the Queen in Right of Canada 2021
C. Stephanidis et al. (Eds.): HCII 2021, CCIS 1498, pp. 357–363, 2021.
https://doi.org/10.1007/978-3-030-90176-9_46

headsets, though interest in MR is quickly increasing. VR has been used for simulation applications that support training (e.g., visualization of a cockpit for pilot training) [1, 2]. VR headsets generally cannot be used in operational environments to perform on-the-job tasks in the real world because they completely occlude the user's view of the real world. In contrast, MR can serve as both a training aid and operational aid to enhance soldier awareness on the battlefield in real time, surgical training and more [3, 4]. The potential of MR for both military training and operations appears to be vast but requires thorough exploration.

We define VR, AR, MR and extended reality (xR), noting the differences between them. We acknowledge that there is still disagreement on exact definitions as these technologies develop and change. The definitions we use are adapted from those found throughout the literature [5–7].

VR. In VR, the Virtual World Completely Occludes the Physical World.

MR. MR integrates graphics with physical properties of the physical environment allowing interactive and integrated use of graphics.

AR. In AR, virtual content is overlaid onto the real world.

xR. xR is an umbrella term for emerging technologies including VR, AR, and MR.

The primary objective of this paper was to present methods to convert VR content developed in Unity to MR content. A second objective was to introduce a graphical user interface (GUI) we developed that allows the user to vary the number of graphically-generated objects in the scene in real time while the user wears a MR headset.

We have identified reports on converting video for VR headset viewing [8–10]. Cross-platform development is supported by a Unity tool called OpenXR - a development environment that is compatible with VR or MR [11]. Therefore, concepts for graphic conversion and compatibility in VR and MR headsets exist in the literature. The novelty of our approach is explicitly outlining the conversion of VR to MR and the ability to scale the number of graphically rendered objects in the scene by the user in real-time using our GUI. This paper resulted from our own need to convert VR to MR for human factors experimentation whereby a physical scene can be reproduced graphically while carefully manipulating the number of graphic vs physical objects in the scene in MR. We were not able to find a conversion method, guidelines, or a GUI for this purpose and therefore developed our own.

A convenient method for VR-to-MR graphic conversion would allow researchers to rapidly modify and compare characteristics of MR to VR (and vice versa) and explore characteristics of both types of scenes in detail. Another potential use for VR to MR graphic conversion is that it would help Unity developers generate content across headset platforms (e.g. VR headset or MR headset) easily, and reduce redundancies in creating similar synthetic environments for different headset platforms. Thus, a scene can first be created in VR, then the graphic content can be scaled to create modified versions of the scene easily for MR. Finally, from a training perspective, VR to MR conversion would allow the end-user to train in a single headset, first showing fully virtually rendered scenes, and then gradually scaling by showing fewer virtual objects. In some cases, the same headset could be used in operational environments. The use of the same headset, virtual environment and GUI from training to operations provides the user familiarity, immersion, predictability, and consistency that support positive transfer of training [12].

2 VR to MR Conversion Scenarios and Guidelines

In all scenarios presented, we used Unity version 2019.4.18f1 with the following packages for VR: OpenVR Desktop 2.0.5 and Oculus Desktop 2.38.4 and the following packages for MR: Windows Mixed Reality 4.2.3, Windows XR Plugin 2.5.2, and MRTK 2.5.3. The OpenXR versions used Unity version 2020.3.2fl with the following packages for MR: OpenXR 1.0.3, MRTK 2.6.1, and Mixed Reality OpenXR Plugin and the following packages for VR: Oculus XR 1.8.1, Open XR 1.0.3, XR Interaction Toolkit 1.0.0-pre.3, and XR Plugin Management 4.0.1. Scripting for the projects was done in C# using Visual Studio 2019. The VR project was developed on a Dell Precision T7600 machine running a Windows 10 Pro 64-bit operating system. The machine has 24 GB of RAM, an Intel Xeon E5-2665 CPU and a Nvidia GeForce GTX Titan graphics card. The MR project was developed on a HP Laptop running a Windows 10 Pro 64-bit operating system. This laptop has 16 GB of RAM, and an Intel i5-7300U CPU. Headsets used for VR to MR conversion assume the Oculus Rift S for VR and the Microsoft Hololens 2 for MR for all conversion scenarios. The five scenarios are summarized in Table 1.

Table 1. Summary of guidelines for 5 Scenarios

Scenario	Steps
2.1 Converting VR to MR Camera	Identify the game objects that make up the VR camera system (for Oculus it is OVRCameraRig) and disable them. Setup the game objects that make up the MR camera system (MixedRealityToolkit and MixedRealityPlayspace)
2.2 Converting to Open XR	Create a new project with Unity version 2020.2 or later and configure the project for Open XR using Microsoft's Mixed Reality Feature Tool. Once the project is setup, import all of the assets to the Open XR project
2.3 Setting up Open XR Camera System	Change the configuration profile of the MixedRealityToolkit object to an Open XR configuration profile
2.4 Converting VR GUI to MR GUI	VR GUIs will be functional in MR but it is recommended to work off of MRTK's menu examples to improve overall user experience
2.5 Placing Objects in MR	Use the spatial mapping, image targets, or a combination of both methods to guide object placement. Place objects in relation to real-world geometry using ray casts, or place objects directly onto image targets

2.1 Converting a VR Camera System to MR Camera System

The camera viewing system is one of the key components that define VR and MR experiences. Different headsets are optimized for different camera implementations in Unity. Oculus VR headsets use a game object called, OVRCameraRig, which holds the primary camera object. Microsoft's Mixed Reality Toolkit (MRTK), uses the default Unity camera object with an Event System and MixedRealityInputModule component attached to it. To change camera systems, first disable or delete all game objects related to the current VR camera system. In Oculus VR, disable the OVRCameraRig game object. Then, add the MR camera components that allow the MRTK camera system to work. This can be done by going to 'Mixed Reality Toolkit' in the top menu in the Unity editor and clicking 'Add to scene and configure'. Additional settings must be changed to ensure for optimized visual quality and hologram stability [13].

2.2 Converting Project to OpenXR

For ease in project conversion from VR to MR, it is recommended that developers use OpenXR, an application programming interface, from the start of the project. However, in the case where a project must be converted from a legacy XR plugin implementation to an OpenXR implementation, we recommend the following steps: To convert a project for it to use the new Unity XR plugin management and OpenXR, extract all of the content from the original project and save it where it can later be imported into a new project. The first step is creating an OpenXR Unity project. This can easily be done using Microsoft's Mixed Reality Feature Tool which performs most of the project setup. Follow Microsoft's documentation in setting up OpenXR for MRTK in Unity [14]. After the new Unity project is setup, import the package from the old project into the new OpenXR project. The final step is to use an OpenXR configuration profile for the MixedRealityToolkit script.

2.3 Setting up OpenXR Camera System

The camera and interaction functions are the main features that differentiate OpenXR and the native Unity XR plugins. There are different ways OpenXR's camera system can be implemented into Unity. In VR, Unity's XR Interaction Toolkit can be used to make a Room-Scale XR Rig. We used a sample input action controller for the rig. In MR, the camera implementation is the same as in legacy MRTK. However, the configuration profile for the MixedRealityToolkit must be swapped to an OpenXR configuration profile. We used the DefaultOpenXRConfigurationProfile for our project. Configuration profiles can be changed in the inspector window of the MixedRealityToolkit object.

2.4 Converting a VR GUI to MR GUI

Camera implementation and UI design are the main differentiating factors between VR and MR GUIs. Unity's default UI system will work with the Hololens 2. However, for an optimal MR experience the GUI should be set up using the MRTK's menu features. To do so, disable the OVRCameraRig and add a Main Camera object with the MixedRealityIn-putModule component attached to it with MixedRealityPlayspace as the parent object. To finish the optimization process for the scene, add a MixedRealityToolkit game object. For user design purposes in MR, it is recommended to lower the opacity of the GUI.

2.5   Placing Graphically Rendered Objects in MR: Three Methods

Spatial Mapping. When converting from VR to MR, the MR headset must register the physical space and map the physical geometry of the real-world environment. This process is referred to as spatial mapping and is critical in MR in order for graphically rendered objects to account for the physical space in which they are presented. The Hololens' spatial awareness system can identify floors, ceilings, walls, and some foreground objects. Spatial mapping is configured through the MixedRealityToolkit game object. Navigate to the Spatial Awareness tab in the MixedRealityToolkit component and tick the 'Enable Spatial Awareness System' box. Microsoft provides default profiles that can be used. These profiles allow for the registration of the surrounding environment. A detailed walkthrough for the spatial mapping process can be found in Microsoft's official MRTK documentation [15].

Object placement can be achieved by instantiating the virtual objects in the desired location using ray casts from the user's position and then using a snapping function to ensure that the objects are placed in the correct position. The snapping function will send rays from the headset to nearby walls to estimate the distance between the object and the walls then place the objects accordingly. This approach is ideal when object placement must be precise and when both the environment and the user position are fixed relative to each other such as in an aircraft cockpit. Spatial mapping allows the developer to build on the project with advanced functionality in the future. A drawback of spatial mapping is that it takes many steps to place objects because techniques like ray casting and MRTK Solvers are required for precise object positioning.

Image Target Setting. Using Vuforia, an AR software development toolkit, place image targets in the physical space to indicate where the virtual object should appear. Object positioning through image targets can be done by designing a unique image target for each object that needs to be placed. For optimal object tracking, image tar-gets should be rich in detail, have sufficient contrast, and limited repetitive patterns. The image targets can be placed in the same positions as their corresponding objects. Upload the image targets to Vuforia's database and import the database into the project. Virtual objects can be mapped to image targets if they are a child of the image target game object.

A benefit to using image targets is that developers will know exactly where virtual objects will be placed relative to their physical environment. A drawback is that it can be time consuming to ensure that the image targets are accurately positioned in the physical space. An additional drawback is that developing and running projects that use Vuforia and MRTK is computationally demanding.

Spatial Mapping + Image Target Setting. A third method to place objects in MR is by combining both spatial mapping and image target placement. The MRTK's Spatial

Awareness system allows the Hololens to register the physical environment around the user and produce a collection of meshes that represent the real-world geometry of the environment. Once the Spatial Awareness system is enabled, we can start placing objects in the scene. The spatial awareness setting registers the dimensions of the physical space to the Hololens. A benefit to using both spatial mapping and image targets is that it gives the developer more tools for object placement methods. A drawback of this Spatial mapping + image target setting combination technique to place objects in MR is that it may be computationally demanding if the project requires both the Vuforia and MRTK packages.

3 XR GUI

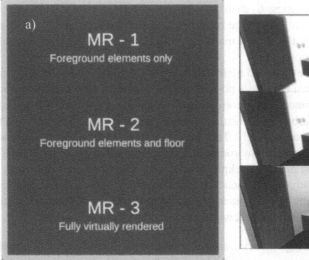

Fig. 1. a) GUI with three MR levels summoned by user hand gesture. The user can select which MR level to view in the MR headset. b) Corresponding visual scene displayed in MR headset based on GUI selection. MR-1 displays foreground objects. MR-2 displays foreground objects and the floor. MR-3 renders floor, walls, ceiling and foreground objects in the scene.

Section 2 outlined steps to convert a VR Unity project to an MR Unity project but this creates separate projects that must be built on separate headset platforms. In this section we present a GUI we developed that allows real-time user-controlled scene conversion from fully virtually rendered to only some elements being virtually rendered in a MR headset. The GUI is activated through an open palm gesture when the user looks at their hand. The menu allows the user to select one of the displayed MR levels in Fig. 1a. The fully virtually rendered MR level must first be built by the developer, then using steps listed in Sect. 2, converted to various levels of MR. We virtually rendered an office space using the same dimensions and furniture as an actual office space to which the authors had access. The various levels of MR shown in Fig. 1b allow the physical space to blend with graphical elements while accounting for their physical properties. This fully virtually rendered display ('MR-3' in Fig. 1b) is translucent. MR levels shown in Fig. 1b are some examples of how a developer may decide to design different levels of MR. The developer may customize each MR level in the GUI as they wish.

4 Conclusions

We described a novel method to convert VR to various levels of MR and present a GUI that allows users to customize the level of graphically rendered objects in the scene in a MR headset. The GUI may be set up by the developer to decide which elements in the scene are graphically rendered. Customization of elements in a scene that are graphically generated and that are real allows flexibility for applications in research, training and operational, on the job use. The conversion concept and methods presented here have vast implications as they allow MR headsets to be an all-in-one platform that can replace VR and AR headsets to be used for training, gaming and operations in the defence industry and beyond. We plan on conducting thorough user testing of this conversion method and automating the VR to MR conversion process outlined in Sect. 2 into a standalone tool.

References

1. Gonzalez, J.: Pilot training next, air force ROTC partner for distance learning instruction. Air Education and Training Command Public Affairs (2020)
2. von Niederhausem, S.: World's First Qualified Device Virtual Reality Training Allows Time to Be Credited Towards Flight Training. VRM Switzerland (2021)
3. Reiner, A.J., et al.: A mirror in the sky: assessment of an augmented reality method for depicting navigational information. Ergonomics 63(5), 548–562 (2020)
4. Douglas, D.B., et al.: Virtual reality and augmented reality: advances in surgery. Biol Eng Med 2, 1–8 (2017)
5. He, Z., et al.: Progress in virtual reality and augmented reality based on holographic display. Appl. Opt. 58(5), A74–A81 (2019)
6. XR Collaboration. XR Glossary. [Web Page] 2021 https://xrcollaboration.com/guide/a-glo bal-resource-guide-to-xr-collaboration/xr-glossary/. Accessed 3 June 2021
7. Milgram, P., Kishino, F.: A taxonomy of mixed reality visual displays. IEICE Trans. Inf. Syst. 77(12), 1321–1329 (1994)
8. Lee, W.T., et al.: High-resolution 360 video foveated stitching for real-time VR. Computer Graphics Forum. 36, 115–123 (2017)
9. Saeed, S., et al.: A high-quality VR calibration and real-time stitching framework using preprocessed features. IEEE Access 8, 190300–190311 (2020)
10. Dickey, R.M., et al.: Augmented reality assisted surgery: a urologic training tool. Asian J. Androl. 18(5), 732 (2016)
11. The Khronos Group (2021). https://www.khronos.org/openxr/. Accessed 3 June 2021
12. Grossman, R., Salas, E.: The transfer of training: what really matters. Int. J. Train. Dev. 15(2), 103–120 (2011)
13. Microsoft. Camera setup in Unity. (2021). https://docs.microsoft.com/en-us/windows/mixed-reality/develop/unity/camera-in-unity. Accessed 3 June 2021
14. Microsoft. Using the Mixed Reality OpenXR Plugin (2021) https://docs.microsoft.com/en-us/windows/mixed-reality/develop/unity/openxr-getting-started. Accessed 3 June 2021
15. Microsoft. Spatial Awareness. https://microsoft.github.io/MixedRealityToolkit-Unity/Doc umentation/SpatialAwareness/SpatialAwarenessGettingStarted.html. Accessed 3 June 2021

A Study on User Interface Design Based on Geo-Infographic and Augmented Reality Technology

Heehyeon Park[✉]

Hanseo University, Seosan-si Chungcheongnam-do, Seosan-si 31962, South Korea
hpark@hanseo.ac.kr

Abstract. The use of augmented reality applications based on location information has increased due to the recent development of smart devices and technological advances. Augmented reality is a technology that displays information on virtual objects in the real world and serves to improve the quality of user experience by providing information based on the user's location. The user interface (UI) in augmented reality requires constant interaction according to the user's location and environment, unlike the existing two-dimensional graphic user interface (GUI). In augmented reality, it is essential to configure the user interface to efficiently and easily recognize appropriate information according to the user's situation. In this paper, we suggested a method that could improve the users' usability and experience by designing a UI based on geo-infographics. Geo-infographics are info-graphics created using location-based information that combines elements such as diagrams, images, and storytelling with information communication techniques to deliver messages quickly and easily. UIs designed using geo-infographics will provide an efficient method for users to intuitively understand the content and acquire the information they want easily and quickly by providing interactions with images and diagrams that match the content's purpose and intent. We produced a prototype for Beonhwa-ro Street in Seosan City in Korea. We introduced the art store on Beonhwa-ro Street and created a AR user interface based on geo-infographics in the Seosan Munhwaro application.

Keywords: Geo-infographic · AR (Augmented Reality) · User interface design

1 Introduction

With the recent development of smart devices and technologies, numerous applications (apps) are being created. Among them, apps that provide geographic information are continuously being developed, and the number is increasing every year. examples include a map app that provides directions and location information, a travel app that provides travel information around the World, an app that provides transportation information, and an app that provides location information on places such as restaurants and hospitals with good ratings in real-time. These applications need to classify vast amounts of information based on the user's location and deliver it to the user quickly and accurately. For this,

© Springer Nature Switzerland AG 2021
C. Stephanidis et al. (Eds.): HCII 2021, CCIS 1498, pp. 364–368, 2021.
https://doi.org/10.1007/978-3-030-90176-9_47

the role of the user interface is very important. The user interface acts as a map to help users quickly and easily obtain the information they want. In this study, we proposed a new type of user interface (UI) design. In the case of an app that provides a large amount of location-based information in real-time, if geo-infographics and augmented reality (AR) technology are applied to the UI design, the users will be able to easily access and quickly obtain the information they need. To verify its effectiveness, we prototyped the Seosan Culture Road app and synthesized users' opinions.

2 Geo-Infographic

First, we need to take a closer look at the definition and meaning of geo-infographics. Geo-infographics is an infographic created using location-based information and refers to a method of easily delivering messages through various communication media such as maps, charts, pictures, storytelling, and interaction [1]. Geo-infographics are not just general maps with location information but contain a variety of images that visually display brands, stories, and specific information about the area.

The term geo-infographics first appeared in 2011. At that time, scholars He, Tang, and Huang defined geo-infographics as a method of fusing traditional maps and infographics [2].

It is necessary to look at the concept of infographics along with the definition of geo-infographics. Infographics is a compound word composed of "information" and "graphics" and is referred to as "explanation graphics." The official definition of an infographic is "the result of visualizing data or thoughts so that complex information can be easily and quickly understood" [3]. But more strictly, "a lot of data is simply moving away from visualizing, having a clear purpose and creating relationships, rules, and structures between information after understanding, the visual result designed with an accurate message through storytelling" can be called an infographic [4].

Therefore, a geo-infographic can be defined as the result of visualizing complex data or thoughts that are intended to be communicated to the public, along with geographical information seen on traditional maps, so that they can be visualized easily, and quickly understood.

3 User Interface Design with Augmented Reality (AR)

The role of the user interface of a smartphone application can be defined as a medium that helps communication between the user and the app. A good UI with high usability helps users to quickly achieve their desired purpose by easily accessing the information they need. Today, with the rapid development of technology, AR is also rapidly developing, which leads to an increase in the use of AR applications. AR is a technology that superimposes virtual objects into the real world. Based on the user's location, various information can be visually displayed easily and quickly. However, AR technology itself should not be the goal, and it is important to use it effectively according to the purpose and intention. Since AR technology-applied apps require constant interaction depending upon the user's location and environment, it is very important to configure the user interface to efficiently and easily recognize appropriate information according to the user's situation. Geo-infographics can be very effectively applied to apps with AR technology. As location-based information is displayed quickly and easily in real-time along with pictures, charts, and interactions, it becomes an efficient means for users to intuitively understand the content and easily acquire the desired information.

4   Case Study

For this study, we prototyped a smartphone app using geo-infographic theory and AR technology. The Seosan Culture Road app, which introduced art shops in Seosan, South Korea, was designed with UIs based on geo-infographics and incorporated image-based AR technology. It was designed to deliver detailed information to users easily and quickly.

For this, location information and geographic situation analysis were first necessary (see Fig. 1). Then, we analyzed the purpose of the app we wanted to create and developed a UI design with geo-infographics applied (see Fig. 2). At this point, the main image or graphic element (building shape, sign image, etc.) that could represent each location was selected. Finally, we incorporated AR technology into the UI, users can instantly get the information they need (see Fig. 3, 4).

Fig. 1. Analyze location information and geographic context

Fig. 2. Maps with geo-infographics applied

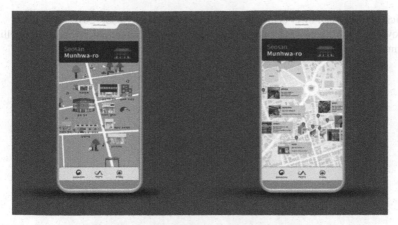

Fig. 3. UI design with geo-infographics applied

Fig. 4. Incorporated AR technology into the UI

5   Conclusion

We decided that location-based smartphone applications needed differentiation from existing GUIs and proposed a new type of UI design, which was a geo-infographics-based UI design that incorporated AR technology into the UI.

To prove its effectiveness, we created a prototype of the Seosan Culture Road app and synthesized user opinions. As a result, 96% of users said their use of geospatial and AR was very effective.

In the future, we would like to use geo-infographic-based UI design for various apps to verify its utility, and also plan to continue research focused on various uses of AR technology.

References

1. Myounghwa, H., Eunsun, I., Sungjae, J.P.: A Study of Developing and Applying Geoinfographics to Improve Communication Capability of Policy Support Mapping. KRIHS, Seoul, Korea (2015)
2. He, M., Tang, X., Huang, Y.: To visualize spatial data using ThematicMaps combined with Infographics. In: Proceedings of the 19th International Conference on Geoinformatics, pp. 1–5 (2011)

3. Smiciklas, M.: The Power of Infographics. Que Publishing, Seoul (2012)
4. Myoyoung, K.: Secrets of things that look good - Infographic: visual storytelling to communicate with information, Gilbut, Seoul, Korea (2014)

Comparing the Impact of State Versus Trait Factors on Memory Performance in a Virtual Reality Flight Simulator

Anya Pejemsky(✉) ⓘ, Kathleen Van Benthem ⓘ, and Chris M. Herdman ⓘ

Carleton University, Ottawa, ON K1S 5B6, Canada
anyapejemsky@cmail.carleton.ca, {kathy.vanbenthem,
chris.herdman}@carleton.ca

Abstract. Situation Awareness (SA) is an important predictor of critical incidents in the aviation domain. Virtual Reality (VR) simulators provide a safe setting for training pilot SA. Despite the necessity of integrating auditory information for SA, it is unknown if the integration of auditory information is impacted by state and trait variables. The present work investigated the utility of a novel state versus trait framework in predicting SA, based on auditory information, in a VR flight environment. It was expected that VR induced states would account for most of the variance found in SA. Using structural equation modeling, causal models were developed to quantify the relationship of VR state, non-VR state, and trait variables to SA during VR flight. VR-induced state, non-VR-induced state, and trait variables predicted approximately two thirds of the variability in SA. VR flight simulation is increasingly integrated into military, commercial, and general aviation. Thus, VR flight training protocols and assessments should consider both state and trait factors examined in this study when recruiting or training new pilots.

Keywords: Situation Awareness · Virtual Reality · Flight simulator

1 Introduction

General aviation (GA), defined as all flight activity excluding scheduled commercial airlines and military related services, has persistently high accident rates [1]. The majority of accidents have been associated with pilot error, rather than mechanical error [2]. Furthermore, historic data shows that 88% of pilot errors are associated with poor situation awareness (SA) [3]. To develop resources for addressing the accident rate in GA, it is crucial that predictive factors which impact SA are better understood. SA is the capacity to monitor radio calls, maintain the call information in auditory working memory, and make predictions about one's future location as well as the future position of other relevant aircraft based on the information in those messages. SA is challenging to examine in an actual aircraft; however, Virtual Reality (VR) environments offer new opportunities for training and studying pilot SA in safe but ecologically robust environments. Little is known regarding how the features of virtual flight environments impact SA. Additionally, aside from expertise and workload, little is known regarding the extent to which

© Springer Nature Switzerland AG 2021
C. Stephanidis et al. (Eds.): HCII 2021, CCIS 1498, pp. 369–376, 2021.
https://doi.org/10.1007/978-3-030-90176-9_48

individual factors might also impact SA in flight. The present study explored the effects of participant VR states, non-VR states, and traits on SA in non-pilots who received training in a VR flight simulator. Due to its intensive experience, it was expected that VR states would account for more of the variability in SA performance than non-VR states and traits.

2 Methods and Procedures

The study was granted ethics approval by the University Ethics Approval Board. Non-pilot undergraduate students were recruited from a research pool. One participant was removed because of crucial data missing due to researcher error, resulting in a final sample of 46 participants. Participant ages ranged from 16–43 years (median age = 20 years, 24 male). The study utilized an HTC Vive VR headset, a simulated Cessna 172 aircraft using Lockheed Martin's Prepar3D flight simulator software, and a custom-built cockpit, which matched the Cessna 172 panel dimensions [4]. Participants listened to radio messages that included aircraft call signs via earphones. Participants flew circuits (oval patterns around an aerodrome) using the simulator. The circuit was marked by nine semi-transparent guide hoops that participants were instructed to fly through.

Participants were provided relevant flight instructions including how to identify pilot call signs within the radio messages, operate the controls, and read the instrument panel. Participants were told that they would hear call signs in the radio messages, and they were to do their best to memorize the three letters associated with each three-letter call sign (e.g., delta, echo, foxtrot). Participants flew the oval circuit three times to practice the tasks and four times during testing. The workload conditions were manipulated such that two circuits were high workload (included the radio message task) and two were low workload (no radio message task). Workload order alternated between circuits and was counterbalanced between subjects. The study was designed to be completed in 2 h. Participants completed pre- and post-study questionnaires related to non-VR states and traits and answered items relating to VR states between circuits.

The relationship between performance on the call sign task and the predictors was undertaken using partial least squares (PLS) structural equation modeling (SEM). SEM is a robust method for analyzing latent constructs and path analysis [5]. PLS-SEM allows users to estimate the direction and strength of the relationships between variables in the model.

3 Variables

3.1 Outcome Variable

SA is an important component in any dynamic and complex system [6]. In aviation, safe flight depends on SA to inform appropriate decision making. Van Benthem measured SA by examining pilot memory for radio call details and status of cockpit instruments [7]. SA performance was shown to be associated with critical incidents, and thus important in training and assessment of pilots. In the present work, accuracy in detecting and recalling call signs served as the measure of SA. Pilot call signs were heard three times during each of the high workload circuits at distinct and consistent points. The SA score for each of the two circuits ranged from 0 to 3, based on the number of call letters participants could recall correctly. Scores from the call sign task from each of the high workload circuits were summed to produce the total SA score and then converted to a percentage.

3.2 Predictor Variables

Virtual Reality Induced States. VR sickness was measured with a 3-item condensed Simulator Sickness Questionnaire, measured using 1 to 6 scale and queried at the end of each of the four circuits [8, 9]. The level of VR sickness was derived by subtracting the final circuit responses from the first circuit responses for each of three key VR sickness symptoms: dizziness, disorientation, and queasiness. The VR immersiveness factors included immersion, interactivity, and telepresence and were measured using a modified questionnaire based on van Baren and IJsselsteijn's questionnaire (see Table 1) [10]. The 6-item questionnaire had two questions for each variable with a scale of 1 (do not agree at all) to 6 (very much agree) scale. The immersion, interactivity, and telepresence items were queried at the completion of each of the four circuits flown.

Table 1. Immersiveness items.

Latent construct	Indicator (queried after each circuit)
Immersion	I had no difficulty concentrating
	I was totally absorbed in what I was doing
Interactivity	The Vive allowed me to interact with the virtual world
	I had the feeling that I could influence the virtual world inside the Vive
Telepresence	The content of the HTC Vive seemed to be 'somewhere I visit' rather than something I saw
	The HTC Vive created a new world for me and this new world suddenly disappeared when the exercise ended

Non-virtual Reality Induced States. All non-VR-induced states were measured using self-report before simulator training. The non-VR states included Nourishment, Fatigue, and Alertness. The variable Nourishment was measured with a query using a Likert type scale, ranging from 1 to 3, which asked participants when they last ate. The options ranged from 1 (within the last hour) to 3 (more than five hours ago). The variable Fatigue and Alertness was measured with a query using a Likert type scale, ranging from 1 to 6.

Traits. In the present study, trait factors were defined as variables that are stable or fluctuate at a slower pace than states. Driver's Experience was measured with a query using a Likert type scale, ranging from 1 to 6, which asked participants how many years they have had their license. The options ranged from 1 (I don't have a licence) to 6 (>5 years). The variable VR Experience was measured with three queries using Likert type scales. The first query asked participants about their previous VR usage. The scale ranged from 1 (never) to 3 (regularly). The second query asked participants how long they had been using VR. The scale ranged from 1 (never) to 6 (>10 years). The third query asked participants to report on the frequency of their VR usage. The scale ranged from 1 (never) to 7 (daily). The variable gender was measured with one query using multiple choice options, male, female, prefer not to disclose, and other. The variable age was measured with one query, which asked participants to report their age as a continuous variable.

4 Results

4.1 Outer Model Development and Testing

In SEM, the outer models represent the structure of the latent constructs (e.g., the indicators used to reflect a construct). The outer models were built and tested individually using confirmatory factor analysis to evaluate relationships between latent constructs and their indicators [11]. The analysis exclusively used reflective models and rank order data transformation to reduce the effects of outliers. The reliability requirements for the outer model structures were that the latent variables have an average variance extracted (AVE) of at least 0.5, a Composite Reliability and Cronbach's Alpha of at least 0.7 and, ideally, the loadings between a construct and its indicators be at least 0.6 (with $p < .05$). If the AVE and reliability coefficients were acceptable, then indicators with loadings between .3 and .6 were retained in the outer model for that latent construct. VR immersiveness variable (Immersion, Interactivity, and Telepresence) met the requirements for construct reliability. The VR sickness construct, constructed using the difference scores for queasiness, dizziness, and disorientation symptoms, met the requirements for construct reliability. The three VR experience indicators (Previous Use, Length of Use, and Frequency of Use) met the requirements to be included in the VR experience construct.

4.2 Inner Model Development and Testing

As shown in Fig. 1, the state versus trait model tested the relative effects of all latent and directly measured predictors on SA. All relationships were tested using the PLS regression mode, whereby the outer models were not affected by relationships in the inner model. The criteria for relevant effects sizes for all predictor variables in the inner models were set to $f^2 > / = 0.02$. Predictor variables that did not meet the f^2 threshold were removed during model refinement. To manage the large number of variables in this study and possible model misspecification, the relationship between VR states, non-VR states, and individual factors and traits with SA was determined systematically by initially building three separate models for each of the predictor categories. Variables that showed no predictive power with regard to SA ($f^2 < 0.02$) were pruned during the inner model testing for each category. Once all three models were determined, a final "State and Traits" model was constructed and the relative predictive power and path analysis beta values for each variable was determined.

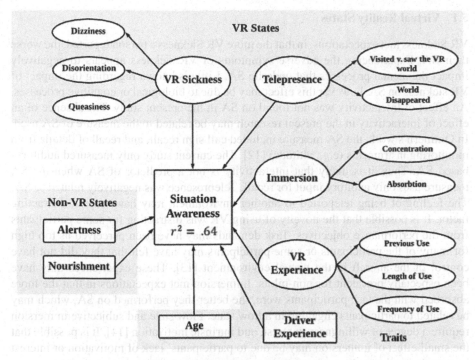

Fig. 1. The final state vs. trait model.

4.3   Final State and Trait Model

The final state and trait model was the combination of the successful variables from the VR state, non-VR state, and traits model. Most of the predictor variables met the relative effect requirements of $f\,\hat{}\,2 > I = 0.02$. The state and trait model accounted for 64% of the total variance in SA performance (see Fig. 1). VR Sickness had the largest relative effect at 0.12 and was negatively related to SA. Alertness had a relative effect of 0.11 and was positively related to SA. Driver's Experience had a relative effect of 0.10 and was positively related to SA. Age had a relative effect size of 0.08 and was positively related to SA. VR Experience, Nourishment, and Immersion all had a relative effect size of 0.07 and were positively related to SA. Lastly, Telepresence had a relative effect size of 0.02 and was negatively related to SA. In accord with the final model, trait variables accounted for the most variance in SA compared to VR and non-VR states.

5   Discussion

The present study aimed to explore the extent to which state and trait factors impacted SA in a VR flight simulator. It was expected that the VR state variables would account for the most variance in SA. Contrastingly, these results showed that the trait variables accounted for the largest amount of variability in SA. However, the three predictor variables that accounted for the most variability in SA (i.e., VR Sickness, Alertness, and Driver's Experience) represent all three categories of predictors.

5.1 Virtual Reality States

VR Sickness met expectations, in that the more VR Sickness a person reported, the worse their SA. Experiencing the adverse symptoms of VR sickness appears to negatively impact the mental processes that underlie SA. Little is known regarding the impact of VR sickness on SA, however this effect may be due to biological or cognitive processes. An effect of Interactivity was not found on SA in the present study. The absence of an effect of Interactivity in the present research may be related to the measure of SA used. In Ommerli's work, the SA measure included call sign recall, and recall of details from monitoring instruments (e.g., altitude) [12]. The current study only measured auditory-based SA. Thus, it is likely that interactivity is not a predictor of SA when the SA measure uses only auditory input for recall. Telepresence was negatively related to SA. The feeling of being teleported to another environment may have been a distracting factor. It is possible that the novelty of using VR was distracting for some participants from the performance objectives. Task demands may have been perceived as too high for many of the participants or some participants may have felt that they did not have control of the aircraft in the virtual environment [13]. These experiences may have been especially prevalent for non-pilots. Immersion met expectations in that the more absorbed with the task participants were, the better they performed on SA, which may be related to participants engaging in a flow state. Flow state and subjective immersion require a degree of willingness, interest, and intrinsic motivation [14]. It is possible that the small effect of immersion may be due to participants' lack of motivation or interest in completing the study.

5.2 Non-virtual Reality States

Higher reported Alertness was associated with better performance on the SA task. Interestingly, Fatigue did not appear to have an impact on SA. Fatigue has been found to be an important predictor for driving and aviation accidents [15]. The distribution of participant scores when responding to the Fatigue query shows that people were rarely very fatigued when completing the study. The majority of participants reported being not fatigued, which is probably why an effect of Fatigue was not found. Alertness, in this case, was more predictive of performance. The distribution of Nourishment by SA scores demonstrated an inverted- U trend. This trend suggests that there is an optimal SA performance between 2 to 5 h after eating. This may be related to rest-and-digest processes, which may take away from attentional resources [16].

5.3 Traits

Individuals with more VR Experience tended to perform better on SA. Individuals with more Driving Experience also tended to perform better on the SA task, which may suggest that SA skills are transferable from driving to flying. An unexpected effect of age on SA was found, in that older participants tended to perform better on the SA task. The effect of age may be related to maturity effects, and perhaps a greater likelihood of driving experience.

6 Future Work

The proposed new framework of predicting SA during flight simulation used in the present research should be of interest to stakeholders in aviation and other complex human-machine systems. Flight training evaluators should take note of trainee alertness and time since they last ate when evaluating performance, given how impactful these factors are on SA. The findings should also inform aviator work shift and breaks policy on the importance of maintaining alertness and timing food breaks for optimal SA. Those who are involved in recruitment and training of pilots should realize that the use of VR may systematically bias against the youngest users, those with little VR experience, and those without driving experience. Given the wide use of SA measuring (e.g., machine operating), it is possible that the state and trait model could be applied to other domains. The present model should be replicated with a larger sample size. Additionally, it would be of interest to confirm the proposed model with licensed pilots. Pilot participant results may provide more information regarding the effects of VR states on SA and the extent to which expertise would impact the explained variance of the state and trait model.

In summary, the novel framework proposed in the present study has promising potential and provides evidence of a broader range of variables that predict SA and, in turn, aviator performance. Although much research has been devoted to VR states, especially VR sickness, further research should be done regarding non-VR states and traits which, based on the present work, account for most of the variability in SA. The present framework has wide applicability to aviation in policy makers, and entry decision making (i.e., GA, commercial, military) and flight simulator development.

References

1. Geske, R.: 27th Joseph T. Nall report: General aviation accidents. AOPA (2015). https://www.aopa.org/-/media/files/aopa/home/training-and-safety/nall-report/27thnallreport2018.pdf
2. Erjavac, A., Iammartino, R., Fossaceca, J.: Evaluation of preconditions affecting symptomatic human error in general aviation and air carrier aviation accidents. Reliab. Eng. Syst. Saf. **178**, 156–163 (2018)
3. Endsley, M., Garland, D. (eds.): Situation Awareness Analysis and Measurement. CRC Press, Boca Raton (2000)
4. Prepar3D Flight Simulator. Lockheed Martin's (2020)
5. Kante, M., Chepken, C., Oboko, R.: Partial least square structural equation modelling's use in information systems: an updated guideline in exploratory settings. Kabarak J. Res. Innov. **6**(1), 49–67 (2018)
6. Vidulich, M., Tsang, P.: Mental workload and situation awareness. In: Savendy, G. (ed.) Handbook of Human Factors and Ergonomics, pp. 243–253. John Wiley & Sons, New York (2012)
7. Van Benthem, K.: Identifying latent cognitive constructs in a comprehensive model of aviation out-comes: the role of the dynamic mental model for pilots (2015). https://doi.org/10.22215/etd/2015-10834
8. Balk, S., Bertola, M., Inman, V.: Simulator sickness questionnaire: twenty years later. In: Proceedings of the 7th International Driving Symposium on Human Factors in Driver Assessment, Training, and Vehicle Design: driving assessment 2013 (2013). https://doi.org/10.17077/drivingassessment.1498

9. Kennedy, R., Lane, N., Berbaum, K., Lilienthal, M.: Simulator sickness questionnaire: an enhanced method for quantifying simulator sickness. Int. J. Aviat. Psychol. **3**, 203–220 (1993). https://doi.org/10.1207/s15327108ijap0303_3

10. van Baren, J., IJsselsteijn, W.: Measuring Presence: A Guide to Current Measurement Approaches. OmniPres, Eindhoven (2004). http://www8.informatik.umu.se/~jwworth/Pre senceMeasurement.pdf

11. Kock, N.: WARP PLS 7.0 User Manual. ScriptWarp Systems, Laredo, TX (2020)

12. Ommerli, C.: Examining the effects of perceived telepresence, interactivity, and immersion on pilot situation awareness during a virtual reality flight exercise (2019). https://doi.org/10. 22215/etd/2020-13923

13. Sheridan, T.: Musings on telepresence and virtual presence. Presence Teleoperators Virtual Environ. **1**, 120–126 (1992). https://doi.org/10.1162/pres.1992.1.1.120

14. Curran, N.: Factors of immersion. In: Norman, K., Kirakowski, J. (ed.) The Wiley Handbook of Human Computer Interaction Set, pp. 239–263. John Wiley & Sons, New York (2018)

15. Caldwell, J., Mallis, M., Caldwell, J., Paul, M., Miller, J., Neri, D.: Fatigue countermeasures in aviation. Aviat. Space Environ. Med. **80**, 29–59 (2009). https://doi.org/10.3357/ASEM. 2435.2009

16. Yazdi, P.: 12 Possible Reasons You May Feel Tired after Eating – SelfHacked. https://selfha cked.com/blog/revealing-6-unknown-reasons-get-tired-eating/.

Co-exploring the Design Space of Emotional AR Visualizations

Sinem Şemsioğlu[(⊠)] and Asım Evren Yantaç

KUAR & Karma Lab, Koç University, Istanbul, Turkey
ssemsioglu16@ku.edu.tr

Abstract. Designing for emotional expression has become a popular topic of study in HCI due to advances in affective computing technologies. With increasing use of video-conferencing and video use in social media for different needs such as leisure, work, social communication, video filters, AR effects and holograms are also getting popular. In this paper, we suggest a framework for emotion visualization for natural user interface technologies such as Augmented or Mixed Reality. The framework has been developed based on our analysis of visualizations formed during a series of emotion visualization workshops.

Keywords: Emotion representation · Abstract visualization · Augmented reality · Human augmentation · Holograms · Design workshop · Speculative design

1 Introduction

Advances in affective computing and integration of Augmented Reality (AR) in our daily lives through 2D image manipulation open up many possibilities in design. One interesting design concept for AR is making what is invisible, visible and this can especially be beneficial during digitally mediated human-human interaction. Our natural communication benefits a lot from non-verbal cues; but transmission of non-verbal information is usually not the focal point while designing communicative services such as video-conferencing tools or AR filters. Therefore; we believe that the inclusion of non-verbal cues in the design of such communicative services can improve the quality of communication in some cases. In this paper, we explore the design space of visualization concepts related to making affective information visible in AR. After collecting visualization ideas from designers through a series of workshops and a focus group; we created a design framework. We then refined the framework with a second series of workshops with designers. This paper contributes to the HCI literature with the resulting framework, for emotional AR visualizations.

2 Background

In this section we review previous HCI studies on relatedness, emotion representation and affective AR.

C. Stephanidis et al. (Eds.): HCII 2021, CCIS 1498, pp. 377–384, 2021.
https://doi.org/10.1007/978-3-030-90176-9_49

There are two dominant emotion models: categorical and dimensional. In the categorical classification model, emotional states are represented by discrete labels, such as anger, sadness, happiness [5] in a manner similar to how we refer to emotions in our daily lives. Although this model is a natural one, it has some limitations such as the inability to express emotional states that do not have a correspondence in the chosen language. In a dimensional model an emotional state is represented by a value in each dimension that the model contains [5]. We chose to work with Russell's circumplex model, as it is one of the most widely used dimensional models. It has two dimensions: valence (pleasant/unpleasant) and arousal (high/low); any emotional state is characterized by the combination of a valence and an arousal value [11].

Relatedness is a sense of closeness and connectedness with people, and is one of the top three human needs along with competence and autonomy [12]. Some of the design concepts based on relatedness enhance existing communication methods. Examples are a hardware plugin for mobile phones to simulate the act of kissing while video chatting, for families and significant others [15], always-on domestic video streaming, for households that closely relate to each other [6], a candle shadow display concept that creates shadows in shape of emojis based on text message context, creating ambient affective representations of their emotional content [7]. Expressivity is identified as a design strategy for relatedness in Hassenzahl et al.'s review [4] and continues to be one of the most common strategies [8]. We think that visualizing emotions in AR can be considered as emotionally expressive.

While it is an option to express emotional states using explicit information such as keywords or emojis, we find ambiguous representations more fitting to the nature of emotions. As put forward by Gaver, ambiguity is a design strategy that involves users in the interpretation and meaning making process [2]. This approach encourages users to reflect on design outcomes they are presented. One place to look while designing abstract visuals is abstract art. The empirical evidence presented in studies investigating the relationship between abstract art and emotions show that some abstract visual properties such as colors (brightness, color pairs, complementary contrasts), complexity and regularity are influential on the elicited emotions [13]. Psychological research also support the evidence on the relationship between colors (as described by hue, saturation and brightness) and emotions (as described by pleasure, arousal, dominance model); researches have found that especially brightness and saturation have a strong connection to emotional dimensions [14].

Emotion detection from facial expressions have become commercially available (Microsoft, Affectiva) and wearables such as Apple Watch also provide emotion detection from physiological signals. In another vein, AR technologies are now a part of our daily lives, with the integration of AR filters in popular platforms such as Instagram, Snapchat, Zoom. Immersive Mixed Reality tools such as HoloLens can also be expected to meet with the general population in the upcoming years. On top of developer tools such as ARKit, ARCore, Vuforia, software such as SparkAR and SnapCamera enable users to create their own filters with minimal programming. More targeted tools also exist; a body-based device-agnostic AR toolkit, BodyLayARs [9] has been developed. Relevant to our work, one example application they present is attaching emotion-based visuals above people's heads [9]. Similarly, demos for providing emotional information [3] and spatial manipulation based on emotions [10] have been presented.

3   1st Phase: Forming the Framework

Our initial aim was to integrate emotion visualizations in an AR system to test their effect on emotional awareness and communication. As a preliminary study to guide our visualization design, we decided to hold a series of designer workshops to see how people would like to see emotions augmented around human body. 15 participants who study or work in design or visual arts related fields (12 females, age: $M = 22.13$, $SD = 1.8$) were recruited by announcement. Each participant produced 3 emotion visualizations: they were asked to imagine themselves studying at a coffee shop and visualize emotional states 1) of a person while studying alone 2) a group of people studying together 3) changing over the course study session. They had 15 min for each visualization task and were provided colored papers, markers, watercolor, fabric, cardboard and daily life material such as egg cartoons and paper bag ropes for constructing the visualizations. During these workshops, we saw that it is not very easy for designers to imagine visual representations of emotions and that there is a large variability in how they choose to express them without any guidance. This showed us that there is a need to make the design process more systematic to obtain design outcome that is more communicable and suitable for implementation in AR. Therefore; we decided to shift our attention in this earlier study to creating a framework to guide the design process. To achieve this, it was important to understand what design decisions were and should be made while designing emotion visualizations.

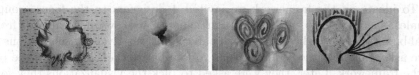

Fig. 1. Four sample visualizations produced by emotion visualization participants

3.1   Analysis and Designer Focus Group

As a starting point for our framework and to aid with the analysis of the visualizations we decided to work with the artwork analysis coding scheme presented in [1] due to the similarity between the visualizations and abstract artworks.

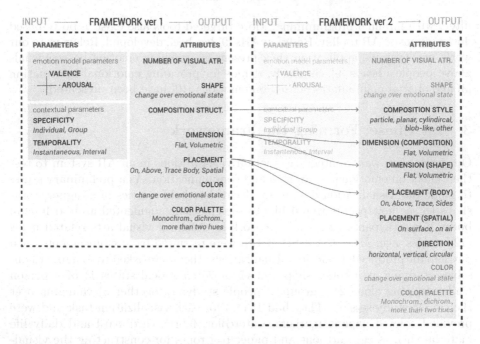

Fig. 2. Two versions of the framework. For some of the fields, we present suggested values based on our results. It should be noted that it was common to use more than one of the presented values in the produced visualizations.

To account for the differences, mainly that the visualizations were produced in a short amount of time, with limited material and without the intention of producing an artwork, we modified the scheme prior to analysis. The refined scheme was applied to all 45 visualizations. Similar to the process described in [1], after the initial labeling, we went over the visualizations and produced labels with a second (shadow) labeling.

To ideate on the framework we invited 4 designers to the focus group (4 females, age: $M = 23.5$, $SD = 4.43$). Participants were awarded giftcards from a local bookstore. In the beginning, each participant was given 5 visualizations and were asked to apply the coding scheme to familiarize themselves with the basis of the framework. Later, they were asked to pick the visualizations they found most appropriate for emotion representation. After the selected visualizations were assembled, a group discussion was held. Analysis results were also shared during the discussion.

3.2   The Framework: Version 1

The framework was formed based on the analysis results and the focus group discussions. It is organized as a list of decisions, prompting a designer to think about the aspects of emotion visualization design that we identified as important. This framework can be found in Fig. 2 under Framework Version 1.

– *Specificity* defines whether the visualization represents an individual's or a group of people's emotional state(s) (individual/group)
– *Temporality* defines whether the visualization represents instantaneous emotional states or those recorded during an interval (instantaneous/interval)
– *Placement* attribute decides where the visualization is placed in relation a body/bodies (on/above/tracing/spatial)
– *Visual Attributes.* The visual attributes that were identified as important were: color, size, fluidity, smoothness, curvature, symmetry, balance and layered structure, randomness, color variation, organic/geometric, opacity, distance of shapes to each other, linearity of composition. Accordingly we decided that the framework should include decisions related to the compositional structure, dimension (flat/volumetric), color palette (monochromatic/dichromatic/more than two hues) and how the visualizations will respond to changes in emotional states. Two common approaches to reflect these differences were manipulating shape and color.

4 2nd Phase: Refining the Framework

We held a second series of emotion visualization workshops with 12 participants (10 females, age: $M = 25.17$, $SD = 8.72$) to test whether our framework (Version 1) helps the design process as intended and to collect feedback. After an introduction; participants were given visualization worksheets that depict interaction of 2 and 4 people. We asked our participants to work on how emotions can be visualized in at least four different configurations (of specificity, temporality, valence, arousal) using the worksheets. They had an hour to work on the visualizations; in the end we held a discussion.

4.1 Coding Scheme

Collected visualizations (59) were coded based on our framework. The categories and subcategories included in this scheme were: specificity (individual/group), temporality (instantaneous/interval), placement (on/above/tracing/spatial), dimension (flat/volumetric), style of shapes (organic/geometric), number of distinct colors (monochromatic, dichromatic, more than 2 hues).

4.2 Expanding the Framework: Version 2

During the coding process we realized that the framework was not sufficient to clearly identify some significant properties of the visualizations; therefore expanded the coding scheme and in parallel, our framework. The expanded version can be found in Fig. 2 under Framework Version 2.

Placement. It was decided that the framework could benefit from including a decision on whether the visualization should be placed in relation to the body or to the surrounding space. In parallel, we realized that there were too many instances of spatial placement which exhibited distinct commonalities and these distinctions were important for our analysis. Therefore, we decided to differentiate between placement in relation to the body and placement in space. The updated coding scheme has the following categories and subcategories: placement in relation to body (on/above/tracing/sides), spatial placement (on surface/on air). Subcategories under placement (other than spatial) were preserved under the placement in relation to body and sides was added as a new subcategory as it was observed frequently in the visualizations.

Direction. Our participants thought that thinking about the motion of visualizations was important. While examining how motion was reflected in the visualizations, we observed that some of the visualizations had a movement direction, while some of them were static. We updated the framework and coding scheme to include direction (horizontal/vertical/circular) subcategory.

Dimension. Our framework differentiated between flat and volumetric visualizations. While evaluating the produced visualizations, we realized that this differentiation was ambiguous and could either relate to the dimension of the composition or its elements. Therefore this decision is separated into two as dimension of composition and dimension of shapes in the framework. Instead of having dimension category, the coding scheme includes: dimension of shapes (flat/volumetric), dimension of composition (flat/volumetric).

Style of Composition. We identified some trends in general composition structure and decided to create a category for these in the coding scheme. The four general stylistic choices were using particle, planar, cylindrical and blob-like structures. The framework and the coding scheme were updated to include style of composition (particle/planar/cylindrical/blob/other) as a decision.

Fig. 3. Sample visualizations from each group

4.3   Analysis of Generated Ideas

Based on the coding scheme discussed in the previous subsection, the principal coder coded all of the visualizations and a secondary coder coded 20% of them (12 out of 59), the intercoder agreement was 86.73%. Before coding, we separated the visualizations into 10 groups based on their general appearance first and then made some adjustments based on their specificity, style of composition and placement values. In Fig. 3 you can find a sample visualization for each group. These groups represent some common tendencies in emotion visualization among our participants and this categorization is important for our future studies as discussed in the Future Directions section. Due to space limitations, we can't share the characteristics of each group but this information can be made available upon request. Using Spearman correlation, we checked whether the subcategories correlate with each other and because the codes were binary (0 or 1) we also checked similarity index (Jaccard). The fields that relate to each other (>0.6) in both of these analyses were: group (temporality) and on air (spatial placement) (*Spearman*: 0.70, *Jaccard*: 0.65), planar (composition style) and flat (dimension of composition) (*Spearman*: 0.81, *Jaccard*: 0.78), volumetric (dimension of shapes) and volumetric (dimension of composition) (*Spearman*: 0.61, *Jaccard*: 0.68).

4.4   Conclusion

While working on the task of visualizing emotional states in AR, we took a co-design approach to account for different ways of expression. During visualization workshops we identified the need for an affective visualization framework to guide the design process. In this paper, we address this gap by providing an emotion visualization framework for AR, that was formed and refined through a series of workshops and a focus group with designers.

We plan to evaluate the framework, in terms of usability and comprehensibility, by publishing it on an interactive website and getting feedback from designers. Moreover, we plan to implement the aforementioned 10 groups of visualizations as social media AR filters and video chat backgrounds to both evaluate how the framework performs when used for design tasks and whether the 10 groups have different effects on emotion communication and awareness when used in different contexts.

References

1. DiBartolomeo, D.J., Clark, Z., Davis, K.: A new method for analyzing data from visual artwork. Visitor Stud. **18**(1), 103–120 (2015). https://doi.org/10.1080/10645578.2015.1016370
2. Gaver, W.W., Beaver, J., Benford, S.: Ambiguity as a resource for design. In: Proceedings of the SIGCHI Conference on Human Factors in Computing Systems (CHI 2003), pp. 233–240.. ACM, New York (2003). https://doi.org/10.1145/642611.642653

3. Hartl, P., Fischer, T., Hilzenthaler, A., Kocur, M., Schmidt, T.: Audiencear - utilising augmented reality and emotion tracking to address fear of speech. In: Proceedings of Mensch Und Computer 2019 (MuC 2019), pp. 913–916. ACM, New York (2019). https://doi.org/10.1145/3340764.3345380

4. Hassenzahl, M., Heidecker, S., Eckoldt, K., Diefenbach, S., Hillmann, U.: All you need is love: Current strategies of mediating intimate relationships through technology. ACM Trans. Comput. Hum. Interact. **19**(4), 252 (2012). https://doi.org/10.1145/2395131.2395137

5. Hussain, M.S., Monkaresi, H., Calvo, R.A.: Categorical vs. dimensional representations in multimodal affect detection during learning. In: Cerri, S.A., Clancey, W.J., Papadourakis, G., Panourgia, K. (eds.) ITS 2012. LNCS, vol. 7315, pp. 78–83. Springer, Heidelberg (2012). https://doi.org/10.1007/978-3-642-30950-2_11

6. Judge, T.K., Neustaedter, C., Kurtz, A.F.: The family window: the design and evaluation of a domestic media space. In: Proceedings of the SIGCHI Conference on Human Factors in Computing Systems (CHI 2010), pp. 2361–2370. ACM, New York (2010). https://doi.org/10.1145/1753326.1753682

7. Lappalainen, T., Colley, A., Beekhuyzen, J., Häkkilä, J.: Candle shadow display for ambient communication delivery. In: Proceedings of the 2016 ACM Conference Companion Publication on Designing Interactive Systems (DIS 2016), pp. 13–16. Companion, ACM, New York (2016). https://doi.org/10.1145/2908805.2908809

8. Li, H., Häkkilä, J., Väänänen, K.: Review of unconventional user interfaces for emotional communication between long-distance partners. In: Proceedings of the 20th International Conference on Human-Computer Interaction with Mobile Devices and Services. ACM, New York (2018). https://doi.org/10.1145/3229434.3229467

9. Pohl, H., Dalsgaard, T.S., Krasniqi, V., Hornbæk, K.: Body layars: a toolkit for body-based augmented reality. In: 26th ACM Symposium on Virtual Reality Software and Technology (VRST 2020) , ACM, New York (2020). https://doi.org/10.1145/3385956.3418946

10. Roberts, J.: Using affective computing for proxemic interactions in mixed-reality. In: Proceedings of the Symposium on Spatial User Interaction (SUI 2018), pp. 176. ACM, New York (2018). https://doi.org/10.1145/3267782.3274692

11. Russell, J.A.: A circumplex model of affect. J. Pers. Soc. Psychol. **39**(6), 1161–1178 (1980)

12. Ryan, R.M., Deci, E.L.: Self-determination theory and the facilitation of intrinsic motivation, social development, and well-being. Am. Psychol. **55**(1), 68–78 (2000)

13. Sartori, A., Culibrk, D., Yan, J.R., Sebe, N.: Computational modeling of affective qualities of abstract paintings. IEEE MultiMedia **23**(3), 44–54 (2016). https://doi.org/10.1109/MMUL.2016.20

14. Valdez, P., Mehrabian, A.: Effects of color on emotions. J. Exp. Psychol. General **123**(4), 394 (1994). https://doi.org/10.1037/0096-3445.123.4.394

15. Zhang, E.Y., Cheok, A.D., Nishiguchi, S., Morisawa, Y.: Kissenger: development of a remote kissing device for affective communication. In: Proceedings of the 13th International Conference on Advances in Computer Entertainment Technology (ACE 2016). ACM, New York (2016). https://doi.org/10.1145/3001773.3001831

Exploring an Immersive User Interface in Virtual Reality Storytelling

Gapyuel Seo(✉)

Hongik University, Sejong 30016, South Korea
gapseo@hongik.ac.kr

Abstract. Virtual reality provides a highly immersive experience as the player's actions interact with the virtual world in real time, and feedback is immediately reflected. We explored a device that could enhance immersion by inducing a natural interaction between the player and the virtual world through VR storytelling. In this study, we mainly concentrated on utilizing affordance in the diegetic UI, which constitutes the virtual world, to increase immersion by inducing natural interaction for the player. To use affordance in VR storytelling, we classified physical affordance, cognitive affordance, sensory affordance, and functional affordance as roles that support diegetic UI. We suggest cognitive affordance and physical affordance to recognize and execute the need for interaction necessary to progress the story. We also suggest sensory affordance and functional affordance to detect the target smoothly and help the player's intentional sequence of actions from a functional point of view. Finally, we suggest that the player's immersion can be improved by supporting affordances so that the story can progress through the diegetic UI and natural interaction with the player.

Keywords: Virtual reality · Affordance · Diegetic UI

1 Introduction

With the development of virtual reality technology, immersive virtual reality (IVR) content is being produced that allows players to immerse themselves in the virtual world more intensively. The use of a head-mounted display (HMD) has the advantage of providing users with a strong sense of immersion. However, it is difficult for players to be immersed in the experience if they do not interact smoothly with the virtual world or are uncomfortable with the reaction speed and feedback [1]. Easy and convenient communication between the virtual world and the player is enabled through the user interface (UI). The UI connects players to the virtual world and is a necessary medium for interaction [2]. The player's field of view is entirely covered by the HMD as the player interacts with the virtual world in the IVR. The player is blocked from information from the real world and plays only with the information provided in the virtual world. We need to facilitate natural interaction between the player and the virtual world through the UI in order to induce immersion in IVR [3]. Natural interaction allows the player to empathize with the characters in the story and actively explore the virtual world. The

C. Stephanidis et al. (Eds.): HCII 2021, CCIS 1498, pp. 385–389, 2021.
https://doi.org/10.1007/978-3-030-90176-9_50

significance of UI in virtual reality is the smooth interaction between the player and the virtual world that allows the player to manipulate the virtual world as in real life [4]. In this study, we suggest using a diegetic UI to provide a better immersive experience to the player in the virtual world. We also suggest an affordance to enhance interactivity with the diegetic UI. The player can proceed with the story by directly interacting with the elements that make up the virtual environment. We enhanced the interaction with diegetic elements, such as all characters, entities, and sounds in the virtual world. We explored supporting affordances so that the story can proceed through natural interactions with diegetic elements and players.

The purpose of this study is to explore ways to enhance immersion by inducing natural interaction to the player by utilizing the diegetic UI elements and affordances that make up the virtual world in IVR storytelling.

2   Diegetic UI in the VR Storytelling

IVR storytelling enables the active participation of players and highly immersive experiences. We implemented the story world in a virtual space and proceeded with the story through direct interaction between the player and diegetic elements. The virtual space wherein the story progresses can show a fantasy world that exists only in fiction or places that the player cannot physically visit. Players can become the main characters in the story and empathize with the characters' experiences through their perspectives. In IVR storytelling, players are placed in the space where the story unfolds and have the freedom to choose what they want to see. In other words, the player is no longer a passive observer but becomes the subject of the immersive experience. However, it is not easy to keep the player focused on the narrative as they can move their gaze freely and get distracted. Therefore, there is a need for a device that will not interfere with the player's immersion and can induce the sense of the natural progression of the story. In this study, the story begins in a room that the player can experience in reality and moves to a fantasy world to proceed with the adventure. Starting from a place that the player can often encounter in real life, the sense of heterogeneity of the virtual world is reduced. The story gradually moves to a fantasy place where interesting events are unfolding [5]. We focused on setting and creating the surroundings by predicting the movement path and leading the player's interest by inducing the interaction necessary for the story's progress with diegetic UI. Diegetic elements exist in the virtual world and are things that the player can see or directly interact with within the virtual world [6]. Players can see the elements that make up the virtual world through the avatar's point of view and directly manipulate them as in the real world. The player intuitively interacts with the environment in the virtual world and is better immersed in the story world through the protagonist's perspective in the story [7].

3   Affordance

Affordance refers to a property that causes an entity to induce action through interaction with the player. We suggest that this entity is the diegetic UI element which will interact with the player in this study. The player can naturally take a specific action by recognizing an entity in a particular situation [8]. When we design entities for interactions, we need to present the possibility of inducing player behavior to induce desired interactions. In addition, the adoption of appropriate affordances in virtual environments provides strong clues to induce specific behavior in players [9, 10]. In this study, we categorized the affordance of the virtual environment into cognitive affordance, physical affordance, sensory affordance, and functional affordance as elements that help the user's behavior from a functional point of view so that diegetic UI design can be applied [11].

Table 1. Summary of affordance type

Type	Description	Example
Cognitive affordance	This element helps the player check and guess what can happen when they interact within the virtual world.	
Physical affordance	This element helps the player intuitively interact with an entity that can open, pull, turn, pick up, or throw.	
Sensory affordance	This element helps the player smoothly recognize the entity to interact with through visual and auditory effects.	
Functional affordance	This element helps the player to interact so that the story can progress sequentially (system design and place transition).	

We presented the cognitive affordance, sensory affordance, and functional affordance to consider the relationship with physical affordance to smoothly interact with the diegetic UI (Table 1).

- Cognitive affordance was provided with clues on posters or blackboards to help the player guess the possible interaction outcomes.

- Physical affordance was placed as a diegetic entity that allowed the player to sense the intent of the interaction quickly. Entities were set where the player could open a box, pick up a book, or rotate the globe.
- Sensory affordance was placed a visual and auditory effects to induce a player's attention to interaction.
- Functional affordance was designed to sequentially interact with the objects that were clues necessary for story progression.

As a cognitive affordance factor, the possibility of player interaction was increased through the guidance of the player's position movement and the interactive entity. As a physical affordance factor, entity manipulation and the player's physical behavior were induced through the use of an entity with increased accessibility for the player. As sensory affordance elements, real-time graphic elements, such as effects and auditory elements, were used to support cognitive affordance and physical affordance. A guide system that sequentially activates the diegetic UI necessary for story progression was supported as a functional affordance element. In addition, the player's experience environment was functionally adjusted as a change in the story development location.

We applied affordances to the diegetic UI design to add cues for players to perform specific actions. Figure 1 shows the correlation diagram between diegetic UI and affordance.

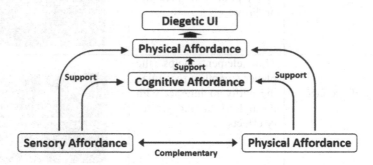

Fig. 1. Affordance diagram

4 Conclusion and Future Work

In this study, we induced players to take action in a specific context and led them to be immersed in the story by supporting affordance in the diegetic UI. We induced the player's action by giving various affordance devices to proceed with the story through natural interaction with diegetic elements, as per the narrative structure. The player's experience is essential in IVR storytelling, and we developed the design of the diegetic UI and affordances to create the optimal experience. The player's experience through the induction of such natural behavior seeks the player's autonomy and prevents them from recognizing that the environment is controlled as much as possible. Allowing the player to explore as much as possible in virtual reality, through interaction with diegetic elements, allows us to respect the player's instinctive desires while providing an immersive experience. However, the utilization of an interface that applies affordances to diegetic elements, constituting the world of virtual reality, will enable natural interaction for the player and lead to a better immersive experience. For future studies, we plan to conduct a user study by analyzing the interaction behavior process.

Acknowledgements. This work was supported by the Ministry of Education of the Republic of Korea and the National Research Foundation of Korea (NRF-2019S1A5A2A01047357).

1. References

1. Tanaka, N., Takagi, H.: Virtual reality environment design of managing both presence and virtual reality sickness. J. Physiol. Anthropol. Appl. Hum. Sci. **23**(6), 313–317 (2004)
2. Schell, J.: The Art of Game Design: A book of lenses. CRC Press, Burlington (2008)
3. Sanchez-Vives, M.V., Slater, M.: From presence to consciousness through virtual reality. Nat. Rev. Neurosci. **6**(4), 332–339 (2005)
4. Bowman, D.A., Kruijff, E., LaViola Jr, J.J., Poupyrev, I.: An introduction to 3D user interface design. Presence: Teleoperators Virtual Environ. **10**(1), 96–108 (2001)
5. Seo, G.: Implementation of immersive virtual reality through the analysis of diegetic user interface. In: Stephanidis, C., Antona, M. (eds.) HCII 2020. CCIS, vol. 1225, pp. 116–121. Springer, Cham (2020). https://doi.org/10.1007/978-3-030-50729-9_16
6. Fagerholt, E., Lorentzon, M.: Beyond the HUD - user interfaces for increased player immersion in FPS games. Master of Science Thesis, Chalmers University of Technology (2009).
7. Dickey, M.D.: Engaging by design: How engagement strategies in popular computer and video games can inform instructional design. Educ. Tech. Res. Dev. **53**(2), 67–83 (2005)
8. Gibson, J.J.: The Ecological Approach to Visual Perception. Houghton Mifflin, New York (1979)
9. Gaver, W. W.: Technology affordances. In: Proceedings of the SIGCHI conference on Human factors in computing systems, pp. 79–84 (1991)
10. Norman, D.A.: Affordance, conventions, and design. Interactions **6**(3), 38–43 (1999)
11. Hartson, R.: Cognitive, physical, sensory, and functional affordances in interaction design. Behaviour & information technology **22**(5), 315–338 (2003)

Developing Spatial Visualization Skills with Virtual Reality and Hand Tracking

Liam Stewart[1] and Christian Lopez[2](✉)

[1] Department of Computer and Electrical Engineering, Lafayette College,
Easton, PA 18042, USA
[2] Department of Computer Science, Lafayette College, Easton, PA 18042, USA
lopebec@lafayette.edu

Abstract. Spatial visualization skills are the cognitive skills required to mentally comprehend and manipulate 2D and 3D shapes. Spatial visualization skills are recognized as a crucial part of STEM education. Moreover, these skills have been linked to both students' capacity for self-monitored learning and GPA in STEM programs. Also, many STEM fields have reported a correlation between spatial visualization skills and the level of academic success of students. Unfortunately, many students have significantly underdeveloped spatial visualization skills. Students traditionally learn spatial visualization skills via the manipulation of 3D objects and drawings. Because Virtual Reality (VR) facilitates the manipulation of 3D virtual objects, it is an effective medium to teach spatial visualization skills. In addition, it has been found that students are more motivated to learn and perform better when taught in an immersive VR environment. Several studies have presented promising results on leveraging VR to teach spatial visualization skills. However, in most of these studies, the users are not able to naturally interact with the 3D virtual objects. Additionally, many of the current VR applications fail to implement spatial presence for the user, which would lead to more effective instruction. The level of immersivity a VR application offers can have a direct impact on the users' "first-person" experience and engagement. In light of this, a VR application integrated with hand tracking technology designed to develop spatial visualization skills of STEM students is presented. The inclusion of a user's hand in the virtual environment could increase the users' sense of spatial presence and first-person experience. In addition, this could act as an intuitive input method for beginners. The objective of this work is to introduce this VR application as well as future work on how to leverage Reinforcement Learning to automatically generate new 3D virtual objects [github.com/lopezbec/VR_Spatia lVisualizationApp].

Keywords: Virtual reality · Spatial skills · Immersion

1 Introduction

Spatial skills are the cognitive skills required to mentally comprehend and manipulate three-dimensional shapes [1]. These spatial skills primarily include the rotating

© Springer Nature Switzerland AG 2021
C. Stephanidis et al. (Eds.): HCII 2021, CCIS 1498, pp. 390–398, 2021.
https://doi.org/10.1007/978-3-030-90176-9_51

and the cutting of three-dimensional shapes. Spatial skills are recognized as a crucial part of STEM education and are directly connected to both an individual's capacity for self-monitored learning and their GPA in STEM programs [2, 3]. Some of the STEM fields that have recorded relations between spatial skills and level of academic success include Chemical Engineering, Civil Engineering, and Computer Science [1, 3, 4]. Unfortunately, many STEM students significantly lack spatial skills when they begin their studies [5].

Whether it is through repetitions of the rotation test or through utilizing building blocks as a toy during their youth, individuals traditionally learn spatial skills via the manipulation of 3D objects [5]. Considering both how virtual reality (VR) facilitates the manipulation of 3D virtual objects, and VR's growing presence as a learning tool, it is an effective medium to teach spatial skills through. In addition, it has been found that students are more motivated to learn and perform better when taught in an immersive VR environment [6, 7]. These benefits would be valuable when used to teach spatial skills. In addition, these benefits are greater the more immersive the VR system is [7]. Currently, there is a multitude of examples of VR being used to teach and assess spatial skills, which include the Purdue Spatial Visualization Test (PSVT) [8] - rotation test, the Paper Folding Test, the Mental Cutting Test, the Mental Rotation Test and Spatial Navigation Test [8]. Within these examples, several limitations negatively impact the technology regarding immersion. The primary limitation is that the display method used is only responsible for a fraction of a student's immersion in a virtual environment. The perceived spatial presence of a user, which is based on the controls used to interact with the virtual environment, plays a much larger factor in the immersion of the user [9]. Many of the current VR applications for spatial skills development fail to implement spatial presence for the user, which would lead to more effective instruction [10]. In order to address this requirement for immersion, this project will implement hand tracking, which enables naturalistic movement to interact with the environment. These naturalistic movements will increase a user's immersion [9].

Another limitation to using VR to teach spatial skills is the novelty effect. The novelty effect is the positive motivational effect that accompanies an individual trying a new device or technology. When the impact of the novelty effect significantly alters a user's mindset toward a task, it would lead to the positive effects of the new device or technology dwindling once the individual becomes accustomed to it [11]. The lack of new content within VR programs can contribute to the significance of the novelty effect [11]. The novelty effect can be mitigated by creating applications with more content and variety. Unfortunately, the cost of creating content in immersive VR has not significantly decreased since it originated [7]. A potential way to avoid this issue is to use procedurally generated content, which this project plans to facilitate using a machine learning agent.

2 Literary Review

2.1 Development of Spatial Skills

An individual's spatial skills are initially developed through the physical manipulation of 3D objects in one's youth [5, 12]. However, it is also known that spatial skills can be taught to individuals beyond this initial learning as a child [8]. The repetitions of spatial tasks such as the Mental Rotation Test (MRT) [8] and stacking blocks can lead to the development of spatial skills in a student [13]. In addition, STEM professionals and teachers all have significantly greater spatial skills than the general population, which further supports the idea that spatial skills can be learned through the repetition of spatial tasks, such as those in STEM fields [14]. The knowledge that spatial skills can be taught via the manipulation of 3D shapes has led to VR becoming an effective tool for educators to use to teach spatial skills.

2.2 VR in Education

Just as with the onset of the internet, as VR technologies became more widespread, they became more integrated into the education system [15]. During this initial integration, from 2000 to 2016, nearly half of all studies regarding VR as a teaching tool were related to engineering [16]. In these studies, VR as an education tool is usually divided into immersive and non-immersive VR platforms, however a standardized use of the term immersive had not yet been established [15] In a modern context, immersive VR first requires the use of a head-mounted display (HMD) and secondly requires the user to be able to interact with the virtual environment they are in [7, 16]. Immersion is valuable in the context of VR as means of learning because many of its benefits correlate to how immersed a user is in the virtual environment. Specifically, how enjoyable a learning experience is, how intrinsically motivated a user is, and a user's long-term behavior retention of material learn are all proportionally correlated to how immersive their learning experience was [7]. All this considered, there are limits to the benefits of VR as a tool for education such as the novelty effect and the cost of generating an immersive VR experience for students. Although the hardware cost of immersive VR platforms has steadily been decreasing, the cost of generating content for those platforms has not significantly changed [17]. With these two flaws in mind, the use of PGC would circumnavigate the cost of generating new content while also generating enough new content to avoid the novelty effect.

2.3 VR for Spatial Skills

VR as a medium for teaching spatial skills has been significantly researched in the past, and there are many studies that detailed its effects [16]. From these studies, there is a consistent result, which is that VR is an effective medium for teaching spatial skills [8, 18]. In fact, there are many advantages to using VR to teach spatial skills. When compared to other technologies like lecture-based learning, and desktop VR, Immersive VR leads to students more effectively learning and retaining spatial skills [8]. Immersive VR has also been shown to increase how much a student can improve their spatial skills from a pre-learning benchmark when compared to control using a traditional method of teaching spatial skills [18]. In addition, users have a greater spatial perception in immersive VR when compared to a conventional workstation.

Some studies have already focused on exploring the value of VR for developing spatial visualization skills [8, 13]. One of these papers [8], was a study of if immersive VR is a better tool for teaching compared to non-immersive VR. This study found that immersive VR was the superior educational tool via the MRT and the PSVT. The application proposed in this study also takes inspiration from the MRT and focuses on using PGC to supply shapes to be used in the assessments of students' skills. This generation of shapes could circumnavigate the novelty effect when compared to the previous study. Another study that utilized immersive VR to teach spatial skills by enabling a user to stack blocks in a virtual environment was presented in [13]. The MRT is used in this study as it is a test that can yield quantitative data about a user's spatial skills, which cannot be gathered from a task like stacking blocks. This study also improves on how a user interacts with the virtual environment by implementing hand tracking as the means of the user interface, which is more intuitive and easier to use compared to the controller-based user interface in the comparative study.

3 VR Application for Spatial Skills

The application introduced in this work has two versions: -(i) The first is designed for a conventional desktop, mouse, and keyboard, and (ii) the other is designed for a VR headset with hand tracking (e.g., Oculus Quest). These two versions will be utilized to further study the effects of VR as a medium for teaching spatial skills. The data collected from the students using VR will be compared to those of the students using the desktop version. Analyzing such data could enable us to draw a conclusion about the effectiveness of VR to help developed students' spatial skills. Readers that are interested in the application, videos of it, or following up in its development, can find more information in the GitHub repo: github.com/lopezbec/VR_SpatialVisualizationApp.

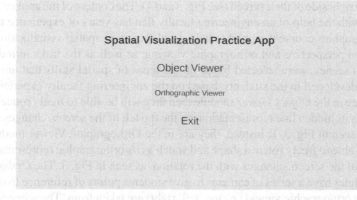

Spatial Visualization Practice App

Object Viewer

Orthographic Viewer

Exit

Fig. 1. Image of the start menu of the application

When the application is started, a user menu, as shown in Fig. 1, appears and prompts the user to select one of the two available modules. The two modules *Object Viewer* and *Orthographic Viewer* focus on teaching and testing different representations of 3D virtual objects. Within the *Object Viewer*, a user will see different 3D virtual shapes and will be rotating them in accordance with the scene in use. Whereas in *Orthographic Viewer*, a user will be interacting with a 3D virtual shape and its orthographic representation. Once a module is selected, the user will see a pop-up introduction window that explains the concepts of either perfective or orthopractic views. The user is then within the "free mode" scene of the module they selected to help them get familiarized with the interface of the module. In the desktop version of the application, they can use their mouse or keyboard to rotate the 3D virtual object in any of the three axes (as shown in Fig. 2 and 3). In the VR version o the application, they can use their hand directly to rotate the 3D virtual object, as shown in Fig. 2.

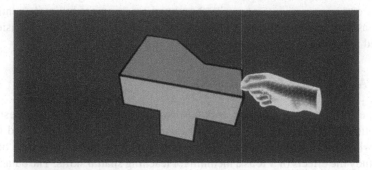

Fig. 2. User in VR uses hand tracking to interact with the 3D virtual shape

Subsequently, they are taken through a series of scenes that presents them with different tasks designed to help them develop and evaluate their spatial skills. These scenes increase in complexity as they advance through the module. The user can also manually select a unique scene they would like to go directly using the scene selection menu on the right side of their screen (see Fig. 3 and 4). The content of the application was developed with the help of an engineering faculty that has years of experience teaching students a graphics course designed to help developed their spatial visualization skills. The focus on perspective and orthographic viewing, as well as the tasks introduced in the different scenes, were selected based on the areas of spatial skills that are usually more underdeveloped in the students, based on the engineering faculty experience.

If they are in the *Object Viewer* module then they will be able to freely rotate a shape and watch as its hidden line representation, on the top left of the screen, changes with the rotation, as seen in Fig. 3. If instead, they are in the Orthographic Viewer module then they will be able to freely rotate a shape and watch as its orthographic representation, on the top left of the screen, changes with the rotation, as seen in Fig. 3. The *Orthographic Viewer* modules have a series of cameras to give students points of reference from where the different orthographic views (i.e., top, left, right) are taken from. The scene selection menu enables our users to select which scene in the module they would like to complete.

Within the *Object Viewer* and *Orthographic Viewer* modules, the scenes, shown in Fig. 4 and Fig. 5, are designed to teach and assess different elements of the user's spatial skills. The first two scenes in the *Object Viewer* module are designed around the concept of a user mimicking the rotations of an additional shape in the display. The following module *"Copy rotation As To"*, reveals the stating orientation and the ending orientation of a shape, and tasks the user with transforming their shape in the same manner as the one rotated by the computer. The third type of scene in the module are the assessment scenes. Within them, either a 3D or 2D shape must be paired with their corresponding

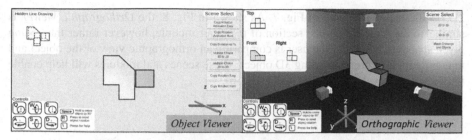

Fig. 3. Free mode of the perspective and orthographic viewer

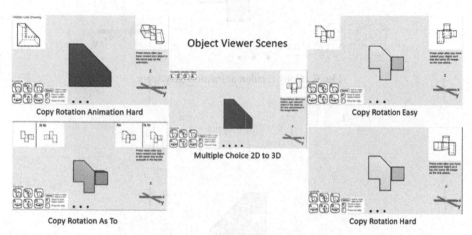

Fig. 4. The scenes in the object viewer module

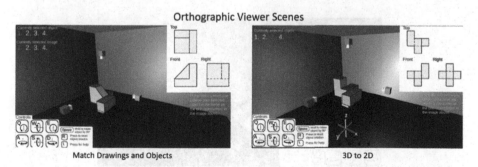

Fig. 5. The scenes in the orthographic viewer module

2D or 3D shape, as shown in Fig. 7. As shown in Fig. 8, the *Orthographic Viewer* is similar to the multiple-choice section of the other module, however rather than being given shapes to compare, the user is comparing an orthographic view of the object and matching it to the corresponding 3D object. These scenes and modules will help enable individuals to developed spatial skills (Fig. 6).

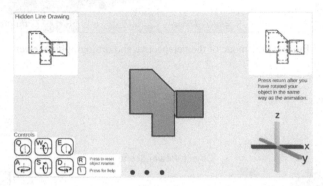

Fig. 6. Copy rotation animation easy scene.

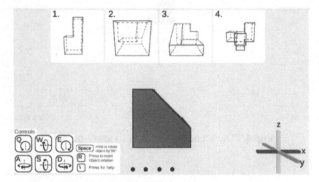

Fig. 7. Object viewer multiple-choice question example

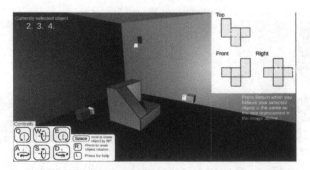

Fig. 8. Orthographic viewer multiple-choice question example

4 Conclusion

With both versions, both modules, and many scenes, this program could not only enable users to determine how large a factor VR is for teaching spatial skills but also be used as a learning tool for those learning spatial skills. In the future, we hope to expand on this project by using Procedural Content Generation to create a wide range of 3D virtual shapes for this program to use, as well as to integrate more modules and scenes to help users developed their spatial skills.

1. References

1. Sorby, S.A., Duffy, G., Loney, N., Perez, L.: Spatial skills and their correlation with engineering problem-solving. In: *29th Australasian Association for Engineering Education Conference 2018 (AAEE 2018)*, p. 10. Engineers Australia
2. Sorby, S., Veurink, N., Streiner, S.: Does spatial skills instruction improve STEM outcomes? The answer is 'yes.' Learn. Individ. Differ. **67**, 209–222 (2018). https://doi.org/10.1016/j.lindif.2018.09.001
3. Roca-González, C., Martin-Gutierrez, J., García-Dominguez, M., Mato Carrodeguas, M.D.C.: Virtual technologies to develop visual-spatial ability in engineering students. Eurasia Journal of Mathematics, Science and Technology Education, **13**(2), 441–468 (2017). https://doi.org/10.12973/eurasia.2017.00625a.
4. Parkinson, J., Cutts, Q.: Investigating the relationship between spatial skills and computer science. In: ICER 2018 of the Proceedings of the 2018 ACM Conference on International Computing Education Research, pp. 106–114, (2018). https://doi.org/10.1145/3230977.3230990.
5. Verdine, B.N., Golinkoff, R.M., Hirsh-Pasek, K., Newcombe, N.S.: I. spatial skills, their development, and their links to mathematics. Monographs Soc. Res. Child Develop.**82**(1), 7-30 (2017). https://doi.org/10.1111/mono
6. Makransky, G., Lilleholt, L.: A structural equation modeling investigation of the emotional value of immersive virtual reality in education. Education Tech. Res. Dev. **66**(5), 1141–1164 (2018). https://doi.org/10.1007/s11423-018-9581-2
7. Makransky, G., Borre-Gude, S., Mayer, R.E.: Motivational and cognitive benefits of training in immersive virtual reality based on multiple assessments. J. Comput. Assist. Learn. **35**(6), 691–707 (2019). https://doi.org/10.1111/jcal.12375
8. Guzsvinecz, T., Orbán-Mihálykó, É., Perge, E., Sik-Lányi, C.: Analyzing the Spatial Skills of University Students with a Virtual Reality Application using a Desktop Display and the Gear VR. Acta Polytech. Hungarica **17**(2), 35–56 (2020)
9. Seibert, J., Shafer, D.M.: Control mapping in virtual reality: effects on spatial presence and controller naturalness. Virtual Reality **22**(1), 79–88 (2017). https://doi.org/10.1007/s10055-017-0316-1
10. Coxon, M., Kelly, N., Page, S.: Individual differences in virtual reality: are spatial presence and spatial ability linked? Virtual Reality **20**(4), 203–212 (2016). https://doi.org/10.1007/s10055-016-0292-x
11. Huang, W., Roscoe, R., Johnson, M., Craig, S.: Investigating the Novelty Effect in Virtual Reality on STEM Learning (2020).
12. Gold, Z.S., Elicker, J., Kellerman, A.M., Christ, S., Mishra, A.A., Howe, N.: Engineering play, mathematics, and spatial skills in children with and without disabilities. Early Educ. Dev. **32**(1), 49–65 (2021). https://doi.org/10.1080/10409289.2019.1709382

13. Lee, M.J.W.: Institute of Electrical and Electronics Engineers. New South Wales Section, IEEE Education Society, University of Wollongong, Charles Sturt University, and Institute of Electrical and Electronics Engineers. In: Proceedings of 2018 IEEE International Conference on Teaching, Assessment, and Learning for Engineering (TALE) : date and venue, 4–7 December, Novotel Wollongong Northbeach Hotel, Wollongong, NSW, Australia.
14. Atit, K., Miller, D.I., Newcombe, N.S., Uttal, D.H.: Teachers' spatial skills across disciplines and education levels: exploring nationally representative data. Arch. Sci. Psychol. 6(1), 130–137 (2018). https://doi.org/10.1037/arc0000041
15. Radianti, J., Majchrzak, T.A., Fromm, J., Wohlgenannt, I.: A systematic review of immersive virtual reality applications for higher education: design elements, lessons learned, and research agenda. Comput. Educ. 147, 103778 (2020). https://doi.org/10.1016/j.compedu.2019.103778
16. Vergara, D., Rubio, M.P., Lorenzo, M.: On the design of virtual reality learning environments in engineering. Multimodal Tech. Inter. 1(2), 11 (2017). https://doi.org/10.3390/mti1020011
17. Román-Ibáñez, V., Pujol-López, F.A., Mora-Mora, H., Pertegal-Felices, M.L., Jimeno-Morenilla, A.: A low-cost immersive virtual reality system for teaching robotic manipulators programming. Sustainability 10(4), 1102 (2018). https://doi.org/10.3390/su10041102
18. Molina-Carmona, R., Pertegal-Felices, M.L., Jimeno-Morenilla, A., Mora-Mora, H.: Virtual reality learning activities for multimedia students to enhance spatial ability. Sustainability 10(4), 1074 (2018). https://doi.org/10.3390/su10041074

The Effect of Avatar Embodiment on Self-presence and User Experience for Sensory Control Virtual Reality System

Huey-Min Sun[✉]

Department Information Management, Chang Jung Christian University, Tainan, Taiwan
prince@mail.cjcu.edu.tw

Abstract. The aim of this study is to explore the factors of virtual character embodiment, self-presence, user experience for the somatosensory control virtual reality (VR) system. We would like to understand the influences of avatar embodiment on self-presence and user experience. According to literature review, we constructed the hypotheses based on a systematic view of thinking from the emotional design theory. In order to efficiently realize the extent to which avatar embodiment, we make use of the quenstionaire of Gonzalez-Franco and Peck (Gonzalez-Franco, M., and Peck, T.C. Avatar Embodiment. Towards a Standardized Questionnaire. Front. Robot. AI, 2018, 5:74. https://doi.org/10.3389/frobt.2018.00074) to assess the embodiment level of subjects. Experimental design shows two kind of task types to understand the effect of avatar embodiment on self-presence and user experience. One is non-verbal behaviour experimental design such as dance practicing, while the other is verbal behaviour experimental design like sing practicing.

Keywords: Embodiment · Self-presence · User experience

1 Introduction

Nowadays, somatosensory interactive technology is gradually maturing and popular, virtual characters are becoming more and more easily to operate, especially in the network generation of virtual character enthusiasts all over the world. Virtual characters influence from the 2D industry gradually expanded to 3D modeling. YouTuber's business model from the Internet also extends to the virtual tuber, called VTuber. This new business mode is constantly innovative technology. In order to stand out from the fierce competition, each VTuber in the virtual character setting has its own story and characteristics, which are to attract different groups of fans and meet the operator's own preferences projection. VTuber first appeared in Japan in 2017 and features anime-like video. There are currently more than 10,000 VTubers, some of whom have their own TV shows or work with international companies [12]. Toshiro from Hitachi of Japan has also shifted from home appliance advertising campaigns for traditional Japanese boy idol ARASHI to digital areas such as personal computers and smartphones where young customers

© Springer Nature Switzerland AG 2021
C. Stephanidis et al. (Eds.): HCII 2021, CCIS 1498, pp. 399–409, 2021.
https://doi.org/10.1007/978-3-030-90176-9_52

watch ads. This led Toshida to develop an original virtual character, Takata, with a new youth-centric form of communication [1].

Therefore, virtual characters applied in the virtual reality systems are increasing with the somatosensory technology and the application involved in user experience is related to the user perception of self-presence extension. These important relationship must rely on that user perceives the extent to which avatar embodiment.

This study uses somatosensory control to construct virtual reality experience of virtual characters for users, and analyzes the positive impact of virtual character embodiment on user experience and self-presence by reviewing the literature of presence and user experience. Role traits can enhance the user experience and identity, the higher the sense of presence in the virtual experience, the higher the feedback of the user experience. Therefore, the virtual character and the user have a link to reach virtual character embodiment on user experience and self-presence. The study is expected to accomplish the following objectives:

1. Establishing the characteristics of the virtual character

Virtual character is set by appearance, gender, values, situation, and so on. User's perception from the setting can enhance the experiencer's perception. We would like to explore whether the extent to which virtual character embodiment will affect the subject's self-presence and user experience. Emotional expression of virtual character through the face recognition technology can be transmitted by the user's facial expression to the virtual character's facial expression. According to past literature, the avatar image characteristics of virtual characters have a significant impact on the user experience and self-presence.

2. Enabled self-presence by the somatosensory control of Microsoft Azure Kinect

Microsoft Azure Kinect provides the somatosensory control characterized by deep sensors that allow for rapid back-to-back, human skeleton tracking, and even spatial 3D scanning for virtual reality system interaction without spending time and effort learning unfamiliar operating instructions. According to the literature review, the higher the sense of self-presence subjects perceive, the more positive the quality of feeling happy they experience.

3. Comparing user experiences with different context tasks

The study will establish two experimental designs for the virtual character situation with non-verbal dance practicing and the other with verbal sing practicing. We would like to observe the impact of user's highly immersive virtual character experience on self-presence and user experience.

2   Literature Review

Depending on the purpose of research objectives, it is necessary that virtual character is personalized by various human characteristics, such as personality, mood (temperament and drowsiness), and motivation. These personality traits, emotions, and motivations are closely related to self-presence. Therefore, this study further explores the composition of virtual characters, self-presence, and user experience.

2.1 Virtual Character

Virtual characters exist in a variety of media, from simple images, images to commercialization of various forms of presentation. What we saw at first was images, but under the competition of many virtual characters in the commercial market, being able to remember in people's minds must be influenced by the setting of "personality" and "characteristic". Zhou [25] studied the famous virtual character, named as Kizuna AI, as a specific and emerging type of Internet celebrity that consisted of controversial definitions, meanings and values, and Kizuna AI' production company, i.e., bilibili.com, a video platform in China, argued that Vtuber was a mobile cultural category, and that the definitions, characteristics, meanings and values of virtual Internet celebrities were constantly changing. Chang [4] proposed that the construction elements of virtual characters must meet styling, personality, central thinking, background, supporting roles, rendering media, and for comic books and other plot-heavy works of the most important story. The author thought if the virtual character was not satisfied by the basic elements to continue vitality, it was only a 2D image and not a 3D virtual character. In addition, Kenji Ito [7] thought that the construction of virtual characters had five elements, such as concept, world view, theme, personality, and naming. According to above literature, the feature of character element is interpreted as Table 1.

Table 1. The basic elements of virtual character

Character element	Original item	Description
Value	Concept or Central thinking	The virtual character wants to convey values with the central idea of the story
Realistic or Science fiction	World view and meaning	An overview of the word in which the virtual character lives
Task type	Theme and background	The setting of task for the virtual character
Character trait	Personality or styling	The personality and styling of the virtual character

Source: Modified by Chang [4] and Kenji [7]

In the development of the network media, users are differentiated by their different age groups, gender, interests, life experiences on their own preferences. If the content information provided by the virtual character is sufficient to arouse the consumer's preferences and increase their impression, more emotional attention and attitude recognition will be invested in the virtual characters [24]. The basic composition of virtual character can be assessed by the user's cognition through the six indicators of the virtual character embodiment questionnaire [5].

In order to understand the experimental subjects for the extent to which virtual character embodiment, we evaluate subjects' feelings about their virtual characters based on the questionnaires by Gonzalez-Franco and Peck [5]. The six indicators are as follows. (1). Body ownership. Participants may still have physical ownership, although they believe they are not in the same position as their bodies. (2). Body agent and motor control. Participants can use device control to reach the mobile part or all of the virtual roles. (3). Tactile. The participants' feelings are enhanced whenever there is a touch or tactile stimulation. (4). Position of the body. Participants must feel that their bodies are in the same position as their virtual bodies in order to experience hallucinations. Participants may feel the effects outside the body, or their body position may have felt drift to the virtual character's position. (5). Appearance. The character is similar to the self-image. (6). Reaction to external stimuli. In many cases during the experiment, such as modifying or threatening the body or body parts of a virtual character, the virtual character reacts.

2.2 Self-presence

In many studies of virtual reality, presence is often used to assess how users feel after the virtual environment experience. The sense of presence is the subjective experience and psychological feeling in a certain environment, when the interaction way or image in virtual reality is synchronized with the real world. The more the sense of presence, the higher users experience.

Witner-Singer [21] pointed out that having a strong tendency to immerse yourself would produce a higher sense of presence. When VR simulates sensory perception with more information in a virtual environment, it creates a greater sense of immersion. Increased collaboration between vision and hearing enhances the entertainment of virtual reality [3]. Presence has been studied by different issues including physical presence, social presence, spatial presence, and self-presence. In this study, we focus on the extent to which subjects connect to their avatars on self-presence. The concept of self-presence describes how the self is extended into virtual environments through virtual character representations. Self-presence includes proto self-presence, core self-presence, and extended self-presence [17, 19].

Self-presence is relevant to all things involving a connection between individuals and their virtual self-representation [18]. Self-presence is a psychological state in which virtual selves are experienced as the actual self (identity and/or body) in sensory and non-sensory ways. Proto self-presence focuses on user's expectation how a virtual character should behave affects behavior, such as confidence in social interactions and negotiations, both within and beyond the virtual environment. Second, core self-presence is an emotional state for the fundamental physiological level generated through encounters between the proto self-presence and the objects in the virtual environment. Finally, extended self-presence is the idea of identity and dependent on memories of past experiences.

2.3 User Experience

The expression of social behavior supports the interaction between players, such as attracting attention and expressing empathy. This comes mainly from the player's personal knowledge of other players in the game [9]. Experiencing the social activities in the real world can be brought into the game and affect the player's attractiveness, expression, and understanding of the game. For example, the "Dance Dance Revolution" study was presented by Hoysniemi [6], the author thought social participation in the social behavior factors was important for people to influence each other. In addition, simulated golf, when the player in the real life was a golfer, naturally this type of game would attract its own eyes, and the understanding of the rules could be quickly familiar, and past experience would be quickly brought in, so that play more hands-on and input. Laugwitz et al. [9] constructed a research framework including perceived attractiveness, perceived ergonomic quality, and perceived hedonic quality. Bianchi-Berthouze [2] proposed the quality of user experience pleasure to meet the user's sense of accomplishment with the influence of user value, including the ability to make people happy after interaction, meet the user's needs, meet the user's social emotional value and friendship, and have the ability to acquire the added value. Sajjadiet et al. [16] believed that the technology of personality-driven embodied conversational agent (PDECA) could mimic the behavior of real people. PDECA facilitated social interaction with users through tips for verbal, non-verbal, and quasi-verbal cues. Therefore, we design two experimental tasks to understand the difference between social participation tasks, especially for verbal and non-verbal social participation. One is non-verbal social participation, i.e., dance practicing, while the other is verbal social activity, i.e., sing practicing.

2.4 Microsoft Azure Kinect

The advantage of somatosensory control lies in its simple operability. Compared with other controllers, the control method of Microsoft Azure Kinect is simpler and clearer. The Microsoft Azure Kinect sensor has three lenses, the middle lens is an RGB color camera, and the left and right lenses are 3D depth sensors composed of an infrared transmitter and an infrared CMOS camera. At the same time, it is equipped with a focus tracking technology that moves with the focused object. The algorithm uses in-depth information, and the device can detect the user's gestures and the position and direction of the limbs.

Part-based human model tracking uses human body part template features for human body tracking, dividing the human body into regions corresponding to the head, torso, and limbs. A segmentation method based on regional shape classification is proposed by Mikolajczyk et al. [13] to use regional features to detect parts of the human body and then combine these parts of the human body with a higher probability function value. Wu and Nevatia [22] proposed the use of side length features for human body detection and extended this method to object detection and design. Mohan et al. [14] proposed to use human body part cutting to train some body part area detectors as a combination requirement. Shet et al. [20] proposed a method based on logical inference and combining human body parts. The above all use the humanoid template to detect whether some humanoids are present in the image.

3 Approach

The analysis of the evaluation indicators corresponding to the self-presence are shown in Table 2. Virtual reality content construction mainly lies in the experimental design of virtual characters to the subjects about the level of reflection, as shown in Table 2, with the emotional design reflection level in the self-presence corresponding to the planning of the content of the actual, the proto self-presence, the core self-presence, and the extended self-presence. Table 3 presents the requirement of experimental system development to complete the experimental design of virtual character with self-presence. In order to evaluate the user experience at the level of reflection of the subjects, the questionnaire is shown in Table 4.

Table 2. The evaluation indicators of self-presence

Self-presence	Evaluation indicators
Proto self-presence	(1) When I use my virtual character in virtual reality, I feel I can completely close to other characters in the virtual reality (2) When I am in virtual reality, I feel that my virtual character is an extension of my body (3) When something happens to my virtual character in the virtual reality, I feel that happening in my body (4) I feel I can extend through virtual character into virtual reality (5) When I feel like my virtual character is part of my body
Core self-presence	(1) I am also happy when happy events occur in my virtual character (2) I am also surprised when something amazing happens to my virtual character (3) I also feel sad when something sad happens to my virtual character (4) I also get angry when something that makes me angry happens in my virtual character (5) I am also excited when something exciting happens to my virtual character
Extended self-presence	(1) It's easy for me to know the gender of my virtual character (2) It's easy for me to make it clear that my virtual character race (3) It is important to depict my virtual character with the characteristics of my own profile (4) I care about my virtual character age (5) I care about my virtual character race (6) I care about my virtual character gender (7) I care how my virtual character looks

- Hypothesis 1. Users' virtual character embodiment has a significant difference between non-verbal and verbal task situations.
- Hypothesis 2. Self-presence has a significant difference between non-verbal and verbal task situations.

Table 3. The experimental design of self-presence for virtual character

Self-presence	Reflection of emotional needs for virtual character
Proto self-presence	(1) Providing VR system to feel that a user's virtual character is with somatosensory control (2) Providing VR system to feel that a user's virtual character is an extension of his body (3) Providing VR system to feel when something happens to a user's virtual character, he feels like it happened to him
Core self-presence	(1) Providing VR system to feel happy when a happy event occurs in a user's virtual character (2) Providing VR system to feel sad when a sad thing happens to a user's virtual character (3) Providing VR system to feel angry when a thing that makes him angry happens in a user's virtual role
Extended self-presence	(1) Providing VR system to feel easy to know the gender of a user's virtual character (2) Providing VR system to feel easy to make it clear that a user's virtual character race (3) Providing VR system to feel a user's virtual character attracted

Table 4. The evaluation indicators of user experience

User experience	The evaluation indicators
Perceived hedonic quality	(1) After the VR task, I feel a sense of accomplishment (2) After the VR task, I feel that the interaction make me happy (3) After the VR task, I feel that it meets my needs (4) After the VR task, I feel that it meets my social emotional value (5) After the VR task, I feel that it is able to obtain the added value

- Hypothesis 3. Users experience has a significant difference between non-verbal and verbal task situations.
- Hypothesis 4. There is a positive influence on self-presence when users perceive higher the extent to which virtual character embodiment.
- Hypothesis 5. There is a positive influence on user experience when users perceive higher the extent to which virtual character embodiment.
- Hypothesis 6. There is a positive relationship between self-presence and user experience.

4   Experimental Design

Experimental system was created by Unity 3D platform integrated with Microsoft Azure Kinect to capture motion information from subjects. We implemented the Azure Kinect application interface in Unity 3D system to provide the user's virtual character with somatosensory control. Figure 1 shows the motion of virtual character synchronized by that of user. The context tasks were designed as non-verbal dance practicing and verbal sing practicing.

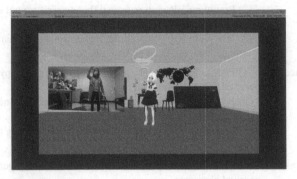

Fig. 1. The synchronization of motion between user and virtual character.

For the virtual character of experimental design, we employed the open tool, called Vroid Studio, from the company Pixiv in Japan. The provided tool could easily create the virtual characters of experimental need. Figure 2 presents the practical operation in the Vroid Studio.

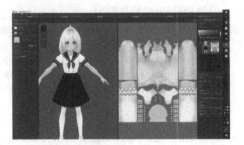

Fig. 2. The interface of Vroid Studio

We made the experimental system of virtual character based on Unity 3D platform. There are important technologies for the requirement of 3D animation including multiple types of animation, different spaces in a 3D scene, translating in local space, and animating models. Unity 3D platform can support these requirements. Figure 3 shows the virtual character experiment system.

Fig. 3. The implementation of the virtual character experiment system

5   Expected Results

From the literature review and discussion, it can be found that the user's operation of the somatosensory control system is affected by cognitive embodiment from the user's virtual character. We think that the extent to which virtual character embodiment will affect the quality of self-presence and user experience. The task experimental design of virtual characters is divided into non-verbal body movement performance like dance practicing and verbal emotional expression like sing practicing for grouping experiments. The study explores whether both self-presence and user experience have significant difference between the two types of virtual character behavior for the subjects. The study wishes to be completed as the results listed below:

1. Using the concept of emotion design theory in the implementation of experimental design, the virtual reality system will be integrated Unity 3D VR with Microsoft Azure Kinect. The two experimental designs, which classify non-verbal dance practicing and verbal sing practicing by virtual character characteristic behavior. The objective is to understand how the relationship between virtual character embodiment, self-presence, and user experience. In addition, we attempt to establish research architecture and hypotheses to carry out questionnaire design.
2. Thinking about the limitations of virtual reality interaction, experimental design will be classify into non-verbal and verbal virtual character behaviors. We will find out which type of task adapts the analysis of self-presence and user experience.
3. We will find out the possible suitable patterns to make the higher extent for the virtual characters embodiment.
4. Under the virtual environment of different virtual character behavior types, we will explore the effect of virtual character embodiment on self-presence and user experience.
5. The development of virtual character will employ the technology of face recognition to transmit the user's expression to the virtual character.

References

1. Hideki, B., Aoi, M.: Debut of official virtual youtuber of Hitachi home appliances: Shirokaden Hakushaku. Hitachi Review **69**(1), 124–125 (2020)
2. Bianchi-Berthouze, N.: Understanding the role of body movement in player engagement. Human-Computer Interaction **28**(1), 40–75 (2013)
3. Emily, B., Paul, C.: A grounded investigation of game immersion. In: Proceedings of CHI2004 extended abstracts on Human factors in computing systems, pp.1297–1300 (2004)
4. Yihui, C.: The study of the image and preference of virtual characters. Master's thesis in Visual Communication Design, National Yunlin University of Science and Technology (2008).
5. Gonzalez-Franco, M., Peck, T.C.: Avatar embodiment. Towards a standardized questionnaire. Front. Robot. AI **5**, 74 (2018). https://doi.org/10.3389/frobt.2018.00074
6. Hoysniemi, J.: International survey on the dance revolution game. Computer in Entertainment **4**(2), 8 (2006)
7. Kenji, I.: How to Create a Character Loved for 100 Years of the Title. Sesame Books Co., Ltd., Tokyo (2006)
8. Lakoff, G., Johnson, M.: Philosophy in the Flesh. The embodied mind and its challenge to western thought, New York (1999)
9. Laugwitz, B., Held, T., Schrepp, M.: Construction and evaluation of a user experience questionnaire. In: Holzinger, A. (ed.) USAB 2008. LNCS, vol. 5298, pp. 63–76. Springer, Heidelberg (2008). https://doi.org/10.1007/978-3-540-89350-9_6
10. Lazzaro, N.: Why we play games: four keys to more emotion without story. Oakland, CA: XEO Design Inc. (2004)
11. Lin, Z., Davis, L.S.: Shape-based human detection and segmentation via hierarchical part-template matching. IEEE Trans. Pattern Anal. Mach. Intell. **32**(4), 604–618 (2010)
12. Liudmila, B.: Designing identity in VTuber era. Virtual Reality International Conference Proceedings (2020). https://doi.org/10.20870/IJVR.2020.3316
13. Mikolajczyk, K., Schmid, C., Zisserman, A.: Human detection based on a probabilistic assembly of robust part detectors. Proc. European Conf. Computer Vision **1**, 69–82 (2004)
14. Mohan, A., Papageorgiou, C., Poggio, T.: Example-Based Object Detection in Images by Components. IEEE Trans. Pattern Anal. Mach. Intell. **23**(4), 349–361 (2001)
15. Pan, X., Gillies, M., Slater, M.: Virtual character personality influences participant attitudes and behavior – an interview with a virtual human character about her social anxiety. Frontiers in Robotics and AI **2**, 1 (2015)
16. Sajjadi, P., Hoffmann, L., Cimiano, P., Kopp, S.: A personality-based emotional model for embodied conversational agents: Effects on perceived social presence and game experience of users, Entertainment Computing **32**, 100313, ISSN 1875–9521 (2019). https://doi.org/10.1016/j.entcom.2019.100313
17. Ratan, R.A., Hasler, B.: Self-presence standardized: introducing the self-presence questionnaire (SPQ). In: Proceedings of the 12th Annual International Workshop on Presence (2009).
18. Ratan, R., Hasler, B.S.: Exploring self-presence in collaborative virtual teams. PsychNology J. **8**(1), 11–31 (2010)
19. Riva, G., Waterworth, J., Waterworth, E.: The layers of presence: a biocultural approach to understanding presence in natural and mediated environments. Cyberpsychol. Behav. **7**(4), 402–416 (2004)
20. Shet, V.D., Neumann, J., Ramesh, V., Davis, L.S.: Bilattice-based logical reasoning for human detection. In: Proceedings of the IEEE Conference Computer Vision and Pattern Recognition, pp. 1–8 (2007)

21. Witmer, B.G., Singer, M.J.: Measuring presence in virtual environments: a presence questionnaire. Presence **7**(3), 225–240 (1998)
22. Wu, B., Nevatia, R.: Detection of multiple, partially occluded humans in a single image by Bayesian combination of Edgelet part detectors. In: Proceedings IEEE International Conference Computer Vision, pp. 90–97 (2005)
23. Wu, B., Nevatia, R.: Simultaneous object detection and segmentation by boosting local shape feature based classifier. In: Proceedings IEEE Conference Computer Vision and Pattern Recognition, pp. 1–8 (2007)
24. Yu, Y., Fang, C.: The importance of consumers' recognition of virtual characters is explored by emotional patterns. J. Des. Res. **7**, 97–111 (2014)
25. Zhou, X.: Virtual Youtuber Kizuna AI: Co-creating human-non-human interaction and celebrity-audience relationship.In: MSc in Media and Communication, Lund University, Sweden (2020)

Presenting a Sense of Self-motion by Transforming the Rendering Area Based on the Movement of the User's Viewpoint

Tomoya Yamashita[✉], Wataru Hashimoto[✉], Satoshi Nishiguchi[✉], and Yasuharu Mizutani[✉]

Faculty of Information Sciences and Technology, Osaka Institute of Technology, 1-79-1 Kitayama, Hirakata City, Osaka 573-0196, Japan
{m1m21a44,m1m21a44,m1m21a44,m1m21a44}@oit.ac.jp

Abstract. Computer graphics is a core technology that can produce realistic images. However, it is difficult to provide sense of movement and immersion using only visual images. In this study, we propose to enhance the sense of self-motion by deforming the rendering area according to the vection illusion which induces a sense of immersion only with images. In general, the body is slouched backward while accelerating forward, and the field of view becomes relatively wide. Therefore, enlarging the drawing area should have a similar effect when the user's viewpoint in the VR accelerates forward. If the user moves backward, the drawing area should be reduced.

We constructed a driving simulation environment to demonstrate the proposed method. The deformation of the drawing area caused VR motion sickness because the expected and the actual deformation differed. It was also confirmed that the transfer of the rendering area enhances the sense of immersion.

Keywords: Vection · Motion sickness · Driving simulation · Sense of immersiveness

1 Introduction

Modern computer graphics can create photorealistic images and generate scenes that look real. Recently, immersive media such as head mounted displays (HMDs) have been used to create interactive environments and enhance the sense of reality. However, it is difficult to enhance the sense of immersion by using only vision. Hence, we propose a method that focuses on vection to enhance the illusion of self-motion. When the viewpoint of a user accelerates forward in the virtual reality(VR) world, the drawing area of the field of view expands. If the viewpoint swings in the right direction, the drawing area moves to the right on the display (Fig. 1). The aim of this study is to enhance vection by forcing the user's gaze to move by scaling/moving the drawing area according to the motion parameters of the character or vehicle moving in the VR space.

© Springer Nature Switzerland AG 2021
C. Stephanidis et al. (Eds.): HCII 2021, CCIS 1498, pp. 410–417, 2021.
https://doi.org/10.1007/978-3-030-90176-9_53

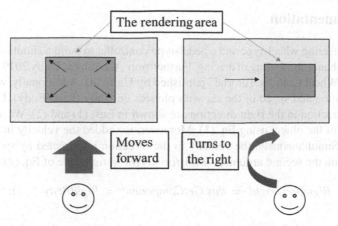

Fig. 1. Examples of transforming the rendering area

2 Prior Work

The illusion of motion when one's gaze is guided by external visual stimuli is called visually induced self-motion sense (vection). Vection can occasionally cause VR sickness. Palmisano et al. reported that the mismatch between perceived and physical head motions contribute to cybersickness [1]. Therefore, it is important to match the perceived motion and physical motion to avoid such adverse experiences related to vection-based content. According to a study, auditory perception can enhance the illusion of self-motion sensation [2, 3]; blindfolded observers were allowed to listen to a rotating sound source while seated on a chair with their feet above solid ground to increase the intensity of self-motion.

3 Basic Idea

The aim of this study is to generate a sense of self-motion by guiding the user's gaze according to change the rendering area of the user's field of view. For example, when a person accelerates forward in a vehicle, the field of view becomes wider because the upper body bends over backward. Therefore, it is assumed that the sense of self-motion is enhanced by enlarging the drawing area as the user's viewpoint moves forward. Similarly, when the user's viewpoint is accelerated backward, the drawing area should be shrunk. When a user turn right in a vehicle, acceleration is generated in the left direction, and the user's gaze is directed to the right direction due to the direction of moving.

We constructed a driving simulation environment to demonstrate the proposed method. We estimate the magnitude of deformation/transfer in the rendering area based on acceleration and velocity parameters of the user's viewpoint such as the first-person view.

4 Implementation

We used a steering wheel-type and a pedal-type controller to build a simulation environment and enhance the feeling of driving. Furthermore, we utilized Unity 2019.3.13f1, and consulted "Wheel Collider Tutorial" published by Unity [4]. Additionally, we extracted the acceleration and speed of the car with physics on Unity (RigidBody). Examples of velocity extraction in the right direction are shown in Eqs. (1) and (2). We assigned the RigidBody of the object using Eq. (1). Moreover, we added the velocity in *RightSpeed* in Eq. (2). Simultaneously, the velocity in the direction is extracted by specifying the direction with the second argument, *transform.right* in right side of Eq. (2).

$$Rigidbody\ rigid\ =\ this.GetComponent < RigidBody > ();\qquad(1)$$

$$float\ RightSpeed\ =\ Vector3.Dot(rigid.velocity, transform.right);\qquad(2)$$

Additionally, we added a script to enlarge/reduce or move the rendering area according to the parameters of the car. Furthermore, we utilized Windows API for transformation. The method, *"MoveWindow"* we applied is expressed in Eq. (3).

$$MoveWindow(x, y, width, height);\qquad(3)$$

For example, we considered a case in which the rendering area moved to the right by a magnitude of *RightSpeed* from Eq. (2). First, we calculated x which is the magnitude of movement in Eq. (4). Using Eq. (4), the magnitude of movement of the rendering area on abscissa axis was calculated. Subsequently, the value of the initial position of the rendering area such as the right hand of Eq. (4) was added and the value was 300. Based on the results of Eq. (4), the rendering area was moved, and its expression is shown in Eq. (3). Then, we added it in the method *MoveWindow()* in Eq. (3). The rendering area moved to the right based on the value of x. In this instance, we assumed that y, *width* and *height* were constant numbers. Accordingly, the rendering area was transformed using the information of the car.

$$int\ x\ =\ (int)RightSpeed\ +\ 300;\qquad(4)$$

Additionally, we projected the rendering area on a 750 mm spherical display to enhance the movement of the user's gaze. Distortion correction was applied while conducting the experiment [5]. Figure 2 shows the experimental setup. A chair and controllers were installed in front of the spherical display. The position of the chair was adjusted according to the height of the user.

5 Evaluation Experiment

Figure 3 shows an image while conducting the experiment. The rendering area moves right when the user turns right.

Fig. 2. Experimental setup

Fig. 3. Experimental image

5.1 Procedure

We verify the effects of the proposed method. The contents of the survey are as follows.

- Has the sense of immersiveness improved?
- Does the user feel sick?
- Does the method improve the temporal performance due to help the user's driving?

The experimental steps are mentioned below.

1. The user drives a lap on the practice course.
2. The user drives on the production course with and without transforming the rendering area.
3. The user answers questions about the immersive effect and sickness.

We measure the time required for one lap to evaluate the temporal performance when the user drives on the production course, with and without transforming the rendering area. The course used for practice is shown in Fig. 4 and the course used for the evaluation is shown in Fig. 5.

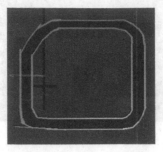

Fig. 4. The course for practice

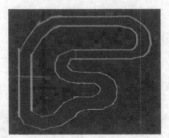

Fig. 5. The course for evaluation

The questionnaire is given below. The Likert scaling method was used to evaluate the answers.

1. Which one is more immersive? (4-step evaluation)
2. Which one made you feel uncomfortable? (Did you feel dizzy/intoxicated?) (4-step evaluation)
3. Why do you think so? (For each question, a short answer and optional)

Sixteen students from Osaka Institute of Technology participated in the experiment.

5.2　Result

First, we created a boxplot as shown in Fig. 6 to compare the temporal measurement result and evaluate the time required to complete one lap. It can be observed that the all participant took more time in the track which transformed the rendering area compared with that of without transformation.

Next, Fig. 7 shows the result of the question asked about the immersiveness of the experience.

A few interesting comments by the participants are mentioned below.

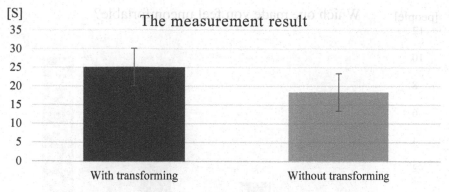

Fig. 6. Boxplot plotted for the temporal measurement result

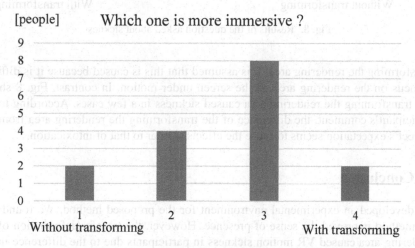

Fig. 7. Results of the question asked about immersiveness

- Because I watched the screen carefully. (Answered 3)
- I will hit the wall if I don't concentrate. (Answered 3)

Next, Fig. 8 shows the result of the question asked about sickness.
An interesting comment by a participant is mentioned below.

- The rendering area shook form side to side more than I imagined, and I couldn't catch up it with my eyes. (Answered 3)

5.3 Discussion

It can be observed from Fig. 6 that the time required for one lap increases in with transforming for all the participants. It is assumed that transforming disrupts driving. However, it was found from Fig. 7 that the sense of immersiveness was improved by

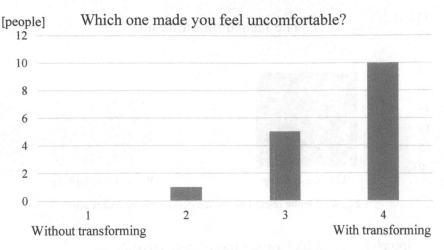

Fig. 8. Results of the question asked about sickness

transforming the rendering area. It is assumed that this is caused because it is difficult to focus on the rendering area on the screen under motion. In contrast, Fig. 8 shows that transforming the rendering area caused sickness in a few cases. According to the participant's comment, the difference of the transforming the rendering area from the subject's expectation seems to cause the effects similar to that of intoxication.

6 Conclusion

We developed an experimental environment for the proposed method. We found that the method improved the sense of presence. However, the transfer/deformation of the rendering area caused VR motion sickness in participants due to the difference in the actual and expected deformation. The proposed method can disturb the user's control behavior as minor decrease in the driving performance was observed. It is crucial to investigate the optimal magnitude of transfer/deformation in the drawing area and further explore the deformation method.

References

1. Palmisano, S., Mursic, R., Kim, J.: Vection and cybersickness generated by head-and-display motion in the Oculus Rift. Displays **46**, 1–8 (2017)
2. Riecke, E.B., Feuereissen, D., Riser J.J.: Auditory self-motion illusions circular vection can be facilitated by vibrations and the potential for actual motion. In: Proceedings of the 5th Symposium on Applied Perception in Graphics and Visualization, APGV 2008, 9–10 August, Los Angeles, California, USA (2008)
3. Riecke, E.B., Feuereissen, D., Rieser, J.J, McNamara, P.T.: Spatialized sound enhances biomechanically-induced self-motion illusion (vection). In: Proceedings of the International Conference on Human Factors in Computing Systems, CHI 2011, 7–12 May, Vancouver, BC, Canada (2011)

4. Unity: Wheel Collider Tutorial, Unity Manual. https://docs.unity3d.com/2019.4/Documenta tion/Manual/WheelColliderTutorial.html. Accessed 18 May 2020
5. Hashimoto, W., Mizutani, Y., Nishiguchi, S.: Projection simulator to support design development of spherical immersive display, HCII 2017. CCIS **714**, 17–24 (2017)

3D User Interface in Virtual Reality

Gu Yue(✉)

Tsinghua University, Beijing, China

Abstract. Three-dimensional user interfaces (3D UI) allow users to interact with virtual objects, environments, or information on the physical or virtual space. With the development of virtual reality technology, Tons of VR products tend to occupy the market quickly. However, the formulation of interface design specifications and the enhancement of user experience always be ignored. More than one-third of the users interrupted their experience during the market research because they did not understand the program operation. 3D UI is fundamental to Interactive in virtual space. Thus, this article introduces the basic overview of virtual reality, focusing on analyzing the main design differences between traditional and three-dimensional interfaces. This study's specific objective was to propose three-dimensional interface construction strategies mainly include: 1) Building a natural harmonious interaction relationship between man and machine; 2) Driving interface experience optimization through mental models. In particular, this research tries to establish the Paradigm of Theoretical Research of 3D user interface, which provides theoretical support for design in the future.

Keywords: Virtual reality · 3D UI · User experience

1 Introduction

With the rapid development of information society, Virtual Reality (VR) has gradually matured. VR Artist Milk (2016) pointed out that VR technology is the ultimate "emotional machine". The sense of immersion created by VR technology can essentially change the audience's emotional acceptance of disseminated content. However, because VR equipment has not been popularized, Tons of VR products tend to occupy the market quickly, resulting from rough designs and bad user experience. More than one-third of the users interrupted their experience during the market research because they did not understand the program operation.

Many empirical studies have focused on immersive virtual reality technology (Slater and Sanchez-Vives 2016). To some extent, immersion was regarded as the "user experience factor, and the user needs at all levels and design methods" (Garrett 2011). Compared to the traditional two-dimensional interface, the 3D interface adds space atmosphere creation and direction control design. 3D UI. increasingly requires the integration of several input modalities and several types of sensory feedback. Together with visual and auditory sensations, haptics is one of the essential types of sensory feedback. In virtual space, users are easy to have negative emotions such as panic and confusion. Considering the process of evaluating traditional virtual environments (VE), previous

© Springer Nature Switzerland AG 2021
C. Stephanidis et al. (Eds.): HCII 2021, CCIS 1498, pp. 418–423, 2021.
https://doi.org/10.1007/978-3-030-90176-9_54

studies focused on VE' usability evaluations and proposed corresponding guidelines (Bowman et al. 2008; Stanney et al. 2003; Bach and Scapin 2004). Above all, the formulation of 3D interface design specifications and user experience enhancement cannot be ignored.

VR technology creates a real immersive three-dimensional environment. It is the result of the digital age and has the characteristics of high technology, immersion, and interdisciplinary. However, it might not be easy to implement design paradigm and analysis practices in VR design, many VR products use the traditional two-dimensional interface directly, which is not friendly to conform to the principle of human-computer interaction design, Even causing virtual reality dizziness (LaViola 2020). Whats more, Further user studies based on carefully selected tasks and task combinations need to examine the advantages and disadvantages of various sensor combinations to further improve 3D UI. Therefore, it is particularly important to establish a virtual reality platform design specification through data collection, experimental testing, user research, and other methods.

Designing 3D interfaces requires knowledge of various disciplines, including psychology, software engineering, product design and many others. The specific objective of this study was to introduce the basic overview of virtual reality, focusing on the analysis of the main design differences between traditional interfaces and three-dimensional interfaces: 1) **The transformation of design tools; 2) The increase of design process links; 3) The transformation of verification methods**. Proposed three-dimensional interface construction strategies mainly include: 1) **Building a natural harmonious interaction relationship between man and machine; 2) Driving interface experience optimization through mental models.** This research try to establishes the theoretical framework of 3D user interface, which provides theoretical support for design in the future.

2 The Concepts 3D UI

2.1 Literature Review of Virtual Reality

The birth of virtual reality can be traced back to the 1960s. At first, it appeared in many literary works and artistic creations in the form of fuzzy fantasy. An early artistic exploration of virtual reality was demonstrated in a 19th-century panoramic fresco by French soldier and painter Jean Charles Langlois. The creation of panoramic paintings such as the *Battle of Borodino* can help the viewer to fill in the vision of the whole scene and have an intuitive feeling of the historical events at that time. The fantasy of virtual reality in literary works is the famous British writer Aldous Leonard Huxley launched the novel *Brilliant New World*. The novel portrays that in a highly technologically advanced future world, human needs can be immediate Satisfaction, but in fact this kind of satisfaction is just an illusion, depicting the use of mechanical civilization in people's future social life (Huxley 1932). The novel *Pygmalion's Glasses* describes the fictional world that wearers experience through vision, hearing, smell, taste, and touch. It mentions and predicts today's VR devices (Stanley 1935). It is currently recognized as the first description of "immersive experience" and is the future of virtual reality. The *Sword of Damocles* designed and displayed what is widely regarded as the first HMD system, which showed for the first time a computer program system in three-dimensional form (Ivan Sutherland and Bob Sproull 1968).

Nowadays, driven by the information age and digital revolution, more and more people recognize and pay attention to virtual reality. People can travel freely between the real and virtual worlds by wearing VR glasses. The combination of technology and computer hardware to create virtual reality will currently involve many fields, such as medicine, entertainment, education, industry, and graphic etc. For example, in 2017 Google launched Tilt brush, a VR painting application based on the HTC Vive helmet. Users wearing a VR helmet can extend the traditional flat painting area to 3D space, giving artists more creative space and making artistic creations more free and efficient.

2.2 From 2D Interface to 3D Interface

Nowadays, the UI and UX theories for two-dimensional interfaces are very mature. In essence, the core theoretical knowledge and methodology applicable to two-dimensional interfaces, such as the user-centered experience-oriented principle, emotional interface design, and consistency principles, are also applicable to three-dimensional interface design. But the difference is that the transition from a two-dimensional interface to a three-dimensional interface requires designers to master interdisciplinary knowledge to a greater extent. Generally, a 2D interface has 2 DOFs (position on the 2 dimensions X and Y), while a 3D interface supports 6 DOFs (position and orientation on the X,Y and Z-dimensions) (Hepperle 2019). At the same time, the design tools, processes, and verification methods after the output results are also changed from the two-dimensional interface:

1. **Design tools:** In traditional UI design, designers mainly use sketches to output design specifications and cut drawings to deliver and develop. The parts related to micro-motion effects need to be carried out in After Effects or other motion design software. In the 3D interface design, the tools required are more diverse due to changes in the design carrier. The most significant increase in interchange is integrating the 3D scene and the physical 3D development engine intervention. 3D scene can be passed through Cinema 4d, 3d Max, Maya conducts production and introduces the designed 3D model scene into entity 3 for interactive development and overall rendering.
2. **The increase in the design process:** the product positioning and user research-related content that needs to be considered in the early design stage is not much different from the 2D UI. Designers need to be more comprehensive in the interactive and visual design due to carrier changes and macro considerations. Compared with traditional design, roles and scene modeling, engine rendering, sound effects, and motion design are added to the process to maximize the immersive experience of VR.
3. **Changes in verification methods:** The verification phase is the analysis, evaluation, and testing of products. The designer should carry out traditional interface and three-dimensional interface design and verification iteratively. After the procedure is verified and the design is modified after confirmation, the cycle can continue to optimize the product to achieve good user feedback. The three-dimensional interface is different from the traditional interface in the physical environment change, with

many more non-traditional input/output devices. Each participating user's gender, height, habits make the verification of the interface more complicated. Therefore, in the early stage of the design, it is necessary to conduct research on the services that the design product needs to provide and the sample of service objects from which the most representative population characteristics are selected. In the design verification, sufficient user samples are also required, and a large amount of experimental data is used to input the equipment. Interface elements and interactive technology to quantify.

3   3D UI Design Strategy

3.1   Expansion of Design Expression—Latitude-Building a Harmonious Natural Interaction Between Man and Machine

3D UI design is a paradigm in the connotation of traditional design and boundary expansion. The MIT Media Lab combining science, Media, art, design, cutting-edge technology, is committed to researching and developing the latest computer from a new cross-subject, be proactive and creative research. With the rapid development of digitalization, designing and creating virtual reality spaces has created a richer and more comprehensive design carrier for designers.

The key of design in virtual reality space is to build a harmonious natural interaction relationship between man and machine. Reasonable natural interaction refers to the interactive instructions that occur when people are in an instinctive state, such as natural avoidance when seeing an object, nodding when expressing recognition, natural arm swinging when moving, etc. When designing specific functions, full consideration should be given to human cognition, perception, and behavior in space, as well as the sensor technology needed to be applied, to ensure that the design results are in line with the target expectations and not burdened by cumbersome wearable devices for users. Designers should get rid of the passive position in the traditional design field, coordinate the resources of various parties, and promote design innovation.

3.2   Mental Model-Driven Interface Experience Optimization

Mind, in psychology, refers to people's storage and precipitation of known things, "mental model" in the form and law hidden behind the behaviour, which affects people's observation, thinking, and action. (Kenneth Craik 1943). Nevertheless, the mental model is not immutable. During the product design cycle, the mental model transfers technological innovation, people's lifestyles, and stereotypical thinking and life habits correspondingly change. People's stereotyped thinking and practices in life will also vary accordingly. At the same time, the user's curiosity and curiosity mentality will also prompt them to break old things and find excitement from new items. For example, we used to buy a New Year's calendar to mark important dates and events at the end of the year. However, with technological innovation, we can directly interact with smart devices by voice to provide us with recording reminder services, and so on. It improves work efficiency and makes ordinary users feel the emotional joy of having a personal assistant. The mental model is a natural iteration. It also a process of introspection, learning, and innovation.

The interface experience optimization driven by the mental model; it is first necessary to determine the target user according to the product positioning and construct the mental model by extracting user needs and analyzing the user's habits. The designer needs to use the constructed mental model to predict user behavior and guide the design; secondly, through Choose corresponding design methods such as quantitative research, qualitative research, interdisciplinary research, and development in 3D interface design to complete the conceptual model design; finally, through the usability test of the design model, calculate the experimental data to obtain the user experience Satisfaction, further optimization, and iterative design. For VR products, usability testing should be carried out after each essential step is completed, even if problems in the development process are solved and improved.

4 Conclusion

People are the yardstick of all things. Since ancient times, both China and the West have emphasized human-centred judgment standards in cultural expressions. The information society is a design that emphasizes humanity. UI designers will focus on displaying page information on the first screen and the priority arrangement of information. In the mark's design to the three-dimensional interface, what needs to be considered is the visual range and the visual focus area, reasonable information layout, and operation instructions. Every technological revolution is not smooth sailing. As a new product of the digital information age, virtual reality products combined with the latest technology have brought users an unprecedented immersive audio-visual experience and brought life, work, education, and entertainment more possibilities post-epidemic.

References

Bowman, D.A., Coquillart, S., Froehlich, B., Hirose, M., Kitamura, Y., Kiyokawa, K., et al.: 3D user interfaces: new directions and perspectives. IEEE Comput. Graph. Appl. 28(6), 20–36 (2008)

Hinckley, K., Pausch, R., Goble, J.C., Kassell, N.F.: "A survey of design issues in spatial input." In: Proceedings of the ACM Symposium on User Interface Software and Technology, pp. 213–222 (1994)

Mel, S., Sanchez-Vives, M.V.: Enhancing our lives with immersive virtual reality. Front. Robot. AI, 3 (2016)

Santos, B.S., Dias, P., Silva, S., Capucho, L., Salgado, N., Lino, F., et al.: Usability evaluation in virtual reality: a user study comparing three different setups. In: Eurographics Symposium on Virtual Environments Posters (2008)

Conn, C., Lanier, J., Minsky, M., Fisher, S., Druin: In: Panel Proceedings AACM Press ACM Siggraph – Boston (1989)

Emadary, M., Metzinger, T.K.: Real virtuality: a code of ethical conduct. recommendations for good scientific practice and the consumers of VR-technology. Front. Robot. AI 19 (2016)

Krug, S.: Don't Make Me Think, Revisited: A Common Sense Approach to Web Usability. New Riders Publishing, Thousand Oaks (2003)

Roy, D., Brine, J.: Design thinking in EFL context: studying the potential for language teaching and learning. Int. J. Des. Educ. 6, 1–21 (2013)

Bach, C., Scapin, D.L.: Obstacles and perspectives for evaluating mixed reality systems usability (2004)

Jacoby, R., Ferneau, M., Humphries, J.: Gestural Interaction in a virtual environment. In: Stereoscopic Displays and Virtual Reality Systems, SPIE 2177 (1994)

Booth, K., Fisher, B., Page, S., Ware, C., Widen, S.: Wayfinding in a virtual environment. Graph. Interf. **32**, 316–329 (2000)

Brock, F.J., Newman, W.A.: Testing recognition of computer-generated icons. J. Inf. Syst. Educ. (1993)

Baddeley, A.D., Hitch, G.: Working memory. In: Bower, G.H. (ed.) The Psychology of Learning And Motivation: Advances In Research And Theory, vol. 8, pp. 47–89. Academic Press, New York (1974)

Cockburn, A., McKenzie, B.: Evaluating the effectiveness of spatial memory in 2D and 3D physical and virtual environments. In: CHI 2002 Proceedings of the SIGCHI Conference on Human Factors in Computing Systems: Changing Our World, Changing Ourselves, pp. 203–210 (2002)

Fetaji, M., Loskoska, S., Fetaji, B.: Investigating human computer interaction issues in designing efficient virtual learning environments. In: Balkan Conference in Informatics, pp. 313–324 (2007)

Manual Preliminary Coarse Alignment of 3D Point Clouds in Virtual Reality

Xiaotian Zhang, Weiping He[✉], and Shuxia Wang

Northwestern Polytechnic University, Xi'an, People's Republic of China
weiping@nwpu.edu.cn

Abstract. The alignment of 3D point clouds consists of coarse alignment and precise alignment. The preliminary coarse alignment must be implemented for point clouds with a significant initial pose difference before time-consuming precise alignment. However, this procedure is normally finished on 2D interfaces manually, which leads to a partial perception of the 3D point clouds. The biased understanding may affect the operation efficiency and alignment accuracy. In this paper, we developed a VR-based prototype for manual preliminary coarse alignment of point clouds. A user study was conducted to compare the efficiency, accuracy, and usability in a controlled alignment task with both the 2D interface and the developed system. The task was graded into three levels based on the complexity of matched points clouds (simple, complex, and incomplete). The result indicated that the prototype system was effective and useful for supporting the preliminary coarse alignment task. It displayed outstanding performance for the coarse alignment of complex and incomplete point clouds.

Keywords: Point cloud alignment · Virtual reality

1 Introduction

The point cloud is a set of discrete points distributed in N-dimensional space, mainly three-dimensional, which is a discrete sampling of the surface of an object. Recently, with the fast development and popularization of high precision sensors such as LiDAR and Kinect, the acquisition of point clouds has become more accessible and more convenient. As a result, point cloud has become the primary data format to represent the 3D world and has been used in reverse engineering, driverless, human-computer interaction, etc.

Due to the limitation of the sensor and the interference of the surrounding environment, most point clouds need to be processed before they can be used. Point clouds alignment is a fundamental processing technology, which estimates the transformation matrix between two-point cloud scans [1]. 3D point cloud alignment includes coarse alignment and precise alignment. Before the time-consuming precise alignment, a preliminary coarse alignment must be performed on the point cloud with a significant initial pose difference to provide a suitable initial transformation. Although there are many algorithms for coarse alignment, manual alignment is still a widespread method

© Springer Nature Switzerland AG 2021
C. Stephanidis et al. (Eds.): HCII 2021, CCIS 1498, pp. 424–432, 2021.
https://doi.org/10.1007/978-3-030-90176-9_55

used in many point cloud processing softwares. This procedure is usually finished on 2D interfaces manually, which leads to a partial perception of the 3D point clouds.

With the development of Virtual Reality (VR) technology, more and more complicated tasks can be done in a 3D virtual space. Virtual Reality can provide not only a more accurate 3D representation but also the high number of degrees of freedom (DoF) used by its input modalities, which can enable the easy perception, interaction, and analysis of complex multidimensional. VR has become a promising platform for 3D data manipulation and analysis because it is easy to explore the data in the VR environment. [2, 3] However, there has been little research on the point cloud alignment task in the VR environment.

Accordingly, in this study, we aim to develop a VR-based prototype that can allow users to browse the point cloud freely and move the source point cloud by the controller for alignment. We refer to the manual coarse alignment techniques in the 2D interface and add some alignment techniques unique to the VR space. Our proposed system can help users get the alignment matrix of point clouds quickly and satisfactorily.

2 System Overview

In this research, we propose a VR-based prototype that can allow users to browse the point cloud freely and move the source point cloud for alignment.

This paper refers to CloudCompare [4], a 2D interface based on 3D point cloud processing open software. It allows users to align point clouds by three methods, 1) matching bounding-box centers, 2) picking equivalent point pairs, and 3) translating and rotating manually.

Therefore, we first developed a simple prototype VR system and migrated the three methods of CloudCompare to the VR environment.

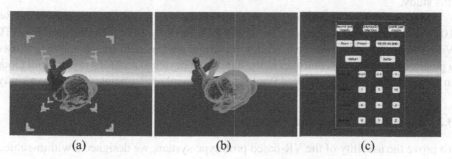

| (a) | (b) | (c) |

Fig. 1. Principle alignment techniques. (a) matching bounding-box centers; (b) matching equivalent points pairs; (c) the UI canvas for alignment.

1) The system will generate a bounding box of the point clouds. The bounding box is the smallest bounding box whose sides are parallel to the coordinate axis. The user can match the centers of the bounding box of the two point clouds by clicking the button in UI canvas.

2) The system allows users to use rays to select equivalent point pairs on the target point cloud and the source point cloud. After the equivalent points are selected, they will be enlarged and displayed, and the equivalent pairs can be matched by clicking the button.

3) The system allows users to rotate and translate the source point cloud by clicking the virtual dangling buttons in front of them.

We then add an extra feature, which can only be realized in the VR environment.

4) Users can press the triggers on controllers to grab the point cloud and apply transformation and rotation by controllers.

The VR system for point cloud alignment is shown in Fig. 1.

3 User Study

We then conduct a user study to explore the detailed effect of different functions and prove the usability of the VR-based prototype system.

3.1 Participants and Apparatus

For this experiment, we invite 12 healthy participants (2 female) with an average age of 23.8 (SD = 2.24) to perform a user study. All participants are right-handed, 2 of them have experience in point cloud alignment, and 11 have experience in VR. The participants in this study were gathered from a university's mechanical engineering department, and all the participants were paid for the one-hour study. The local ethics committee approved this study.

This experimental platform was on a 4.00 GHz Intel Corei7 PC running Windows 10. The experimental scenes were built by VRTK in Unity 2019.3.13. We used the HTC Vive VR headset as the device to render the virtual environment for users. We also used a position-tracked Vive controller as the hand-held device to control a ray or point cloud in virtual reality. Finally, we used Pcx [5] to import and render point cloud data in Unity.

3.2 Experiment Design and Tasks

To prove the usability of the VR-based prototype system, we designed a within-subject experiment with factors system and complexity of point cloud. There were two systems: 2D interface (we use Cloudcompare) and VR environment (our VR-based prototype system). There were three different complexities of point cloud: simple, complex, and incomplete, as shown in Fig. 2. The simple point cloud is a cube point cloud with one of its corners cut off. The complex point cloud is the Stanford Bunny, which is frequently used in point cloud research. Because the sensors can only capture scans within their limited view range, the incomplete point cloud is most common in real-life alignment. To simulate the worst case in real life, we cut off several most distinguishable features

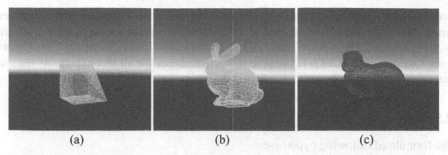

| (a) | (b) | (c) |

Fig. 2. Three different complexities of point cloud: (a) simple; (b) complex; (c) incomplete.

of the Stanford Bunny, such as its ears, tails, and feet, to get our final incomplete point cloud.

Our user study consisted of six different scenes, including the simple, complex, and incomplete point clouds under 2D and VR systems. The source point cloud and target point cloud are the same for the alignment of simple and complex case. For the alignment of incomplete point clouds, the source point cloud for alignment is incomplete, and the target point cloud is complete.

The initial position of the point cloud with the same complexity is identical for the 2D interface and VR system so that they will have the same difficulty for alignment. We also make sure the coordinates and Euler angle for source cloud and target cloud are different so that the participants cannot finish the alignment with simple steps. The sequence of the three tasks is fixed to ensure the same difficulty but the order of two interfaces is randomized to eliminate possible error due to participants' familiarity with the tasks.

3.3 Measures

This passage introduces two objective measures to evaluate the effectiveness of point clouds alignment.

Performance Time: We calculate the time spent on each alignment task for every participant. The alignment time is the elapse between the time when participants start alignment and when they think the alignment is precise enough.

Error: We use the average distance between each point in the source point cloud and its nearest point in the target point cloud to measure the alignment accuracy, which is also the definition of distance between point clouds in CloudCompare and similar to RMS measurement in ICP algorithms.

3.4 Experiment Procedure

At first, we introduced the experiment and guided the participants to get accustomed to 2D and VR systems. After the participants could handle the devices, they were asked to finish three tasks consecutively under 2D interface and VR system. We stopped timing when they think the source point cloud is close enough to the target point cloud. After finishing the same point cloud alignment under two different interfaces, the participants were asked to take a break. The whole experiment took about one hour. After the experiment, the participant was required to fill a questionnaire based on System Usability Scale (SUS) [6], The NASA Task Load Index (NASA-TLX) [7], and the User Experience Questionnaire (UEQ) [8] to give subjective scores for all techniques. At last, we interviewed the participants and collected their experiences and preferences.

3.5 Hypotheses

We formulated following hypotheses:

H1. 2D interface will have faster alignment and precision for simple point clouds.

H2. VR system will have faster alignment and precision for complex point clouds and incomplete point clouds.

H3. VR system will have higher usability than the 2D interface.

H4. VR system will exert a smaller workload on participants than the 2D interface.

H5. VR system will have a better user experience than the 2D interface.

H1 was formulated since simple point clouds contain more distinguishable features which can be easily selected and compared. H2 was developed because the complex and incomplete point cloud has few distinguishable features, and the 2D interface will lead to biased cognition of the 3D point cloud. H3, H4, and H5 were formulated because we consider VR system conforms to human operation preferences.

4 Results

4.1 Performance Time

Table 1. The mean performance time and alignment accuracy for three types of point cloud.

Complexity	Simple		Complex		Incomplete	
System	2D	VR	2D	VR	2D	VR
Performance time (s)	173 ± 99	77 ± 33	182 ± 142	68 ± 42	192 ± 94	67 ± 52
Alignment accuracy ($\times 10^{-2}$m)	0.73 ± 0.80	0.89 ± 0.40	0.58 ± 0.26	0.56 ± 0.25	3.50 ± 1.75	0.80 ± 0.38

Performance time of three different complexities of point cloud in 2D interface and VR system was shown in Table 1. A pair-samples T-test was conducted to compare the meantime for participants to complete three separate tasks. The one-sided $p = 0.004$ for simple point cloud, $p = 0.006$ for complex point cloud and $p < 0.001$ for incomplete point cloud. Results showed the mean time spent on the 2D interface is significantly greater than that in the VR system in all three tasks.

4.2 Alignment Accuracy

The alignment accuracy of three types of the point cloud in 2D interface and VR system was shown in Table 1. Again, a pair-samples T-test was conducted to compare the mean error for participants to complete three separate tasks. The one-sided p-value is 0.281 for simple point cloud, 0.442 for complex point cloud, and < 0.001 for the incomplete point cloud. Results showed no significant difference in Alignment accuracy between 2D interface and VR system for both simple point cloud and complex point cloud alignment tasks. However, for the incomplete point cloud alignment task, the alignment error of the VR system is significantly smaller than that of the 2D interface.

4.3 Usability

The usability of the interface was measured with three indexes: the System Usability Scale (SUS), The NASA Task Load Index (NASA-TLX) and the User Experience Questionnaire (UEQ).

The mean SUS score for the 2D interface is 47.1, below the average score (68), indicating that the 2D interface has poor usability. However, the mean SUS score for the VR system is 79.6, entirely above the average, thus displaying excellent usability. A pair-samples T-test was also conducted to compare the mean score between the two systems. The one-sided p-value < 0.001, indicating the VR system's SUS score, is significantly more significant than the 2D interface.

The mean NASA Task Load Index for 2D interface and VR system is 58.33 and 36.58. A pair-samples T-test was conducted to compare the index from two systems. The one-sided p-value is 0.002 < 0.05. Therefore, the workload for VR system is significantly smaller than that of 2D interface.

The scores of the User Experience Questionnaire between 2D interface and VR system was shown in Fig. 3 and Table 2, showing that VR system has more excellent user experience in all six dimensions. Pair-Samples T-tests were also conducted to compare the difference of scale means between two interfaces. All p-values are less than 0.05, indicating a significantly better user experience for the VR system over the 2D interface.

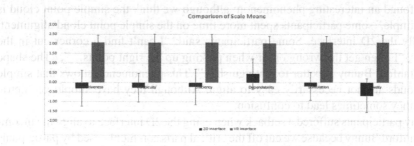

Fig. 3. Result from UEQ in six dimensions

Table 2. P-values for UEQ in six dimensions

Category	Attractiveness	Perspicuity	Efficiency
P-value	0.0004	0.0004	0.0004
Category	Dependability	Stimulation	Novelty
P-value	0.0024	0.0024	0.0024

5 Discussion

In this section, we discuss the results in relation to the hypotheses.

5.1 Align Times and Accuracy

Table 1 summarizes the analysis results. With respect to the alignment time on three complexity of point cloud, the VR system takes much less time than the 2D interface. This can be explained using the simplicity and convenience of alignment in VR systems. In a VR environment, we use the controller as an embodied object with point cloud location information, and users can translate and rotate the point cloud by moving the controller. This unique technique in the VR environment is much faster than other techniques when aligning. Concerning the accuracy, for simple and complex point cloud, 2D interface and VR system do not yield significant difference, but for the incomplete point cloud, VR system is significantly better than the 2D interface. This can be explained using features of the point cloud. Features of the simple point clouds are richer and easy to select, and features of the complex point cloud are rich but difficult to select. However, the incomplete point cloud features are sparser and more difficult to determine. The 2D interface's alignment depends on features, so it is challenging to align the incomplete cloud in the 2D interface. Users prefer to align point cloud based on shape rather than features in the VR environment, so the point cloud features have little effect on alignment in the VR environment. The results of the user study partly support our hypotheses H2 but reject our hypotheses H1.

We found an interesting phenomenon: although we think the simple point cloud is more "simple," some participants spent more time on the simple point cloud alignment, especially the 2D interface. Some participants said: "I can't find a corner cut in the cube…", "I often get the wrong order when picking up the right points…", "The shape of the Stanford Bunny is better to distinguish…". This phenomenon shows that simple point clouds are not necessarily easy to align. Although they have simple geometric shapes, they sometimes lead to confusion.

Many participants suffered a setback when using the 2D interface to align the incomplete Stanford Bunny because we cut off the critical parts commonly used by participants during alignment. Although this operation also impacts the alignment of the VR environment, the impact on the 2D interface is more annoying. Most participants could not do as well as when aligning simple and complex point clouds. Some participants said: "I can't find the feature for alignment," "It's so difficult that I want to give up."

5.2 Usability of System

For usability, workload and user experience, the VR system was better than the 2D interface. Ten participants commented, "We find alignment in VR system is easy to learn." Seven of them also mentioned that they could quickly move the point cloud to the place they want. Therefore, H3, H4 and H5 are supported.

6 Conclusion and Future Work

We proposed and evaluated a VR system for manual preliminary coarse alignment of 3D point clouds with four alignment techniques: matching bounding box center, matching identical point pairs, translate and rotate point clouds via UI buttons, and translate and rotate point clouds via controllers. We also compare with traditional 2D interfaces under simple, complex, and incomplete alignment scenarios. Based on our user study, the VR system has a shorter alignment time for all three scenarios and is more accurate for most common incomplete point clouds. VR system also has significantly better usability, workload, and user experience than the 2D interface. The overall result indicates that the VR system behaves better than the traditional 2D interface for manual preliminary coarse alignment of point clouds, with faster speed, greater accuracy, and better usability.

Our work has some limitations. First, we did not complete the entire point cloud alignment process, only performed a manual initial coarse alignment. A transitional interface can be developed in the future to improve usability. Secondly, the effect of migrating the 2D interface alignment method to the VR environment is not good, and it is challenging to select point clouds accurately. The migration alignment method can be improved in the future. In addition, we only align a pair of point clouds whose size is moderate in each scene. In the future, we should add the scaling function and try aligning point clouds with different scales.

Acknowledgements. This work is partially supported by the National Key R & D Program of China (Grant No.2019YFB1703800), Natural Science Basic Research Plan in Shaanxi Province of China (Grant No.2016JM6054), the Programme of Introducing Talents of Discipline to Universities (111 Project), China (Grant No.B13044).

References

1. Huang, X., et al.: A Comprehensive Survey on Point Cloud Alignment. ArXiv Preprint ArXiv: 2103.02690 (2021)
2. Montano-Murillo, R.A., et al.: Slicing-volume: hybrid 3D/2D multi-target selection technique for dense virtual environments. In: 2020 IEEE Conference on Virtual Reality and 3D User Interfaces (VR), pp. 53–62 (2020)
3. Wagner, J., et al.: Comparing and combining virtual hand and virtual ray pointer interactions for data manipulation in immersive analytics. IEEE Trans. Visual. Comput. Graph. **27**(5), pp. 2513–2523 (2021)
4. http://www.cloudcompare.org/.
5. https://github.com/keijiro/Pcx.

6. Brooke, J.: SUS: a 'quick and dirty' usability scale. In: Usability Evaluation in Industry, pp. 207–212 (1996)
7. Hart, S.G.: NASA Task Load Index (TLX), vol. 1.0; Paper and Pencil Package (1986)
8. Bangor, A., et al.: An empirical evaluation of the system usability scale. Int. J. Hum. Comput. Interact. 24(6), 574–594 (2008)

Games and Gamification

Agrihood: A Motivational Digital System for Sustainable Urban Environments

Antonio Bucchiarone[1]($\boxtimes$) (iD), Giulia Bertoldo[2], and Sara Favargiotti[2] (iD)

[1] Fondazione Bruno Kessler, Trento, Italy
bucchiarone@fbk.eu
[2] University of Trento - DICAM, Trento, Italy
giulia.bertoldo-1@alumni.unitn.it, sara.favargiotti@unitn.it

Abstract. Extreme industrialization and globalization have turned cities into the most voracious consumers of materials and they are overwhelmingly the source of carbon emissions through both direct and embodied energy consumption. Newly created cities and the urbanization process in rural areas replicate a lifestyle based on consumerism and the linear economy, causing destructive social and economic impact while compromising the ecology of the planet. To reduce this phenomenon, we need to re-imagine cities and the ways they operate, with the perspective of making them locally productive and globally connected. The purpose of this contribution is to make the citizens more aware about their consumption, ecological footprint, visible and invisible fluxes to suggest a new trend in the urban context. We propose a method to plan the city of tomorrow in a dynamic way, where the active participatory process and the gamification techniques are the core pillars of our vision. We analyze the issues of a pilot city (Trento) and report one of the possible outcomes: Agrihood. The provided solution shows how a physical temporary space and digital tools can be integrated and can interoperate to drive a more sustainable urban environment through citizens engagement and participation. If you create an Agrihood network for the whole city the system begins to have major impacts on it: new green spaces that become real lungs for the city, new interactions between neighborhoods, new production and savings in economic terms for each individual family.

Keywords: Gamification · Citizen participation · Open data · Metabolic urbanism · City visioning

1 Introduction

Unites Nations projections suggest that 75% of the human population will be living in cities by 2050[1]. New methods, new equipment, new way to think about process and life, are basics to let the organism of a city productive again, able

---

[1] https://population.un.org/wup/.

© Springer Nature Switzerland AG 2021
C. Stephanidis et al. (Eds.): HCII 2021, CCIS 1498, pp. 435–442, 2021.
https://doi.org/10.1007/978-3-030-90176-9_56

to monitoring and improving itself. Using *Open Data*, parametric software to let the cognitive system and evaluation systems stronger could be a possibility [5]. Nowadays, open data are not only part of an elite sphere, but every person could contribute to monitoring the city. This could be done exploiting the organization of *participatory processes* to engage and motivate users to design sustainable urban planning solutions.

For example Smart Citizen[2] and Superbarrio[3] are two projects that use data analysis and gamification to collect data and engage the citizens in the design of the public space. They overcomes the limits of conventional methodologies and used also to collect data about the citizens' needs, desires and proposals, to educate to sustainability and inclusiveness.

Gamification has demonstrated to be a possible solution to engage people on changing their habits and contributing to the society [8]. *"Through play there is a profound relationship to culture to society, there is a profound material component, there is a profound relationship to our technologies and how we evolve these ecosystems"*[4]. Gameful applications have been successfully exploited for encouraging sustainable or healthy behaviors [6,9]. This interest is testified by the availability of hundreds of gamification development platforms, that offer pre-packaged templates to build-up gameful applications. *Could citizen participation, open data and gamification help the urban planner in design dynamic city?* The aims of this contribution is to explore how open data can become tools to offer a real time figure for understanding and influencing urban dynamics in space and fluxes. With the help of the Fab City approach and gamification, our contribution wants to suggest a novel urban design, studying the impacts of the project on the analyzed data.

The Metabolic Urbanism concepts will be introduced in Sect. 2, then Agrihood will be explained in Sect. 3, based on a experimentation in the city of Trento. Finally, some remarks and open issues will be prensented in Sect. 4.

2   Metabolic Urbanism

The Fab City is an innovative model for re-imagining cities [4]: it is an international initiative started by Institute for Advanced Architecture of Catalonia (IAAC)[5], the MIT's Center for Bits and Atoms (CBA)[6], the Barcelona City Council and the Fab Foundation[7] to develop self-sufficient cities that are at once locally productive and globally connected. The project is connected to the global network of Fabrication Laboratories[8], or Fab Lab, and made up of an

---

[2] https://smartcitizen.me/.
[3] http://superbarrio.iaac.net/.
[4] Ann Pendleton-Jullian, TEDxColumbus, 2009 http://www.tedxcolumbus.com/speakers-performers/2009-global-speakers-performers/ann-pendleton-jullian/.
[5] https://iaac.net/.
[6] http://cba.mit.edu/.
[7] https://fabfoundation.org/.
[8] https://fabfoundation.org/global-community/.

international think thank of civic leaders, makers, urban planners and innovators working on changing the operates in a linear fashion, importing products and producing waste. It foresees a new economy based on *distributed data* and manufacturing infrastructure. The aim of the Fab City research is to arrive at a globally connected system but which remains locally productive in the individual poles.

In the XXI Century, internet and the technology revolution allow people to reach every kind of information, and this one could create knowledge if it is well discretize. We went from a centralized to distributed process, from a static to a variable model. But *how could cities become able to convert information into resources?, What kind of knowledge come from this new technology and what could be helpful for? How cities could become productive again?* According to the Fab City models, a change of paradigms is required: from a *"Product in, Trash out"* paradigm, typical of a linear metabolism of cities, where we pass from extraction, to production, to use and then waste, to a more efficient *"Data in Data out"* system* where the metabolism is circular, where we can find a constantly exchange of data and knowledge not only from cities to cities but also from citizens to citizens.

Urban Metabolism refers to the "collection of complex socio-technical and socio-ecological processes by which flows of materials, energy, people, and information shape the city, service the needs of its populace, and impact the surrounding hinterland" [10]. We want to understand how technology (such as open data, artificial intelligence, 5G and so on) could help this revolution [11]. But first of all we have to think about people: *How citizens could be part of this process?* We have to inform and empower them because they are the most important and relevant activator of the change. This is a bottom up revolution, which starts from the behaviour of people and could be a possible solution to re-think they way we live.

The limits of the Fab City initiative are in the outcomes because a city revolution takes time. We should try to follow the Fab City strategies also trying to use urban acupuncture to make it work immediately. To overcome these limitations we propose a metabolic way to concept the city and the urban fabric. We think about our city like a human body, with all its systems working together, and closely. The strength of this approach is that there isn't a specific project dependent and closely connected to a single city: it is a method, a new urban tool, a new way of thinking.

3 Agrihood: Gaming the City, Cultivating the Future

The purpose of this research is to envision a new approach in the urban context. We want to take care about all the fluxes that go through the city, material and immaterial ones, that most of the time we don't see. We present our motivational digital system called *Agrihood* with its life-cycle (depicted in Fig. 1) and an installation in the city of Trento. The life-cycle we envisioned exploits three components (i.e., topics in Fig. 1): (1) Open Data Analysis, (2) Participatory

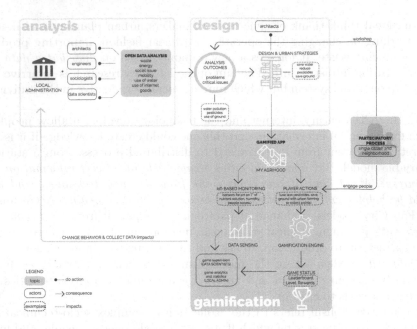

Fig. 1. Agrihood life-cycle.

Process, and (3) Gamification, all collaborating to gaming the city and cultivating the future. Our approach caters to three principal stakeholders. The (i)
Local Administration, the (ii) *Urban planners*, and the (iii) *Single Citizen and
Neighborhood*. We will now look more in details each component and how they
have been concretely instantiated in the Trento city context.

*__Open Data Analysis.__ The use of *open data* to do a faithful mapping of the
anatomy of the city is the basis of this research. The first step of this method
is mapping and analyse the fluxes of the city (i.e., `Analysis` phase in Fig. 1)
to have a real time image of the urban fabric (e.g., waste, energy, social issue,
mobility, use of water, use of internet, goods). It is possible thanks to new technologies [1] and the attention paid by the *Local Administration* to them. After
all the `Analysis Outcomes` will show us pros and cons of each city, the *critical
issues* and the strong points of the urban fabric. Based on this, the aim of the
`Design` phase is to design a *tool* and a *urban strategy* that could be useful for
the population but at the same time try to solve some problems highlighted
by the analysis. The City of Trento has a huge amount of data collected in
a open source online platform called *Opendatatrentino*[9]. Analysis and interaction between these data is useful to understand numerous dynamics of the city,
an example is that the water of Trento river is polluted mostly by substances

---

[9] https://dati.trentino.it.

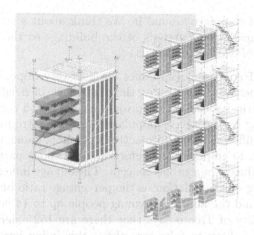

Fig. 2. Agrihood design.

deriving from the washing of agricultural soils: ancient agricultural techniques and waste of water are serious problems[10].

According to the waste chain is possible to understand how 76% of the waste produced follows the paths of separate collection (Trento is the Italian city with the highest percentage of differentiated collection: 80%) and the remaining 25% is partly sent to waste-to-energy plants, part sold to private entities capable of using waste to produce energy and the remaining is stored in landfills.[11,12]

Talking about water (and referring to 2008 data), 74.3% of the resource water invoiced by the water service operators is destined for civil utilities; a further 23.1% is destined for industry and for other economic activities and the remaining 2.6% belongs to the uses agricultural and livestock. It is a huge amount of water because new agricultural techniques (such as hydroponics, aeroponics and drip irrigation systems), are still underdeveloped[13].

Based on this kind of analysis and outcomes we want to try to give an answer to find solutions able to provide impacts in the short time. The aim of the Design phase of Fig. 1 is to think about a structure that brings back nature and agriculture to our cities: we are talking about innovative way to concept agriculture to save water and save ground, pay attention in the use of pesticides that are the major pollutants of Trento's river in the name of the Fab City approach. The idea of the Agrihood project has been the result of Design phase.

Agrihood is a modular façade prototype (see Fig. 2) of vertical farming that lets the city locally productive and globally connected, but at the same time the aim is to try to understand how this structure could be important for the

---

[10] https://www.isprambiente.gov.it/it/pubblicazioni/rapporti/rapporto-nazionale-pesticidi-nelle-acque-dati-2015-2016.-edizione-2018.

[11] https://www.tn.camcom.it/.

[12] http://www.statistica.provincia.tn.it/.

[13] https://adep.provincia.tn.it/, https://www.isprambiente.gov.it/it.

climate comfort of the place around it. We think about a scaffolding structure anchor in blind facades or flat roofs of the buildings so the theme is also the reuse and recycle of existent materials.

*Participatory Process. Social issues are also very important to investigate because in this specific city (Trento) there is a lack of neighborhood identity, hence an hypothetical social design project as Agrihood could be rejected by citizens. According to the age of population we can introduce a *participatory process* based on different levels: interactive workshop, game, using software and IoT. We need also to empower and inform people about participatory process, necessary to introduce a new urban concept. The old age index, which represents the degree of aging of a population, is the percentage ratio between the number of over sixty-five and the number of young people up to 14 years old.

The municipality of Trento says that there are 162 elderly people per 100 young people[14]. We have to take care about this index because tells us what kind of population we are dealing with. We want to make citizens an integral part of the innovation process and building a sense of relatedness with the rest of the community fosters a motivation to use the system, thus pursuing a positive behavior change. This is particularly relevant for those citizens that are sensitive to sustainability issues and whose motivation can be leveraged to social project impact and reach thousands of users. This can be achieved through a continuous dialogue with end-users and a participatory co-design approach [3,12]. Thanks to the citizen feedback and suggestions, this component can have a prominent role in the enhancement of Agrihood.

*Gamification. Most of the time the limitations of urban projects are in the outcomes. These are too theoretical, because the scale is to big, there is a huge amount of topics and the city revolution takes time. We have to empower citizens, let them involved in this transformative and adaptive urban process. Also cities have to change their way to think and to work, so this innovation takes time and a lot of resources. To make this possible we use gamification to enhance and increase the participatory process after its definition. The gamification tool could be the theme that is able to put together all the different goals of the project and at the same time encouraging the population to be part of the change.

To make the Agrihood idea a reality, we exploit existing gamification techniques [7] in a dedicated gamified mobile app. Using this app we want to be able to improve urban qualities, making citizens feel part of the system. Through a set of sensors (i.e., IoT-Based Monitoring task in Fig. 1) the application is able to monitor the cultures, the pollution in the air, the noise, giving at the population a real time snapshot of the city status. At the same time the application is able to engage citizen asking to join the city life with the goal to improve urban qualities, making citizens feel part of the system. It is only though their *activities* and *actions* that this impact becomes tangible. We introduce also a way to make citizen active exploiting gamification mechanisms as *rewards, levels and leaderboards*. A snapshot of the My Agrihood gamified app is depicted in Fig. 3.

---

[14] http://dati.istat.it/.

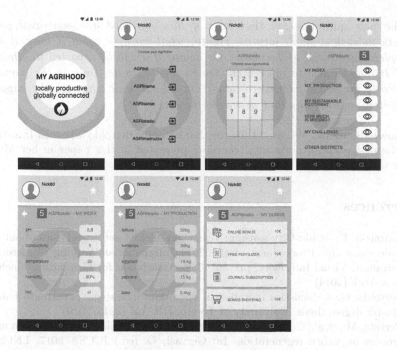

Fig. 3. My Agrihood app

The user could monitor index of water (like the level of nutrients, the pH of the solution which is very important to let the plants survive, the temperature of water), how much vegetables have produced, how many days left for harvest, the ecological footprint (like the amount of oxygen your module produced, how many pesticides you saved) and then there is the gamified system with ranking and challenge between different neighborhood.

4 Open Questions to Play the City

The research presented in this paper guided the process towards a locally productive and globally connected city in terms of urban agriculture production, bringing nature back to the urban fabric to ensure not only food, but also improvements in the social dynamics like: citizen participation and engagement, thermal comfort of the indoor and of the surrounding environment (outdoor). We propose a gamification-based methodology that can be used in any city, based on in-depth analysis via open data, that will give different responses depending on the urban fabric internal organization, the functioning of the flows and the existing connections between them.

Agrihood is the result of a targeted analysis, on its potentials and its problems. If we move the analysis to another city, the problems can change, and we will have to sew a specific project on that city.

The new questions are therefore: *if this Agrihood has generated positive impacts in such a small city as Trento, what impacts could it have if it will be implemented in all of Trentino? Or again, if it will be exported to other realities? It may be able to offer a change in mentality not only to the population but also to the public administrations? On a large scale what are the impacts of this system on the flows that permeate the city?*

Acknowledgement. We would like to thank Giulia Bertoldo who has investigated first the design and experimental concepts presented in this paper in her Master's degree thesis [2].

References

1. Antonelli, F., et al.: City sensing: visualising mobile and social data about a city scale event. In: Proceedings of the 2014 International Working Conference on Advanced Visual Interfaces, pp. 337–338. Association for Computing Machinery, New York (2014)
2. Bertoldo, G.: Urbanistica metabolica: open data e strategie per Trento Fab City. Master degree thesis, University of Trento, DICAM (2018/2019)
3. Cerreta, M., et al.: Community branding (Co-bra): a collaborative decision making process for urban regeneration. In: Gervasi, O. (ed.) ICCSA 2017. LNCS, vol. 10406, pp. 730–746. Springer, Cham (2017). https://doi.org/10.1007/978-3-319-62398-6_52
4. Diez, T.: Fab City: the mass distribution of (almost) everything. Institute for Advanced Architecture of Catalonia (2018)
5. Galli, A.: Urbanistica Parametrica. Open data, strumenti e tecniche per la progettazione della città di domani. Ph.D. thesis, Master thesis in Ingegneria Edile, Politecnico di Torino (2013)
6. Johnson, D., et al.: Gamification for health and wellbeing: a systematic review of the literature. Internet Interv. **6**, 89–106 (2016)
7. Kazhamiakin, R., Loria, E., Marconi, A., Scanagatta, M.: A gamification platform to analyze and influence citizens' daily transportation choices. IEEE Trans. Intell. Transp. Syst. **22**(4), 2153–2167 (2021)
8. Koivisto, J., Hamari, J.: The rise of motivational information systems: a review of gamification research. Int. J. Inf. Manag. **45**, 191–210 (2019)
9. Marconi, A., Schiavo, G., Zancanaro, M., Valetto, G., Pistore, M.: Exploring the world through small green steps: improving sustainable school transportation with a game-based learning interface. In: Proceedings of the 2018 International Conference on Advanced Visual Interfaces, AVI 2018, pp. 24:1–24:9 (2018)
10. Musango, J., Currie, P., Robinson, B.: Urban metabolism for resource efficient cities: from theory to implementation, p. 12 (2017). Book of Abstracts
11. Offenhuber, D., Ratti, C.: Decoding the City: Urbanism in the Age of Big Data. Birkhäuser (2014)
12. Vassileva, J.: Motivating participation in social computing applications: a user modeling perspective. User Model. User Adap. Interact. **22**(1–2), 177–201 (2012). https://doi.org/10.1007/s11257-011-9109-5

A Study on the Integration Method of Sports Practice and Video Games

Sakuto Hoshi[1]([✉]), Kazutaka Kurihara[2], Sho Sakurai[1], Koichi Hirota[1], and Takuya Nojima[1]

[1] The University of Electro-Communications, Tokyo, Japan
s.hoshi@vogue.is.uec.ac.jp
[2] Tsuda University, Tokyo, Japan
http://www.nojilab.org/

Abstract. It is difficult for recreational players to continue practicing sports, which they know is important to improve their technique and get more enjoyment. Therefore, we propose utilizing a concept of "toolification of games", which enables players to perceive the effect of practicing while playing a game. Few papers have focused on sports training while playing a video game, but some sports players benefit from a training strategy similar to playing particular video games. This benefit suggests the possibility of using a video game for sports training. The proposed method will contribute to making monotonous training more enjoyable by "improving their sports skill while playing a game." In this study, we focused on badminton training and playing Tetris together. When practicing badminton, the player is often required to hit the shuttlecock to different parts of the court anywhere they want to. This way of practicing is similar to a general strategy used when playing Tetris—the player attempts to distribute Tetriminos (block units in the Tetris game) to every row without bias. This paper describes experimental results from badminton training practice using Tetris compared with practice using conventional visual feedback methods.

Keywords: Sports training methods · Serious video games · Skill development · Gamification · Toolification of games

1 Introduction

1.1 Background

It is difficult for recreational players to continue practicing sports, which they know is essential to improve their technique and get more enjoyment while playing it. Therefore, we propose utilizing a concept of "toolification of games", which enables players to perceive the effect of practicing while playing a game. Video games help improve physical activity enjoyment, demonstrated in several studies that have integrated video game concepts into physical activities to motivate

C. Stephanidis et al. (Eds.): HCII 2021, CCIS 1498, pp. 443–450, 2021.
https://doi.org/10.1007/978-3-030-90176-9_57

people to be more active. However, in most instances, only the video game–related concepts, not video games themselves, are used. The primary purpose of the activities is still practice.

When practicing a sport, players often need to perform basic motions repeatedly. This method of practice is often dull, and players quickly lose motivation to continue the activity. Thus, game elements are integrated into the practice action to reduce dullness to solve the issue. However, when considering the effect of practice, it is essential to perform the basic motions without alteration repeatedly. Though the player's interest and consequent attention when completing the motion may have positive effects, the most critical aspect is the actual repetition of the practice action. Thus, a person's positive attitude toward practicing is not mandatory. For example, suppose a person plays a physical game consists of basic "practice actions" of a particular sport. In that case, the person could perceive the effect of "practicing" as long as they play the person plays that physical game repeatedly, although the physical game is not the specific sport itself. Even if the person does not have any motivation for practicing that sport, the sport's skill will improve by playing the physical game. In this situation, the necessary motivation is to play the physical game, not to practice. This is the concept called the Toolification of Games [1], i.e., the person obtains the effect of practicing the sport without knowing it while playing the game. The Toolification of Games (ToG) involves "achieving non-game purposes in the redundant spaces of existing games. ToG is that the task is attached a posteriori after the host existing game becomes popular in our society, and makes harmonious coexistence with the host" [1].

In this research, our goal was to achieve a situation in which a person could achieve the effects of practicing badminton without focusing on playing the physical practice. In this paper, we propose using a modified Tetris game that uses basic badminton motion as game inputs—playing our proposed modified Tetris would lead to improved badminton skills. Some sports have training strategies similar to those used in playing a particular video game; therefore, the video game can be integrated into sports training and contribute to visualizing the effects of practice and increasing motivation. This method is also considered to improve enjoyment in monotonous training.

From among various skills recommended to play badminton better, we focus on hitting the shuttlecock accurately anywhere on the court. Badmintonplayers recommended to become capable of hitting every part of the opponent'scourt and hit in the right way for each location [2].

On the other hand, when playing the Tetris game, players focus on repeatedly putting Tetoriminos to the field's specific point. From this consideration, we propose using the badminton practicing method as a game input of Tetris. Then, it will contribute to achieving a situation that a player can "practice badminton" while "playing Tetris".

2   Related Work

Gamification refers to the application of game elements to things of non-game activity. For example, by using the gamification method, monotonous sports training can be changed into a game [4]. It contributes sports training become much enjoyable activity. It also reveals that gamified training can improve participants' skills. Mueller et al. focus on the benefits of combining game elements and physical activity, then he summarizes how to design sports using such concept [7].

Toolification of Games (ToG) [1] also combines game and non-game activities. The most crucial difference between gamification and ToG is what the purpose is. Gamification has a task as its primary objective, and the game elements are only used to help achieve the main objective. ToG, on the other hand, has the game as the main objective, and the task is completed on its own while playing the game. Kurihara et al. showed an example of ToG as an application of their proposed system [3]. The user of the system plays the popular Nintendo game Super Mario Brothers with fundraising by using their proposed technology. This system allowed users to donate much money as they earned in coins within the game. As shown in this example, the ToGames allowed a game to be played to complete another task without realizing it.

3   Prototype System

As a preliminary study, a prototype system was developed based on the idea described above, that capable of practicing badminton while playing Tetris game as shown in Fig. 1.

Key features important to this concept are as follows:

- It must capable of playing an existing game.
- It must capable of playing a physical sport, or training.

Fig. 1. Proposed Tetris with badminton

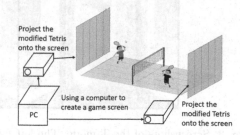

Fig. 2. The system configuration diagram

Each player can watch screens behind the opponent player. Then modified version of Tetris game is displayed on the screen. Two short focus projectors are used to cast the game image onto the screen (Fig. 2). In this system, the location of the player at the time of hitting the shuttlecock corresponds to the falling position of the tetromino. For example, if the player hits the shuttlecock back at the rightmost side of the field, the tetriminos will fall on the rightmost row.

4   Experiments

4.1   Procedure of the Experiment

To evaluate our proposed method, an experiment was conducted. Under the situation of wide spreading of COVID-19, a web-based experiment was performed to avoid physical contact among participants. Then, all activity including badminton aspect are done in VR space. In this experiment, we prepared the following three modes:

- T mode: a mode in which the impact of the practice is visualized as a game (proposed method, Fig. 3)
- N mode: a mode without any visualization (Fig. 4 Left)
- G mode: a mode in which the effect of the practice is visualized as a bar graph (Fig. 4 Right)

T mode is a game based on the system described above. When players hit a flying ball back with players' mouse-operated racket, tetriminos fall.

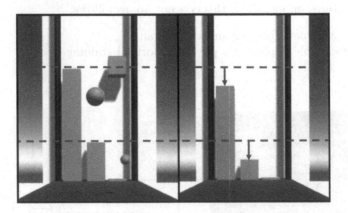

Fig. 3. Screenshots of the T mode. The left figure shows a screenshot just before the Tetriminos disappears in a row. The right figure shows the same screen just after the Tetriminos disappears. A dotted blue line was added to emphasize the difference in the height of the bars. (Color figure online)

Fig. 4. A snapshot of N mode (left) and G mode (right).

The position of the tetrimino changes depending on which part of the racket players hit back with. As in Tetris, one line disappears when one line is aligned and Two types of tetriminos appear: square and elongated. Two types of tetriminos appear: square and elongated. The actual playing screen just before and just after the disappearance is shown in Fig. 3. It also imposes a condition that the game ends if more than ten pieces end or if the player hits back 30 times. Balls are made to fly once every 1.5 s in unity. This requires players to hit the ball evenly across the three rows to keep eliminating tetriminos and hit the ball back 30 times as far as possible.

In contrast to T mode, G mode uses bar graphs for visualization, and the end condition is that the game ends when there are more than ten balls in a row. N mode is a mode without any visualization and has the same end condition as G mode.

T mode and G mode were compared with N mode respectively to evaluate the proposed method. Participants accessed the web application with their PC browser for this experiment. The detailed procedure goes as follows:

1 The URL for this experiment was shown to the participants. By accessing the URL by their environment, they begin the experiment. Informed consent was obtained electrically via the page before starting the application.
2 The participants are asked to play N mode followed by G mode or T mode randomly assigned by the application. Each pair (N and G, N and T) was done three times.
3 After all the experiments were completed, the participants were asked to answer questionnaires.

Participants' whole action and hit back result is recorded and stored in the network-connected database.

4.2 Evaluation of the Practicing Effect

We recruited eight adult participants from inside of the university community who were able to use computers at a general level. Most of them spent playing

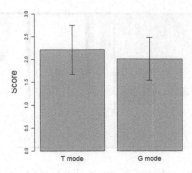

Fig. 5. Result of hit score

games between 3 and 7 hours per week. They prefer action games, role-playing games and puzzle games. Each participant was asked to hit the ball equally in the court.

The court was divided into three areas: left, center and right. The number of balls being hits into each area was counted. For example, we assume the situation that the participant plays G mode. The number of hits into the court's left area is denoted as H_{lG}. H_{cG} denotes the that of the center area, H_{rG} indicates that of the right area. Then, a set of H_{lG}, H_{cG} and H_{rG} was perceived after playing one game. After each game, the standard deviation was calculated and denoted as S_G. After playing three sets of the pair of the game modes, the average of S_{Gs} was calculated and denoted as AvS_G.

When the series of the experiment was completed, eight sets of AvS_G and AvS_T were obtained. Average and standard deviation of the result is shown in Fig. 5. Smaller score indicates the participant could hit back the ball more equally on the field. Mann–Whitney U test was performed to find the difference between AvS_G and AvS_T to evaluate the effect of the proposed method. The p-value was 0.3823, which means that there was no significant difference between T mode and G mode.

4.3 Questionnaire

After the series of trials, questionnaires are performed. Participants were asked to compare N mode and G or N and T to answer questions. In this questionnaire, five-point Likert scales were used to answer. The list of questions as follows:

a) How evenly did you hit the ball into the court? (EQUALITY)
b) How much does the provided visual information help you to determine where to hit back? (DECISION)
c) How much fun did you have? (ENJOYMENT)

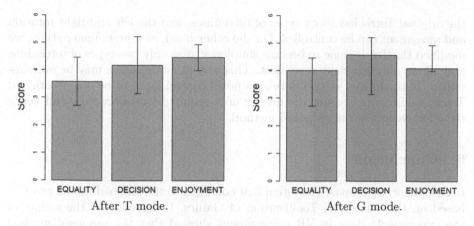

After T mode.   After G mode.

Fig. 6. Result of the questionnaire.

Table 1. Average score of each questionnaire

	EQUALITY	DECISION	ENJOYMENT
T mode	3.58 (p-value = 0.04404)	4.17 (p-value = 0.01717)	4.46 (p-value = 0.006607)
G mode	4.00 (p-value = 0.017)	4.58 (p-value = 0.006664)	4.08 (p-value = 0.005988)

The results of the questionnaire are shown in Table 1, Fig. 6. Each value in Table 1 is the average of all subjects' responses to the questionnaire. Since the sample size was small this time, a one-tailed Wilcoxon signed rank test, one of the non-parametric tests, was conducted with the population mean set at three. From this result, we could find a significant difference between N and T mode. We also could find a significant difference between N and G mode.

5 Discussion

According to the questionnaire (Table 1, Fig. 6), visual information improve subjective evaluation in both T mode and G mode. However, the hit score results (Fig. 5) show no significant difference between T mode and G mode in terms of practice efficiency. This suggests that propsoed T mode does not have distinct effect on practice compared to G mode. At the same time, this also should indicate that the T mode used in this experiment is not difficult to operate, at least compared to the simple visualization of G mode.

One reason for the lack of significant differences between T mode and G mode is that the experimental conditions, such as visual representations and control inputs, might be too simple. In actual badminton, it is recommended to practice to hit the shuttlecock back to eight separated areas in the court: one near the net, one is at the back of the field, two (back and front) by three (left, center and right) areas in the center. In contrast, the experimental environment has only three rows (left, center, and right), limiting the area of play. In addition, the original Tetris has seven types of tetriminos, and the left and right rotation and movement can be controlled. On the other hand, as a preliminary study, we modified the Tetris game to become simpler; it uses only two types of tetriminos and allows only left-right movement. This way of modification may be oversimplified. In the future, we will develop a novel control input to be able to original Tetris, taking into account the hitting area required for badminton, and verify the effectiveness of the proposed method.

6   Conclusion

In this paper, we proposed a system that combines Tetris and badminton practice based on the concept of Toolification of Games. Unfortunately, the results of the experiments done in VR environment showed that the proposed method was not effective enough compared to the conventional visualization method. However, the results of the questionnaires showed that the proposed method was acceptable to the participants and more enjoyable than the conventional method.

Acknowledgments. This work was supported by JSPS KAKENHI Grant Number 19H01129.

References

1. Kurihara, K.: Toolification of games: achieving non-game purposes in the redundant spaces of existing games. In: Proceedings of the ACE 2015, pp. 31:1–31:5 (2015)
2. Pelton, B.C.: Badminton. Prentice-Hall, Englewood Cliffs (1971)
3. Kurihara, K., Itaya, A., Uemura, A., Kitahara, T., Nagao, K.: Picognizer: a JavaScript library for detecting and recognizing synthesized sounds. In: Cheok, A.D., Inami, M., Romão, T. (eds.) ACE 2017. LNCS, vol. 10714, pp. 339–359. Springer, Cham (2018). https://doi.org/10.1007/978-3-319-76270-8_24
4. Jensen, M.M., Rasmussen, M.K., Grønbundefinedk, K.: Design sensitivities for interactive sport-training games. In: Proceedings of the 2014 Conference on Designing Interactive Systems, pp. 685–694 (2014)
5. Anthony, W., Hannah, J., Nicole, N., Jo, W.: Exergame effectiveness: what the numbers can tell us. In: Sandbox 2010: Proceedings of the 5th ACM SIGGRAPH Symposium on Video Games, July 2010, pp. 55–62 (2010)
6. Kathrin, M.G., Jonas, S., Maic, M.: Exergame design for elderly users: the case study of SilverBalance. In: ACE 2010: Proceedings of the 7th International Conference on Advances in Computer Entertainment Technology, November 2010, pp. 66–69 (2010)
7. Florian, F.M., et al.: Designing sports: a framework for exertion games. In: CHI 2011: Proceedings of the SIGCHI Conference on Human Factors in Computing Systems, pp. 2651–2660 (2011)

Development of a Board Game Using Mixed Reality to Support Communication

Shozo Ogawa[1(✉)], Kodai Ito[2], Ryota Horie[1], and Mitsunori Tada[2]

[1] Shibaura Institute of Technology University, 3-7-5 Toyosu, Koto-ku, Tokyo, Japan
af17028@shibaura-it.ac.jp
[2] National Institute of Advanced Industrial Science and Technology,
2-3-26 Aomi, Koto-ku, Tokyo, Japan

Abstract. Ice break has been attracting attention as a tool for enhancing communications during the first encounter. Previous research showed that collaborative tabletop games are effective for ice break. However, few research discuss the factors of these games that influence this enhancement. In this research, we developed a tabletop game where a piece on a board is manipulated by inclining the board with four levers to navigate the piece to follow the predefined path. Our hypothesis is that communication may be enhanced by counter-intuitive behavior of the piece, such as climbing up the slope that is against the laws of physics on the earth. Though what the players manipulate is the real levers, what they see is virtual board and piece rendered through MR device (HoloLens2). In this research we have implemented two behaviors of the piece, one is normal gravity behavior where the peace goes down the slope while the other is anti-gravity behavior where the peace climbs up the slope. To evaluate the effect of the counter-intuitive behavior on the enhancement of the communication, we have conducted experiment where the pair of players played the game under two different conditions. The results of the five-point Likert scale questionnaire demonstrated that the counter-intuitive behavior had positive effect on the freshness and interestingness of the game while it had no effect on the difficulty of the cooperation. However, it was confirmed that the verbal communication between the players increased 6.7% in average which partially support our hypothesis.

Keywords: Cooperative control · Mixed reality · Interactive system · Communication · Manipulation · Augmented reality · IMU

1 Introduction

Ice break has been attracting attention as a tool for enhancing communications during the first meeting. Sundari et al. showed that collaborative tabletop games are effective for ice break [1]. It is an educational tabletop game to enhance mutual understanding of jobs through tasks related to various jobs. However, few research discuss the factors of these games that influence this enhancement.

© Springer Nature Switzerland AG 2021
C. Stephanidis et al. (Eds.): HCII 2021, CCIS 1498, pp. 451–458, 2021.
https://doi.org/10.1007/978-3-030-90176-9_58

While tabletop games have enhanced the effect of ice break, it isn't known what elements of that.

And in the research of Sasaki and Igarashi et al. on the subject of cooperative tabletop games such as SlideQuest that are fully digital including input interfaces such as levers, they analyzed the selfish and altruistic cooperative skills using machine learning [3]. However, they didn't talked about activation of cooperation. In this research, we evaluate the enhancement of coordination using a cooperative tabletop game that combines analog and digital systems. We use physical levers as the evaluation target because we are interested in the enhancement of cooperation.

In this research, we examine whether the tabletop game "Slide Quest [2]" by Blue Orange can be used as an ice break. This is a multi-player tabletop game in which players manipulate the pieces on the board by inclining them with four levers to navigate the pieces to follow a predetermined path. Lowering the levers to incline the board is a very intuitive operation. Therefore, the player can unconsciously understand what the opponent wants to do. The game system, which requires both players to cooperate with each other, creates a conversation opportunity for cooperation. On the other hand, since it is easy to understand, the amount of conversation required for cooperation isn't large enough.

Therefore, we presented a counter-intuitive operation to increase the amount of conversation for cooperation. The counter-intuitive operation is an operation that can't be obtained in daily life. Therefore, it takes time to understand the counter-intuitive operation, and the amount of conversation for cooperation is expected to be larger than that for the intuitive operation.

In this research, we developed a tabletop game using mixed reality to support communication, based on the hypothesis that communication can be activated by presenting elements unique to digital games, such as counter-intuitive operations that behave against the laws of physics on earth.

2 Proposal System

2.1 Summary of the Proposal System

In this research, we used levers as the input interface of Slide Quest which is an analog board game by Blue Orange. Slide Quest is a multi-player cooperative tabletop game in which players must move frames to the goal through designated positions on a map. The borad is inclined by operating the lever with several people. The controls are very intuitive in that pressing a lever causes the board to incline. It is also an input interface in which the operations strongly influence each other.

In this research, we superimposed a virtual world board on a real world board in order to present counter-intuitive operations. In this research, counter-intuitive operations are the operations when the behavior is against the physical laws on the earth. We used Microsoft's HoloLens2 as a visual presentation device to display a virtual space on the board that realizes the behavior against the laws of physics. The HoloLens2 is a device that realizes mixed reality (MR),

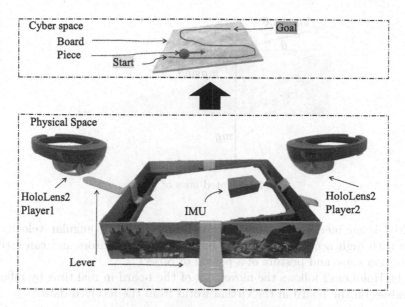

Fig. 1. System configuration

a technology that combines virtual space information with real space through visual presentation [4].

In order to bring the slope information of the board in the real world into the virtual world, we need to measure the slope of the board in the real world. In order to draw the board and pieces in the virtual world with HoloLens2, sharing the positional alignment between the real world and the virtual world and real-time object changes are necessary. When using multiple HoloLens2 , there are problems that the coordinates of objects will be spatially different among players due to different world coordinates.

We show below how to solve these problems.

2.2 Configuration of the Proposal System

The configuration of this system is shown in Fig. 1. In this system, a piece moving uphill in the opposite direction instead of downhill according to gravity was drawn on the SlideQuest board using HoloLens2 as a behavior that is against the laws of physics.

We applied a force equal to twice the inverse vector of the gravitational force parallel to the slope of the piece in order to change the laws of physics.

The applied force is shown in Fig. 2. The angle θ in Fig. 2 is measured by an inertial measurement unit (IMU, DhaibaDAQ [5]). In the proposed system, one inertial measurement unit is mounted on the board, measures the angle, and transmits it to HoloLens2 via UDP/IP communication with Wi-Fi serial communication.

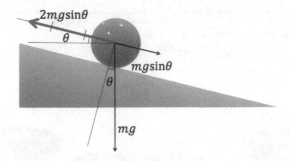

Fig. 2. Adapted laws of physics

IMU is an inertial measurement unit that measures angular velocity and angle with high accuracy. The IMU integrates some sensors and can estimate the motion state and posture of a person or object.

The HoloLens2 follows the movement of the board in real time by reflecting the values on the board in the virtual world from the received data.

3   Experimental Details

We conducted an experiment to confirm the influence of counter-intuitive operations on communication. In this experiment, a pair of subjects each manipulated two levers and were tasked with picking up an object placed along the path while moving a piece along the path from the start to the goal. The experiment was conducted under two different conditions: one in which the pieces move down the slope according to gravity, and the other in which the pieces move up the slope against gravity.

The experiment was conducted in an within-subject design and counterbalanced. A questionnaire on a 5-point Likert scale was administered to the subjects to determine whether the operation of going up the hill was new to them, whether the operation of going down or up the hill was more cooperative, interesting, or easy to operate. We will compare and verify the influence of counter-intuitive operations on communication. We investigate the time, frequency, and content of conversations during the experiment by recording video.

4   Results and Discussion

Preliminary experiments were conducted on three sets of subjects (six subjects in total).

4.1   Average Time to Complete the Task

Figures 3 and Fig. 4 show the average time taken to perform each condition of the experimental task. The horizontal axis shows the condition of each trial.

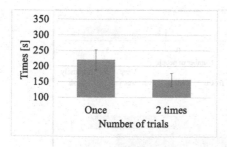

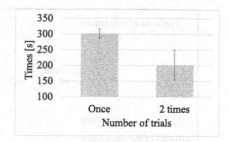

Fig. 3. Average time to complete the task under normal gravity conditions

Fig. 4. Average time to complete the task under anti-gravity conditions

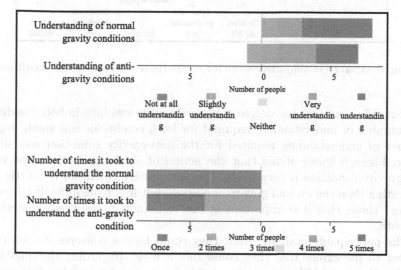

Fig. 5. Average of subjective score for understanding of the experiment

The vertical axis shows the average time taken to perform the task. The average time to complete the task in the normal gravity condition is about 80 s shorter than that in the anti-gravity condition, in which the pieces go down the slope.

4.2 Average of Subjective Score

Figures 5, Fig. 6 and Fig. 7 show some of the average values of the questionnaire results. The horizontal axis shows the five-point rating scale for each questionnaire item. The vertical axis shows some of the questions in the pre- and post-experiment questionnaires, and the questions are grouped according to the rating scale on the horizontal axis. Figure 5 summarizes the questions on the level of understanding of the experiment. Figure 6 summarizes the questions about the comparison of experimental conditions. Figure 7 summarizes the questions about the content and degree of recognition between subjects.

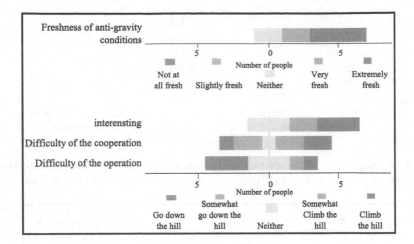

Fig. 6. Average of subjective score for comparison of experimental conditions

Figure 5 shows that the degree of understanding was high in both conditions. The number of understanding required for both conditions was small, but the number of understanding required for the anti-gravity condition was slightly larger. Figure 6 shows shows that the action of climbing up the slope in the anti-gravity condition is very fresh. The anti-gravity condition is a little more interesting than the normal gravity condition, but it is more difficult to control. Figure 7 shows that it is important or not to be able to see the opponent, but not both.

The participants evaluated that they could have a conversation with their partner to the extent that they could talk a little. Regarding the question of whether they would like to use the system for ice-breaking with a first meeting person, they tended to be somewhat willing to use the system and neither. The results showed that the participants felt a little familiarity with the experimental subjects. In addition, some of the subjects answered verbally that they didn't find the operation of going down the slope fresh at all.

4.3   The Content and Duration of Speech Were Confirmed from the Video Recording

The content and duration of the conversations were confirmed from the video recordings made simultaneously during the experiment. The average conversation rate during the experiment is shown in Fig. 8. The average conversation rate was calculated by dividing the conversation time by the time to complete the task in each experimental condition. The conversation rate was increased by about 6.7% in the anti-gravity condition compared to the normal gravity condition. The conversation rate in the anti-gravity condition was larger than that in the normal gravity condition. The reason for this was to discuss how to move the object and what route to take, according to the free description in the questionnaire.

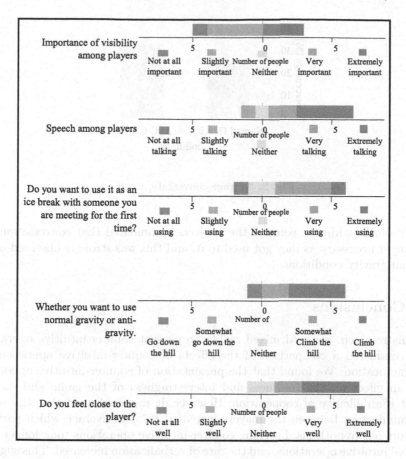

Fig. 7. Average of subjective score for perception between subjects

According to the video recording, there was little surprise or confirmation under normal gravity conditions. However, in the anti-gravity condition, the conversation was not only at the beginning but also at the end, discussing how to move each lever for each operation. Surprise and impatience were also observed in the anti-gravity condition in addition to manipulation.

4.4 Discussion

Counter-intuitive operations such as behaviors that are contrary to the laws of physics may have affected the freshness and interestingness. Climbing up the slope in the anti-gravity condition was evaluated as very fresh, which may be one of the reasons why the motion of climbing up the slope in the anti-gravity condition was evaluated as somewhat more interesting than the motion of going down the slope in the normal gravity condition. It seems that it took more time to talk to the participants in the anti-gravity condition than in the normal gravity

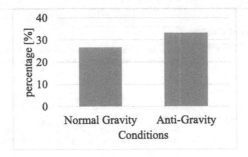

Fig. 8. Average conversation rate

condition. In addition, some of the subjects commented that conversation was no longer necessary as they got used to it, and this was strongly observed under normal gravity conditions.

5   Conclusions

In this research, we used mixed reality to present counter-intuitive operations and conducted a comparison of the effects of counter-intuitive operations on communication. We found that the presentation of counter-intuitive operations had an effect on the freshness and interestingness of the game and did not affect the difficulty of cooperation. However, it was confirmed that the verbal communication between the players increased 6.7% in average which partially support our hypothesis. Learning counter-intuitive operations took longer than normal intuitive operations, and the rate of verbalization increased. This suggests that the counter-intuitive operation may have triggered the conversation. In the future, it is important to verify whether freshness and other factors contribute to the activation of communication.

References

1. Joseph, S., Diack, L.: Playing interprofessional games: reflections on using the Interprofessional Education Game (iPEG). J. Interprof. Care **29**(260), 2 (2015)
2. Slide Quest: Blue Orange Editions (2019)
3. Sasaki, G., Igarashi, H.: Analyze the cooperative skills of leadership and followership using machine learning. In: JSME Annual Conference on Robotics and Mechatronics (Robomec), 2020, 2A1-I04 (2020)
4. HoloLens2, Microsoft
5. Tada, M.: Wireless Sensor and display modules for on-site motion measurement and intervention. J. Comput. Inf. Sci. Eng. **22**, 418–422 (2018)

The Creative Design-Engineer Divide: Modular Architecture and Workflow UX

Brian Packer[1]([⊠]) [iD], Simeon Keates[2] [iD], and Grahame Baker[1]

[1] University of Greenwich, Chatham Maritime ME4 4TB, UK
B.W.Packer@greenwich.ac.uk
[2] University of Chichester, Bognor Regis PO21 1HR, UK

Abstract. There are competing priorities between creative freedom and the need for robust, stable software frameworks to facilitate the rapid implementation of creative ideas in game development. This may result in a disparity between system and user requirements. Qualitative data extracted from seminars at the Game Developers Conference informs the design of several interviews with veteran game-system designers to explore this phenomenon. A survey of modular software plug-ins from the Unity Asset Store then validates the interview findings and explores the benefits of modular software architectures. Findings indicate that modifications to the native user experience (UX) design of Unity and plug-ins that reengineer for different workflows are most popular. The most popular workflows provide for data, asset, and project management. Discussion reflects on how modular architecture can alleviate points of failure within a game engine's architecture whilst providing customized usability for different user needs.

Keywords: Game design · Workflow · User experience · Qualitative analysis

1 Introduction

Video game development stands at the intersection between the disciplines of creative design, system design and software engineering [1]. The software used to develop games must provide a robust framework by which ideas and content can be rapidly implemented. So-called "game engines" (also called "Integrated Game Development Environments" (iGDEs), so as to not conflate the development software suites with the extrinsic (primarily graphical rendering) libraries that compile and execute a game) must provide a flexible software architecture to facilitate this with maximum technical accessibility for less technically trained system/art designers.

The artistic nature of games demands that neither limit nor consensus be enforced on what defines "a game" [2, 3], yet this poses a unique challenge to the design management of such software and the traditional requirements gathering process for identifying how to deliver an intuitive user experience (UX) for uninhibited implementation. Furthermore, developing video games is a multi-discipline task, demanding a range of artistic and technical skills which may benefit from varied UX needs [4].

Until the emergence of more purposefully accessible "all-in-one" visual editors in the early 2010s [5], common practice was to build toolchains to interface third-party

© Springer Nature Switzerland AG 2021
C. Stephanidis et al. (Eds.): HCII 2021, CCIS 1498, pp. 459–470, 2021.
https://doi.org/10.1007/978-3-030-90176-9_59

tools and bespoke development environments (Fig. 1). But the advent of, and shifting publication/access rights to, engines like Unity and Unreal have opened the discussion of whether it is better to build an engine for a game or build a game using engines that comes with much of the engineering precompiled and abstracted.

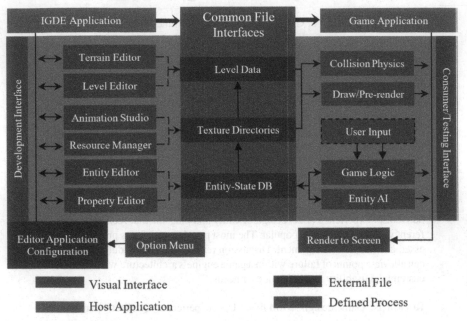

Fig. 1. An example architecture of a so-called "Game Engine", highlighting the distinction between the iGDE and Game presentation layers.

This investigation sought to profile 3 sources of qualitative data from game designers relating to tool engineering by using content analysis. Whilst each source has limits in isolation, cross-referencing 3 distributed sources to inform generalized findings about tool engineering was thought to allow for a better understanding of the specific modules game designers most need engineers to reflect upon. The first analysis looks at seminars presented at the Game Developers Conference, the second analyzes transcript data from interviews with 3 veteran game system designers and the third is a survey of the tools and plug-ins commercially available on the Unity Asset Store.

2   Game Developers Conference Content Analysis

Prior requirement analysis derived from content analysis of "Game Tool" case-studies indicated that tool engineering with a focus on quality assurance (QA) and iterative design was a major concern amongst both game designers and tool engineers on small to medium-sized development teams [6]. The findings were generalized and only identified broad trends between disciplines of game developers and different studio structures.

This prompted further investigation to better identify specific functional requirements and possibly identify aggregate trends in game engine design management. Replicating these methods and cross-referencing for either tooling or production key-phrases resulted in some indicative observations, including:

- "Editor" was the most repeated key word, appearing 8.9 magnitudes (V) of standard deviation above the average frequency ($5.1 + 6.3V$) across all 701 meaningful key words or phrases. This indicates it is the "inductive generic", the word most descriptive of the sample.
- Tool-engineering key phrases: "Script(ing)" ($\mu + 7.9\sigma$) and "Code" ($\mu + 1.7\sigma$), "Data" ($\mu + 5.1\sigma$), "Animation" ($\mu + 4.3\sigma$) and "Kinematic" ($\mu + 2.9\sigma$) and "Modular" ($\mu + 1.8\sigma$), were also notably repeated above average across the sample.
- Iterative design and QA key phrases included "Iteration", "Bug", "Debug(ging)", "QA" and "Test", and these made up 33.2% of all key phrase distribution.
- Collectively, the sample of key phrases relating to users, user-experience, creativity, productivity, and workflow comprised 36.3% of all key phrases.
- Some seminars were in the context of utilizing general-purpose game engines (Unity, Unreal, Frostbite) combined with bespoke modules/libraries to support their specific design requirements. Other seminars discussed entirely proprietary ("in-house") game engines or bespoke, self-contained, and automated tools built to support the development, or even procedural generation, of specific games.

It is difficult to validate generalized knowledge from one sample of content analysis. These key phrases could, however, be used to inform the design of further investigation. Combined, each investigation could then be cross-referenced with these preliminary findings to build a better representative aggregate of user needs.

3   Industry Interviews

Triangulation is the process of sampling multiple relevant data sources and cross-referencing the findings of each analysis. This can be used to confirm theoretical models and add detail to those models [7, 8]. Since, by nature, archival footage cannot provide elaboration on any findings observed, interviews with suitably experienced participants may provide stronger evidence to inform better design of game tools.

3.1   Interview Design

Interview questions were designed to use sentiment-evoking keywords to pre-contextualise the participant's answers towards different categories of observation, as described in Table 1. Responses could then be codified as independent variables [9]. The selection criteria of the candidates can be considered multiple factors of linear regression, with the most common sentiment mined from semantic coding of each response serving as a dependant variable which can be measured. Participant selection criteria act as coefficients of regression, adding to the experiment power, meaning a small number of interview participants can be used to strongly contribute to the observable criteria for a third investigation [10, 11]. The selection criteria for participation included:

1. Primary discipline of system designer (as opposed to Artists)
2. AAA Studio and Small-Medium Enterprise (SME) studio work experience
3. Professional experience shipping a game using a proprietary engine.
4. Professional experience with either Unreal or Unity engines.
5. Worked on the development of at least 1 released game either operating as a service for at least 5 years or perpetual open-access development for 5 years.

Table 1. Open-ended interview prompts and their respective semantic context-clues.

Q1	What technical limitations have you found most limiting when trying to implement new ideas?
Semantic Keywords: Technical, limitation, implementation, ideas	
Q2a	What do you feel is the biggest loss in efficiency, sometimes referred to as bottlenecks, in your development and iteration process?
Semantic Keywords: Efficiency, iteration	
Q2b	What do you feel is the biggest loss in efficiency in training new designers?
Semantic Keywords: Efficiency, training, designers	
Q3a	With 7 being high and 1 being low, what impact do you think this issue has on your creative expression?
Semantic Keywords: Creative expression	
Q3b	(Optional) What are your thoughts of contextual development interfaces?
Semantic Keywords: Context-sensitive, interfaces	
Q4	What does creativity mean to you as a systems designer?
Semantic Keywords: Creativity, system design	

The reason system designers were selected over artists is due to the lack of constraints on the scope of what system designers do within game design. It was thought this would give the broadest perspectives on many tools, rather than the specialized tools different disciplines of artists tend to use. The need to have worked at both AAA and smaller studios was informed by the findings that tool needs and priorities differed depending on the expectation that a studio will have more general-purpose roles or the scope for large-staffed dedicated departments. Experience working with both proprietary and modular, general-purpose engines helped to control the bias towards one or the other. Finally, the requirement to have such extensive development experience on a single game was to control for participants who may have used tools still in early-development or not reasonably functional for fair measure.

3.2 Interview Analyses

After removing interviewer interjection or clarification there was 47 min and 35 s (2855 s) of participant data at an approximate average rate of 2.67 words per second. Continuing to replicate the methods used in the Interpretive Content Analysis model; Layers

1, 2 and 3 (Literal, Contextual and Observational) were supplemented using 3 methods of content analysis: Lexicography, Coding and Distillation. Layer 4 (Meta-factor Analysis) was predetermined by the design of the interview questions and participant criteria.

Lexicographical Analysis. There are some limitations to using the same word-pair analysis used on the GCD data for interviews. The open nature of the interview questions resulted in more topical variance than GCD seminars. This, combined with the smaller sample of word data, means the data distribution was weaker with fewer impactful trends. Furthermore, the context-clue keywords from the question design had to be removed from the data to avoid inflating their value: "Technical", "Ideas", "Limitation", "Implementing", "Efficiency", "Iteration" and "Context" are "leading" words. The transcriptions removed the interviewer's speech to further mitigate this effect. Words were grouped by how many magnitudes of standard deviation they appear above the average (Table 2).

Table 2. Frequency (f) of which key words or word-pairs occurred in the interview transcripts, grouped by prominence as determined by magnitudes of standard deviation from the mean.

Very prominent ($f > = \mu + 3\sigma$)		More prominent ($f >= \mu + 2\sigma$)			Prominent ($f >= \mu + 1\sigma$)			
Key phrase	f	Key phrase	f	Key phrase	f	Key phrase	F	Key phrase	f
Game	59	New	36	Interesting	19	Space	14	Character	12
Engine	52	Make more	27	Context	19	Working	13	Animation	11
Tool	46	Time	26	Creativity	18	Developer	13	Level	11
Work	41	Team	24	Feel	17	Unity	12	End up	10
Different	39	Designer	23	WoW	17	Object	12		

"Game Engine", "Engine" and "Tool(s)" are again a primary focus by a large margin. This is reflective of the GDC findings and highlights concurrency between data. Strong focus on "team" and "designers" indicating a level of generalization reflective of experienced collaborative designers. "Making more" and "time" reflect the main metrics by which productivity is measured. "Context" and "Feel" were almost exclusively used in the context of tool user experience. The phrase "Space" lacks context in abstraction, but reviewing the source data showed that it was often used as short-hand for "3D Space", "head space" (sic) and "work space" (sic). "3D space" references usability or functionality within a level or scene, whereas "headspace" and "workspace" allude to concepts of user experience or productivity [12, 13], whilst "Object", "Character", "Animation" and "Level" each represent different workflows for game designers (Level Design, Animation and Character, and System Design). Finally, the phrase "end up" typified a sentiment of resignation with systems that do not work as expected, or desired, but can be used imperfectly to achieve a goal.

Finally, "WoW" was used as short-hand for the MMORPG "World of Warcraft" and was the context for a bespoke game engines with a relatively long product life cycle, 18 years, maintained for a single game-as-a-service. For comparison, Unity is mentioned slightly less and represent a more modern modular engine. Unreal was rarely mentioned.

Interview Coding. Coding is the process of assigning meaning to qualitative data in a systematic way. Distillation is the process of recursively categorising semantic data into less discrete groups of data, inferred from commonality between the meaning of key phrases [14]. The data was reviewed, and timestamps placed denoting interview structure (breaks, questions, clarifications) and subject categorisations (Fig. 2).

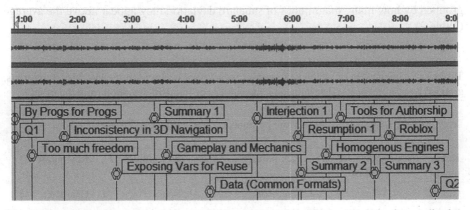

Fig. 2. Example of the coding process, starting with cataloguing the raw interview audio data labelling and chaptering.

These codes were then assigned to 1 of 5 categories and given semantic tags. For example, "3D Navigation" may be the subject, but this may be discussed in the context of the task of prototyping "3D Block-Outs". If a specific feature was discussed in this context, it was noted, with either affirmative (positive) or contradictory (negative) statements assigned to the given statement [15]. Word-association was used to divide participant responses into discrete "chunks". This is known as "open coding" and allowed the most accurate model representation of the interview data (Table 3).

Once "open coding" was complete, a process of abstraction called "recursive coding" sought to consolidate semantically similar codes into broader groups. These chunks are then consolidated and measured for reoccurrence to give a better measure of the weight assigned to topic across all participants. Continuing with the previous example, multiple participants may discuss specific problems with "3D Block Outs" but they may each discuss different tools or aspects that clarify their responses. An aggregate of the task category would come under the discipline of "Level Design", whereas the tools may not semantically relate (Table 4).

Given coding is an intermediary step between literal and interpretive analysis, the results expectedly reflected the lexicographical analysis. Each category of coding had between 79 and 96 chunks assigned across all interviews. *Affirmative sentiments* were

Table 3. An extract of the table used during the "open coding" stage of interview reviews. Each row is self-contained by code category. Each column represents each expression of sentiment.

Task	3D block-out	Pre-art implementation	Rapid implementation	Reengineering assets	...
Affirmative Sentiment	Abstract proportions	Fast concept testing	Consistent UI, by context	"Pro-mode" 3D designer UI	...
Contradictory sentiment	Too much freedom	Features prioritised over UX	Abstract relative scaling (2D/3D)	Snapping overrides	...
Experience or reflection	Inadequate requirements analysis	Requirements vary by discipline	Too much access to incidental vars	Not enough accessibility to data structures	...
Feature highlight	Relative scaling	Snapping	Sandbox testing	Prefabrication	...

Table 4. An extract of the "selective coding" stage of interview distillation.

Task	Level design	System design	System design	System design	...
Affirmative sentiment	User familiarity	System testability	User profiling	User profiling	...
Contradictory sentiment	Data accessibility	User profiling	Navigation accessibility	Navigation accessibility	...
Experience or reflection	User profiling	User profiling	Data accessibility	Data accessibility	...
Feature highlight	Controls	Controls	Prototyping	Prototyping	...

focused on designing tools for workflows and "contextual interface" design (47%). *Contradictory sentiments* were split between two smaller trends, "data accessibility" (24%) and "collaborative design" (17%). "Data abstraction" tools, including scripting and data visualization, were the most discussed *feature highlights* (37%).

Interview Distillation. Much debate has been presented across most scientific fields engaged with any analysis of naturalised (human) data about the validity, and practicality, of presenting comprehensive depictions of nuanced user behaviour and opinions [16–18] The more data is abstracted from a verbatim transcription, the more an observer's "theoretical priori" orientation may influence their neutrality [19]. With due consideration to this, some summary findings from the interviews are presented here to provide context for the data previously presented in abstraction, taken verbatim where possible:

Question 1. On technical limitations on creative development:

- Engines are built "by programmers, for programmers", with too much access to variables without the ability to expose only what is meaningful.
- There is "inaccessibility to common tools/formats [in favour of proprietary ones]".
- "All in wonder" tools (like Unity) limit accessibility by making anything possible only once you know how to setup and build the underlying game systems.
- Technical limits on live collaboration prevents consistency in design intent between disciplines.

Question 2. On losses of efficiency, both in a HCI and team-work context:

- Lost context, or noisy UIs, break the comfortable and intuitive headspace of design task. This can overwhelm new users, distract experienced users, and slow down proficient users.
- Learning how to do a new task is a huge limit. Especially in proprietary engines where documentation is limited, and enquiries cannot be crowdsourced externally.
- Game data concurrency, especially in the context of live collaborative development, can throttle the iterative cycle of design, implement and testing game "feel".
- Repetitive or chain-tasks often require specific replication of inputs or task sequences. Losing interface focus during these sequences often means starting over.

Question 3. The impact on creative expression returned a mean score (μ) of 6 out of 7, with a standard deviation (σ) of 1.4, suggesting general agreement that responses to question 2 heavily impact creativity.

Question 4. On the definition of creativity from the perspective of system design.

- Creativity is working within the constraints of a system(s) to develop novel application of, or interactions between, those system(s).
- Creativity is about communicating a system to a player through the design and presentation of data in a way that is immersive and accessible.

4   Unity Asset Store Survey

Most content on the Unity Asset Store provides prefabricated art resources, not functionality-adding components. A quick analysis of that repository provided no unexpected results. 3D art was more prominent than 2D art, with Sound and Visual Effects (VFX) being considerably less in supply (Fig. 3).

**DISTRIBUTION OF ART
ASSETS ON THE UNITY
STORE**

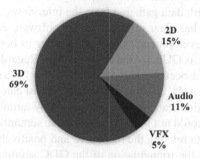

Fig. 3. Distribution (%) of art plug-ins on the Unity Asset Store, by art sub-disciplines.

Tools and plug-ins (modules) are a distinct category unto themselves and are further sub-divided by a moderated tagging system. These tags tend to reflect distinct work-flows or disciplines within game development, though some describe specific tasks or functionality standard to most game engines. The distribution of these plug-ins provides much more relevant data to the design of engine architecture than the artistic plug-ins, as well as specific (and independently assigned) semantic grouping.

Table 5. Distribution of the sum number of plug-ins (f) in each category.

Category	(f)	Category	(f)	Category	(f)
Utilities	1638	Game Toolkits	315	Sprites control	209
GUI	1248	Animation	314	Level design	150
Integration	1104	AI	297	Visual scripting	145
Particles & effects	593	Network	270	Video	89
Input management	455	Camera	263	Localization	78
Physics	387	Audio	257	Painting	49
Modelling	385	Terrain	234	Version control	18

There were several categories listed separately to the tool/plug-in that bear inclusion:

- Templates (2774 (f) plug-ins), which includes precompiled Unity project structures, data configurations, databases which support certain common game systems, tutorial projects for learning to use Unity, and finally, resources packs by game genre.
- Services (21 (f) plug-ins), which mainly included plug-ins for connecting game systems and interfaces to financial transaction services or instant messaging APIs.
- Machine Learning (17 (f) plug-ins), which provide a variety of neural net and competitive agent libraries for programming AI for games.

Across all tool categories, "Utilities", "GUI" (including Unity GUI Managers) and "Integration" tools were the most prominent categories (Table 5), occurring 2.9, 2.0 and 1.7 standard deviations above the mean frequency of all tool categories, respectively, which was concurrent with data gathered from the interviews.

Whilst "Integration" has clear relevance to the software engineering and compatibility aspects of game development, "GUI" could refer to both the implementation of GUIs into games, as well as GUIs for the Unity Engine. Regardless, GUI still has a clear association relative to an aspect of game-design. "Utilities" is a semantically vague term, despite it being (speculatively, causing it to be) the largest category of plug-ins. Deeper investigation of the "utilities" category was carried out by sampling the 50 most reviewed 5* plug-ins. Whilst this could not give a representative semantic assignment to the category, it could provide data relating the most used and positively received plug-ins. This can be used to complete the triangulation of the GDC seminar data and the interview data. Some observations included:

- 80% provided modular GUIs to provide functionality not native to Unity.
- 63% re-engineered GUI elements native to Unity or extended/overwrote the functionality of existing Unity interfaces or tools.
- 28% provided interfaces or functionality for managing, reviewing, or controlling game data and data connected to game-assets. 4% were script-driven.
- 60% delivered work-flow enhancement for a given task or discipline, with 24% specifically cited increasing developer productivity as a feature. Most examples being interfaces or scripts adding functionality to improve workflow for tasks including: pooling and asset inspection (9), programming (6), level design (5), debugging (5), security and data obfuscation (4), and quality assurance, texturing, animation, and particle effect management (1).
- 54% provided methods and interfaces for game project file and asset management, particularly for optimization.
- 28% provided functionality or interfaces for optimization of render and compute performance, primarily through asset dependency calculation and asset pooling, though some provided for the implementation of level-of-detail control on art.
- 6% provided tools for procedural generation for either 2D or 3D level design.

Reviewing rating to price ratio found that, of the 100 most expensive plugins in each category (including any plug-ins of equivalent price to the price floor), 36–37% of each of the 3 top categories did not have ratings, indicating insufficient reviews and (implicitly) sales. Utilities had the most favorable ratings (62.7%, 4–5 star ratings), but favorability was level across all 3 categories (62.7%, 56% and 57%, respectively).

Notably, quality assurance (excluding performance optimization) was a focus of very few plug-ins; 1 in the sample of most popular tools, and 10 across all tool categories. The "Testing" tag also yielded only 34 results. This is less than anticipated given the relative focus on QA from SME developers at GDC.

Finally, in two samples taken 8 months apart (October 2020, June 2021), there was a significant reduction in the number of System Templates (−24%, 878 to 667). Filtering for version-compatibility shows that much of this reduction came from deprecated support due to versioning. This highlights that the problems with legacy systems, alluded to in the interviews, are not isolated to long-life proprietary systems/engines.

5 Conclusions

To summarize, across 3 investigations into different sources of game system designer behavioral patterns and perspectives, there was repeated evidence in favor of designing game engine user experiences that favor contextual design and optimizes for discipline-aligned workflows.

The first analysis indicated that Editor design was the most referenced topic across professional seminars reflecting on tooling or production issues. Scripting, Data, Animation and Modular (design) were key tasks of focus for tools, but phrases connected to concepts of productivity, users and usability, creativity and workflow were the most prominent phrases across all seminars.

The second analysis supported these findings and incorporated them into designing interviews with seasoned game system designers. Those interviews emphasized contextual design for given tasks is greatly preferable and that exposing too much data to the point of over-accessibility is destructive to the user experience of any engine or tools, with the caveat that controlling what is or is not exposed is preferable to not being able to access essential data under any circumstances.

The third analysis highlighted the tools and utilities most used and reviewed by game designers using the Unity Asset Store. These plug-ins largely override the functionality and user experience of the Unity engine in favor of workflows optimized for given tasks or aspects of game development. The most common of these was project and data/asset management, primarily for performance optimization and project refactorization.

Modular architecture is common in both proprietary and general-purpose game engines as it allows for the agile assessment of the game system designer's needs. When development of these modules can be aggregated across larger audiences (such as the Unity Asset Store) there is an almost evolutionary "survival of the fittest" effect that delivers enhanced usability. However, data management and abstraction are major restrictions on meeting these needs, and further research is needed to understand how data and creative design can be better interpolated to free up experienced designers and increase accessibility to initiate designers.

References

1. Lightbown, D.: Designing the User Experience of Game Development Tools. 1st edn. A K Peters/CRC Press, Boca Raton (2015)
2. Wolf, M.: The Medium of the Video Game Republished edn. University of Texas Press, Austin (2001)
3. Palazzi, C., Roccetti, M., Marfia, G.: Realizing the Unexploited potential of games on serious challenges. Comput. Entertain. 8(4), 1–4 (2010). https://doi.org/10.1145/1921141.1921143
4. Meyer, A., Zimmermann, T., Fritz, T.: Characterizing software developers by perceptions of productivity. In: 2017 ACM/IEEE International Symposium on Empirical Software Engineering and Measurement (ESEM), pp.105–110 (2017). https://doi.org/10.1109/ESEM.2017.17

5. Haas, J.: A History of the Unity Game Engine. Worcester Polytechnic Institute, Worcester, March 2014
6. Packer, B., Keates, S., Baker, G.: Game Developers in the Wild: Trending Perspectives on Software Limitations. Multimed Tools Appl (2021). Publication Pending.
7. Gibson, W., Brown, A.: Working with Qualitative Data. SAGE, Los Angeles (2009)
8. Renz, S., Carrington, J., Badger, T.: Two strategies for qualitative content analysis: an intramethod approach to triangulation. Qual. Health Res. **28**(5), 824–831 (2018). https://doi.org/10.1177/1049732317753586
9. Wilson, C.: Chapter 2 - Semi-structured interviews. In: Interview Techniques for UX Practitioners: A User-Centered Design Method, pp. 23–41. Morgan Kaufmann, Boston (2013). https://doi.org/10.1016/B978-0-12-410393-1.00002-8
10. Pribeanu, C., Balog, A., Iordache, D.: Measuring the perceived quality of an AR-based learning application: a multidimensional model. Interact. Learn. Environ. **25**(4), 482–495 (2014). https://doi.org/10.1080/10494820.2016.1143375
11. Hariyanto, D., Triyono, M., Koehler, T.: Usability evaluation of personalized adaptive e-learning system using USE questionnaire. Knowl. Manag. E-Learn. **12**, 85–105 (2020). https://doi.org/10.34105/j.kmel.2020.12.005
12. Kress, G., Hoster, H., Chung, C., Steinert, M.: Headspace: the stanford imaginarium. In: Proceedings of the 2nd International Conference on Design Creativity, Glasgow (ICDC 2012), vol. 2, pp. 261–268 (2012)
13. Ali-Babar, M.: The application of knowledge-sharing workspace paradigm for software architecture processes. In: Proceedings of the 3rd International Workshop on Sharing and Reusing Architectural Knowledge, Leipzig (SHARK 2008), pp. 45–48 (2008). https://doi.org/10.1145/1370062.1370074
14. Rowley, J.: Using case studies in research. Manag. Res. News **25**(1) (2002). https://doi.org/10.1108/01409170210782990
15. Weston, C., Gandell, T., Beauchamp, J., McAlpine, L., Wiseman, C., Beauchamp, C.: Analyzing interview data: the development and evolution of a coding system. Qual. Sociol. **24**(3), 381–400 (2001). https://doi.org/10.1023/A:1010690908200
16. Dave, K., Lawrence, S., Pennock, D.: Mining the peanut gallery: opinion extraction and semantic classification of product reviews. In: Proceedings of the12th International Conference on World Wide Web (WWW 2003), Budapest, pp. 519–528 (2003). https://doi.org/10.1145/775152.775226
17. Suddaby, R.: From the editors: what grounded theory is not. Acad. Manag. J. **49**(4), 633–642 (2006)
18. Leroux, J., Rizzo, J., Sickles, R.: The role of self-reporting bias in health, mental health and labor force participation: a descriptive analysis. Emp. Econ. **43**, 525–536 (2012). https://doi.org/10.1007/s00181-010-0434-z
19. Flyvberg, B.: Five misunderstandings about case-study research. Qual. Inq. **12**(4), 219–245 (2006). https://doi.org/10.1177/1077800405284363

Training of Drone Pilots for Children with Virtual Reality Environments Under Gamification Approach

Cristian Trujillo-Espinoza[1] , Héctor Cardona-Reyes[2](✉) ,
José Eder Guzman-Mendoza[1] , Klinge Orlando Villalba-Condori[3] ,
and Dennis Arias-Chávez[4]

[1] Center for Research in Mathematics, Zacatecas, Mexico
{cristian.trujillo,jose.guzman}@cimat.mx
[2] CIMAT, Zacatecas, Mexico
hector.cardona@cimat.mx
[3] Universidad Católica de Santa María, Arequipa, Peru
kvillalba@ucsm.edu.pe
[4] Universidad Continental, Arequipa, Peru
darias@continental.edu.pe

Abstract. Today, drones have become one of the most desired technological products by children and adolescents. Unlike console or table games, the game based on learning to pilot a drone allows them to work on their problem-solving skills. Many parents look for activities to share with their children in their free time. However, in big cities, this can be tricky. Learning to pilot drones in virtual reality environments can be a hobby that can be fun for young and old, that can be shared as a family and that can also be useful to improve their learning capacity and their skills and knowledge. Under this situation, it is where gamification and virtual reality environments can be used to generate drone training scenarios for children and adolescents from a fun and safe environment. The work presents a design model of reality environments based on gamification and the design of the user task associated with the flight information guides. A case study is presented in which a proposed virtual reality environment is launched for the training of recreational drone pilots and the preliminary results obtained are presented.

Keywords: Virtual reality · Gamification · Interactive environments · Drone

1 Introduction

Nowadays the use of drones has a wide variety of applications, ranging from civilian and agricultural applications to educational and entertainment purposes.

H. Cardona-Reyes—CONACYT Research Fellow.

© Springer Nature Switzerland AG 2021
C. Stephanidis et al. (Eds.): HCII 2021, CCIS 1498, pp. 471–478, 2021.
https://doi.org/10.1007/978-3-030-90176-9_60

One of the main benefits offered by the use of drones is the reduction of associated costs, due to their efficiency and reliability with which they can perform various tasks, even involving a risk factor [1].

Under this context, it is currently common for inexperienced users to have access to these devices due to their low cost and variety of models for various user needs. This is an area of opportunity to offer strategies that allow inexperienced users such as children and teenagers to acquire the necessary skills to pilot their drones safely and that the knowledge acquired is based on the regulations of the region, the type of drone to be used and the user's profile.

Emerging technologies such as virtual reality in simulated environments oriented to drone pilot training can be very useful, as they allow pilots (children and adolescents) to reduce the learning curve by obtaining prior knowledge before flying a drone physically and in an environment free of risk of accidents.

If these virtual environments are also produced under the gamification approach, the mechanics of the games are transferred to the virtual environment to achieve the best possible results [5]. The reason why it is important to incorporate the gamification technique in the entertainment of children and adolescents in the handling of drones is because they can learn by playing and thus acquire knowledge constantly, and this makes children stay predisposed and alert to develop flying skills in a shorter time.

This work proposes the application of virtual reality environments under a gamification approach as a support tool to train children and adolescents taking into account their skill level and flying needs, from beginner to expert levels. As a result of this work, the first results of the implementation of a virtual reality environment in children and adolescents in which they perform obstacle avoidance and drone control tasks are presented.

This work is composed of 5 sections, Sect. 2 presents the types of users and a classification of drones available in the literature. The proposal for the production of virtual reality environments is presented in Sect. 3, Sect. 4 presents a case study where a proposed virtual reality environment is tested and some preliminary results are presented. Finally, the conclusions and future work section is presented in Sect. 5.

2   Drone Types and Users

Drones are divided into two large groups, those that are considered autonomous because they do not require human intervention during operation, and those with remote control, which are those that require a pilot to act permanently in the operation [1]. Zakora and MolodChik [6] in Table 1 present a categorization of drones according to the characteristics of their designation, such as their flight range and weight.

In terms of the types of users, the drone industry is mainly composed of three sectors [1]. Recreational users, which are those who are usually new to drones and use them for photography and video, tourism, recreational and leisure applications; the most commonly used drones are those that are accessible and

Table 1. Drone categorization proposed based on weight and flight range, by Zakora and Molodchik [6].

Designation	Weight range	Flight range
Micro and mini UAVs close range	$W \leq 5\,\mathrm{kg}$	$25\,\mathrm{km} \leq R \leq 40\,\mathrm{km}$
Light UAVs small range	$5\,\mathrm{kg} < W \leq 50\,\mathrm{kg}$	$10\,\mathrm{km} = R = 70\,\mathrm{km}$
Light UAVs medium range	$50\,\mathrm{kg} < W \leq 100\,\mathrm{kg}$	$70\,\mathrm{km} \leq R \leq 250\,\mathrm{km}$
Medium UAVs	$100\,\mathrm{kg} < W = 300\,\mathrm{kg}$	$150\,\mathrm{km} = R = 1000\,\mathrm{km}$
Medium heavy UAVs	$300\,\mathrm{kg} < W \leq 500\,\mathrm{kg}$	$70\,\mathrm{km} \leq R \leq 300\,\mathrm{km}$
Medium heavy range UAVs	$500\,\mathrm{kg} \leq W$	$70\,\mathrm{km} \leq R \leq 300\,\mathrm{km}$
Heavy UAVs heavy endurance	$1500\,\mathrm{kg} \leq W$	$R \leq 1500\,\mathrm{km}$
Unmanned combat aircraft	$500\,\mathrm{kg} < W$	$R \leq 1500\,\mathrm{km}$

low cost. Professional users, are those who already have experience in handling drones and their use is more complex and refers to commercial applications and therefore already have some technical and regulatory knowledge in terms of drones. Finally, there are the training users, which are those who belong to organizations and technical schools or universities and who are certified to train personnel in drone operation. As presented in Fig. 1.

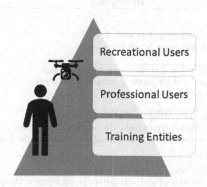

Fig. 1. User classification for drone operation [2]

3   Production of Virtual Reality Environments Under the Gamification Approach

This section presents the production of virtual reality environments for the training of drone pilots under the gamification approach. These virtual reality environments produced will be oriented to the different types of users identified and the regulatory, safety, technical and technological aspects are considered to allow the proper representation of the various types of drones and scenarios in an immersive environment considering aspects of gamification characteristic of video games in a playful context in which the motivation of users can be increased to achieve the objectives of training as drone pilots and offer a rewarding experience [9]. Following the steps of the production process of virtual reality environments are presented.

3.1 Analysis

In this stage, the necessary elements are identified so that the virtual reality environment complies with the characteristics according to the type of user to which it will be oriented. In this sense, the user tasks to be performed within the simulation environment are identified, the drone characteristics for its correct representation in virtual reality and the guidelines according to the training standards are identified. The training tasks include those activities defined by the regulatory institutions related to aviation safety. These activities are practical activities that aspiring pilots must pass in order to obtain a certification. Table 2 presents an example of the exercises applied by the State Agency for Aviation Safety (AESA) of the Government of Spain to recreational pilot candidates [3].

Table 2. Recreational drone pilot training exercises, source AESA Spain [3]

Exercise	Description	Image
1	Take off the multicopter 10 meters away from you, raise it to eye level, and hover for 10 seconds.	
2	Steer the drone forward in slow flight and 20 meters high. During its trajectory, make it zigzag (S-shaped trajectory) by making a minimum of 4-course changes.	
3	Same as exercise 2, but making the drone fly backward (towards you / the pilot). Try to make the aircraft face towards you, so that the controls are reversed if the drone does not have the headless mode.	
4	Steer the multicopter laterally, both left and right, making it reach a distance of up to 30 meters on each side of the pilot.	

3.2 Design and Implementation

In this stage, the design elements for the production of virtual reality environments are defined, together with the components and tools necessary for the generation of prototypes that can be implemented with the users in the training sessions. This stage mainly proposes the following:

- Define the activities that the user will perform within the virtual reality scenario, ranging from the instructions to interact with the scenario and the objectives to be covered when executing the training tasks.
- Determine the characteristics of the simulation scenario to be recreated.

- Define and design the virtual reality elements, such as drone model, the physical characteristics and behaviors within the simulation scenario, the objects with which the user will interact and the objects that will be static within the scenario.
- Define the gamification elements to make the virtual environment playful, pleasant and motivating for the user (Fig. 2).

Fig. 2. Gamification aspects proposed for the production of virtual reality environments [5]

At this stage the incorporation of gamification strategies is determined. These strategies aim to maintain the user's interest and raise motivation when using the virtual reality environment. Some of the gamification aspects proposed are: [2,9].

- Accumulation of points: a qualitative value is assigned to certain actions and points are accumulated as they are performed.
- Level scaling: a series of levels is defined that the user must overcome to reach the next one.
- Obtaining prizes: as different objectives are achieved, prizes are awarded to be collected.
- Gifts: these are goods that are given to the player free of charge when an objective is achieved.
- Classifications: users are categorized according to the objectives achieved, highlighting the best ones in a list or ranking.
- Challenges: it encourages competition among users, the best one gets the points or the prize.
- Missions or challenges: to solve or overcome a challenge or objective.

The objective of incorporating aspects of gamification is to guarantee the quality of the virtual reality environment, the quality of the platform in which it will be executed and the mechanics of the interaction [4]. In order to achieve this, this stage takes into account the principles established by Akihiro Saito [10], which are described below:

- An intuitive user interface.
- Avoid user confusion about what to do and how to do it.
- Define interfaces that help overcome the traditional learning curve.
- Provide the user with familiar interaction mechanisms to ensure integration with the virtual reality environment.

3.3   Evaluation

It is important to have evaluation strategies that allow obtaining feedback information to offer improvements to users and evaluate the user experience. The incorporation of gamification aspects in the previous stage allows to establish indicators that allow to obtain from the user, the amount of points obtained, the fulfillment of tasks, unlock levels, etc. Regarding the evaluation of the user experience, it is important to consider evaluations that consider the perception of use and usefulness of the system (User Experience Questionnaire (UEQ) [11]) in addition to aspects such as ease of use (Computer System Usability Questionnaire (CSUQ) [8]), and how in general the user perceives using it in their training activities (AttrakDiff [7]), among other evaluations that can be proposed. The result of these evaluations will allow the improvement of virtual reality environments in order to increase the acceptance by users and trainers.

The following section presents as a case study the design and implementation of a virtual reality environment proposed for the training of recreational drone pilots.

4   Case Study

This section presents the prototype and preliminary results of a virtual reality environment proposed for the training of recreational drone pilots implemented in 24 students. This virtual environment is intended primarily for users who have little or no knowledge of drones and can practice the exercises related to the recreational level (see Table 2) in a simulation scenario which they can run on their mobile device.

The proposed virtual reality environment consists of an instructional design that consists of a set of instructions for use presented in audio form, at the end of the instructions an option is enabled on screen to start with the activities and the basic operation controls of the drone are shown. At that moment, an audio indicates to the user the instructions related to exercise 1, after being completed, the indications to perform exercise 2 are given, until completing the 4 exercises established for a recreational user presented in Table 2. Within the exercises the main objective is to collect a series of coins placed in such a way that the user can practice the indicated movements to achieve his goal. As presented in Fig. 3.

Fig. 3. Interface of the virtual reality environment for recreational users.

For the development of the virtual reality environment, the Unity 3D videogame engine was used because it allows the reuse of 3D models and has a wide range of freely available resources. As for the development aspects of the 3D scenarios, it allows the creation of 3D scenarios, interfaces and coding the behavior of the objects in the scene and assigning them a specific behavior.

The procedure for testing the virtual reality environment consisted of providing students with the APK file to be installed on their Android mobile device and they were asked to follow the indications that the system gave until completing the four exercises for training recreational drone pilots. During the execution, the system recorded the times in minutes of each of the activities performed by the user to subsequently make an analysis of the user's preromania, as presented in Table 3. It is worth mentioning that the exercises were designed under the practices that are performed to train drone pilots for recreational users, as shown in Table 2.

Table 3. Average time for each exercise and total time in minutes.

	Exercise 1	Exercise 2	Exercise 3	Exercise 4	Total time
Mean	*0.73*	*1.94*	*2.73*	*3.85*	*3.95*
Std. Dev.	*0.50*	*1.11*	*1.72*	*2.35*	*2.40*

Once the virtual environment test was completed, the students answered a survey in which it was found that approximately 70% of the students have no experience in handling drones, only 30% stated that they had flown one at some time. Regarding the students' comments on the design of the virtual environment, they stated that their preference lies in the fact that the training scenario is visually more attractive due to the 3D objects present, the design of the scenario that resembles a training field. Regarding the basic control interface of the drone, most of the students stated as an additional comment in the survey, that they are difficult to use at the beginning because of the sensitivity with which the drone moves, but as time goes by and they perform the exercises they acquire the ability to control the drone.

5 Conclusions and Future Work

This work proposes the use of virtual reality environments as an alternative for the training of drone pilots considering aspects of gamification in order to maintain the user's interest and raise the motivation to use the virtual reality environment and that the knowledge is acquired in a playful and fun way taking into account the existing rules and regulations of safety and aircraft. Some stages are presented for the production of these virtual reality environments where aspects of gamification are considered that can be incorporated into training exercises and that can raise the motivational factor and the fulfillment of objectives within the virtual reality environment. Finally, a case study is presented in which a virtual reality environment oriented to recreational users is implemented, a set of exercises is defined and a mobile user interface for basic drone operation control is presented, and some preliminary results are presented on the performance of the system use and the user experience obtained after using the system. Future work includes the incorporation of new exercises for professional and recreational users, the incorporation of new types of drones and the generation of new scenarios, as well as the incorporation of new user experience evaluation strategies that can provide feedback for the production of these virtual reality environments.

References

1. Beers, G.: Documento del plan estratégico de drones (2018). http://www.gisandbeers.com/documento-del-plan-estrategico-de-drones/
2. Blohm, I., Leimeister, J.: Gamification. Bus. Inf. Syst. Eng. **5**(4), 275–278 (2013). https://doi.org/10.1007/s12599-013-0273-5
3. de España, G.: Agencia estatal boletín oficial del estado, real decreto 1036–2017 (2017). https://www.boe.es/buscar/doc.php?id=BOE-A-2017-15721
4. Francisco-Aparicio, A., Gutiérrez-Vela, F.L., Isla-Montes, J.L., Sanchez, J.L.G.: Gamification: analysis and application. In: Penichet, V., Peñalver, A., Gallud, J. (eds.) New Trends in Interaction, Virtual Reality and Modeling, pp. 113–126. Springer, London (2013). https://doi.org/10.1007/978-1-4471-5445-7_9
5. Gaitán, V.: Gamificación: el aprendizaje divertido. Recuperado el 15 (2013)
6. Hassanalian, M., Abdelkefi, A.: Classifications, applications, and design challenges of drones: a review. Prog. Aerosp. Sci. **91**, 99–131 (2017)
7. Hassenzahl, M., Burmester, M., Koller, F.: AttrakDiff: a questionnaire to measure perceived hedonic and pragmatic quality. In: Mensch & Computer, vol. 57, pp. 187–196 (2003)
8. Lewis, J.R.: Measuring perceived usability: the CSUQ, SUS, and UMUX. Int. J. Hum. Comput. Interact. **34**(12), 1148–1156 (2018)
9. Marczewski, A.: Gamification: a simple introduction. Andrzej Marczewski (2013)
10. Saito, A.: Gamenics and Its Potential. Game Usability: Advice from the Experts for Advancing the Player Experience, pp. 357–381. Morgan Kaufmann, San Francisco (2008)
11. Schrepp, M., Hinderks, A., Thomaschewski, J.: Construction of a benchmark for the user experience questionnaire (UEQ). IJIMAI **4**(4), 40–44 (2017)

The Interaction Design of AR Game Based on Hook Model for Children's Environmental Habit Formation

Qitong Xie[✉] and Wei Yu

School of Art Design and Media, East China University of Science and Technology, No. 130, Meilong Road, Xuhui District, Shanghai, People's Republic of China

Abstract. Human beings are facing the crisis of deteriorating ecological environment. To strengthen the cultivation of children's environmental awareness and make them develop the habit of environmental protection life are important parts of ecological environment improvement and protection.

This study investigate and analyze the current situation of children's environmental awareness education which had found that the limitations of it is the main reason why it's so difficult for children to form environmental awareness and habits. The purpose of this study is to conduct an interactive design which based on AR technology, to enhance children's environmental protection awareness, to further enable them to form eco-friendly habits in their daily lives. Based on Hook model, the study designs an AR game mechanics by considering children's psychological characteristics so as to trigger children take actions. The design of game interaction mode adopts the Hook model. This study attempts to build an ecosphere management model in the game and the main interaction mode of the game is that players can use AR scanning function based on image recognition technology to obtain virtual models of plants and animals to build their own unique ecosphere. Players can experience the actions of cognizing and managing their own ecosystem.

Keywords: Hook model · Children's environmental cognition and behavior development · Interaction design · AR technology · Embodied cognition

1 Introduction

The Emissions Gap Report 2020, published by the United Nations Environment Programme, shows that in 2019, global greenhouse gas emissions increased for the third consecutive year to 52.4 billion tons (excluding ±5.2) and 59.1 billion tons (including ±5.9), including greenhouse gas emissions from land use changes). [1] China, as the world's first total carbon emissions and the world' s fourth economy per capita, is facing great pressure to reduce emissions. In addition to carbon emissions, the water pollution, soil pollution and air pollution coming with industrialization also bring great challenges to the sustainable development of the ecological environment (Fig. 1).

© Springer Nature Switzerland AG 2021
C. Stephanidis et al. (Eds.): HCII 2021, CCIS 1498, pp. 479–485, 2021.
https://doi.org/10.1007/978-3-030-90176-9_61

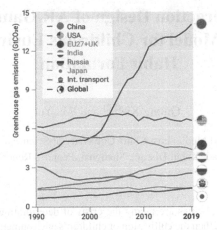

Fig. 1. Absolute GHG emissions of the top six emitters (excluding LUC emissions)

The importance of environmental education is self-evident, raising awareness of environmental issues and environmental action. In addition to the accumulation of knowledge, it also values people's participation and action [2]. The purpose of this research is to use AR games to study the interactive strategy based on the Hook model, to cultivate children's environmental awareness, and then to form environmental behavior habits.

2   Current Situation of Children's Environmental Protection Education

This study used an interview method to understand their ecological and environmental awareness and daily environmental behavior habits through communication with 20 children aged 7–12. In addition, through issuing 110 questionnaires for teachers and parents, they investigated the ecological awareness cultivation. The following problems exist in children's environmental education.

(1) Poor effect of the traditional education model

According to the research, the main model of environmental education that children receive on campus is the teachers' single theoretical introduction. This way makes the children feel boring. Simple theoretical indoctrination cannot get good behavior feedback, and the education effect is general. Through communication, children know that they should save food, not littering, but according to parents' observation of their children, they cannot practice environmental behavior in daily life.

(2) Insufficient environmental action force of children

According to the research, some schools have made a lot of efforts in the form of environmental education. The main forms are musicals, campus environmental protection activities, children's comic books, etc. These forms are more novel than the traditional environmental protection education, easy to arouse the interest of children [3]. It was found that while these forms make boring theories interesting, children are still less expressive throughout the study.

According to children's interviews, children were interested and curious about AR games, and 60% of the children interviewed knew or were exposed to AR products and expressed their willingness to try more AR games. Parents and teachers are also agree with the teaching methods with fun. AR has been widely used in children's teaching research, such as child safety education, space cognition, language teaching, and traditional learning methods have improved with the help of AR [4–6]. AR plays an important role in cultivating students 'interest in learning. Its visualization of virtual and reality improves students' content understanding, long-term memory retention, learning motivation and collaboration [7].

3   Embodied Cognition Enhances Environmental Awareness

Before cultivating children's environmental behavior habits, children need to form an awareness of ecological protection. Games start from the embodied cognition to help children understand the importance of environmental protection. The core concept of embodied cognitive theory is that human beings interact and communicate with themselves and the outside world, that is, body structure, nervous system, sensory organs, combined with the corresponding activity methods, to gain understanding of themselves and the outside world, and form cognition of the world in the brain. Cognition is the result of the body's interaction with objects in our living world in the appropriate way, that is, the proper and effective interaction between cognition, body and environment enables learning to occur [8]. In the AR game, children's players can not only form cognition on the senses, but also practice environmental behavior in the living environment through their own bodies. In the game experience, children constantly gain experience to form the cognition of ecological and environmental protection.

4   Eco-friendly AR Game Design

4.1   Children's Environmental Game Mode Design

The design of AR games is to comply with the cognitive development of children. 6–12-year-old children are more suitable for regular game forms [9]. In this study, the main rules of the game are to let each child build their own ecosystem. In the game, some small environmental tasks will be completed in reality, and children will receive certain game rewards, such as the reduction of the carbon emission. During the course of the game, children also realized the knowledge of what carbon emissions are and how to reduce carbon emissions. In addition, children can also build a wider ecosystem with other players. In the game, children can use image recognition technology to identify animals and plants in their surrounding environment which can be transformed into game models to build an ecosystem unique to the player. Players build the ecosystem with the things around themselves, and when the ecosystem is damaged, they can also feel deeper about how important it is to protect the environment around them.

(1) Game for the development of children's environmental awareness

The game lets children through the ecological crisis to feel the potential hazards that the environment breaks the ring. For example, the game ecosystem of players may face greenhouse crises, air pollution and sea eutrophication. These crises will be reflected by the rising sea level of the islands, haze, and a large number of fish deaths in the ocean, so that children can intuitively feel the harm of environmental damage. To eliminate the crisis in the game, children need to make real-world environmental actions to protect their ecosystem. After children practice environmental behavior, such as the carbon emissions of the game ecosystem will be reduced, and the greenhouse effect crisis will be solved. The video in the game will further explain to children what carbon emissions are, what the greenhouse effect is, what the consequences of this phenomenon will cause. In the whole process of solving the crisis of the game ecosystem, children's awareness of ecological and environmental protection is based on their personal practice of children.

(2) Game helps children develop environmentally friendly behavioral habits

Children in order to protect their own ecosystem, fight with the ecological crisis, it needs them to complete in real life within the power of environmental tasks, such as not littering. Players in reality, through photos uploaded to the game, so as to protect their own ecosystem. Out to protect the emotions of the game ecosystem, players will continue to invest in daily environmental behavior, promote the formation of children's environmental behavior (Fig. 2).

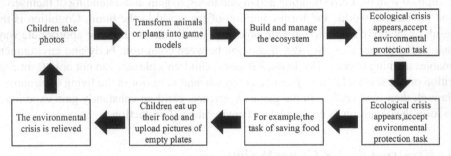

Fig. 2. The game process

4.2 Hook Model Application of the Model in the Cultivation of Children's Environmental Habits

The AR game interactive design strategy is based on the Hook model, proposed by Neil Yal, Ryan Hoover, author of Addiction, focusing on the four major product logic that allows users develop use habits, including four elements: trigger, action, reward, and investment [10]. The use of the Hook model is not to make children addicted to the game, but not to delay their study and life. The research aims to use Hook models to develop AR games, to attract children to continuously participate in games, so as to cultivate their ecological awareness and promote the formation of environmental behavior habits.

(1) Trigger

The game, dominated by internal triggers, internally triggers children's curiosity and the psychology of loving the game and everyday scenes in their lives, drawing interest from children and enabling them to form good behavior habits in happy games.

(2) Action

Action is the behavior that the product wants to complete after it reaches the user. Considering the scope of children's cognitive ability, the interactive design of the game needs to be easy to operate, reduce learning costs, and improve their mobility while also avoiding children spending a lot of time in the game. Depending on the age of the children, the difficulty of the tasks they need to complete in the game will also vary.

(3) Reward

The game offers random rewards and continuous updates, in addition, children can unlock new things step by step, increase the freshness of children, and keep them enthusiastic about the game.

(4) Investment

The focus of the game is not to give children a lot of time and money in it, but on the emotional input of children to realize that their environmental behavior can change the natural environment and protect the home on which humans live.

4.3 A Study on Interactive Strategies of Children's Environmental Games

(1) Sensory level

In order to establish a good immersive experience, the current augmented reality games on the market usually add pictures with strong light and dark contrast and sound effects with high intensity and high recognition, to attract the attention of users. However, the visual nerve and auditory nervous system of minors are still in the development period. Compared with adults, the corresponding threshold value of external stimulation is lower, and it is correspondingly more likely to produce damage due to excessive stimulation. From the perspective of maintaining the physical and mental health of minors, the production of design games for such groups, especially before the secondary sexual development, should appropriately reduce the picture saturation and contrast, and avoid too harsh sound effects [11].

As a supplement to attract users 'attention, it can be adjusted for the target group's preferences in the art design. Specifically, avoid complex art materials, and highly abstract and summarize the virtual image prototype. The overall color style adopts high lightness and low saturation, in order to reduce the sinking cost consumed by users in understanding the game.

(2) Interface and operating system

Considering the nature of the product and the target population, in order to reduce the risk of missed touch, too complex setting is not suitable to be set on the primary interface of such games. The appropriate addition of similar language effects can effectively attract the attention, with the appropriate changes of the screen to improve the efficiency of the understanding of the game. Considering the play platform and the target population, in order to avoid the excessive icon density, less operations should be done at the same interface than the common game. At the same time, when predicting the user behavior according to the operation logic, it should be unified with the overall art style in the icon design, and avoid forming the abrupt feeling between the picture and the operation experience during the process of playing [12].

(3) Immersive design

Considering the limitations of the mobile terminal platform in display technology, we can adopt fine model and optimization of real-time algorithms to improve the integration of the picture and real environment. In addition to the technical methods, we can also improve the immersion of the game from the psychological level. According to the principle of uncanny valley, within a certain range, the closer the nonhuman image approaches to humans, the lower the inhuman feeling, but after the similarity reaches a certain extent, people will dislike it. In the process of art practice, we found that the more in a certain range of the image of the art increases the head and body ratio, reduce the ratio of the limbs and the length of the trunk, increase the proportion of the eye in the face or the closer to the "baby" image, the more likely to be favored by the audience. In the collection target virtual image of art design, can be in the above highly abstract summary concept, the virtual image to a certain degree of personification, or its "baby", to create intimacy, so as to enhance the user's immersion in the process of interaction.

5 Conclusion

This study based on the Hook model discuss interactive design strategies for environmental protection-class children's games and Analyses the behavioral mechanism of constructing "trigger-action-reward-investment" in the game to cultivate children's environmental behavior habits. At the same time, a specific plan is proposed to improve their experience in visual and hearing, interface and operating system, and immersion. It provides a theoretical basis for the next practice of developing environmental education games for children.

References

1. UNEP.Emissions Gap Report 2020.UN environment programme (2020) .https://www.unep.org/emissions-gap-report-2020
2. Ye, Y.-H., Shih, Y.-H.: Environmental education for children in Taiwan: importance, purpose and teaching methods. Univ. J. Educ. Res. **8**(4), 1572–1578 (2020)
3. Wang: The role of children's musical in environmental education tries to compile environmental theme children's musical. The New Emperor **26**, 98–99 (2017)
4. Tarkkanen, K., Lehto, A., Oliva, D., Somerkoski, B., Haavisto, T., Luimula, M.: Research study design for teaching and testing fire safety skills with AR and VR games. In: 11th IEEE International Conference on Cognitive Infocommunications, CogInfoCom 2020-Proceedings, Paper Number 9237831, pp. 167–172 (2020)
5. Zhu, Y., Palsha, S.: Build our town-using an augmented reality game to enhance young children's spatial cognition. In: ICCE 2016–24th International Conference on Computers in Education: Think Global Act Local-Workshop Proceedings, pp. 1–5 (2016)
6. Barreira, J., Bessa, M., Pereira, L.C., Adao, T., Peres, E., Magalhaes, L.: MOW: augmented reality game to learn words in different languages-case study: learning English names of animals in elementary school. In: Iberian Conference on Information Systems and Technologies, CISTI, Paper No. 6263236 (2012)
7. Hassan, S.A., Rahim, T., Shin, S.Y.: ChildAR: an augmented reality-based interactive game for assisting children in their education. Universal Access in the Information Society (2021)
8. Xiuli, W., Xiao, J., Danling, Z., et al.: Research on intelligent toys. Packag. Eng. **40**(16), 165–170 (2019). https://doi.org/10.19554/j.cnki.1001-3563.2019.16.025
9. Rui, H.: Interactive design of child educational class APP based on immersion theory. Packag. Eng. **39**(10), 177–181 (2018)

10. Liu, L., Jun, Y.: Pay-for APP interactive design research for knowledge based on the addiction model. Art Technol. **34**(2), 4–6 75 (2021)
11. Xueying, C.: The design studies of simple style in the APP interface for children's games. Art Educ. Stud. **1**, 95 (2016). https://doi.org/10.3969/j.issn.1674-9286.2016.01.065
12. Junjie, Z.: Characteristic analysis based on child user mobile interface. Hubei Acad. Fine Arts **2**, 140–141 (2014). https://doi.org/10.3969/j.issn.1009-4016.2014.02.040

Conflicts: A Game that Simulates Cognitive Dissonance in Decision Making

Morgan Spencer Yao[✉], John Casey Bandiola, John Michael Vince Lim,
and Jonathan Casano

Ateneo de Manila University, Quezon City, Metro Manila, Philippines
morgan.yao@obf.ateneo.edu

Abstract. This research aims to develop a game that accurately simulates situations that would cause cognitive dissonance to the player. Cognitive dissonance is a psychological concept that involves situations of conflicting attitudes, beliefs, or behaviors that result in feelings of mental discomfort. The game is a visual novel with choice-based decisions that will influence the ending of the story. The player will have to make choices that will satisfy either their family for their happiness or their boss for money to spend on their family. In order to assess and measure the player's cognitive dissonance, the investigators used a modified scale derived from Sweeney, Hausknecht, and Soutar's research which uses three dimensions to measure dissonance after a major decision. The questions were in the form of a 7-point Likert scale and were integrated within the game itself and presented after the participant makes a major decision. The data was averaged for analysis. Results had shown that the game developed was only able to simulate average levels of cognitive dissonance.

Keywords: Digital games/online games · Game and flow/game immersion · Game psychology · Impact of game play · Player personality · Characteristics and demographics · Simulation games · Video games

1 Introduction

Cognitive dissonance is a psychological concept that involves situations with conflicting attitudes, beliefs, or behaviors which result in feelings of mental discomfort. This mental discord results from a contradiction between two separate thoughts [1]. Someone who experiences cognitive dissonance may alter their attitude or behavior towards a certain situation to relieve themselves of the discomfort they experience [2]. Festinger claims that people have an inner drive to stick with their attitudes and behaviors to avoid disharmony within themselves which he calls cognitive consistency [3]. When an inconsistency is present, something needs to change within that person in order to counteract the dissonance [4]. Festinger and Carlsmith also found, in their theory of induced or forced compliance, that a person that acts against their initial belief typically changes their belief into what they acted as [5].

Moral choices are increasingly being used as plot tools in video games [6] which makes them interesting to examine in a psychological context. These games involve

© Springer Nature Switzerland AG 2021
C. Stephanidis et al. (Eds.): HCII 2021, CCIS 1498, pp. 486–493, 2021.
https://doi.org/10.1007/978-3-030-90176-9_62

making the player choose a choice both directly, where the game explicitly tells the player to make a choice, and, indirectly, where the game may take in the player's actions and give it a consequence without telling the player that an event had occurred. In a game made to induce cognitive dissonance titled Spec Ops: The Line, the player is tasked to locate an army colonel and other survivors in a post-apocalyptic world. But throughout the game, the player is forced to shoot and kill many innocents and supposed allies in a game that involves saving them [7]. This causes cognitive dissonance in the player as they become confused about whether they are the protagonist or antagonist of the game and if what they're doing is even right.

Given the above aspects of cognitive dissonance, the aim of this study is to develop a game that would simulate situations that would cause cognitive dissonance. Cognitive dissonance was measured using a questionnaire taken by participants after making a major choice. Specifically, this study aims to answer the following questions:

1. How can a game be designed to incorporate choices that would have the player experience cognitive dissonance?
2. To what extent does the game measure cognitive dissonance?
3. How does the participant resolve the discomfort brought about by cognitive dissonance?

This paper presents an attempt to raise awareness and knowledge of cognitive dissonance among the players who played Conflicts. Raising awareness of cognitive dissonance is important because recognizing the conflict between personal beliefs and behaviors can lead to an understanding of personal values [8]. A better understanding of values facilitates decision-making skills [9]. This paper also contributes a novel attempt at representing cognitive dissonance through a visual novel game.

2   Review of Related Literature

The goal of this study is to develop a game that would analyze how players make decisions when put in a position of cognitive dissonance. This section discusses previous studies that measured the concepts on cognitive dissonance and its effects in decision making, how different types of games integrated these effects in their stories and mechanics, and the effects of a player's morality in making choices within games.

Shultz and Leveille of McGill University and Lepper of Stanford University explained that cognitive dissonance arises when a person is forced to choose between imperfect options, leading to the weighing out of imperfect options against each other [10]. Festinger defined three ways on how to resolve cognitive dissonance. The first one is to simply just change one's beliefs. Second, by adding new beliefs that would help outweigh the conflicting choices. And third, reducing the importance of the beliefs would mean that people "rationalized" their actions to persuade themselves to choose one of the choices [3].

2.1   Influence of an Individual's Morality in Making Choices in Video Games

Holl, Bernard, and Melzer's research aimed to gain insights on player perceptions of morality in video games using a qualitative approach. They concluded that emotional or moral engagement and meaningful play are strongly connected with each other. One of the framing characteristics they mentioned, consequences through rewards and penalties, is relevant to this research as the researchers used this method to elicit cognitive dissonance in players. This study shows that moral engagement is needed for the player to actually be able to relate and use their personal beliefs and opinions in the game they play [11].

Furthermore, the researchers Joackel, Bowman, and Dougruel, wanted to find out if a person's sense of morality plays a role in their games that might indicate how that person may play other certain games [12]. They found that players do not get morally disengaged when faced with moral issues in virtual environments but rely on their moral intuitions to act accordingly.

These studies points are important for this research as they mentioned that participants need to be emotionally invested and act as if making decisions in the game were in real life in order to get reliable results for the research. Participants need to be morally engaged for them to use their personal morals and absorb the emotion coming from a virtual environment.

2.2 Cognitive Dissonance in Video Games

Many video games available today use decision-making mechanics to inject cognitive dissonance triggering scenarios. An example of such a game is Papers, Please which lets the player simulate a border guard in a fictional communist country in war with its neighbors. The player would need to decide whether to let people with invalid passports and documents into the country. Narratives are used to convey why the people with outdated travel papers want to get in to expose the player to imperfect options. Player morality and judgement is needed here as punishments and consequences can occur if you let in someone illegally [13]. Another example is Fallout: New Vegas which allows the player to do what they want to do in an open world which includes making choices and decisions that affect their karma or faction reputation. Conflicts uses this form of reputation system to put player's in a state of cognitive dissonance as they would have to make conflicting choices between opposite factions.

2.3 Assessing and Measuring Cognitive Dissonance

Sweeney, Hausknecht, and Soutar developed a reliable scale to measure cognitive dissonance. Their research focused on dissonance induction, which is the dissonance customers felt after making a major purchase [14].

Sweeney et al.'s 22-item questionnaire measures cognitive dissonance using three dimensions: emotional, wisdom of purchase, and concern over deal. The two cognitive dimensions, wisdom of purchase and concern over deal, tackle a customer's doubt over their purchase and if they believe that they have been swayed by external factors, while the emotional dimension deals with the negative emotions customers felt right after their purchase. The researchers assumed that customers with higher dissonance would have "greater difficulty in judging the quality of the product" and "lower levels of satisfaction" which were supported by the 22-item scale built around the three dimensions [14]. Sample items from the questionnaire include "I felt disappointed with myself.", "I felt

I'd let myself down.", and "I wondered if I had done the right thing in making this decision.", among others.

This study uses a modified version of this questionnaire to assess dissonance after making a decision in Conflicts. We have used the three dimensions of cognitive dissonance to assist in designing choices and situations that would induce the feeling of cognitive dissonance.

3 Methodology

A game was created with decision-making checkpoints with the goal of making players experience cognitive dissonance. Below is a brief description of the game concept and design followed by the testing procedures.

3.1 Game Concept

Conflicts is a visual novel, story-based game that would put players in a state of cognitive dissonance. The game design, theme, and gameplay on the puzzles were adopted from the simulation game Papers, Please. The game also took inspiration from the Karma System of Fallout: New Vegas by tweaking it to indicate Family and Boss Satisfaction instead. Players were given rewards and penalties based on their in-game choices in the form of Family and Boss Satisfaction and in-game currency [13].

The researchers prioritized the storyline and the choices the players would make as the game concludes with different endings based on the player choices. Prioritizing work will yield more Boss satisfaction while prioritizing family will yield more Family satisfaction. The players would do missions every day in the form of minigames. After each mission, the players can choose among different options that will increase or decrease the Family and Boss Satisfaction. The player is given a salary every end of the week which they may use to buy their family's needs and wants. All dialogue in the game was written in Filipino. As the game is set in an alternate Philippines, having the dialogue in Filipino would increase immersion and relevance to this setting.

Story. The game is set in an alternate Philippines with an abusive government who is hungry for more power. In the first week, the story introduces the player to this setting, the characters, and basic gameplay. The player plays as an investigator trying his best to provide needs for his family. The second week introduces the corrupt government and police force who are trying to get evidence to incriminate an anti-government group who the government labels as terrorists. The player would get a major choice of tampering with the evidence or submitting the work done properly. In the third week, your son mysteriously runs away from home which was then discovered by your character as the leader of the rebellious group. By this point, the player would need to decide whether to help his son in his work or continue helping the government in stopping their group. In the fourth and last week, the police conducts a raid to finally catch and detain the members of the rebel group wherein you can decide to apprehend your son or let him go. After this, the last choices would either a.) ask you to officially help your son by releasing him from custody or proceed to take your son in or b.) lie about your son's whereabouts to your boss or tell the truth about there he went. To avoid repetitiveness and stale gameplay, the game also implemented mini-games that also act as choices. The mini-games to be played are relevant to the current part of the story to allow the player to still feel like they are affecting the story and therefore, feel more immersed.

Endings. The game features multiple endings depending on the satisfaction meters you achieved at the end of the game. The endings include a high Family Satisfaction ending which is for our context, the only morally good ending. The low Boss Satisfaction ending and low Family Satisfaction ending are the low morality endings where the character would suffer bad consequences. And lastly, the in-between ending also provides a bad outcome.

3.2 Testing

In order to answer research questions 2 and 3, players were asked to play the game and answer the modified Sweeney, Hausknecht, and Soutar questionnaire at certain points in the game. After making a major in-game decision, the player had to indicate their level of agreement to the statements using a 7-point Likert scale with 1 being the lowest and 7 being the highest. Major decisions are to be made at the end of each week starting with the second week. As the game implemented varying choices that satisfy two different sides of the game, having the survey, in both English and Filipino, right after the week they made the choice would provide a more accurate result when the decision is still fresh on their minds. Data gathered from the game was uploaded into a Google sheet using an integration with Unity. Collected data were then analyzed.

A total of 15 participants play-tested the game. The participants were all current Ateneo de Manila University students between the ages of 19–23. The participants answered the cognitive dissonance survey once for each major decision in the game for a total of three times.

4   Results and Discussion

The choice from week 2 caused the highest amount of dissonance among the players with that choice having the highest averages for all 3 dimensions in all weeks. Week 3 came next ranking 2nd in all the dimensions except emotional. Lastly, week 4 averaged the lowest in all dimensions except the emotional. The average ending satisfaction the participants got for the family meter was 95.67 while it was 55.67 for the boss meter (Table 1).

4.1   Analysis

A drop in overall dissonance can be seen among the participants week after week. The week 2 choice had the highest dissonance felt but is only considered as average to above-average strength in the Likert scale. The major choice from week 3 and 4 gave even lower dissonance to the participants. Based on their answer to how they resolved the dissonance

Table 1. Results gathered from the testing of 15 participants using a 7-point Likert Scale

Dimension	Week 2	Week 3	Week 4
Emotional	3.1939	2.8359	2.9180
Wisdom of choice	4.8222	3.8222	3.6222
Concern over deal	4.2222	2.7555	2.6222

felt, for the first major choice in week 2, most players said that they were just doing what they "felt was right" and they were still trying to get a feel of the game and the story. A player stated that they still did not understand the implications of their choice so they were just testing things out to see the effects of it by trying to find a middle ground in the choices. Many players also mentioned choosing what they personally believe in to resolve the dissonance. The next two week's essay answers made it clearer as to why lower dissonance was felt overall by the players. By this point, the players stated that they had already gotten a feel for how the game gives out its rewards and consequences. The players also stated that they had already made up their mind in protecting a character which meant that the choices moving forward were no longer hard decisions. This can be clearly seen in the last major choice wherein most players had already fully accepted which side they were going to take and fully believed in their choices.

As each player's playthrough progressed, they tunneled into a side and no longer thought much about the consequences of going against the other side. They put a lot of belief in themselves thinking that their choice was the correct one no matter what happens. It is also interesting to note that an overwhelming majority of the players sided with the family and not the boss. This can be seen in the high average of the family satisfaction and a middling average boss satisfaction. The researchers speculate that this comes from the Filipino's family orientedness which makes the testers more likely to side with family overwork which can also be seen in the participant's responses to how they resolved their dissonance.

5   Conclusion

This study developed a game that would simulate situations that cause cognitive dissonance among the players of Conflicts. Using insights gathered from the playtesting through a questionnaire embedded into the gameplay. We draw the following conclusions.

First, to answer RQ1, the design of the decision mechanics within Conflicts was created such that the player is presented with imperfect options. The narrative forces the player to choose between increasing his Boss satisfaction or his Family Satisfaction. The story-driven visual-novel design made for an immersive experience that reinforced the weight of choosing between the imperfect options.

To answer RQ2, The results of our testing showed that Conflicts was able to simulate situations that caused cognitive dissonance but only to an average extent based on the modified instrument of Sweeney et al for measuring the degree of cognitive dissonance. It was observed that the game was not able to keep cognitive dissonance high all throughout the game, as supported by the decreasing cognitive dissonance scores as the players progressed through the weeks in the game.

To answer RQ3, the answers to the open-ended questions given via the embedded data collection page within Conflicts revealed that, the participants resolved their cognitive dissonance discomforts by deciding to trust in their choices once they were able to get a feel of the game's reward and punishments mechanics while playing the game.

5.1 Recommendations

The researchers recommend future researchers craft a lengthier, slower-paced, and more engaging story to enhance the player's immersion in the Conflicts game world. We feel this would sustain high levels of cognitive dissonance throughout the game.

It is also important to incorporate more complex choices and unpredictable effects so the player is not simply choosing one or the other for each choice. Introducing more minigames of escalating difficulty might keep the player engaged. Having more audio and visual cues might also be helpful in providing players with a more gameful experience.

The researchers found that using a visual novel shifts the brunt of simulating cognitive dissonance to how the game's story is crafted instead of the mechanics or gameplay elements present in the story. Perhaps other genres could provide a way to simulate cognitive dissonance through the gameplay elements directly (instead of through the narrative) to provide a higher level of dissonance to the player.

Acknowledgements. The researchers would like to thank the Ateneo Laboratory for the Learning Sciences for generously funding this research. We would also like to thank our panelist and advisers Dr. Jenilyn Agapito and Jose Alfredo De Vera III for their valuable comments and suggestions that provided us with a different perspective in the work we did. Lastly, we would like to thank the Department of Information Systems and Computer Science, Dr. Marlene De Leon, the Office of the Registrar, Jessica O. Sugay, and Dr. Ma. Mercedes T. Rodrigo for their help in making this paper possible.

References

1. Psychology Today. Cognitive Dissonance (2020). https://www.psychologytoday.com/us/basics/cognitive-dissonance. Accessed 21 July 2020
2. Dunning, D., Balcetis, E.: Cognitive dissonance and the perception of natural environments. Psychol. Sci. **18**(10), 917–921 (2007). https://doi.org/10.1111/j.1467-9280.2007.02000.x
3. Bohren, A.: Cognitive Dissonance: How Does it Influence How We Think? March 2018. https://blog.cognifit.com/cognitive-dissonance/. Accessed 21 July 2020
4. Festinger, L.: A Theory of Cognitive Dissonance. Stanford University Press, Stanford (1957)
5. Carlsmith, J.M., Festinger, L.: Cognitive consequences of forced compliance. J. Abnorm. Soc. Psychol. **58**(2), 203–210 (1959). https://doi.org/10.1037/h0041593
6. Weaver, A.J., Lewis, N.: Mirrored morality: an exploration of moral choice in video games. Cyberpsychol. Behav. Soc. Network. **15**(11), 610–614 (2012). https://doi.org/10.1089/cyber.2012.0235

7. Hannaford, J.: Cognitive Dissonance in Video Games – Spec Ops: The Line. Video. (Jan. 2015) (2015). https://www.youtube.com/watch?v=ahOWbixhr2U. Accessed 21 July 2020
8. Tavris, C., Aronson, E.: The Role of Cognitive Dissonance in the Pandemic, July 2020. https://www.theatlantic.com/ideas/archive/2020/07/role-cognitive-dissonance-pandemic/614074/. Accessed 26 July 2020
9. Lawler, M.: Cognitive Dissonance Is Part of Every Decision We Make, February 2018. https://www.everydayhealth.com/neurology/cognitive-dissonance/every-decision-we-make/. Accessed 25 July 2020
10. Léveillé, E., Lepper, M.R., Shultz, T.R.: Free choice and cognitive dissonance revisited: choosing "Lesser Evils" versus "Greater Goods". Pers. Soc. Psychol. Bull. 25(1), 40–48 (1999). https://doi.org/10.1177/0146167299025001004
11. Melzer, A., Holl, E., Bernard, S.: Moral decision-making in video games: A focus group study on player perceptions. Hum. Behav. Emerg. Technol. 1–10 (2020). https://doi.org/10.1002/hbe2.189
12. Dogruel, L., Bowman, N., Joeckel, S.: Gut or game? The Influence of moral intuitions on decisions in video games. Media Psychol. 15(4), 460–485 (2012). https://doi.org/10.1080/15213269.2012.727218
13. Whitehead, D.: Papers, Please Review (2013). https://www.eurogamer.net/articles/2013-08-09-papers-please-review. Accessed 25 July 2020
14. Hausknecht, D., Soutar, G., Sweeney, J.: Cognitive dissonance after purchase: a multidimensional scale. Psychol. Market. 17(5), 203–210 (2000). https://doi.org/10.1002/(SICI)1520-6793(200005)17:5<369::AID-MAR1>3.0.CO;2-G

Development of 'School Nocturnble': A Sensitive Game with Eye Trackers

Subeen Yoo⬤, Dain Kim⬤, Seonyeong Park⬤, and JungJo Na(✉)⬤

Duksung Women's University, Seoul 132-714, Korea
jungjona@duksung.ac.kr

Abstract. This paper presents "School Nocturnble," a new type of eye-tracking game, and explains about the development process.

Recently, the game industry has been actively applying various new technologies into games. It's because gamers, who want more realistic and new experience through game, have been reacting positively towards the industry's new attempts. One of the field that the industry tries to innovate through new technology is a gaming controller. Eye-tracking technology is one of many technological innovations in development of gaming controllers.

"School Nocturnble" is a 2D side-scrolling puzzle adventure game that uses eye-tracker as an assisting gaming controller. A single player can control the protagonist with a keyboard while they can also control the assist character with the eye-tracker, solving puzzles and participating turn-based battles to save the magic school "School Nocturnble" from its curse. The game was developed with Unity 2019, Visual Studio 2019(C# code), and Tobii Unity SDK Version4. This game can be played in Windows PC and requires Tobii Eye Tracker5.

The development of "School Nocturnble" focuses on providing new game mechanics for gamers who prefers various experience and contents. At last, it's a meaningful attempt in both the gaming and eye-tracking field to use the Eye-tracker as an assiting gaming controller, since it's not as commonly used as its potential.

Keywords: Video game · Eye-tracking · Game controller · Unity

1 Introduction

Recently, the game industry has been actively applying various new technologies into games. It's because gamers, who want more realistic and new experience through game, have been reacting positively towards the industry's new attempts.

One of the field that the industry tries to innovate through new technology is a gaming controller. Eye-tracking technology is a technology that utilizes the user's sight as an interface. Eye-tracker, an Eye-tracking HW, is different with existing controllers that use hands because it can control by only using eyes. A player can experience new and special experience by using eye-tracker in game. With this potential, project "School Nocturnble" decided to use the eye-tracker as an assiting controller.

© Springer Nature Switzerland AG 2021
C. Stephanidis et al. (Eds.): HCII 2021, CCIS 1498, pp. 494–499, 2021.
https://doi.org/10.1007/978-3-030-90176-9_63

2 Program Design and Production

2.1 Game Summary

"School Nocturnble" is a 2D side-scrolling puzzle adventure game that uses eye-tracker as an assisting gaming controller. A single player can control the protagonist with a keyboard while they can also control the assist character with the eye-tracker, solving puzzles and participating turn-based battles to save the magic school "School Nocturnble" from its curse. The game was developed with Unity 2019, Visual Studio 2019(C# code), and Tobii Unity SDK Version4. This game can be played in Windows PC and requires Tobii Eye Tracker5.

2.2 Production Objective

- Introduce the new gaming controller, eye-tracker, to users who want new experience and make them experience the potential of eye-tracker.
- Suggest new direction of gaming controller for disabled players.
- Provide aesthetical experience through cute graphics and story.
- Provide various gaming experiences through puzzles and battles.

2.3 Game Design

Game Objective
Players travel through stages to lift the curse from students and discover how the magical stone that protects the school was destroyed.

Game Story
In the middle of Aster, a village shrouded in eternal darkness and curse of nightmare, resides a school for magicians named the School Nocturnble. Nocturnble has a magical stone that protects the village from curses, which have been protecting the villagers from darkness and nightmares with light magic. After a long time, when the magical stone has weakened, the protagonist joins Nocturnble as a freshman. After a short excitement of going to the school for the first time, the weakened magical stone finally breaks and the school is shrouded in curse. The protagonist begins the adventure with a glowing creature to restore the broken stone.

Game Character
Players can control the protagonist with a keyboard while they also control the assist character with the eye-tracker. Protagonist is a freshman that just got into the magic school. Assist character is a glowing creature that has been sleeping on top of the watchtower. There are 6 other important NPCs (Fig. 1 and 2).

Game Stage
Stages are based on the magical school "School Nocturnble." School Nocturnble is divided in 3 different areas: Sweven Hall of the West, Remental Hall of the East, and the Main Hall in the middle. The Main Hall's top floor is connected to the watchtower and an underground cellar (Fig. 3).

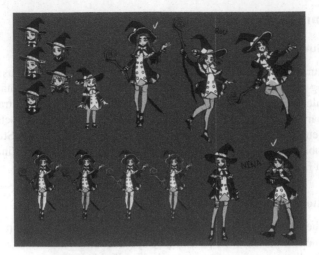

Fig. 1. Protagonios and NPC sketches

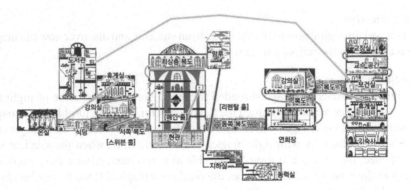

Fig. 2. Game stage structure

Fig. 3. Tobii eye tracker 5 that is used in-game

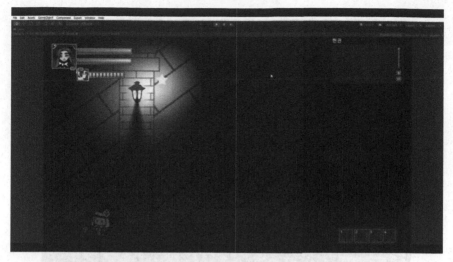

Fig. 4. Using eye-tracker to interact the assisting character and object

Application of Eye-Tracker. In this project, the eye-tracker is used to control the assisting character, solving puzzles, and battling. The code above is a code that allows to implicate the eye-tracker in game environment. If there is no main camera, or has no gazeOnScreen value, it returns Vector3.zero (Fig. 4).

Controlling the Assisting Character. Player can activate the eye-tracker with a Tab key and move the assisting character. The code above connects the location of the eye-tracker with the location of the assisting character. _gazePoint checks for most recent data and reflects as the character's movement).

Puzzle (See Figs. 5 and 6).

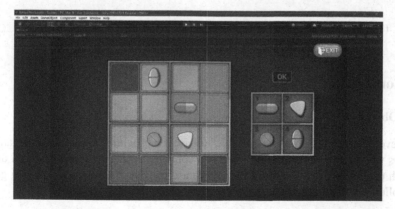

Fig. 5. Puzzle screens that can experience eye-tracker

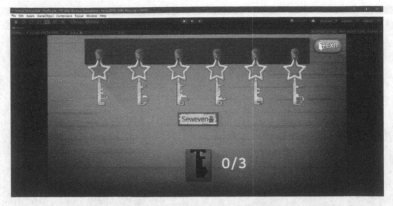

Fig. 6. Puzzle screens that can experience eye-tracker

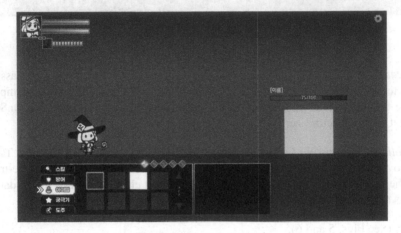

Fig. 7. Battle screen sample

Battle (See Fig. 7).

3 Conclusion

3.1 Objective

The development of "School Nocturnble" focuses on providing new game mechanics for gamers who prefers various experience and contents. At last, it's a meaningful attempt in both the gaming and eye-tracking field to use the Eye-tracker as an assiting gaming controller, since it's not as commonly used as its potential.

3.2 Benefit

Players can discover new potential of eye-tracking controls by playing the game. Furthermore, through fine graphics, detailed characters, and effects, players can go through an experience that is different from common PC games.

4 Future Plans

We will finish the production of the game and display "School Nocturnble" in an exhibition by October.

Reference

1. Brown, M.A., Kehoe, A., Kirakowski, J., Ian Pitt, F.: Beyond the gamepad: HCI and game controller design and evaluation. In: Evaluating User Experience in Games, pp. 197–219, December 2010

HCI in Mobility, Transport and Aviation

Disruptive Technology in the Transportation Sector (Case in Indonesia)

Pahmi Amri[1]([⊠]) [iD], Achmad Nurmandi[2] [iD], and Dyah Mutiarin[2] [iD]

[1] Universitas Muhammadiyah Yogyakarta, Universitas Islam Riau, Pekanbaru, Indonesia
Pahmi.amri@soc.uir.ac.id
[2] Universitas Muhammadiyah Yogyakarta, Bantul, Indonesia

Abstract. Online transport regulatory policies are critical to the success of this new type of transport. Tariff setting is a problem for online transportation users and drivers who are considered unfair. The zoning of operational areas that need to be underlined is the gap between conventional drivers and online drivers. This study looks at online transportation users' responses and drivers to tariff and zoning policies for operational areas. The method used in this research is qualitative analysis. This research uses Nvivo 12 Plus software to analyze qualitative data, which presents cross tab analysis and visual analysis. The stages in using Nvivo have five stages including; data collection, data import, data coding, data classification, and data presentation. The data that Nvivo had processed was then continued for qualitative analysis. The data source was obtained from the Twitter data set. This study's findings indicate that the tariff setting has not provided a solution to the gap between users and drivers of online transportation. The zoning of online transportation operations does not yet have a solid legal umbrella to enforce so that it still causes polemics between conventional and online transportation. This research's limitation is that this research only discusses the tariff and red zone for online transportation. Recommendations for further research are grouping online transportation problems in all urban areas in Indonesia.

Keywords: Online transportation · Policy · Technology

1 Introduction

Online transportation has existed since 2015 in Indonesia. The presence of online transportation was started by Uber, followed by an Indonesian company, PT. Gojek and Grab. Online transportation that uses ordering through applications can simplify the service process. This online application-based transportation is a unity of ojek and communication technology [1]. The demand for online transportation in Indonesia is very high. The data obtained show that 21.7 million Indonesians use online transportation [2].

Online transportation has both positive and negative impacts on the environment. Online transportation's positive impact provides convenience in ordering, lower costs, and a more practical e-Money payment system. Comfort and safety are guaranteed because online transportation provides complete information on the rider's identity,

© Springer Nature Switzerland AG 2021
C. Stephanidis et al. (Eds.): HCII 2021, CCIS 1498, pp. 503–510, 2021.
https://doi.org/10.1007/978-3-030-90176-9_64

such as name, contact, and driver [3]. Also, online transportation opens up new jobs for Indonesian residents [4]. The negative impact of online transportation can be a nuisance for conventional taxis [5].

The advantages and disadvantages of online transportation have not resolved the problems in its operation. Setting tariffs is considered high and does not go through fair arrangements by absorbing passengers' and drivers' interests. Then, zoning red, yellow, and green without precise regulation from the government is considered detrimental to drivers and passengers.

Tariffs and zoning for online transportation can generate public reactions in the form of opinions. Social media, such as Twitter, most readily discern online travel customer views. Some of the previous research results using Twitter data include analyzing public opinion sentiment towards Gojek Indonesia [6]. Analysis of netizens' perceptions of government policies on online motorcycle taxis uses twitter analysis [7]. Analyze the social media feelings on Twitter using the Naive Bayes classification technique on online transportation [8]. From these studies' results, the researcher is interested in analyzing online transportation from a different perspective, namely analyzing tariff setting and zoning policies for online transportation operations using user opinions via Twitter. This study utilizes user opinions on the homepage @Gojekindonesia, @grabid, then searches with the keywords "Ojek Online" and "ojol." The Nvivo 12 Plus software for viewing processed data in the visual format helps Twitter data analysis.

2   Literature Review

2.1   Online Transportation Arrangement

Online transportation regulatory policies are fundamental in supporting modern transportation. Indonesia has issued a presidential regulation regarding the implementation of online transportation. The regulation regulates that online transportation technically requires cooperation with public transportation companies. It is mainly related to technical matters such as payment mechanisms, restrictions, and requirements, using digital facilities. It is obligatory to report it to the Minister of Transportation, governors, regents, and mayors of all the technicalities. This is an attempt to track the online movement [9]. Furthermore, one of the Ministry of Transportation regulations is implementing online transportation to cooperate with established transportation companies and is not allowed to use the Online application individually.

As the holder of power, the government has the right and authority to regulate and create harmonious public transport policies. The government needs to present a suitable policy by accommodating input from users and online transportation drivers [10]. The Indonesian government has regulated this transportation sector innovation by issuing regulations that have been challenged for judicial review and amendments and formulating an accommodative regulatory format by equating online transportation with special rental transportation [11].

From online transportation until the emergence of regulatory policies, Indonesia is still polemic in online transportation [12]. The published policies have not fulfilled the interests of the various elements involved in it. The policies expected for online transportation can provide benefits by paying attention to conventional transportation interests [13]. In this case, policymakers such as the legislative and executive, and online transportation drivers can synergize supporting online transportation policy [14].

2.2 Online Transportation as a Disruptive Technology

The transportation sector revolution is underway, requiring us to think about doing business and taking advantage of disruptive technology and innovation. Technological developments can trigger changes that have never happened before so that they have the potential to become a disruptor in the goods and services sector [15]. *Disruptive technology* is a technology that uses a strategy by changing work patterns in competition [16]. Because competitor companies are under tremendous pressure, requiring agile and complex governance management [17].

Clayton Christensen found out about the bully invention hypothesis [18]. Various definitions have defined the meaning of disruptive technology. First, disruptive technology is a combination of new technology with existing technology. The combination can be seen from the dimensions of the system or operation [19]. *Disruptive technology* is a technology that dominates specific markets. Several technologies that arise automatically can interfere with the existing regulatory regime [20]. Failure The existing market is due to the inability to embrace these disruptive technologies [21].

Innovations in the urban mobility sector, such as online transportation, have been proliferating. However, online transportation's legality is unclear because transportation that uses the internet network is a bully to the previous conventional taxi companies [22]. This type of online transportation company is disruptive innovation. This can be seen from its ability to exploit digital technology to threaten the traditional taxi industry [23]. Online transportation technology has a disjointed line because it has upset an established market [24]. This type of technology can cause conflicts related to regulations [25]. Not only that, online transportation innovation can exhibit significant levels of disruption and can potentially destroy the traditional taxi industry [26]. It is challenging for the government as the regulator to overcome his arrival. The law to regulate the taxi industry has not been able to regulate this type of online transportation.

3   Research Methods

This research uses the Nvivo 12 Plus software. Nvivo 12 Plus is used to analyze qualitative data that presents crosstab analysis and visual analysis. The stages in using Nvivo have five stages including; data collection, data import, data coding, data classification, and data presentation. The data that Nvivo has processed is then continued for qualitative analysis.

4   Discussion and Results

Diverse Dynamics of online transportation developments always occur in Indonesia. Via Google Trends, headlines from 2018–2019 have always been a subject for online communication media discussion. Issues that often arise in its development are tariff settings [27], zoning of operational areas (Fig. 1).

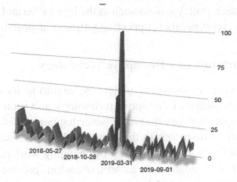

Fig. 1. Trends in online transportation topic in online media from 2018–2019. Source: [34]

4.1 Polemic of Online Transportation Arrangements

Problems in the workplace also involve those linked to wages and benefits that are not what an enterprise offers. Like transportation sector companies, in practice, Online transportation drivers earn inappropriate income from the company/platform. The fare setting system for drivers is very burdensome because of the revenue-sharing system, with 80% for drivers and 20% for companies. A study found related wages given by the company. Gojek is unfair and is not under Law Number 13 concerning labor, emphasizing that workers' wages must meet a decent living [28]. Furthermore, the provisions in determining fees imposed by online transportation companies are not based on regulations because they are not in the law [29] (Table 1).

Table 1. Guidelines for calculating service fees for using motorbikes with applications. Source: [35]

Area	Tariff lower limit	Tariff upper limit	Service fee
Zone I (Sumatra, Java, apart from Jakarta, Bogor, Depok, Tangerang, and Bekasi, Bali)	IDR. 1,850/km	IDR. 2,300/km	IDR. 7000–11,000
ZONE II (Jakarta, Bogor, Depok, Tangerang and Bekasi)	IDR. 2,250/km	IDR. 2,650/km	IDR. 9000–10,500
ZONE III (Kalimantan, Sulawesi, Nusa Tenggara Islands, Maluku Islands, Papua)	IDR. 2,100/km	IDR. 2,600/km	IDR. 7000–10,000

The online rate calculation has been provided for in the Decree KP 348 of 2019 by the Minister of Transport. The regulation describes the provisions of tariffs regulated based on the region's zoning, in which it regulates lower and upper tariffs. However, the Minister's decision did not provide a solution to the problem of determining tariffs. Below can be presented opinion data of online transportation users on social media (Twitter) (Fig. 2).

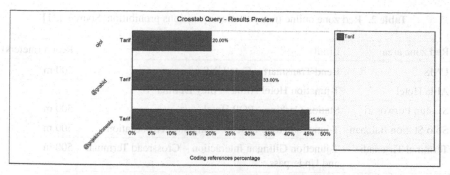

Fig. 2. The response of drivers and online transportation users via Twitter

The above graphic gives the views of Twitter users and drivers of online transport. On the @Gojekindonesia twitter homepage, 45% of public opinion is seen regarding tariff issues. Then on the Twitter homepage @grabid, we can see 33% of users' tweets regarding tariffs. Furthermore, using the search term "Ojol," it can be seen that 20% of users' tweets are related to tariffs. The tariff setting for driver-partner transportation ideally tariff is determined by considering the system's weight on the factors affecting the rate to calculate an accurate figure by the government [30].

4.2 Online Transportation Operational Zone System

Operating Zoning System In different towns, online travel has been carried out [31]. Like conventional transportation activists, the city of Bandung has boycotted online transportation by creating a no-operate zone [32]. The operating prohibition zone is divided into three zones, including the red zone, which prohibits online transportation to pick up, pick up and wait for passengers in the area. The yellow zone is allowed for Online transportation to drop off and pick-up passengers but not allowed to wait for passengers. The green zone is the safest area for drivers to deliver, pick up passengers and wait for orders. The zoning aims to avoid conflicts between online and conventional transportation [33]. Supporting data relating to the operational prohibition zone in Solo City, Indonesia, can be seen in the following table (Table 2);

Zoning of the operational prohibition area for online transportation has been implemented for solo cities. The table above shows that there are eleven red zone points prohibited from operating, each of which is 200 to 500 m apart. The provisions are enforced based on a joint agreement between conventional transportation activists with the government and online transportation. Responding to the establishment of an operational prohibition zone for online transportation in Indonesia, several opinions were seen through social media twitter as follows (Fig. 3);

Opinions of users and online transportation drivers via social media Twitter can be seen in the graph above. Through management assisted by NVivo 12 plus with the data source for the account @gojekindonesia, user opinion regarding the zone is 11%. Then on the @grabid account homepage, the user's opinion regarding the red zone is 55%. Furthermore, Twitter data using the search for the word "Ojek Online" shows that user

Table 2. Red zone online transportation operations prohibition. Source: [31]

Red zone area	Limits	Reach (meters)
UMS	Bend Transmart – Gate UNS	200 m
Alila Hotel	T-junction Hotel Alilla - Alley Delima II	
Stasiun Purwosari	Station Oarking - POP Hotel	500 m
Solo Station Balapan	T-junction Hotel Pose in - Balapan Petrol Station	500 m
Terminal Tirtonadi	T-junction Gilingan Interaction – Crossroad Terminal and Underpass	500 m
Jebres Station	Bend SMP 14 - Cross Front Station	500 m
RSUD Moewardi	Kimia Farma - East Moewardi Hospital	300 m
RS Hermina	The Exit Mom milk Jebres - Motor Stage	300 m
UNS	Main Gate of UNS - UNS Gas Station	200 m
Legi Market	Intersection Road Sultan Syahrir - Road S. Parman Intersection	500 m
Market Klewer	Park parking alun-alun North Square - Hasyim Ashari Street intersection	500 m

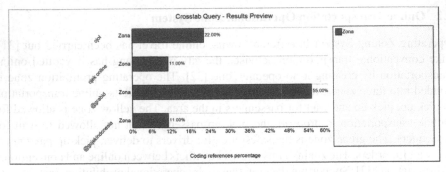

Fig. 3. User responses related to rates via twitter social media

opinions related to the red zone are 11%, and the search for the word "ojol" user opinions is 22%.

5 Conclusion

Online transportation tariff setting policies and operational zoning have become a long polemic. Central and local government regulations have not been able to provide solutions to solve these online transportation problems. User opinion regarding tariff setting and operational zoning always appears on social media, Twitter. This research concludes that the determination of tariffs and operational zoning has not provided a solution. The limitation of this research is that firstly, this research only uses Twitter social media data.

Both of these studies focus on discussing tariff and zoning issues for online transportation. For future research, a cluster study is proposed on matters of online transport across Indonesia.

References

1. Damayanti, S.A.S.: Transportasi Berbasis Aplikasi Online: Go-Jek Sebagai Sarana Transportasi Masyarakat Kota Surabaya. Universitas Airlangga (2017)
2. Astutik, Y.: 21,7 Juta Masyarakat Indonesia Pakai Transportasi Online, CNBC Indonesia (2020). https://www.cnbcindonesia.com/tech/20200317150135-37-145529/217-juta-masyarakat-indonesia-pakai-transportasi-online. Accessed: 25 Jan 2021
3. Anindhita, W., Arisanty, M., Rahmawati, D.: Analisis Penerapan Teknologi Komunikasi Tepat Guna Pada Bisnis Transportasi Ojek Online (Studi pada Bisnis Gojek dan Grab Bike dalam Penggunaan Teknologi Komuniasi Tepat Guna untuk Mengembangkan Bisnis Transportasi). In: Prosiding Seminar Nasional INDOCOMPAC (2016)
4. Rifaldi, R., Kadunci, K., Sulistyowati, S.: Pengaruh Kualitas Pelayanan Transportasi Online Gojek Terhadap Kepuasan Pelanggan Pada Mahasiswa/i Administrasi Niaga Politeknik Negeri Jakarta. Epigram 13(2) (2016)
5. Avinda, S.P.: Analisis dampak ojek online terhadap pangkalan ojek konvensional Griya Pasteur (2017)
6. Syahputra, H., Basyar, L.K., Tamba, A.A.S.: Sentiment analysis of public opinion on the Go-Jek Indonesia through twitter using algorithm support vector machine. J. Phys. Conf. Ser. 1462(1), 12063 (2020)
7. Ramdhani, A., Muzadid, B.K., Alamanda, D.T., Fahruroji, F.: Persepsi Netizen Terhadap Kebijakan Pemerintah Pada Ojek Online Menggunakan Twitter Analysis. Seminar Nasional Teknologi Informasi 2, 82–91 (2019)
8. Sari, D.F., Kurniawati, D., Prayitno, E., Irfangi, I.: Sentiment analysis of Twitter social media to online transportation in Indonesia using naïve bayes classifier. J. Int. Conf. Proc. 2(1), 31 (2019)
9. Adhani, H.: Controversy, legality and constitutionality of online public transportation in Indonesia. In: ICIB 2019, pp. 431–437 (2020)
10. Oshima, R., Fukuda, A., Fukuda, T., Satiennam, T.: Study on regulation of motorcycle taxi service in Bangkok. J. East. Asia Soc. Transp. Stud. 7, 1828–1843 (2007)
11. Hadi, H., Tejomurti, K., Imanullah, M.N., Nurhidayatuloh: Online Transportation: violation of privacy rights and vulnerability to sexual violence by drivers in digital platform based work. vol. 358, November 2017, pp. 241–246 (2019)
12. Djuyandi, Y., Hidayat, A.: Political space competition between online and conventional transportation in Jakarta, Indonesia. J. Soc. Dev. Sci. 10(1)(S), 1–10 (2019)
13. Sekar Bidari, A.: The political law of government in responding to the development of online transportation in Indonesia. In: SHS Web Conference, vol. 54, p. 06012 (2018)
14. Ambarwati, O.C., Nugroho, R.A., Suharto, D.G., Setyowati, K.: Narration of stakeholder perspectives on online transportation policy. In: ICSTCSD 2019, vol. 389, pp. 80–84 (2020)
15. Arnold, V.: The changing technological environment and the future of behavioural research in accounting. Account. Financ. 58(2), 315–339 (2018)
16. Danneels, E.: Disruptive technology reconsidered: a critique and research agenda. J. Prod. Innov. Manag. 21(4), 246–258 (2004)
17. Brennan, N.M., Subramaniam, N., van Staden, C.J.: Corporate governance implications of disruptive technology: an overview. Br. Account. Rev. 51(6), 100860 (2019)

18. Limba, T.: Industry 4.0 and national security: the phenomenon of disruptive technology. vol. 6, no. 3, pp. 1528–1535 (2019)
19. Kostoff, R.N., Boylan, R., Simons, G.R.: Disruptive technology roadmaps. Technol. Forecast. Soc. Change **71**(1–2), 141–159 (2004)
20. Cartwright, M.: Historical institutionalism and technological change: the case of Uber. Bus. Polit. **2017**, 1–24 (2019)
21. Ganguly, A., Das, N., Farr, J.V.: The role of marketing strategies in successful disruptive technologies. Int. J. Innov. Technol. Manag. **14**(3), 1–20 (2017)
22. Bick, G.: Uber SA: disruption of the local taxi industry? Emerald Emerg. Mark. Case Stud. **9**(2), 1–9 (2019)
23. Nazir, M.S., et al.: No Title 膠原病 · 血管炎にともなう皮膚潰瘍診療ガイドライン. Spectrochim. Acta - Part A Mol. Biomol. Spectrosc. vol. 192, no. 4, pp. 121–130 (2018)
24. Geissinger, A., Laurell, C., Sandström, C.: Digital disruption beyond uber and Airbnb—tracking the long tail of the sharing economy. Technol. Forecast. Soc. Change **155**, 1 (2020)
25. Laurell, C., Sandström, C.: Analysing Uber in social media—disruptive technology or institutional disruption? Int. J. Innov. Manag. **20**(05), 1640013 (2016)
26. Schwalbe, U.: Schneider Henrique: Creative destruction and the sharing economy: Uber as disruptive innovation. J. Econ. **124**(1), 93–96 (2017). https://doi.org/10.1007/s00712-017-0589-6
27. Azizah, A., Adawia, P.R.: Analisis perkembangan industri transportasi online di era inovasi disruptif (Studi Kasus PT Gojek Indonesia). Cakrawala-Jurnal Hum. **18**(2), 149–156 (2018)
28. Harahap, A.M.: DETERMINATION OF GO-FOOD WORKERS' WAGES IN THE VEW OF YUSUF QARDHAWI: CASE STUDY OF PT. GOJEK MEDAN. Int. J. Lang. Res. Educ. Stud. **4**(1), 44–53 (2020)
29. Latifah, L.: Analisis hukum islam terhadap penerapan tarif layanan jasa PT. Ojek Syar'i Indonesia di Surabaya. EKNIS J. Ekon. Islam dan Ekon. Pondok Pesantren **7**(1) (2018)
30. Atletiko, F.J., Rakhmawati, N.A., Ts, H.: Determination of freight rates based on package dimension and distance of delivery using fuzzy logic system in Angkotin application. Procedia Comput. Sci. **161**, 527–534 (2019)
31. Rozdianda, M.: PERSEBARAN ZONA MERAH OJEK ONLINE DI SURAKARTA. Universitas Muhammadiyah Surakarta (2019)
32. Rusyadi, M.K., Fajarwati, A.: Dampak Transportasi Online Terhadap Keberlanjutan Angkutan Kota (Angkot) Sebagai Transportasi Umum Perkotaan Di Kota Bandung. J. Bumi Indones. **9**(3) (2020)
33. Ristanti, N.S.: Smart Mobility dalam Pengembangan Transportasi Berbasis Aplikasi Online Di Indonesia. Ruang **4**(3), 237–246 (2018)
34. Google.com: Trends in online transportation topic in online media from 2018–2019 (2021)
35. Ministry of Transportation: Decree of the Minister of Transportation Number KP.348 of 2019 GUIDELINES FOR CALCULATION OF SERVICE COSTS FOR USE OF MOTORCYCLES USED FOR THE INTEREST OF THE COMMUNITY DONE WITH THE APPLICATION (2019)

Collaborative Workspace – Concept Design and Proof of Concept of an Interactive Visual System to Support Collaborative Decision-Making for Total Airport Management

Mandra Bensmann[1]([⊠]), Alicia Lampe[1]([⊠]), Thomas Hofmann[1], and Steffen Loth[2]

[1] Industrial Design, Hochschule Osnabrück, Sedanstraße 60, 49076 Osnabrück, Germany
{mandra.bensmann,alicia.lampe,t.hofmann}@hs-osnabrueck.de
[2] German Aerospace Center, Institute of Flight Guidance, Lilienthalplatz 7,
38108 Braun-schweig, Germany
steffen.loth@dlr.de

Abstract. The future of aviation should be safe, efficient, measurable, collaborative, fair and transparent. New concepts like Collaborative Decision Making and Performance Based Management at airports address these challenges demanding human centered workspace approaches. Centralized and remote solutions have taken into account and technical realization has been addressed. Conventional widget based solutions, as well as gamification ideas are considered for the design of the future workplace in a multi-stakeholder environment at airports. The work results in possibilities to present complex data sets into a uniform and clear interface design that meets the needs of the operators. Design elements were used to ensure that the user will experience the most pleasant working atmosphere and will be able to perform their activities effectively and in a goal-oriented manner.

Keywords: Performance based airport management · Collaborative decision making · User interface design

1 Introduction

With more and more automation and digital assistance supporting humans in their work, the need of a user centered interface and optimized work environment is growing. This is also true for airports, that have significantly developed to multi-stakeholder environments [1], with complex structures, data information flows and new operational processes. New concepts like Total Airport Management (TAM) [3] and Performance Based Airport Management (PBAM) [2] have been introduced to further improve operations. As a central element to these concepts, a collaborative decision-making approach, involving the different stakeholders at airports, is defined. Work has been done regarding interface design and cooperation of these stakeholders as well as user requirements for future APOC operators in [4] and [5] have been evaluated by DLR. To support the existing

© Springer Nature Switzerland AG 2021
C. Stephanidis et al. (Eds.): HCII 2021, CCIS 1498, pp. 511–516, 2021.
https://doi.org/10.1007/978-3-030-90176-9_65

approaches the following paper addresses the topic from a user design perspective and details aspects for the future workplace of operators.

In collaboration between the University of Applied Sciences Osnabrück and DLR, two workspace solutions are being developed to be used in an airport operation center environment with a timeframe 2025 to 2030. With challenges of huge amount of different data as well as to quickly identifying critical situations and their reasons, the goal is to design a User Interface (UI) in combination with a workspace solution that creates a collaborative decision-making atmosphere in order to optimize overall airport operations (user experience design) [6].

2   Design Concept

The focus of this work is on the holistic view of the users and their relationship to the technical system and interface design, which are combined to a future vision of a workspace in APOC. The design process behind the workspace solution can be found in [7].

Due to different initial situations at airports, in terms of financial resources, size and infrastructure [1], two concepts for a workspace in a centralized and decentralized control center are being developed. The resulting onsite and remote solutions are based on the same UI and shown on different hardware devices. In addition, an approach for the use of object-oriented representations in three-dimensional space has been developed for better visualization of complex data correlations. Therefore, emerging technologies, such as Mixed and Virtual Reality, has been used to display these correlations in virtual and real environments. Moreover, the design options for the work environment and ergonomic requirements for the workplace are also considered in order to create a human-centered business workspace in terms of interaction and collaborative decision making. Out of these three aspects (interface, VR/MR-application, workplace), this poster addresses the design of an interface for an interactive visual system in an APOC.

3   Prototypical User Interface

For the design of the interface the results from the Airport2030 project, carried out in 2014, have been used [8]. An APOC setup with a prototype interface was used with airport operators in an operational environment working in shadow mode (see Fig. 1). The idea of an APOC UI was generally considered useful as a predictive tool. However, the design makes decision making difficult because the UI was very extensive and confusing because of a complex and for the user not familiar visualisation, which made interaction time consuming. Based on this user feedback, the design in this work should be created from a user-centered and application-oriented perspective [8].

In addition to the DLR results, cross-industry research was conducted to become aware of future workplace design trends. In the wake of digitalization and globalization, emerging technologies show great potential for collaborative workspaces in terms of natural communication, decision making and less complex visualisation. Parallel to

Fig. 1. Exemplary APOC setup [8]

this, the desire of the workforce for more individualization and a human-centered workplace design is increasing. Accordingly, technological and social innovations must be combined to a holistic workspace design.

For this purpose, suitable hardware devices for the two work environments (on-site/remote) were selected as examples:

– Multi-touch display. The multi-touch display is to be used in an on-site workspace in a central airport control center, where there is an increased need for coordination. It is hoped that this will lead to a more intuitive handling of the hardware. For the presentation of the UI, a 58-inch display was used as an example.
– Curved Monitor. At smaller airports, a lower coordination effort is expected, which is why operators might have two different jobs. Accordingly, a 49-inch curved monitor is used as an example in the remote workspace of a decentralized control center. This enables the control of two computer sources and a seamless design. In the event that various tasks are combined, the monitor enables the content to be flexibly displayed in one HMI.

For the concept of the workspaces, a prototypical user interface was created based on responsive design elements. The behavior of the design is exemplarily simulated on a multi-touch display (see Fig. 2) and a curved monitor (see Fig. 3).

Due to the complex airport structures and the resulting large fluctuating amounts of data, the UI should show a situation-adaptive behavior. Widget application are used, as they are variable in their number, size, arrangement and depth of information. Information is prepared in a partially redundant manner, allowing users to grasp and assess the

Fig. 2. UI multi-touch   **Fig. 3.** UI curved screen

complex environment. This is intended to create a holistic situational awareness. The individual widgets are unified into a coherent UI through a uniform interface design.

The aim of the prototypical UI is the adaptation of complex data sets into a uniform and clear interface design that meets the needs of the operators in the airport control center (see Fig. 4). Moreover, it should create a common platform for joint decision-making processes. In addition, communication can be initiated by means of the UI, which can enhance collaboration and social exchange.

While widgets can be configured individually, there are recommended arrangements based on the physiological characteristics of humans. Widgets that require the user's attention most, should be placed in the center of the interface. There, the highest sharpness and colorfulness can be perceived by the human eye. Inactive or less used widgets should be placed at the edge of the display. However, if they change or show deviations, motion or strong contrast changes are used to draw attention to this element [9].

In general, animations were used to locate workflows in time and to optimize the user's understanding of the processes. Thus, the overarching situational awareness can be strengthened.

Under the gamification approach, users should be motivated in their work by more emotionally designed UI elements in order to maintain their attention and increase their work performance and quality [10]. Therefore, numerical values are visualized and supported in the interface with the help of graphical elements. Color coding and multiple content loading of individual elements are intended to create connections between the widgets and help users understand the interrelationships of processes and workflows.

4   Design Evaluation

The UI design of the remote and on-site workspace was placed into an application context by simulating an exemplary user journey. The design- and interaction design mockUp showed that the interface in the user journey scenario was structured logically and purposefully. Complex processes were designed and visualized in a simplified way. Consequently, it can be assumed that it was made more accessible for the user. Critical situations are visually highlighted, which can potentially lead to faster recognition. The interface offers the possibility to join conferences and thus shows a way for joint decision making and provides space for collaborative work. Thus, it can be assumed that the

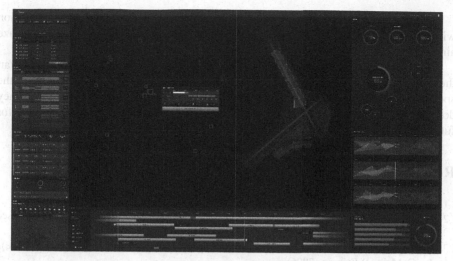

Fig. 4. Prototypical APOC UI

previously used experimental interface setup is now designed in a more user-friendly way in terms of situation awareness, situation overview and decision making.

By simulating the UI in a remote and on-site workspace, the responsiveness of the design concept could be tested and adapted. Despite the different screen formats, all content could be conveyed correctly without loss of information. Instead of multiple screens, modern hardware solutions were used. Multi-touch and curved-screen technologies bring new impulses to the workplace design of an airport control center. They show potential for the application area of this work. The evaluation could only be done partially. A proper validation has to be tested with the responsible operators.

5   Conclusion

In this extended abstract, a design approach of an UI for a workspace in a future airport control center is shown. This approach was tested and iteratively optimized with the help of simulations and design MockUps. In the future, usability testing have to be conducted with airport operators under real circumstances to evaluate the concepts [11].

For the first time, designers were involved in the development process as support for visualizing the concept around the use cases TAM and PBAM which had the advantage that HCI were examined from a design development perspective and adapted to users' needs.

The merger of interdisciplinary institutions for the research of HCI and its workspace environment can be seen as novel and enriching in this context and provide new impulses for future research.

The project presented here is supporting the strategic research topic of an Integrated Airport Management of the DLR Institute of Flight Guidance. The aim of this work was to propose solutions from the point of view of design and UI methodology and to discuss them for validity.

In addition, the project was to design a possible user interface (UI) in combination with a workspace solution that creates a collaborative work situation in order to optimize airport operations as a whole.

Due to complex interdependent airport processes and the lack of test options so far, the results of this project must be seen as a hypothesis. The results are based on the specialist knowledge from design and usability research, but at this point in time they do not claim to be operational. They serve as a basis for discussion and development for future HMI in an APOC environment.

References

1. Günther, Y.: Airport2030, HAP 3 (AP 3.1), Leitstandkonzept (2014)
2. Helm, S.: Advancing total airport management - an introduction of performance based management in the airport context. In: ATRS World Conference (2015)
3. Günther, Y., et al.: Total airport management (operational concept & logical architecture)., In: C. Meier, P. Eriksen (2006)
4. Jipp, M., Schaper, M., Günther, Y., Papenfuss, A.: Ecological interface design and its application to total airport management. In: IEEE Conference on System, Man, and Cybernetics, 09–12. October 2011, Anchorage (2011)
5. Papenfuss, A.: Konzeption einer Anzeige zur Unterstützung von Verhandlungsprozessen: Methodik und erste Validierungsergebnisse. In: Kooperative Arbeitsprozesse DGLR-Bericht 2009–02, 2009–10, pp. 107–123, Braunschweig (2009)
6. Hofmann, T., Jakobi, J., Blessmann, C., Reuschling F., Kamender, T.: Design and implementation of a virtual workstation for a remote AFISO. In: Proceedings of: 22nd International Conference on Human Computer Interaction (HCI 2020), Copenhagen (2020)
7. Bensmann, M., Lampe, A., Hofmann, T., Loth, S.: Collaborative workspace – concept design of an interactive system for total airport management. In: Proceedings of 12th International Conference on Applied Human Factors and Ergonomics (AHFE 2021), New York (2021)
8. Papenfuss, A.: Airport2030, Evaluierungsbericht Leitstand, Braunschweig (2014)
9. Windel, A., Bleyer, T., Bux, K., Brockt, G., Lafrenz, B., Lazarus, H.: Kleine Ergonomische Datensammlung. TÜV Media TÜV Rheinland Group (2019)
10. Kumar, J.M., Herger, M.: Gamification at work: designing engaging business software. In: Marcus, A. (ed.) DUXU 2013. LNCS, vol. 8013, pp. 528–537. Springer, Heidelberg (2013). https://doi.org/10.1007/978-3-642-39241-2_58
11. Barnum, C.M.: Usability Testing Essentials: Ready, Set...Test! Morgan Kaufmann, Burlington (2011)

From a Drones Point of View

D. L. Dolgin[1]([⊠]), D. Van Der Like[2], J. London[3], and C. Holdman[3]

[1] LLC, Pensacola, USA
[2] Hellcat Productions LLC, Pensacola, USA
[3] London Arts Acting Studio, New Haven, USA

Abstract. Drones* are on every horizon. They are an essential part of military defense, telemedicine, agriculture, construction, security, firefighting, search and rescue operations, NASA space exploration and Hollywood film production.

Drones are referred to by many different names. Whether referred to as Uninhabited Autonomous Vehicle (UAS), Unmanned Combat Air Vehicle (UCAV or Remotely Piloted Vehicle (RPV), the reference is to an aircraft piloted from the ground. The importance of psychomotor abilities (stick and rudder) in drone operations is a diminishing one. Considerations for autonomous flight success include the operator's willingness to rely on a computer for decisions. This may be a particularly important factor for Uninhabited Air Systems (UAS) war fighting efficacy [1].

*Drones, UAS, UAV and RPV are synonymous terms used interchangeably.

Keywords: Drones · Autonomy · Human autonomy teaming · Military operations

What can be expected of future military drone missions was suggested by DARPA (Defense Advanced Research Projects Agency) in "In the Sky and on the Ground, collaboration vital to DARPA's CODE for success". [2] Modern drones are dependent on satellites. The most obvious is through GPS, which has in a few decades moved from cutting-edge military enabler to an integral part of daily life for both military and civilian communities. GPS enables far more complex and accurate navigation than the high error tolerances of inertial management before it, but GPS signals can be jammed or, in a worst scenario, the satellites in orbit could be destroyed. Besides GPS, military drones can be remotely piloted with signals relayed through a permissive electromagnetic spectrum and sometimes even carried by satellites in orbit.

The result is a new software infrastructure enabling drones to work together. Mission goals are accomplished without the need for a dedicated human pilot to remotely control each drone. Autonomy is designed primarily as a way to overcome jamming and continue operations in denied environments.

Autonomous swarms refer to dozens of drones overseen by the same crew it once took to pilot a single aircraft. This technology has significant implications for the future of aviation warfare. Civilian drone applications appear limitless. NASA drones and Rovers lead the way for space exploration and our future.

C. Stephanidis et al. (Eds.): HCII 2021, CCIS 1498, pp. 517–520, 2021.
https://doi.org/10.1007/978-3-030-90176-9_66

Military advantages of drones are numerous:

1. Compared to drones, equipping fighter jets and training pilots is expensive
2. Drones are expendable. Drone waves can be launched with acceptable losses far greater than anything acceptable using manned aircraft
3. Drones can swarm. As drones become less costly hundreds of them could be deployed into aerial battlefields, quickly overwhelming the Air defense of any opponent. Even sophisticated anti-aircraft systems would fall victim as there would be too many targets for them to engage successfully
4. Drones could potentially achieve air superiority within minutes of an attack. By destroying an enemies Air Force and completely overwhelming their air defenses with numbers, drones could obtain air superiority so quickly that an opponent may choose to surrender rather than leave their ground forces and installations open to destruction from the air
5. Drone pilots are protected from harm. Since military drones can be operated from bases on other continents, losing pilots may become a thing of the past. For example, no g-forces and related aviation hazards for aviators to contend with

Pilots transitioning to remote control requires adjustment. For example, pilots in manned aircraft can see outside, hear the engine noise and feel the turbulence. A pilot's situational awareness is immediate whereas drone data is limited. Student drone pilots quickly learn where to access drone information that in a manned craft would be at their fingertips. For example, in the case of a lost data link, a drone is programmed to return to either a pre-programmed location or its original launch point. When that happens, a pilot needs to know what the programming is and change it if needed.

Boredom an Issue. Drones are so sophisticated that they need less flying than minding. Flying a drone does not require continual focus when at the controls. Pilot's report that hovering a craft while waiting for a target makes it difficult to be fully alert when needed. This makes boredom a unique but genuine problem among pilots that can affect performance and create difficulties when pilots need to respond quickly

There is some evidence suggesting that pilots with less flight experience behind the drone controls is a better strategy than the other way around. A report examining drone accidents showed that pilots with real flight experience made more mistakes than operators with no flight experience. That's because "pilots learn to rely on a set of cues non-existent in the management of UAS (Uninhabited Air Systems) so it is unclear that pilots are the best qualified drone operators [3].

Lt. General David Deptula reported that the Air Force has "experienced a 600% increase in demand for unmanned missions in the past decade. They are very important and very effective". According to General Deptula, "drones hit what they are aiming at 95% of the time" [4]. DARPA's CODE program is focused on the capability of groups of drones to synchronize under a single "drone pilots" supervision. The drones would continuously evaluate themselves and their environment while presenting recommendations to a UAS team for approval. Drones designated for military combat require a high technology support base. At a minimum, secure long range communications and advanced computer technologies are minimal requirements for supporting drone flight

Fig. 1. Image of an Army Predator drone (courtesy of DARPA)

operations. Additionally, as drone technology improves, the support team flying them requires advanced training. When flying a drone configured with expensive cameras, sensors and weapons, the margin of error is non-existent.

We have stressed the military applications of drones. However, civilian industrial applications are increasingly using drones to improve and optimize industrial processes as well as enhance operational efficiencies. For example in sea ports, drones can perform applications such as mapping, surveying, operational oversight, port monitoring and traffic control. Additionally, agricultural, insurance and real estate industries are benefiting from drone utilization. Drones are also used for medication and prescription delivery, blood donation delivery, laboratory sample collection and delivery, vaccine storage and delivery and organ transport.

As technology improves and manufacturing costs decline, the focus on the human factor and developing predictive measures of team compatibility becomes significant to mission success.

If the postulate of compatibility is correct we need to focus not only on selecting well-qualified individuals, but we also need to select individuals who can be compatible within a group. Compatibility refers to "the relations between two or more persons that leads to mutual satisfaction of interpersonal needs and harmonious existence." [5]

There is increasing recognition of the role of compatibility in a variety of operational environments. Maximizing interpersonal effectiveness is a goal of cockpit resource management (CRM). In some operational environments, such as in Special Forces Teams, and for teams functioning in isolation and confinement (e.g., long duration space flights, Antarctic winter-over and space exploration) compatibility is particularly critical.

In these environments we recognize the crucial role that interpersonal factors play in operational performance. Investigators are looking closely at interpersonal issues in these environments [6].

Selection of individuals tends to focus on screening out psychopathology and screening in intelligence and cognitive processing capacity. Very little attention is paid to selecting individuals based on their non-pathological interpersonal characteristics. The best person for the job may not necessarily be the best person for the team.

The question remains open: Can self-report personality measures be used to form groups of individuals who are likely to be maximally compatible. Field studies and group/team simulation activities provide a direct means of observing teams engage in task-related activities. These studies also allow for the measurement of the team's productivity. However, the field-study approach to team assessment has considerable costs and doesn't easily permit the evaluation of all possible permutations of team member groupings. A validated measure of interpersonal compatibility would be far less costly and time consuming. Additionally, a (self-administered) test would allow for the modeling of all possible groupings of potential team members.

Clearly, we need to match our advances in the selection of individuals with advances in methods for selecting and forming effective teams. It is likely that the instruments that work with one population or for one type of activity will not be effective elsewhere. With the inevitable advent of manned planetary deep space exploration, our measurement of interpersonal characteristics will need to be better understood. The role of situational variables and their interaction on the characteristics of teams will likely include biological and psychological predictors.

References

1. Kay, G., Dolgin, D.L.: Team compatibility as a predictor of team performance: picking the best team. In: NATO Research and Technology Organization (RTO), RTO Meeting Proceedings 4, December 1998
2. Collaborative Operations in Denied Environment (CODE) (Archived): Mr. Scott Wierzbanowski
3. Nethus, T.E., Schiflett, S.G., Eddy, D.R., Whitmore, J.N.: Comparative Effects of Antihistamines on Aircrew Performance of Simple and Complex Tasks Under Sustained Operations. Armstrong Laboratory, US Air Force Systems Command, AL-TR-1991-0104, December 1991.
4. Interview With Lt. Gen. David Deptula, USAF (Ret.) https://www.defensemedianetwork.com
5. Schutz, W.: The Interpersonal Underworld: FIRO A Three-Dimensional Theory of Interpersonal Behavior. Science and Behavior Books, Inc., Palo Alto (1966) (ISBN:0-8314-0011-0)
6. Schutz, W.: Beyond FIRO-B-three new theory-derived measures-element B: behavior, element f: feelings, element s: self. Psychol. Rep. **70**, 915–937 (1992)

Desirable Backrest Angles in Automated Cars

Martin Fleischer(✉) [ID] and Nikko Wendel

Chair of Ergonomics, Technical University of Munich, Boltzmannstraße 15,
85747 Garching, Germany
martin.fleischer@tum.de

Abstract. This study was conducted to explore the effects of NDRTs (nondriving related tasks) on driving posture. For references on seating postures, the seat back angle was the examined measure. The objective of this study was to conclude if certain NDRTs, like reading and eating, result in specific NDP (nondriving postures). Another aspect of this study was to compare NDPs by drivers doing the same NDRTs when a steering wheel and pedals were present to when there were none. This was done, as in future scenarios there will be no more need of steering wheels and pedals in HAD (highly automated driving) vehicles. Therefore, the seat angle of 30 participants doing ten NDRTs in a modular driving simulator were examined. All NDRTs were performed twice by the participants. Once with the steering wheel and pedals present and once without. The seat angles were collected and analysed using a 2-way factorial repeated measures ANOVA. Following that, a pairwise *t*-test was conducted to explore correlations between the NDRTs and the differences in having a steering wheel and pedals present or not. The results showed that the absence of a steering wheel and pedals did not have a significant impact on the seat angle. Whereas NDRTs showed a big influence on the seating angle, of which the NDRT "*relaxing*" resulted in the highest seat back angles and therefore had the strongest influence on the seat back angle within all tasks.

Keywords: Automated driving · Non-driving related activities · Non-driving related tasks · Human factors · Backrest · Seatback

1 Introduction

With the rise of automated driving the interior of vehicles is subjected to change. When the driver becomes a passenger, customers' needs shift from those related to the driving task to those related to non-driving activities. Being no longer optimized for the driving task the parameters of the adjustment fields of the car need to be more like those in other transportation means. Airplanes, buses, trains or luxury cars driven by professionals for the costumer can serve as role models for the designers of highly automated vehicles. If the intended use case is focusing on productivity activities, such as working with paper or with a laptop, regular office guidelines can be consulted. In trucks this might pose a feasible way. In cars the limitations in the z-axis complicate invalidate these approaches.

Besides the prominent H30 measurement for the design of vehicles, the A40 is one of the features that define the seating posture of the occupants. In accordance to [1] A40

© Springer Nature Switzerland AG 2021
C. Stephanidis et al. (Eds.): HCII 2021, CCIS 1498, pp. 521–526, 2021.
https://doi.org/10.1007/978-3-030-90176-9_67

is defined as the angle between the vertical line through the H-Point and the torso line of the driver. In conventional vehicles A40 is around 27°, in trucks the angle is sharper up to 10° [2]. Porter and Gyi [3] found that smaller participants preferred steeper backrest compared to taller persons.

[4–8] have gathered various A40s for non-driving-related activities. While [6–8] considered the relaxing activity only, [4, 5] reviewed more activities. When taking all numbers reported for sleeping and relaxing in these publications into account, it leads us to an average backrest angle of 44.7° (SD = ±16.3°). For other tasks the publications do not provide a consistent set of activities, thus the individual values are to extract from the original sources.

2 Methodology

A study with 30 participants was conducted in a simple setup (Fig. 1). One participant had to be taken from the sample. The participants were asked to perform ten non-driving related tasks (Table 1) and they got 10€ for the participation in the experiment. A conventional car seat with a H30 of 350 mm was adapted to measure A40. Similar to [9] two different scenarios were presented to the participants. One scenario included a steering wheel at the usual position in the car, the second one did not include a steering wheel at all. The participants were asked to take seat in the mock-up and perform each of the ten tasks in both scenarios. The backrest angles were adjusted by the subjects until a favorable perceived configuration was found. The A40 was then recorded and the next activity was started. The participants' height ranged from 1.60 m to 1.89 m with an average of 1.76 m (SD ± 0.07 m). The gender of the participants was not surveyed.

Fig. 1. Experimental setup scenario with steering wheel

Table 1. List of non-driving related tasks

Task	Description
Reading	Reading a magazine
Eating	Eating of a pretzel and sweets
Observing landscape	Looking around the room
Talking to another passenger	Talking to the investigator, who is sitting on the co-driver's seat
Relaxing	The participant takes a comfortable resting posture
Smartphone	Texting and surfing on the smartphone
Tablet	Playing a game on a tablet
Paperwork	Filling out a questionnaire (part 1)
Laptop	Filling out a questionnaire (part 2)
Talking on the phone	Holding the cell phone to the ear for a phone call

Two hypotheses were tested using a two-way ANOVA ($\alpha = .05$) carried out with JASP:

$H_{0,1}$: The non-driving related task has no significant influence on the backrest angle
$H_{0,2}$: The scenario has no significant influence on the backrest angle.

3 Results

The ANOVA results (see Table 2) show no significant effect of the scenario on the backrest angle. However, the tasks have a highly significant effect on A40. The mean angles and standard deviations for each task are shown in Table 3.

Table 2. ANOVA results

ANOVA - A40						
Cases	Sum of squares	df	Mean square	F	p	η^2
Task	12760.130	8	1595.016	33.737	<.001	0.346
Scenario	0.000	1	0.000	0.000	1.000	0.000
Task * Scenario	242.483	8	30.310	0.641	0.743	0.007
Residuals	23827.931	504	47.278			

Table 3. Means and standard deviations of A40 for each task

	Eating	Observing landscape	Paperwork	Reading	Relaxing	Smartphone	Tablet	Talking on the phone	Talking to another passenger
Mean A40	24.3°	25.5°	25.1°	28.2°	41.8°	29.5°	29.2°	27.8°	26.5°
SD	5.0°	4.7°	7.5°	6.6°	10.1°	6.9°	5.8°	7.4°	5.7°

Looking into the differences between the specific tasks using a Bonferroni-Corrected Post Hoc Test it can be seen that there is the consistently highly significant difference between relaxing and the other tasks as shown in (Table 4). For the other tasks only Paperwork-Smartphone (mean difference $= 4.3°$, $p = .028$), Eating-Smartphone (mean difference $= 5.2°$, $p = .002$) and Eating-Tablet (mean difference $= 4.9°$, $p = .006$) show significant differences.

Table 4. Post Hoc comparison of relaxing to the other activities

95% CI for mean difference							
	Tasks	Mean difference	Lower	Upper	SE	t	Pbonf
Relaxing	Talking to another passenger	15.3	11.3	19.3	1.277	11.991	<.001
	Observing landscape	16.3	12.3	20.2	1.277	12.734	<.001
	Paperwork	16.7	12.7	20.6	1.277	13.044	<.001
	Smartphone	12.3	8.3	16.3	1.277	9.641	<.001
	Tablet	12.6	8.6	16.6	1.277	9.871	<.001
	Talking on the phone	13.9	10.0	18.0	1.277	10.951	<.001
	Eating	17.5	13.5	21.4	1.277	13.679	<.001
	Reading	13.5	9.6	17.5	1.277	10.600	<.001

Figure 2 shows the boxplots for A40 in correlation to the tasks and without the influence of the scenario. It is to be noted that Relaxing leads to many outliers in the range between 60° and 70°.

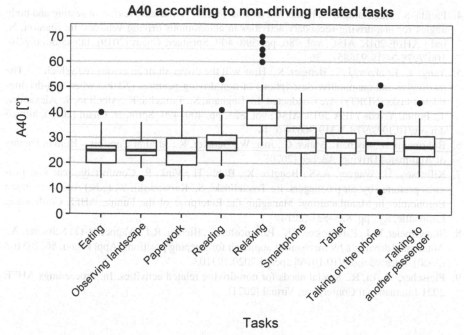

Fig. 2. Backrest angle (A40) in correlation to the non-driving related tasks performed by the particitpants

4 Discussion

Similar to the literature described, the observed A40 lies around 40° for a relaxing posture. It must be emphasized, that [5] reported angles around 60°, which can also be observed as outliers in the newly gathered data. The rather high number of outliers during Relaxing might hint to a binominal distribution as the sample gets bigger.

For the other tasks, it can be said, that the desired A40s largely show no significant differences.

Acknowledgements. This study was conducted in the context of the project INSAA funded by the Federal Ministry of Education and Research of the Federal Republic of Germany.

References

1. Human Accom and Design Devices Stds Comm. Motor Vehicle Dimensions. 400 Commonwealth Drive, Warrendale, PA, United States: SAE International. https://doi.org/10.4271/J1100_200911
2. Bubb, H., Bengler, K., Grünen, R.E., Vollrath, M.: Automobilergonomie. Springer Fachmedien Wiesbaden, Wiesbaden (2015)
3. Porter, J.M., Gyi, D.E.: Exploring the optimum driver posture for driver comfort. Int. J. Veh. Des. **19**(3), 255–266 (1998)

4. Parida, S., Mallavarapu, S., Franz, M., Abanteriba, S.: A literature review of seating and body angles for non-driving secondary activities in autonomous driving vehicles. In: Stanton, N. (ed.) AHFE 2018. AISC, vol. 786, pp. 398–409. Springer, Cham (2019). https://doi.org/10. 1007/978-3-319-93885-1_36

5. Yang, Y., Klinkner, J.N., Bengler, K.: How will the driver sit in an automated vehicle? – The qualitative and quantitative descriptions of non-driving postures (NDPs) when non-driving-related-tasks (NDRTs) Are Conducted. In: Bagnara, S., Tartaglia, R., Albolino, S., Alexander, T., Fujita, Y. (eds.) IEA 2018. AISC, vol. 823, pp. 409–420. Springer, Cham (2019). https://doi.org/10.1007/978-3-319-96074-6_44

6. Bohrmann, D., Koch, T., Maier, C., Just, W., Bengler, K.: Motion Comfort – Human Factors of Automated Driving, Aachen (2020)

7. Kilincsoy, Ü., Wagner, A.-S., Bengler, K., Bubb, H., Vink, P.: Comfortable rear seat postures preferred by car passengers. In: Trzcieliński, S., Karwowski, W. (eds.) Advances in the Ergonomics in Manufacturing: Managing the Enterprise of the Future. AHFE Conference, Louisville, Ky., pp. 823–831 (2014)

8. Stanglmeier, M.J., Paternoster, F.K., Paternoster, S., Bichler, R.J., Wagner, P.-O., Schwirtz, A.: Automated driving: a biomechanical approach for sleeping positions. Appl Ergon. **86**, 103103 (2020). https://doi.org/10.1016/j.apergo.2020.103103

9. Fleischer, M., Li, R.: Spatial needs for non-driving related activities. In: Proceedings AHFE 2021 International Conference; Virtual (2021)

Identifying Mobility Pattern of Specific User Types Based on Mobility Data

Tobias Gartner[✉], Waldemar Titov, and Thomas Schlegel

Institute of Ubiquitous Mobility Systems, Karlsruhe University of Applied Sciences,
Moltkestr. 30, 76131 Karlsruhe, Germany
iums@hs-kalrsruhe.de

Abstract. To better understand users and their information demands, it is useful to divide them into user groups. These user groups can be assigned characteristics and mobility preferences. With the help of these parameters, the individual user can be better addressed. In this work a user model was created for the commuter and validated with mobility data. Based on this model, an analysis tool for mobility data was developed. The mobility data analysis tool was designed to identify commuter routes in the dataset. The analysis tool was tested using daily mobility data collected by student in 2018 using the app "MobiDiary". The results of the analysis show that filtering the trips with the criteria "trip purpose" and "start time" can be a first approach identifying commuter trips. However, a more precise filtering of commuter routes is much more complex. The general findings of this work indicate, that the model trained on the labeled data set, where the participants provided trip purposes, needs to be aware of more parameters for being able to identify commuter trips only based on not labeled trip data.

Keywords: Mobility pattern · Mobility data · Analysis tool · User model

1 Introduction

The best possible and constant information of a user is the goal of apps for travel assistance. Particularly in local public transportation, this is an important component for increasing the attractiveness of the service. In order to be able to inform users more precisely, different user groups must be described in models. With the help of these models, the information systems can be better adapted to the users. According to the study "Mobilität in Deutschland" 23% of trips are for work and education [4]. Commuter routes are assumed to have more comparable characteristics to leisure routes, for example. Furthermore, commuters are an important user group for public transport.

Therefore, in this paper, a user model for a commuter was created. Based on this model, an analysis tool was developed to analyze mobility data and to filter commuter routes from this data. The analysis tool was then tested with mobility data from students at Karlsruhe University of Applied Sciences. Finally, these results were analyzed and discussed.

© Springer Nature Switzerland AG 2021
C. Stephanidis et al. (Eds.): HCII 2021, CCIS 1498, pp. 527–534, 2021.
https://doi.org/10.1007/978-3-030-90176-9_68

2 State of Research and Technology

2.1 Introducing Commuter Model

In order to better describe a user, it is useful to assign him or her to a user group. A user profile can then be created for these user groups, describing the characteristics and mobility preferences of this group. This profile data includes information such as demographic data, availability of and familiarity with transportation, available tickets, preferred means of transportation, preferred distances, preferred total duration, desired comfort and acceptable delay, purpose of the trip, date and time, weather, traffic situation, current schedules, luggage, fellow riders [8]. For illustration purposes, personas can also be created for the user groups, which describe this user group as an example. The described mobility preferences can also be assigned to these personas, resulting in different scenarios and use cases. This makes it possible to derive requirements for software solutions [2]. One way to create a commuter model would be to analyze smart card data. Smart cards require users to hold their card up to a terminal when entering and exiting a public transportation system. This check-in/check-out process stores when a card was held up to a terminal at which station. Here, analogous to the analysis of tourists that has already been performed, a classification of stops could be performed and thus the volume of commuters at this stop could be inferred [7]. The problem with this approach is that smart cards are not that widespread in public transportation, especially in Germany.

2.2 Introducing Mobility Data

In order to describe the user group as accurately as possible, the characteristics of these groups should be derived from as much data as possible. Electronic route diaries are ideal for this purpose. There, users can have their paths recorded via a Global Navigation Satellite System (GNSS) and specify a path purpose. Requirements for data processing are error detection and filtering of the measured data, path recognition, automatic mode recognition and user verification of the recorded paths [5]. An electronic trip diary can already be used to determine the most important mobility preferences such as the purpose of the trip, date, means of transport used, duration and distance.

3 User Model

With the help of the mobility preferences, a user model can be created for the commuter user type. This user model, shown in Fig. 1, illustrates which data can be used to describe a commuter. On the one hand, it can be viewed from the user's perspective. A lot of information can be obtained from users, especially with the help of their smartphones. Important data here are movement data from route diaries. Information about which ticket is being used can also be important. Smart cards with check-in and check-out offer very good evaluation options for public transportation. An evaluation with classic monthly and annual passes is much more difficult to implement, since not all journeys are registered here. With classic monthly and annual passes, an additional survey or an additionally kept trip diary is necessary. It is important to work out the habits of the individual user: Which route is his commuter route? At what time of day does he travel? From where to where is he traveling? What means of transport does he use? Does he have to change trains? On the other hand, information about commuters can be obtained via the infrastructure. The central question here is to work out what the destinations of commuters are. Such commuter destinations could be stops in city centers, near industrial areas or train stations. The long-term goal is to develop a system that can recognize from supplied data whether the user is a commuter. A self-learning system can link the two areas of user and infrastructure described above and classify them using the following questions: When does a commuter drive? What route does a commuter take? Which ticket does a commuter use? Where does a commuter go?

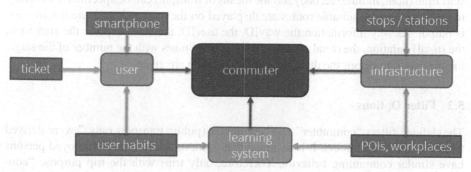

Fig. 1. Commuter model

4 Mobility Data Basis

In this work, path data from students of the Karlsruhe University of Applied Sciences from 2018 were available for the analysis. The students recorded their daily trips under two different questions. From 10.10.2018 to 16.10.2018, the students observed their general mobility behavior, and from 17.10.2018 to 23.10.2018, they were to avoid using motorized individual transport in their mobility. The routes were collected with the app "MobiDiary". This data was chosen because a unique user ID was stored here in addition to a path ID. This makes it possible to assign routes to a user. In addition to the pure route data, the routes stored via the app contain extensive information such as weather information and "nearby places" [1, 6]. "Nearby Places" refers to important locations near the GNSS coordinates. This information was not used extensively in the present work, but in the further development described in the outlook there is the possibility to include this data. In order to be able to analyze the path data in the analysis tool, they had to be converted into a certain format. After the conversion, 308 paths from 24 users were available for evaluation.

5 Analysis Tool MobiDiary

5.1 User Interface

The input menu was arranged on the left side, the map display on the right side. The user interface is built up step by step for better clarity. First, route data can be read in JSON format. After reading in, a user can visualize all paths on the map or filter the paths. Further, he gets all users with the number of paths per user output. The user can choose whether he wants to make the further filter options for all users or for a certain user. Afterwards it can be selected whether all ways of a user or all users are to be represented or a defined filter for the user type "commuter" or "commuter (only public transport)" is to be used. Alternatively, the user can set his own filter options. Here, the trip purpose, the start time (hour, minute, second) and the means of transport can be specified. According to the selection, the suitable routes are displayed on the map and the route information is output. As way information the wayID, the userID, the way purpose, the start time, the (total) duration, the (total) distance and the wayStages with the number of the stage, the means of transport, the duration and the distance are given.

5.2 Filter Options

The defined filters "commuter" and "commuter (public transport only)" were derived from the commuter model. It is assumed that trainees, students and employed persons have similar commuting behavior. Therefore, only trips with the trip purpose "education", "work" and "home" are selected. Further, commuters are assumed to travel primarily during the morning and afternoon rush hours. The rush hour times used in this tool are based on times collected in a study using smart card data. There, it was found that in the morning, the rush hour is between 6:30 and 9:30 am, and in the afternoon the time window is longer, from 4:30 to 8:00 pm [3]. However, in this tool, the time periods were adjusted to 6:00 to 10:00 in the morning and 16:00 to 20:00 in the afternoon. This adjustment was made because of the specific data used. The filter for the morning rush hour was extended to 10:00 a.m. because the start of the second lecture block is at 9:50 a.m. and trips made by students who live close to the university should also be included. In the filter "Commuter" all means of transport are shown, in the filter "Commuter (only public transport)" only the means of transport bus, streetcar, suburban railroad and subway. The criterion "ticket" described in the commuter model is not taken into account in this analysis tool.

6 Analysis of Collected Mobility Data

6.1 Hypotheses

The analysis and evaluation of the data focused on the following hypotheses:

1. The defined filters can be used to determine a user's commuting paths.
2. With the filtered paths, conclusions can be drawn about the behavior of a commuter.

6.2 Procedure

To test the hypotheses, the mobility data described above were analyzed. For this purpose, of the 24 users, the paths of the seven users with the most paths were examined in more detail. These seven users together completed 241 of the total 304 paths. It was examined in more detail, which paths were output via the filter option "all paths of the user" and which paths were output via the filter "commuter". Here it was analyzed whether and if so which paths the filter "commuter" did not select and for which reasons. For comparison, the result outputs from the analysis tool of the routes drawn in each case were compared and the criteria route purpose and start time were compared with each other. Routes that were not present in both result outputs were marked. Finally, an attempt was made to identify outbound and return trips from the commuting trip data. For this purpose, the route information was evaluated and the routes were compared on the map display. A query of path data with the commuter filter can be seen in Fig. 2.

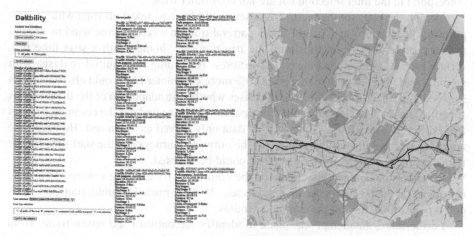

Fig. 2. Analysis tool MobiDiary

7 Results

The seven users with the most trips completed 241 of the 304 trips. Of these 241 trips, 63 trips were selected as commuter trips, representing 26.14% of the trips.

The user with the most trips completed 53 trips, of which 11 trips were selected as commuter trips by the "Commuter" filter. The user with the seventh most trips has completed only 12 trips, of which three trips were selected as commuter trips by the filter "Commuter". The proportion of commuter trips is relatively similar between 20.00% and 36.36% for all users considered.

When analyzing the selected routes, it was found that some routes with the purpose "education" or "work" were not selected as commuter routes. Here it could be determined that these routes were not selected because the start time of these routes did not fit into the specified time window of 6:00 to 10:00 and 16:00 to 20:00. However, since these routes clearly also count as commuter routes, they should also be selected by the filter. In developing the analysis tool, the "classic" commuter was initially assumed. For the "classic" commuter who travels to work in the morning and home in the afternoon, this filter would presumably provide good results. However, the data at hand are students whose commuting behavior differs from this. Students have a schedule with different times for the start and end of lectures, so commuting trips are also made during the day. In the analysis tool, only a later lecture start time of 9:50 a.m. was taken into account. Therefore, trips made by students whose lecture does not start until 11:30 or 14:00 were not selected by the filter. For this particular data set, the filter would have to be adjusted to consider these time windows as well.

Another problem is that the trip purpose "home" is used as a return trip for all other trip purposes. The filter used selects all trips with this trip purpose in the specified time window. However, these do not necessarily have to be return trips from the lecture/work. The filter incorrectly selects a certain number of trips as commuter trips, since they correspond to the filter selection but are not commuter trips.

Ideally, the filter for the present data set would have to select all trips with the trip purposes "education" and "work" and an arrival time in a certain time window around the start of lectures or all trips with the trip purpose "home" with a start time in a certain time window around the end of lectures. According to an initial analysis, with an improved filter for each user, a good 20% more commuter trips could also have been selected as such. However, the question arises whether an adaptation of the filters to this specific data set is at all reasonable. The goal should be to find out the commuter routes from different user groups. The available data only served as a first test. However, the approach of checking the arrival time for the outward journeys and the start time for the return journeys in a specific time window could be adopted.

It was also examined how many of the commuter routes were covered by public transport. Of the 63 commuter routes selected, 25 were made by public transport. This corresponds to 39.68% of the commuter routes.

Furthermore, an attempt was made to identify the outward and return routes from the route data of the commuter routes. For evaluation, the trips were sorted based on trip purpose, start time, duration, distance, and mode, and predictions were made about potential trip pairs. These predictions were verified by displaying the potential path pairs on the map in the analysis tool and comparing the paths with each other. (Shown in Figs. 3 and 4.)

Fig. 3. Outward route

Fig. 4. Return route

8 Conclusion and Outlook

In this work, an analysis tool for path data was developed from a commuter model. This tool was intended to detect commuter routes from a set of path data. The analysis of the path data showed that the user behavior of the students of the considered path data deviated from the assumptions in the commuter model. Paths that met the defined filter criteria were identified as commuter paths. However, a relatively high proportion of commuter trips were not selected in this particular data set. Furthermore, it was found that for the trip purpose "home", the criterion start time alone is not sufficient to identify return trips of commuter trips.

The first hypothesis that the defined filters can be used to identify a user's commuter routes could only be partially verified. The identification of commuters from trip data cannot be mapped by the trip purpose and start time criteria alone. An analysis tool that can identify commuter routes must be more complex in design than the present prototype. However, the analysis has provided insights to improve the analysis tool. Therefore, the second hypothesis, that filtered paths can be used to draw conclusions about a commuter's behavior, can be considered verified.

A filter for commuter trips would have to select all trips with the trip purposes "education" and "work" and an arrival time in a certain time window, respectively all trips with the trip purpose "home" with a start time in a certain time window. It should be noted that trips could not be selected because a user mistakenly entered the trip purpose "education" or "work" for the return trip instead of the trip purpose "home" when recording the trip. It could be shown that commuter routes do not necessarily have to include a public transport mode. Filtering for commuter routes that only contain means of public transport is not mandatory for identifying commuter characteristics.

A next step would be to adjust the filtering of start or arrival time. The filter can be further developed so that it can find a return trip for an outbound trip similar to the analysis performed manually. In addition to the start time, the date must also be evaluated here. Furthermore, the GNSS coordinates must be used in addition to the criteria of route length, route duration, and means of transport used. Thereby an area around start and destination could be defined. In addition to the GNSS coordinates, the "nearby places" stored in the route data could also be used. "Nearby Places" are used to compensate for inaccuracies in GNSS coverage by evaluating the "nearby Places" of the start and destination points of the paths in addition to the GNSS coordinates. A corridor can be defined between the start and destination areas along the as the crow flies line between the areas. This corridor would allow a user to not necessarily use the same route on both paths.

References

1. Böhm, F., et al.: Toolbox for analysis and evaluation of low-emission urban mobility. In: Krömker, H. (ed.) HCII 2020. LNCS, vol. 12213, pp. 145–160. Springer, Cham (2020). https://doi.org/10.1007/978-3-030-50537-0_12
2. Keller, C., Titov, W., Schlegel, T.: SmartMMI Analyseergebnisse. Modell- und kontextbasierte Mobilitätsinformationen auf Smart Public Displays und Mobilgeräten im Öffentlichen Verkehr. Hg. v. Hochschule Karlsruhe – Technik und Wirtschaft (HSKA). Institut für Ubiquitäre Mobilitätssysteme (IUMS). Karlsruhe. Online verfügbar unter (2018). https://smartmmi.de/smartmmi-leaflet-analyseergebnisse/. zuletzt geprüft am 18 Dec 2020
3. Lathia, N., Froehlich, J., Capra, L.: Mining public transport usage for personalised intelligent transport systems. In: 2010 IEEE 10th International Conference on Data Mining (ICDM), Sydney, Australia, 13 December 2010–17 December 2010, pp. 887–892. IEEE (2010)
4. Nobis, C., Kuhnimhof, T.: Mobilität in Deutschland – MiD. Ergebnisbericht. BMVI, infas, DLR, IVT, infas 360. Bonn, Berlin (2018). Online verfügbar unter http://www.mobilitaet-in-deutschland.de/pdf/MiD2017_Ergebnisbericht.pdf. zuletzt geprüft am 10 Jan 2021
5. Stephan, K., Köhler, K., Heinrichs, M., Berger, M., Platzer, M., Selz, E.: Das Elektronische Wegetagebuch – Chancen und Herausforderungen einer Automatisierten Wegeerfassung Intermodaler Wege. In: Schelewsky, M., Jonuschat, H., Bock, B., Stephan, K. (eds.) Smartphones unterstützen die Mobilitätsforschung, pp. 25–45. Springer, Wiesbaden (2014). https://doi.org/10.1007/978-3-658-01848-1_3
6. Trefzger, M., Titov, W., Keller, C., Böhm, F., Schlegel, T.: A Context Aware Evaluation Tool for Individual Mobility. Karlsruhe University of Applied Sciences, Moltkestr. 30, 76133 Karlsruhe, Germany. Institute of Ubiquitous Mobility Systems (2019)
7. Xue, M., Wu, H., Chen, W., Goh, G.H.: Identifying tourists from public transport commuters. In: Macskassy, S. (Hg.) Proceedings of the 20th ACM SIGKDD International Conference on Knowledge Discovery and Data Mining, New York, NY, USA, 24–27 August 2014, KDD. Association for Computing Machinery; ACM SIGKDD International Conference on Knowledge Discovery and Data Mining; Annual ACM SIGKDD Conference, pp. 1779–1788. ACM, New York (2014)
8. Entwicklung kontextadaptiver Erfassungsmethoden von Mobilitätspräferenzen der Fahrgäste im öffentlichen Verkehr. Karlsruhe University of Applied Sciences, Moltkestr. 30, 76133 Karlsruhe, Germany. Institute of Ubiquitous Mobility Systems (2020)

How to Find My Ride? Results of an HCI Expert Workshop for AR-Aided Navigation

Fabian Hub[1]([✉]) and Michael Oehl[2]

[1] German Aerospace Center (DLR), Rutherfordstraße 2, 12489 Berlin, Germany
fabian.hub@dlr.de
[2] German Aerospace Center (DLR), Lilienthalplatz 7, 38108 Braunschweig, Germany
michael.oehl@dlr.de

Abstract. In order to increase acceptance of automated mobility on-demand (AMoD) it is essential to provide high usability along the whole user journey. The user's challenges of getting to flexible pick-up locations and the identification of the booked shuttle need to be addressed from a user-centered perspective. A workshop was conducted with HCI experts to create user-centered smartphone interface design solutions and elicit means of augmented reality (AR) for three scenarios: 1) navigation to the pick-up location, 2) identifying the pick-up location, and 3) identifying the SAV. Post-hoc fundamental AR information elements that provide users with high usability to overcome the aforementioned challenges were identified and visualized. Results of the workshop serve as a starting point to iteratively develop AR-aided user interfaces of virtual ride access points that cover the user journey of AMoD.

Keywords: Virtual ride access point · Automated mobility on-demand · User-centered design

1 Introduction

1.1 Motivation

In future mobility, the transition from conventional fixed route public transportation to demand responsive transportation solutions, like on-demand ride pooling (ODRP), is a foreseeable scenario. Especially, in combination with shared automated vehicles (SAV) ride pooling services show great potential in terms of reduced resource consumption, traffic congestion, and convenience for its customers [1, 2]. These innovative forms of automated mobility on-demand (AMoD) services are characterized by the utilization of flexible pick-up locations that are set up spontaneously by the service providers' algorithms when customers book a ride [3].

New requirements in terms of human-computer interaction (HCI) and user experience of the novel mobility service arise. Research has shown that predominantly usability aspects of the vehicle are critical for user acceptance of automated mobility on-demand [4]. However, in order for AMoD to be utilized by the majority of the users addressed,

© Springer Nature Switzerland AG 2021
C. Stephanidis et al. (Eds.): HCII 2021, CCIS 1498, pp. 535–542, 2021.
https://doi.org/10.1007/978-3-030-90176-9_69

it is essential to provide high usability along the whole user journey. This paper focuses on information that needs to be provided to users of AMoD prior to boarding the SAV. It is crucial that the user's challenge of getting to flexible pick-up locations and the identification of the booked SAV are also addressed from a user-centered perspective.

Taking these aspects into consideration the concept of virtual ride access points (VRAP), as a specific form of smartphone HCI with means of augmented reality (AR) in the context of AMoD, helps users to seamlessly encounter the SAV at flexible pick-up locations. An early stage prototype of a VRAP had been introduced in a previous user study and meaningfulness of the HCI concept was evaluated positively [5].

However, it remains unclear which exact AR information items are helpful to users to master the aforementioned challenges most efficiently. By conducting a workshop with HCI experts the authors were able to identify fundamental AR information elements that help users to overcome specific pain points in the AMoD user journey prior SAV boarding, i.e., navigation to the flexible pick-up location and identification of pick-up location and identification of SAV.

1.2   Virtual Ride Access Points and Augmented Reality

The concept of VRAP is of importance when users of ODRP are guided to a pick-up location to await the shuttle. In pooled ride situations vehicles are dispatched in real time to pick-up/drop-off customers at flexible locations. Fares are bundled in one vehicle and routes are adjusted accordingly. Customers have to walk the first and last part of the journey and share the same vehicle with other customers who want to go into similar direction. Providers try to balance efficient pooling and vehicle detours.

As users book a ride with a smartphone, the ODRP provider determines a pick-up location and shuttle. The users receive information about the vehicle (e.g., plate number, vehicle type), the pick-up time, and are guided by information on the smartphone to the meeting point to board the shuttle. There is no physical cue to identify the flexible pick-up location on site. When arrived at the meeting point, the user is awaiting the vehicle to get picked-up. Already at the beginning of the user journey three main challenges arise for the user: firstly, to navigate to the pick-up location; secondly, to identify the exact meeting point where the user can expect the vehicle to stop; and, thirdly, to identify the right pick-up vehicle. It is likely that the user is in a foreign city and has to solve the tasks under time pressure. All challenges are common in state of the art ODRP services with flexible pick-up locations and are expected to become even more difficult with the deployment of SAVs.

By providing users of AMoD with meaningful information elements in reference to the street environment VRAPs will address the aforementioned challenges with means of AR. Human-centered design of AR interfaces for smartphones will potentially lead to more efficient information processing for the user. A more efficient solving of the given tasks, due to more efficient information processing, will foster usability of AMoD services. This work gives insights into results of an HCI expert workshop that aimed to generate basic AR information elements of VRAPs.

2 Method

2.1 Participants

In order to further develop an early stage VRAP prototype and gain understanding about which information information elements should be presented to the user with means of AR an expert workshop was conducted. Due to the covid-19 pandemic the workshop was conducted online with a browser-based collaboration tool and video conferencing software. 11 experts (4 female) from the domain of human-computer interaction (HCI) and computer science participated in this workshop. All participants had an affiliation to the German Aerospace Center (DLR) and conducted their respective work within the context of transportation systems and automated vehicles. Age (21–46 years; M = 31.64; SD = 7.95) and vocational experiences (about 1 to 18 years; M = 5.27; SD = 5.48) varied widely among the participants. The group can be considered as semi-heterogeneous as attendees academic backgrounds varied: three participants had a degree in computer science, four in psychology, two in human factors, and one in engineering. One undergraduate student was part of the workshop, too. Three workshop participants had experience with ODRP services themselves. All participants were familiar with the concept of VRAPs.

2.2 Procedure

Goal of the workshop was to conceptualize a possible AR solution for hand held devices (HHD) from a human-centered point of view. The AR solution eventually should provide users of automated ODRP with efficient information and high usability. The workshop was held on two days with the duration of about two hours on each day. The agenda was structured into four chapters. Each chapter had specific goals and specific methods of convergent and divergent thinking. All used methods were design thinking related and participants were engaged to work collaboratively within small groups [6].

The first part of the workshop focused on facilitating the participants with a deep understanding of the research topic of VRAP design. Personas of typical ODRP users, considerably early adopters, were presented. Furthermore, the user journey of ODRP, from booking a ride until entering the vehicle, was outlined. Information requirements and pain points from user's perspectives were portrayed and existing interface solutions (smartphone screenshots of various ODRP provider apps) were shown. This approach was chosen to highlight applied information strategies and state of the art HCI in the context of ODRP services.

In the second part participants were split up into three similar sized groups and focused on synthesizing key aspects from an HCI perspective of the before presented subject matter. Goal of this phase was for each group to determine relevant user pain points in each user journey scenario. The scenarios were the following: 1) navigation to the pick-up location, 2) identifying the pick-up location, and 3) identifying the SAV.

In the following part, solutions for the previously identified user pain points were sought. The method of 6-3-5 brain writing was adapted to the workshop conditions [7]. Consequently, all ideas were grouped, clustered and presented in the plenary.

The next part of workshop focused on idea selection and rapid prototyping [8]. Each group was assigned to focus on one scenario. The groups selected the most valuable ideas in terms of desirability for the user, feasibility, and radicality. Low-fidelity prototypes were created, using the online collaboration tool. Predefined smartphone wireframe templates with AR-view simulation of the respective scenario were given. With this approach a quick visualization of the generated ideas was possible. Finally, all low-fidelity prototypes were presented in the plenary.

Subsequently to the expert workshop, all prototype sketches and ideas were analyzed post-hoc. Basic AR information elements were extracted for every single scenario. By following this approach, a profound understanding of expedient HCI strategies for each scenario was gained. Visual HCI strategies for displayed information were determined. To eventually assure congruent HCI solutions, all scenarios were taken into consideration. Differences of AR information elements were discussed with participants of each workshop group in order to assure that user pain points were addressed properly. Essential AR interface elements that help to master the user pain points efficiently were realized for each scenario with basic geometric abstraction and rapid prototyping manner.

3   Results

3.1   Scenario 1: Navigation to the Pick-Up Location

The first scenario addressed was the user wanting to navigation to the pick-up location. Assuming being in a foreign city the determined user pain points in this scenario were identification of the correct direction and walking to the pick-up location effortlessly. Key aspect in this scenario is the fact that the user needs to find the pick-up location under time pressure on a first try, otherwise the SAV could be missed. Accordingly, the HCI solution should foster awareness regarding correct/incorrect orientation and provide information about which way the user should go efficiently. Other information like, pick-up time and distance to pick-up location and whether the user will make it in time were also identified to be necessary. The group came up with two AR interface solutions to solve the user pain points.

A first AR solution focused on providing familiar navigation system elements in AR. The prototype mainly showed the direct path that users would have to walk to reach their pick-up location. The whole sidewalk which was shown through the smartphone was highlighted. The next turning point at an intersection close by was indicated with a symbol pointing in the turning direction, also showing distance information. Orientation was shown permanently with an arrow on the bottom of the screen. Additionally, users would be warned if they are deviating from ideal path or may arrive lately at the pick-up location (e.g., by change of pathway color from blue to red).

Another AR solution was inspired by video game analogies and showed an AR overlay-like frame on the smartphone screen. This prototype focused specifically on solving the orientation issue users have when located in a foreign city. By distinctive frame coloring and use of symbols the user would notice intuitively whether he/she is on the right path (green = follow this direction; red + arrow = turn). The distance to the next turn and next turning direction was shown. Goal of both HCI concepts was to provide the users with information intuitively so they would also take down their smartphone while walking.

After analyzing both prototype sketches, basic information elements for AR implementation derived. Each element can be seen as standalone solutions to solve the navigation task. The following three AR information elements were determined: 1) orientation element (i.e., a compass like function to show direction to the user), 2) path element (i.e., directly showing the straight way to walk), 3) node element (i.e., showing where and in which direction to turn next). Other information such as pick-up address, remaining time and distance were identified to be sufficiently realizable with conventional interface design (see Fig. 1).

Fig. 1. AR information elements to navigate to the pick-up location (in blue). From left to right: orientation, path, node. (Color figure online)

3.2 Scenario 2: Identification of the Pick-Up Location

The second scenario assessed was identifying the pick-up location in the roadside environment. The group identified the challenge of clear identification of the position where the user will be picked-up by the SAV. Especially, the pain point of being uncertain whether he/she is positioned correctly, which could potentially cause missing the SAV, was determined. The idea to virtually show the stop location and allow bidirectional communication to assure certainty was targeted by the group. A low fidelity prototype combined display of information with gamification aspects. The position of the pick-up location was presented with a huge cone shaped object in the street. The color of the object would turn green when the user arrives. The user could also ask "am I right?" and will be assured to be positioned correctly (e.g., by comparison of GPS data). Additionally, the system would reward the user with virtual credits when arriving in time. Purpose of the credits was not defined further.

The subsequent discussion focused on the display of information. Four basic information elements were identified. Again, each AR element can be seen as standalone solutions to solve the task of identifying the pick-up location. The basic AR information elements are: 1) orientation element (i.e., showing the direction to the pick-up location), 2) area on the floor (i.e., showing the location by highlighting the floor), 3) floating symbol (i.e., showing the pick-up location from afar), 4) 3D object (i.e., to identify the pick-up location with object analogies). Again, other information such as remaining time and distance for pick-up were identified to be sufficiently realizable with conventional interface design (see Fig. 2).

Fig. 2. AR information elements to identify the pick-up location (in blue). From left to right: orientation, area on the floor, floating symbol, 3D object. (Color figure online)

3.3 Scenario 3: Identification of the SAV

The third group focused on the scenario of identifying the SAV. In this scenario the determined user pain point was confusion which vehicle to board in case when multiple similar looking SAVs (e.g., same AMoD service provider) are stopping at the pick-up location or just are around. Given information of vehicle number plate was seen as not efficient and users could mistakenly board the wrong vehicle and miss the actual SAV.

Therefore, pairing of vehicle and smartphone by highlighting the correct SAV through the smartphone AR interface was targeted. In one approach the whole vehicle was illuminated digitally to stand out. In a second approach personalized information (e.g., initial letters of the user) were floating above the SAV. A third approach highlighted the door to board the correct vehicle. An arrow would show up in all prototype sketches to give orientation to the user if the device was not pointed at the SAV.

Analysis of the prototypes lead to the identification of four types of information elements. The basic AR information elements to identify and board the right SAV are: 1) orientation element (i.e., showing the direction to the SAV), 2) vehicle highlighter (i.e., the vehicle is directly highlighted), 3) vehicle stopping area (i.e., the position where the vehicle will stop is highlighted on the street), 4) customer boarding area (i.e., the position where the user can directly board the SAV is highlighted on the sidewalk). Other information such as remaining time for pick-up, number plate and picture of the shuttle were identified to be sufficiently realizable with conventional interface design (see Fig. 3).

Fig. 3. AR information elements to identify the SAV (in blue). From left to right: orientation, vehicle highlighter, vehicle stopping are, customer boarding area. (Color figure online)

4 Discussion

4.1 Discussion of the Results

An expert workshop was conducted aiming to elaborate on user-centered HCI and AR interface design of VRAPs. Understanding about which fundamental AR information elements need to be presented to the users was gained. Information concepts for three specific AMoD user journey scenarios were created in small groups. AR functionality fostered new and different approaches to VRAP design. Building on the groups' initial concepts, basic information elements for high usability were identified post-hoc.

Concluding, orientation information was consistent throughout all scenarios. Other information elements were rather specific for each use case, but main information strategies that promised high usability were distilled. Information that needs reference to the environment was considered beneficial to be displayed in AR. With the results an early stage VRAP concept can be iterated to cover all scenarios of the AMoD user journey.

Overall, the workshop succeeded in working out fundamental AR information elements that provide high usability for users of AMoD.

4.2 Limitations and Further Research

The workshop based on an early stage VRAP design prototype and results of interviews with users of ODRP (early adopter). Accordingly, a very selective group of users was chosen to look at and, hence, no generalizability of the determined user pain points can be made. Real users were not involved to check on assumptions or clarify questions during the workshop. Only three participants had experienced ODRP services before. However, this approach did fit the purpose of a user-centered design. Another limitation to the results is the focus on visual information elements. Although the groups developed holistic approaches during rapid prototyping, synthesis of AR components was prioritized. Other aspects like communication strategies with the service, gamification, personalization or behavior of an interface like right/wrong feedback were not further elaborated. This workshop's goal was to generate AR information elements of an HCI interface for HHD. Further valuable facets for VRAP design that the experts conceptualized should be tackled in later development phases.

Single use of identified AR information elements is helpful to the users. However, it is expected that combination of certain information elements will further increase usability. Therefore, further research needs to be conducted to identify combinations and density of presented information elements for efficient HCI. Eventually, a real-life exposure study needs to be conducted in order to evaluate the AR interface against conventional smartphone interface solutions that are currently used by ODRP providers.

4.3 Conclusion

With the aim of developing an AR-aided HCI concept for smartphones to provide users of AMoD with information efficiently, an expert workshop was conducted. Three scenarios of the user journey of ODRP were investigated and essential AR information elements were identified: 1) navigation to the pick-up location (identified elements: orientation, path, node, 2) identifying the pick-up location (identified elements: orientation, area on the floor, floating symbol, 3D object), and 3) identifying the SAV (identified elements: orientation, vehicle highlighter, vehicle stopping are, customer boarding area). Consequently, basic visualization of each element was realized in form of smartphone wireframes. Workshop findings help to further investigate on AR-aided user interfaces of VRAPs.

References

1. Ke, J., Yang, H., Zheng, Z.: On ride-pooling and traffic congestion. Transp. Res. Part B Methodol. **142**, 213–231 (2020). https://doi.org/10.1016/j.trb.2020.10.003
2. Salonen, A., Haavisto, N.: Towards autonomous transportation. passengers' experiences, perceptions and feelings in a driverless shuttle bus in Finland. Sustainability **11**(3), 588 (2019). https://doi.org/10.3390/su11030588
3. Hahn, A., Pakusch, C., Stevens, G.: HMD Praxis der Wirtschaftsinformatik **57**(2), 348–365 (2020). https://doi.org/10.1365/s40702-020-00589-9
4. Distler, V., Lallemand, C., Bellet, T.: Acceptability and acceptance of autonomous mobility on demand. In: Mandryk, R., Hancock, M., Perry, M., Cox, A. (eds.) The 2018 CHI Conference, Montreal QC, Canada, pp. 1–10 (2018). https://doi.org/10.1145/3173574.3174186
5. Hub, F., Wilbrink, M., Kettwich, C., Oehl, M.: Designing Ride Access Points for Shared Automated Vehicles - An Early Stage Prototype Evaluation. In: Stephanidis, C., Antona, M., Ntoa, S. (eds.) HCII 2020. CCIS, vol. 1294, pp. 560–567. Springer, Cham (2020). https://doi.org/10.1007/978-3-030-60703-6_72
6. Tschimmel, K.: Design thinking as an effective toolkit for innovation. In: ISPIM Conference Proceedings, p. 1 (2012)
7. Rohrbach, B.: Kreative nach regeln: Methode 635, eine neue Technik zum Lösen von Problemen. Absatzwirtschaft **12**, 73–75 (1969)
8. Hardtke, F.: Rapid prototyping for user-friendly and useful human machine interfaces. In: Proceedings of SIMTECT 2001, Simulation Industry Association of Australia (2001)

Smart Mobility: How Jakarta's Developing Sustainable Transportation to Connect the Community

Mohammad Jafar Loilatu[1]([⊠]) [iD], Dyah Mutiarin[1] [iD], Achmad Nurmandi[1] [iD], Tri Sulistyaningsih[2] [iD], and Salahudin[2] [iD]

[1] Department of Government Affairs and Administration, Jusuf Kalla School of Government, Universitas Muhammadiyah Yogyakarta, Bantul, Indonesia
[2] Department of Government Studies, Universitas Muhammadiyah Malang, Malang, Indonesia

Abstract. This paper aims to analyze the implementation of Trans-Jakarta (Bus Rapid Transit) in realizing smart, sustainable transportation. As a strategic area of mobility in Jakarta is very high, with community productivity reaching 71%, another factor that causes Jakarta's density is the number of private vehicles. Intelligent transportation management deploys APS to ICT and infrastructure. The research uses a qualitative approach by analyzing the amount of infrastructure, and this theory of approach is seen as growth and phenomenon. Based on the analysis results, the study responded that the increase in BRT Jakarta users' number is based on improved infrastructure and integrated planning. The number of BRT Jakarta users in 2015 (102,950,384), 2016 (12,3706,857), 2017 (1 44,859,912), 2018 (178,565,827) and 2019 (265,160,290). The procurement of BRT Jakarta infrastructure encourages an increase in BRT users, restricting private transportation, and the separation of routes between BRT and private transportation with a route range from 280.5 km^2 to 438.8 km^2 encouraging people to switch to using BRT. The increasing number of BRT users has a correlation between social sustainability and smart mobility, where both influence each other if the infrastructure is adequate so that the community can choose which route to go.

Keywords: Smart transportation · Sustainable transportation · Smart mobility · Trans-Jakarta

1 Introduction

The population density in Jakarta results in high mobility of the community. The mobility is based on Jakarta's people's age of productivity, meaning most Jakarta residents work outside the home. Based on the bps report of household work, as many as 1.9 million people while 1.7 million people have not worked, meaning more than 10.4596 work outside the home. Work activities in Jakarta are done outside the home, so they use transportation to do activities. However, not all workers in Jakarta use public transportation as means of transportation. Based on the bps report, the number of vehicles

C. Stephanidis et al. (Eds.): HCII 2021, CCIS 1498, pp. 543–551, 2021.
https://doi.org/10.1007/978-3-030-90176-9_70

registered in Jakarta is dominated by motorcycles as much as 13 million or 73.92%, passenger car usage is 3.5 million units or 19.58%, while special vehicles are only 0.79% (katadata.com).

Jakarta's productive age causes high mobility, 71% of productive age consisting of 5.22 million women, 5.24 million men. The density factor is also caused by the number of private transportation in Jakarta. The number of private vehicles passing through Jakarta every day reaches 20 million, while Jakarta's population is only 10 million. There are 3.5 million cars, 13.3 million motorcycles, and 4.7 million special vehicles passing through Jakarta. Jakarta's high population, with a small area as a province, and high private transportation users result in overcrowding and congestion in Jakarta.

Addressing the increasing population and faster mobility of the community, the Jakarta Government provides public transportation to overcome traffic density, air pollution, and community mobility. Mass transportation such as Bus Rapid Transit (BRT), Light Rapid Transit (LRT), and Mass Rapid Transit (MRT). BRT is a transportation system with shorter mileage and fewer passenger capacity than LRT or MRT with a large capacity with transportation types such as trains. BRT in Jakarta has been operated since 2004. However, the people do not request experienced challenges, starting with the management system, bus quality, range of operations and infrastructure that does not support, so this transportation of Jakarta, so the People of Jakarta prefer private transportation that is comfortable and safe even though it takes time. BRT is intended for Jakarta to move from private transportation to public transportation and reduce Jakarta's increased air pollution.

Jakarta's transportation management has progressed, starting with policy synchronizing between private transportation users and applying odd-even systems for people to take advantage of public transportation. Good infrastructure starts with rest area, information center, disability access, cleanliness, the accuracy of the schedule, and good information delivery supporting BRT Jakarta transportation to be better and increasing the number of Jakarta transportation users. In 2019, Jakarta was named one of the cities with the best transportation innovation system globally. The governance between Jakarta Transportation and the Jakarta Government became one of Jakarta's drivers, named the city with the best transportation innovation. Similarly, in 2020 Jakarta was awarded as a city with innovative public transportation, meaning that Jakarta has received two transportation awards. Smart transportation developed by the Jakarta Government has created a new Jakarta society culture so that public transportation users in Jakarta increase. This study aims to see Bus Rapid Transit (BRT) Jakarta's development in realizing intelligent, sustainable transportation. Jakarta is a strategic area, the center of government, economy, and industry so that the mobility of the community is high and results in congestion and population density.

2   Overview of the Literature Review

Smart transportation as a traditional transportation solution, promoting modern transportation using information communication and technology [1], technology becomes a determinant factor in sustainable transposase. As modern transportation, sustainable transportation is designed with the community's socio-culture [2], to that sustainable transportation can answer the publicity in the city. By definition, research on intelligent transportation is defined as; intelligent transport system ITS [3, 4], which becomes a model of sustainable public transportation, or as future public transportation by understanding the socio-culture conditions of society and change [5]. Sustainable transportation is designed to be integrated with public infrastructure [6]. Through a control system conducted by public transportation service providers [7] and ensuring services on public transportation run well, it is necessary to maintain a public transportation system [8]; the services provided can be categorized as sustainable transportation. In recent studies, sustainable transportation was developed to reduce, emission, and impact public transportation [9]. Furthermore, as public transportation, sustainable transportation is designed for friendly and comfortable public transportation [10].

Other aspects that encourage sustainable transportation are infrastructure; sustainable transportation planning needs to see roads, routes, stops sidewalks, and other supporting facilities [11]. Smart transportation does not stand alone needs a transportation integration system with other supporting infrastructure [12]. [13] The jam was ICT as a tool to integrate the transportation infrastructure [13], such as location termination, traffic light, electronic road directions, CCTV, and internet connection through project sustainable transportation management. Peng et al. (2017) intelligent transportation infrastructure such as; mobile connected vehicles, intelligent buses, and intelligent traffic lights; besides, transportation infrastructure includes; length of the transportation network and the division of bus lanes stops [15]. This infrastructure is a physical form on the road to facilitate the activity of public transportation. It is not included in the infrastructure IoT or ICT Transportation infrastructure functions to directly integrate services, thus smart transportation to solve congestion and traffic density [16].

3 Method

This study uses a descriptive qualitative approach by analyzing Trans-Jakarta's annual report. This approach was chosen to describe the intelligent transportation model developed. This study describes sustainable transportation based on the framework [17], using agency reports Trans-Jakarta or secondary data [18]. The findings are elaborated with the concept of sustainable transportation.

4 Finding and Discussion

Public transportation is a sustainable transportation model, innovative transportation design Jakarta (BRT) to integrate with other transportation modes such as commuter line, rapid mass transit, and light rapid transit. Currently, Jakarta has developed mass transportation to reduce the congestion and congestion on the road. Through the development of transportation by increasing the amount of infrastructure and cooperating with public transportation service providers. In 2004 Jakarta developed public transportation that connects one point to another with close mileage to introduce trans Jakarta or Bus Rapid Transit (BRT). In five years, Trans-Jakarta developed BRT Jakarta to solve congestion problems and the use of private transportation. From 2014 the number of Trans-Jakarta infrastructure procurement is still low, and there has been an increase starting in 2015, with the number of procurements reaching 369 procurement consisting of infrastructure procurement and services.

The number of procurement as part of public transportation infrastructure, the number as one of the benchmarks in sustainable transportation, with consistent procurement, can be predicted [19, 20] addition of transportation infrastructure to facilitate Trans-Jakarta users. To promote sustainable transportation, infrastructure aspects such as ICT and logistics [1], or smart infrastructure [6].

Consistent procurement of goods and services conducted by Trans-Jakarta encouraged increased Trans-Jakarta users in the last five years. In 2014, Trans-Jakarta (11,969,896), 2015 (102,950,384), 2016 (123,706,857) 2017 (144,869,779), 2018 (118,933,489), 2019 (246,653,712). within five years, Trans-Jakarta users increased from the growth of the use every year. The increase in Transjakarta customers encouraged the community's changes and behavior and switched to using public transportation. Besides the increase in Transjakarta users each month, the picture below shows the increase of Transjakarta customers every month in the last five years. The increase explains that technology is the dominant factor for improving transportation users (Figs. 1 and 2).

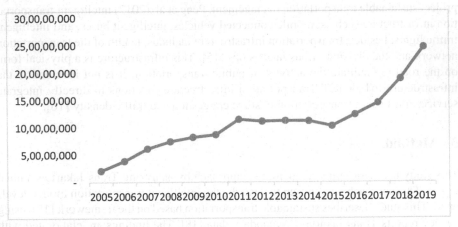

Fig. 1. Trans-Jakarta users year 2005–2019. Source: Trans-Jakarta, 2020.

The innovation of services provided by Trans-Jakarta and the Government of DKI Jakarta by changing the infrastructure of roads, pedestrians, bus stops, wayfinding has attracted Jakarta's interest to switch to using environmentally friendly transportation. One of them is by providing free services for public transportation users with special service categories, the goal is for people with specific routes to enjoy the free service, in addition to the trans-Jakarta holidays and religions provide free transportation services; length of the transportation network, division of bus lines [15] (Fig. 3).

Trans-Jakarta in 2015 coverage is only (280.5 km^2) from Jakarta area of (661.5 km^2). In 2016 (361.7 km^2) 2017 (394.6 km^2), and 2018 to (438.4 km^2). Trans-Jakarta's wider reach shows that Trans-Jakarta users are thorough, calling it an inclusive service; every one with different backgrounds feels inclusive service. In 2019 Trans-Jakarta's reach became (5046 km^2) with Trans-Jakarta population coverage in the last three years of

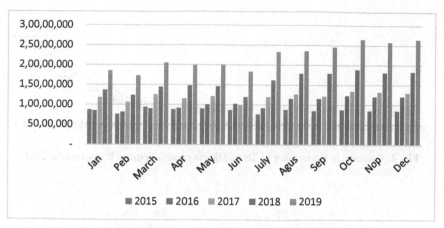

Fig. 2. Number of Trans-Jakarta users in five years. Source: Trans-Jakarta, 2019.

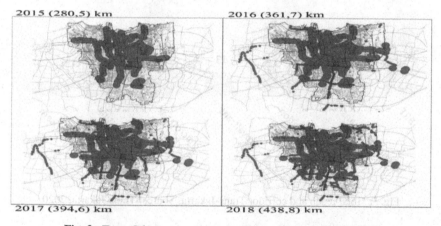

Fig. 3. Trans-Jakarta coverage area. Source: Trans-Jakarta, 2020.

2017 (62%), 2018 (67%), 2019 (83%), from Trans-Jakarta passenger coverage, Trans-Jakarta users in the last five years have increased to reach the population of Jakarta (10.57 million), the increase is an integrated form of service and using the modern infrastructure (Fig. 4).

The area of Trans-Jakarta coverage and the number of Trans-Jakarta routes in the last four years, and the number of routes since 2004–2019. From 2004–2014 the addition of low routes did not reach 50 routes, but that number rose in the last five years of 2015 the number of routes increased (39), 2016 (80), 2017 (109), 2018 (160), and 2019 (247). In 2017 the number of routes rose to 109 and increased by 100% in 2019 with the number of routes (247), the addition of routes, and the expansion of trans-Jakarta routes from both data related to the addition of transportation infrastructure, consisting of stops, integration routes, and corridors [11], with the benefit of the transportation integration system (Fig. 5).

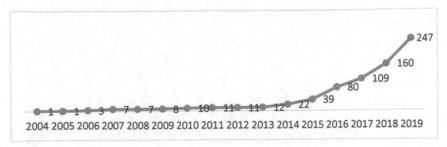

Fig. 4. Increase in the number of Trans-Jakarta routes. Source: Trans-Jakarta, 2020

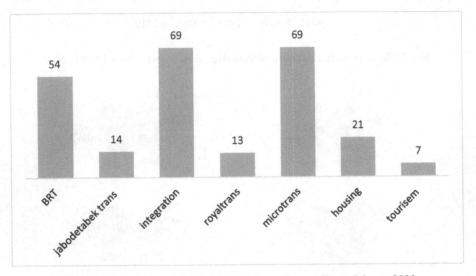

Fig. 5. Total reach and corridor Trans-Jakarta. Source: Trans-Jakarta, 2020.

Trans-Jakarta coverage the number of reaches determines the number of Trans-Jakarta passengers; from the chart, the range with the largest number is Micro-trans (69) and Integration (69), both BRT (54), flats (21), Royal-trans (14), Jabodetabek (13), Tourist Transportation (7). The number of reaches based on stop and stop location, in the chart below, is the accumulation of Trans-Jakarta coverage in recent years. Trans-Jakarta is time transportation with a smaller size than MRT or LRT with more cargo capacity, but the Trans-Jakarta model is designed to connect with strategic locations that are not too far from each other. The service is a grouping based on Trans-Jakarta users' purpose; with an integrated transportation system and using one trip one pay, Trans-Jakarta strives to take line connecting Jakarta's life (Fig. 6).

The Government of DKI Jakarta uses CCTV to secure and supervise public activities, including transportation mobility. CCTV in Jakarta is managed by 17 different organizations, including CCTV public transport. CCTV transport Jakarta is divided into four, namely, Trans-Jakarta, department of transportation, IBS, and Forte; besides, the

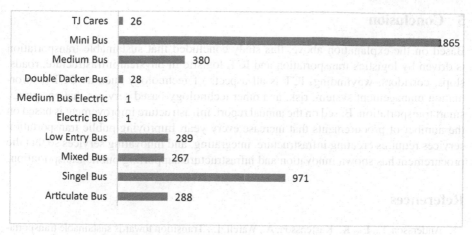

Fig. 6. Number of Trans-Jakarta fleet by buss type. Source: Trans-Jakarta, 2020.

Government of Jakarta also cooperates with CCTV service providers to monitor conditions in Jakarta. The operators with the highest number of CCTV are Bali Tower with the number (4373), IBS (746), Forte (706), Mitral (689), Delta Art Star (184), and department of transportation (180). CCTV installed by operators surrounds Jakarta with strategic areas such as highways, offices, buildings, and other public facilities. CCTV distribution in Jakarta, based on the overall CCTV distribution map then there is (7723) CCTV with active (7069) and non-active (680). Sustainable public transportation model using surveillance system through ICT [7], and transportation information system management [8] thus the service leads to sustainable service by connecting people from one point to another [9] (Fig. 7).

Fig. 7. Distribution of CCTV Jakarta and Trans-Jakarta. Source: Smart City Jakarta, 2020.

CCTV other providers also support the distribution of CCTV Transportation Jakarta. Therefore the information is not only equalized by the trans-Jakarta transportation supervisory camera but also others. This function shows that ICT infrastructure is the primary driver of intelligent transportation [16]. Therefore public transportation needs to combine two or more aspects to fructified sustainable services [2] and ITS system [3, 4].

5 Conclusion

Based on the explanation above, this study concluded that sustainable transportation is driven by logistics transportation and ICT, logistic in physical infrastructure, roads, stops, corridors, wayfinding. ICT is all aspects of technology such as CCTV, information management system, risk, and other technology-based services that encourage smart transportation. Based on the annual report, infrastructure improvement is based on the number of procurements that increase every year. Improving public transportation services requires creating infrastructure, integrating, and innovating services so that the procurement has shown innovation and infrastructure supporting public transportation.

References

1. Andersson, L., Ek, K., Kastensson, Å., Wårell, L.: Transition towards sustainable transportation – What determines fuel choice? Transp. Policy **90**, 31–38 (2020). https://doi.org/10.1016/j.tranpol.2020.02.008
2. van den Buuse, D., Kolk, A.: An exploration of smart city approaches by international ICT firms. Technol. Forecast. Soc. Change **142**, 220–234 (2019). https://doi.org/10.1016/j.techfore.2018.07.029
3. Khazraeian, S., Hadi, M.: Intelligent transportation systems in future smart cities. In: Sustainable Interdependent Netwokrs III, Studies in Systems and Network, Decision and Control, vol. 186, pp. 109–120 (2019)
4. Mohanty, S.P., Choppali, U.: Everything you wanted to know about smart cities: the internet of things is the backbone. IEEE Consum. Electron. Mag. **5**(3), 60–70 (2018)
5. Batty, M., Axhausen, K.W., Giannotti, F., Pozdnoukhov, A., Bazzani, A.: Smart cities of the future. Eur. Phys. J. Spec. Top. **518**(214), 481–518 (2012). https://doi.org/10.1140/epjst/e2012-01703-3
6. Chourabi, H., et al.: Understanding smart cities: an integrative framework. In: Proceedings of Hawaii International International Conference on Systems Science, pp. 2289–2297 (2012). https://doi.org/10.1109/HICSS.2012.615
7. Albino, V., Berardi, U., Dangelico, R.M.: Smart cities: definition, deminsion, and performance. J. Urban Technol. **22**, 3–21 (2015). https://doi.org/10.1080/10630732.2014.942092
8. Shi, Y., Arthanari, T., Liu, X., Yang, B.: Sustainable transportation management: Integrated modeling and support. J. Clean. Prod. **212**, 1381–1395 (2019). https://doi.org/10.1016/j.jclepro.2018.11.209
9. Buwana, E., Hasibuan, H.S., Abdini, C.: Alternatives selection for sustainable transportation system in Kasongan City. Procedia Soc. Behav. Sci. **227**, 11–18 (2016). https://doi.org/10.1016/j.sbspro.2016.06.037
10. Wey, W.: Sustainable urban transportation planning strategies for improving quality of life under growth management principles. Sustain. Cities Soc. (2018). https://doi.org/10.1016/j.scs.2018.10.015
11. Korczak, J., Kijewska, K.: Smart logistics in the development of smart cities. Transp. Res. Procedia **39**, 13–14 (2018). https://doi.org/10.1016/j.trpro.2019.06.022
12. Ammon, D., Stiller, C.: Automated driving. At-Automatisierungstechnik **63**(3), 153–154 (2015). https://doi.org/10.1515/auto-2015-0008
13. Aamir, M., Masroor, S., Ali, Z.A., Ting, B.T.: Sustainable framework for smart transportation system: a case study of Karachi. Wireless Pers. Commun. **106**(1), 27–40 (2019). https://doi.org/10.1007/s11277-019-06259-4

14. Peng, G.C.A., Nunes, M.B., Zheng, L.: Impacts of low citizen awareness and usage in smart city services: the case of London's smart parking system. IseB **15**(4), 845–876 (2016). https://doi.org/10.1007/s10257-016-0333-8
15. Caragliu, A., Del Bo, C.F.: Smart innovative cities: the impact of Smart City policies on urban innovation. Technol. Forecast. Soc. Change **142**, 373–383 (2019). https://doi.org/10.1016/j.techfore.2018.07.022
16. Garau, C., Masala, F., Pinna, F.: Cagliari and smart urban mobility: analysis and comparison. Cities **56**, 35–46 (2016). https://doi.org/10.1016/j.cities.2016.02.012
17. Cornet, Y., Gudmundsson, H.: Building a metaframework for sustainable transport indicators review of selected contributions. Transp. Res. Rec. **2531**, 103–112 (2015). https://doi.org/10.3141/2531-12
18. Hox, J.J., Boeije, H.R.: Data collection, primary vs. secondary. In: Encyclopedia of Social Measurement, pp. 593–599 (2004). https://doi.org/10.1016/B0-12-369398-5/00041-4
19. Banister, D.: The sustainable mobility paradigm. Transp. Policy **15**(2), 73–80 (2008). https://doi.org/10.1016/j.tranpol.2007.10.005
20. Curtis, C.: Planning for sustainable accessibility: the implementation challenge. Transp. Policy **15**(2), 104–112 (2008). https://doi.org/10.1016/j.tranpol.2007.10.003

Analysis of the Daily Mobility Behavior Before and After the Corona Virus Pandemic – A Field Study

Waldemar Titov[✉] and Thomas Schlegel

Institute of Ubiquitous Mobility Systems, Karlsruhe University of Applied Sciences,
Moltkestr. 30, 76133 Karlsruhe, Germany
`iums@hs-kalrsruhe.de`

Abstract. In 2020, the world have seen a global spread of the corona virus. Various measures were undertaken to slow down the spread so that the national healthcare systems will be able to treat infected people. This included lockdowns and restrictions of before common activities of public life such as visiting relatives, going to cinemas and theaters or even commuting to work or school. All off these activities allowed people to be mobile and caused traffic. In our research, we analyze to what extent the outbreak of the COVID-19 pandemic and the introduced counter measures in Germany influence the mobility behavior of students at the Karlsruhe University of Applied Sciences. In our mobility behavior analysis we compare collected mobility data from October 2018 being collected before the corona virus pandemic and October 2020, collected after the outbreak of SARSCoV-2. In both measuring periods, students were asked to record their daily mobility over a two-week period with our mobility evaluation tool "MobiDiary".

Keywords: Mobility pattern · Mobility data · User model · Analysis tool

1 Introduction

Mobility analysis is about collecting, evaluating and assessing traffic data correctly. Usually, this is easy to accomplish. The cross-section or intersection under consideration is first surveyed, i.e. every movement of a road user is documented and evaluated at the end. With the help of this data, statements can then be made about traffic quality and safety. If necessary, changes can be made to the geometry of the intersection, the right-of-way, or the signalization, depending on the results of the survey and the needs that need to be addressed.

In the past, traffic analysis was mainly used to ensure optimal management of private motorized traffic. Nowadays, both bicycle and pedestrian traffic are increasingly taken into account in traffic analysis, so that the existing infrastructure can also be adapted to their needs.

Currently, March 15, 2021, it is somewhat more difficult to conduct meaningful surveys here in Germany, as the modal split has changed due to the COVID-19 pandemic. Due to SARS-CoV-2, the Virus responsible for the pandemic, many people are

C. Stephanidis et al. (Eds.): HCII 2021, CCIS 1498, pp. 552–557, 2021.
https://doi.org/10.1007/978-3-030-90176-9_71

avoiding public transport and switching to individual means of transport such as cars [1]. Transportation companies are also adjusting their schedules to the circumstances [2] and offering reduced services. To protect drivers, in Berlin, for example, passengers are only allowed to board buses through the rear door and cannot buy tickets from the driver [3]. Furthermore, many employees are encouraged to work from home, which also further reduces the daily commute.

Due to the state decree of the local government in March 2020 [4], there are many facilities in the state of Baden-Württemberg that have ceased operations due to the pandemic and some prohibitions or measures that must be followed:

- closure of schools and day care centers for children,
- interruption of face-to-face classes at universities,
- prohibition of meetings and other events,
- closure of cultural, educational institutions and baths,
- restriction of the operation of restaurants,
- protection of endangered persons,
- prohibition of entering and
- further measures according to the Infection Protection Act

All these measures change and reduce the volume of traffic. First, it is to be expected that the share of public transport will decrease, since the government recommends that a distance of at least one meter be maintained, which cannot be guaranteed in buses and trains at full capacity. This share will largely migrate to MIV. Therefore, it can be assumed that the total number of journeys made by private motor vehicle will initially remain the same, despite the general reduction in the total number of journeys.

How long the restrictions on the population will remain is unclear. It is also uncertain whether the existing restrictions will be extended, which would lead to a further reduction in traffic.

2 Analysis of Selected Mobility Evaluation Methods

Navigation services such as Google Maps, for example, use the GPS data of their many users to detect traffic congestion on busy routes. The so-called floating car data is obtained from every user who uses the in-house navigation and congestion warning system. In contrast to classic traffic jam alerts, this data is constantly updated and refers to the current traffic situation on all stretches of road. An alternative to GPS localization is the use of radio cell data. However, this data is less accurate and requires the cooperation of one or more mobile communications companies. With both systems, anonymization of the data is important [5].

Bluetooth tracking can be used to identify mobility and movement behavior in another way. Places where many people are present can be evaluated in an area-wide observation. The method accesses activated Bluetooth interfaces of mobile devices without the observed persons having to use additional devices or apps [6].

Since some sharing providers of, for example, bicycle or scooter rental systems make their vehicle data available live, it can be determined how often vehicles are currently used and on which relations they move. On the one hand, the general usage figures can be used to determine whether mobility has increased or decreased overall, and on the other hand, it can be observed whether the routes and destinations traveled change over time.

3 Evaluating Daily Mobility Behavior with Our MobiDiary

With our prior introduced mobility evaluation tool "MobiDiary" an instrument for multi modal mobility analysis, we conduct annual mobility analysis of student's mobility [7]. Following the standardized method for accessing travelers mobility designed by the German ministry of traffic and infrastructure [8] our android application captures start time, chosen transport mode, transfer time, time of arrival and the purpose of the taken route.

Other researchers also saw the possibilities of using Smartphones for data acquisition and developed several solutions. Schelewsky et al. developed such an application and examined the chances and challenges of using mobile devices for automated acquisition of intermodal routes [9]. They report that the feasibility of smartphone tracking is very high, because most routes can be determined more precisely than with classic methods. Safi et al. employed their system SITSS (Smartphone-based Individual Travel Survey System) as a pilot in the national household survey of New Zealand [10]. They conclude that the application reduced the required human and financial re-sources for the data collection. Patterson et al. created "Itinerum" a smartphone travel survey platform that allows researchers to customize the Itinerum app with their own questions and prompts, distribute these surveys, monitor, visualize and process the collected data without a background in programming [11]. All these projects show the demand and benefit of those apps.

Nonetheless, we were missing some key features in the developed solutions. That is why we created our own android application for mobile devices called "MobiDiary". What differentiates our App from the Apps mentioned above is the possibility to track additional context information. The App queries the current weather and links the Information to the recorded routes. The App also checks the audio jack, and records, if headphones are connected. That enables to verify multiple hypotheses like:

- when its sunny people are more likely to ride to work by bike and
- people listen to their headphones while riding a train rather than while riding a bike

The app also captures factors like start time, travel path, the chosen mode of transport, the transfer time, the time of arrival and finally, yet importantly, the purpose of the trip. The data acquisition is based on existing and time-proven methods like the "Mobilitätspanel", which is a standardized questionnaire for accessing travelers mobility designed and conducted by the German ministry of traffic and infrastructure [8]. The app asks the user to state their mode of transport after each stage of their way. Simultaneously, the Google Awareness API automatically identifies the modes. This makes it possible to verify the provided data from the users and vice versa, the identification Google provides. Similar we handle the purpose of the route. As stated above the user can give us the purpose of the route. Additionally, we also use the Google nearby Places API to identify the purpose automatically. Furthermore, the App enables the users to add a description of the situations in which they made a transport change decision. We use this information to validate the specifications on the purpose of a trip given by the app users. If for example, a user indicated that the route purpose is free time when being located in a university building, the given information might be wrong. To record a trip, the user has to actively start the recording. After finishing the trip, the data is stored on the local device and can be shared by the user. The device uploads the data to our server as soon as a Wi-Fi connection is established.

3.1 Mobility Evaluation Study Set-Up

In our mobility behavior analysis we compare collected mobility data from October 2018 being collected before the corona virus pandemic and October 2020, collected after the outbreak of SARSCoV-2. In both measuring periods, students were asked to record their daily mobility over a two-week period with our developed MobiDiary tool. The first mobility evaluation from October 2018 were described in more detail in [12].

3.2 Mobility Evaluation Study Results

The mobility data set collected in 2018 contains data from 38 students. Overall, 308 ways with a sum of 4.954 km in over 89 h of travel time were collected. The density of tracks traveled around campus and the outposts is clearly visible (Fig. 1). In 2020, the number of participants rose by three person up to 41. However, the collected data decreased by more than 50% down to 150 ways. The distance of collected tracks decreased by over 63% to the amount of 1.760 km in 74 h travel time. Due to online and distance lectures, the necessity of visiting lectures at the campus disappears (Fig. 2).

Fig. 1. Visualization of recorded tracks over a two-week period in October 2018 – **before** the corona pandemic outbreak

Fig. 2. Visualization of recorded tracks over a two-week period in October 2020 – **after** the corona pandemic outbreak

4   Limitations and Outlook

We evaluated our mobility evaluation approach in to studies. In the first study, 38 student subjects participated in 2018 in the second 41 student subjects participated in 2020. In both studies, participants used the app to record their daily mobility behavior over two weeks in October 2018. Additionally, to the pure location tracking the acquisition of context-based information enabled us to evaluate more scenarios than it would have been possible using only traditional surveys. However, we also found some flaws in our approach. One challenge we encountered was that user often forgot to mark in the app that they finished a trip. This resulted in the app still recording the trip while the users were already at their destinations. For this reason, we want to implement a feature that detects inactivity and asks the user by means of a notification if they have finished their journey. Despite these initial difficulties, the advantages of electronic route recording using apps clearly outweighed the disadvantages of conventional methods.

In conclusion, the current situation under the prevailing mobility restrictions is new for everyone and the traffic analysis has to adapt to it first. With the help of our introduced tool, the short-, medium- and long-term mobility behavior in crises can be considered. Such data can then help to make the right decisions in the future to better deal with such a crisis. For this reason, it is also advisable to collect as much data as possible in order to evaluate it, since such a situation will hopefully not come back too soon.

The evaluation of the choice of means of transport in such a time is very interesting, because it also shows the fear of the population of a contagion by strangers. Overall, it can be said that digital methods can be used to monitor the impact of the Corona epidemic and the measures taken can also be evaluated for comparative values. Unfortunately, these questions and data can only be answered or revealed after the crisis is over.

References

1. Haberland, D.M.: 20 March 2020. https://www.mobil.org/. https://www.mobil.org/auto-rue ckgrat-unserer-mobilitaet-in-corona-krise/
2. Mainz, R.-M.-B. i.: 20 March 2020. https://www.mainzer-mobilitaet.de. https://www.mai nzer-mobilitaet.de/corona
3. RBB, R.E.: 20 March 2020. https://www.radioeins.de/. https://www.radioeins.de/programm/ sendungen/die_sonntagsfahrer/_/auswirkungen-des-corona-virus-auf-die-mobilitaet.html
4. Baden-Württemberg, D.R.: 17 March 2020. https://stm.baden-wuerttemberg.de/. https://stm. baden-wuerttemberg.de/de/service/presse/pressemitteilung/pid/landesregierung-beschliesst-massnahmen-gegen-die-ausbreitung-des-coronavirus/
5. Grün, G.-c.: Stauforschung: Der beste Staumelder ist das eigene Handy. In: Zeit, D., 21.06.2012 (2012). https://www.zeit.de/digital/mobil/2012-06/staudaten-handy/komple ttansicht . Accessed 20 Mar 2020
6. Ellersiek, T., Liebig, T., Hecker, D., Körner, C.: Analyse von raumzeitlichen bewe-gungsmustern auf basis von bluetooth-sensoren.na (2012)
7. Trefzger, M., Titov, W., Keller, C., Böhm, F., Schlegel, T.: A Context Aware Evaluation Tool for Individual Mobility. Karlsruhe University of Applied Sciences, Moltkestr. 30, 76133 Karlsruhe, Germany. Institute of Ubiquitous Mobility Systems (2019)
8. BMVI: Article describing the inquiry of mobility data by the German ministry of traffic and infrastructure (2019). https://www.bmvi.de/SharedDocs/DE/Artikel/G/deutschesmobili taetspanel.html. Accessed 27 Mar 2020

9. Schelewsky, M., Bock, B., Jonuschat, H., Stephan, K.: Das elektronische Wege-tagebuch: Chancen und Herausforderungen einer automatisierten Wegeerfassung inter-mo-daler Wege (2014). https://www.researchgate.net/publication/259897501_Das_el-ektronische_Wegeta gebuch_Chancen_und_Herausforderungen_einer_automatis-ierten_Wegeerfassung_inte rmodaler_Wege

10. Safi, H., Assemi, B., Mesbah, M., Ferreira, L., Hickman, M.: Design and implementation of a smartphone-based travel survey. Transp. Res. Rec. **2526**(1), 99–107 (2015)

11. Patterson, Z., Fitzsimmons, K., Jackson, S., Mukai, T.: Itinerum: the open smartphone travel survey platform. SoftwareX **10**, 100230 (2019)

12. Böhm, F., et al.: Toolbox for analysis and evaluation of low-emission urban mobility. In: Krömker, H. (ed.) HCI in Mobility, Transport, and Automotive Systems. Driving Behavior, Urban and Smart Mobility. HCII 2020. LNCS, vol. 12213, pp. 145–160. Springer, Cham (2020). https://doi.org/10.1007/978-3-030-50537-0_12

Research on Interaction Design Promote Aesthetic Changes in Car Styling Under the Background of Intelligent Driving

Mangmang Zhang[✉]

Tsinghua University, Beijing, People's Republic of China
zhmm@mail.tsinghua.edu.cn

Abstract. With the development of digitalization and networking of automobiles, the focus of car styling has gradually shifted from the study of three-dimensional modeling to the design of Driving & Riding Experience centered on human-automobile interaction. The motor drive greatly simplifies the internal structure of the car, saves more space, and brings more styling possibilities. At the same time, intelligent driving has changed the entire driving mode, and the new relationship between people and the car has brought unprecedented changes to the space layout of the car. All of these have had a huge and long-term impact on the aesthetics of the current car design and are changing the methods of the entire car design and people's perception of the aesthetics of the car. From the perspective of interaction design, this article discusses the changes and trends in the aesthetics of car styling in the context of intelligent driving from several aspects.

Keywords: Interaction design · Intelligent driving · New travel lifestyle · Aesthetic · Styling design

1 Introduction

In the past more than a century, due to the limitations of engines and transmission gears, as well as the constraints of driving behavior patterns, the appearance and interior design of automobiles have not undergone essential changes. In the iterative accumulation of the styling of internal combustion engine vehicles in the past hundred years, the traditional functional design paradigm has become the mainstream choice, forming the aesthetic consciousness of the social group.

Traditional cars have been offline since they were produced. The conservative driving and limited entertainment and navigation functions cannot be synchronized with the latest data. These basic functions have very limited interactive operations. In the process of replacing fossil energy with new energy represented by electric power, digitization and networking have become the beginning of technological changes in automobiles. The chain reaction of the advancement of new energy technology has triggered the rapid development of intelligent and digitized automobiles, and automobiles have become a moment. The online mobile information platform and digital terminal, the driving mode and the way of using cars have all caused tremendous changes.

© Springer Nature Switzerland AG 2021
C. Stephanidis et al. (Eds.): HCII 2021, CCIS 1498, pp. 558–563, 2021.
https://doi.org/10.1007/978-3-030-90176-9_72

New energy vehicles no longer rely on traditional mechanical drive and transmission structures, and the space saved gives designers a brand-new creative space, which can completely break the concept of traditional automobile styling. Autonomous driving technology has completely changed the driving mode, liberating people from the mechanical labor of driving. More interactivity and possibilities are generated during the driving process, giving birth to new relationships between people and vehicles, and also completely changing the interaction mode between people and the car, as well as the relationship between the occupants in the car. New user needs and usage scenarios have bred completely different internal spatial layouts. Automobiles have produced new attributes and values outside of transportation, changed the business practices of many different industries, and quickly affected people's work and life [1]. Intelligent driving derives new modes of travel, new human-vehicle relationships, new business opportunities, and socio-economic models.

This article discusses the changes and trends of automobile styling aesthetics in the digital age from the following aspects.

2   Family Design Language, Emotional Identification from Car Styling to Digital Design

The family-oriented design language of the car or the design gene is to control the overall style and establish a guiding framework to unify the aesthetics of appearance, interior and interactive design, so that the brand's series of products have consistent subjective feelings and experiences. Output and strengthen a consistent brand experience. The family-oriented design language is not just the use of styling elements, but a memory and inner feeling that has been accumulated through history and is deeply rooted in the minds of consumers.

Traditional car design reflects the family characteristics of products through the symbolic inheritance of internal and external shapes. In the digital age, this memory will become a digital asset to be preserved and passed on.

For example, after 73 years of development, the Porsche brand born out of the Beetle gene can still find the shadow of the typical Beetle on the first 356'No.1' Roadster produced in 1948 and the latest Taycan models, such as the evolution from the original model. The coming "Hood's topography" shape retains Porsche's unique curved body as one of the classic stylized elements. Together with the inclined round lamp shape, sleek body, and Powerful shoulders, it has become a family identification feature that lasts for 73 years. They Together they define Porsche's brand image [2] (Fig. 1).

Similarly, Taycan inherited the classic Porsche ring-shaped instrument panel shape, replacing the tachometer in the middle, which is regarded as the Centre of Power (as shown in Fig. 2), with a power meter representing electric vehicles, which was regarded as the engine heart rate from the internal combustion engine era. The tachometer in the picture, to the power meter that represents electric vehicles, from mechanical entities to digital displays, continue to strengthen Porsche's "Brand Emotional Value" in the hearts of consumers (see Fig. 2).

Whether it is the ability to transform the external styling or the interior style into the user's memory, a strong brand appeal is required. People must experience their own

Fig. 1. The styling design of the Porsche Taycan is in the same line as the first generation 356'No.1' Roadster.

Fig. 2. From the classic instrument panel of 911 to the semi-digital instrument of the 992, to the new digital instrument cluster of Taycan.

existence and self-recognition through the feedback of the sensations and sense organs they feel constantly [3]. For consumers, this kind of cognition and experience can come from the curves of appearance, the touch of materials, the feedback of the vehicle to the body during driving, the operation logic and interactive experience, the form of user interface, the pattern icon, and even the sound and Internal smells, etc., these details that can trigger emotional memory, cross-domain models and ages, together constitute an overall brand impression.

3   Emotionalization of the Branding

NIO's NOMI in-Car AI System is the first intelligent digital in-car robot applied to mass-produced cars in China's self-owned brand cars. The concept of NOMI has expanded from a simple robot to partners and friends during driving. This kind of psychological role transformation has further shortened the emotional distance between users and cars, and has also given technology more vitality. NOMI has a simple expression ability, and will give different expression feedback to users according to different functional states, scenes, and events. For example, it will present a dynamic expression of triumph with music during driving. This kind of lovely emotional expression, It closes the distance between people and cars, hiding various complex operations in the fun, harmony and pleasure brought by NOMI, and the emotional experience it brings to users has far exceeded its specific functional value.

In the future, the car's AI will customize different subdivision functions according to the different needs of each user, and constantly learn the user's preferences, so that the voice and the tone of the conversation are more in line with the user's own taste and habits, and the information provided by the intelligent partner It is highly personal, reducing user choice and judgment. Personalized characteristics can most arouse consumer's emotional empathy and Cognitive empathy [4]. The emotionalization of the brand will use the brand DNA to unify the human-computer interaction logic and the visual presentation style of the user interface, and establish a family-oriented interactive experience system. The more interactive experience with strong brand characteristics and family style, the more identity of values can be generated, allowing users to invest more emotions in smart partners, and also allowing users to have more emotional sustenance for the brand (see Fig. 3).

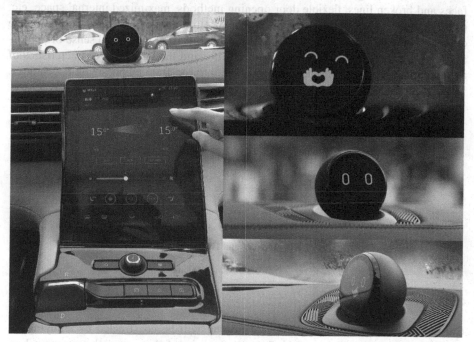

Fig. 3. NIO's NOMI in-Car AI System transforms a car from a travel tool into a travel partner.

4 Platform and Modular Design

The aesthetic cognition of traditional automobile styling is based on the shaping of three-dimensional space by human vision, emphasizing the power, speed and functionality of appearance styling. It is influenced by fluid mechanics, mechanical structure, ergonomics, and visual perception. Dynamics and the influence of brand family design language. For example, BMW's body styling design is a functionally dominant result of the typical aerodynamics and engineering structure.

With the advent of the era of intelligent driving, when driving is no longer the main contradiction of the relationship between humans and cars, the current layout of the car's interior space has lost its basis, and the steering wheel and numerous control devices are no longer necessary. The journey from point A to point B can be used to rest, appreciate the scenery, communicate, shop, study, work and so on. The diversification of people's space behavior in the car will lead to a revolution in the design of space layout in the car and the transformation of the car's own attributes. Car design will move from physical modeling to interaction design, user experience and service design.

Therefore, many concept cars launched by companies facing the future of unmanned driving technology have adopted platform-based and modular design, and adopted similar forms in shaping: sleek and concise appearance, reducing unnecessary Curved surfaces and broken lines, flexible door opening methods, maximized internal space, etc. (see Fig. 4). This shows that people's values of automobiles will undergo qualitative changes in the future. Consumers' attention will shift from the formal sense of appearance to the experience and feelings of travel life, and the individual characteristics of automobiles will shift from the exterior to the interior, from emphasizing appearance. The styling shifted to human-computer interaction design as the new value driver.

Fig. 4. Concept cars of Kia, Toyota, and Bosch all use similar appearances.

5 Conclusion

Car design in the context of intelligent driving will be constructed by studying the dynamic development and mutual influence of a series of elements such as users, behaviors, scenarios, services, and experiences, combining smart cities, smart transportation systems, and smart public facilities. A new travel lifestyle. In this context, automotive design will inevitably produce new design languages and design methods.

At the same time, people's needs for cars have changed, and the aesthetic perception and aesthetic needs of cars have also changed. Car design has moved from a visual aesthetic perception of styling to a comprehensive aesthetic perception with interactive design as the core and the combination of virtual and reality. At this stage, the multi-channel human-computer interaction reform began to build a new user experience and a new automotive aesthetic cognitive model. In the car design facing the future, there will be a new symbiotic relationship between car styling design and human-computer interaction design. When L5 autonomous driving is approaching, the interactive operation between humans and cars will not only bring more free space layout and digital operation methods, but also change people's aesthetic perception of the entire shape of the car. Gives new development space and vitality to automobile design.

Acknowledgement. This research was supported by 2019 National Social Science Foundation Art Project "Interaction Design Method Research based on AI", the number is 19BG127.

References

1. Lipson, H.: Driverless, p. 301. Wenhui Press, Shanghai (2017)
2. Mission, E.: Porsche design of the future [EB/OL], 24 February 2016. https://newsroom.porsche.com/en/products/porsche-mission-e-design-michael-mauer-movie-12252.html. Accessed 05 June 2021
3. Lei, L.I.: The Daily Aesthetic Era, p. 23. Social Sciences Literature Press, Beijing (2014)
4. Wispe, L.: History of the concept of empathy. Empathy Dev. **2**, 17–37 (1978)

Author Index

Aciar, Silvana II-233
Adhikari, Nayan II-3
Aguirre, Joel I-44
Akbar, Paisal II-359
Albin, Aaron II-272
Albright, Liam II-115
Alimardani, Maryam I-223
Alp, Demir II-249
Altıntoprak, Nektar Ege II-515
Amri, Pahmi I-503
An, Qingfan II-125
Aoyagi, Saizo I-271
Arias-Chávez, Dennis I-471
Asafo, Seth M. II-115
Ask, Torvald F. II-545
Attah, Dzifa A. II-115

Babaian, Tamara II-134
Baker, Grahame I-459
Balmaceda Castro, Iván II-233
Bandiola, John Casey I-486
Becking, Dominic II-383
Beckmann, Armin II-242
Ben Zeev, Dror II-115
Bensmann, Mandra I-511
Berry, Yapah I-107
Bertoldo, Giulia I-435
Bevilacqua, Roberta II-139
Bhurtel, Samip I-3
Bienhaus, Diethelm II-23, II-56
Blessmann, Christian I-37
Bollmann, Marc II-242
Borja, C. II-325
Bouchriha, Zineb II-522
Bowers, Margaret A. I-257
Brenner, Daniel II-272
Bucchiarone, Antonio I-435
Buchholz, Tim II-242
Bui, Michael II-80
Büyükyazgan, Zeynep II-249
Byrne, Kaileigh II-197

Cabrerizo, Alejandro I-91
Cadier, Agnes I-11

Camps, Jean-François II-258
Cao, Zhiwei I-311
Capiola, August I-257
Cardona-Reyes, Héctor I-471
Casano, Jonathan I-486
Casler, James II-564
Chaisirithanya, Kamolmal II-163
Chandwadkar, Apurva I-51
Chang, Albert I-239
Chaudhry, Beenish I-126
Chen, Chih-Yung II-425
Chen, Guang-Dah II-527
Chen, Li-Hsin II-147
Chen, Ningxi II-258
Chen, Shuyi II-64
Chen, Shu-Yi II-73
Chen, Zhangyi I-332
Chiang, Ying-Yu II-73
Chiu, Jen-I II-302
Chopade, Pravin II-272
Civerchia, Patrizia II-139
Clarkson, Jeffrey D. I-17
Collins, Pamela Y. II-115
Conrad, Jan II-242
Costa Mesquita, Sandro II-11
Cripe, Curtis II-564
Croft, Bryan I-17
Cui, Jingyi II-347

da Rocha, Victor Hazin II-11
Dai, Yihang II-215
Densmore, Tucker I-99
Devkota, Sujan II-433
Dey, Romi II-266
Diógenes de Araújo, Tiago II-11
Divekar, Rahul R. II-272
Dolgin, D. L. I-517
Dong, Jeyoun I-234
Drozdal, Jaimie I-239
Du, Jiachun I-214, II-441
Duan, Hanyue I-214, II-441
Ducao, Arlene I-107
Duffy, Vincent G. I-99
Duran, Sonia II-286

Eren, Arda   II-249

Fahey, Will   I-239
Falconi, Fiorella   I-44
Fan, Hsiwen   II-527
Fan, Jiaxu   II-93
Fang, Tianhong   II-64
Farid, Sabra   II-522
Favargiotti, Sara   I-435
Felici, Elisa   II-139
Felix, Odalis   I-17
Feng, Shuo   I-206
Fleischer, Martin   I-521
Fujii, Ayaka   I-249
Fukasawa, Raita   II-39, II-107
Funke, Gregory J.   I-257

Gadelha, Mikhail R.   I-349
Gado, Sabrina   II-80
Gambella, Elena   II-139
Gartner, Tobias   I-527
Geiser, Rafael   II-242
Gilbert, Stephen B.   I-341
González, D.   II-325
Gračanin, Denis   I-165
Grunitzki, Ricardo   II-463
Guevara Mamani, Joseph   I-288
Guzmán, M.   II-280
Guzman-Mendoza, José Eder   I-471

Han, Han   II-317
Harriott, Martin   I-357
Harris, Maggie   II-197
Hashimoto, Naohisa   II-17
Hashimoto, Wataru   I-410, II-489
He, Weiping   I-206, I-311, I-424
Heracleous, Panikos   I-115, II-88
Herdman, Chris M.   I-369
Hernández-Sánchez, Irmina   II-286
Hidayati, Mega   II-207
Hirao, Kentaro   II-39, II-107
Hirota, Koichi   I-443
Hofer, Julien   I-24
Hoffman, Robert R.   I-144
Hofmann, Thomas   I-37, I-511
Holdman, C.   I-517
Hoover, Melynda   I-341
Horie, Ryota   I-451
Horie, Sachio   I-31
Horsburgh, Sheri   II-184

Hoshi, Sakuto   I-443
Hou, Zhenghang   I-206
Hsu, Yu-chen   I-318
Hu, Linwei   II-390
Hu, Xiangyuan   I-119
Hu, Yupeng   I-206
Huang, Hsin-An   II-446
Huang, Hsuan-de   I-318
Huang, Siao-wei   I-318
Hub, Fabian   I-535
Hung, Hsu-Wen   II-155

Inaba, Masayuki   I-249
Inoue, Fumiya   II-535
Irawan, Bambang   II-359
Ishihara, Makio   II-535
Islam, Muhammad Usama   I-126
Ito, Kodai   I-451

Jacke, Luka   I-324
Jalil, Miftahul Jannah   II-454
Jamieson, Peter   I-91
Ji, Ru   II-93
Jia, Weiwei   I-332
Jiang, Jiujiu   II-390
Jiang, Lijun   II-93
Jiang, Ting   II-572
Jing, Lei   I-151
Johnson, Landon   I-107
Jubba, Hasse   II-207

Kakuta, Nobuhito   II-17
Kalu, Chidinma U.   I-341
Kang, Dongyeop   I-234
Kang, Namgyu   II-339
Kaplan, Alexander   II-101
Kawakami, Guto   I-349
Keates, Simeon   I-459
Kelley, Marjorie M.   II-125
Kelly, Jonathan W.   I-341
Kerpen, Daniel   II-242
Khaliq, Sehar   I-58, I-279
Khurshid, Aasim   I-349, II-463
Kim, Dain   I-494
Kirchner, Elsa Andrea   I-324
Kirollos, Ramy   I-357
Knothe, Svenja   I-37
Knox, Benjamin J.   II-545
Ko, Ju-Ling   II-368
Kobayashi, Fumiya   I-271

Koen, Ilias   I-107
Konomi, Shin'ichi   I-119
Kozanoğlu, Elif Selin   II-249
Kreutzer, Michael   II-23, II-56
Kumagai, Daisuke   II-31
Kuo, Pei-Yi   II-368
Kurihara, Kazutaka   I-443
Kurniawan, Danang   II-375, II-454, II-472, II-480
Kwon, Wookyong   I-234

Laak, Matti   II-383
Lampe, Alicia   I-511
Le, Hoa   II-115
Lee, I.-Jui   II-155
Leithe, Wasana   II-539
Lepp, Haley   II-272
Li, Haicui   I-151
Li, Jianghong   I-311
Li, Jiawei   II-215
Li, Jinze   II-163
Li, Mingzhu   II-414
Li, Ning   I-135
Li, Xiaofang   I-183
Li, Xiaoling   I-332
Li, Zhellin   II-93
Lim, John Michael Vince   I-486
Lin, Minling   II-317
Lind, Pedro G.   I-3, II-3, II-433
Lingelbach, Katharina   II-80
Liu, Lili   II-176, II-390, II-414
Liu, Xuhong   I-135
Loilatu, Mohammad Jafar   I-543, II-375
London, J.   I-517
Loosen, Christian   II-56
Lopatin, Sergej   II-23
Lopez, Christian   I-390
Loth, Steffen   I-511
Lugo, Ricardo G.   II-545

Maag, Simone   I-294
Malherbe, Billy   II-368
Mamun, Tauseef Ibne   I-144
Manjhi, Kailash   II-266
Manzanilla, P.   II-280
Maranesi, Elvira   II-139
Martínez, J.   II-280
Maurus, Michael   I-324
Mei, Ramaini   II-480
Meller, Suzanne   II-115

Méndez, A.   II-325
Miller, Brent   I-257
Misran   II-207, II-472
Mitchell, Tommy   I-107
Miyake, Shin   II-550
Mizutani, Yasuharu   I-410, II-489
Mogilisetty, Lehar   I-239
Mohammad, Yasser   I-115
Mohsin, Zehra   I-58, I-279
Moquillaza, Arturo   I-44
Moreno e Mello, Gustavo B.   I-3, II-3
Moreno, Maria   II-286
Morgenstern, Holger   II-294
Muallidin, Isnaini   II-454, II-480
Mueller, Shane T.   I-144
Murthy, Nikhilas   I-239
Mutiarin, Dyah   I-503, I-543

Na, JungJo   I-494
Nagata, Noriko   I-271
Nakamura, Kanako   II-31
Nam, Seung Woo   I-234
Namatame, Takashi   II-550
Navarro, Isidro   II-331
Nayak, Jitesh   I-51
Neve, Lisa   I-223
Nishiguchi, Satoshi   I-410, II-489
Nishizawa, Yuri   II-39
Nithaworn, Mike   I-17
Nojima, Takuya   I-443
Núñez, A.   II-280, II-325
Nurmandi, Achmad   I-177, I-503, I-543, II-207, II-359, II-375, II-399, II-454, II-472, II-480

Oehl, Michael   I-535
Ofori Atta, Angela   II-115
Ogawa, Shozo   I-451
Ohshima, Hiroyuki   II-558
Okada, Kei   I-249
Oswal, Lohitvenkatesh M.   II-47
Oswal, Sushil K.   II-47
Otake, Kohei   II-550
Ouiddad, Smail   II-522

Packer, Brian   I-459
Pàmies, Carles   II-331
Paolini, Susi   II-139
Park, Heehyeon   I-364
Park, Seonyeong   I-494

Parra, Margel   II-286
Pasquini, Sara   II-139
Paz, Freddy   I-44
Pejemsky, Anya   I-369
Pelliccioni, Giuseppe   II-139
Pinto, Pablo Pari   I-288
Pohling, Kevin   I-294
Powell, Curtis   I-239
Presas, Daniel   II-184

Qodir, Zuly   II-207

Ramanarayanan, Vikram   II-272
Ramírez, Javier   II-286
Rector, Terry   II-564
Redondo, Ernest   II-331
Ren, Shanjiao   II-176, II-390
Ren, Xiangshi   I-300
Riccardi, Giovanni R.   II-139
Rieger, Jochem W.   II-80
Rinn, Klaus   II-23
Robayo, Adriana del Rosario Pineda   II-307
Rodríguez, Alex Alberto Castellar   II-307
Rodríguez, Harold Gamero   II-307
Rössler, Marc   I-294
Rothman, Seana   I-17
Roussel-Fayard, Adrian   II-258
Ruh, Paulina   II-294
Rusu, Cristian   II-233

Sakuma, Kasumi   I-151
Sakurai, Sho   I-443
Salahudin   I-543, II-375, II-399, II-454,
    II-472, II-480
Sánchez Riera, Alberto   II-331
Sanderson, Norun Christine   II-433
Sandnes, Frode Eika   II-539
Scanlon, Matthew   II-189
Schaefer, Emily   II-189
Schlegel, Thomas   I-527, I-552
Schmitz, Anne-Kathrin   II-383
Seelmeyer, Udo   II-383
Şemsioğlu, Sinem   I-377
Seo, Gapyuel   I-385
Seo, Ryan   I-159
Sheu, Scott   I-107
Shewaga, Rob   II-184
Shi, Yueyang   I-332
Shibata, Ryuichi   II-489
Shimada, Shigenobu   II-558

Shimizu, Soichiro   II-39, II-107
Silva Vidal, Yuri   I-288
Six, Stephanie   II-197
Snyder, Jaime   II-115
Sohail, Maarif   I-58, I-279
Standfield, Benjamin   I-165
Stewart, Liam   I-390
Strobel, Simon   I-294
Su, Hui   I-239
Sugimoto, Masashi   I-271
Suid, Taima Z.   I-66
Sulistyaningsih, Tri   I-543
Sulla Espinoza, Erasmo   I-288
Sun, Huey-Min   I-399
Sun, Winnie   II-184
Sunray, Jody   I-239
Supo Colquehuanca, Elvis   I-288
Suri, Dia Meirina   I-177
Suswanta   II-359
Sutan, Arissy Jorgi   II-375, II-399
Sütterlin, Stefan   II-545
Swaid, Samar I.   I-66
Syamsurrijal, M.   II-207
Syrov, Nikolay   II-101

Tabarant, Charlotte   II-258
Tada, Mitsunori   I-451
Takahashi, Yuka   II-339
Takai, Kohichi   II-88
Takaoka, Alicia J. W.   II-407
Taki, Rana   II-249
Takinami, Yusuke   II-17
Tanaka, Hisaya   II-39, II-107
Tang, Hsien-Hui   II-73
Tao, Qianru   II-414
Tao, Qianyi   II-176
Tapia, T.   II-280
Taufik, Mohammad   II-359
Tezza, Dante   I-191
Tian, Ruihang   I-214, II-441
Titov, Waldemar   I-527, I-552
Tolston, Michael T.   I-257
Trujillo-Espinoza, Cristian   I-471
Tsuei, Mengping   II-302
Tsugawa, Akito   II-39, II-107

Uetake, Tomofumi   II-550
Uribe-Quevedo, Alvaro   II-184

Van Benthem, Kathleen   I-369
van Bergen, Tania   I-107
Van Der Like, D.   I-517
Vasilyev, Anatoly   II-101
Vella, Frédéric   II-258
Verkaart, Anouk   I-223
Vigouroux, Nadine   II-258
Vilcapaza Goyzueta, Denilson   I-288
Villadiego Rincón, Derlis Aminta   II-307
Villalba-Condori, Klinge Orlando   I-471
von Zabiensky, Florian   II-23, II-56
Voncolln, Eric   I-17
Vukelić, Mathias   II-80

Waag, Philipp   II-383
Wagner-Hartl, Verena   I-294
Wang, Chunhui   II-572
Wang, Fei   II-497
Wang, Jing   I-71
Wang, Long   I-332
Wang, Shuxia   I-206, I-311, I-424
Wang, Wei   II-515
Wang, Xiaoju   I-197
Wang, Yuanlu   I-183
Watermeyer, Markus   I-24
Webb, Joshua   I-191
Wei, Bingzhao   I-311
Weinhardt, Marc   II-383
Wendel, Nikko   I-521
Werner, Nicole   II-189
Winterlind, Emma   II-197
Wright, Thomas   I-91
Wu, Jiang   II-215

Xia, Yunguo   II-414
Xie, John   II-224
Xie, Qitong   I-479
Xu, Maoqi   II-505

Yalçın, Sedat   II-249
Yamamoto, Michiya   I-271

Yamashita, Tomoya   I-410
Yang, Cheng-Han   II-368
Yang, Zhou   II-64
Yantaç, Asım Evren   I-377
Yao, Morgan Spencer   I-486
Yasuda, Keiji   II-88
Yen, Po-Yin   II-125
Yoneyama, Akio   I-115, II-88
Yoo, Subeen   I-494
Yoshida, Kohei   II-107
Yu, Hongqiang   II-572
Yu, Wei   I-81, I-197, I-479
Yuan, Chieh   II-368
Yuan, Xiaojun (Jenny)   I-300
Yuan, Yuan   II-215
Yue, Gu   I-418

Zepeda, S.   II-280, II-325
Zeurcher, Will   I-91
Zhang, Jie   I-311
Zhang, Lixia   I-332
Zhang, Mangmang   I-558
Zhang, Ruoqi   II-414
Zhang, Shaohua   I-206
Zhang, Shuo   II-414
Zhang, Xiaotian   I-424
Zhao, Huan   I-135
Zhao, Nan   I-214, II-441
Zhao, Wei   I-214
Zhao, Weijia   II-505
Zheng, Meng-Cong   II-147, II-425, II-446
Zheng, Shuai   I-332
Zhou, Bingxian   II-572
Zhou, Jie   II-347
Zhu, Yifei   I-81, II-64
Zhu, Yongyi   II-93
Zong, Mingming   II-163
Zurlo, Francesco   II-317